CANADA

P. T. Babie and Charles J. Russo

The World Today Series®
2025–2026

40th Edition

BLOOMSBURY ACADEMIC
Bloomsbury Publishing Inc, 1359 Broadway, New York, NY 10018, USA
Bloomsbury Publishing Plc, 50 Bedford Square, London, WC1B 3DP, UK
Bloomsbury Publishing Ireland, 29 Earlsfort Terrace, Dublin 2, D02 AY28, Ireland

BLOOMSBURY, BLOOMSBURY ACADEMIC and the Diana logo are trademarks of Bloomsbury Publishing Plc

First published in the United States of America 2026

Copyright © Bloomsbury Academic Publishing, 2026

Cover design: Chloe Batch
Cover images: © iStock.com/sorendls and iStock.com/Gile68

All rights reserved. No part of this publication may be: i) reproduced or transmitted in any form, electronic or mechanical, including photocopying, recording or by means of any information storage or retrieval system without prior permission in writing from the publishers; or ii) used or reproduced in any way for the training, development or operation of artificial intelligence (AI) technologies, including generative AI technologies. The rights holders expressly reserve this publication from the text and data mining exception as per Article 4(3) of the Digital Single Market Directive (EU) 2019/790.

Bloomsbury Publishing Inc does not have any control over, or responsibility for, any third-party websites referred to or in this book. All internet addresses given in this book were correct at the time of going to press. The author and publisher regret any inconvenience caused if addresses have changed or sites have ceased to exist, but can accept no responsibility for any such changes.

Library of Congress Cataloging-in-Publication Data Available

ISBN: PB: 979-8-8818-0243-1
ePDF: 979-8-8818-6281-7
eBook: 979-8-8818-0244-8

Series: World Today

Typeset by Sue Murray
Printed and bound in the United States of America

For product safety related questions contact productsafety@bloomsbury.com.

To find out more about our authors and books visit www.bloomsbury.com and sign up for our newsletters.

ACKNOWLEDGMENTS

It is with great gratitude that we thank Dr. Wayne C. Thompson and James Kent Donlevy, former editors of this volume for their stellar work in the preparation of the text. We have relied heavily on their good work. We have also depended on the various official federal and provincial websites as well as major Canadian media sources to update this book.

We also thank Ms. Rhiannon Jones at the University of Calgary for her assistance in the preparation of previous editions of this volume.

Charlie Russo would like to offer his deepest love, now, always, and forever, as well as his thanks, to his wife and best friend, Debbie, for her loving support over the years.

Courtesy of iStock.com/Orchidpoet

CONTENTS

Map of Canada	vi
Canada Today	1
Culture	3
Geography	17
People	26
History	39
New France	41
The Conquest (La Conquête)	43
British North America	45
The War of 1812	46
The Road to Independence	48
Confederation	50
Tightening the East–West Link	52
Loosening the Apron Strings	55
World War I	55
The Interwar Years	57
World War II	59
After 1945	61
The "Quiet Revolution" in Quebec	62
Meech Lake Accord	72
A New Constitution for Canada?	72
Political System	76
Constitution	78
Governmental Structure	80
The Monarch	80
The Governor General	82
The Political Executive	86
Parliament	90
Senate	93
The Legal System	95
The Charter of Rights and Freedoms	100
Federalism and the Provinces	101
Provincial Governments	103
Newfoundland and Labrador	104
Nova Scotia	107
Prince Edward Island	107
New Brunswick	109
Quebec	110
Ontario	117
Manitoba	118
Saskatchewan	120
Alberta	122
British Columbia	124
Yukon, Northwest Territories, and Nunavut	128
Parties and Elections	134
2004 Federal Elections	148
2006 Federal Elections	149
2008 Federal Elections	150
2011 Federal Elections	151
2015 Federal Elections	153
2019 and 2021 Federal Elections	154
Foreign Policy	155
Defense	173
Economy	183
Future	210
Web Sites and Bibliography	212

Their Majesties King Charles III and Queen Camilla
Photo credit: Hugo Burnand/Buckingham Palace

**The Rt. Hon. Mark Carney
Prime Minister of Canada**
Photo credit: Government of Canada

**Her Excellency the Right Honourable
Mary Simon, C.C., C.M.M., C.O.M., O.Q.,
C.D., Governor General and Commander-in-
Chief of Canada**
Photo credit: Sgt Johanie Maheu, Rideau Hall © OSGG-BSGG, 202

Aerial view of Parliament Credit: First Light Associated Photographers

Canadian Prime Ministers since Confederation

Rt. Hon. Sir John A. Macdonald	(C)	July 1867–Nov. 1873
Hon. Alexander Mackenzie	(L)	Nov. 1873–Oct. 1878
Rt. Hon. Sir John A. Macdonald	(C)	Oct. 1878–June 1891
Hon. Sir John J. C. Abbott	(C)	June 1891–Nov. 1892
Rt. Hon. Sir John S. D. Thompson	(C)	Dec. 1892–Dec. 1894
Rt. Hon. Sir Mackenzie Bowell	(C)	Dec. 1894–Apr. 1896
Rt. Hon. Sir Charles Tupper	(C)	May 1896–July 1896
Rt. Hon. Sir Wilfrid Laurier	(L)	July 1896–Oct. 1911
Rt. Hon. Sir Robert L. Borden	(C)	Oct. 1911–Oct. 1917
Rt. Hon. Sir Robert L. Borden	(U)	Oct. 1917–July 1920
Rt. Hon. Arthur Meighen	(U–L & C)	July 1920–Dec. 1921
Rt. Hon. Wm. Lyon Mackenzie King	(L)	Dec. 1921–June 1926
Rt. Hon. Arthur Meighen	(C)	June 1926–Sept. 1926
Rt. Hon. Wm. Lyon Mackenzie King	(L)	Sept. 1926–Aug. 1930
Rt. Hon. Robert B. Bennett	(C)	Aug. 1930–Oct. 1935
Rt. Hon. Wm. Lyon Mackenzie King	(L)	Oct. 1935–Nov. 1948
Rt. Hon. Louis Stephen St. Laurent	(L)	Nov. 1948–June 1957
Rt. Hon. John G. Diefenbaker	(C)	June 1957–Apr. 1963
Rt. Hon. Lester B. Pearson	(L)	Apr. 1963–Apr. 1968
Rt. Hon. Pierre Elliott Trudeau	(L)	Apr. 1968–June 1979
Rt. Hon. Charles Joseph Clark	(C)	June 1979–Mar. 1980
Rt. Hon. Pierre Elliott Trudeau	(L)	Mar. 1980–June 1984
Rt. Hon. John Napier Turner	(L)	June 1984–Sept. 1984
Rt. Hon. Martin Brian Mulroney	(PC)	Sept. 1984–June 1993
Rt. Hon. Kim Campbell	(PC)	June 1993–Nov. 1993
Rt. Hon. Jean Chrétien	(L)	Nov. 1993–Dec. 2003
Rt. Hon. Paul Martin	(L)	Dec. 2003–Feb. 2006
Rt. Hon. Stephen Harper	(C)	Feb. 2006–Nov. 2015
Rt. Hon. Justin Trudeau	(L)	Nov. 2015–Mar. 2025
Rt. Hon. Mark Carney	(L)	Mar. 2025–present

(C) Conservative
(L) Liberal
(U) Unionist
(PC) Progressive Conservative

Canada

Canada Today
Against All Odds

It has often been said that Canada is a "geographic improbability" a huge, sparsely settled country whose diverse people have only two things in common: a map and a preference not to be absorbed by the United States. As poet Al Purdy put it, it is "an opposite nation talked into existence." Because of Canadians' enormous differences in language and cultural heritage, it is difficult to call its people a "nation." Nor is it politically correct, in the opinion of journalist Andrew Coyne: "The very idea that we are a nation . . . has disappeared. The Parliament of Canada may be so bold as to recognize 'the Québécois' as a nation, but it would not dare to say the same of Canada. We are a superstructure, a federation, perhaps a country—but never a nation." Indeed, many disagree with what Prime Minister Justin Trudeau said after the 2015 national election: "There is no core identity, no mainstream in Canada,' [but] there are shared values—openness, respect, compassion, willingness to work hard, to be there for each other, to search for equality and justice." He started that Canada was a "post national state."

Whatever the case, Canadians have shaped a democratic, peaceful, and prosperous country seemingly against all odds. Canada was created in the middle of the nineteenth century from the remnants of the British empire in North America which managed to escape the United States' momentous revolution in the 18th century and its exuberant "Manifest Destiny" in the 19th century which harbored dreams of the "Stars and Stripes" flying all over North America. Canada was a country born of patience and compromises, not of violent revolution whose unity has been preserved through the years by forbearance and concessions, not by civil war.

For residents of the United States (U.S.), Canada is no longer a region for expansion or merely for recreation. Rather, they see Canada as a vibrant sovereign, country with a British governmental system and characteristics that should be studied and understood. Canada is a neighbor, a very desirable neighbor at that. Former Prime Minister Brian Mulroney was right when he said not long after his 1984 election victory that "if I were the President of the United States, I'd wake up in the morning and probably look at the events around the world—Americans under attack here, U.S. Embassy attacked there, acts of terrorism and violence—I'd look at all that, and I'd look at Canada and say, 'Thank God I have Canada for a neighbor. Now, what can I do for Canada today?'" Canada and the U.S. conduct the world's largest bilateral trade agreement, are each other's best trading partners and are each other's most preferred country for foreign investments.

Population: 41,465,298 in 2024
Capital City: Ottawa (Pop. 1,072,000 in 2022).
Other Principal Cities: Toronto (6,202,225 in 2022), Montreal (4,291,000 in 2022), Vancouver (2,642,825 in 2022), Calgary (1,481,806 in 2022), Edmonton (1,418,118 in 2022), Winnipeg (834,678 in 2022).

Climate: Varying climatic regions from moderate to bitterly cold Arctic, with generally mild summers in the southern areas and long, cold winters.

Neighboring Countries: Canada is bordered by the United States and shares maritime boarders with Russia, Greenland (an autonomous territory of Denmark) and the French Territory of the island St. Pierre and Micuelon. A portion of the United States is also within Canada due to a 1700s error in mapping: the Minnesota Northwest Angle; this land is part of the Northern Lake of the Woods County of Minnesota but is in Canada.

Official Languages: English and French.
Other Tongues: A broad spectrum of languages spoken by immigrants from Europe and Asia with many primary languages and dialects being of First Nations and Inuit Peoples.

Major Religions (2022):

Rank	Percent-Population
No religion	(34.6%)
Catholic Church	(29.9%)
United Church	(3.3%)
Anglican Church	(3.1%)
Eastern Orthodoxy	(1.7%)
Baptist	(1.2%)
Pentecostalism	(1.1%)
Other Christians	(13.0%)
Islam	(4.9%)
Hinduism	(2.3%)
Sikhism	(2.1%)
Buddhism	(1.0%)
Judaism	(0.9%)
Other religions	(0.8%)

Note(s): Religion refers to the person's self-identification as having a connection or affiliation with any religious denomination, group, body, sect, cult or other religiously defined community or system of belief. Religion is not limited to formal membership in a religious organization or group. Persons without a religious connection or affiliation can self-identify as atheist, agnostic or humanist, or can provide another applicable response.
Source(s): Census 2021: Statistics Canada/Statistique Canada (October 26, 2022)

Chief Commercial Products: Canada is a highly industrialized nation producing a wide variety of sophisticated goods; it is also rich in natural resources. Canada's leading exports are natural resources, especially crude petroleum and natural gas, metal ores, diamonds, wheat, lumber, paper and pulp along with automobiles and parts, machinery and equipment, and high technology products.

Major Trading Partners: Below is a list showcasing 15 of Canada's top trading partners, countries that imported the most Canadian shipments by dollar value during 2018. Also shown is each import country's percentage of total Canadian exports.

United States: US$439.6 billion (78% of total Canadian exports)
China: $22.6 billion (4%)
Japan: $11.68 billion (2.1%)
United Kingdom: $10.49 billion (1.9%)
Mexico: $6.49 billion (1.1%)
Netherlands: $5.50 billion (0.97%)
South Korea: $5.14 billion (0.91%)
Germany: $5.13 billion (0.91%)
India: $3.78 billion (0.67%)
Hong Kong: $3.60 billion (0.64%)
Switzerland $3.54 billion (0.63%)
France: $3.16 billion (0.56%)
Brazil: $3.02 billion (0.54%)Belgium: $2.93 billion (0.52%)
Australia $2.33 billion (0.41%)
Norway: $2.25 billion (0.4%)Italy: $1.99 billion (0.35%)
Over nine-tenths (94.65%) of Canadian exports in 2024 were delivered to the above 17 trade partners.

Currency: Canadian Dollar. Its nickname is the "loonie" or "loon" ("toonie" or "toon" for the two-dollar coin) because of the aquatic bird depicted on it.

National Holiday: Canada Day (July 1). In Quebec, the main holiday is June 24, the Fête Nationale, formerly called St-Jean Baptiste Day.
Head of State: His Majesty King Charles III of Great Britain and Canada (since 8 September 2022).
The Queen's Representative: Her Excellency the Right Honourable Mary May Simon (from July 26, 2021).
Head of Government: The Rt. Hon. Mark Carney, Prime Minister (Leader of the Liberal Party), since March 14, 2025.
National Flag: A stylized red maple leaf on a white square flanked by red bars one half the width of the square.

Moreover, the two Nations are close allies in the North Atlantic Treaty Organization (NATO) and the North American Aerospace Defense Command (NORAD).

Canada

What other country but Canada would have harbored the six American diplomats for three months after the escaped from their Embassy in Teheran, Iran, on the fateful day in 1979 when scores of their colleagues were taken hostage and held captive for more than a year? At great risk to their own diplomatic personnel, the Canadians and their ambassador, Ken Taylor, worked with the Central Intelligence Agency to devise an escape plan, issued diplomatic passports to the Americans, closed their embassy in the Iranian capital, and escorted the nervous Americans through the checkpoints and controls onto an airplane bound for home.

The United States accurately conveyed the Nation's gratitude for protecting its diplomats when its government ordered that a sign be posted on a giant billboard overlooking the border into Canada reading, "Thank you, Canada!" This daring rescue was partly fictionalized in the Ben Affleck film, *Argo*, which won the Oscar for best movie in 2012. Responding to charges that the film gave Canada and its ambassador too little credit for the escape, actor/director Affleck publicly stated that the "Canadians did absorb the risk."

After the terrorist attacks of September 11, 2001, that claimed the lives of 24 Canadians as well as over 3,000 Americans and persons from other nations, hundreds of flights were diverted to Canada, including 224 over the Atlantic and 90 over the Pacific; 250 more flights had enough fuel to return to Europe). Communities housed and fed the stranded passengers, mostly Americans. Transport Minister David Collenette remembered: "I felt an immense pride in what Canada was doing to help our American friends. . . . No one complained or argued about financial compensation. Canadians were pulling together in a remarkable way. . . . No one held back. . . . Thank God we got it right." The residents of Gander, Newfoundland, who extended their generosity to 6,700 travelers are commemorated in a successful Broadway musical, "Come from Away."

More than 100,000 Canadians gathered on Parliament Hill in Ottawa to raise American and Canadian flags to honor the victims of 9/11, the largest gathering there ever known. The American embassy was deluged with flowers, and charter buses carried thousands to New York for a grand "Canada Loves New York" weekend in December 2001. Vancouver firefighters raised $535,000 for their fallen comrades and a fourth of them traveled to New York at their own expense to pay their respects at funerals.

Only two weeks after the tragedy, more than 60 skilled tradesmen from Ontario and Alberta went to help rebuild the stricken city. New Yorkers on the sidewalks stopped to shake their hands with one businessman speaking for an entire nation when he told them: "This has been so hard for us all, but because of people like you, we'll all get through it. You have no idea what this means to us. As your neighbor, I thank you." Then Prime Minister Jean Chrétien received the "Statesman of the Year Award" in New York the following year. In 2013, the US gave to Appleton Peace Park in Newfoundland a piece of steel wreckage from the World Trade Center to recall Canadians' help to stranded Americans on 9/11.

Corporal Doug Ford and Constable Diane Bérubé of the Royal Canadian Mounted Police

John F. Kennedy said about Canada: "Geography made us neighbors. History made us friends. And economics made us partners." A quarter century later, President Ronald Reagan made no secret about his reasons for meeting with the Canadian prime minister in March 1985, a practice usually repeated twice a year: "No other country in the world is more important to the United States than Canada, and we are blessed to have such a nation on our northern border." In both of his terms in office, Reagan's first foreign trips were to Canada, as was President Barack Obama's first foreign outing in February 2009.

The first non-citizen of the United States to fly into space with American astronauts was a Canadian, Marc Garneau, later the Liberal party spokesman in the House of Commons. Garneau worked at NASA the rest of the century, flying his third shuttle mission in 1999. Two other Canadians served in the space station: Julie Payette, who made a return visit in May 2009, and Chris Hadfield, who walked in space and commanded the International Space Station.

Canada is the only foreign country that is permitted to locate its embassy on Pennsylvania Avenue. Former Canadian Ambassador Derek Burney had this to say about the modern building, opened in 1989 and situated halfway between the White House and the Capitol: "It conveys the message that I want to convey: Canada counts." Ottawa extended the same privilege to the United States by allowing it to open its new embassy in 1999 on the last vacant lot on Parliament Hill. The site

Canada

is prominent on Sussex Drive, the ceremonial parade route between Parliament and the Prime Minister's residence. When the U.S. embassy was opened in Ottawa, it was the first time a sitting president, Bill Clinton, left the U.S. to do so. Alas, the architecture of the bomb-resistant, four-story steel and concrete structure with 3-inch glass, situated near the National Gallery and Chateau Laurier Hotel, was not universally praised by aesthetically minded Canadians.

The United States and Canada are different countries, but perhaps no two other nations in the world need to remind themselves so often of this fact. As of 2021, Canada had a population of more than 38 million as compared to that of the U.S. with a population (332 million) and an economy ten times larger. However, the land mass of the US is 10% smaller than Canada's. The relationship between the two countries is therefore lopsided and sometimes difficult for the smaller of the two. Former Prime Minister Pierre Elliott Trudeau once remarked that sharing a border with the US is like "sleeping with an elephant. No matter how friendly or even-tempered is the beast, if I may call it that, one is affected by every twitch and grunt!"

Nevertheless, Canada is that country with which the U.S. is most successful at settling differences; the frictions existing between the countries are always manageable. The most important reason for these good relations is the common-sense and good will they are inclined to show toward the other. In fact, Americans and Canadians have been well practiced at "splitting the difference" yet with the end of the North American Free Trade Agreement (NAFTA) and of the U.S.-Mexico-Canada Agreement (USMCA), some discord has occurred. Enacting only minor changes, however, the USMCA took effect and replaced the NAFTA on July 1, 2020.

CULTURE

Canadians tend to focus on the differences between them and persons from the US even though, as Pierre Berton admitted, they are often "tongue-tied" when asked to define these distinctions. "We know we're not the same but we can't express it succinctly." Americans are inclined to emphasize the similarities. Canadians do not appreciate it when their neighbors to the south view them as "just like us," not considering Canada a foreign country. Still, there is, to be sure, an extraordinary degree of military and economic interdependence between the two countries.

According to a 2005 SES Research poll, Canadians and Americans still find their countries to be defined more by their similarities than by their differences. Asked which country in the world is most like Canada in terms of human rights, Canadians chose the U.S. more than any (43%), while 51% of Americans chose Canada. Two thirds of Canadians (67%) had a generally positive attitude toward the U.S. The sincere and constant references to Canada as the U.S.' "partner" and "good neighbor" help erase in Americans' minds the sharp line that usually appears between "us and them." In fact, U.S. residents traveling in Canada see people who dress almost exactly as they do. Canadians wear baseball caps, jeans, jogging shoes, sweatshirts, and T-shirts with writing on them—basically the same things that are in style in the United States.

People from the U.S. also meets people who, by and large, speak English as they do except those 22% who speak French as a mother tongue and who therefore might speak English with a French accent. The English that Canadians speak much more closely resembles that spoken in the United States than in the United Kingdom. This is understandable in an age of radio and television, quick travel and strong trade ties. A few British usages do linger on in Canada, though. Most say "aluminium," with the accent on the third syllable, "controversy" with the accent on the second syllable, and "schedule," as if there were no "c" in the word. "Been" is pronounced like "bean," and "again" like "a-gane." A "lieutenant" is addressed as "leftenant." Also, the "i" in the last syllable of words ending in "-ile" is likely to be pronounced distinctly, rather than to be swallowed, as most Americans do. "Out" and "house" are spoken more like "ute" or "whuse."

Perhaps the most distinctive sign that a Canadian is speaking is the "eh?," pronounced as a long "a," which is frequently tacked onto the end of sentences. There is a rough French equivalent in Quebec: *hein*. In addition, writing in Canada is slightly different: not all Canadians have dropped the "u" when writing such words as "labour" or "colour." "Centre," "cheque," "theatre" and "connexion" are not American spellings, and "defense" is still spelled with a "c," as is the custom in Britain.

French-speakers, called "francophones" in Canada, in contrast to "Anglophones," English-speakers, have opened the gates to let in hundreds of English words, such as le *fun, dialer* ("to dial"), *la potate* ("potato"), *le smoked beef, le hamburger, les king pins, le brake drum, un party,* or *une shop*. An example of this usage can be seen in an advertisement for an *Atelier Mecanique-Machine Shop Crankshaft* which once appeared in the yellow pages of the Montreal telephone book: *Moteur nettoyé et testé. Moteur grindé all surfaces. Crankshaft nettoyé et testé with sonoflux process. Crankshaft grindé with micro finish*.

The mixture of the two languages to form what is often derisively referred to as "Franglais" or "Frenglish" has perhaps reached its height among Acadians in New Brunswick. One francophone from Moncton provided *Maclean's* with an example of the "chiac" dialect: *J'ai drivé mon friend à l'airport, but la plane a také off à dix minutes de quatre. Too bad que j'avais pas findé ça out avant*. The French spoken elsewhere in New Brunswick sounds little different from that in Poitou and Brittany, France, from whence their ancestors hailed. Yet, the pronunciation and slang of the French spoken on the streets of Quebec and Acadia are intriguingly different from Parisian French.

Totem poles at Museum of Anthropology, University of British Columbia
Credit: Province of British Columbia

Canada

In recent years, there has been a tremendous improvement in the quality of French spoken in Quebec due to the provincial legislation on the use of French on Radio Canada; TV is also a good example of international French. Nevertheless, Candice Bergen's French-language Sprint ads were taken off the air in 1995 because her French was "too Parisian."

Americans also find that most Canadians know far more about the United States than Americans know about Canada. For instance, a 1995 Louis Harris poll revealed that a mere 1% of residents of the U.S. knew that Jean Chrétien was prime minister. Conversely, only 11% of American university students surveyed in 1989 knew which city Canada's capital is; only 1% knew the name of the premier of Quebec, a province much larger than Texas, bordering three New England states, and the United States' sixth-largest trading partner in the world.

Further the results of a 2011 survey published in Canada's National Post revealed "that fewer than half of all Americans can name Canada's capital and that close to two-thirds of our neighbours to the south admit they learned nothing about this country's history in school."

In another example of how little residents of the U.S. knew about their neighbor to the north, almost twenty years ago, entertainer Rick Mercer became famous by producing TV specials such as *Talking to Americans* that brought howls of laughter to Canadians. He asked people on the streets of America, including Congressmen and Harvard professors, ludicrous questions highlighting just how little they knew about their northern neighbor.

Canadians watch more American television than Canadian, and what Canadian news programs they watch bring incomparably more news about the United States than American newscasts bring about Canada, despite the penetration into the American broadcasting elite of such Canadians as ABC's former anchorman Peter Jennings, Kevin Newman (formerly of ABC's Nightline), and CBS's Morley Safer. Controversial talk-show hostess Jenny Jones hails from Canada, as does Robert (AKA Robin) MacNeil of the earlier MacNeil-Lehrer Report. McNeil, who has had a summer home in his native Halifax, the setting of the first of his novels, *Burden of Desire*, confesses to "a sense of sentimental curiosity" about Canada, but admits: "The Canada I grew up in was white bread, dominated by Anglo-Scots and Quebec. Now Canada is a wondrously multi-coloured, multilingual country. It's fascinating, but it's not the Canada I grew up in." This is why he became an American, as he described in *Looking for My Country. Finding Myself in America*.

Canadians often read such newsmagazines from the U.S. as *Time*, while few Americans have ever even held a Canadian magazine, such as *Maclean's*, in their hands, let alone read one. Insofar as 88% of all residents in the U.S. live farther than 100 miles from the Canadian border and cannot see or hear Canadian programs by simply switching on their dial, Americans must make a more concerted effort to become informed about Canada, and few do.

The imbalance as to what U.S. residents know about Canada is slowly changing. Major American newsmagazines and newspapers carry much more news about Canada. In the past, few American institutions offered Canadian studies courses; now, this is a popular field of study for undergraduates, especially those attending colleges and universities in proximity of the Canadian-U.S. border. Moreover, as of 2022, the Association for Canadian Studies in the United States (ACSUS) has more than 500 individual and institutional members from the United States, Canada, and other countries. The *Toronto Star* even complained: "Curse those Americans. They are taking away one of our great Canadian preoccupations. They are not ignoring us anymore." In any case, visitors from the U.S. can still chat with Canadians about a wide variety of subjects ranging from the president's difficulties with Congress and midwestern farmers' financial problems to the World Series, Super Bowl, and Academy or Grammy Award nominations, forgetting in the process that he is talking to a foreigner.

The popular culture on both sides of the border is strikingly similar. One hears rock, country-western and gospel music, in rock or traditional form. either blaring out from car radios or softly channeled

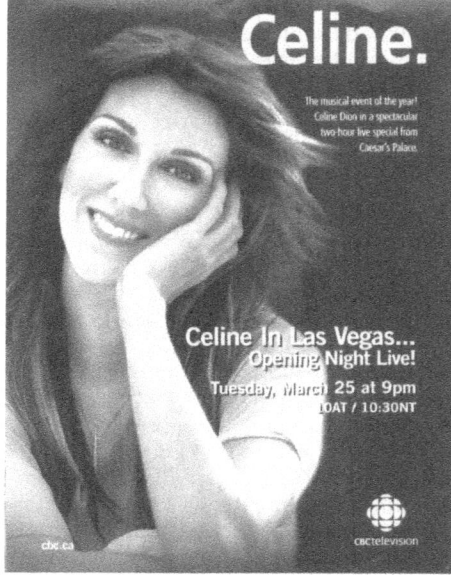

into homes by radio. Hank Snow, Gordon Lightfoot, Neil Young, Anne Murray, Bryan Adams, Michelle Wright, Buffy Sainte-Marie, a native North American who wrote the Oscar-winning theme song for the film, "An Officer and a Gentleman," Sarah McLachlan (who has starred both as rock singer and women's rights advocate), rhythm and blues diva Deborah Cox, jazz pianist and singer Diana Krall from Nanaimo, British Columbia (BC), the rock groups Crash Test Dummies, Barenaked Ladies (a fun-loving male quintet), Drake, Bublé and Nickelback are all Canadians who have been popular on both sides of the border.

In 1997 Ottawa rocker, Alanis Morissette, who won the favorite album and female artist awards at the American Music Awards along with Justin Bieber

Nia Vardalos in *My Big Fat Greek Wedding*

Canada

are Canadian artists who have done well in the U.S. Ontario native, Shania Twain, was named best female country artist. Her "The Woman in Me" surpassed "Patsy Cline's Greatest Hits" as the best-selling female country album ever. By 1999, she had become history's top-selling country singer and was named the entertainer of the year at the 2000 Academy of Country Music Awards. Quebec superstar, Céline Dion, who is the top-selling singer of all time in France, won top album and best pop album at the Grammys in 1997. By 2007, she had sold 200 million records, and her Las Vegas show, "A New Day," had grossed more than US$400 million during its four-year run. Because Morissette, Dion, and Twain each won two Grammy awards in 1999 and Joni Mitchell of Saskatchewan received the U.S. National Academy of Recording Arts and Sciences lifetime achievement award in 2001, few persons disputed *Maclean's* claim that "Canadian divas virtually rule the world of female pop."

Canadians laugh at the same comedians, such as Dan Aykroyd, Bob and Doug McKenzie, Jim Carrey, and "Wayne's World" star Mike Myers, all Canadians. One of the biggest box office hit in the history of screen comedy, *Ghostbusters*, was a product of Canadian filmmaker Ivan Reitman. His Montreal-born son, Jason Reitman, directed one of 2008's hottest movies, *Juno*, which was filmed in Vancouver and starred two Canadians—Ellen Page and Michael Cera. Two years later, his football film, *The Blind Side*, was a blockbuster; its female lead, Sandra Bullock, won the best actress Oscar. Even Warner Brothers was founded by Canadians.

Quebec's cinema is thriving, and Quebecers produce excellent French-language films which are of a different style than those viewed by Americans. An example is *Maria Chapdelaine*, based on Louis Hemon's classic 1914 novel, a moving portrait of the restricted life led by Quebec women in the frontier.

While residents of the U.S. anglophone Canadians usually go to the same movies, Canadians watch more Hollywood films than films produced in Canada, and English Canadian filmmakers must search hard for audiences. In fact, only 2% of box office revenues are derived from Canadian films. Canadians have far less money to spend. Additionally, Canadian producers have trouble getting some of their films shown on Canadian screens because U.S. companies largely control distribution of movies in Canada. In order to stimulate the industry, an annual Whistler Film Festival awards prizes for promising Canadian feature films.

Some films to which Americans flock are Canadian, often unbeknownst to Americans. Winnipeg's Nia Vardalos took the cinema world by storm in 2002 with her award-winning film, *My Big Fat Greek Wedding*, which was filmed in Toronto and was the year's fifth-highest grossing movie. Norman Jewison, one of the world's most successful directors as a result of such blockbusters as *Fiddler on the Roof* and *Moonstruck*, much of which was filmed in Toronto, is Canadian. In 1999, Jewison, who received a special Academy Award for lifetime achievement, founded the Canadian Film Centre in north Toronto, an elite institution for ten highly selected filmmakers annually and the only film school in the world that produces its own features.

James Cameron, born in Kapuskasing, Ontario, and raised near Niagara Falls, studied physics at Fullerton College, specializes in gargantuan high-tech films of mass destruction, such as *The Terminator*, *Judgment Day*, *Aliens*, *The Abyss*, *True Lies*, and *Titanic*. In 2010, his three-dimensional *Avatar* broke all records for box office receipts to date. In the words of Fox's president, Cameron "has taken Hollywood by the throat and they do what he says."

The 1997 Academy Award for best film was given to *The English Patient*, based on the best-selling novel by Canadian author Michael Ondaatje. Assisted in his research by a grant from the Canada Council, in 1992 Ondaatje shared the Booker Prize, the world's most prominent English-language literary award. His *Anil's Ghost* won him both the Governor-General's Award and the Prix Médicis, France's highest prize for a foreign novel, in 2000. Later, in 2007 Ondaatje's *Divisadero* won him his fifth Governor General's Literary Award for English-language fiction, tying the record of the late Hugh MacLennan.

In 2004, Canadian director Denys Arcand made history when his film, *The Barbarian Invasions*, became the first Canadian movie to win an Oscar for best foreign-language film. In 2007, Indian-born Canadian director, Deepa Mahta, won a best foreign-language Oscar nomination for her extraordinarily successful Hindi-language film, *Water*. This was the first non-French-Canadian film to receive such an honor. In the same year, Mahta's *Partition* opened, depicting the tragic carnage following the division of India in 1947.

Many American films and TV shows are filmed in Canada. With the average cost of film-making in the U.S. having soared to $76.9 million by 2000, and close to double that today, it is small wonder that producers are attracted to Canada with its generous provincial and federal tax breaks to foreign and domestic film companies and its film crews. To lure more American filmmakers back to Ontario in the wake of a rising value of the Canadian dollar, which has scared off some Hollywood productions, the province offered even greater tax inducements.

Toronto has become the third-largest film-producing center in North America after Los Angeles and New York City. Two of the 2006 Oscar nominations were filmed in the Canadian West: *Brokeback Mountain* near Calgary and *Capote* in Winnipeg, Manitoba. U.S. TV networks, including ABC and CBS, buy Canadian police serials like "Rookie Blue" and "Flashpoint" at the discount rate of $350,000 per episode, far cheaper than the typical license fee of well above $1 million an episode.

Vancouver and Montreal also attract more and more American moviemakers. British Columbia boasts of $1 billion annual revenues from film production, two-thirds of which comes from the U.S. This can also cause problems for Canadian filmmakers because high-cost American productions inflate the prices that Canadian film crews charge. However, the "runaway productions" are an unmistakable boon for Canadian film people. Yet, some union actors in the U.S. call Canada a scab country for aggressively courting American film, television and advertisement production with tax rebates and other incentives. Films of the past have featured Canadians such as Genevieve Bujold, Margot Kidder, Christopher Plummer, William Shatner, Raymond Massey, Michael J. Fox (the "all-American boy"), Keanu Reeves, and Donald Southerland.

Canadians and U.S. residents read much of the same literature, by such authors as Jack Kerouac, Will Durant, Saul Bellow, Arthur Hailey, Robertson Davies, Mordecai Richler, Brian Moore, Morley Callaghan and Alice Munro. All are Canadians. Both countries also sometimes forbid the same

Canada

books. In 2005, Nova Scotia's education department banned Harper Lee's *To Kill a Mockingbird*.

Alice Munro, who hails from southern Ontario, is one of the greatest short-story writers of all time. With her stories focusing on Canadians and their peculiarities, Munro is praised for her exploration of large themes in small-town settings of Ontario. Having won her second Giller Prize for her collection of eight stories entitled *Runaway*, which appeared on the *New York Times'* bestseller list as well as on Canada's, in 2009 she became the first short-story writer to win the Man Booker international prize. The judges called Munro's body of work "practically perfect." In 2012, at age 81, Munro published her fourteenth volume, *Dear Life* and a year later she became the first Canada-based author to win the Nobel Prize in Literature, being cited as the "master of the contemporary short story."

Other authors focus on their native Canada and are read and admired in both countries. Perhaps the best-known Canadian author is Lucy Maud Montgomery, whose precocious, pert, and lovable book about *Anne of Green Gables* has delighted children and adults from scores of nations since its publication in 2008.

Hugh MacLennan's *Two Solitudes* is the classic study of the separate worlds in which the *Québécois* and anglophone Canadians live. In 2001, Alistair MacLeod became the first Canadian to win the world's richest literary prize, the International IMPAC Dublin Literary Award, for his debut novel, *No Great Mischief*, a work later translated into 14 languages. Pierre Berton was perhaps Canada's most prolific writer, producing best-selling books on the country's history and people almost on an annual basis. When he died in 2004, writer June Callwood said of him: "It's as if the biggest tree has fallen down."

Margaret Atwood writes about the lives and challenges of modern women. In her view, "survival" is the "single unifying and informing symbol . . . which holds the country [Canada] together and helps the people in it for common ends." Atwood also points to the search for identity: "Canadians are forever taking the national pulse like doctors at a sickbed; the aim is not to see whether the patient will live well but simply whether he will live at all. . ." Attwood's ninth novel, *Alias Grace*, a murder mystery, was a global sensation in 1996, winner of the Giller Prize that was made into a TV miniseries. A televised adaptation of her novel, *The Handmaid's Tale*, won the 2018 Golden Globe for best TV drama.

Many of Attwood's books had been translated into other languages and in 2000 she became only the second Canadian to win Britain's highly competitive Booker Prize for *The Blind Assassin*, an epic tale about a once-wealthy family in Ontario. Attwood's sly, operatic and feminist retelling of *The Odyssey* from the perspective of the dutiful wife of Homer's hero in her 2005 *The Penelopiad: The Myth of Penelope and Odysseus*, was an instant success. Attwood's 2003 novel, *Oryx and Crake*, followed in 2009 by *Year of the Flood*, a story of a totalitarian dystopia, led in 2013 to the last book in a trilogy, MaddAddam.

By 2006, Attwood's popularity was such that that she began using an electronic pen to activate a remote robotic arm that replicated her autograph for fans thousands of miles away. In 2016, Atwood moved to a different genre, co-authoring a superhero comic book series Angel Catbird, with illustrator Johnnie Christmas. The central character in these graphic novels, scientist Strig Feleedus, is victim of an accidental mutation that left him with the body parts and powers of both a cat and a bird.

In 2002, Saskatoon novelist Yann Martel beat out two other Canadians on the short list, Rohinton Mistry and the late Carol Shields, to win the Booker Prize with his novel, *Life of Pi*, a magical fable of a young man ship-wrecked with a Bengal tiger. In 2012, it was made into a movie and captured multiple Oscars, including best director. Clearly Canada's book business is thriving.

Stephen Leacock was one of the most famous Canadians of his time and in his heyday from 1910 to 1925 was the world's best-selling English-language humorist. His stories bring alive the early Ontario of his childhood. Rudy Wiebe's writings, including The Temptations of Big Bear and *The Scorched-Wood People*, describe with great vision and understanding the lives of Indians, Métis and white settlers in the Canadian West. Northrop Frye, who hailed from Ontario and taught his entire career at the University of Toronto, is widely acclaimed as perhaps the greatest literary critic of our time. American-born Carol Shields, who moved to Canada in 1957 and died in 2003, won the 1995 Pulitzer Prize for her novel about sexual and family values, *The Stone Diaries*. In 2013, the Ontario-born and New Zealand-based Eleanor Catton was presented the Man-Booker Prize for The Luminaries; at 28 she was the youngest writer ever to win this award.

Quebec also boasts authors of international renown. Anne Hebert, who died in 2000, became famous in 1970 through her great novel, *Kamouraska*, which was later made into a film in Quebec. Gabriele Roy wrote Quebec's first urban, socially aware novel, *Bonheur d'Occasion*, known to anglophones as *The Tin Flute*, just after the Second World War. This novel, like *Maria Chapdelaine*, deals with survival and a young girl's rejection of a glamorous lover who could have taken her out of the narrow French Canadian world in which she lived. Also, like *Maria Chapdelaine, The Tin Flute* was made into a movie in Quebec in 1983.

Roch Carrier has written perceptively and humorously about the gulf between the *Québécois* and anglophone Canadians. In *La Guerre, Yes Sir* he describes Quebecers' negative attitudes about fighting in the two world wars. In a short story, "The Hockey Sweater," the mother of a young boy in rural Quebec orders a Montreal Canadiens hockey shirt from a Montreal department store, which in error sends a Toronto Maple Leafs jersey instead. The boy is panic-stricken. But with no other hockey shirt to wear, he goes out to play with his friends, only to be shunned with the parish priest ordering him from the ice. The boy is devastated and goes to the parish church and prays that moths will descend from heaven and consume the shirt so that his mother will buy him another. In an interview with *Maclean's*, Carrier implied that the wall which once separated Quebec from anglophone Canada has become much more porous: "When my books were first translated, everybody felt it was a kind of treason, giving my books to the rest of the country. But today everybody wants to be on the other side of the frontier."

Translation into English can today be indispensable for a French-language novel, as Gil Courtemanche discovered. His first novel, *A Sunday at the Pool in Kigali*, was a modest success in Quebec when it was published in French in 2000. But after Knopf Publishers had it translated into English in 2003, it quickly won him international fame and was translated into 13 more languages. How many more nuggets might there be in the Quebec literary scene?

If residents of the United States do not want to go to films, read books or listen to music, they can simply sit at home and immerse themselves in Americana by playing "Trivial Pursuit," a game invented by two Canadians, Chris Haney and Scott Abbott. Or they can pick up a telephone, invented by Canadian Alexander Graham Bell in Canada before moving to the U.S. If they are hungry, they can go to McDonalds, founded by Canadians. One gradually begins to wonder whether what is sometimes called the "Americanization" of Canadian culture might, in some cases, be better called the "Canadianization" of American culture.

American films, television and radio broadcasting, reading material, music, slang and styles do continue to pour northward across the border because

Canada

these are attractive to most Canadians. Canadians are usually the first to admit that American culture is produced primarily for domestic consumption and that no American can ever force it on Canadians. Nevertheless, Canadians worry about the massive influx of American customs and usages. It is therefore Canadian policy to encourage and to subsidize Canadian cultural products in order to avoid being engulfed by American culture and to make it possible for talented Canadians to work in Canada rather than seeking their fame and fortune in the United States. The government wishes to help offer the population an alternative.

As of 2022, the federal budget devotes $500 million for the recovery of the arts, culture, heritage, and sports sectors as well as to support community-level festivals and other in-person cultural events, a, sums lower than in most western European countries. These cuts come at a time of intense upheaval in many spheres of the arts. A communications minister in the federal cabinet disperses money through a variety of institutions which enjoy a high degree of autonomy from the federal government and which have become powerful lobbying groups when their freedom or budgets are trampled on as the National Film Board and Telefilm financially support Canadian cinema. Provincial governments also help finance the production of films, and their censorship can prevent "X-rated" movies from being shown in Canadian theaters.

The Canadian film industry had created an Academy Awards ceremony of its own called the "Genie Awards" that were given out between 1980 and 2012. In 2012, the Genie Awards combined with the Gemini Awards, the equivalent of the Emmy Award in the U.S., creating the Canadian Screen Awards. These new awards are conferred annually by the Academy of Canadian Cinema & Television to recognize excellence in Canadian film, English-language television, and digital media productions.

The National Arts Centre in Ottawa, which began operating in 1969, contains stages of various sizes entertaining audiences of all ages. The semi-independent Canada Council dispenses grants to a wide array of professional artists and organizations including writers, publishers, translators, musicians and composers, dancers, painters, sculptors, photographers and film makers. Government money was instrumental in building and maintaining the National Ballet Company in Toronto, *le Theatre du Nouveau Monde* and *les Grands Ballets Canadiens* in Montreal, the Canadian Opera Company, the Stratford Shakespearean Festival in Ontario, and more than 160 theater groups

Typical road sign in English and French

across the country. Cirque du Soleil, founded in 1984, and based in Montreal received initial funding from the government; the largest theatrical producer in the world, it offers shows on all six inhabited continents.

Canadians, most of whom live along the U.S. border, listen freely to American radio and watch much American television. The most heavily cabled country in the world, Canadians are among the most generous donors to American public television stations along the U.S. border. The Canadian federal and provincial governments do nothing to prevent their citizens from tuning in to U.S. stations, but do go to great expense and effort to provide Canadian alternatives and to reinforce a sense of Canadian community by making it possible for Canadians everywhere in the country to learn about each other.

Canada's first television stations, CBLT in Toronto and CBFT in Montreal, began operations in 1952, under the banner of the leadership of the government-created Canadian Broadcasting Corporation or CBC, called *Radio Canada* in Quebec. The CBC operates radio and television networks in French and English, as well as in many native languages, throughout the country. CBC sponsors a 24-hour all-news channel in English—*Newsworld*—while *Radio Canada* does the same in French through RDI. To strengthen its bottom line, CBC carries advertising on its TV networks and two it its four radio networks.

There are two rapidly proliferating, privately-operated networks: Canadian Television (CTV) in anglophone Canada and *Reseau de Television* (*TVA*) in francophone Canada. Since 1998, TVA, Quebec's most popular French-language TV network must be included in the mandatory cable-TV selection across Canada. In 1997, CTV launched Canada's first round-the-clock headline news service—CTV News 1. Demonstrating its reach, CTV outbid CBC for the 2010 and 2012 Olympic Games. There are many private radio stations and a proliferation of specialty channels on cable. A variety of Canadian channels beam into American homes through DirecTV, setting a trend to bring more Canadian programming to viewers in the U.S.

Public money enables the CBC to offer more elevated and experimental programming. However, the CBC is not freed from the constant battle over ratings as the country entered a 500-channel universe. The beleaguered service has tried to compete with private broadcasters by imitating their programming in some ways, but this has weakened the public's willingness to continue to support it. It seems that only the lucrative *Hockey Night in Canada* keeps them alive; CBC and Radio-Canada face a continual identity crisis: do they offer a service or a product?

In order to ensure that Canadian networks, private or public, do not simply buy cheaper American programs, the Canadian Radio-Television and Telecommunications Commission establishes "Canadian Content" guidelines. "Canadian Content" is defined by means of a complicated formula involving whether the cast, singers, songwriters or production team are Canadian citizens. This applies even to pornography films. The exact quotas change according to the political winds. Radio stations must devote 30% of their airtime to Canadian music, even though only 13% of music purchased in record stores is Canadian. Further ownership of TV and radio stations, newspapers and magazines is restricted to Canadians or Canadian companies.

The government's efforts notwithstanding, Canadian television programs claimed only a fraction of the audience share when compared with programming from the U.S. This has led many Canadians to wonder whether the nation has a national culture distinct from the culture of the U.S. While Canada does have a culture of its own, many find it difficult to preserve insofar as such a culturally magnetic country as the U.S. is so close. Of course, it is difficult for Canadian culture to remain distinct in light of the facts that about 80% of magazines on newsstands, more than 60% of books, 90% of recordings, 64% of TV programs, and 94% of films are foreign, overwhelmingly from the U.S.

In order to "have the means to communicate with our own people," in the words of ex-Prime Minister Chrétien, Canada insists on exempting cultural industries from its two free-trade agreements with the U.S. Such Canadian governmental decisions as slapping an 80% excise tax on *Sports Illustrated Canada* and other "split-run" magazines (which have Canadian editions and advertising, but mostly American editorial content) and withdrawing Country Music Television's broadcasting license and awarding it to a Canadian-owned country channel, are

Canada

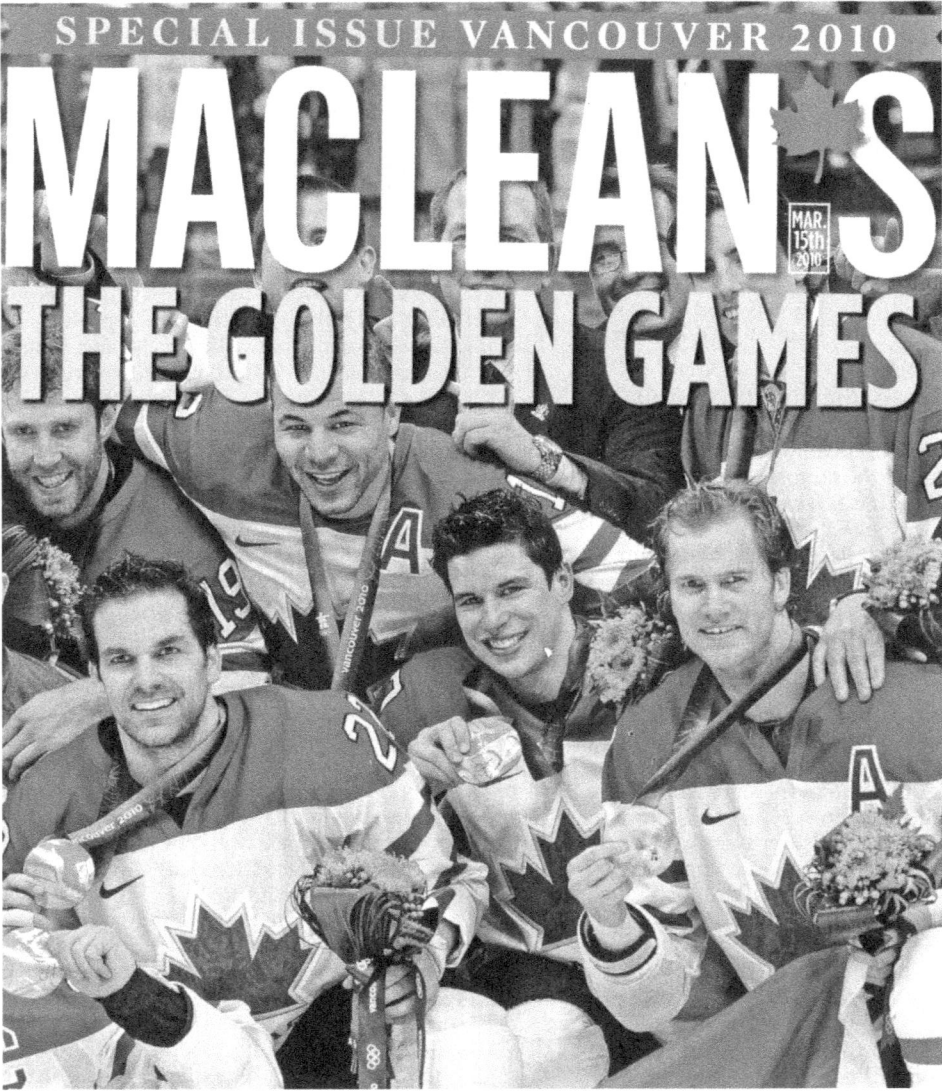

Olympic Gold in 2010!

bound to antagonize Americans. In 1997, the U.S. sought and won a ruling from the World Trade Organization: Canadian punitive taxes on split-run magazines, as well as postal subsidies to Canadian magazines, violate international trade rules. The dispute was resolved in 1999.

Canada's next moves were to convene a summit meeting of 20 culture ministers (excluding Americans) to discuss international misgivings about the "onslaught" of U.S. films, TV, and music. Then, in 1999. Parliament passed legislation prohibiting Canadians from advertising in split-run magazines; negotiations between Ottawa and Washington were commenced to head off a conflict, and the dispute was resolved. For the first time, the U.S. accepted the principle that countries can take steps to limit imports in order to protect the viability of local culture. The Canadians agreed to allow American publishers to produce special Canadian editions as long as less than 18% of its advertising pages are from Canadian advertisers aimed at Canadian readers. The Canadian government would provide annual operating subsidies to the Canadian magazine industry. In cultural terms, the border is not undefended. In 2005, Canada approved in UNESCO the first international treaty designed to protect music, movies and other cultural treasures from foreign competition; the U.S. found itself in a minority of two.

The American sports fan notices a few unfamiliar sports in Canada, such as curling, but most are strikingly similar. Ice hockey, reportedly invented at Kingston's Tete du Pont Barracks on a Christmas day in 1855 by a group of bored soldiers, who tied blades to their boots and used field hockey sticks and an old lacrosse ball, is a Canadian export to the world. As of 2018, Canada leads the world with 3,000 indoor and 5,000 outdoor rinks, compared with 584 and 2665 in Russia, respectively, and 1,535 and 500 respectively in the United States.

The National Hockey League (NHL) is, in fact, *international*, with more professional teams in the U.S. than in Canada. Six Canadian teams faced serious financial difficulties and threatened to relocate in the U.S. The Winnipeg Jets left in 1995, and the Quebec Nordiques went to Denver a year later. In 2001, 80% of the fabled Montreal Canadiens, once known as *Les Glorieux*, and all of the Molson Centre where they play were bought by a Colorado businessman, George Gillett. The Canadiens remain in Montreal, and Gillett respects the Canadiens' spirit, which he calls "truly a religion and a passion." In 2003 the Ottawa Senators filed for bankruptcy protection, and fears were openly expressed that half the Canadian teams might not exist a year later.

Canada produced the first woman in the NHL, Mamon Rhéaume, backup goalie for the Nashville Knights. One had to admire a 122-lb Québécoise wearing size 5 skates and children's-sized equipment who shared the ice with players almost twice her size. Along with other female stars, she helped inspire thousands of Canadian girls to take up ice hockey. In the 2002–03 season, a record 61,000 females registered for teams across Canada, 7,000 more than the previous season and five times more than a decade earlier. In rural areas ,some former boys-only squads are filling their rosters with girls. The payoff came in the 2006 Olympic Games in Turin, where the Canadian women took gold; they repeated this feat in the 2010 Vancouver Games.

American teams are well-stocked with Canadian players; in fact, 45% (down from 96.7% in 1967) of the NHL players are Canadian. Priceless hockey property such as Wayne Gretzky, the "Great One" who retired in 1999 and later coached the Phoenix Coyotes, and widely considered to be the greatest to ever play the game (and ranking among the pantheon of Canadian hockey greats: Maurice "The Rocket" Richard, Gordie Howe, and Mario Lemiuex), is known and admired almost as much in the United States as in Canada and helped make professional hockey so popular in the U.S. One mystery remains unexplained in this cross-border sport: most Canadian players (including Gretzky) shoot left-handed, while most Americans shoot right-handed.

The 2010 and 2014 Winter Olympics in Vancouver and Sochi brought Canada glorious victories over the Americans in both men's and women's hockey, a sport many Canadians think they own. After all, what other country in the world puts the sport

Canada

on its currency? The five-dollar bill shows kids playing hockey on a pond with a quotation from Roch Carrier's beloved short story, "The Hockey Sweater: "The winters of my childhood were long, long seasons. We lived in three places—the school, the church and the skating rink—but our real life was on the skating rink." Canadian writer Adam Gopnik asserted: "the way that you show yourself to be authentically Canadian is by engaging with hockey." In what other country would a sitting prime minister write a detailed history of the sport, as Stephen Harper did: *A Great Game: The Forgotten Leafs and the Rise of Professional Hockey.*

Even Canadian troops in Afghanistan put down their weapons to view their teams' triumphs. They were joined by 85% of Canadians at home who reportedly watched their men's hockey team defeat the American players 3–2 in a sudden-death overtime thriller in the last event of the games. Sidney Crosby, captain of the NHL's Pittsburgh Penguins and the youngest captain ever to lift the Stanley Cup in victory, fired the magic shot. This was Canada's eighth Olympic men's hockey gold medal since 1920, and it ignited an outburst of Canadian patriotism few people could have ever imagined in this divided country. There were red maple leaves all over, on flags, signs and clothing, and *O Canada* could be heard everywhere. Even many normally modest Canadians were taken aback by their own public outpouring of pride in their athletes, who in 2010 won the most gold medals any country had ever won in any Winter Olympic Games—fourteen—capturing medals in nine different sports.

The success of the national team was the result of a program to finance the Olympic athletes' preparation to the tune of $117 million. The motto was controversial: "Own the Podium." Some found this too arrogant, too boastful, yes, too American. But it worked. The Vancouver Games were a smashing success from beginning to end. Three billion persons watched the opening ceremonies, and 3.5 billion tuned in to the Games at some point during the 17 days to see what a winter sport superpower Canada had become.

Canadians' winning ways continued at the Sochi Olympics in 2014, where they captured 24 medals, including 9 golds. The first gold and silver medals were won by two sisters from Quebec in mogul skiing: Justine and Chloé Dufour-Lapointe, with big sister Maxime finishing 12th. Only Russia, the U.S. and Norway earned more. Their men's and women's hockey teams captured gold at Sochi. The men became the first team to win back-to-back titles since 1980. The

Canadian women take Olympic hockey gold in 2006 and again in 2010 and 2014.

Source: *Maclean's*

Canada

women won a barn burner against their American rivals 3–2.

A troubling aspect of professional hockey in Canada came to light in 1997. To claw their way into the NHL, many adolescent Canadian boys enter an intense and regimented system, which has deep roots in Canada. It culminates in 49 "major junior" teams divided into three leagues and lumped together under an umbrella organization called the Canadian Hockey League (CHL). Talented players as young as ten are drawn into the system and beginning at age 14 top prospects hire agents and are aggressively pursued by the top clubs. At age 16 or 17 players often move away from home and are billeted with families paid by the clubs. Attending unfamiliar high schools where they do not play on school teams, they become so dependent on their all-powerful coaches that they are easy prey for abuse, sexual and otherwise. The NCAA, to which only Simon Fraser among Canadian universities belongs, considers CHL teams to be professional, so its players are barred from college athletics on both sides of the border.

Fifty-two percent of NHL players come through the CHL system, and over the years it has produced more professional hockey players than any other organization in the world. Only 10% come from college or high school teams although 30% of NHL players went to college. But since only 6% of players coming out of major junior or college teams ever play in the NHL, more and more young players weigh their options between the CHL and intercollegiate hockey that results in a college education.

Players who do not survive the CHL are unable to continue playing on American or Canadian university teams. With this in mind, Dave Dupuis turned his back on the CHL and became the first Inuit to play NCAA hockey. His coach at Skidmore asked: "How many kids who go to a private liberal arts college can say they've hunted a wolf, a walrus, tracked a polar bear or set up a fishing net on a fall salmon run to help feed his community?" Unlike their American counterparts, Canadian universities do not offer athletic scholarships.

It is no wonder that enrollment in the CHL system is declining steeply. Even the number of young Canadians playing hockey is going down as more now play soccer than hockey. It is a problem that the high costs of maintaining ice rinks have caused a distressing number of them to close. One way to deal with this is the introduction at some rinks of artificial ice made with a plastic polymer. Nobody is happy with this alternative since it makes stopping and turning harder, and experts admit it is only "80% like a real ice surface." One small aboriginal community in northern Alberta, Fort Chipewyan, opened the first such rink.

Although two-thirds of Canadians say that hockey is important for the country, according to a 1999 poll, 60% think the player development system needs change; 85% believe the sport needs to be overhauled. One player put it this way: "There's too much emphasis on size and hitting, and not enough on finesse and skill." A March 6, 2000, *Maclean's* cover story was entitled "Blood Sport," and the magazine reported in 2003 that a third of the 33,000 referees in minor-league hockey quits every year because of abuse from parents, players and coaches. Its message: "Relax, it's just a game."

One would not have known that in 2004 when the NHL's Todd Bertuzzi brutally attacked Steve Moore from behind and broke his neck in an internationally televised game. Bertuzzi was banned for the rest of the season. Nevertheless, the NHL cannot bring itself to ban fighting even though a 2011 poll showed that 60% of Canadians favored banning it and another 9.5% were "torn" over the issue. Nor can it draft tougher rules on violence; regrettably, fighting seems to sell tickets. It is said only half in jest that the only time Canadians' politeness ends is when they strap on skates. Rules are selectively enforced as frontier justice of revenge and retribution is encouraged, not just tolerated.

That "rink rage" is a continuing problem was demonstrated in 2006 when a father, who was furious that his son had been benched, choked the coach until the latter lost consciousness. Another dad slammed a referee's head against a metal door, while a mother threw coffee in the face of a player who had cross-checked her son from behind. Forgiving judges gave them all light fines and temporary bans from rinks.

One observer noted: "Outside the rink, hockey adults can be the nicest people. It's almost like they check their brains at the door." In Vancouver fan rage ran out of control after the Stanley Cup playoffs in June 2011. The defeat of the Vancouver Canucks ignited one of Canada's worst ever experiences of rioting. Mobs went on a four-hour rampage through the heart of the city leaving much property damage and many terrified citizens in their wake.

On January 2, 2009, the inevitable happened: York University student Donald Sanderson was killed when his head slammed against the ice after his helmet came off during the fight. It takes a long time to change the rules in a sport that Canadians have long claimed teaches values like respect, discipline and grace under pressure. Polls in 2011 revealed that 30% still believed that fighting is an integral part" of the sport; 60% thought pro hockey had become more violent in the past five years, and four out of five (79%) believed the NHL had not done enough to protect its players from head injuries. But only a minority (41%) thought that hockey would be better off if fighting were banned. One exasperated Canadian said: "I can see a time when hockey will be like a Roman circus: no referees and lots of body bags."

It remains to be seen if automatic ejections, escalating fines and suspensions, and prohibitions on removing helmets and gloves become a part of Canadian hockey. A small but welcome step was taken in 2010 to ban blindside hits to the head in order to curb the many concussions in the NHL. Also head injuries are no longer treated on the bench with mere smelling salts, but any player suspected of having a concussion will be removed

O Canada

O Canada!
  Our home and native land!
True patriot love
  in all of us command.
With glowing hearts
  we see thee rise,
The True North
  strong and free!
From far and wide,
  O Canada,
We stand on guard
  for thee.
God keep our land
  glorious and free!
O Canada,
  we stand on guard for thee.
O Canada,
  we stand on guard for thee.

Ô Canada

Ô Canada!
  Terre de nos aïeux,
Ton front est ceint
  de fleurons glorieux!
Car ton bras
  sait porter l'épée,
Il sait porter
  la croix!
Ton histoire
  est une épopée
Des plus
  brillants exploits.
Et ta valeur,
  de foi trempée,
Protegera nos foyers
  et nos droits,
Protégera nos foyers
  et nos droits.

The Canadian National Anthem

Canada

from the game and evaluated by a doctor. Putting pressure on the NHL clubs to do more to protect its players are some powerful corporate sponsors, such as Air Canada, which threatened to end its sponsorship arrangements. Governor General David Johnston, a former two-time hockey All-American at Harvard, worries about a culture of violence: "we're teaching our children things that are contrary to the Canadian character."

By 2015 violence on ice had declined by a third since 2000. The thirst for victory is increasingly trumping the desire to see blood. All feeder programs for the NHL are taking steps to eliminate fighting and it is hoped that it will disappear from the sport.

Asked in 1996 what professional sports they preferred, 60% of Canadian respondents said hockey, 16% baseball, and only 6% basketball. Ten years later that had changed remarkably: 19% preferred Canadian football and only 13% favored hockey, 13% baseball and 7% basketball. Three years later, though, a 2019 report, in the World Atlas, without percentages, listed hockey, followed by lacrosse, football and baseball as the most popular sport in Canada. Nevertheless, the unique contribution that hockey makes to national identity is that it bridges English- and French-speakers, native and non-natives, eastern and western Canadians.

With the highest paid stars commanding $14 million pay packages, the NHL teams are in some economic trouble despite a US$50.3 million team salary cap. Overall their profit margin is a razor-thin 4%. But by 2011, because sponsorship revenues were up by a third, the NHL signed seven-year deal for $400 million with Molson Coors making it the "official beer" on both sides of the border.

Canadians also play basketball, although as a winter sport it must always take the back seat to hockey. One NBA team remains in Canada, the Toronto Raptors, after the Vancouver Grizzlies moved to Memphis. Americans can thank a Canadian, Dr. James Naismith, who devised this game in a Springfield, Massachusetts, YMCA in 1891 as a more interesting indoor alternative to calisthenics. Canada reached its basketball pinnacle in 2006 when Steve Nash, a dazzling point guard who came from Victoria, BC, and starred at Santa Clara before joining the Phoenix Suns and then the Los Angeles Lakers, won the NBA's most-valuable player award two consecutive years. This put him in the company of such greats as Michael Jordan, Magic Johnson, Larry Bird, Wilt Chamberlain, and Bill Russell. He is said to be the greatest pick-and-roll point guard of his generation.

Football was also first played in Canada and brought to the United States about a century ago when a group of McGill University students came down to Harvard to teach a few of its people the new game. With team names like, the "Winnipeg Blue Bombers," the "Ottawa Rough Riders," the "Calgary Stampeders" or the "B.C. Lions," and with Americans composing 45% of the professional players on the nine Canadian teams, American football fans feel right at home in Canada (at least until they count 24 players on the field, notice scores on the board like "four to one," and see teams punting on third down from the fifty-three yard line!) Even the cheering sections chant familiar yells, such as "Give me a "B," an "l," a "u," an "e," "what do you have?! . . ."

Canadians were asked in a 1999 poll which icons and institutions helped most to define Canada. The Canadian Football League placed third behind the Order of Canada and the beaver and just ahead of health care, maple syrup, and beer. Polls in 2006 indicated that more Canadians (19%) preferred their professional football than their pro hockey (13%).

Due to insurmountable financial difficulties, the American teams in the Canadian Football League (CFL) disappeared. Some Canadian teams in the league teeter on the brink of bankruptcy. Despite average annual salaries of only $89,000 and team salary caps, American players still play in the cash-strapped CFL. With no mandatory drug testing, the CFL attracts American players who have the talent to play in the NFL.

Baseball and softball are played everywhere in Canada. Even the legendary Babe Ruth hit his first home run in organized baseball in Toronto's Hanlan's Point Stadium on September 5, 1914 and blasted his longest homer (600 feet) at Montreal's Guybourg Grounds in a 1926 exhibition game. His first wife (Helen Woodford) was from Halifax, and his favorite hunting and fishing destinations were New Brunswick and Nova Scotia. Jacky Robinson first broke the sport's race barrier in Montreal's de Lorimier Grounds with the Royals in 1946.

Although the Expos packed their bags in 2005 for a move to Washington D.C., with a new name—The Nationals, major league teams still play "America's favorite pastime" against the Blue Jays in Toronto. Canadian professional teams in all sports face daunting financial problems which drive more and more of them south. They are usually located in smaller towns that are not as willing as American cities to subsidize stadiums and arenas or to reduce property taxes. The popular resentment against millionaire players discourages governments from assisting clubs.

Fans at Blue Jays home games are treated with the usual major league fare: hot dogs, peanuts, cokes and beer, organ music and comic figures both on huge electronic boards and in costume running around the sidelines and into the crowd. Games are begun, though, by playing two national anthems, not just one. In 1985, New York Yankees fans booed when *O Canada* was heard in Yankee Stadium prior to a game against the Toronto Blue Jays. That incident was so embarrassing that the American ambassador in Ottawa formally apologized to the Canadians. During the 1992 World Series, the president of the United States himself had to do the same after a Marine honor guard unfurled Canada's flag upside down in a pre-game ceremony. Within days T-shirts could be seen all over Canada bearing the inverted Stars and Stripes and the words, "Sorry, eh?"

A similar international incident occurred before a key playoff hockey game between the Edmonton Oilers and the San Jose Sharks on May 14, 2006, when San Jose fans loudly booed the singing of the Canadian national anthem. During the next game, played in Edmonton, the singer of the national anthem held up the microphone to allow the crowd to loudly sing part of the anthem; this is a tradition that continues to this day in Canadian arenas.

Horrified Canadians had sweet revenge when the Blue Jays captured the series in a six-game thriller. To rub salt in the wounds, the Blue Jays won again in 1993. In 1997, Larry Walker of the Colorado Rockies became the first Canadian to win the National League's most valuable player award. The next year he led the league in batting and won the Lionel Conacher Prize. In 2003, the Blue Jays ace, Roy Halladay, was the American League's Cy Young winner, while Montreal's Eric Gagné won the National League's Cy Young Award for best pitcher. The National League's Most Valuable Player in 2010 was Toronto-born first baseman for the Cincinnati Reds, Joey Votto. He was the third Canadian to win an MVP award in "America's favorite pastime."

In the first decade of the 21st century, more than a dozen Canadian players filled All-Star roster spots. In the 2011 season, 20 Canadians played in the major leagues, double the number only a decade and a half earlier. Over 70 were in the minor leagues, and another 600 played American college baseball. Every year about 30 young Canadians are drafted by big league clubs.

The American fan was confronted with intriguing language differences when attending a home game of the Montreal Expos. In Montreal, *O Canada* had to be sung in two languages. Announcers used both languages, and the American experienced

Canada

RCMP mourning death of four comrades Source: *Maclean's*

such play-by-play accounts as this: "The situation is tense for the Expos; there are already two *retraits* (outs). The *frappeur* (batter) steps up the plate. The *lanceur* (pitcher) receives the signal from the *receveur* (catcher) and uncorks a mighty pitch. The *frappeur* is undaunted, though. He swings and, hurray, slams a *circuit* (home-run)!" This vocabulary is no longer needed in Washington, D.C.

The American motorist also notices few differences, except that road signs show distances in kilometers, are in French in Quebec and are often in both French and English outside of the French-speaking regions. The chances are that he will not notice that he is paying more for gasoline (though not as much as if he were driving in most other foreign countries), since it is measured in liters (spelled "litres" in Canada), not in American gallons. Even when a Canadian speaks in terms of "gallons," he means an imperial gallon, which contains a fifth more than an American one. Canada has already adopted the metric system, although many Canadians still talk in terms of inches, feet, miles, pints, quarts, pounds and tons. It cannot be denied that a system of measurement which makes a mile equal the distance a Roman legion could march in 1,000 double steps, a yard equal to the distance from Henry I's nose to his fingertips and an inch as equal to the width of three barleycorns laid side-by-side, is not as logical as the metric system.

Canadian roads are good, unless, of course, he wants to drive deeply into the far northern parts of the country. He sees American-looking cars and pickup trucks everywhere. In 1995, the young racing sensation, Jacques Villeneuve, became the first Canadian to win the Indianapolis 500, snatching victory in the final laps from another Canadian, Scott Goodyear. In 1997, he became the first Canadian to clinch the world Formula One championship. In 2011, another Canadian race driver, Alex Tagliani, won the pole position at the Indianapolis 500.

What the American may not know is that all major North American automotive producers have plants in Canada and that completely free trade in automotive vehicles and parts exists between the two countries. In 2004, for the first time, Ontario produced more vehicles than Michigan. The American tourist may, in fact, be driving a Canadian car, rather than an American one.

Most cities have a North American look, with the full rundown of fast-food chains, gasoline stations and convenience stores. There are some charming exceptions, such as Quebec City and Victoria, BC. There are far fewer slums and less litter and graffiti; concern grows over the noticeable increase of homeless Canadians in its chilly cities. But the cores of cities remain vital and have been largely spared the kind of urban deterioration that afflicted some American cities.

Canadian cities are still somewhat safer than their American counterparts. In a 2003 World Health Organization report, five Canadian cities were listed as among the safest in the world—Sault Ste. Marie, Brockville and Rainy River in Ontario, as well as Calgary and Fort McMurray in Alberta. A 2019 *Maclean's* report stated that 29 out of the 50 sleepiest crime spots are in Ontario, and the other eight are in Quebec. The chances of being murdered are four times lower than in a U.S. city. An Internet definition of a Canadian is not far off the mark: "An unarmed American with health insurance."

There has been a decline in violent crime in Canada from the mid-1990s, and the overall crime rate by 2015 had fallen to its lowest level since the 1970s. Nevertheless, nearly as many Canadians reported encountering violent crime as did Americans (21% to 26% in 2007). Fear of street violence is widespread: a third (36%) of Canadians (and half the women) said in 2006 that they "would not walk alone at night within one kilometer of my own home." The percentage is down from 40% in 1975 and about the same for American respondents.

Since the mid-1990s, there has been a threefold growth in gang-related killings. It is not only rising, but it is overwhelming authorities. One out of five persons killed in Canada is the victim of a gang hit, and there are few arrests and very few convictions. Vancouver has the spotlight, but Saskatoon, Winnipeg and Regina are the cities most plagued by violent crime. It is often connected to the drug trade. This is not only in organic drugs, such as cocaine and heroin, but increasingly also in synthetic drugs, such as methamphetamine and ecstasy. It has become North America's leading producer and exporter of these synthetic substances.

Quebec experienced one of the longest and bloodiest gang wars in North American history as the Hell's Angels showed shocking brutality in seeking to gain control of the province's drug trade. More than 160 had died by 2003. In May 2009, a long overdue OperationSharQc, planned for four years and involving more than 1,200 police officers from 20 different forces, arrested 111 Hell's Angels and their hangers-on in Quebec. This ended the infamous biker club's stranglehold on Quebec's drug trade. Admitted illegal drug use in Canada is high, according to the UN's "World Drug Report 2007": it has the highest percentage of marijuana users among developed countries (16.8% in 2004 vs. 6.1% in the Netherlands), and 2.3% use cocaine. The attitude toward marijuana use hardened with the Conservative victory in 2006. One of Prime Minister Stephen Harper's first acts was to terminate the laws liberalizing the use of marijuana.

The omnipresence of potential violence was seen in tragic killing rampages in schools since 1999. In that year, a ninth-grade dropout terrorized a rural high school in Taber, Alberta, killing one student and seriously wounding another with a 22-caliber rifle. A year later three teenage boys were shot and wounded by a fellow student at a Toronto high school, Emery Collegiate Institute. Some argued that Canada's tighter gun control measures made these senseless attacks less deadly: instead of accumulating an arsenal of guns and explosives, as in Columbine, Colorado, the Taber boy could only get his hands on his father's rifle. But in

Canada

2006 a young man was able to arm himself with a Baretta semi-automatic rifle, a Glock .45 pistol, a shotgun and a tote bag with 1,000 rounds of ammunition. He walked into Montreal's Dawson College, the province's biggest junior college, and proceeded to kill one student and wound 19 others before turning his gun on himself. Only a brilliant police response prevented the carnage from being much worse.

Guns are increasingly used in such violence; they were involved in two-thirds of Toronto murders in 2005, twice the rate from previous years. Police gun seizures in British Columbia rose by 50% from 2002 to 2005. Controls on the sale of handguns are stricter than in the U.S., but they are not banned. There is a 28-day waiting period to buy a handgun, and one must have the support of two people vouching for him. According to the world population review, in 2020 the number of guns per 100 people was 34.7 in Canada and 125 in the U.S. The overall murder rate per 100,000 persons was 1.6 in Canada and 5.3 in America, and gun murders per 100,000 was 0.61 in Canada and 4.46 in the U.S. In the two decades to 2013, two people died in five shootings inside a Canadian elementary or secondary school. During the same period in the U.S., more than 230 died in 70 school shootings.

Many of the guns used in the kind of violent incidents that are now alarming Canadians are smuggled in from the U.S. Canadian crime experts claim that half come from south of the border, a figure that American authorities dispute although nobody denies that many guns find their way north into Canada. Canadian border agents seized 5,400 firearms from the U.S. in the five years since 2000, and that is only a fraction of the true number. Canadian gun orders reached such a high volume in 2000 that the U.S. federal government suspended the export of handguns, rifles and ammunition to Canada. Canada had been at the center of one of the largest firearms-smuggling operations in North American history. In 2000, nearly 23,000 vintage U.S. military guns, which are legal in Canada but not in the United States, were seized in Toronto and Montreal gun shops before they could be shipped south of the border.

High-powered hunting guns, including semiautomatics, are widely available. A fourth of all households possess firearms. In 1995, the Liberal government enacted a stricter gun law, banning some small handguns and requiring registration of firearms. In 2000, it tightened the law by requiring registration of all guns by 2003. There was a powerful lobby against gun registration, including by six provinces and two territories that contend that this is an unconstitutional intrusion into their authority. The federal auditor-general criticized its large cost, and the four Western provinces and Newfoundland opted out of administering the program. But the Supreme Court of Canada ruled in June 2000 that both laws had been "passed in the spirit of protecting the public" and were therefore valid.

At the same time that gun- and gang-related crime is dangerously increasing, there are worries that the legendary Royal Canadian Mounted Police (RCMP) is no longer up to the job of maintaining peace and order. The RCMP is a federal force that is contracted by 200 cities and every province and territory but Quebec and Ontario (which have their own provincial police forces) to help enforce the law. It also patrols the Great Lakes and St. Lawrence River. Thus it is caught between the need to meet the growing demand for sophisticated federal policing services, such as immigration, weapons enforcement, counter-terrorism and commercial and white-collar crime, and the "contract policing" at the provincial and local level, which requires that well-trained officers patrol the streets of small towns and answer citizens' calls. It is not performing either duty as effectively as it could.

The force is struggling to cope with the challenge of replacing many baby-boom officers while fewer young Canadians are interested in law-enforcement careers. There are only 183 policemen per 100,000 people, compared with 238 in the U.S. and 211 in Britain. The RCMP began recruiting women in 1974; ; they now constitute 21.7% of its 30,092 officers.

The eight provinces and three territories that use the Mounties' services have little interest in creating their own police forces since Ottawa pays up to 30% of the policing tab, 10% for municipalities. By and large, Canadians still trust the RCMP so much that its occasional use of phone buggings, wire-tappings, break-ins, use of general search warrants, forgery of income-tax forms, mail tampering, planting of incriminating evidence on innocent persons and harassing left-wing political groups—actions that would seldom be tolerated by American courts or the public if they were known—are generally accepted by Canadians. However, the public's tolerance has its limits. This was shown in 2007 when four RCMP officers at Vancouver International Airport killed an innocent, unarmed, and distressed Polish traveler who spoke no English by shooting him with a taser stun gun when he did not understand and respond to their orders. This lamentable incident was captured on video. Two years later a 200-page report concluded that such use of the electronic weapon was both premature and inappropriate.

Canadians go about their daily lives in a way similar to Americans, with a few minor differences. As in the U.S., schools are run by local school boards under the overall authority of the individual provinces. Their aim is now mass education in comprehensive schools, not academically tracked education in separate schools, as in most European countries. Depending on the province, children begin school at age six or seven, generally attending elementary school for six years, junior high school for three and senior high school for three. In Quebec, pupils enter a two- to three-year *college d'enseignement general et professionnel* (college of general and professional instruction) to prepare either for the university or a specific occupation.

Canadian pupils score very well in international comparisons. On the darker side, there is an alarmingly high dropout

Dinnertime at the Royal Military College of Canada

Canada

Alberta's lake and mountain landscape.

rate for black high school pupils: at 40% it is almost double the rate for the student population as a whole.

A lower percentage of Americans age 25-34 (43%, including community colleges) have a college education than in Canada (54.0%); the percentage is much higher for Asian students (ca. 70%) but lower for Caribbean (12%). Canadian universities have strictly meritocratic admission policies, and Canadian-born and foreign Asian students have the reputation for studying the hardest and having the most success. The immigration process attracts highly educated parents, who pass on their high aspirations to their children. Immigrants are an answer to the country's slowing birthrate and aging population; they constitute three-fourths of the annual net growth in the work force.

More students are being admitted, and over the decade before 2003 university enrollment increased by 20%. Following a trend also noticeable in the U.S., 60% of undergraduates in Canadian universities are women, and this can be as high as 79% at such institutions as Mount Saint Vincent University in Halifax. This is especially pronounced in medicine: the majority of students at 13 of Canada's 17 medical schools are women, and at the Université Laval the percentage rises to 70%. No wonder 52% of doctors under age 35 are women.

Those who wish to study have a wide variety of universities from which to choose. There are elite research universities, such as McGill, University of Toronto, University of British Columbia, University of Alberta, and Université de Montréal. These five institutions alone enroll 22% of undergraduates and produce 45% of doctorates. They receive 46% of all the public monies distributed for research and innovation. In the global Shanghai rankings of the top 100 universities, four Canadian institutions and 54 American ones are included. There are also fine primarily undergraduate institutions, such as Mount Allison, Acadia, Brandon, Lethbridge, Mount Saint Vincent, St. Thomas, Moncton, Bishop's, St. Francis Xavier, Wilfrid Laurier and the Royal Military College of Canada (RMC).

These universities and colleges, all public with a few exceptions in Ontario and BC, are not as expensive as equivalent American institutions. Tuition in 2020-2021 ranged from $7,938 in Ontario, $7,829 in New Brunswick, $8,757 in Nova Scotia, and $3,036 in Newfoundland, to $3,500 in Quebec. Tuition is much higher for international students. Canadian institutions are severely cash-strapped and overcrowded because the federal government reduced its transfer payments to the provinces. In 1999, Canadian universities spent 60% per pupil of what large public universities do in the U.S. In the final five years of the century, state allocations to U.S. universities increased by 28% (50% in California) while they dropped by 6% in Canada.

In a 2010 survey, two-thirds of parents said they could not afford the four-year average cost of $60,000 to send their children to university. Three-fifths of all students have to take loans to finance their studies, and the average debt on graduation stood at $26,680 in 2015, roughly the same as the average college debt in the U.S. Many wonder if college is worth the price. In the U.S., a college education enables men to earn $365,000 more in a lifetime; in Canada only $169,000. A third of those with doctorates have employment that does not require a PhD. The tough job market goes a long way to explaining why 42% of Canadians between age 20 and 29 live with their parents.

Canadian universities are learning how to raise private funds, but it will be years until they catch up with their American counterparts. For example, the university with the largest endowment is Toronto, with only $1.3 billion, less than one-twentieth of that of Harvard and Yale.

In 2017, nearly 27,000 Canadians went to the U.S. for their post–secondary education, a decrease in approximately 1,000 since 2005. They constitute the largest group of foreigners at Harvard (150 or 2.3%) being 787 (2018). This educational migration is particularly true of Ph.D. students. The word that many would-be professors hear in Canada is that an American Ph.D. may give one an edge. American-trained professors are in the majority in many departments, especially at leading Canadian research universities. Canada confers fewer than 10% as many doctorates as does the much larger U.S. Nevertheless, Canadians still earn five times as many Ph.D. degrees in Canada as they do in America.

Approximately 10,000 (2018) Americans attend Canadian universities. This may well be due to the much lower cost of attending a Canadian university due to the difference in the Canadian and American currencies' values notwithstanding a higher tuition paid by non-Canadians attending Canadian universities. In fact, when considering currency differences and cost of living in Canadian university cities other than in British Columbia, the cost is approximately 50% less than that paid at an American college. At the same time, some Canadian universities are aggressively recruiting American high school students, promising gun-free schools, good ski possibilities and quality education for less tuition. Also popular are branch campuses of American universities in Canada, primarily for teachers and other professionals. By 1990, seven U.S. universities (including Niagara and Central Michigan) offered extension programs for about 500 students in Ontario alone, and such operations are expanding in Alberta and British Columbia. Despite the higher tuition costs, these programs offer study opportunities at night and on weekends.

Five provinces provide state support for religiously affiliated schools. Also, the federal government is directly responsible for educating Indians and Inuit children and indirectly involved in education through financial support for higher education and bilingual teaching throughout Canada. Canadian public schools, which 95% of children attend, are suffering under the strain of funding cuts, labor strife and the needs of an increasingly diverse student body. Since 1995 the percentage of provincial wealth spent on education has declined dramatically.

Canadian-American Images

Americans are quick to recognize Canadians as a friendly, open and pragmatic people. Canadians are a bit more reserved than Americans. As Pierre Berton noted, "we are not a back-slapping race" and Canadians themselves admit to being somewhat embarrassed by public displays of emotions. A publication of the Royal Bank once encapsulated how many Canadians react to their more ebullient neighbors: "Americans prefer first to second names, and, in conversation, they seem to use yours in every sentence or two . . . They belong to clubs and lodges named after animals. They talk to strangers on street corners and at lunch counters. As they themselves would put it, they're friendly as hell."

Polls consistently reveal that Americans have a positive impression of Canadians: friendly (29%), peaceful, polite, helpful. Canadian's viewed Americans as more "dangerous" than "compassionate." Americans use the words "tolerant," "compassionate" and "funny" to describe Canadians. Only 1% of Canadians thought Americans are "funny" or "humorous."

A *Maclean's* poll asked Americans what country they liked after their own, and they said Canada, favored by 90%, followed by Britain. Only 3% had a negative view of Canada. A quarter of Canadians and Americans indicated that they would accept citizenship in the other country, and a third of *Québécois* said they would accept an offer to become U.S. citizens. A resounding 91% of Americans agreed in 2007 that they would have a better quality of life if they moved to Canada.

Many people argue that there is no such thing as Canadian patriotism because there is no such thing as a Canadian nation. Although Canadians are patriotic, they feel uncomfortable when they display it too much in public. In his 1988 book, Peter C. Newman wrote that "becoming a Canadian never required conversion to a burning faith or even a salute, since we had no distinctive flag during the first 98 years of our existence."

The two countries' standing in the world is very different. Reflecting on the differences between his Canadian and American students, Northrop Frye said: "American students have been conditioned from infancy to think of themselves as citizens of one of the world's great powers. Canadians are conditioned from infancy to think of themselves as citizens of a country of uncertain identity, a confusing past and a hazardous future." That seems to resonate as Prime Minister Justin Trudeau has called Canada the first postnational state. Toronto academic

Former *New York Times* bureau chief in Toronto, Andrew H. Malcolm, reported an example of the differing manifestation of patriotism. At the start of a stock car race in Calgary, the announcer asked the crowd to stand for the national anthem. A few seconds after a record of "O Canada" had begun to play, he stopped the music with a wrenching scratch and said, "You all know the rest," as the racecars' engines began to roar. Such an incident would be unthinkable in the United States.

Asked at the end of the century about factors that are important parts of what makes them Canadian, 80% named the flag (60% in Quebec) and only 41% named the British Queen (20% in Quebec). Nevertheless, rather than pledging allegiance to the flag, most Canadian pupils make their pledge to the Queen. In May, they are released from school for a day in order to celebrate Victoria Day, in honor of Queen Victoria, despite the fact that she never visited Canada during her long reign. The birthday of Canada's "founding father," Sir John A. Macdonald, is not a federal holiday, but school children observe Martin Luther King Jr. Day in January. Thanksgiving comes the second Monday in October, almost six weeks earlier than in the United States. There is certainly no Fourth of July celebration in a country which remained loyal to Britain during the American Revolution and which was a haven for Loyalists who either left or were driven out of the Thirteen Colonies. Canadian school children still learn about such heroic men of principle as *Benedict Arnold*, who demonstrated their devotion to order and the English sovereign. Canadians' national holiday is July First, the day on which both the country's constitutions were enacted in 1867 and 1982.

Canada has its own history, has been shaped by more challenging geographical conditions, has different cultures and languages, and has a different political heritage. Its political system is British by origin, even though it has been powerfully influenced by political practices in the United States. And Canadians have tended to place a greater emphasis on order than have Americans, who tend to treasure liberty above all else. Canadian-born sociologist, Seymour Lipsit, gave an

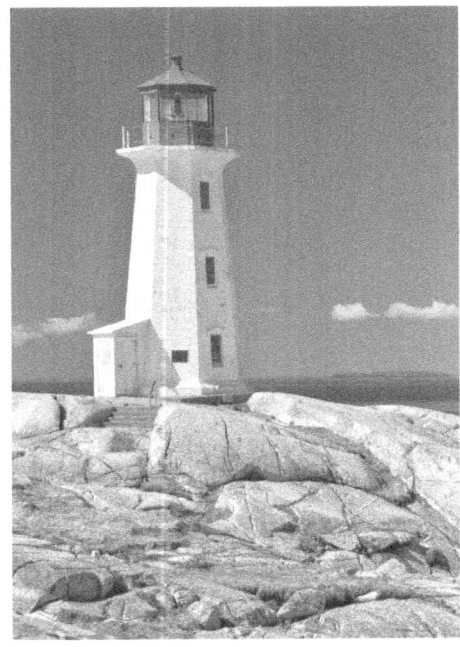

Courtesy of iStock.com/onepony

Canada

example: "Canadians were told to go metric and they did. Americans were told to go metric and they didn't."

Canada's first constitution, the British North America Act (BNA) of 1867, set up the objectives of "peace, order, and good government" rather than "life, liberty and the pursuit of happiness." Canada never had a "Wild West" because, unlike in America, organized society in the form of the mounted policeman, the railway agent, the bank manager, the missionary and agents of the Hudson's Bay Company usually arrived before or along with the settlers. Therefore, there has always been less violence and greater respect for authority in Canada than in the United States. What other country in the world uses a policeman (the Mountie) as a national symbol?

Canadians know that their emphasis on order makes them seem boring to the rest of the world. In a "boring headline" contest held in 1986 by the U.S. magazine, *The New Republic*, the winner was: "Worthwhile Canadian Initiative." In an interview with *The Economist* in 2003, one Canadian compared Canada to a "boring party where the guests are too polite to leave." The book titles of two earlier bestsellers were: *Canada on the World Stage: Is Anyone Listening* and *The Future of Canada: Does Nationalism Even Matter?* Some Australians call Canadians "frozen Yanks." Nevertheless, when asked in which country they would rather live other than their own, Australia was Canadians' first choice (18%), followed by the U.S. (14%).

In a 1992 editorial, "Boring, and proud," *The Globe and Mail* countered: "The reason Canada is considered boring is because nothing apocalyptic ever happens here—no civil wars, no nuclear disasters, no famine. On a global scale, Canada just can't cut it when it comes to violence and tragedy. We discuss our possible national break-up over lunch beside a lake. Blame our Canadian forefathers for the cruel hand we've been dealt. Didn't they realize that when they founded this country on the principles of Peace, Order, and Good Government that it would never make CNN?"

Although they are changing, Canadians have tended to be less assertive of their rights than have Americans. Peter Newman put it this way: "In dramatic contrast to the individualism of the United States, the idea was to be careful, to be plainly dressed, quiet-spoken and, above all, close with one's money and emotions . . . You could immediately spot a Canadian at any gathering: he or she was the one who automatically chose the most uncomfortable chair."

The *Maclean's*/CBC end-of-century poll provided ample evidence that Canadians believe they have a unique identity, separate and distinct from all other countries, as 90% of respondents indicated. Fully 77% believe it is based on a strong sense of their own history and appreciation of what they have accomplished as a nation, rather than simply a desire not to be American; 81% hold the view that they can thrive in the twenty-first century by keeping their own values and not trying to become more like Americans. A subsequent *Maclean's* poll published on July 1, 2006, concluded that the endless and mostly futile search for a single national identity and vision had been replaced by a growing sense that Canada's greatest asset is its diversity of lifestyles, beliefs and opinions. Former Prime Minister Jean Chrétien expressed this confidence: "We are North Americans but not Americans. We are different because of history and geography, but basically we have built a different society." Further, a 2016 study by Angus Reid revealed that almost eight in ten Canadians (79%) say they are either "very proud" (52%) or "proud" to be Canadian, though this sentiment is lower in Quebec.

Events from the 1960s on tended to sharpen Americans' and Canadians' awareness of the differences between their countries and objectives. The United States' seemingly endless involvement in the Vietnam War became unpopular in Canada, where an estimated 50,000 or more Americans fled to avoid military service; all but 20,000 returned to the U.S. after a 1977 amnesty. Those who stayed include several judges, scores of university professors, a popular radio host, a music promoter, a well-known film critic and numerous politicians. Less known is the fact that as many as 40,000 Canadians fought in that war, and more than a hundred Canadians' names are etched on the Vietnam Memorial in Washington, D.C.

In 2004 four American soldiers deserted their Iraq-bound units and fled to Canada, where they requested refugee status. But unlike in 1969, when Prime Minister Pierre Elliot Trudeau declared his country to be "a refuge from militarism," the Canadian government, backed by a board that hears refugee cases, opposed their applications, arguing that they were not persecuted and that the war was not illegal. Canada is no longer an open-armed sanctuary despite the fact that three in five Canadians thought American deserters should be granted permanent residency. Parliament approved nonbinding resolutions in 2008 and 2009 to stop the deportation of deserters, but the government refused to do so. In July 2008, the first American soldier was deported, and more followed. There are still more Canadians serving in the U.S. military forces than any foreign nationality.

From 1968 to 1984, Trudeau felt freer to criticize American foreign policy in public, and many Canadians agreed with him. Also, racial violence in America and the disillusionment stimulated by the Watergate scandal sullied the image of America in Canadian eyes. Further, Canadians

Canada

began to feel a surge of nationalism and sought to lessen their country's economic dependence on the United States in ways that greatly irritated American businessmen and their government.

More and more Americans began to take notice of the fact that Canada is a sovereign country that defines its own interests. As Americanized as Canadians might have become, they seem determined to be a different kind of society, which tries to avoid the kinds of problems the United States faces. One young Canadian, Neil Bishop, noted, "It's not that U.S. civilization is bad; on the contrary, it is truly great. But one U.S.A. is surely enough."

GEOGRAPHY

Canada is the second-largest country in the world; only Russia is larger. Covering almost four million square miles, it is 10% larger than the United States (including Alaska) and 40 times bigger than Great Britain; it is roughly the same size as the entire European continent and occupies 46.6% of North America. It is bracketed by huge islands, such as Newfoundland, Vancouver and Baffin, the world's fourth largest island, with 16,000 miles of crinkled coastline.

Canada stretches 4,545 miles east to west and almost 3,000 miles north to south, and it spans one fourth of the world's time zones. Its three coasts, when combined, are the world's longest coastline, with an enormous store of offshore riches. Inland Canada has more than a million rivers, streams and lakes, containing over a fifth of the world's fresh water supply. Manitoba alone has one lake for every 10 inhabitants. It also shares the world's largest body of fresh water, the Great Lakes, with the U.S. Canada possesses a fourth of the world's wetlands and 15% of its forests. Even though it occupies the "winter half" of North America, it has a wide range of climates, and there are regions in Canada that experience one-hundred degree drops of temperature in the wintertime.

Almost one-half of Canada is located on a massive shield of ancient Precambrian rocks hewed and scraped by a gigantic prehistoric glacier. It covers the bulk of six provinces and most of the Northwest Territories. It is a sparsely-populated physical environment of forests, wilderness, lakes and rocks jutting from the earth. This landscape differs remarkably from the lowlands south of it and keeps Canadians hemmed in close to the U.S. border, where most of them live. This Shield has always been a formidable barrier to settlement, to the building of roads and railways and to the movement of Canadians from east to west or from south to north.

Former Governor General visiting Parliament in Ottawa

Because so much of it is practically uninhabitable, Canada cannot be compared to the United States. A thousand miles of rocks, eroded mountain chain and bogs placed a wall between the Prairie provinces (the West) and the settled portion of Ontario, which belongs to Canada's East, even though Toronto is closer to such Midwestern cities as Cleveland, Detroit and Chicago, than to New York and Boston. It has always threatened to cut off the Canadian West from the East and has contributed to a greater feeling of separation from each other on the part of westerners and easterners than is felt in the United States.

It has helped to create and perpetuate a western dependence on eastern financial power that has always been resented in the West. Finally, it has strengthened Canadians' reliance upon government and has helped shape the Canadian character. As Pierre Berton wrote, "if we are a solemn people, it is partly because the Shield and the wilderness bear down upon us, a crushing weight, squeezing us like toothpaste along the borders of your country."

Nevertheless, the rugged Shield also contains treasures that help make Canada a natural resource powerhouse. It was an ideal habitat for beavers, which had almost single-handedly attracted European attention to Canada three centuries ago and provided the first important economic stimulus to Canadian settlement. Beaver fur was so popular that the animal faced extinction in the 19th century. One result is that Canada is the only country in the world with a rodent for its national animal: the beaver. Its image was on the first Canadian postal stamp in 1851 and is on today's nickel; in 1971 the government made it the official emblem. No wonder there was such a furious outcry in 2011 when Senator Nicole Eaton dared propose that the polar bear replace the beaver as the national animal. Calling the beaver, a "dentally defective rat," she argued that the white beast is "the world's largest terrestrial carnivore and Canada's most majestic and splendid animal."

The beaver is an amazing creature, which can cut down 216 trees a year with its bare teeth. But it suffered a horrible indignity in 2010. In 1920, the Hudson Bay Company had founded a journal of popular history called *The Beaver*. On its ninetieth birthday, the editors felt compelled to change its name to the dull *Canada's History* because the iconic animal's name had become a slang carnal term referring to a certain location on a woman's body. The death krell was rung by the internet. If spam filters did not bury it, users of its website were often disappointed to discover that the content was history rather than something else, and they clicked out on average after only eight seconds. Editors hope the publication's new name will expand its 50,000 circulation.

Today, much of the Shield remains richly endowed with nickel, cobalt, zinc, copper, gold and silver; it is the source of 40% of Canada's mineral production. It contains the trees that make Canada one of the two major pulp and paper producers in the world, the uranium mines in northern Saskatchewan and the huge Ungava iron ore deposits. It is a major source of waterpower, which supplies Canada with 70% of its electricity and enables it to export hydroelectricity to the United

Canada

States, especially to the Northeast.

The Shield's rugged landscapes, scenery and wildlife, particularly multitudes of birds including millions, even billions, of ducks and geese, have inspired some of Canadians' best painting, especially since the 1920s, when seven talented Canadian artists (known as the "Group of Seven") captured its majestic beauty on their canvases. It also attracts vacationers from all over North America and helps to perpetuate that erroneous image which some Americans have of modern Canadians: as lumberjacks or rugged frontiersmen who carve a precarious living out of a beautiful, but hostile, land. As can be seen, Canadians are predominately city-dwellers who have learned to exploit the riches of the Shield in order to create and maintain a comfortable standard of living similar to that enjoyed by most Americans.

Canada is a very sparsely settled land, with an overall population density of only 3.7 people per square kilometer, compared with 36 in the United States. Even Saudi Arabia has a higher population density than Canada. The most densely populated provinces are in the Maritimes: New Brunswick, Nova Scotia, and Prince Edward Island: pointedly Newfoundland/Labrador is not part of the Maritimes. The Maritimes climate and geography have powerfully influenced settlement patterns. The Shield and climate compressed Canadians to close proximity to the U.S. border. There were further incentives to settle in the extreme south. Many settlers to Canada came from the United States and wanted to remain close to that country. Many Canadian manufacturing facilities were owned by Americans or were intentionally located close to the American market, which is the world's largest and the target for 75% of Canadian exports. Also, in the level plains between the southern rim of the Shield and the U.S. border are fertile farmlands and a fortuitous string of lakes and rivers connected in places by canals that provide inexpensive transportation and water power.

The result of these forces is that three-fourths of all Canadians live within 100 miles of the U.S. border, and 90% live within 200 miles. In fact, three-fourths of all Canadians live *south* of the northernmost point of the 48 contiguous United States. By contrast, most Americans live far away from Canada, and only 12% of them live within 100 miles of the Canadian border. This percentage is decreasing as more and more Americans move south within the U.S.

If one regards only population distribution, Canada more closely resembles the snake-shaped country of Chile, rather than the well-proportioned geographic configuration that Canada is. It could be seen as a country 4,545 miles wide and a hundred miles tall, albeit with a hinterland which stretches straight to the permafrost, the ice pack and the North Pole. Even within this thin band of settlement, Canadians are not dispersed evenly. Four out of five Canadians live in cities; 31% live in the three largest—Toronto, Montreal, and Vancouver—and half of new immigrants settle in these three cities. One-third of Canadians live in communities with fewer than 10,000 inhabitants. Political pollsters detect an urban-rural split on such issues as gun control and gay rights, and the economic disparity is growing. Differing lifestyles are also reflected in the facts that rural Canadians are more likely to smoke, drink underage, and be obese.

Urban concentrations are strung out from east to west, "an archipelago of population islands walled off from each other by the terrifying obstacles of Precambrian rock, muskeg (bogs), mountain barriers, storm-tossed waters," to quote Pierre Berton. The bulk of Newfoundland's people have to cross the Gulf of St. Lawrence to get to the Canadian mainland. French-speaking Acadia and Quebec separate anglophones in the east from those in Ontario. Distance and the southern extremity of the Shield, which juts through western Ontario, separate most inhabitants of On-

tario, the most populous Canadian province, from the prairie provinces of Manitoba, Saskatchewan, and Alberta. Finally, the Rocky Mountains provide a majestic separation of the prairie region from British Columbia.

These sharply divided regions are, in many ways, northward thrusts of the North American continent. Indeed, a serious challenge to Canada has always been that only man-made barriers separate Canadian from American regions, whereas daunting natural barriers divide most of Canada's regions from each other. This has made the forging of unnatural east–west links and the overcoming of the natural north–south ties absolutely essential if Canada were to become and to remain a unified country. A closer look at these distinct regions will demonstrate why this has always been difficult and why author Arthur Malcolm described Canada as a "puzzling collection of frequently feuding fiefdoms."

THE ATLANTIC PROVINCES: In the East are the Atlantic Provinces, composed of the three Maritime provinces of Nova Scotia, Prince Edward Island (Canada's smallest province although twice the size of Rhode Island) and New Brunswick (40% of whose population is French-speaking Acadian) plus Newfoundland and Labrador, Britain's first overseas colony. Officially renamed Newfoundland and Labrador in 2001, this is Canada's most recent province. It had Dominion status equal to Canada's from 1907 to 1933, when it lost its self-rule. Not until 1949 did it join Canada, after a very close (52%) vote by its people. It still remains remote from the rest of the country and even has its own time zone 30 minutes ahead of the Maritime provinces. Less urbanized than Ontario and Quebec, this region is covered by forested hills and low mountains. Water is everywhere. These provinces are largely encircled by rocky coastlines, coves, isolated fishing villages and port cities, such as St. Johns and Halifax.

With about 2.3 million inhabitants, 7% of the country's population, Atlantic Canada is the most ethnically homogeneous region of Canada. Acadians, remnants of those ten thousand hardy pacifist folks brutally rooted out and resettled by the British in 1755 for trying to stay neutral in the war between England and France, are immortalized in Longfellow's moving poem "Evangeline." No longer discriminated against because of their French language, they now live along New Brunswick's northern border and eastern shore and are sprinkled around in other parts of the region, especially in the southwest corner of Prince Edward Island and on Cape Breton in Nova Scotia. On August 15, 2005, thousands of them assembled at the site of their ancient village of St. Pré in the heart of their lost homeland to celebrate their survival of that deportation 250 years earlier, now referred to as *le grand dérangement* (the Big Inconvenience).

About 80% of the Atlantic Provinces inhabitants are of British descent (higher in Newfoundland), especially Scottish, by whom Nova Scotia, meaning "New Scotland," was named. Perhaps the most famous Scotsman to grow up and live here was Alexander Graham Bell, who invented the telephone. It is reported that more people speak Gaelic in Nova Scotia today than in Scotland itself. One still hears a distinctive Scottish burr when many Nova Scotians speak English, especially in Cape Breton, which is expe-

Canada

riencing a revival of Gaelic cultures and language.

This predominantly British population has long valued its transatlantic ties with Great Britain, and it has always maintained thriving trading relations with the northeastern seaboard cities south of the border. Because of its window to the Atlantic, it has always been strategically important. During the two world wars its ports were assembly points for convoys of ships carrying troops and supplies from North America to Europe. It is no surprise that Canada's small navy is headquartered in this part of the country. In fact, Halifax, the capital of Nova Scotia, is the home of Canada's largest defense establishment, which provides employment for almost a fourth of the city's work force.

Despite their strategic location, the Atlantic Provinces have always been the poorest of Canada's provinces. They have been excessively reliant upon fishing and timbering. A greater percentage of their jobs are dependent upon the extraction of primary resources and increasingly upon tourism, and this has resulted in a large number of single-industry towns. They have too little arable land, population and industry to have a more balanced economy and be prosperous on their own. They are just now finding reliable alternatives to their former economic mainstays of fishing, lumber and military bases. Average wages were until recently only two-thirds of the national figure, but they are now rising. Their population is aging rapidly, and unemployment is well above the national average. Numerous attempts to form a Maritime union to combat these problems more effectively have failed.

Their present economic hopes and success stem from discoveries of natural gas and oil off the coasts of Nova Scotia and Newfoundland and Labrador. These capital-intensive industries do not generate many jobs directly, nor do they spread cash around as cod fishing once did. But they boost government resources and trickle down to others. The importance of these discoveries explains the history of bitter struggles with Ottawa over the question of who owns or controls these valuable resources: Canada or the individual provinces. The people in these provinces are proud of their more relaxed, less urbanized life, but they have also tended to resent the economic and political domination of Canadian life by provinces to the west. In 2000, the region's four premiers formed a joint council to lobby in Ottawa. By 2009, Newfoundland had become a "have" province, sending more financial assistance to other provinces than it receives from them.

Although the region lacks a very large urban center, Halifax is an important

and interesting city. With a population of around 280,000, it is a showcase of 19th century architecture with the leisurely air of a small, tree-lined community. Its significance as Atlantic Canada's most important port city suffered with the opening of the St. Lawrence Seaway, which enabled ships to bypass Halifax and churn their way directly into the Great Lakes.

ST. LAWRENCE LOWLANDS: The two provinces of Quebec and Ontario form the heartland of the Canadian Confederation. They were formerly two separate colonies, called Lower Canada (Quebec) and Upper Canada (Ontario). Their merger in 1840 signaled the imperfect wedding of Canada's "two founding peoples" in one country. Although very large portions of these two provinces are covered by the Canadian Shield, they share in the south the St. Lawrence Lowlands, which form the most heavily populated, most industrialized and, therefore, traditionally the richest part of Canada. It contains 60% of Canada's entire population. It has more cities of over 100,000 inhabitants than any other region, and it includes Canada's two largest cities, Toronto and Montreal, as well as the federal capital, Ottawa.

About three-fourths of the total value of Canada's manufactured goods are produced in this region. Its moderate climate and excellent agricultural lands attracted many settlers in the 18th and 19th centuries, and farms here still help feed the country's most densely populated region. A further blessing for this region is the waterway formed by the St. Lawrence River, the Great Lakes and connecting canals and locks, the last of which were completed in 1959. The economic importance of the Great Lakes cannot be underestimated: the eight American states and Ontario that share the lakes account for 30% of North America's employment and output and 36% of manufacturing jobs.

This entire waterway is ice-free about nine months a year and gives this inland area enviable access to the Atlantic Ocean and from there to the rest of the world. For example, although located 1,000 miles from the sea, the port of Toronto receives

ocean-going ships and is the same shipping distance from Britain as is New York City. Also, many vessels can travel almost 2,000 miles from the Atlantic Ocean all the way westward to Thunder Bay, the railhead for products and grain from the West and located on the northern shore of Lake Superior, and then return to the high seas.

QUEBEC: While the St. Lawrence Seaway binds the eastern half of Canada, it could never erase the crucially important cultural differences of the people who live close to its banks. This Canadian heartland is sharply divided into francophones in Quebec and anglophones in Ontario. With a land area three times larger than France, Quebec is Canada's largest province and is as wide at its widest point as the distance between Dallas and Washington, D.C.

Home to about 22.5% of Canada's population, it is a French-speaking island in the midst of an anglophone sea in which francophones are outnumbered by fifty to one. About 87% of Quebec's 8.1 million people speak French as a mother tongue, 7% speak English at home, 6% speak another native language, and 16% of the total population is fluent in a third language. A relatively small percentage (20.6%) of the

Railway magnate William Van Horne points westward, Banff, Alberta

Canada

francophones speak only French, especially those living outside the larger cities of Montreal and Quebec City. In Montreal, two-thirds speak both French and English. A 2013 poll revealed that 85% of Quebecers think it is important to be bilingual. The *Québécois*, as they are now called most of the time even outside of francophone Canada, have a distinctive language, culture, and heritage.

In the past they tended to consider themselves more as *Québécois*, than as Canadians. In the 1994 *Maclean's*/CTV poll, only 45% of Quebec respondents identified themselves as "Canadian." By 2001 that figure had risen to 75%, and in *Maclean's* 2003 year-end poll an unprecedented 69% claimed they were "proud to be Canadian." That percentage continues to go up: *La Presse* published a poll in 2007 showing that 85% were proud to be Canadian, a 20-year high. Due largely to a serious Liberal Party scandal in Quebec, the number of *Québécois* who considered themselves "very proud to be Canadian" fell from 65% in 1985 to only 32% in 2006 (in Anglophone Canada the percentage fell from 80% to 61%). Nevertheless, a former separatist (PQ) premier, Bernard Landry, said in 2007 that "being Canadian isn't dishonorable." That was high praise from a man who once called the Canadian flag "a piece of red rag." In the wake of Canada's superb Olympic performance in 2010, fewer than one-third of *Québécois* supported the notion of having their own Olympic team.

Québécois still regard themselves as a nation, even though they are linked politically with the rest of Canada. For the first time the Canadian parliament gave this formal expression by declaring in November 2006 that *Québécois* are "a nation within a united Canada." Constituting almost a fourth of all Canadians, they have always doggedly resisted assimilation with the English-speaking world around them. They have successfully asserted their right to manage most of their own affairs and largely to determine their own destiny. They have their own national day on June 24, a week earlier than Canada Day on July 1. The Quebec government officially renamed it the Fête Nationale, but *Québécois* still refer to it as Fête de la St-Jean-Baptiste, or "La St-Jean."

A dramatic change had taken place by 2004. *Québécois* seem to accept Canada more than they used to. Only 2% of them considered national unity a major issue. As the most socially liberal Canadians, *Québécois* like the social experimentalism they see in Canada, such as gay marriage, abortion and legalization of marijuana: 69% endorsed the statement that they are proud of what Canada is becoming "because it shows what a socially progressive and diverse country we live in." The figure in the rest of Canada was 54%.

The *Québécois* also now share anglophone Canadians' views on the nation's place in the world. *Québécois* were more critical of the 2003 war in Iraq; 90% opposed it, and some of the world's largest anti-war rallies had been held in Montreal. Thus, from being the most pro-American Canadians, *Québécois* have become perhaps the most skeptical of the foreign and social policies pursued by the United States—60% said their attitude toward the U.S. had become more negative in recent years, compared with just under half of Canadians as a whole. A broad dislike for President George W. Bush and the war in Iraq had much to do with this. A final reason for this unprecedented *Québécois* embrace of common Canadian values is the confidence *Québécois* now have that their language and culture are more firmly entrenched than ever before.

A third of all *Québécois* live in metropolitan Montreal, a city of about 4.2 million people and the world's third-largest French-speaking city after Paris and Kinshasa, Congo. This city dominates the economic and cultural life of Quebec. Quebec's major newspapers are published here: the one with the largest circulation is the unabashedly sensational tabloid, *Le Journal de Montreal. Le Devoir* is the influential French-language daily. *La Presse* occupies the middle ground between those two dailies and is the voice for Canadian unity. The *Montreal Gazette* is the major English-language daily. The newsmagazine, *L'Actualité*, the French-language sister of *Maclean's,*is published in Montreal. All major Quebec political parties have their headquarters in the city, even though the provincial political capital is Quebec City.

At one time Montreal was the cultural and economic heart of Canada. Its population doubled from 1941 to 1971. Most of that growth came from the migration of unilingual Quebecers from the solidly-French countryside into this city, which offered hope for advancement and a better standard of living. Urbanization greatly changed the culture and outlook of the Quebecois and brought about a "Quiet Revolution" in the 1960s and 1970s. The influx also greatly altered the city of Montreal by bringing unilingual Quebecers to live side by side with anglophones, who dominated the city's economy. Nowhere else in the province was there such contact. Montreal became more and more French and again became the focus of Canada's most divisive debates, as it had been during the conscription controversies in both world wars.

It has experienced terrorism, so rare in Canadian history, and serious political tension resulting from the vigorous assertion of French-language rights. An increasing number of anglophones and major corporate headquarters abandoned the city, and investments in the city dwindled. During the 1970s its economy and population declined, as Toronto overtook it as Canada's major city. Although that economic and population decline was halted in the mid-1980s, Montreal's position as Canada's primary city was lost perhaps forever. Today it is corruption and organized crime that drive the citizens of Montreal into the suburbs and head offices elsewhere. In the six years to 2008, more than 20,000 city residents left for the suburbs.

In the 21st century, Montreal has become a leading high-tech center. A 2000 Price Waterhouse Coopers study of large North American metropolitan areas ranked the city fourth in concentration of high-tech jobs on a per-capita basis. *Wired* magazine also singled it out as the only Canadian city on a list of 46 global high-tech hubs to watch. Bombardier Aerospace, which built the high-speed train for the Washington-Boston run in 2000 and produces rail engines and cars for the European market, is in Montreal.

ONTARIO: In the middle of the 19th century, Queen Victoria located the federal capital of Ottawa on the banks of the Ottawa River, presumably because it was a safe distance from the United States insofar as the War of 1812 was still a fresh memory and because it was on the boundary separating English and French Canada. Ottawa remains Canada's most determinedly bilingual city. It is a pretty, comfortable city of 1,407,928 (2021) inhabitants, making Ottawa Canada's fourth largest metropolitan area. Ottawa is distinguished by its scenic drives, the Rideau Canal, its colorful downtown market district, and, of course, its stately gothic architecture which houses Parliament, the Supreme Court and other government institutions. This capital city is resplendent with pomp and pageantry, with scarlet-

Canada

coated Mounties guarding Parliament Hill on horseback and Canada's Guards wearing bearskin hats, red coats and black trousers performing rituals before Parliament and the residence of the governor general.

Bruce Phillips, a television correspondent and former aide to the prime minister, remarked: "most people who live outside Ottawa see it as a place peopled with fat-cat civil servants with bullet-proof jobs." Some Canadians look down on Ottawa as a boring, bureaucrats' city with little nightlife (other than that which takes place in the bars and nightspots in Gatineau, across the river in Quebec, after Ottawa's citizens have gone to bed). A typical crack at the town was made by one of Trudeau's ministers, who contended, "the best thing about Ottawa is the train to Montreal." Some people also complain that the cultural life is not what one would expect in a federal capital. That is now changing, and, to quote Phillips again, "the city is sprouting a few cultural wings." In 2008 a *Maclean's* cover story named Ottawa Canada's "smartest city" and the fourth "most cultured" after Calgary, Victoria and Gatineau, Quebec.

Ottawa has long had a National Arts Centre near parliament, which houses a chamber orchestra, theaters and facilities for touring opera companies and shows. In 1988, a dramatic neo-Gothic glass and granite palace for the National Gallery, with a panoramic view of the city and Ottawa River, was opened. Designed by the Israeli-born Montreal architect Moshe Safdie, this gigantic magnificent edifice, which is a third larger than the National Gallery in Washington, finally relieves a major embarrassment of having a national collection of art, established in 1880, with no permanent home for it. In 1988, a new structure for the Canadian Museum of Aviation was also completed.

In 1989, a Museum of History (previously named Museum of Man and Museum of Civilization) across the river in Gatineau, Quebec (known until 2002 as Hull), connected to the Ottawa side and the National Gallery by a footbridge. The construction of two connecting museums in English and French Canada symbolizes the strengthening of fragile bonds that tie together Canada's two founding nations. In 2005, on the 60th anniversary of VE Day, a remarkable War Museum opened on the LeBreton Flats, a short distance from Parliament. Its primary architect, Raymond Moriyama, is a Japanese-Canadian who was interned in Canada during the Second World War. A National Holocaust Monument was opened in Ottawa in 2017.

The economic and cultural power of Toronto reflects the weight of Ontario within

Flatiron Building and CN Tower, Toronto, Ontario *Courtesy: Tourism Canada*

Canada. This province alone is three times as large as Japan. It occupies the entire northern shores of the Great Lakes, while eight American states are washed by their southern shores. No American state has such a commanding position within the American republic as does Ontario within the Confederation. Its predominance would be even greater if Quebec were ever to separate from Canada; Ontario would then become half of Canada, and it is uncertain whether any federal state could bear this. Because of the leading rank that Ontario has traditionally enjoyed, it tends to be most satisfied with the status quo. Just as some Americans once believed that "what is good for General Motors is good for America," people in Ontario tend to believe that "what is good for Ontario is good for Canada."

With almost 15 million inhabitants, Ontario is not only the most populous province, but it is ethnically the most diverse. About 5% of its population, concentrated basically in the eastern part of the province, speaks French as a mother tongue, and in 1989 Bill 8 improved government services to Ontario's half million francophones. Non-British immigrant groups from a variety of European and Asian countries have settled here.

Greater Toronto has 6.4 million inhabitants and lively ethnic neighborhoods, restaurants, and small businesses that are reminiscent of New York or Chicago a half century ago. The idea of neighborhood is strong, and in 1996 *Forbes* magazine rated Toronto as the best place in the world to balance work and family. Of its residents, half are immigrants, and Toronto is the favorite urban destination for newcomers to Canada. A fourth of the country's immigrants live there. A fifth of its people arrived in Canada after 1981 and a tenth after 1991. By 2007, 49% of its population had been born outside the country, the second highest figure in the world after Miami. Almost half (43%) of the overall population belongs to a visible minority. In fact, Toronto at the turn of the century was home to 42% of Canada's non-whites. Since 1967 the largest Caribbean festival in North America, Caribana, takes place in Toronto. A tenth of the population is either Chinese or Filipino by ethnic origin. The airwaves are filled with a Babel of foreign languages; one radio station beams programs in 30 languages, while one television station shows films in many different languages.

The city government prints official notices in six languages, including Portuguese, Italian, Greek, and Chinese. Drivers' tests are given in 12 languages. Half the children in state schools speak a native language other than English. Nevertheless, Ontario has maintained a fundamentally British air and sentiment. Its provincial flag still has a Union Jack prominently in the upper left-hand corner, and the word "Loyalist" has wholly positive connotations here.

Along with Alberta and British Columbia in the West, Ontario is one of Canada's high growth areas. Indeed, that cluster of cities around the western end of Lake Ontario extending from Niagara Falls and St. Catharines (north of Buffalo, New York) westward through Hamilton and Oshawa (the center of Canada's automotive industry) to Windsor (Detroit's twin-city) is called Canada's "golden horseshoe." While Canada's population between the 1996 and 2001 census takings grew by 4%, the population of the "golden horseshoe" had increased by 9.2%; 59% of Ontario's people and 22% of Canada's live there. Here is the center of gravity for Canadian industry, and its heart is Toronto, the country's capital of finance, culture, publishing and fashion. It is home to one out of seven Canadians. Almost 10 million people live within 75 kilometers (50 miles) of Toronto. The city has not only been spared the mountains of litter, the hundreds of square miles of graffiti and a high crime rate, but it has remained freer of the racial tensions which have plagued some American, British, and Canadian cities.

Canada

Vancouver, B.C.

There has been a long-simmering feud with Michigan over the trucking of Toronto's trash to dump sites south of the border. Even presidential candidate John Kerry, fishing for votes in that important swing state, declared in 2004: "It's time to end the Canadian trash-dumping in Michigan!" He was supported by the Canadian-born ex-governor of Michigan, Jennifer M. Granholm. The U.S. Supreme Court has repeatedly ruled that garbage is a commodity that is as subject to free trade as any other product. It also travels on a two-way street. An American company, Clean Harbors Environmental Services, operates a hazardous-waste landfill incinerator in Ontario that treats the contaminated remains primarily from U.S. auto plants around the Great Lakes. In fact, the trucks pass each other at the border.

Toronto did not have the European sophistication of Montreal or the natural beauty of Vancouver, and for a long time it was called "Hogtown." That has all changed. Profiting from the shift of wealth from Montreal and fighting off the challenge of Calgary in the West, Toronto remains the financial heart of Canada. Its Bay Street is the equivalent of Wall Street in America, even though the Toronto Stock Exchange and most brokers and investment houses have moved to more spacious, modern quarters on other streets. Toronto is the home of the University of Toronto (Canada's largest and arguably most renown). The headquarters of ten of the 20 leading corporations are domiciled there. The next in order are Calgary (6), Vancouver, and Montreal. It is the center for hundreds of suburbs and satellite towns involved in a broad range of economic activities and which economically nourish and are nourished by Toronto.

Asked in a 1989 Gallup poll "which province has the greatest future?" half of Canadian respondents said Ontario. That changed as economic and political influence moved westward, especially toward oil-rich Alberta. A 2010 poll revealed how uncertain Ontarians have become: half responded that Ontario's influence in national affairs is declining and that the province is not treated with the respect it deserves.

Most of Canada's leading English-language publications are produced in Toronto. According to the *New York Times*, the *Toronto Star* is the largest newspaper in Canada by circulation as of 2021. It also introduced a weekly section of articles from the *New York Times*, as well as a reduced version of the *Times Book Review*. The *Globe and Mail* (ca. 291,571 daily [2013]) is owned by Canada's richest man, Ken Thomson and is one of Canada's most influential dailies. In 2010, it introduced a slightly smaller size and became the first major daily Canadian newspaper to print high-quality color on every page.

To compete with it, in 1998, Conrad Black, a peer of the British House of Lords and, in 2007 convicted in an American court on criminal charges related to company matters, founded the somewhat rebellious *National Post* (ca. 186,000 daily in 2015), which is willing to sneer at some of Canada's traditional values. The *National Post* still survives despite the determined efforts of the *Globe and Mail* to crush it. The *Post* is deeply in debt and has never made a profit. It filed for bankruptcy in 2010, but it emerged from it and competes in the market. The *Financial Post* is the equivalent of the *Wall Street Journal* in the U.S. Other dailies in Canada are regional newspapers, with the exception of the *Ottawa Citizen*. Unlike their counterparts in the U.S., Canadian papers have largely avoided precipitous financial decline and have not been quite as overwhelmed by digital competitors.

By century's end, Black already controlled more than half of Canada's dailies from his corporate headquarters in Toronto, and he was the world's third-largest newspaper publisher. But he sold most of them, including his 50% stake in the *National Post*. That left most major English-language newspapers in the hands of five TV or telecom giants. CanWest, owned by Canada's most powerful media mogul, Izzy Asper, bought the *National Post* and 135 other daily newspapers from Black for $2.2 billion. This was the largest media deal in Canadian history. University of Toronto journalism professor, Vince Carlin, asserted, "This is not a healthy situation. There is competition in the United States. There is no competition here." Nevertheless, a 2002 study by Reporters Without Borders found that Canada ranked fifth in the world in terms of press freedom; the U.S. placed seventeenth.

Canada's second oldest magazine and most-read news magazine with three million readers, *Maclean's*, is produced in Toronto. It emphasizes Canadian news, but it gives some coverage to events in the U.S. as well. Reacting to slumping sales, it overhauled its management in 2005 and became livelier and more provocative. It seeks to avoid the criticism often leveled at the Canadian press and broadcasters that they are bland and politically correct. Financially strapped, it is largely online; its hard copies are reduced to one issue per month. Its French-language sister version is *l'Actualité*. Also published in Toronto is *Saturday Night*, a monthly that covers a multitude of subjects and is perceptive and well informed. It closely resembles *Harper's* and *Atlantic* in the United States. Finally, the women's monthly, *Chatelaine*, whose English- and French-language editions sell about 1.3 million copies, is produced in Toronto.

Toronto is filled with art galleries, museums, opera houses and more than 40 independent theater companies. It is a frequent location for first-run openings, and the Toronto Film Festival is a major event

Canada

in North America. Its major league baseball team, the Blue Jays, and other athletic teams play in the SkyDome, renamed in 2005 the Rogers Centre, a 60,000-seat indoor-outdoor stadium with a unique

retractable roof. By century's end, it was insolvent, but for a while it symbolized a new era of urban dynamism, as did the CN Tower, which is twice as high as the Eiffel Tower. Torontonians no longer have to say that the best thing about their town is that it is close to New York City.

PRAIRIE PROVINCES: Manitoba, Saskatchewan and Alberta could generally be described with the words "flat, prairie, wheat and petroleum." They form a region of new economic opportunity and wealth. The West is the fastest growing part of Canada. The discovery of oil and natural gas primarily in Alberta in 1947 greatly helped to diversify the prairie economy. This region always was and still is Canada's "breadbasket." Half of its area is covered by forest, but much of the other half is occupied by large farms, which are responsible for making Canada the world's second largest exporter of grain, behind the U.S.

The Prairie provinces have a very diverse ethnic mix. A resilient knot of francophones, some of them descendants of the Métis (a mixed race of French and Indian), have survived in Manitoba. Although they constitute only 6% of that province's population, they have been very successful in reasserting their rights to be schooled and to be spoken to in French. In this region, a quarter of the population is made up of non-Anglo-Saxon immigrants from Germany, Eastern Europe, Ukraine, and Russia. Entire villages or sections of towns are inhabited by persons whose every-day language is other than English, and one sees almost as many onion-shaped domes of Russian and Greek Orthodox churches in this region as grain elevators.

This region was never a frontier area, as was the American West, because of the different ways in which the two Wests were won. The American West was won by "six-shooters" and by settlers advancing before the American flag and the forces of "law and order." The Canadian West was largely organized by Mounted Police. Settlers attracted by governmental policies and land-grants traveled to their new homesteads on transcontinental railways, rather than in covered wagons.

Canada's Westerners are an independent-minded people with a strong sense of regional identity. They long felt that Ottawa's policies favored central Canada, whether that favoritism be expressed in dictated freight rates on the railways, high interest rates set by banks headquartered in Montreal or Toronto, the high price tags on goods manufactured in the East which result from protective tariffs and federal subsidies, or attempts to force bilingualism on a people who, despite the many different languages they speak at home, wish to see English remain as Canada's only official language.

These Westerners have been confidently assertive in federal-provincial relations during the past decades. In 1979, for the first time, a westerner (Joe Clark, leader of the Conservative Party) became prime minister although he remained in office less than a year. They have been inclined to form protest parties, such as the New Democratic Party (NDP), the Social Credit Party, or the Reform Party (renamed in 2000 the Canadian Alliance and in 2004 the Conservative Party, whose leader, Stephen Harper, became prime minister in February 2006). All have played very important roles in both regional and federal politics. Thus, one sees in the Prairie provinces a bastion of both conservative politics and of Canada's brand of socialism.

Since cities in the prairies were settled mainly in the 20th century, they have a slightly different appearance than those in the East. They have fewer old buildings and narrow winding streets, but newer construction and broad thoroughfares. They also are very spread out, as are many cities in the American West. Winnipeg, the capital of Manitoba, resembles Denver. Here is Canada's commodity exchange, where buyers and sellers determine the price of grains. One can hear French spoken in the streets, especially in the suburb of St. Boniface. Also, one can visit the monument to and home of Louis Riel, the leader of the French-speaking Métis. He led a rebellion against Ottawa in 1885 but now receives a hero's homage because he fought for the rights of francophones in the West. Moreover, on May 24, 2019, Prime Minister Justin Trudeau apologized and provided an exoneration of the First Nations Chief, Poundmaker, of his 1885 convictions for "treason-felony" for his allegedly instigating violence in the 1885 Northwest Rebellion. Canada has no difficulty owning up to past injustices—although it seems to take many years to do so.

Another major metropolis in the prairies is Calgary. Perhaps no city in Canadian history ever experienced such a boom as this city. In 1947, large reserves of oil were discovered. The Leduc oilfield was North America's largest at the time. The world energy crisis beginning in 1973 made Alberta's oil extraordinarily precious, and the entire province's economy felt the immediate benefit of swollen oil revenues. Almost overnight, Calgary became Canada's second-largest head office city, and easterners

Baffin Island, Nunavut, with stone marker ("Inukshuk") at left built by the Inuit
Courtesy: Michael J. Hewitt

Canada

moved westward in one of the country's most massive migrations.

At one point, Calgary was growing at the astonishing rate of 2,500 newcomers a month. Americans joined this massive influx and now constitute a fifth of the city's population. Practically no new construction was necessary to accommodate the 1988 Winter Olympics in Calgary. With the recovery of Alberta's oil industry in the 1990s, prosperity returned to the city. However, with the fall of oil prices and the inability to build oil pipelines to the east and west of Canada and south to the United States a recession has overtaken Alberta. Yet, it remains a magnet for high tech companies and corporate head offices.

Alberta has displaced Montreal and Vancouver as Canada's biggest business and financial center after Toronto. Indeed Alberta, with a population of 4.3 (2018) million, is a magnet for residents of other provinces. Some speak of "an internal brain drain to Alberta," and the vice president of the Business Council of British Columbia noted: "It's almost as if we are creating a small version of the United States built right here into Canada."

The Calgary-Edmonton corridor has become the fasting growing economic region in Canada, boasting a per-capita GDP 40% higher than the national average. The Prairie provinces and BC have replaced Ontario as the engine of Canada's economic growth. The West's combined GDP surpassed that of Ontario for the first time in 2008. Taken together, Alberta and British Columbia now have a higher population (ca. 7.5 million) than Quebec. Statistics Canada projects that the West will have almost a third of Canada's total population by 2031. The West is younger, has more babies, attracts more migrants, is more open to change, displays a higher degree of egalitarianism and shows less deference to authority.

With the election of Albertan Stephen Harper as prime minister in 2006, the country's political and commercial centers of gravity shifted westward. However, Al-

berta is vulnerable to the ups and downs of oil prices. The plunge below $30 per barrel in 2015 cast the province into recession. The price of oil has increased since then but Alberta has not yet recovered from the downturn and due to the lack of support from British Columbia and Quebec, as well as the blockage of the pipeline to the USA. The current (2019) Bill 12 in the Canadian parliament promises to land lock Alberta's oil again causing great concern in that province.

BRITISH COLUMBIA: This is Canada's window to the Pacific and the Far East, with which Canada maintains a growing volume of trade. Vancouver, Canada's largest port, is 350 miles closer to Tokyo than to Halifax. British Columbia (or "BC," as it is called) is a third larger than Texas. It is cut off from the rest of Canada by the Rocky Mountains, whose various ranges cover most of the province, forcing three-fourths of the province's people into the southwest corner around Vancouver. Because of its isolation and great distance from the rest of Canada, BC has an even more pronounced sense of regional pride than do the Prairie provinces. It shares the Canadian West's traditional distrust and hostility toward the East. It also has traditionally felt a certain kinship with the northwestern states in America, which it considered joining in the 19th century and with which it does a large volume of trade. The unnaturalness of east-west ties is felt more strongly in BC than in any other Canadian province. A cross-border alliance, called "Cascadia," encompasses an array of cooperative links between BC and the states of Washington and Oregon.

BC, with a population of 3.8 million, is a relatively prosperous province within the Canadian Confederation. It has very little arable land, but it possesses a panoply of mineral resources, almost unlimited hydroelectric power and huge forests, which provide its major product: timber. Its waters also produce a rich harvest of fish, including salmon. However, one does not see the countless quaint fishing villages along its coast, as one does in the Maritimes. The introduction of modern, long-range fishing vessels, and the existence of a few major processing and canning plants along a few rivers, especially the Fraser and the Skeena, have enabled the province's fishing industry to become centralized. BC's broad resource base has enabled the province to have considerable industrial growth and diversified production.

Victoria, the capital of BC, located on Vancouver Island. It is a city with a distinctive British air, complete with red double-decker buses and statues of the great 19th century queen for whom it was named. In 2010, *Maclean's* placed it on top of its ranking of Canada's "smartest" and most cultured cities. With only 78,000 in-

Canada

habitants, it has two universities and two smaller colleges, its citizens are well-read, half its residents visit local museums, and it sustains a symphony, two ballets, an opera and a philharmonic choir.

The most important city in this province is Vancouver, with a population estimated to cross 2.4 million by the end of 2022 (up from its current 2.26 million), making it Canada's third largest city. It has a very mild climate by Canadian standards, and is, without question, one of the world's most beautiful cities. It boasts a magnificent physical setting of mountains and sea, and it has a dazzling city center and Canada's first domed stadium. In 2019, Mercer's Quality of Living Survey ranked Vancouver third in the world (after Vienna and Zurich) in terms of quality of life. No U.S. city was in the top 25, but Toronto, Ottawa, Montreal and Calgary joined Vancouver in that category. A 2009 examination by *Maclean's* named Vancouver the best-run city in Canada, and the Economist Intelligence Unit's business travel index placed it first in the world as a desirable business meeting location, followed by Toronto. Its image is being tarnished by rising brutal gang violence and drug and gun trade.

Vancouver is truly a world city. One fifth of its residents work for American companies. It has an ethnically diverse population, 30% of whom are immigrants and 40% of whom are of Asian origin. Half of the Asians are Chinese, giving rise to one of the city's controversial nicknames: Hongcouver. With only about 13% of Canada's population (2016), BC absorbs almost a fourth of all immigrants; 80% of those are Asian. Non-Whites comprised more than 40% of the city's population by 2005. It is one of the world's most integrated cities with 13% of young couples being inter-racial.

Its school system must struggle with the problem of teaching 55,900 pupils, 61% of whom speak a first language other than English. Almost half the school children in 1997 required English as a Second Language (ESL) courses. Such ESL instruction demands a growing share of shrinking education budgets. Pupils in Vancouver's Richmond School District represent 75 distinct languages and cultures. In Lord Strathcona Elementary School, 90% of the children are of Asian descent, and Chinese Cantonese interpreters must be present at PTA and parent-pupil meetings. In Grandview/Uuqinak'uuh Elementary School, 52% of the students are First Nations (Indians), and 30% are recent immigrants or refugees.

With the Chinese community comprising a fifth of the population, Vancouver has Canada's most vibrant Chinatown, covering eight square blocks. This concen-

tration has made the Chinese-language media—four newspapers, three radio stations and two TV stations—influential players in provincial and national politics. In the past, the predominant dialect in the city was Cantonese. But newcomers and visiting dignitaries now largely speak Mandarin.

All eyes were on Vancouver in February 2010 when it hosted the Winter Olympic Games. Canada emerged with more gold medals than any other country. These Games were a grand success by any definition.

THE NORTH: The Yukon, Northwest Territories, and Nunavut are vast, covering about 40% of Canada's land area. They are wild, cold, isolated, ruggedly beautiful and almost entirely uninhabited. Its few residents have to adjust to long, dark winters and short summers. The northern parts are Arctic regions of packed ice, frozen fjords, icebergs, countless islands and glaciers, 70% of which are melting. Living there is a hardy people, whom Americans call "Eskimo," meaning "meat-eaters," but who prefer to be called "Inuit," meaning "the people." About 51,000 of the world's Inuit live in Canada. They represent less than half the Arctic's aboriginal people, who in turn account for only 10% of the region's population. Their communities tend to be located on bays, river mouths, inlets or fjords; this reflects the fact that their lives were always tied to hunting, fishing and gathering.

During the past quarter century, the isolation of the Inuit has been decreasing, and mainstream Canadian life-styles have penetrated their communities. Traditional hunting and fishing activities are not as important for their economy as they once were. The Inuit have grown dependent on the comforts and conveniences of Canadian life: kayaks and dog sleds have by and large been replaced by canoes, motorized toboggans, snowmobiles, trucks and airplanes as their major means of transportation. Electricity, oil stoves and furnaces, schools, hospitals, films, television and radio (which beam some programs in their language—Inuktitut, for which

Chinese-Canadians in Vancouver

there is no uniform alphabet or spelling, and which has more than 40 words for "snow") have greatly changed life in the extreme North. Unfortunately, some of these changes have so disturbed or destroyed traditional roles and ties within the communities that alcoholism, drug abuse and suicide have become frighteningly commonplace among the Inuit.

South of this Arctic area is a vast region of tundra and permafrost, covered by forests, filled with wild animals, and inhabited mainly by Indians, called aboriginals or "First Nations" in Canada, who value their traditional identity. There are few roads and railways running northward into these areas, and the few cities there, such as Whitehorse, Yellowknife and Iqaluit, are small frontier towns, whose residents must become accustomed to paying high prices and having all but air links severed during much of the bitter winter.

As a whole, the Canadian North contains important natural resources. These are not distributed evenly over the entire area. The extremely high costs of extraction and transportation, as well as the impact of mining and drilling on native cultures, greatly limits the extent to which they can be exploited.

That this vast, sparsely populated northern expanse had to be defended necessitated close defense links with the United States. American defense planners were well aware that Canada lies directly between the U.S. and Russia. They were therefore more than willing to cooperate with the Canadians in creating NORAD and in maintaining a costly Distant Early Warning (DEW) line of radars in the Ca-

Canada

nadian North in order to be able to detect any hostile penetration of North American airspace. The shortest distance between U.S.-based missiles and the strategic cities of the former Soviet Union—and vice-versa—was via Canada over the North Pole. This route is only 3,600 miles versus 8,000–10,000 miles parallel to the Equator.

To ensure that Arctic concerns are given a higher priority, the Chrétien government appointed the first aboriginal ambassador of Circumpolar Affairs, Mary May Simon, a longtime Inuit activist, to spearhead federal efforts to protect Arctic ecology. In 1996, an eight-nation Arctic Council was created, consisting of Canada, the United States, Russia, Denmark (Greenland), Finland, Iceland, Norway and Sweden; it has a permanent secretariat at Tromso in northern Norway. In addition, non-voting membership in the council with the same status of sovereign states has been granted to six indigenous Arctic peoples and the Inuit Circumpolar Conference (ICC), a non-governmental group that draws together Inuit representatives from Alaska, Greenland, Canada and Russia every three years to develop common policies. In 1989, it agreed to develop a standardized script. In April 2009, the ICC declared "sovereignty" over the Arctic's natural resources.

The ICC has become a vigorous lobby and has resisted efforts by the U.S., Russia and environmental groups to declare the polar bear an endangered species. It argues that this would hurt the local economies by, among other things, deterring American hunters from paying millions of dollars a year for the right to shoot them. The killing continues in Greenland and Canada under quotas set by territorial governments. Two-thirds of the world's estimated 25,000 polar bears roam the Canadian Arctic.

The Arctic Council also includes the Sami Council (representing Scandinavian aboriginals), the Association of Indigenous Peoples of the North of Russia, and the Aleuts on the islands between Alaska and Russia. The first foreign ministers' meeting of the members was held in Nunavut's capital, Iqaluit, in 1998. Canada is implementing its goal of a "Northern dimension" to Canadian foreign policy that strives to gain input from the peoples of the North rather than imposing "southern" values on them. Simon noted, "Northerners are really the pioneers of circumpolar cooperation."

PEOPLE

Unlike the United States, Canada is often described as a "mosaic," rather than a "melting pot." In many ways, this is accurate. In Canada, there are many population groups that speak different lan-

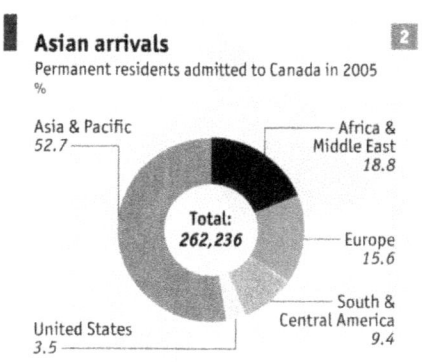

Source: *The Economist*

guages, or that are ethnically distinct from one another. Many vigorously resist assimilation with other Canadians; they are less inclined to lose their former identity in a larger "Canadianism," than have been most ethnic groups in the United States. The Canadian government recognizes this diversity by having an official policy of multiculturalism administered by a minister of state with cabinet rank.

Given the specific conditions of the country, this is an enlightened approach. It should be recognized, though, that this policy makes a virtue out of a necessity. Few British Canadians in the 18th and early 19th centuries foresaw that French Canadians would struggle so successfully against assimilation and that, one day, ambitious anglophone children would be flocking to French-immersion schools in order to get a leg up on those who cannot speak French. Multiculturalism in Canada grew out of the need to conciliate francophones and has been broadened to include other ethnic groups as well. Many francophones were uneasy about such broadening because it seemed to undercut their view of Canada as a union of *two* peoples, rather than as a collection of ethnic minorities in which francophones are merely one of many. Yet it was Quebec nationalism that necessitated the official policy of multiculturalism, which is of such benefit to other minorities as well.

Some Canadians need reminders that Canada is multicultural and multilingual whether they like it or not. When in 1983 the unilingual John Crosbie challenged the completely bilingual Brian Mulroney and Joe Clark for leadership of the Conservative Party, he declared that Canada's 3.7 million bilingual Canadians should not regard themselves as "some sort of aristocracy" from which the country's prime ministers would be drawn. The fact is, though, that no unilingual Canadian does have the chance to become prime minister any more. Crosbie's unfortunate utterance completely destroyed his bid for leadership; Canada never was, is not and

will not become a homogeneous, wholly English-speaking country.

Of course, terms like "mosaic" and "melting-pot" are over-simplifications in the case of both neighbors, even though they are not "myths," as some persons claim. Some suggest that Canada is really a "mosaic of mosaics." The goal has never been to transform Canada into a land of isolated communities, but to accommodate cultural differences in a way that newcomers can be integrated into a shared civic space.

Since the 1960s many countries have experienced ethnic revivals, including the United States. The number of black, brown and yellow faces, "hyphenated Americans," bilingual schools and Spanish-language documents and signs reveal the limits of cultural and ethnic assimilation in the United States. American blacks have successfully demanded *group* rights for people of their race, as opposed to the traditional American emphasis on *individual* rights, which has been an American creed since the country's founding. Thus, the United States has also moved in the direction of a "mosaic" society.

Any implication that each "stone" in the Canadian "mosaic" shares equally in the overall product is misleading. To use Orwellian language, some Canadians "are more equal than others." A Canadian's race, language and/or ethnic background are still socially relevant. For instance, only slightly over 3% of all Canadian marriages and common-law unions are mixed race, and most of them are likely to be between Asian-Canadians and Caucasians. Political, economic and social power is still held by people of European heritage. For example, of the 200 top corporate chief executives surveyed by the *Financial Post* in 1997, only seven were non-white, and they were all Asian.

Nevertheless, there is something remarkable about the way the parts stick together. Former Saskatchewan Premier Roy Romanow described it this way: "Each province, territory and region, plus our many cultures and different stories, can be likened to individual pearls making up a beautiful necklace, connected to each other by the strand of shared destiny. That strand, however, is fragile and requires constant attention."

Population Groups

The largest "stone" in the "mosaic" is the British one. By the mid-1980s, Canadians of British ancestry made up a little more than 40% of the total population, a proportion which has steadily decreased over the years, even though 76% of all Canadians claimed in the 1981 census to have at least one British ancestor. By 1997, the UK had fallen to tenth place as a

Canada

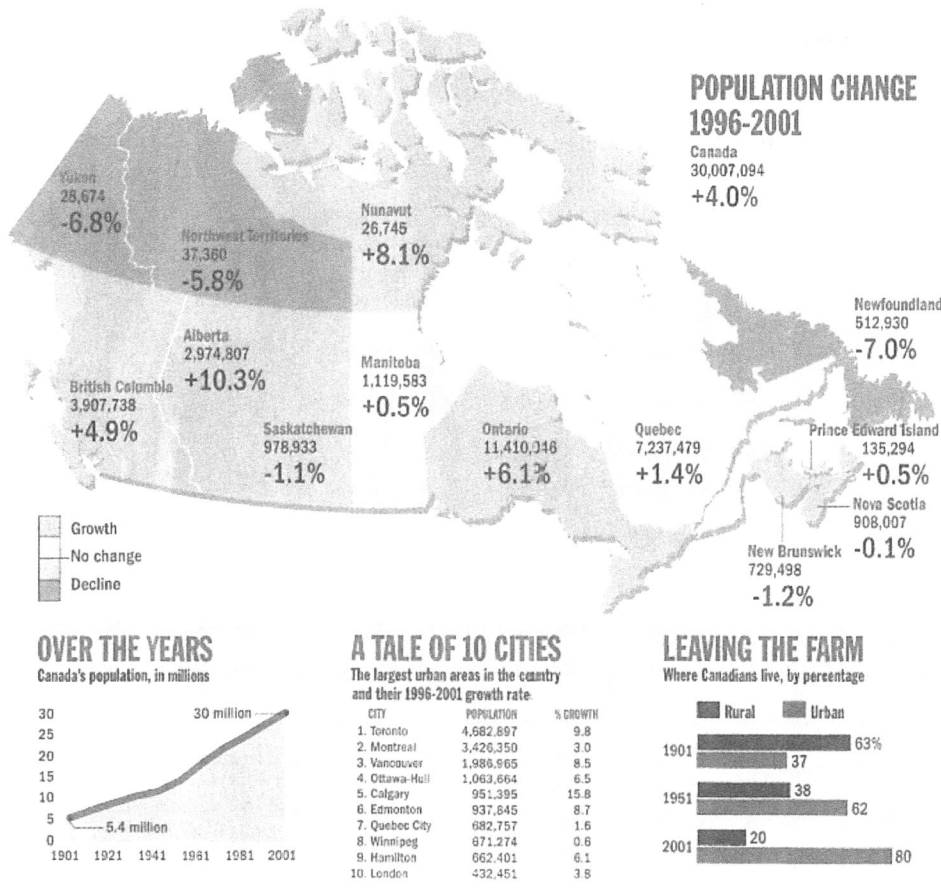

Source: *Maclean's*

source country for Canadian immigrants. Of course, this grouping is not as homogeneous as it might seem at first glance: it includes Scots and Welsh, who are not English, and it encompasses Irish Protestants from Ulster and Catholics from the rest of Ireland, groups which are by no means interchangeable.

The second largest "stone" is the French one, which makes up 22.9% of the total population (2001) and is declining. The French were the first Canadians, and they now constitute the overwhelming majority of Quebec's population, about 40% of New Brunswick's, 5% of Ontario's, and 6% of Manitoba's. Because of Quebec nationalism since the 1960s and the federal government's response to it, francophones' opportunities within the entire Canadian Confederation have been markedly improved. Its oil-based economy attracts immigrants from all over Canada. Therefore, Alberta is experiencing the country's greatest growth in francophone population—12.6% each year. It is the only province since 1996 to experience an increase in francophone children under age 5. The country as a whole is experiencing an uptick in the number of French moving to Canada.

The third largest group of Canadians is of German ancestry, constituting 3.3% of the total. This group is perhaps the most fully assimilated minority in all of Canada, although there is a notable exception to this generalization: the Hutterites in the Prairie provinces, who came to Canada from South Dakota during the First World War because of their refusal to serve in the armed forces. They are a religious sect similar to the Amish and Mennonites, except that they believe in the communal ownership of property and rearing of children. They shun contact with the outside world as much as possible. On grounds of faith, they object to being photographed for their driver's licenses. Then come Italians, who make up 2.8% of the population and whose numbers have grown enormously since the Second World War. One Canadian citizen, Gino Bucchino, even won a seat in the Italian parliament in 2006.

In fifth place are Ukrainians, who make up 1.5% of all Canadians. Canada has the world's third-largest Ukrainian population after Ukraine itself and Russia. During the First World War about 5,000 Ukrainian Canadians were interned in a fit of ethnic fear, their property was confiscated, and many were forced to perform hard labor. Former Prime Minister Paul Martin acknowledged that this was "a dark day in Canadian history" and offered both a formal apology and $25 million to Ukrainians and other groups for educational exhibits and memorials. Roy Romanow, whose father left Ukraine in the 1920s, remembered growing up in Saskatoon: "Our family's universe was comprised of the Ukrainian hall, St. George's Ukrainian Greek Catholic Cathedral, our schools, and the shopping area of 20th Street just a few blocks away. We could go to church, visit friends and neighbours and buy our necessities without using either one of Canada's two official languages." Ukrainian communities in Canada were deeply concerned for, and acted to support those still living there in light of the horrendous destruction caused by the Russian invasion in early 2022.

The same was true of many other immigrants, including Icelanders, whose descendants in Canada outnumber the population of Iceland itself. The largest congregation of Finns outside of Scandinavia lives in Canada, especially in Thunder Bay, Ontario.

Canada was always a land of immigration. Today there are over 200 immigrant groups there, and more than a fifth of Canadians were born outside the country; the figure is 12.2% in the U.S. and 4.8% in the United Kingdom. Forty members of the 2006 parliament were born outside Canada. The 2016 census confirmed that Canada now has the highest proportion of foreign-born persons since 1931. In 2016, the foreign-born population represents 21.9% of the total population, the highest proportion of G8 countries. When the data of the 2021 census are updated, these percentages may change.

Immigrants, only 44% of whom come with the ability to speak English or French, were responsible for the 4% growth of the Canadian population between 1996 and 2002. In 2016, however, 93.2% could conduct a conversation in French of English. Nevertheless, Canada's population is aging: 37% are over 45, increasing to 43% in 2011.

An important demographic trend in Canada is the decreasing percentage of citizens of European heritage, from 79.7% in 1971 to only 66.9% in 1981, and 13.7% in 2011 and 11.6% in 2016. The reason for this is a decreasing birth rate (1.66 children per woman in 2011) and a change in the composition of immigrants to Canada. In the 1960s, the Canadian Parliament liberalized the country's immigration policy, opening the door to Asians, Africans, Caribbean islanders, Latin Americans and other groups from the third world, which make up more than three-fourths of all immigration to Canada. Their percentages of Canada's total population changed noticeably from 1971 to 1981: Asians grew from 4.2% to 14%. In 2006, Asia accounted

Canada

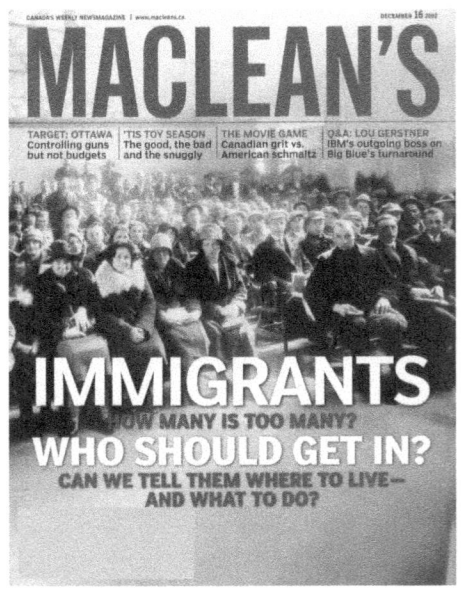

for 52.7% of new arrivals, while 15.6% were from Europe, 18.8% from Africa and the Middle East, 9.4% from Latin America and the Caribbean, and only 3.5% from the U.S. Those coming from the Caribbean have fallen sharply.

The top countries of origin for immigrants during the past five years (2011-2016) are Asians (including those from the Middle East), who made up 61.8% of newcomers, which is slightly higher than the 2006 census. Immigration from Africa, Caribbean, and Central and South America increased slightly. Asian countries accounted for seven out of ten of the immigrant countries which included: the Philippines, India, China, Iran, Pakistan, Syria, and South Korea. They bring with them much university education and potential for high-paid occupations.

By 1996, the number of European immigrants had for the first time fallen below 50% of the total immigrant population. As of 2016, only 27.7% of immigrants were from Europe. The vast majority of the foreign-born population live in four provinces: Ontario, Quebec, British Colombia and Alberta (2016). Seven out of ten lived in the largest census metropolitan areas: Toronto, Montreal and Vancouver (2016). The magnets are Toronto (46% of immigrant in 2016), Vancouver (40.8%) and Montreal (23.4%), making these three metropolitan areas increasingly distinct from the rest of Canada. Only 6% of newcomers chose to live outside major urban areas, and Canada's immigration policy seeks to attract young, large foreign families to rural Canada. Toronto is now home to 62 different ethnic groups numbering more than 10,000 people and 15 groups with more than 100,000. Geography professor Larry S. Bourne of the University of Toronto admits: "We just don't know how a Toronto of the future, which is 60 percent nonwhite with 110 different ethnic groups and languages, is going to relate to the rest of Canada."

The first Chinese came to Canada in 1858 to work as laborers in the gold mines that had begun to be opened during the Fraser River gold rush. From 1881 to 1884, they were used as laborers to construct the Canadian Pacific Railway. Many died doing their dangerous work, and from 1923 to 1947 they were banned from entry altogether. By 2004, they constituted 16% of Canada's immigrants and more than 3% of the total population (1.1 million). The Philippines is now Canada's largest source of immigrants, followed by China. Chinese wield considerable political and economic influence, and they form a crucial link in the country's growing trade with China. Acceding to a long-standing demand in 2006, the Canadian government offered both an apology and compensation for their past mistreatment.

During World War II, as in the U.S., thousands of Japanese who immigrated were suspected of disloyalty and received the same undignified treatment as Japanese-Americans: the 22,000 Japanese-Canadians, 17,000 of whom had Canadian citizenship, were forced to resettle in internment camps deep in the interior of the country, "to safeguard the defences of the Pacific coast of Canada." Their property was disposed in an attempt to prevent them from returning.

Most Canadians today regret that action, which Brian Mulroney called "one of the greatest blots on civil liberties ever inflicted on citizens of this country," and in 1988 the government agreed to pay about $291 million in compensation. From 1933 to 1945 Canada accepted only 5,000 Jewish refugees from Nazi Germany, compared with 200,000 by the U.S. and 15,000 by Bolivia.

Asians poured in from war-torn Indochina, including thousands of "boat-people" from Vietnam. At the end of the 1990s an organized attempt to smuggle Chinese into the country sparked angry demands for tighter controls. Chinese-based gangs receive down payments of up to $60,000 to drop Chinese onto Canada's shores. They are moved through an underground network to eastern Canada or the United States, where they are forced to work off their debts through low-paying jobs or prostitution. Canada's large Chinese community denounces these illegal Chinese as queue-jumpers.

In the past, Canadians have viewed each successive wave of immigration with suspicion; however, the fact that most newcomers are now non-white makes their reception even frostier. Pollster Allan Gregg noted, "you do not have to scratch too deep to find racist views." Despite Canadians' growing uneasiness about the goal of a "cultural mosaic," Ottawa passed a multiculturalism act in 1988 making Canada "in essence a microcosm of the world." Officials talk about Canada as a "community of communities," and the government provides more money to ethnic societies than it spends to encourage immigrants to become Canadians. Nevertheless, anglophone Canadians regard multiculturalism as central to their national identity. According to a 2014 poll, they rank it below universal health care and the Canadian flag, but above ice hockey, the Mounties, and the Queen.

Polls in 1994 indicated that 72% of Canadian respondents believed at that time that the multicultural mosaic was not working and should be replaced by an American-style cultural melting pot, which insists that immigrants put their ethnic differences aside and embrace American values and customs. Some Canadians fear that the waves of newcomers will alter their way of life.

An example of this attitudinal change was the outcry against the decision to permit male Sikhs, who are required to wear turbans, to continue wearing them after becoming Mounties, as Sikhs were already allowed to do in the Canadian armed forces, unless safety is an issue. In 2006, the Supreme Court of Canada struck down the Montreal school board's ban on Sikh ceremonial daggers (kirpans), citing freedom of religion. It did allow the boards to restrict the size of such daggers and require that they be sheathed and out of sight. Sikhs make up 2% of Canada's population. Justin Trudeau's cabinet has four Sikh members including the defense

Canada

An Eastern Orthodox church, Thunder Bay, Ontario

minister. The leader of the opposition New Democratic Party, Jagmeet Singh, is also Sikh.

In 2007, a debate broke out in Quebec over how specific Canadians are willing to give advice and set rules and guidelines concerning how immigrants should live. Some Canadians argued that one should be able to expect "reasonable accommodation" of newcomers, especially Muslims, who constitute only 3% of Canada's population (6% by 2050), in adapting to the language, attitudes and lifestyles of the majority population. A 2018 government online survey conducted by the Privy Council Office found that Canadians feel that they are being asked to change and adapt too much and 59% believed many immigrants don't adopt "Canadian values." Further, a 2017 Angus Reid Survey poll found that 53% of Canadians thought the country did too much to accommodate religious diversity. For example, Muslim parents in Toronto requested that their children be exempted from mandatory music classes, citing Islam's ban on listening to or playing musical instruments.

There were geographic differences: 77% of Quebecers thought that immigrants should fully adapt, compared with 49% in Ontario. These results were confirmed two years later, in 2009, when 62% of Canadians believed that laws and norms should not be modified to accommodate minorities (74% in Quebec). In 2017, Quebec banned women from wearing face coverings when providing or receiving public services. In rare cases, hatred can get the upper hand. In Ste-Foy in 2017, a Québécois student entered Quebec City's largest mosque and murdered six Muslims.

The Quebec government sponsored a long series of sometimes inflammatory public hearings on the subject and concluded that conflicts between lifelong Québécois and immigrants are rare, even if highly publicized in the media. Nevertheless, in 2010 the Quebec government passed legislation requiring woman to take off their veils and show their faces when receiving government services. Bill 94 was the first legislation in North America to ban face coverings in any government building, including schools and universities. A poll revealed that 95% of Quebecois and three-fourths of non-Quebecers approved of the law. Support for accommodation was highest in the Atlantic provinces, the Prairies and Alberta. In 2012, Canada's immigration minister, Jason Kenney, banned face veils worn by immigrants taking the citizenship oath. However, the Supreme Court of Canada ruled later that year that female witnesses could under some circumstances cover their faces for religious reasons when testifying in court.

There are some doubts as to whether the traditional pattern of assimilation works any more. In the past, immigrants tended to congregate in enclaves, and then their children and grandchildren mastered English or French, moved out and integrated with Canadians. That does not always work these days. Incomes and employment rates are lower for immigrant families, and offspring of visible minorities reportedly tend to feel less Canadian and experience more racism than their parents.

Now constituting roughly a fifth of the population (about twice that in the U.S.), the numbers of immigrants allowed to enter Canada each year had risen from 84,000 in 1985 to over 300,000 in 2019, including 44,610 Syrian refugees. Those with job offers are favored. More than half are skilled workers and their dependents picked for their potential contribution to the economy. Half have college degrees (only 27% in the U.S.). Family reunification accounts for 28% of immigrants (compared with almost two-thirds in the U.S.). Canada now takes in .85% of its population in new immigrants every year (compared to .6% for Australia and .3% for the U.S.), and most of them head for the three largest cities: Toronto, Vancouver and Montreal. Most learn a good deal about Canadian history, politics, culture and geography. This was tested in 2009 by the Dominion Institute: given a mock examination that mirrored the citizenship test, 70% of immigrants passed it, but only 40% of Canadians were able to do so. Asked what Canada's defining symbols were, both immigrants and Canadians ranked the maple leaf and hockey at the top.

A majority of immigrants now admitted are members of visible minorities, particularly South Asians, Arabs and Blacks. They join the 11.47% of Canada's population that, according to the 2011 census, were visible minorities. This varied from 25.9% in BC, 19.1% in Ontario (where some communities, such as Markham, had as many as 53%) and 18.4% in Alberta to only 11% in Quebec, .9% in PEI and .8% in Newfoundland. Prime Minister Justin Trudeau named a refugee, Ahmed Hussen, as "immigration czar."

The government ordered that greater priority be given to immigrants with high job skills and competence in English or French than to those joining families. In 2002, a point system was introduced that assigned points for such things as years

Miss Universe Natalie Glebova

Canada

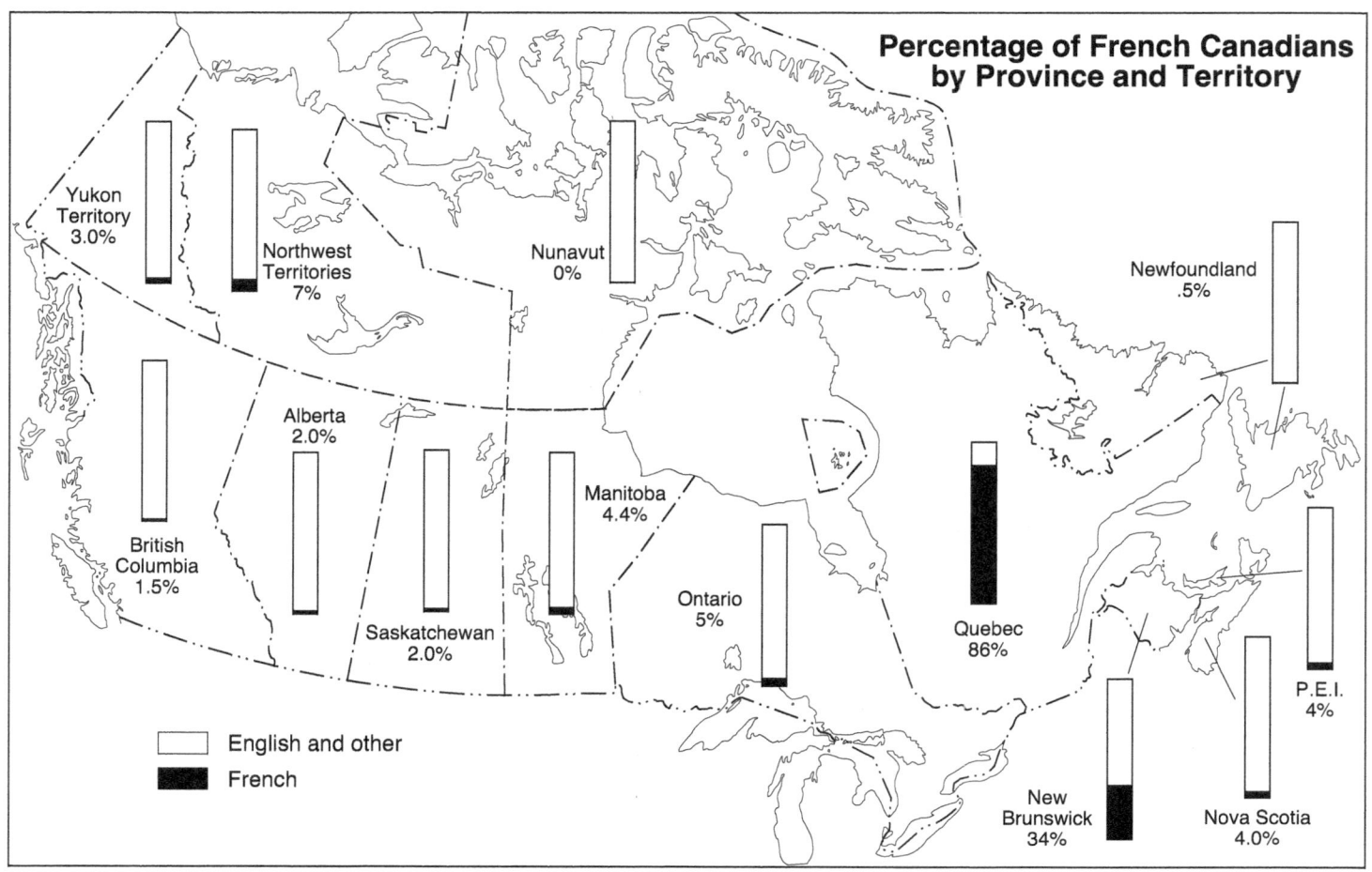

in school, numbers of university degrees, age, working experience and language skills; it favors higher-skilled and higher earning persons. This created problems since foreigners with trade skills needed in the labor market often do not qualify. This made certain labor shortages even worse and sparked discussion on how to make immigration reflect the country's new economic and demographic needs. Also some who get in through the point system have difficulties applying their education due to discrimination, language handicaps or the problem of having their credentials recognized. By 2007, four-fifths of skilled immigrants to Canada had a university degree, but their earnings lagged behind those of native Canadians. By contrast, immigrants to the U.S. with college degrees earn more than their American counterparts. Nevertheless, immigrants to Canada managed in 2012 to send an estimated $23.4 billion in remittances back to their families overseas. In 2017, fearing deportation from the U.S., a storm of Italians illegally crossed unguarded border areas in upstate New York seeking asylum. Authorities had to create temporary tent encampments and open the Montreal Olympic Stadium to house them. Half the applicants were rejected.

A stunning and successful immigrant is Natalie Glebova. A shy 12-year old who stepped off a plane from Russia in 1994 speaking only a few words of English, Glebova's family settled in Toronto and she graduated in IT from Ryerson University. In 2005, she was crowned Miss Universe, the second Canadian to wear the crown after Karen Baldwin in 1982. In 2012, Jenna Talackova, who had undergone a sex change at age 19, failed to win the Miss Universe crown, but the Canadian beauty captured the title of Miss Congeniality. Canada's Miss World candidate in 2016, Chinese–Canadian Amastasia Lin, infuriated China by publicly criticizing its human rights abuses.

The July 2006 war in Lebanon prompted a lively discussion over what it means to be a citizen and what responsibilities Canada has toward its dual citizens living abroad; 15,000 Canadian passport holders were evacuated from that war-torn country to safety at a cost to the Canadian taxpayer of almost $100 million. How is it that 50,000 "Canadians" lived in Lebanon? They constitute about 1.3% of the total population and more citizens than the U.S., Britain, and Germany combined have living there.

Canada permits dual citizenship since 1977. Among the best known dual citizens is former Governor General Michaëlle Jean (Haitian). All that is required to get a Canadian passport is three-years of residency. Many then leave the country and become what critics call "Canadians of convenience," with no ties to the country except an additional passport. Indeed, 40% of the Chinese who went to Canada in their working years during the late 1990s left the country for higher-paying jobs in Hong Kong or the U.S. Many Indo-Canadians also moved on. As many as half the Canadians who move to the U.S. are born outside of Canada.

They can vote in overseas elections, as well as in Canadian. Unlike American citizens, Canadians are not required to pay Canadian taxes no matter where they live. Therefore, Ottawa has no idea how many dual citizens live abroad, or even inside of Canada. The Asia Pacific Foundation of Canada calculates that there are 2.7 million overseas passport holders, roughly 9% of the population. That would represent proportionally the world's fourth-largest Diaspora, and it includes some of

Canada

Asia's wealthiest people. An estimated quarter of a million reside in Hong Kong alone. Close to a million live in the U.S.

Canada faces a tormenting dilemma about what kind of help it can offer to the world's 21.5 million political refugees and who precisely is a "political refugee." For example, after 2007 the number of claimants from former communist countries in Europe shot up. The top source were Roma (Gypsies) from Hungary, who maintain that they face life-threatening discrimination at home. Only 2% were accepted in 2010. The backlog of individual applicants for visas, the increase in the number of refugees around the globe, and the tighter immigration controls in other nations all contribute to an illegal stampede to Canada—not unlike what the US. is experiencing at its southern border.

Every year about 25,000 persons claim refugee status in Canada. Once the claim is made, the newcomers are entitled to all the legal rights and benefits of Canadian citizens. They are allowed to work for at least four years and receive free medical care and social assistance for years while their cases are processed and appealed. As in the U.S., more than half of refugee claims are approved, compared with only about 15% in most countries. Even if they are ultimately rejected, they have a good prospect of never being removed. In 2007, there was a backlog of about 50,000 unexecuted deportation orders. All Canadians agree that they need an orderly and selective infusion of immigrants in order to keep their country strong and healthy. But critics are divided over whether too many or too few illegal newcomers are being permitted to stay. Many Canadians think that the country's present immigration system is unable to handle the problem.

Attitudes hardened after the September 11, 2001, terrorist attacks in New York and Washington. They destroyed the prior assumption that all newcomers to Canada shared its fundamental values. Ottawa expanded police powers and the use of preventive arrests to deal with immigrants or refugees who might be involved in terrorist activities. These measures especially worry Canada's diverse population of more than 600,000 Muslims (about 3% of the population) from dozens of nationalities, upwards to 44 different ethnicities, and many different languages, cultures, economic and political backgrounds. Roughly half were born in Canada. Of those born abroad, about a third is Arab-Muslim, and another third is from Pakistan and India. More than 148,000 speak Arabic as their mother tongue.

One third of Canada's Muslims said in 2004 that their lives had changed for the worse after September 11, while 22% thought their lives had changed for the better because they now have the opportunity for greater dialogue and debate. An opinion survey in 2009 revealed that 45% of Canadians believed that mainstream Islam encourages violence. In a 2017 poll, 62% of respondence agreed that Islamaphobia is a problem. At the same time, B'nai Brith Canada reported that an unfortunate consequence of the post-September 11 tension was an increase in anti-Semitic violence usually involving young Arab and Muslim men.

In 2011, voters in Calgary elected Naheed Nenshi, a visible-minority Muslim academic as the first Muslim mayor of a major Canadian city. The son of immigrants, he won a scholarship to do graduate study at Harvard after graduating from the University of Calgary. This city's dynamic economy and cosmopolitan character have attracted more immigrants per capita than Montreal; one out of four inhabitants is a visible minority.

Hate crimes are also rising against Muslims, even at universities. Sometimes compromises would lessen tensions. An example was the request by Muslim art students at the University of Western Ontario to be given an alternate assignment instead of having to sketch nude models. The university rejected this. At the same time, more than 80% of respondents in a 2007 CBC poll of the Muslim community said they are broadly satisfied with their lives in Canada; 73% were "very proud" to be Canadian, and only 17% sensed that Canadians were hostile to Islam. In another poll, a mere 6% of Canadians claimed to be uneasy about the idea of a Muslim living next door. Rapid change is often most difficult to absorb. From 1991 to 2001 Canada's Muslim population doubled. This makes Islam the country's fifth largest religion and the second largest in every big city except Vancouver. This will rise even more with the influx of at least 25,000 Syrians fleeing violence in their country.

One immigrant group that is shrinking in Canada is Americans; from 1971 to 1981 their percentage of the Canadian population dropped from 9.3% to 8.06%. Canada's immigration laws make it more difficult to enter. In the 1980s, two times more Canadians moved to the U.S. than *vice versa*. Nevertheless, Canada remains the favorite destination for American expatriates, followed by Mexico and Britain. In 2019, the number of Americans settling in Canada—10,800—was more than double the number in 2000 (5,800) and a 30-year high. The most common reason was the labor market. Their challenges in adjusting were such that the first American ex-pat support group was formed in Vancouver. The 60 or so regular members not only socialize with each other but discuss Canadian pet peeves, such as Americans' habits of talking loudly and neglecting to take off their shoes when entering a Canadian's house.

A visible portion of those former Americans is black. While it is true that the Underground Railway before the American Civil War extended all the way into Canada and that abolitionism was strong in Canada during the first half of the 19th century, slavery did exist there for more than 200 years. It had been introduced in New France in 1628 and was not abolished until the British Emancipation Act of 1833.

Even after emancipation, blacks in Canada continued to suffer discrimination and tended to be confined to all-black ghettos in the larger cities. Further black immigration from the United States was never officially barred, but blacks were normally prevented from crossing the border on all kinds of specious grounds, such as disease or inability to withstand Canada's harsh climate. Reports reveal that black children suffered violence and abuse in a Halifax orphanage. Discrimination has declined now, but it still exists in employment and housing, and racial prejudice has not been purged from Canadian social life. Festering racial tension in Montreal, Halifax and Toronto confirm that. Of course, not all Canadian blacks, who make up 4% of the population, are from the United States. Many have poured in from Africa, the U.K., and the Caribbean. Some, such as Haitians, do not speak English, and those who settled in Montreal have had difficulties in becoming equal citizens in Quebec society. Such diversity has meant that blacks remain the least cohesive of Canada's minority groups; they form distinct communities whose members arrived at different times.

**Ex-National Chief Shawn Atleo
Assembly of First Nations**

Canada

Individuals can rise to prominence. A notable example was Ontario's former lieutenant general, Lincoln Alexander, who passed away in 2012. Born in Toronto, he was the son of Caribbean immigrants. He became Canada's first black member of parliament, first black cabinet minister (of labor), and first black lieutenant governor. Ex-Governor General Michaëlle Jean, who subsequently became secretary-general of La Francophone, was born and raised in Haiti. The stunning world record in the 100-yard dash set by Ben Johnson in 1987 focused attention on Canadian blacks. An immigrant from Jamaica, he especially did Canadians' hearts good by beating the brash, flag waving American, Carl Lewis, whose cocky manner epitomized that which irks many Canadians about Americans. However, Olympic gold turned to dust when a urine test following his 1988 victory revealed that the now-disgraced Johnson had used performance-enhancing steroids. The 1996 Olympic Games produced a new hero: Donovan Bailey, who won the 100-meter sprint without the aid of drugs. He did manage to ignite a national furor when he said to a *Sports Illustrated* interviewer that Canada is as racist as the U.S.

Aboriginal Peoples

One minority of particular importance to Canadians and their governments is the native Inuit, Métis and Indian population, which constitute only 1.4 million (about 4.3%; in BC 17%) of all Canadians. It is growing six times the rate of the general Canadian population. In fact, the Aboriginal population increased 42.5% from 2006 to 2016. No one questions the fact that they were the first humans to settle what is now Canada, having migrated at least 12,000 years ago over the Bering Strait, a narrow stretch of water, about 50 miles wide, separating Siberia from Alaska. The Inuit remained in the Arctic North, while other tribes moved southward to the more temperate climate. Anthropologists still do not agree upon exactly when they came and how they crossed the Bering Strait, nor can they find any lingual connection between the 58 Indian languages and dialects spoken in Canada and languages spoken in Asia today.

When the first Europeans began to settle Canada in the 16th century, there were already an estimated 200,000 Indians and a few thousand Inuit living rather evenly distributed there. Culturally none had advanced beyond the stone-age. Most sustained themselves by hunting and fishing, but a few tribes, such as the Iroquois, had begun to establish semi-permanent settlements and had begun to derive a part of their livelihood from agriculture. They were indispensable to the first Europeans, teaching them how to survive in the rugged and cold North American setting.

There are about 553,000 "Status Indians" (also called "First Nations people") registered under the Indian Act of Canada. They belong to 633 different bands (tribes, averaging 650 persons, with the largest numbering 18,600—the Six Nations of the Grand River in Ontario), and about 326,000 of them live on 2,300 reservations, which are largely self-governing. Ontario has the largest native population, and BC has the greatest number of bands—197. There are also about 405,000 "Non-Status Indians," who do not enjoy special benefits. Many women married non-Indians, and other Indians gave up their status as Indians. Of registered Indians living off reservations who have children, 70% have their kids with non-status partners thereby relinquishing their registration entitlements.

The Canadian government's policy since 1970 of encouraging Indians to assimilate with Canadian society has led to no dramatic changes. Since the birth rate on reservations is about the same as Indians who leave, the reservations' populations are remaining stable. Forty-four percent of natives live in cities. Because of their high birth rate (twice the national average), aboriginals are Canada's youngest and fastest-growing ethnic group. About two-thirds are younger than 35, and half are under 25.

The federal government runs schools on Indian reserves. By 2004, one in four schoolchildren in Manitoba and Saskatchewan were aboriginal. The infant mortality rate is double the Canadian average, and half the children live in poverty. The high school graduation rate for aboriginals in 2013 was 36%, about half that of non-natives. A depressing statistic is that a First Nation boy is more likely to go to jail than graduate from high school. Compared with the national average in 2004, aboriginals on reservations have only half the national average income, a lower life expectancy (68 years vs. 80 for men, 75 vs. 84.2 for women), and greater dependence upon social assistance; 40% are on welfare. Canada as a whole is always ranked toward the top of the UN's annual Human Development Index, but its aboriginals alone would rank only 63rd.

Nevertheless, comparisons of the 1981 and 2001 census figures show that there has been some improvement in the social conditions of urbanized aboriginals. From a half to two-thirds of aboriginal youths age 15 to 24 attended school in 2001, as opposed to only a third to a half two decades earlier. The high school dropout rate in 2011 for urbanized aboriginals was 43% versus 60% for Inuit and reservation aboriginals and only 10% for other Canadians. More attend and graduate from institutions of higher learning although only 9% of Métis, 7% of First Nations and

Stanley Park, Vancouver, BC Credit: Province of British Columbia

Canada

4% of Inuit have university degrees, compared with one-quarter of non-aboriginal Canadians. More of those in urban areas are employed, and fewer depend on welfare assistance.

Not only do Indians occupy huge tracts of Canadian territory, but they have a wide variety of special relations, both by treaty and by legislation, with the rest of Canada. About half the registered Indians, mainly those living in the three Prairie provinces and Ontario, receive treaty payments as a result of prior agreements with the British Crown. Those rights were incorporated in the 1982 constitution. Still, the Canadian government continues to face difficult challenges from Indian and Métis (French-Indian) groups stemming from unsettled claims, the problems of defining who should be considered as a registered Indian, and what precisely the natives' rights should be. So controversial are some of these questions that Canadians were not yet prepared in 1982 to spell out native rights in their new constitution.

Native frustration exploded in 1990, only weeks after the rancorous Meech Lake debate designating Quebec as a "distinct society" had already laid bare the inter-communal fractures in Canadian society. It had failed to be ratified because a Cree Indian representative in Manitoba's legislative assembly, Elijah Harper, had single-handedly prevented that body from voting for it because it ignored native rights.

In Oka, Quebec, 18 miles west of Montreal, Mohawk Indians from the nearby Kanesatake reserve, joined by warriors from the United States, protested a proposed expansion of a local golf course into what they claimed was their ancestral land. Ottawa agreed to buy the land and turn it over to the Mohawks, but militants seized upon the situation to publicize wider native grievances, including demands for sovereignty. Mulroney categorically stated that "native self-government does not now, and cannot ever, mean sovereign independence."

A fatal clash on July 11, 1990, was tinder for a massive escalation, as the violence moved to Montreal, where Mohawks blocked the Mercier Bridge, one of the main arteries connecting the island of Montreal with the southern shore of the St. Lawrence, creating immense inconveniences for commuters. All over Canada, Indians showed their support by mounting demonstrations and blockades of roads and rail lines. The Quebec police were unable to control the violence, and the provincial government requested Ottawa to send troops to quell the uprising. After 90 days of skirmishes and negotiations, the Indians surrendered, leaving Canadians perplexed about how to deal with the dilemma of native claims to more than half of Canada's land.

After that standoff, the Quebec police, RCMP and politicians stayed out of the Kanesatake community of 2,000 Mohawks, located at the far edge of northwest Montreal. This left a void that, according to elected Grand Chief James Gabriel, was filled by three dozen or so organized criminals, who traffic in cigarettes, alcohol, drugs, weapons and illegal immigrants. Mohawks do not regard themselves as Canadian. In 2010, they evicted 25 non-natives from their reserve just south of Montreal. First Nations have the right to determine who can live on their reserves.

Natives demand respect in symbolic ways as well. They blocked the naming of a road in Whitehorse, Yukon, after the author Jack London, who had once traveled in the territory. He was charged with having written insulting observations about aboriginals and having advocated white supremacy, charges that some literary experts dispute. In 2006, violence again erupted, this time in Caledonia, 80 km (50 miles) southwest of Toronto. When a new housing development broke ground on land claimed by the Six Nations Iroquois Confederacy, aboriginals occupied the site.

Much more peaceful protests began the end of 2012. Indians blocked roads and railways, performed impromptu dances in shopping malls and chanted outside the office of ex-Prime Minister Harper, whom they accused of neglect. One female Cree chief, Theresa Spence, pitched a tepee near the parliament and went on a partial six-week hunger strike, refusing solid food. Canada spends over $11 billion a year on its aboriginal population.

As a whole, Indians and the estimated 153,000 surviving Métis are among Canada's poorest citizens despite the various forms of state assistance available. They are plagued by unemployment, and many live on welfare. Their alcoholism rate is 13 times that among whites, their life expectancy is eight years less, infant mortality is twice as high, and their suicide rate is three times higher (six times among youth). Aboriginals account for as much as 8% of HIV infection, a higher percentage than any other ethnic group. About a quarter of new cases involve the native population. One reason is the large numbers of young aboriginals who travel from inner cities to rural communities and reservations carrying infections back and forth. They are also disproportionately represented in prisons, a known breeding ground for disease. Only half of all Métis reach the ninth grade in school. Métis males are eight times more likely to be jailed than non-Métis; aboriginals as a whole are seven times more likely to be incarcerated. Winnipeg's problem of gang violence stems largely from Métis and native youths.

PURSUIT OF BILINGUALISM

The percentage of students enrolled in French immersion in 1998-1999

B.C.	4.6%
ALTA.	5
SASK.	4.8
MAN.	9.2
ONT.	7.3
QUE.	37.3*
N.B.	23.6
P.E.I.	13.4
N.S.	7.5
NFLD.	4.4
YUKON	6.6
N.W.T.	2.8

*English school boards only

Source: Statistics Canada

In 1992, a breakthrough occurred in native (called "aboriginal") standing. Aboriginals were admitted to the negotiating table to work out a new constitution and were granted the "inherent right of self-government." The Canadian government is attempting to settle the hundreds of land claims made by native groups. It spends C$9 billion each year on aboriginal programs. But the problems are mind-boggling. The 553,000 status Indians and 51,000 Inuit have different demands than the half million Métis and non-status Indians, who have no land base and often live in inner-city poverty.

The Assembly of First Nations (AFN), led by Perry Bellegarde, is made up of the chiefs of over 600 reserve communities and is divided between moderates and radicals. They disagree on how to respond to settlement offers. Native groups' land claims often overlap each other. The AFN presses such key issues as resource-revenue sharing and education. Aboriginals can tie resource projects up in legal knots for years. Another organization, the Congress of Aboriginal Peoples (CAP), represents off-reserve natives. In 2017, the government gave these aboriginal organizations the former U.S. embassy building facing parliament.

Self-government is difficult to define, especially before the thorny issue of boundaries is settled. Native leaders demand that aboriginals live only under their own laws, but this would create a patchwork of differing legal zones across Canada. Finally, although there are some

33

Canada

female chiefs, women in the male-dominated bands might have fewer rights than those guaranteed them by the Charter of Rights and Freedoms.

In 1997, the Supreme Court of Canada ruled that native people can have clear, definable title to their land based on their oral histories and that governments have a moral duty to negotiate with them. This ruling has profound ramifications, especially in British Columbia, where most native groups have never signed land treaties and where more than 230 of them are pursuing land claims that cover the entire province.

On January 7, 1998, the Canadian government apologized to all aboriginal peoples for decades of mistreatment. The "Statement of Reconciliation" dealt with an array of offenses, including the hanging of Métis leader Louis Riel in 1885. Finally, the statement was linked to a federal initiative called "Gathering Strength" to work with the provinces, territories and aboriginal groups to give native peoples more control over their land, government, and economic development. Hundreds of land claims throughout the country are being negotiated. The federal government claimed in 2007 that there were 790 outstanding claims, but the AFN said the number is 1,100. Around eight are settled every year.

The "Statement of Reconciliation" included earlier policies that had sought to stamp out native culture through "aggressive assimilation" by confining Indian children to government schools. Beginning in 1920 attendance at such schools was mandatory for Indian children between ages 7 and 16. About 150,000 were forced to do so. Half of them were physically or sexually abused, and 6,000 died. Most were closed by the mid-1970s, and the last one shut its doors in 1996. They were secluded from their families and forbidden from speaking their own languages. At that time about 100,000 native children also were separated from their parents to attend a hundred or so residential schools operated by the major Christian churches all over Canada from the 1880s to 1996; 60% were run by Catholic orders. The children were often poorly fed and clothed, compelled to work long hours, whipped if they spoke their native languages, and sometimes subjected to physical or sexual abuse. The former national chief of the Assembly of First Nations, Phil Fontaine, claimed that he had suffered sexual mistreatment.

A royal commission documented these offenses in 1996, and by 2000 more than 6,200 aboriginals had sued the federal government and the churches. The government has settled out of court and paid a few hundred claims. The churches, which publicly apologized and begged forgiveness, the last one being the Catholic Church during former Pope Benedict's April 2009 visit, fear bankruptcy if they are pressed too far. Native leaders show little sympathy. They blame the traumatic experiences in those schools for much of the alcoholism, sexual abuse, suicide and divorces in their communities. One in seven of the 90,000 former students still alive launched abuse claims against Ottawa and various churches, and new claims continue to pour in.

In 2002, the federal government and the Anglican Church of Canada agreed to divide liability for the increasing number of abuse claims by Indians, capping the Church's liability at $16 million and thereby saving it from insolvency. In 2006, the federal government announced $2 billion in payments to 80,000 natives who were abused in these residential schools. By 2015, twice this amount had been paid. The sum includes about $120 million for a foundation to promote traditional native healing therapies and finance a "truth and reconciliation commission" to hear victims' testimony. The churches involved also agreed to open up their archives.

In June 2008, then Prime Minister Stephen Harper offered a second public apology: "Today we recognize that this policy of assimilation was wrong, has caused great harm and has no place in our country." The apology was combined with an agreement to pay an additional $Can1.9

Hockey game at the Royal Military College, Annual Classic against West Point.
Begun in 1923, the standing in 2004 was West Point 37, RMC 28.

billion to the surviving students. In a seldom break with tradition, native leaders were permitted to speak from the House of Commons floor, some in their native languages. In 2015, the governments of Manitoba (where Métis' claims include the land on which Winnipeg is located) and Alberta also officially apologized, and a new report was published by the Truth and Reconciliation Commission. In 2021, thousands of unmarked graves were discovered on the former grounds of many residential schools across Canada, compounding the ongoing deep trauma suffered by Canada's First Nations Peoples.

In this era of truth, Canadians are discussing the emotionally charged subject of how to regard the country's founder, John A. MacDonald, who called native peoples "savages" among other racist terms. What should be done about the hundreds of statues, schools, and streets that were named after him?

In 1998, Ottawa, BC and native leaders initialed the Nisga'a land claim. The settlement, approved the following year by Parliament, gave that northern British Columbian tribe self-government, land, resource rights, and $253 million over 15 years. Fifty other BC claims are under negotiation.

In 1999, the Federal Court of Appeal handed the Mi'kmaq of New Brunswick a victory by ruling that the National Energy Board had not satisfactorily dealt with native interests when it granted a private company rights to build the Sable Island natural gas pipeline. There have been numerous cases where the tide is turned by aboriginal insistence that their rights be acknowledged and that there be assurances of job creation, revenue-sharing, and land ownership before industrial development is permitted to proceed. Companies put pressure on governments to reach a deal.

Only a month earlier, the Supreme Court of Canada had decided that a 1760 treaty gave the Mi'kmaq and other Maritime natives year-round fishing rights. The Mi'kmaq thereupon claimed the right to control their own lobster fishing. This sparked conflict and violence with non-native fishermen, who are obligated to observe limitations on their fishing. Shots were fired, boats were rammed, and fishing traps were destroyed in the months of scuffling. Finally, in 2000, the Mi'kmaq agreed to remove a substantial number of their lobster traps from the water, to shorten their fishing season, and to cooperate with federal authorities to maintain peace.

Aboriginals have become increasingly involved in politics as Canada's fast economic expansion has pushed forestry, mining and hydroelectric companies deeper into their living area in the resource-rich wilderness. By 2012, there were a record seven aboriginals with seats in Parliament in Ottawa and five in the Saskatchewan legislature. In 2015, 54 aboriginals ran for federal seats. In March 2012, Quebec Cree member Romeo Saganash, who represents a sprawling parliamentary constituency extending over the northern half of Quebec, became the first aboriginal to run for the leadership of a national political party: the NDP.

Quebec recruits immigrants from Europe

Demographic Characteristics

The 2021 census and subsequent demographic surveys provide a good snapshot of Canadians today. Canadians are one of the few peoples in the world who are even more mobile than are Americans. Almost one out of three Canadians changed provinces during the 1970s, and many more move either from one city to another or from the city centers to the suburbs or small towns. Canada is heavily urban today, with 80% living in towns of more than 10,000 people (compared with 56% in 1956). In fact, in the 21st century the most visible division in Canada is not between francophones and anglophones, but between five large urban areas that are dynamic, successful and appealing and the rest of Canada that is mainly rural with declining economies, high unemployment and heavy dependence on federal assistance.

The most noticeable regional shift is from the East to the West, a movement that continues in the 21st century. The Calgary-Edmonton corridor in Alberta has seen its population grow by 12.3% since 1996 and now has more people than the four Atlantic provinces combined. These shifts in population also brought a westward shift in economic and political power. Central Canada has lost some of its economic pre-eminence. Since seats in the House of Commons are distributed according to population, those regions that increased in population grew in political clout. The Atlantic Provinces have slipped significantly, and Ontario, where more than half of immigrants have settled since 1996 (two-thirds of whom in Toronto), has increased. The biggest gains in political power were made in Alberta and British Columbia.

The efficient distribution of medical services and the amenities of life enable Canadians to live longer (80 years for men and 84 for women) and to lower the infant mortality rate to 10.4 per 1,000, compared with 12.5 per 1,000 in the United States. Their family lives have also changed dramatically. Social changes, a decline in religious beliefs and liberalized divorce laws have meant that the proportion of marriages ending in divorce was frighteningly approaching one-half by the mid-1980s. Therefore, more Canadians are living alone than used to be the case.

It can hardly be doubted that the decline in religious belief is one contributor to the growing divorce rate. In a 2006 *Maclean's* Canada Day poll, only 34% of Canadians admitted that they attended a religious service "once a month or more," down from 41% in 1975. It is lowest in Quebec and BC. Two years later, only one in five Canadians identified themselves as "regular churchgoers."

Nevertheless, God is not dead in Canada: 81% believe in God, 62% in heaven,

Canada

62% in angels, and one third in hell. Two-thirds believe Jesus Christ is God's divine son. A third believes earthlings can communicate with the dead. Three out of ten (28%) say "religion plays an important part in my life" (down from 61% in 1992), compared with 60% in the U.S. (down from 83%). In the 2005 annual *Maclean's* poll, almost a third of Canadians defined themselves as born-again Christians or evangelicals, but two thirds also said that political leaders should never use their religious beliefs to guide their actions. Only 3% claim to be out-and-out atheists (1% in the U.S.).

Sociologist Seymour Martin Lipset noted from diverse polling results, Americans are more inclined to believe in God, attend church regularly or adhere to religious beliefs than are either anglophone or francophone Canadians. They are also more inclined to apply their religious beliefs to politics than are Canadians. Canadians therefore often perceive American political views as too moralistic and uncompromising. This may seem surprising, given the fact that although Canada has officially separated church and state, the state in Canada does provide more support to religious institutions, particularly schools. Such support is understandable in the Canadian context, however; unlike the majority of Americans, most Canadians have belonged to the Roman Catholic or Anglican churches, both of which are hierarchically organized and historically linked with and supportive of the state.

According to the last published census numbers on belief, Catholicism is the biggest denomination, with 43% or 11.2 million members, followed by the United Church of Canada (formed in 1925 by the merger of the Presbyterian, Methodist, and Congregational faiths, 3.8 million), the Anglican Church (2.5 million), and a myriad of conservative Christian denominations (2 million), the largest being the Pentecostal Assemblies of Canada, with a quarter million adherents. In all, Protestants account for 29%. The Eastern Orthodox Church claims 1.5%, most of Ukrainian ancestry, while 1.1% of Canadians are Jewish, a percentage that is growing slowly. Roughly 1% each are Hindus, Sikhs or Buddhists. Muslims make up 2%, while 16% of Canadians claim no religion.

Women are leaving their homes in large numbers to enter the work force. In 1951, 24% of Canadian women worked; in 2004 the figure was 57% (63% of mothers with children under age 3). Although the most blatantly discriminatory laws have been off the books for years and though Canada's new constitution spells out equality before the law, women in the work force still earned only about 60% as much money as males. This is in part because 28% of working women are part-timers compared with 11% of working men. This wage differential does not exist to any extent, however, in the professions and managerial positions into which women have poured. Since 1971 the number of female lawyers increased six-fold, engineers five-fold and accountants three-fold. Three-fourths of female executives in 2004 believed that commitments to family hinder advancement. Nevertheless, in its gender equality rankings in 2005, the World Economic Forum placed Canada seventh in the world, ahead of the U.S. in 17th place.

Even though the Canadian population had steadily grown to 33.9 million by 2013, the Canadian birth-rate has declined rapidly. In 1971, the average woman who was past childbearing age had statistically given birth to 3.2 children. In 2011, that figure was down to 1.66, well below the 2.1 needed to maintain a constant population (and which the U.S. maintains). These changes in birth-rate differed regionally. In the Atlantic Provinces, it remained high, whereas it was lowest in British Columbia and Quebec.

In Quebec, where families used to be large because of the strength of Catholicism and because of the determination to maintain the Quebec nation in the face of a perceived anglophone threat, the birth-rate plummeted, reaching 1.5 children per woman past childbearing age in 1992, below the country's average and below the 2.1 necessary to maintain Quebec's 6.5 million population in 1990. In an attempt to reverse this downward trend, the Quebec government adopted policies in 1988 and 1989 to create 60,000 more day care spaces and to make tax-free cash payments to parents of $500 for the first child, $1,000 for the second, and $4,500 for each additional child. These measures have helped raise Quebec's birth rate since 2001. Upon taking office in February 2006, Prime Minister Stephen Harper promised parents $1,300 in cash annually to help defray the costs of day care.

Fewer women are marrying in their teens. The average marrying age for a Canadian woman was 28.5 in 2008 (compared with 25.1 in the U.S.). More are waiting to have their first child. The proportion of Canada's population under age 15 has decreased and over age 65 has increased. The result of this drop in births is noticeable in declining school enrollments. More and more parents are not marrying at all: in 2008, 25.6% of children (38.5% in the U.S.) were born out of wedlock. This figure was higher in Quebec, where 30% of all couples have common-law relationships, compared with 14% in Canada as a whole. More Canadians cohabit (18.4% of all couples) than Americans (7.6%).

The low birth-rate does not help Canada deal with the consequences of the baby-boom of the 1950s and 1960s, described by John Kettle in his book, *The Big Generation*: "Something extraordinary happened in Canada between 1951 and 1966. It has already wreaked havoc in our lives and will go on echoing down the years into the middle of the next century, disrupting and reshaping and rebuilding most of our society and economy in the process." This boom, which poured large numbers of young people into the job market in the early 1980s was more than the Canadian job supply could bear. It is a major factor in Canada's unemployment problem.

Although this swollen younger generation has gradually worked its way through the employment bottleneck, it will ultimately cause a different kind of problem in the 21st century. As a result of the declining birth-rate now, by the year 2030 there will be one pensioner for every two Canadians in the work force. The country's 240,000 immigrants each year help to boost the fertility rate in the short term, but they will not be able to solve the problem in the long run. This future reality cannot help from putting pressure on Canada's pension and social welfare system. To help alleviate this, the federal government eliminated the mandatory retirement age in 2007, but only 6% work past age 65.

Despite the problems with employment, the work ethic remains essentially intact. Canadians want to work, but they are compelled to find jobs in an economy that is changing and modernizing. Fewer and fewer Canadians are working on the land or in factories, and more and more are working in the service sector, including the public service.

Bilingualism

According to the 2016 census, Canada is an increasingly multilingual society, with more than five million inhabitants having a mother tongue other than English or French. Called "allophones," these people now constitute one out of six Canadians, up 12.5% from 1996. More than 100 languages are spoken in Canada. According to the 2016 data, 57% of Canadians speak English while 22% say French is their mother tongue of 22.9%, while 22% speak some other language, with Chinese is the third most common native language

One change since the early 1970s is that more Canadians have become bilingual in both of the languages proclaimed to be equal by the country's Official Languages Act in 1969: French and English. Today 17.7% of the population (9% of anglophones and 43.4% of francophones, according to the 2001 census) have become bilingual in French and English, up from 13.5% in 1971. Traditionally, the great majority of bilingual Canadians were francophones who needed to learn English to get ahead in an anglophone country. Even in the mid-1980s, 60% of bilingual Canadians were francophones. But the remarkable development is the percentage increase of anglophones who had acquired French: 56.7% for English as opposed to 13.4% for French speakers. In other words, anglophones are becoming bilingual at a quicker pace than are francophones. Westerners, who have shown considerable resentment to the conversion of Canada into a country with two official languages, have led the way toward bilingualism.

In Quebec, where most francophones live, the percentage of anglophones has steadily declined since the 1960s and now numbers 750,000 representing less than 10% of the population; 83% and rising are francophones, 11% speak English at home, and 6% speak other languages as their mother tongue (and are referred to as "allophones"). Thee anglophones who remained in Quebec are now far more likely to be able to speak French and therefore feel more comfortable in their surroundings; 61% and rising of Quebec's anglophones now consider themselves to be functionally bilingual (up from 36% in 1971); 32% of Quebec francophones are bilingual (up from 26%).

A minority of anglophones in Quebec has even begun to speak French at home. This means that for the first time in Canada's history, English-speakers are assimilating into the French-speaking world. By 2005, a surge in marriage and coupling outside the communities was underway: 40% of anglophones have non-anglophone partners, and a fourth have paired with a francophone. There are economic incentives as well. Without French, an anglophone in Quebec is twice as likely to be unemployed; if employed he would earn only two-thirds as much as if he were bilingual. Enrollment in English-language schools has declined by 60% since the 1960s, and they are closing or switching to French instruction by the dozens. This has significant implications for Quebec politics since the fortunes of the independence movement were always dependent upon language tensions that are now slowly disappearing.

An "estates general" set up by the Quebec government in 2001 concluded that French is no longer under threat in the province. Although it did not recommend any loosening of the language laws, it saw no need to make them stricter. The problem, it found, was the poor quality of French spoken in Quebec. Perhaps that was embarrassingly demonstrated in 2001 when 20% of 8,055 prospective French-language teachers failed a written French test that is a prerequisite for employment by most francophone school boards.

This assimilation has affected the English which Quebec anglophones speak. So many French words, such as *depanneur* (convenience store) have seeped into their English that some worried observers are warning against "Frenglish." The Montreal *Gazette* decided to test the extent to which this process has gone by printing an article filled with Frenglish: "The work conflict has been a long one and the main revendications of the syndical militants have been for lower cotisations, more subventions for prestation beneficiaries and better social advantages." In standard English, this means: "The strike lasted a long time, and the principal demands by union representatives were for lower dues, more grants for social benefit programs and better working conditions." For better or worse, all readers understood the report perfectly.

Seeking to strengthen its French character, Quebec spends almost twice as much per capita on cultural activities as does Ontario. Despite the outcry against the policies of the Quebec government during the past quarter of a century designed to protect and strengthen the French-speaking character of the province, Quebec remains the only province in Canada that requires the study of a second language in school. Beginning in 2001 francophone pupils started English in Grade 3 instead of Grade 4 in order to improve their skills. Although 98% of *Québécois* children study English, there are no English-immersion schools in Quebec; 37.3% of anglophone children in the province educated under the authority of English school boards were registered in French immersion by the year 2000.

A 1993 study of secondary education in Montreal concluded that anglophone Quebecers are leaving school more or less competent in both languages, while most francophones are not. Even though a majority of *Québécois* still speaks French only, there are a fifth more bilingual francophones in Quebec than there were in 1971. Quebec nationalists encourage individual bilingualism while opposing institutional bilingualism. Indeed, 56% of young Québécois age 19 to 34 were bilingual in 2014. A perfectly bilingual Jacques Parizeau proclaimed in 1992: "By God, I'll boot the rear end of anyone who can't speak English. A small people like us must speak English."

How have so many Canadians become bilingual so quickly? Some have buckled down and learned French out of necessity. Over a quarter of the federal civil service jobs now require *both* languages, and that percentage slowly rises every year. Thus, government employees have taken advantage of state-financed extra language courses. Also, many of the top jobs in politics, the judiciary and some of the professions, including journalism, public relations and economics, require proficiency in both languages. The federal capital of Ottawa has been proclaimed a bilingual city, so almost *any* job that involves dealing with the public demands facility in both tongues. The result, complained Mark Steyn, is that about 83% of Canadians are ineligible for the country's most prominent jobs. Therefore, night schools and crash language courses have experienced a boom.

Perhaps the most significant innovation in the long run is French-immersion schools for the children of English-speaking parents. They are largely funded by the provinces, which control education. During the 1990s Ottawa reduced its contribution by half, leaving it to the provinces to pick up the slack. In these schools, anglophones learn all or part of their subjects totally in French. The programs vary, but most enrollees study exclusively in French for two to four years and then take about half their courses in French as long as they remain in the program. They enter "early" immersion beginning in kindergarten or "late" immersion, usually starting in the sixth or seventh grade.

This concept swept the country, and the supply of such state-financed schools and qualified teachers cannot keep pace with the demand. Some ambitious parents reportedly wait in line through the night in order to get their children signed up for such programs. One such parent was former PEI premier Joe Ghiz, who himself took French lessons in 1988 to improve his prospects for higher federal office. He and 122 other applicants stood in line all night in 1989 to enroll their children in French language kindergarten. The tired premier grumbled: "There must be a better way to get your child into French immersion." His favor helped young Robert Ghiz's political career; at age 29 he led his father's Liberal Party to victory in the 2003 PEI provincial elections and was later reelected.

These schools hardly existed before the 1970s. By 1979, they had an enrollment of 38,000, a figure that topped the 100,000 mark by 1983 and 342,000 by 2011. It is still rising, thanks in part to the fact that Ottawa remains a major booster of the program. Its annual budget for official-language education grew to $219 million in 2000, and it requires provinces to develop a formal action plan for such schooling. By 1989, immersion teaching and conventional French instruction reached roughly half of all anglophone elementary and high school pupils.

Canada

The stampede to bilingual schools has tended to drown out the criticism that has been leveled against them. Some purists claim that these schools make pupils "little butchers of French despite the fact that 42% of high school seniors in the program achieve the marks of "advanced or higher." While it is true that many of the graduates of these schools do not speak French perfectly, they understand it and are wholly functional in standard (called "international") French, that form which is spoken and written by educated *Québécois* and Acadians in business, schools, newspapers and on the air. Acadian and Quebec dialects, such as *Joual*, that French spoken in the streets of Montreal and which contracts syllables and drops sounds, remain largely incomprehensible to outsiders, even to visitors from France. In fact, English-language films dubbed in Quebec must be re-dubbed for audiences in France. Other critics claim that these schools contribute to the creation of a "new cultural and economic elite."

The kinds of children who tend to enroll in these schools already come from middle-class or upper-income families, and their acquisition of French language competency in a country which lays so much stress on that enhances even further the social and economic advantages they already had. A survey in 1997 to determine the reasons parents chose early French immersion for their children revealed that the chief motives were "future employment enhancement," "a more stimulating learning environment," and "a better student-teacher ratio," in that order.

To some extent they serve the same purpose as private schools in other countries, such as the U.S. In other words, the social gap between Canadians from upwardly mobile families and those who are not becomes even wider. Statistics bear this point out: bilingual graduates entering the work force, especially the professions, do earn more on average than their unilingual counterparts outside of Quebec, bilingual men earn on average 3.8% more and women 6.6% more. There are problems: there is a shortage of French teachers and the dropout rate is high.. Most Canadians find the value of bilingualism indisputable. In a 2000 poll, 87% of respondents said they believe the ability to speak a second language is important. Employers agree. Some Canadians see bilingualism, not as a cultural fetish, but as the glue for a unified Canada. Nuclear physicist, John Madden, asserted: "If you believe in Canada as an entity, then you speak both of its official languages. It's as simple as that."

It is possible that Quebec's influence in Anglophone Canada will diminish over time. Given the composition of immigration to Canada, each future generation of francophone Canadians living outside of Quebec and Acadia will be half the size of the previous one. Among the fourth of all Canadians outside of Quebec who speak a different mother tongue than English, there are almost as many who speak Chinese as speak French. Soon the Chinese-speakers will surpass the francophones. This is already the case in British Columbia, where they outnumber French-speakers 15 to 1. With francophones shrinking as a minority outside of Quebec and Acadia, their claims for special treatment might become weaker.

Despite intense efforts and expense by the federal government, only 17.7% of Canadians are truly bilingual, and even fewer use both languages on the job. The truth is that few Canadians outside Quebec need French because its use has not spread appreciably. In Ontario, dozens of communities have declared themselves as officially English-only, sending a powerful symbolic message across Canada and reflecting the deep divisions between the country's two language communities.

Nevertheless, one cannot speak of the failure of bilingualism. In fact, support for it reached an all-time high by 2006: 64% of Canadians favor it, while 89% of *Québécois* do. This continues to grow, rising to 49% in British Columbia and 47% in the Prairies. By 2017, the favorable percentage had risen to 78%. Only 12% of Canadians consider the state of English-French relations as a very serious problem. The percentage that thinks Quebec will one day separate from Canada fell to 8% (25% and declining in Quebec).

Canada

17th century French map of eastern Canada—*New France*
Public Archives Canada/C42132

HISTORY

Identity, Unity, Survival

Canadian history has been decisively influenced by three concerns: identity, unity, and survival. The problem of identity, of defining what it means to be Canadian has never been satisfactorily resolved. Is there such a thing? Right up into the 20th century, anglophone and francophone Canadians tended to regard each other as "racially" different.

Québécois still view themselves as a separate nation, referring to their provincial parliament as the "*National* Assembly." In any case, the concept of nationhood is problematic in a country that makes a virtue out of describing itself as a "mosaic," rather than a "melting pot."

To what extent does being Canadian simply mean not being British? Francophones have always resented the English connection, and for a long time, anglophones were ambivalent about how much they should share in Britain's institutions and destiny. In past wars, any call by the federal government to Canadians to go to the aid of Britain as the "mother country," inevitably divided Canadians. In 1982, Canadians severed most of their constiututional/legal ties with Britain when they finally revised and repatriated their constitution: the British North America Act, 187—renamed the Constitution Act, 1867 and the Canada Act. The latter acts were passed by the British Parliament. However, the British monarch is still the head of state in Canada and the country's political system continues to resemble that of the United Kingdom.

Canadians on the whole are more inclined than Americans to try to define their own identity as a people. Most Canadians tend to describe themselves in terms contrasting themselves to Americans. When asked what it means to be a Canadian, many preface their answer with such words, "well, unlike Americans, we . . ." Even Pierre Berton's work, *Why We Act Like Canadians. A personal exploration of our national character*, is written in the form of letters to an American friend named "Sam." The Canadian state took shape in a context of distrust toward the American Revolution and republicanism. As Northrop Frye once said, "historically, a Canadian is an American who rejects the revolution." Looking south, many Canadians saw too much democracy which seemed to create unacceptable instability and violence. While Canadians can all agree that they are not Americans, such a negative definition of their own identity is barely strong enough to withstand the forces of division that often plague Canada. At the same time, though, many Canadians have always been irresistibly attracted to certain aspects of the United States (U.S.) and have come to resemble Americans.

The second concern in Canadian history is unity. Canada has often been accurately described as a "geographic improbability." Distance and rough terrain have always made communication and transportation

Canada

difficult. Canada was occupied by the aboriginal peoples then settled by many different European and other peoples with differing national backgrounds, languages and cultures. Geography aided Canadians in preserving these differences. Regional diversity was always a salient fact in Canadian life with politics always characterized by a tug-of-war between the center being the capital of Canada Ottawa and the provinces which have often regarded themselves almost as separate legal entities – which of course they are in a federalized state.

Third, Canadian history has been shaped by the continual struggle for survival as a unified state. Canadians have viewed the threat as having different sources. For the *Québécois, la survivance* meant the survival of their language and culture which they feared were vulnerable to the ever-growing power of anglophone culture in Canada. The powerful melting pot to the south also potentially threatened to destroy the Quebec nation. Anglophones, who were always a minority in the province of Quebec, have feared that their survival was threatened by the francophone majority, especially since the 1960s.

Anglophone Canadians have usually perceived the primary threat as emanating from the U.S.. At every step in Canadian history, the dynamic, expanding, populous and economically powerful U.S. was a challenge and entered mightily into Canadian deliberations. Canadian governments were always on guard against potential annexation. Moreover, American culture's overwhelming presence has threatened to destroy whatever distinctive characteristics existed in Canadian culture. In the past, Canada's leaders have often been so busy maintaining their country's independence from the U.S. that they had little inclination to count their blessings at having such a democratic, tolerant and basically friendly country with which to share their 5,524-mile border.

Canada's first inhabitants were, of course, the indigenous peoples, First Nations, Inuit and Metis. The white man's presence in the new world permanently changed the lives of Canada's native population. The story of the colonization and the attempt to assimilate indigenous peoples into Canadian society is fraught with shame and crystalized in 2015 with the report of the Truth and Reconciliation Commission of Canada. That report represents a defining moment in Canadian history and its many recommendations have been embraced by both the federal and provincial governments as well as Canadian society as being essential for a true reconciliation with Canada's indigenous peoples. The Truth and Reconciliation Commission of Canada was a truth and reconciliation commission active in Canada from 2008 to 2015, organized by the parties of the Indian Residential Schools Settlement Agreement.

In the 10th and 11th centuries the first Europeans set foot on Canadian shores. Norsemen such as Leif Ericson set out from Iceland and Greenland to explore the uncharted West, and after perilous sailing sighted the Labrador coast. For 30 harsh years off and on, a small winter basecamp of Vikings eked out an existence at L'Anse aux Meadows in what is now Newfoundland. Its main purpose was to supply the larger Viking settlement of about 500 people in Greenland. The Vikings struck out from L'Anse aux Meadows as far as what is now New Brunswick. This is known because the butternuts they brought back were only to be found there. Based on archeological excavations, these temporary Viking settlers averaged five feet ten inches, very tall by the standards of their time. The European average was only five feet five inches. The Vikings wore cone-shaped helmets, not the horned models one sees in Hollywood films. Despite their reputation for fighting and pillaging, they mainly survived by raising livestock and cutting hay. The Vikings were also innovative shipbuilders and skilled artists who decorated woodwork and cast-metal ornaments with sophisticated designs.

Lacking both numbers of potential settlers and fire-arms necessary to subdue

Champlain trading with the Indians
Public Archives Canada/C103059

Canada

Quebec in 1640
Public Archives Canada/06492

the Indians, the Norsemen withdrew from North America. A millennium later, in 2000, a replica of a Viking ship, accompanied by a flotilla of other Viking vessels, sailed from Iceland for a six-week voyage to L'Anse aux Meadows on the northern tip of Newfoundland. There they were greeted by hundreds of onlookers who remain fascinated by the mysterious Nordic mariners.

The New World remained hidden in Norse legend until three Spanish galleons under the command of the Italian mariner Christopher Columbus bumped into a Caribbean island in 1492 while searching for a passage to the riches of China and India. As soon as Columbus reported his discovery to an enthused Europe, a stream of hardy French and English explorers began steering their ships toward Canada. In 1497, the Italian seaman John Cabot (who lived in England) rediscovered Newfoundland.

In a series of three daring voyages in 1534, 1535, and 1541, Jacques Cartier sailed into the Gulf of St. Lawrence and up the St. Lawrence River as far as the present city of Montreal. On one such voyage, he reportedly went ashore to inquire as to his whereabouts. Believing that he was asking about their village, the Indians answered "Kanata," which was the Huron-Iroquois term for "a small fishing village." On returning to France, Cartier used this word to refer to the land he had seen, and the name, "Canada," stuck. In 1610 the Englishman Henry Hudson discovered the Hudson and James Bays, gigantic waterways that gave the English relatively easy and inexpensive access to the very heart of the vast Canadian half-continent. Between 1609 and 1615 Samuel de Champlain penetrated what is now eastern Ontario and pointed in the direction where the lucrative fur trade would develop.

These explorers were driven by a burning spirit of gain. Even though they did not succeed in finding a direct sea route to China, the fur trade provided fortunes for anyone who could move beaver pelts from the dense North American forests to the chic shops of London and Paris. Following in the wake of these explorers and frontier entrepreneurs came a different brand of Europeans: settlers.

NEW FRANCE

The first permanent European settlers to move to this new land were French and they dominated most of what is now Canada until 1760. In 1604, they established a short-lived settlement on the island of St. Croix, and one year later French pioneers established a community at Port Royal, now Annapolis on Nova Scotia. But the explorer and soldier, Samuel de Champlain concluded that these two early sites were too exposed militarily and too unpromising economically. Therefore, he moved up the Gulf of St. Lawrence to the narrows guarded by the imposing cliffs of Cape Diamond. Here de Champlain founded the city of Quebec and befriended the Algonquin Indians, thereby establishing a secure and well-placed base in the heart of the continent. Soon thereafter an outpost was established up the river at Trois Rivières.

In 1642, a Catholic mission to the Indians was established at Montreal. This outpost was situated on an island near the points where the Ottawa and Richelieu rivers flow into the St. Lawrence but was subjected to constant Indian attacks. The fiercest assault occurred in 1660 but was stopped by Adam Dollard and a small band of Jesuit followers in a legendary struggle to the death. Once secured, Montreal became the natural control point for the fur trade and for westward expansion. Because of a brief but vigorous French governmental immigration policy initiated in 1666, the number of inhabitants in New France rose to 6,705 by the year 1672 when the French court ceased supporting emigration. The population ultimately climbed to between 60,000 and 70,000 by 1760, when the English conquered the French in North America.

The French settlers' motives were varied. The Reformation in Europe divided Europeans religiously with intolerance that resulted in some of the most bestial and bloody conflicts known to civilized man. Thousands escaped religious persecution by coming to the New World. Others, especially the Jesuit Order, came to North America in order to try to preserve the French Catholic tradition and to convert the Indians to Catholicism. From 1625, when the first Jesuits landed at Quebec, right up until the 1960s, Quebec province was a hostile place for French Protestants. No Huguenots were permitted to emigrate to New France. Thus, not only were some of the most industrious and imaginative elements of French society

Canada

kept out, but the French population in the New World remained religiously homogeneous and conservative.

Settlers were also attracted to Canada by the longing for a new life and for economic gain. The northern half of America possessed all the basic economic resources for settlement: fish, furs, timber and agricultural land. Throughout the 17th and 18th centuries the most important of these resources by far was the fur trade which ultimately provided the financial basis for the government and the church. From their bases in the north and south, the British hemmed in the French fur trade in the 17th century.

In 1670, the British monarch, Charles II, granted to the Hudson's Bay Company not only a trade monopoly but also the privilege of ruling all the land draining into that gigantic bay. The British trading posts, which were established along the edge of the most lucrative fur-producing territory, had the enormous advantage of being supplied by sea and were therefore economical. To the south of New France, the British replaced the Dutch in the Hudson River Valley and had established a powerful base in Albany. Having inherited the Dutch alliance with the Iroquois Indians, the British could challenge the French bid for control of the Ohio Valley fur trade.

The English pincers to the north and south forced the French to push into the interior of the continent in search of the beaver. The French forged into the Great Lakes and into the Saskatchewan and Mississippi Valleys. The Jesuit priest Jacques Marquette and the trader-explorer Louis Jolliet joined efforts in 1673 and paddled from Green Bay on Lake Michigan all the way down the Mississippi to the confluence with the Arkansas River.

In 1682, Robert Cavalier de la Salle pressed on to the mouth of the Mississippi River and in 1699 the French founded a colony on the Gulf of Biloxi, close to what is now the Gulf of Mexico. Bby the dawn of the 18th century, French *voyageurs* had established a far-flung network of trading posts embracing the entire Mississippi Valley and Great Lakes region. *Coureurs de bois*, literally "runners of the woods," gathered furs from the Indians deep in the Ohio Valley, as far north as Hudson Bay, and as far west as the plains.

This huge fur trading network brought great wealth to New France but it also created severe problems. The French had to build a string of forts over a massive area in order to protect their share of the fur trade from the English, a process calling for large expenditures for soldiers with long supply lines into the interior that were both vulnerable and expensive to maintain. Also, the fur trade retarded development in other economic sectors and prevented New France from diversifying its economy. Perhaps worst of all, the fur trade forced the French to make territorial claims which continually brought them into conflict with the British, whose population in the New World soon far exceeded that of New France. From the early 17th century on, the French and English were rivals for control of North America and the undefined borders between their colonies were a constant source of war.

From 1627, New France was governed by private, chartered companies, such as the Company of New France which performed governmental services in return for trade monopolies and control of land. In 1663, the status of New France changed, becoming a royal French province, with all the trappings of French provincial law and government. In typical French fashion, all institutions, from the government and church to the fur trade, were highly centralized.

The government was dominated by three offices: the governor was usually a military man and was appointed by the King to oversee defense and foreign relations. The *intendant*, a lawyer and administrator, was appointed by the King to maintain royal power, regulate the economy, and administer justice. For a while, these people were assisted by an appointed council, but its influence shrank quickly. New France was unable to develop an effective form of representative government at any level as the British had done.

The third pillar of power was the Catholic Church. Due largely to the personality and force of the first Bishop of Quebec, Francois Laval, no major governmental decisions were made without the influence of the Bishop being involved.

At the communal level, the two top leaders were the *curé* or pastor, who represented the Church, and the *seigneur*, or Lord, a powerful and wealthy figure appointed by the governor. The *seigneur* was not necessarily a nobleman, but he had control over a feudal estate to whom peasants rendered feudal services in the form of rents and work.

Montreal in 1720
Public Archives Canada/06497

Canada

View of Louisbourg in 1731
Public Archives Canada/C23082

The system was not as rigid as in France because of the peasants' possibility of escaping by merely running away into the woods. Also, because the captain of the militia provided military protection, the *seigneur* did not bear the feudal responsibility for protecting the peasants. Nevertheless, this communal order left important legacies for French Canada. The form of land ownership which was granted by the governors under the influence of the Church, and which was *not* bought and sold in a free market, greatly irritated and thereby limited English settlers to Quebec, who desired the kind of freer economic activity to which they had become accustomed in the British colonies. Clearly, politics in Quebec involved from the beginning a close link between Church and state.

Slavery existed for almost two centuries in Canada until it was abolished in the 19th century. During French rule, about 1,500 black slaves were imported and 2,000 more were brought north by loyalists fleeing the American Revolution. Most slaves belonged to urbanized elites.

THE CONQUEST or *LA CONQUÊTE*

While the French established an early permanent presence in what is now Canada, the English first settled in what is now the U.S.. Even so, the line between French and British America was not clearly defined, a factor that caused continuous tension. Because New France was unified, and British North America was divided up into many separate colonies, New France could mobilize its resources more effectively and compete well, even though by 1760 it had only 10% of the British colonial population. Yet, throughout the 18th century Britain whittled away at the French possessions in North America. The origins of the conflicts were often to be found in momentous events in Europe such that, for instance, the War of the Spanish Succession of 1702–13 brought skirmishes in North America that influenced the Treaty of Utrecht in 1713.

The settlement of the War of Spanish Succession required the French to renounce their claims to the Hudson Bay, Newfoundland, except the French shore, and all of Acadia, except Isle Royale, now known as Cape Breton Island. Acadia had been an area of French settlement that encompassed at that time most of the present-day provinces of Nova Scotia and New Brunswick. The British were also granted the right to trade with the western Indian tribes. Because the scales were thus tipped in favor of the British, only their inability to coordinate an effective attack against Quebec enabled the French to survive in North America for another half century.

Determined to prevent further losses of territory to the British and to try to secure their vital exits from the St. Lawrence, the French built a further series of forts, including the magnificent Louisbourg. This elegant and imposing fortress was constructed on Isle Royale according to plans drawn up by the great French military engineer, Sebastien Vauban, and could accommodate 1,400 regular soldiers, the governor and his retinue, merchants, craftsmen, and fishermen. The British seized the fort in 1745 during the War of Austrian Succession, only to return it reluctantly to the French at the Peace of Aix-la-Chapelle in 1748 in exchange for Madras in far-away India. The French diplomatic victory was a short-lived one, though. The British intended to rid North America of their perennial French rival.

The decisive conflict soon began in the Ohio Valley, which the French regarded as crucial for maintaining communications with their colony in Louisiana and for protecting their fur trade in the west. In 1753, the French sent a force into the Ohio Valley. Virginia responded by sending a wealthy planter by the name of George Washington to inform the French that they were treading on British territory. Rebuffed, Washington returned with an army in 1754, but his army was defeated at Ft Necessity. Establishing Fort Duquesne, now Pittsburgh, and successfully conducting guerrilla warfare with their Indian allies, the French were resolved to make good their claim to the Ohio and to prevent the restless Virginians from pressing into the western side of the Allegheny Mountains.

Of four principal attacks on New France in 1755, only one succeeded, the one against French positions in French-speaking Acadia. The 13,000 Acadians had announced their decision to remain neutral in all struggles between the British and French and not to swear loyalty to the British Crown, even though they had fallen under British rule in 1713. Equally disturbing to the British was the fact that a few Acadians helped the French to construct a fort on the isthmus separating Nova Scotia and mainland Acadia, now New Brunswick.

In 1775, a jittery British colonial government in Nova Scotia chose to deal with this looming danger in a brutally effective way, reflecting just how serious the British were at seeking to eliminate their French rival from the New World. The British hunted Acadians down in Nova Scotia, expelled them from their towns and villages, and dispersed 10,000 of them to France as well as among the English-speaking colonies to the south. In his moving poem, "Evangeline" Longfellow immortalized this tragic diaspora, remembered as *"le Grand Dérangement,"* The Big Inconvenience; the poem was also the inspiration for Antonine Maillet's play, *La Saguine*.

A few Acadians escaped expulsion and hid in the forests, fled to the French islands of Saint-Pierre and Miquelon, or took refuge in New Brunswick along the Restigouch and Miramichi rivers and along the shores of the Bay of Chaleur. Some returned from exile in the late 1700s

Canada

and joined those Acadians who fled to New Brunswick.

In northern Nova Scotia and northwestern New Brunswick, their offspring and the Quebecers who immigrated to New Brunswick more than a century later continue to form a French-speaking minority distinct from the Quebecers and still noticeably neutral in the present debates between Quebec and the rest of Canada. In its final cabinet meeting in December 2003, the government of former Prime Minister Jean Chrétien approved a proclamation acknowledging the historic wrongs done by the British Crown between 1755 and 1763 when about 10,000 Acadians were expelled from the Maritimes.

Hostilities in the New World broadened rapidly, and both contenders were set on a collision course when in 1756 the Seven Years War erupted in Europe between the two mother countries. Known in North America as the French and Indian War, this grave struggle demonstrated the extent to which the colonial conflict was influenced by events in Europe as much as by concerns of the North Americans themselves. Determined to crush the French in the New World, William Pitt, the British

minister of war, sent fresh land and naval reinforcements to America. The French court could send their colony little more than feeble moral support after 1756. One fortress after the other around the Great Lakes and Lake Champlain and along the Ohio River fell to the British onslaught. The most significant prize was Louisbourg, whose capture in 1758 opened up the St. Lawrence to Britain's formidable naval power.

In the summer of 1759, British ships entered the St. Lawrence and set their sights on the cornerstone of French power in America: the commanding fortress at Quebec City. After a nerve-wracking siege and a prolonged military cat and mouse game around Quebec, the British commander, General James Wolfe, succeeded in landing his army in the darkness of night. The army scaled the cliffs to appear on the Plains of Abraham, just outside the fortress walls in the early morning light of September 13, 1759. The surprised French commander, the Marquis de Montcalm, hastily assembled his army to face the British army outside the security of the fortress.

For the first time during the entire French and Indian War, the French unwisely chose to engage the British according to the European rules of battle rather than employing the irregular manner of guerrilla warfare which had often been so successful. Within ten ferocious minutes of

General Wolfe mortally wounded on the Plains of Abraham, September 1759
Public Archives Canada/C12248

fateful fighting, both armies suffered more than 2,000 casualties, including both the commanding generals. The French army was routed but not captured. Not until it was crushed at Montreal a year later did the final British "conquest," as French Canadians have called it ever since, occur.

The financial cost to Britain of the Seven Years War was so high that Britain had to raise taxes on its American colonies, thereby ultimately precipitating the American revolution 17 years later. Thus, the foundations of both Canada and the U.S. were laid that day on the Plains of Abraham. Further, the terms of surrender drafted by General Wolfe, who died on the battlefield, established the protection of Quebec's unique culture, language, law, and religion that has since become the hallmark of modern Canada's identity.

The memory of the *Conquête* has continued to nourish and invigorate French Canadian nationalism. In 2009, the long-scheduled re-enactment on the occasion of the 250th anniversary of the most important battle ever fought on Canadian soil had to be canceled because Quebec separatist groups, some hinting at violence, claimed such an event would be humiliating and evidence of federal propaganda. Canadian history has been politicized.

In the Treaty of Paris, the French lost to Britain all their North American holdings east of the Mississippi, except the two small islands of Saint-Pierre and Miquelon, which were needed as stations for the French naval and fishing fleets and which remain in French possession to this day. In addition, the French relinquished all of their holdings west of the Mississippi to Spain. In 1801, Napoleon secretly forced Spain to cede these western lands to France. But before he repossessed them, he sold them to the U.S. for $15 million in the Louisiana Purchase of 1803.

BRITISH NORTH AMERICA

By 1763, the British controlled of all land east of the Mississippi, but the magnitude of the problems facing them soon cut short their celebration of this great imperial victory. The British faced the problem of how to rule the newly conquered French citizens in Quebec, which at that time was called "Canada." Some of the leading French political leaders returned to France, but there was no mass French exodus from Quebec. The Catholic clergy remained and, absent the former French political leadership, the Catholic Church retained a leading position in Quebec life that lasted for two centuries. British law and administration, which was newly introduced, forbade Catholics from holding public office. Therefore, those citizens who clung to that faith were barred from participation in the political life of the province.

The new masters viewed the application of this law as an incentive for the French to give up their language and religion. Hoping that many French would emigrate and that those remaining would be swallowed up by an influx of English-speaking Protestants, the British assumed that the new French minority would be simply digested into British North America. The French viewed this design as a dangerous threat to their culture and identity, and to this day they have never lost their fear of such assimilation. This danger made the French more resistant than ever and continues to harden the backbone of the *Québécois* when facing anglophone Canadians.

By 1774, the British realized that their earlier hopes for a rapidly Anglicized Quebec had been naive and that it would be necessary to deal with a resilient French-speaking community through the leaders who remained: the *seigneurs* and the clergy. The Quebec Act of 1774 reflected this realization by declaring that: French Canadians need not take an anti-Catholic oath; the Church could continue to take tithes; French civil law could be practiced, although criminal law had to be English; the seigniorial land system would be permitted, in contrast to the British freeholding system; Quebec would be governed through an appointed council, as opposed to a representative council, as in other British colonies; and, the boundaries of Quebec would be extended to include much of the old French empire between the Ohio and Mississippi Rivers where Montreal fur traders continued to dominate the economy.

This 1774 Act was good news to most French leaders who saw it as protecting many of their former practices. However, the Act stimulated nervousness or downright anger in the minds of many Americans to the south who saw it as evidence of shaky British commitment to representative government; they also viewed it as an unacceptable limitation on their westward expansion. As a response to that nervousness, two American armies led by Richard Montgomery and Benedict Arnold marched on Canada in 1775, capturing Montreal and besieged Quebec City before withdrawing in 1776. But the year 1776 was only the beginning of the major threat to British North America posed by the American Revolutionary War.

In that struggle few Quebecers took up arms for the British, a refusal which was to be repeated in later conflicts, including the two world wars in the 20th century. Still, few French Canadians supported the American war effort either, even though France had openly sided with the Americans. The U.S. clearly had its eye on all the British holdings to the north. The Americans convened a Continental Congress, and their Articles of Confederation contained a section that was a door through which other British North American colonies could enter the newly independent country.

In the peace treaty of 1783 Britain retained its holdings north of the Thirteen Colonies while granting the Americans a peace so conciliatory that many Canadians still consider it an "astonishing giveaway" which allegedly severely crippled Canada's prospects for future growth. In the peace talks the American negotiator, Benjamin Franklin, asked for Quebec, Nova Scotia, Newfoundland, and the Hudson Bay territory. The British negotiator did not consider this proposal to be unreasonable but was overruled by George III and parliamentary leaders in London, who insisted on maintaining Halifax and Quebec as rampart against the northern expansion of the U.S. as well as a refuge for loyalists from the Thirteen Colonies. Consequently, the northern half of the continent was to remain separate from the southern half.

The British were probably inclined to make a lenient peace with the U.S. in order to woo the Americans away from their alliance with France. The British conceded the entire Ohio country, the great triangle west of the Appalachian Mountains between the Mississippi and Ohio Rivers, even though it was still controlled by the British and it was a traditional dependency of Canada which, when populated, could ultimately changed the power and economy of Canada.

The northern boundary was also generous to the new nation as it followed the St. Lawrence River where it intersects with the 45th parallel, through the Great Lakes to the Lake of the Woods, from which it aimed straight westward to the Mississippi River. This boundary was imprecise at important points and provided a constant source of tension between Britain and the U.S., particularly because Britain decided to maintain its string of forts, such as Michilimackinac, Detroit, Niagara, and Oswego, which were located on territory granted by the treaty to the new nation. Also, some Indian tribes refused to recognize the new boundaries and looked to the British to back up traditional Indian claims. Finally, the Americans were given access to the inshore fisheries of Nova Scotia and Newfoundland.

There were many consequences of the peace settlement of 1783 that helped shape the future development of Canada. First, Canada's contacts with the far West could no longer run through the Great Lakes and the shorter and less hostile lands to the south. Instead, they had to

Canada

be maintained over the rugged terrain of the Precambrian Shield north of Lake Superior. This ultimately necessitated the construction of a coast-to-coast railway in order to weld together the different parts of Canada.

Second, 32,000 loyalists, mainly city-dwellers from the eastern seaboard who sought refuge in New York, Charleston, and Savannah, sailed in British ships from the newly independent U.S. into Nova Scotia, trebling the population there and ultimately prompting the founding of New Brunswick. Many of the 8,000 free blacks who gained their freedom by fleeing their patriot owners for the British promise of emancipation for those who took up arms for the king, settled in Nova Scotia. A smaller number of loyalists, who were to form the nucleus of what would later become Ontario, trekked across the wilderness of northern New York to Niagara and Kingston and across the northern shore of Lake Ontario. Some even penetrated into the valley of the Ottawa River.

As loyalists, these settlers brought with them an aversion to the particular American variety of republican democracy even though they were former Americans who still had emotional and personal links with the U.S.. Like the rebels, they too desired a new relationship between the colonies and the mother country. The settlers later pressed successfully for the expansion of representative assemblies and democratic reforms in what became Canada.

About 8,000 loyalists, chiefly from Pennsylvania and New York, moved into Quebec north of the St. Lawrence, Lake Erie, and Lake Ontario, for the first time creating a sizable English-speaking minority in the province and demanding to live under British political institutions. They received support from London after the French Revolution in 1789. The momentous changes wrought by that first democratic revolution in Europe stiffened British views on the subject of representative democracy.

At the same time, most French-speaking Canadians were critical of the democratic revolution in France which led to a bloody onslaught against the Catholic Church and clergy there. The French Revolution drove a powerful wedge between revolutionary France and conservative Quebec. Not until the 1920s did Quebecers begin to look again toward Paris. A final important consequence of the French Revolution was that it ultimately produced a European war that so loosened the ties which France had to the New World that the U.S. was able to acquire the huge Louisiana territory from Napoleon Bonaparte in 1803. This ultimately greatly enlarged and strengthened the energetic and ambitious southern neighbor.

British General Sir Isaac Brock enters Queenston, 1812
Public Archives Canada/C46958

With a mixed population in British North America, in 1791 London saw a need to divide Quebec into two separate provinces: Upper Canada, later Ontario, and Lower Canada, present-day Quebec, then called lower because it was closest to the point where the St. Lawrence met the Atlantic Ocean. English common law and freehold land tenure were established in Upper Canada. In that new province, then, considerable tension arose between small freeholders and an elite around the governor.

On the other hand, Quebec was permitted to retain French civil law, a decision which infuriated the largely English-speaking merchants in Montreal who nevertheless continued to control the economic life of the province and who forged close links with the senior clergy and wealthy seigneurs. This "Chateau Clique," which included some anglophones, stimulated French nationalist opposition from the bulk of ordinary Quebecers. As such, the Canada Act of 1791 left both new provinces with simmering social and political tensions and left to the north of the U.S. a variety of British colonies with no links to each other. Separated by geographical barriers, language, and customs, each had its own governor or lieutenant governor, an appointed council, and an elected legislative assembly with limited powers.

THE WAR OF 1812

The British masters of these loosely connected colonies continued to have tense relations with the young and restless U.S. The flashpoints were many: the British possession of such forts as Niagara and Detroit on American territory continued to be a bone of contention

Canada

Bytown in 1830, later renamed Ottawa
Public Archives Canada/C607

until the British finally relinquished the western posts in Jay's Treaty of 1794–5. Continuous Indian wars in Indiana and Ohio kept alive American suspicions that the British were actually encouraging and supporting the Indians.

The American defeat of some western tribes in 1795 enabled the state of Ohio to be founded in 1803. The Americans, led by future president William Henry Harrison defeated at Tippecanoe in 1811 an alliance of Indian tribes forged by the prodigious Shawnee orator, warrior and chief, Tecumseh, and his brother, the Prophet, Americans living in the West continued to be convinced that there were many Canadian traders and British officials who were prepared to stir up and arm the Indians for profits and politics. Finally, Americans strongly objected to British violations of neutral rights on the high seas involving the boarding of American ships and the conscription of sailors on the grounds that they were still British subjects.

For a while these disputes could be settled peacefully, but that possibility diminished as time passed. Any armed struggle between the U.S. and Britain could only be fought on Canadian or American soil with Canada vulnerable. Canada had only a fraction of the American population; by 1812 there were a half million persons living in British North America, compared to 7.5 million in the U.S. Also, many loyalists had emigrated from the U.S. after the Revolutionary War, and subsequently many more Americans had emigrated to Canada, especially to what is now Ontario, for economic, not political, reasons. Therefore, it could not be known at that time how enthusiastically many Canadians would fight for Britain. Further, British hands were tied by the struggle in Europe against Napoleon, and they could spare few troops and material for a war in North America. The 5,000 British troops in North America would have to be used primarily to defend Quebec and Montreal, while the areas to the west seemed to lie wide open to attack.

By 1812, many Americans in the western part of the country saw the British colonies as ripe pieces of fruit waiting to be picked. They prevailed on President James Madison and a majority in Congress to declare war on Britain even though the latter offered to rescind its hated practice of intercepting American shipping to enforce its blockade against Napoleon. A confident Henry Clay declared that "I verily believe that the militia of Kentucky are alone competent to place Montreal and Upper Canada at your feet." The American war effort was, indeed, mainly a Kentucky affair, and two-thirds of the American casualties were from that state as Clay soon learned how badly mistaken he had been. The U.S. was poorly prepared for the War of 1812, and from the beginning there was little enthusiasm for actually conducting the fighting.

Most state militiamen refused to fight outside the borders of their own states with the New England states refusing to participate in the war as they kept their ports open to British shipping throughout the conflict and regularly traded with the enemy. In this way, the British did not even have to mount a defense for a large portion of the frontier separating the U.S. and their colonies to the north and could therefore concentrate on American attacks in the west.

The American campaigns into Canada in 1812, 1813, and 1814 were dispersed, and ineptly conducted. American hopes that French speakers and settlers from the U.S. would side with them were in vain. The American forces were composed largely of Indian fighters and backwoodsmen, who did not fight according to the "rules of the game." Instead of standing shoulder-to-shoulder and advancing politely and openly toward the enemy, the American forces ran through the woods with their squirrel rifles and hid behind rocks and trees. Frustrated British regulars screamed, "Show us our enemy!" This was a different kind of American than the easy-going farmers who had immigrated earlier into Canada, and they helped change Canadians' image of Americans.

The well-trained British regulars, supported by Indians, blunted all American attempts to seize and hold territory. The charismatic and energetic General Sir Isaak Brock, who had a mere 1,200 troops under his command supported sporadically by natives and settlers, won three stunning victories in the first months of the conflict. Brock captured the U.S. Fort Mackinac before the garrison was even aware that war had been declared. He then bluffed the nervous American General William Hull into surrendering his whole army in Detroit without firing a shot. Brock died on the battlefield at Queenston Heights, near Niagara Falls after repelling another U.S. force. American forces did gain control of the Great Lakes, and they captured and burned to the ground the capital at York, now (Toronto.

Both sides plundered and murdered civilians, engaging in brutal guerilla combat and tit-for-tat retaliatory strikes on both sides of the border. The governor of Michigan Territory ordered Brigadier-General Duncan McArthur to create "a desert between us and them." The burning of York

Canada

prompted the British in 1814 to seize the American capital of Washington and to burn much of it in retaliation. Only the specter in Europe of a Napoleonic resurgence in 1814 saved the Americans at the eleventh hour as it inclined the British to accept a quick peace settlement with the U.S. The Treaty of Ghent confirmed the 1783 boundaries between British North America and the U.S. but did not mention maritime law, the original reason for the war. Even so, Britain never again interfered with American ships.

The War of 1812 was the last American attempt to expand northward into Canada east of the Rocky Mountains, but it was also significant for the two countries' relationship in other ways. The war stimulated among most Canadians a sense of distinctiveness and separateness from the American nation and created the beginnings of a definite, though still weak, Canadian identity. Unlike General Wolfe's victory against the French at Quebec City in 1759, which divided Canadians, the outcome of the War of 1812, in which British and French Canadians fought together, helps to unite them. The war also ultimately helped Americans and Canadians develop a tolerance for each other.

To make sure that there would always be an alternative route between Toronto and Montreal in case the Americans ever seized control of the St. Lawrence, Canadians dug by hand the 123-mile Rideau Canal with 47 locks between Kingston and what is now Ottawa. By 1832, it was completed, after only six years of work. This canal is one of the first examples of the state-sponsored mega-projects that have helped to build and to bind Canada together. Fortunately, the canal never had to be used for military purposes and today is a beautiful placid waterway flowing right through the middle of Ottawa.

The memory of the War of 1812 ultimately led in 1858 to Queen Victoria's decision to establish the Canadian national capital in Ottawa, a tiny backwoods lumber town called Bytown, which grew into the "city of saws and laws." Located on the Ottawa River, which now separates the provinces of Ontario and Quebec, Ottawa was therefore a symbolic cord linking Canada's two founding peoples. More important, though, it was safely located out of reach of possible American attacks. The war stimulated on both sides a desire for more peaceful relations. One of the first steps in that direction was the Rush-Bagot convention of 1817, which limited naval armament in the Great Lakes to police vessels. This was an important beginning for the establishment of what until September 11, 2001, was the longest undefended border in the world.

Leaders also established diplomatic machinery to facilitate the peaceful settlement of disputes among the neighbors. This machinery has functioned ever since. An 1818 convention established the northwestern boundary along the 49th parallel all the way to the Rockies. Unfortunately, this convention was unable to settle conflicting claims on the Pacific Coast and provided for joint occupation of that area for the time being. Tempers were again to flare over this territory a quarter of a century later, with some Americans defiantly screaming "Fifty-four forty or fight!", meaning that the U.S. should have all the land west of the Rockies up to the fifty-four forty parallel.

After 1814 these neighbors were never to fight again over disputes, and the boundary was firmly established in 1846 along the 49th parallel, with only a minor southward dip to the Strait of Juan de Fuca so that Vancouver Island would remain entirely within British North America. After the northern border had been agreed nn, the U.S. could concentrate on its western destiny, and Canada could turn its attention to creating a unified nation in the less hospitable northern part of the American continent.

THE ROAD TO INDEPENDENCE

The period from 1815 to the rebellions of 1837 was one of adjustment to rising demands for more democracy and for responsible government, a government responsible not to a monarch or his governors, but to a popularly elected legislature. The revolutions in America and France had contradictory effects on many Canadians. These convulsions caused some Canadians to fear instability resulting from too much democracy. Canadians tended to see British institutions as the best bulwark against such instability and saw American democracy as offering too little order, an impression later greatly strengthened by the American Civil War. At the same time, the revolutions fanned the desire for more representative self-government in British North America.

During those years the immigration patterns changed so that the make-up of the Canadian population also changed. Following the War of 1812 the British showed less tolerance toward American immigration into their Canadian colonies. Therefore, the influx of Americans practically stopped until the end of the century. At the same time, economic and social distress in the British Isles led to a flood of emigration to the New World. Most went to the U.S., but between 1815 and 1850 approximately 800,000 went to Canada. About 100,000 settled in the Maritime Provinces, strengthening the British character of that area with most moving into the uncleared portions of what is now Ontario, whose population by 1850 had practically reached a million.

These settlers left a motherland which was experiencing significant reform movements; some brought British progressive ideas with them and enthusiastically supported democratic reform in Upper and Lower Canada such as William Lyon Mackenzie and Louis-Joseph Papineau. While both admired British institutions, they opposed aristocratic rule and favored the popular election of executive officers, as had long been practiced in the U.S.

In 1837, followers of both men rebelled in Toronto and Montreal, but their uprisings were promptly crushed. Both leaders were forced to make hair-raising escapes to the U.S., where they hoped to gain the support of the American government for their causes. However, American leaders were not willing to risk conflict with Britain by granting assistance. Even though Canadians have never experienced as much domestic violence as their American neighbors, the rebellions of 1837 were among the few incidents of political violence there. While they failed in the short term, these uprisings did succeed in prompting the British to sit up and take notice of political conditions in Canada as they launched an investigation that ultimately led in 1867 to a largely independent Canada.

The British remembered the futility of attempting to erect dams against the democratic tide in the U.S. six decades earlier. In 1838, they dispatched John Lambton, the first Earl of Durham, to Canada to serve as Governor General of all the provinces and to investigate the grievances of the rebels. Because of his hand in the passage of the Great Reform Bill in Britain in 1832, Durham earned the nickname of "Radical Jack." Soon after his debarkation at Quebec City, Durhm became embroiled in quarrels with his government at home.

Canada

He returned to England only five months later and submitted his now famous Durham Report early in 1839. While the report dealt with a wide range of North American problems, Durham's most important recommendations were the establishment of responsible government, the union of Upper and Lower Canada, ultimately aiming toward the union of all British North American provinces, and the practice of permitting the provincial governments to make most decisions, reserving only a few important matters, such as defense and foreign policy, for the imperial government.

Ultimately, all of Lord Durham's proposals were enacted and it became a major milestone in the transformation of the British Empire into a Commonwealth of self-ruling nations and in the evolution of democratic government in Canada. In 1841, the provinces of Upper and Lower Canada were united as the first step toward a unified Canada. A single legislature was created with each former colony having equal representation, even though initially only English could be spoken in the debates. By the end of the decade responsible government had been established.

Durham noted the gulf that divided anglophones from francophones: "I found two nations warring within the bosom of a single state; I found a struggle, not of principles, but of races." He had developed a low opinion of French Canadians, believing them to be "an utterly uneducated and singularly inert population . . . destitute of all that can invigorate and elevate a people." Durham therefore believed it to be a "vain endeavor to preserve a French-Canadian nationality in the midst of Anglo-American colonies and states." He mistakenly believed that unity would ultimately anglicize the French. Such remarks understandably stung French Canadians who openly opposed the Durham Report. Further, these remarks and attitudes also hardened their determination to resist assimilation at all costs and to survive as a cultural entity as they were convinced to demonstrate that Canada could not be ruled without French cooperation. Through tolerance, solidarity, and constructive parliamentary work, the French showed in the years that followed that Canada could be ruled with their collaboration.

The political union of the two provinces proved to be cumbersome, resulting in frequent elections and changes of government. By the 1850s, it was clear to many that a new and different kind of political framework, still linked with Britain, would ultimately be necessary in order to enable Canada to face the challenges posed by economic development and the ever-present dynamism of the U.S. The need to compete with the U.S. for business investments and immigrants, as well as to ward off the powerful American force of manifest destiny, stimulated Canadian determination to develop the West, to improve transportation within the colonies, and to steer toward national unity.

Letter dated October 3, 1840, in the hand of the Governor of Nova Scotia, Viscount Lucius Bentinck Cary Falkland (1840–46), to a London merchant requesting lamps plus sherry and claret glasses, ending the hasty request with "I am, gentlemen, your obed[ient] servant, FALKLAND."

The growing pressures for self-government also pointed toward greater unity. While the American political experience helped to whet many Canadians' own appetite for self-rule, the actual political model in the U.S. had considerably less appeal. In Canadian eyes, the American Civil War of 1861–1865 revealed serious weaknesses in the decentralized regime with excessively powerful states and no mature mother country to act as a stabilizer. Nevertheless, 40,000 Canadian fought in the Civil War, participating in every major battle, and 29 were awarded the Congressional Medal of Honor. In fact, a Canadian led the troops who captured Lincoln's assassin, John Wilkes Booth.

More and more Canadians wanted self-rule, but few wanted complete independence from Britain. What the reformers who were ultimately successful wanted was a large measure of self-rule under the British constitution and within the British Empire. The American Civil War further stimulated some talk in America of acquiring Canada. For years some Americans were angry about the fact that Canada was the last station of the "Underground Railway" for 30,000 run-away slaves. To this end, Harriet Beecher Stowe based *Uncle Tom's Cabin* on an escaped slave residing in Canada. Canada had abolished slavery in 1833.

Others were irritated by the fact that Britain tolerated Confederate raids on the northern states launched from Canadian soil during the Civil War. President Lincoln's Secretary of State, William H.

Canada

The Charlottetown Conference, September 1, 1864
Public Archives Canada/C733

Seward, was reported to have been an interested listener to talk about taking possession of Canada, but Lincoln turned a deaf ear to it.

CONFEDERATION

By 1864, the forces supporting Canadian unity really began to gain momentum. Legislative deadlock had been created over such explosive issues as "representation by population," or "Rep by Pop" for short, which would have awarded legislative seats according to the size of population, thereby discriminating against Quebec. The reformist governing coalition since 1854 led by John A. Macdonald, who came to dominate Canadian politics until his death in 1891, and by the *Québécois*, George-Etienne Cartier, could no longer rule. In 1864 these two helped form a broader coalition which initiated discussions among the colonies and London aiming toward some form of confederation.

It is characteristic of Canadian politics that this coalition rejected all forms of coercion to muscle unwilling provinces into a new confederation or to maneuver a province into a situation where it could simply be outvoted by the majority. Canada is very much a compact among powerful provinces so that even today politicians address many important issues in semi-annual "summit conferences" involving the prime minister and the ten provincial premiers.

The "Fathers of Confederation," as they later came to be known, found the greatest resistance to union in Quebec and the Maritimes. In September 1864, representatives of the Maritime provinces assembled in Charlottetown, Prince Edward Island, to discuss the possibility of uniting the four Atlantic provinces. This Charlottetown Conference is reverently regarded in Canada as the first step toward Canadian unity.

The Charlottetown Conference was only a first step because the astute John A. Macdonald mobilized a delegation to attend and to persuade the Maritimers to consider a larger vision of Canadian unity. The latter agreed to postpone their decision and to attend a conference of all provincial leaders in Quebec City in October where they met behind closed doors for two weeks. The delegations thoroughly discussed the ever-explosive Canadian question of the relationship between provincial and central authority as they sought a way to create a central government sufficiently strong to hold the confederation together and to block possible American northward expansion without being so strong that it could crush the important cultural differences in the individual provinces.

In the end, the delegates could agree on the general shape of confederation, and the "72 Quebec Resolutions" were a detailed outline of the structure of government and the division of powers and financial responsibilities which became the basis for Canada's first constitution in 1867. Obtaining the approval of all the provincial legislatures proved to be considerably more difficult. There was relatively little opposition in what is now Ontario, the most populous part of Canada and well poised to benefit economically from westward expansion that was sure to follow unification.

Francophone Canadians were much more skeptical, fearing that union would make them an even smaller minority and therefore threaten their survival as a distinct cultural entity. Cartier was able to persuade a slim majority of *Québécois* that they would face a greater danger of extinction by remaining outside, rather than inside, the new union. He pointed out that a solitary Quebec would risk annexation by the U.S. There, the force of the "melting pot" would surely destroy French Canadian culture, as was actually demonstrated in the case of most French-Canadian emigrants to the U.S. Cartier stressed that confederation would leave the provinces authority over educational and religious matters, that French civil law would remain in Quebec, and that French would be one of two official languages in both the federal parliament and the province. Most importantly, Cartier maintained that confederation would recreate the separation of Lower from Upper Canada and create a province of Quebec in which there would again be a French-speaking majority.

The greatest resistance was found in the Atlantic provinces, which always had closer ties with Britain and New England than with the provinces farther west. The Atlantic provinces viewed the new constitutional scheme as favoring the more populous and economically powerful central Canada. Prince Edward Island and Newfoundland rejected union, with the latter not reconsidering its action until 1949, when its people chose in a close referendum to become a part of Canada. Because Britain wanted a united Canada and put great pressure on Nova Scotia and New Brunswick. While both chose to join, Nova Scotia almost backed out of the union nine years later.

The next step took place in London in 1867, where a delegation of Canadians met British leaders to draw up the British North America Act (BNA). This act differed little from the Quebec Resolutions except that it contained some compromises sought by the Maritimes. The British Parliament accepted the BNA without

Canada

serious opposition and it served as Canada's constitution until 1982. The differences in the way Canada and the U.S. adopted their first constitutions is revealing. Because there was no constitutional convention in Canada, there was much less haggling over details.

Some of the constitution's terms or concepts were stated in general terms, and, in good British style, some important political practices were left entirely unwritten. The document explicitly provided that Canada should have "a constitution similar in principle to that of the United Kingdom" but it also revealed an awareness of the special difficulties of ruling a vast federation with sharp racial, cultural, and regional differences. The constitution left much room for the Canadian political system to evolve and to adapt to such a diverse and far-flung country.

On July 1, 1867, the Dominion of Canada, composed of Ontario, Quebec, Nova Scotia, and New Brunswick, came into existence. This date remains Canada's main national holiday. To soothe *Québécois* feelings after the 1960s, the federal government officially renamed the holiday "Canada Day," but some Canadians still call it "Dominion Day."

Canadians did not regard themselves as being independent of Great Britain, but only as being self-governing in their own domestic affairs. Indeed, as Pierre Berton noted, "we did not separate violently from Europe but cut our ties cautiously in the Canadian manner—so cautiously, so imperceptibly that none of us is quite sure when we actually achieved our independence." The tie with Britain, insofar as foreign and defense policy were concerned, was still considered to be of great importance in assisting this loose collection of provinces in defending their interests against the more powerful and self-confident American republic, which, Canadians feared, still had territorial ambitions north of their border. They saw evidence of this only four months before the Confederation was founded in 1867 when the U.S. purchased Alaska from Russia.

A transcontinental Canadian confederation was visibly taking shape, despite formidable obstacles. One of the first hurdles cleared was the Canadian government's 1869 purchase of the Hudson's Bay Company's charter and trade monopoly in the West and Northwest. The company had, in a sense, held the Canadian West in trust until Canada became ready to develop it. The company relinquished a huge expanse of land with a settled population of only about 7,000 people, concentrated mainly around Fort Garry, now Winnipeg, in the Red River Colony (now Manitoba).

The Canadian acquisition of the Hudson's Bay charter was not good news to most of the inhabitants of the Red River Colony. Most residents were Métis, a racial mixture of Indians and French and British fur traders who spoke both French and English. The Métis had few contacts with or interest in Eastern Canada, and over the years developed a strong sense of their own identity. They feared that their traditional way of life would be destroyed, leading to clashes with the new government in Ottawa. Under the leadership of the legendary Louis Riel, the Métis formed a provisional government and prepared to resist Ottawa's authority.

The Canadian government was torn over how to respond. In Ontario there was outrage at Riel's order to execute a Canadian official who had been sent to the colony. On the other hand, Quebecers sympathized with the French-speaking Métis. Faced with such differences, the infant Canadian government developed a two-pronged strategy: it sent troops to Fort Garry, forcing Riel to flee to Montana, where he became a poverty-stricken schoolteacher for the next 15 years; it also received a delegation from the Red River Colony in Ottawa to discuss terms for entry into the Canadian federation.

Ottawa conceded all the essential rights which Riel sought, especially demands for religious schools and the equality of

The British North America Act, July 1, 1867
Public Archives Canada/C104073

Canada

French and English as official languages. The Colony entered the federation as the province of Manitoba in 1870, but the problems of ensuring the French language rights that were granted in 1869 continue to plague Manitoba and Ottawa today.

The next step in building Canada was to induce the colony of British Columbia to join the federation. Heavily attracted to the U.S., not until 1869 did the sentiment to join Canada outweigh the inclination to enter the American union. Finally, in 1871 Ottawa struck a deal with British Columbia. As a price for the colony's entering Canada, Ottawa promised to assume its accumulated debt and to build a railway all the way to the Pacific. This latter promise proved an exceedingly difficult one to keep.

In 1871, British Columbia entered Canada. Also in 1871, the new country entered into difficult negotiations with the U.S. in which many specific disputes were settled. The major significance of this Treaty of Washington was that the U.S. officially recognized the facts that the American continent north of Mexico was forever to be divided between the two countries and that Canada was a federation extending from coast to coast. In 1873, Prince Edward Island, which saw union as the only solution to its desperate financial problems, joined Canada.

Leaders in Ottawa skillfully hammered together a unified Canada by enticing wavering colonies into the federation through promises of economic benefit. This tool was particularly important and effective because of a severe world-wide economic downturn which began in 1873 and lasted until the mid-1890s. This seemingly endless economic depression was the longest and worst the modern world has ever known. It greatly hampered the construction of a northern transcontinental railway which the Canadian government had promised the new provinces in the East and West. The crucial importance of the railway, which would staple together all the far-flung provinces of Canada and attract investments and immigrants from Europe, was revealed in a letter which Prime Minister Macdonald wrote to London: "Until this great work is completed, our Dominion is little better than a geographical expression."

TIGHTENING THE EAST–WEST LINK

Short railways had begun to be built in the 1840s and 1850s to link trading terminals and to connect with the rail networks which were being constructed in the U.S. Macdonald knew that in order to prosper, though, Canada had to establish an East–West transportation and trade axis to counteract the more natural North–South trade axis. Voted back into power in 1878, Macdonald proclaimed a "national policy," which called for raising the protective tariff to shelter Canadian companies from excessive competition by bigger and financially stronger American firms. Such protectionist economic measures were vigorously debated at that time.

One of the ironies of such a lasting protectionist policy is that American companies circumvented it by establishing their own subsidiaries in Canada. They thereby created what many observers and critics would later call the "Americanization" of the Canadian economy. Indeed, the large degree of foreign, especially American, ownership of the economy remains an unsolved and perhaps insoluble dilemma.

Macdonald's policy also called for the fulfillment of the Dominion's promise to British Columbia to complete the railway to the Pacific. He was also determined that this railway be constructed entirely within Canada, rather than to extend partly through the less foreboding American landscape. This was a daunting task. In light of Canada's immense size, formidable terrain, extremely variable climate and sparse population, economic development depended far more on gigantic projects and close cooperation between the government and business leaders than was ever considered necessary or desirable in the U.S. This pattern of a large governmental hand in the nation's economy continues to this day.

In order to persuade British and Canadian businessmen to take the great risks of building a transcontinental railway, the government offered an assortment of cash subsidies, special privileges, and huge land grants in the unsettled areas through which the rail lines would run; much of this land is still owned by the Canadian Pacific Railway Company (CPR). The opposition Liberal Party strongly criticized the generosity of the contract offered to the CPR. Every dollar the CPR could lay its hands on was needed to build the railway through the twisted, rocky countryside of western Ontario, across the Prairies and though the treacherous Kicking Horse Pass in the Rocky Mountains. On November 7, 1885, Macdonald received a telegram informing him that the railway was finally completed.

The central government in Ottawa moved energetically to secure order and to enlarge its powers throughout Canada. The Royal Canadian Mounted Police (RCMP) controlled the western settlements more tightly than their counterparts did in the U.S., so the shooting iron and the violence that characterized much of life in the early American West were largely absent. Hollywood helped to create a myth about the Royal Canadian Mounted Policeman that is misleading. Pierre Berton noted in his book, *Hollywood's Canada*, that Hollywood made 575 movies about Canada between 1907 and 1975, and in 256 of them the "Mountie" always "got his man," a name and a slogan the RCMP dislikes today.

Although the Mountie's guns blazed in the movies, he, in fact, seldom drew his weapon. He did enforce the law, but also dispensed social services, helped persons get to far-away hospitals, tried to secure food for the settlers and Indians in his area in time of need, and sometimes even sorted and delivered the mail. His patient, tactful paternalism helped to prepare Canadians' receptivity to the idea of the state as the generous dispenser of social services like family allowances and universal medical treatment. This is a notion less firmly implanted in the minds of most Americans.

Trying to avoid the bloody Indian wars the American settlers had experienced, the Canadian government negotiated what it thought at the time were fair treaties with the Indians, with some allowing themselves to be relocated on reservations. Indeed, there were fewer Indian wars and massacres of natives in Western Canada than in the U.S.. However, in the late-20th century Indians began to challenge many of those treaties as well as their status as second-class citizens in modern Canadian society.

The last two decades of the 19th century were not a golden age of harmony for the young dominion. Most of the provinces resented the growth of Ottawa's power, resulting in one crisis after the other. Western farmers resented both the high freight prices caused by the CPR's monopoly and the high price of goods manufactured in the East which resulted from the country's high tariff policy.

In the territory that is now Alberta and Saskatchewan, the mainly Indian and Métis inhabitants resented the intrusion of government agents into their lives. They feared a radical disruption of their traditional way of life. The great Cree Indian chief, Big Bear, was attempting to unify the Indians to renegotiate the treaties with the white men. Also, the Métis in the Saskatchewan River Valley were pressing for surveys of their land claims in order not to be dispossessed of their farms again, as they had been in Manitoba after the government had allegedly broken its promises to them. In short, the region was ripe for a rebellion.

Because the Macdonald government showed little interest in these concerns, in 1884 the Métis asked Louis Riel to return from his American exile in order to lead them in their resistance to Ottawa. He

Canada

Lord Strathcona drives in the last spike completing the Canadian Pacific Railway, November 1885
Public Archives Canada/C3693

proclaimed the provisional government of Saskatchewan on March 19, 1885. Aided by his able adjutant general, Gabriele Dumont, he led an ill-fated uprising, known as the Northwest Rebellion of 1885, which pitted a guerrilla force of 600 Métis and Plains Indians against a poorly trained Canadian army of 8,000 men. The war opened with a Métis victory at Duck Lake, with Riel, a self-proclaimed "Prophet of the New World," riding unarmed within range of the Canadians waving a crucifix and yelling, "Fire! In the name of the Son and the Holy Ghost! Fire!"

The brave natives ultimately lost to the railway which carried thousands of green Canadian troops to the West in 10 days. After 51 days of fighting, including an indecisive battle at Fish Creek and a stinging loss at Batoche, the uprising was crushed. The last human barriers to white settlement of the West were thereby eliminated.

Dumont escaped and fled to the U.S., where he later joined Buffalo Bill's Wild West Show as a sharpshooter on horseback and the "hero of the half-breed revolution." Riel was captured, and despite vigorous protests by Quebecers, who regarded him as a staunch defender of French and Catholic rights, he was hanged on November 16, 1885, in the Mounted Police barracks at Regina, Saskatchewan.

Macdonald, who said that "Riel shall hang, though every dog in Quebec bark in his favor" and his Conservative Party suffered greatly from Riel's execution one of the most significant events in Canadian history. English Protestants at the time viewed Riel as a common criminal, but francophones saw him differently. His execution reignited French Canadian nationalism and exacerbated the animosities between anglophones and francophones.

The debate over Riel was the first time since Confederation that anglophones and francophones were diametrically opposed, paving the way for the Liberal Party's acquisition of national power in 1895, five years after Macdonald's death. In addition, it was the beginning of the Conservative Party's almost complete political exclusion from Quebec which continues to the present. Quebec has consistently reacted to any perceived attack on the rights of French speakers anywhere in Canada in the same way as it did to Riel's execution.

In 1985, the centennial of the Northwest Rebellion, many Canadians were still uncertain that a war had to be fought in order to deal with the Métis' and Indians' grievances. The fight seems to symbolize the basic tensions that still exist in Canadian life: the struggle for minority rights and for regional autonomy. With the resurgence in the 1970s of various forms of nationalism in Canada, many Western Canadians came to regard Riel as a defender of Western interests, socialists see him as a staunch opponent of imperialism, and francophones still view him as the champion of French language rights. Riel's home and grave in Winnipeg are

Louis Riel in front of Manitoba's legislature

Canada

maintained as befitting a hero, not a rebel to be despised.

In 1992, the House of Commons, which was desperately trying to keep Quebec in Canada and placate the West, officially recognized Riel's "unique and historic role as a founder of Manitoba." This act was, in former Prime Minister Joe Clark's words, "an indication that we have matured as a nation." In 1998, the Canadian government apologized to all aboriginal peoples for past mistreatment and offenses, including the hanging of Riel. Nevertheless, the Métis National Council regretted that the apology fell short of an official pardon. The fact that most Canadians want Riel exonerated was revealed in a 1999 poll that showed Riel as the most popular Canadian politician; his "approval rating" was 75%, the same percentage of respondents who believe it was wrong to hang him as a traitor.

In 1999, the first overt political act of Governor General Adrienne Clarkson was to attend a ceremony honoring Riel, calling him "the founder of Manitoba" who "played a key, vital role in opening up Canada's West." On the occasion of Canada's 150th anniversary in 2017, the Canadian Opera Company again staged the opera "Louis Riel." The opera explores in musical form Canada's mistreatment of its indigenous people and its efforts to take away their rights and land.

Within months of leading his party to electoral victory 1891, John A. Macdonald died. He had made the role of prime minister a powerful centralizing force. Without him Canada would have become a different country. Five years later the era of Conservative Party dominance in Canada came to an end. In the three decades of that era, Canada had survived the initial challenges of self-government. Canada had expanded its borders from coast to coast.

As a young country with only four million citizens in 1885, it had tied the country from East to West with a railway; the U.S. had completed its first transcontinental railway a quarter of a century earlier, but America's population and market were ten times larger than Canada's at that time, and its terrain is much more amenable to railroad construction than is that of its neighbor to the north. Canada had survived the effects of the world-wide recession which had begun in 1873 and which had seemed interminable. Moreover, Canada had worked out a national economic policy, which had foreseen not only the expansion of the railways, but also increased immigration and the erection of a tariff barrier to encourage the growth of Canadian manufacturing.

In 1896, Sir Wilfrid Laurier led the Liberal Party to victory in the federal elections and launched practically a century

Louis Riel addresses the jury before his conviction, Regina, Saskatchewan, 1885
Public Archives Canada/C1879

of almost continuous Liberal Party rule in Canada. Laurier was a handsome, urbane, superbly educated man, who was equally articulate and elegant in both his native French and in English, which he spoke with an appealing French touch. Laurier was regarded as a master of rationality and compromise whose skill at finding the middle ground enabled him to govern as prime minister for 15 years.

Laurier helped to unify both French and English concerns, calling on all his countrymen to remember that "your duty is simply and above all to be Canadians." He gave his party something of a basic philosophy. Because Laurier believed that his party was heir to British, not continental European liberalism, he thought that cultural toleration should be a guiding rule in which anti-clericalism, the view that organized churches have no place in political affair,) should have no part. Laurier did expect the Catholic Church to restrain itself, though.

By the time Laurier became prime minister, Canada had already begun to pull out of the economic crisis. In fact, for decades the Liberal Party benefited from this fortunate coincidence of gaining power at the threshold of a long period of prosperity and development. The Conservative Party would not be so lucky as it would have to bear much of the blame for the suffering that World War I and the Great Depression of the 1930s would inflict on Canadians.

Canada was beginning to take full advantage of the world-wide rise in grain prices. Canadian wheat began to represent in the economy what fur had once been in the French-Canadian economy: it played the dominant role until well into the 1930s. Gold was discovered in the Yukon in 1898. The headlines unleashed a stampede north, but only a few became wealthy. This was followed by rich mining strikes elsewhere in Canada.

This was also a time of robust industrial development; the net value of manufacturing production grew by more than two and one-half times from 1901 to 1911. A new mood of optimism, which began to attract hundreds of thousands of immigrants from the United Kingdom, continental Europe, and the U.S., emerged. Most came to the Canadian West where there was still free land to be had. By the 1890s most of the free land in the U.S. had already been claimed. With the practical closing of the American frontier, Canada had become the place for landless people with dreams. In 1896, almost 17,000 immigrants came, but by 1913 this inflow became a floodtide of a half million annually. From 1896 to 1911, over two million persons poured into Canada. From 1897 to 1930 almost a million and a half American farmers from Minnesota, the Dakotas and other border states crossed the line into the Prairie provinces.

Such an explosive migration into Canada was an important boon to the young country. Even so, the boon did bring social, political and economic changes that would trouble Canada. A multitude of new, relatively short, railroads were constructed west of Winnipeg to provide transport for the produce of new farms which were opening up. The financing of these lines, obtained in Canada, New York, and London from private sources, was a high risk, as the investors would find out within a few decades. Because almost none of the immigrants came from France, despite the higher birth-rate in Quebec, the percentage of French in the overall Canadian population continued to decline.

Canada

This decline was aggravated by the steady stream of French Canadians who left Quebec and the Maritimes for New England during the second half of the 19th century. From the late 1800s to the early 1900s, almost a million French Canadians poured across the border to work in textile and shoe mills. In 1881, one Massachusetts official called them "the Chinese of the eastern states." Even more English Canadians moved south, with peaks in the 1880s and 1920s and ending with the Great Depression.

By 1900, the number of Canadians residing in the U.S. equaled 22% of Canada's entire population. Today at least two million of their descendants live in Maine, New Hampshire, Vermont, and Massachusetts. These population trends and patterns disturbed Quebec's leaders, who were angrily watching French language rights being whittled away not only in Manitoba but also in Saskatchewan and Alberta, which had become provinces in 1905. Despite legal assurances to francophones in 1875, separate French Catholic schools and the status of French as an official language alongside English were largely abolished. French Canadians have often shown that they have long memories, and the recollection of these actions at the end of the 19th century would in the 1970s and 1980s again spark bitter conflict over French language rights in Manitoba.

More than a fourth of the newcomers came from Central Europe and the Ukraine. Settling in the prairies, they faced ethnic and cultural condescension and resentment from settlers of British descent. These Central European and Ukrainian people had, and still hav,e an important cultural influence in the West, but they were forced to earn the respect they now enjoy. Distressing to the Quebecers was the fact that when these non-British immigrant groups finally became integrated, they integrated into English, not French language and culture, whether they settled in Quebec or not. With this phenomenon in mind during the 1970s, the Quebec government required by law that immigrant children in Quebec province be schooled in French, not English.

Almost none of the immigrants stayed in the Maritime Provinces, and the economic boom of this era touched these provinces less than elsewhere, thereby helping to deepen the economic distress that still exists there. Further, the journey of some of the less fortunate immigrants stopped in the urban slums of major cities in Quebec and Ontario with their restlessness for social and economic improvement bringing ferment into urban politics and labor union activity.

LOOSENING THE APRON STRINGS

The 1898 Yukon gold rush in the Klondike fields sparked another of many border disputes with the U.S. This one involved the eastern border of the Alaska Panhandle, through which supplies to the Klondike had to pass. Russia had obtained Alaska from Britain in 1825 and had sold it to the U.S. in 1867. The U.S. insisted on the border that was recognized in 1867. Insofar as the British government wanted time to defuse disputes with the U.S., it agreed to have the question adjudicated in 1903 by a commission composed of three Americans, two Canadians and one Englishman. When the Englishman sided with the three Americans in accepting the American claim, Canadians were incensed against both the U.S. and Britain.

This 1903 incident was a helpful reminder to Canadians that their interests were by no means identical to those of the U.S. and that Britain could no longer be relied on energetically to back up Canadian demands in the face of American opposition. Of course, this realization had not come suddenly. Macdonald believed that Canada's independence in the face of "American Manifest Destiny" depended on its ties with Britain; he also was convinced that the colonial apron strings must gradually had to be cut if Canada were to fully mature as a nation.

Macdonald began sending ambassadors to London after 1880. Despite a strident Quebec nationalist stance early in his career, because Laurier was a great admirer of many things British, he accepted a knighthood. Nevertheless, he, like many of his countrymen, feared a more active British imperial policy in the world, and he had staunchly opposed the creation of a permanent Imperial Council which could have imposed tariffs and military measures on all of the colonies.

This controversy, and the entire series of negotiations since 1867 with the Americans on a wide variety of issues ranging from commerce, fishing, waterways, and boundary lines persuaded both neighbors that an International Joint Commission (IJC), composed of three representatives each from the U.S. and Canada would be a useful permanent body to settle bilateral disputes, particularly ones dealing with waterways. This commission has worked effectively since its creation in 1909. That same year the Canadians also decided that because it had to look out for its own interests, leaders should create a Department of External Affairs through which a Canadian foreign policy could be conducted. This began as little more than an archive and it would be more than a decade before Canada could truly handle its own foreign affairs.

Foreign policy disputes created a strong anti-American sentiment in Canada, which boiled to the surface in the federal elections of 1911 when voters rejected the aging Laurier because he dared to negotiate tariff reductions with Washington. Anti-British feeling had also become a greater force to be reckoned with, as Canada's leaders were to make the painful discovery at the time of the outbreak of the World War I in 1914.

WORLD WAR I

When Britain entered the war in September 1914, many Canadians and most Britons considered Canada automatically to be at war also. Yet, many Canadians, particularly francophones, who saw this matter differently. An early warning of

Panning for gold in the Yukon, 1898
Public Archives Canada/C16459

Canada

francophones' reaction to a British war effort had already been given 15 years earlier when the Boer War had broken out in South Africa. In 1899, while the Laurier government faced emotional demands from English-speaking Canadians to stand by Britain during this conflict, francophones made it equally clear that their sons should not be called on to die for Britain in far-away wars unrelated to the defense of Canada. Laurier's compromise, that volunteers could be sent to fight for Britain, prompted his brightest follower in Quebec, Henri Bourassa, to break with him.

Bourassa became a rallying point for dissident francophones. In 1907, he declared: "There is Ontario patriotism, Quebec patriotism or western patriotism, but there is no Canadian patriotism." Bourassa laid the groundwork in Quebec for the bitter resistance to Canada's participation in World War I.

As a member of the British Empire, Canada found itself legally at war in 1914. Canada was sparsely peopled, overwhelmingly rural, mired in an economic recession, and divided by language, faith and region. A majority of Canadians favored national involvement but not all shared a willingness to sacrifice blood and resources for a European dispute. This split was evident in the makeup of the First Canadian Contingent that was raised and sent overseas within two months of the war's outbreak. Of its 36,267 volunteers, only 1,245 were francophones, only 10,880 had been born in Canada, and over 23,000 were British born with close ties to the old country.

Many anglophones felt retained loyalty to Britain. However, *Québécois*, who represented three of the eight million Canadians at the time, neither shared that loyalty nor had a sentimental attachment to France, where the bloodiest battles of the war were fought. The France of the 20th century was no longer the France to which the *Québécois* ancestors belonged. The French Revolution had beheaded the king and his family, proclaimed a republic, decapitated 25,000 persons, and brutally attacked the Catholic Church. The Jacobin regime even went so far as to proclaim, for a brief time, a worship of reason, instead of God, renaming the Cathedral of Notre Dame the "Temple of Reason."

During the entire 19th century, the controversy over the role of the Church in French society had been a dominant issue in French politics. This was shocking to a people like the *Québécois*, who until the 1960s were a deeply Catholic people and who accepted the Church's active hand in politics. Also, French society had become socially experimental in ways that shocked many Quebecers, who until the 1960s, were socially conservative. As McGill historian Pierre Boulle noted: "The name of Quebec as a special, protected entity—very different from nasty revolutionary France—essentially existed until the 'Quiet Revolution' in the 1960s." In short, *Québécois* did not regard Frenchmen in 1914 as brothers in distress who should be saved.

The turmoil that followed entry into the "Great War" in 1914 revealed the lack of unanimity concerning how much Canada should be integrated in the British Empire and how much the nation should have contributed to the war effort. The uneasiness about the war increased as casualties piled up and as Canadians began to realize that this war was going to be much longer than they had initially thought. The Canadians' first major engagement was the Second Battle of Ypres in April 1915, where gas was first used as a weapon. This bloody battle inspired Canadian doctor John McCrae to write the war's most famous poem: "In Flanders Fields."

On Easter morning, April 9, 1917, the Canadian Corps fought together under their own commanders for the first time. It was also the first time that all four divisions of the Canadian Army came together. In a fierce battle lasting four bloody days, they defeated the Germans at Vimy Ridge, near Arras, France, after suffering terrible casualties: 3,598 killed and 7,004 wounded. Of the 15,000 Canadians who "went over the top," one-third were killed or wounded.

Many argue that the Canadian nation was born on that day. The victory also made the Canadians the sharp point of the Allied spear. Joined by the Australians, they broke through the German lines at Amiens on August 8, 1918, and helped set off the drive that would win the war three months later. This ugly four-year conflict would claim 66,000 Canadian lives (12,000 more than the U.S.). One out of ten Canadian soldiers died in the conflict. The nation called 619,636 Canadians to arms, all but 75,000 of whom for overseas duty.

Canadian troops performed extremely well, showing themselves and the world that their country was capable of things undreamed of before 1914. The last Canadian veteran of this "Great War," John Babcock, died in February 2010 at age 109. Then Prime Minister Stephen Harper called him "the last living link" to a conflict "which in so many ways marked our coming of age as a nation."

After the war bogged down in the trenches, unimaginative mass suicidal assaults against the well-entrenched enemy claimed more and more lives. The demands on Canadian manpower became so great that leaders reached politically explosive crossroads. Recruiting declined dramatically in 1916, endangering the Canadian commitment to maintain four divisions on the Western front. Therefore, in 1917 the Canadian government felt compelled to present legislation to introduce conscription, just as the Americans did on entering the conflict in April of that year. This decision ushered in the greatest threat to Canada's internal harmony since confederation almost a half century earlier.

The most prominent French-Canadian politician, Sir Wilfrid Laurier, vigorously opposed the draft, although he continued to support the war effort. Other Quebec leaders had greater difficulty understanding why the Canadian government justified its calling for greater sacrifices. After all, a considerable number of *Québécois* had volunteered for military service, and with a few exceptions, they had served in English-speaking units. A notable exception was the highly decorated Twenty-Second Regiment of Quebec called the "Vandoos." In the midst of the struggle, an affront that deepened the antagonism was the elimination of bilingual schools in Manitoba and severe restrictions on French-language instruction in Ontario.

The actual introduction of conscription in June 1917 ignited intense emotions in Quebec as many Quebecers openly protested the measure or went into hiding to avoid the recruiters. In March and April 1918 serious riots protesting Canada's war policy took place in Quebec City.

The conscription issue split the Liberal Party. Quebec Liberal membership was solidly opposed the draft. In a bitter and virulently racist federal electoral campaign in December 1917 over the issue of conscription and the formation of a united government, one which would include all the country's major parties, the Liberal Party won all but three seats in Quebec but captured only 20 seats outside of Quebec. The Conservative Party, under Prime Minister Robert Borden, won the hard-fought contest. Borden's majority Unionist government introduced measures that would have been unthinkable a few years earlier: the vote for women, railway nationalization, the income tax, and prohibition. Yet, this election decisively altered party alignment and effectively banished the Tory Party to English Canada for decades. Not until the federal elections of 1984 were there signs that the Liberal Party lock on *Québécois*' votes in federal politics had broken.

Borden and his Conservatives, which had been in office throughout the war, paid a high price for willingly aiding the victorious allies. The war widened the gulf between English and French-speaking Canadians. Voters presented the Conservatives with the bill in the first post-war election on December 6, 1921,

Canada

Rt. Hon. William Lyon Mackenzie King
Public Archives Canada/C86772

handing them a stinging defeat as they won only 49 seats, 37 of which were in Ontario. Thus, the Conservative Party, which in 1917 was practically eliminated from Quebec politics, was banished to the wilderness in federal politics as well.

THE INTERWAR YEARS

World War I sparked a huge expansion of the central government and bureaucracy in Ottawa. Its end saw a problem identical in both Canada and the U.S. Almost all railroads had gone broke. In the U.S., they went into receivership under the Railroad Administration, later to be returned to private ownership. In Canada, all but the Canadian Pacific were bankrupt. The government, which made generous grants of land and money for their construction held the first mortgage, with priority over the private sector investors.

Ultimately, the government took permanent control of these lines in 1923, combining them into the Canadian National, which remains its property today; this includes what used to be the venerable Grand Trunk Railroad, running from Portland, Maine, via its subsidiary, the Central of Vermont, and the Grand Trunk Pacific, with a line to Prince Rupert, British Columbia. A few privately-owned lines remained in operation, but the government was permanently in the railroad business, combining lines it already owned into a massive system stretching from the Maritime Provinces to Vancouver and Prince Rupert.

The 1921 election ushered in a long era of Liberal Party domination in federal politics, first under the leadership of William Lyon Mackenzie King, who governed Canada for most of the rest of his life, until his death in 1950. King, who received a Ph.D. from Harvard and served for years as an industrial relations consultant for the Rockefellers in the U.S., remained a bachelor all his life, and is widely regarded as the strangest, but largely respected, politician in Canadian history.

King who was deeply immersed in spiritualism, had a kind of psychopathic devotion to his deceased mother, and thought he had worked out a way to talk to her. This might sound odd, but a *Maclean's* poll on Canada Day 2006 revealed that about half, or 55%, of Canadians believed in psychic powers, and a third thought that earth-bound human beings can communicate with the dead. Despite all his personal quirks, though, King was responsible for making the Liberal Party an effective and attractive "all-things-to-all-men" grouping which could gather together Canadians of many different persuasions.

In addition to renewed Quebec nationalism and division between anglophones and francophones, the World War I brought other important changes to Canada. The heavy demand for military production stimulated Canadian industry. With Britain's hands tied, Canadians turned to the U.S. for investment capital. New York replaced London as Canada's chief source for outside capital, and during the war American investment in Canada increased more than threefold. The rate of such investment grew steadily thereafter, until it became a matter of grave concern to Canadians after the World War II. Moreover, the war sparked a renewed wave of immigration from Europe into Canada.

The "Great War" boosted Canadian nationalism and the determination to become an entirely self-ruling country. During the war the Canadian government made an important assertion of independence by insisting that a Canadian, Sir Arthur Currie, not an Englishman, command Canadian troops. The government also demanded that Canada be treated as an ally, not a colony. Accordingly, in 1917 all the prime ministers of the dominions, the British colonies settled primarily by whites, were included in the Imperial War Cabinet.

At the 1919 Versailles Conference, which patched Europe together again, Canada was represented as a separate country, signing the treaty as an independent land. Professor Margaret MacMillan, great-granddaughter of British Prime Minister Lloyd George and former Trinity College provost at the University of Toronto, described the conference in her prize-winning study, *Paris 1919: Six Months that Changed the World*. Asked how she could be so even-handed in her treatment, MacMillan answered: "When you're a Canadian, you're looking at great events from a distance."

Unlike the U.S., Canada joined the League of Nations, which had sprung from the imagination of American President Woodrow Wilson. Like the U.S., though, Canada remained largely aloof from European affairs during the interwar years, and it was not actively supportive of the League.

There was much disagreement within Canada about how quickly the country should move toward autonomy from Britain, but while the debate was going on, the government took concrete steps. In 1922 Prime Minister King notified British leaders that Canada could no longer be committed in advance to military actions on the basis of its association with the British Empire. In 1923 Canada assumed the right to negotiate and sign treaties and to make its own foreign policy. It did promise Britain the courtesy of keeping it informed about what Canada was doing. In 1927 Canada sent its first ambassador to the U.S.

At a large gathering of nations within the British Commonwealth in 1926, leaders of Britain and the dominions proclaimed that they were "equal in status and in no way subordinate one to another." This understanding became law when the British Parliament passed the Statute of Westminster in 1931. This statute formally deprived the British Parliament of the right to legislate for the dominions. There remained a few apron strings, though. In Canada's case, the British Parliament retained the exclusive right to amend Canada's constitution, the British North America Act (BNA), whenever the issue involved the distribution of political powers between the central government and the provinces. Canada would probably have obtained this right also if the various provincial governments in Canada could have agreed on a formula for doing so.

It was not until 1982, though that the parties reached an agreement regarding constitutional amendments on all subjects. Finally, the Judicial Committee of the Privy Council, which is lodged in the British House of Lords, remained the highest court of appeal for Canadians until 1935 for criminal cases and until 1949 for civil cases.

Even though the decade following the end of the war was relatively prosperous when compared with the 1930s, it was a time of political radicalization. Canadians were confronted with a wave of labor agitation and strikes throughout the land. Canadian labor unions had doubled their membership during the war, but with re-

Canada

turning veterans vying for jobs, unemployment grew and union leaders feared that their power and influence would become weakened. Employers were especially resistant to demands for collective bargaining and workers resented what they saw as employers' excessive profiteering and conspicuous consumption. Frustration increased due to high inflation, which was stimulated during the war. Frustration also grew due to the perennial perception on the part of Westerners that the government in Ottawa, supported by industrial and financial powers in Eastern Canada, regulated the economy to the advantage of the East and at the expense of the West. On top of this catalogue of concrete economic grievances, some labor leaders espoused socialist convictions and syndicalism, a radical trade unionism to achieve political objectives.

The unrest came to a dramatic crescendo in the Winnipeg General Strike which lasted from May 15 until June 25, 1919. At first, only workers in the building and metal trades struck to protest their employers' refusal to grant either higher wages or collective bargaining. Yet, weeks later the Winnipeg Trades and Labour Council struck in sympathy, paralyzing the economic life of the city within a few hours. Unionists in Vancouver and other Western cities then joined the strikers.

For a time the strike remained free of violence, but many employers and members of the federal and provincial government were inclined to see it as a deliberate attempt by Bolsheviks to undermine the democratic order in Canada. In the U.S. a similar "Red Scare" was afoot in 1919. The Canadian government had sent 4,400 troops to Russia after the overthrow of the czar in 1917. Although public opinion and the government turned against this deployment, it was not until April 1919 that the last Canadians withdrew from the Soviet Union.

A particularly unfortunate event occurred when Mounties and militia troops in Winnipeg broke up a banned march by strikers. In the confused situation that developed, one person was killed and 30 were injured. This tragic development prompted the government to arrest the leaders of the strike on charges of sedition and to patrol the streets of Winnipeg with soldiers. Finally, on June 25 the strike was called off after the government promised to look into the underlying causes of the strike. A governmental commission concluded that the aim of most of the strikers had been to achieve collective bargaining and better working conditions.

The commission's findings notwithstanding, the jailed union leaders were tried, convicted of seditious activities and given jail sentences from six months to two years. This strike created bitterness in Winnipeg and elsewhere that took decades to remove, stimulating the creation of protest sentiments and movements, which, through many twists and turns, continue to survive today.

Canada's social and economic problems became desperate in the aftermath of the New York stock market crash in 1929. Canada was vulnerable to the severe and prolonged worldwide economic depression that set in. The country always depended on foreign capital and on the exportation of raw materials to industrial nation which now could no longer buy the things that Canada had to sell.

By 1933 almost a fourth of Canada's labor force was unemployed and one was confronted everywhere with the same images as in the U.S.: bankruptcies and evictions, farm foreclosures, tent cities, soup-kitchens, and itinerant Canadians desperately looking for work. Government officials spent much of their time and attention on maintaining law and order. The terrible economic situation sparked bitter labor unrest with the government responding by sending in Mounties to disperse demonstrations, infiltrating union meetings with agents, and censoring literature the government perceived to be radical.

Such a charged political atmosphere was an ideal greenhouse for diverse populist protest parties. They were heirs to the defunct Progressive Party which reared up against the dominance of the eastern financial centers, but which lost all its strength by the early 1930s. Two of these parties, which still have a role in Canadian politics, sprang up in the West. The Social Credit Party, headed by a fiery radio evangelist, William Aberhart, aimed its appeal to ranchers and farmers and excoriated the eastern bankers, who allegedly manipulated credit, freight rates and tariffs for their own selfish interests. This party won the Alberta provincial elections in 1935. Although most of its anti-banking legislation was struck down by the Supreme Court, it managed to establish a foothold in Albertan politics which remained firm for decades. It always rejected socialism and became an increasingly conservative party, which seeks to protect "the little guy" and Western Canadian interests. Today the party rules in British Columbia as it cooperates with the Conservative Party in federal politics.

The second party that was, from its beginning, socialist in nature was the Cooperative Commonwealth Federation (CCF). It set out to organize laborers and farmers in order to "eradicate capitalism and put into operation the full programme of socialized planning which will lead to the establishment in Canada of the Cooperative Commonwealth," as its Regina Manifesto proclaimed in 1933.

As doctrinaire as it program seems to be on first reading, the CCF never sought to abolish private property; it promised the "security of tenure for the farmer on his farm." Also, unlike many radical parties, the CCF strongly favored parliamentary government and reform by legal, nonviolent means, gaining ground among urban intellectuals and trade unionists while becoming a permanent fixture in Canadian politics, although it never established firm roots in Atlantic Canada or Quebec. The CCF's electoral fortresses were always in the West, and in 1944 it became the ruling party in Saskatchewan. The CCF changed its name to the New Democratic Party (NDP) in 1961.

A third party that rose up at this time was the Union Nationale or the UN in Quebec. In 1935, under the leadership of the former Quebec Conservative party

Winnipeg General Strike, June 10, 1919
Public Archives Canada/C26782

Canada

The Great Depression: unemployed men board a train for Ottawa, June 1935
Public Archives Canada/C29461

leader, Maurice Duplessis, it gathered together the scraps of that province's Conservative and Liberal parties. As in almost all times of adversity, Quebec nationalism flared up again during the depression. No doubt nationalism was aggravated by the fact that almost all of the major employers in the province were anglophones, while an overwhelming majority of unemployed were francophones.

Claiming that the provincial government was ridden with corruption and that reform was needed in Quebec, Duplessis became premier in 1936. Despite repeated charges that he and his ruling clique were as corrupt as the leaders they replaced and that they were not genuine reformers, the UN gained a hold on Quebec politics that would not be broken until 1970 as it pursued a conservative policy and maintained close relations with the Church. In addition, the UN opened the door widely to foreign investment. Until it was finally swept aside by a new breed of Quebec nationalists and reformers who gained momentum in the late 1960s, the UN could always reap a rich harvest of votes by championing Quebec provincial rights in opposition to the government in Ottawa.

Economic depressions often spark energetic governmental intervention in the economy, especially in Canada, where the state's role in the economy was always larger than in the U.S. Amid so much anxiety and human misery, a Conservative Party government was elected. The new prime minister was R. B. Bennett, an energetic and competent lawyer from Calgary, but an authoritarian manager, was was elected by promising social welfare and employment for hard-pressed Canadians.

In January 1935, Bennett introduced a far-reaching "New Deal" to Parliament which proposed no less than "modifications of the capitalist system to enable that system more effectively to serve the people." He advocated state-supported farm credit, unemployment insurance, minimum wages and maximum hours of work. Bennett's program stunned many of his fellow Conservatives as his Liberal opponents charged that the measures were unconstitutional on the grounds that they infringed on provincial powers, a charge which the Supreme Court of Canada largely upheld in an important decision a year later. The prime minister had already become so unpopular that he and his party were thrown out of power by a landslide in October 1935; the Liberal Party won a stunning 171 seats to the Tories' 39, with Mackenzie King again assuming the helm.

The discredited Conservative Party, which had had the misfortune of being in power during the depression, was banished to the political wilderness for most of the next half century. Even so, in the long run, the party did not repudiate the strides Bennett took. Today, the Conservative Party in Canada still advocates a wider social welfare net and a more activist government than do most Americans, Democrat, or Republican. Also, the federal government's intervention in the economy continued, despite the 1936 Supreme Court decision.

In 1934, the Bank of Canada was established, and in 1938 it was fully nationalized. In 1935, the government created the Wheat Board, a body which still exists to stabilize prices. The Canadian Radio Broadcasting Commission was created during this time and renamed the Canadian Broadcasting Corporation (CBC) in 1936. The CBC continues to provide and regulate radio and television broadcasting with a heavy Canadian content. Moreover, the Bennett government began the process of establishing a state-controlled air transport system, which in 1937 became the Trans-Canada Air Lines, a nationalized "Crown" corporation and forerunner to Air-Canada. Clearly, the government's hand was in the economy to stay.

WORLD WAR II

Canadian economic life remained wretched throughout the 1930s. However, in 1939 an event came which not only led Canada out of the depression, but ushered in momentous political, diplomatic, and military challenges and changes for the nation: the outbreak of World War II. Canada had pursued a basically isolationist foreign policy during the 1920s and 1930s.

Until 1939, Canada resisted any efforts to involve itself in any collective security arrangement stemming from its membership either in the League of Nations or the British Empire. Further, Canada remained neutral in the Spanish Civil War from 1936–9 although 1,700 Canadians defied the law and formed the Mackenzie-Pap-

Canada

ineau Battalion to fight on the republican government's side; over 400 were killed.

In 2013, Canada's last veteran of that conflict, Jules Paivio, died at age 96. Because Canada had done little to keep up the size and quality of its armed forces prior to 1939 it was unprepared for war.

Unlike in 1914, when Canada become automatically involved in the war on Britain's entry, in September 1939 the government and Parliament deliberated for a week after fighting commenced before declaring war on Britain's side. Also, the King government felt free to negotiate a defense agreement with the U.S. at Ogdensburg in 1940.

In August 1940, Prime Minister King and President Roosevelt agreed to a Permanent Joint Board on Defense, which could design defense arrangements for the North American continent. In 1941 these two leaders penned the Hyde Park Declaration, which provided for the sharing of defense production and for increased trade in defense equipment. These were measures that deepened the meshing of the two countries' economies while serving as a clear indication that Canadian defense was no longer linked exclusively with that of the British Empire.

World War II created a potentially dangerous domestic political situation for Canadians and threatened to open up the terrible wounds of 1914–18. Parliament adopted the declaration of war almost unanimously, but support from French-speaking Canadians stemmed largely from the King government's promise not to draft Canadians into the armed forces for service abroad. Most Canadians understood that their country's contribution was to be mainly economic. Canada was indeed a crucial source of supplies for Britain in the 27 months before the U.S. entered the war. Throughout the war, Canada's eastern ports continued to be important points of origination for convoys that churned back and forth across the submarine-infested Atlantic bringing indispensable supplies to the Allies.

The government assured Canadians that their fighting forces would be composed exclusively of volunteers. The contribution of these soldiers was considerable during the war: almost a million Canadians served admirably in all theaters of operation. Following the disaster on the Belgian beaches at Dunkirk, Canadian soldiers formed the primary armed forces defending Britain, while that island nation caught its breath and reequipped itself for the onslaught which lay ahead. In addition, Canadians bore many casualties in the unsuccessful attempts to defend Hong Kong from the Japanese in December 1941.

On August 19, 1942, 5,000 Canadians led an allied force that included 1,000 British to probe the European coastal defenses at Dieppe. It was long believed that the objective was to demonstrate that a fortified port could be seized from the sea. The attack was a disaster: 907 Canadians were killed and 1,154 were wounded while 1,954 were captured. Later research revealed that the main goal was to provide assistance and cover for a top-secret British Royal Marines commando unit to steal highly valuable intelligence material, including Ultra coding secrets, from the German naval headquarters inside the town. Due to faulty planning and preparation, the raid was an epic failure.

Three months after D-Day 1944, the 2nd Canadian Division liberated Dieppe. Canadian divisions were heavily involved in the invasion of Sicily in 1943 and the subsequent liberation of Italy. An elite integrated Canadian-American commando unit, the First Special Service Force (FSSF), fought at the bloody Anzio beachhead. In addition, Canadian soldiers played an important role at the Normandy beaches in June 1944. Numbering 15,000 they dominated the landing at Juno Beach. One can still visit the fortified beaches in northern France which they were assigned to conquer. One out of ten soldiers who went ashore on June 6 was Canadian, as were 350 of the 4,500 Allied dead, of which 2,500 were American, on D-Day. Canadian troops moved inland quickly and were the only ground unit to attain all of its assigned D-Day objectives.

Another 7,600 Canadians were killed liberating the Netherlands in the closing months of the war, something the Dutch have never forgotten. To this day schoolchildren tend the graves of fallen Canadians. By war's end, 42,000 Canadians had lost their lives.

Another Canadian contribution was its development and administration of the British Commonwealth Air Training Plan which provided airfields and training schools on Canadian soil for more than 131,500 airmen and air mechanics from Britain and the Dominions. Canadian pilots flew in Britain's Royal Air Force and in 41 Canadian squadrons which protected the sea lanes and which joined in the air attack against Germany.

It is scarcely surprising that the massive Canadian participation in the world war would put intense pressure on the government's commitment not to draft soldiers into the armed forces. Conscription for duty inside Canada had already begun in the summer of 1940. However, by April of 1942, the mounting casualties and the lagging of volunteers from Quebec forced the government to hold a controversial plebiscite asking Canadians whether they would free the government of its pledge not to introduce conscription for over-

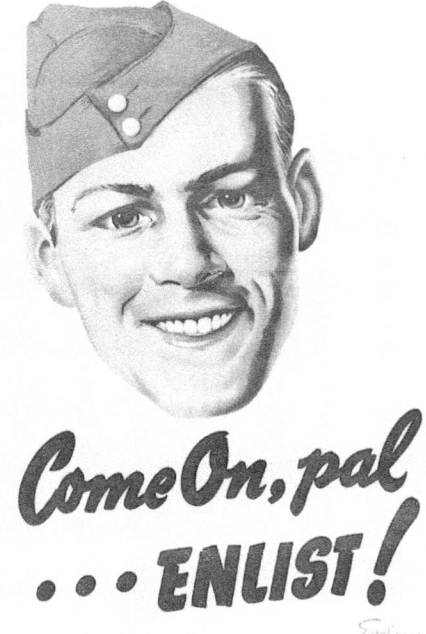

Recruitment poster for World War II
Public Archives Canada/C87427

seas duty. The results of the vote revealed clearly how divided the country was over this historically explosive issue. In English Canada 80% of the voters said "yes," but 72% of *Québécois* said "no."

Even though Germany occupied and controlled France, French-speaking Canadians were inclined to perceive the conflict as a "British war." Two *Québécois* who later become prominent in Canadian politics were among the many French-speaking Canadians who avoided military service. Pierre Elliott Trudeau managed to avoid ever putting on a uniform while René Lévesque served as a public information officer in the American army and wore an American uniform.

Because Prime Minister King unmistakably sensed the danger, he resisted sending conscripts to war zones until November 1944, when he finally ordered 16,000 draftees overseas. Angry riots broke out in Quebec province, and some *Québécois* came close to mutiny in some military bases. Victory in Europe in May 1945 fortunately defused this gathering domestic political storm, and a relieved Canada proceeded to demobilize its draftees as quickly as possible.

In 1997, a panel of 25 scholars of Canadian history evaluated and ranked Canada's 20 prime ministers. They especially valued a leader's coherent vision of the country and well-articulated goals in domestic and foreign policy. In their opinion, William Lyon Mackenzie King was the best. They were impressed by his great political skills, his devotion to unity, his establishment of Canada's international identity, his steps towards establishing the social welfare safety net, and the brilliant way he ran Canada's enormous war effort. On May 8, 2005, the sixtieth anniversary of Victory in Europe (VE) Day, a spectacular new War Museum was opened on LeBreton Flats upriver from Parliament Hill in Ottawa to commemorate the sacrifices of Canadian soldiers.

AFTER 1945

World War II and its aftermath changed the face of Canada and its people. The end of the most destructive war the world has ever known churned up a wave of immigration into Canada, as millions of persons in war-torn Europe sought security and a more promising life in this huge and sparsely populated land. The massive influx helped to more than double the country's population from 11.5 million in 1941 to 25 million in 1985. These modern immigrants tended to settle in cities, joining the masses of native-born Canadians who were leaving the countryside, changing the country almost overnight into one that was, and is, predominantly urbanized. Moreover, because only a third of the newcomers were of British stock, citizens of British heritage no longer constitute a majority of the population, falling to less than 45% in the 1990s.

It is true that the newcomers, who often continued to speak a wide variety of languages in their homes and churches, almost invariably adopted English, not French, as their new language, even if they settled Quebec. This distressed francophones, who already had dramatically lowered their own birth-rate; their percentage among the Canadian population dropped from 31% in 1945 to under 23% today. While these demographic shifts meant that every Canadian had become a member of a minority within Canada, they stimulated an anxiety in francophone Canada that would ultimately find a Quebec nationalist expression.

While the Canadian population underwent significant alteration, four other developments that were set in motion in the 1930s and 1940s were to demand much of the country's attention right into the 1980s. First, the economic depression and the war significantly increased the power of the central government at the expense of the provincial governments. Second, the war demonstrated Canada's almost total independence from the apron strings of the mother country and had made even more glaring the anachronism of having to request a foreign parliament to amend some important parts of its constitution. It seemed to more and more Canadians that a country that still could not amend its own constitution was not yet entirely sovereign.

Third, Canada accumulated far more wealth than it had expended during the war. It had become even more highly industrialized and had emerged from the war as one of the world's major industrial and trading nations. The war had fostered a more intense interrelationship between the economies of Canada and the U.S., and, as had been the case in 1918, had brought another burst of American capital investment across the border. Canadians did absolutely nothing to stem that flow, and in the 1960s they woke up to find that much of their economy and natural resources were in the hands of a single foreign country, its neighbor to the south. Fourth, despite ugly riots that took place in Quebec in the closing months of the war, Canada had emerged from the armed struggle far more unified as a country than it had in 1918.

All four developments sparked further changes in the post-war era. The provinces energetically reasserted themselves and challenged Ottawa's hold on a wide variety of powers from taxing to the pricing of natural resources extracted within their borders. Moreover, the long and bitter disputes over the shape of the new constitution revealed just how muscular the provinces have become. The result of those prolonged disputes was a new constitution, signed into effect in 1982 by the British Queen and the Canadian prime minister, which left Canadians as the undisputed political masters in their own house. The only symbolic link with the mother country that remains is that the British monarch is still formally the Canadian head of state.

Moving on to the next armed conflict, 20,000 Canadians fought with their allies in the Korean War of 1950–53, with 516 of them killed. An additional 7,000 remained as peacekeepers for two years after the armistice. However, the war in Vietnam (1965–1974) forced Canadians to reexamine their relationship with the U.S. Canada's participation in the International Control Commission in Indochina from 1954 until 1973, along with Poland and India, caused some friction when American leaders sometimes thought that the Canadians, who had been appointed with the expectation that they would be biased toward the American view while Poland was selected to provide the opposite bias, did not show enough sympathy toward the U.S. position. There was evidence that these charges were untrue most of the time, but the Vietnam War was indeed a landmark in Canadians' appraisal of America's leadership in the world.

As was true of many of the U.S.' other allies, Canadians were uneasy about American policy in Indochina, even though up to 40,000 Canadians served as volunteers in the American armed forces in Southeast Asia. Canadians were more skeptical of containment of communism based on military force and were more inclined to see the roots of third-world instability in poverty and social problems rather than in Soviet or Chinese meddling.

Prime Minister Lester Pearson spoke for most of his countrymen when he delivered a speech at Temple University, in Philadelphia, in 1965 calling for a bombing halt in North Vietnam. President Lyndon B. Johnson was livid. What angered him was not only that Canada departed from its usual quiet diplomatic style to criticize the U.S. publicly in a time of crisis but also that he did so on American soil. Johnson put it unofficially in his typically crude way: Pearson had "pissed on my rug."

Pearson was the best diplomat Canada ever produced. He played a pivotal role in creating NATO and the United Nations and he was elected president of the UN General Assembly in 1952. For his negotiation skills, he was awarded the Nobel Peace Prize in 1957. More than any other, Pearson popularized the image of Canadians as an understated, compassionate and peacemaking people.

Perhaps Pearson was wrong to deliver such a speech in Philadelphia. Perhaps also Canadians do not fully appreciate the difficulties of America's position as a superpower. Even so, the speech and Canadians' general support of its basic message revealed at least two things: Canadians do view the world somewhat differently than do Americans and no Canadian government could support every American policy, regardless of its nature.

Canada thus experienced a birth or rebirth of two forms of nationalism in Canada: first, because Canadians grew nervous about the extent to which foreigners controlled their economy, the nation developed a sense of economic nationalism that was strongest in English Canada. The economic nationalism visible in Quebec was directed as much against English Canada's penetration of the Quebec economy as against that of the U.S. Second, the dramatic assertion of political and cultural nationalism in Quebec from the 1960s on represented the greatest threat to Canadian unity since confederation in 1867. At times, one could not be sure that Canada as a country would survive into the 21st century.

Indeed, the election of President Donald J. Trump in November 2024, joining Grover Cleveland as only the second president of the United States to serve non-consecutive terms (Messier, 2024), ushered in significant changes in American trade and foreign policy, brining to the fore some of the concerns about Canada's survival. The forty-fifth and now forty-seventh presidents, oldest ever to be elected, Trump

Canada

was buoyed by a victory in which he ran on a campaign in large part relying on a platform calling for an "America First" strategy. Trump's "America First" strategy included, among other items, helping to secure the border by preventing individuals from entering into the United States illegally along with stopping the large flow of fentanyl that is causing the deaths of many Americans and to end existing trade imbalances with other nations. In line with that policy, Trump announced the imposition of 25% tariffs on various imports from Canada, and other nations, in an effort to help revive the economy in the United States. Combined with this economic policy, Trump also made repeated comments about making Canada the 51st state of the United States. The initial 25% tariffs went into effect on March 4, 2025, after Canadian and American officials were unable to reach an agreement to pause or end their being imposed. In response, Canadian Prime Minister Justin Trudeau announced that Canada would impose its own tariffs on goods from the United States. Also in early March, Trump rescinded what he promised would be even larger tariffs on Canadian steel and aluminum after Ontario Premier Doug Ford walked back a planned 25% surcharge on electricity exports to Michigan, Minnesota, and New York. Not surprisingly Trump's actions has caused significant conflict.

On March 23, 2025, after being in office for only nine days, Prime Minister Mark Carney, who to date neither served in public office nor ran a political campaign, called for a snap election on April 28, 2025. Carney explained that he had called an election because with the tariffs and annexation calls, Canada is "facing the most significant crisis of our lifetimes." Tensions thus remain high as this book heads to press as Canadians are responding with am "elbows up" attitude, a phrase coined by all-time hockey Great Gordie Howe who "used his elbows to defend himself when opposing players crowded in" on the ice, meaning that he was willing to use his physical strength as a means of self-defense. It can only be hoped that cooler heads will prevail and a mutually acceptable compromise that is beneficial to both nations can be worked out soon to preserve the long-standing good relations between the governments and people of Canada and the United States.

THE "QUIET REVOLUTION" IN QUEBEC

The "French fact" had, of course, existed in Canadian life for more than two centuries, despite the illusions of many

Rt. Hon. Louis St. Laurent, 1949
Public Archives Canada/C20048

anglophones that the *Québécois* would become absorbed into the Anglo-Saxon mainstream, as had been so many other groups in North America. All too often, *Québécois* were viewed condescendingly "as priest-ridden, traditional-bound, backward, clannish and occasionally sullen or riotous," in the words of sociologist Jane Jacobs.

Francophones resented what they interpreted as an arrogant sense of superiority on the part of anglophones, who indeed did dominate much of Quebec's economy, and, in the opinion of many *Québécois* sought to destroy their culture. In times of crisis, Quebecers repeatedly demonstrated that they could not be expected to react as anglophones thought they should. Quebecers were Canadians, but they were distinct and intended to remain that way. Profound disagreements could always be papered over by compromise. Yet each side often thought that the necessary compromises had been foisted on it by the other, reactions that intensified into festering resentment giving rise to yet other grievances.

Quebecers had always proved to be an extraordinarily resilient people who would never permit their language and culture to die. The French nobleman and politician, Alexis de Tocqueville, had discovered their traditional secret for survival during his trip to North America in 1831–1832, a journey that resulted in a seminal work, *Democracy in America*. The *Québécois*, he noted, "is tenderly attached to the land which saw his birth, to his church tower, and to his family."

Traditionally, Quebecers turned their backs on the cities which threatened their families and society by placing them at the mercy of English employers and customs. For a long time, Quebecers tended to remain in rural areas, where the Catholic Church shielded them from alien influences, provided a firm guiding hand and administered an educational system which shunned commercial and technical subjects, and reinforced traditional values and French language and society.

The Québécois were prodigious procreators, responding to the threats, often described vividly from the pulpit, presented by an almost total absence of immigrants from France, and by a constant emigration to northeastern U.S. of young Quebecers

Flag of the Province of Quebec

Canada

who were unable to find farmland or employment in their own province. Between 1851 and 1931 over 700,000 Quebecers left for the melting pot south of the border. To help stem this tide, the Church sponsored colonization drives to channel Quebecers into the formerly anglophone Ottawa Valley and Eastern Townships or into the Quebec interior around Lac St. Jean and in the Laurentian Mountains. The best defense, though, was the *revanche des berceaux*, "revenge of the cradles." Until the post-1945 era, Quebecers maintained the highest birth-rate in Canada.

Like all Canadians, Quebecers have always been concerned with survival. even so, their worries were a different kind of survival from that of their English-speaking compatriots. For English Canadians, it meant survival of the union against the hostile forces of geography, climate, internal diversity, and the dynamic southern neighbor, with a population ten times the size of Canada's. It meant coping with these challenges and reconciling the diversities in order to preserve the whole. For the *Québécois, la survivance* meant the preservation of their separate *nation*, against domination or, worse, absorption by anglophones in both English Canada and the U.S.

An important motto in Quebec has been *Exister c'est survivre!*: To exist is to survive!." This nation has always been held together by a common memory of Quebecers' past and a separate language and culture. On every Quebec license plate today are the words, *Je me souviens*, "I remember." They are an allusion to a poem with the bitter line, "I remember that I was born under the *fleur-de-lis* and grew up under the [English] rose." They underscore the importance of Quebec's past for the present values and feeling of community. Survival as Quebecers' goal cannot be denied. The question now is how survival can be guaranteed when the traditional supports of religion, rural isolation and educational and economic backwardness have broken down.

Quebec nationalism was clearly visible during the World War II, but it was prevented from boiling over by the timely end of the war, by the election of Maurice Duplessis, who had been returned to the Quebec premiership in 1944, and by the accession of a French Canadian Liberal, Louis St. Laurent, to the prime ministry of Canada when Mackenzie King retired in in 1948. On the death of King's chief lieutenant, Ernest Lapointe, in 1941, he appointed St. Laurent, a successful bilingual lawyer from Quebec City with close connections with the leading Montreal and Toronto businessmen.

As a conservative French Canadian and as King's loyal lieutenant during World

Quebec Premier Jean Lesage, April 1964
Public Archives Canada/PA108147

War II, St. Laurent earn the gratitude of many anglophones and the criticism of ardent Quebec nationalists who accused him of "selling out" to the English. This well-educated, silver-haired statesman became so well liked in English Canada that he was dubbed "Uncle Louis" by the English-language press. St. Laurent quickly came to symbolize Canada's post-war stability and affluence, thereby gaining respect in both anglophone and francophone Canada. Until his retirement in 1957, St. Laurent provided a psychologically important French presence in Ottawa, even though he was a conservative French Canadian, much in the mold of Sir Wilfrid Laurier.

Another French-Canadian conservative, Maurice Duplessis, remained Quebec's premier until his death in 1959 and his Union Nationale ruled uninterruptedly for the next 16 years as well as for one last term from 1966 to 1970. Duplessis and his party resorted to Quebec nationalist rhetoric at every opportunity. In two important cases Duplessis followed his words with concrete steps: he introduced a provincial income tax to make Quebec somewhat less dependent financially on Ottawa. Additionally, he adopted a new Quebec flag that underscores the province's French character: the *fleur-de-lis* which portrays a white cross on a blue field and a white *fleur-de-lis* in each quadrant. This flag still flies over the National Assembly building in Quebec City and is far more visible throughout the province than the Canadian maple leaf flag which was adopted in the 1960s to placate Quebec sensitivities by purging all traces of the British heritage.

Nevertheless, Duplessis was an older, more conservative form of nationalism. By raising the specter of integration with English Canada, he maintained the support of the Catholic Church in the province, which in return retained its hold over the education of the Catholic French majority. By the 1950s many Quebecers were beginning to call on the government to follow the example of other provinces and become more active in the fields of education, health and welfare, and even to wield the state's power in the economic sector in order to loosen anglophones' grip and to stem the inflow of investment capital and companies from English Canada and the U.S.

Before the "conquest" of 1763, the state in New France always intervened heavily in economic affairs. Yet, for the next 200 years energetic state activity had not been a part of the Quebec political tradition. Under British rule, Quebecers were suspicious of the state, even including the province's political system, which had originally been modeled on British governmental practice.

Quebecers considered it to be safer to rely on traditional French-Canadian institutions, especially the Catholic Church, to educate the young and to provide any additional health or welfare assistance that individuals might need. Duplessis respected these traditions as he still clung to the belief that the Quebec nation was and always would remain essentially rural and agrarian.

The Union Nationale merely papered over temporarily the momentous social, economic, and attitudinal changes that were occurring in Quebec. Quebec was already becoming rapidly industrialized and urbanized; by 1945, less than a third of Quebecers lived in rural areas, as opposed to three-quarters in 1900. Also, the bitter Asbestos strike of 1949 revealed how militant some of Quebec's trade unions had become. As René Lévesque, who would later be Quebec's premier, noted, modern *Québécois* had become "city dwellers, wage-earners, tenants. The standards of parish, village, and farm have been splintered." More and more articulate reformers began to criticize the conservative and, they claimed, corrupt Quebec government while calling for fundamental changes in the way the province was ruled. These critics were at first centered at Laval University and the University of Montreal.

Laval was established in 1852 as an outgrowth of the Jesuit seminary of Quebec City, been inspired in part by the desire to have a French-language alternative to McGill, the venerated English-speaking university in Montreal. Later, the University

Canada

of Montreal was created, first as a French-language branch of Laval and then in 1920 as a university with its own charter.

No critic was more prominent than a young, brilliant, and wealthy law professor at the University of Montreal, Pierre Elliott Trudeau. Born into a prominent Montreal family of a Scottish mother, from whom he learned to speak perfect English, and a *Québécois* father, Trudeau was given a first-rate classical education at the Jesuit-operated College Jean de Brebeuf in Montreal.

Trudeau rounded off his education at the University of Montreal Law School, the Sorbonne, the London School of Economics, and Harvard University. Deftly managing to elude the recruiters during World War II, Trudeau instead, spent an enviable youth reading philosophy and traveling both to Europe and to exotic places such as the Holy Land, China, and Tibet, unreachable at the time to young, or any, people without sizable private means. Always eccentric, Trudeau often wore gaudy and intentionally inappropriate clothing and drove his sports car to the site of the 1949 Asbestos strike to show his support for the strikers. Nevertheless, he always had at his disposal one of the most powerful minds ever produced in Canada.

In his many articles in the journal *Cite Libre*, or, "Free City," for which he was the principal contributor and editor, along with Gerard Pelletier, Trudeau used his powerful logic and language to attack his fellow Quebecers' notions of authority. Trudeau called for the use of political power as a positive instrument of the people's will to bring about social and economic progress. Trudeau advocated a kind of social democracy, free from the Church and centered in the city, rather than in the villages and farms. He and increasingly more Quebec intellectuals wanted a modern, forward-looking Quebec, in step with the times, while retaining its French character.

The year 1960 was a watershed in Quebec history. In 1960, the Quebec Liberal party, under the leadership of Jean Lesage, toppled the conservative Union Nationale government and ushered in a wave of reform that unalterably changed the province and the attitudes of its people. So momentous were the changes that everyone began speaking of a *revolution tranquille* or "quiet revolution." This term was first coined by an English Canadian journalist, but was well suited to the character of the people to whom it applied. René Lévesque, one of its most important proponents, explained that the "quiet gives us to understand that Quebec could not change radically. Nonetheless this same old Quebec, where a system of values had broken down, was trying to organize itself to face the modern world."

The change was indeed revolutionary. From the early 1960s on, the most fundamental assumptions and beliefs of Quebecers about politics, religion, economics, and society were being carefully scrutinized and, to a large extent, discarded. Rather than viewing technology, business, industrialization and urbanization as a threat to their unique culture, *Québécois* began to regard them as instruments for elevating and improving their people. Instead of turning to traditional social institutions, such as the Catholic Church, to protect them from the modern world, they became more secular in their outlook and began to take a more positive view of the state as a tool to help Quebec develop itself to catch up with the rest of Canada.

During the "quiet revolution," Quebecers drew a much sharper boundary around their conception of the Quebec "nation" to fit the geographical boundaries of the province. Although they were to remain sensitive to the treatment of francophones in other parts of Canada, Quebecers no longer felt a national link with them; the term "French Canadian" fell into disfavor in Quebec. Most importantly, *Québécois* gained the self-confidence that they could change things if they really wanted to do so, acquiring a mood of optimism that they could be progressive and modern, while still being completely French in outlook, institutions, and language.

At first, anglophones greeted these developments as signs that Quebecers were finally developing a pragmatic Anglo-Saxon outlook which would help bring about a greater unity of Canada's two founding peoples. It was not long, though, until the opposite became obvious. Rather than becoming more attached to Canada, Quebecers were becoming more attached to Quebec. The Quebecers developed the courage, not only fundamentally to challenge Canadian federalism, but perhaps even to question the very existence of Canada as a unified country.

The Liberal Lesage government was determined that Quebec would make more of its own decisions, meaning that the provincial government would have to wield many of the powers which had long been exercised by the federal government in Ottawa. This was a direct challenge to the prevailing distribution of powers between Ottawa and the provinces. It was a matter that no government in the country's capital could ignore because it went to the core of the Canadian political system.

In coming years Ottawa made some important concessions. It agreed to give Quebec, without strings or conditions, funds which the federal government would have used to administer and finance a program in the province. The province could then design and execute the policy in its own way. An example of this so-called "opting-out" possibility was the hard-fought Quebec Pension Plan, which protects Quebecers, while other Canadians are covered by the Canada Pension Plan. By aggressively seeking out political terrain into which exclusive Quebec governmental authority could be extended, the province's political leaders were able to take advantage of numerous such "opting out" opportunities in a variety of areas, including health, education and welfare. By doing this, Quebec secured for itself a *de facto* special status within the Canadian federation.

The Lesage government, which was re-elected in 1962 under the slogan *Maitres chez nous*, "masters in our own house," was able to act decisively in the field of education, which has always been a provincial prerogative. Although it was often a controversial matter, Quebec schools had always been in the hands of the Catholic Church which was regarded as the chief protector of Quebec's values and culture. One of the most dramatic changes during the Quiet Revolution, though, was the weakening of religious sentiments that occurred almost overnight. Quebec author Roch Carrier, who was living in France at the onset of the Quiet Revolution, recalled that what surprised him most when he returned to Quebec in the early 1960s was that so few people seemed to go to church.

Two decades later, during a visit to the province, Saint Pope John Paul II went so far as to call Quebec a "dechristianized society." Polls in 1994 revealed that only 19% of *Québécois* attend religious services at least "once a week or so," the second lowest percentage among Canadian provinces; only 56% said that maintaining Christian values "is very important to me," the lowest percentage in Canada outside British Columbia. It had become secularized, and this fact was bound to affect the schools and almost everything else in Quebec society.

Many changes were introduced in rapid order, perhaps the most important of which was the creation in 1964 of a provincial Ministry of Education and a non-denominational Advisory Committee to replace the separate Catholic and Protestant Committees. The practice of appointing only Catholic clergymen as rectors of Laval and the University of Montreal was eliminated, as both universities completely severed their ties with the Catholic Church.

In 1968, a new University of Quebec, with branches all over the province, was founded with no ties to the Church. Tuition-free state high schools were created to compete with Catholic-operated schools and to break the Church's stran-

Canada

France's President de Gaulle: "Vive le Québec libre!"
Public Archives Canada/C6013

glehold on university admissions. This deemphasis on religion and secularization of the province's schools occurred at all levels of the school system and dramatically affected the preparation and the attitudes of the students who emerged from Quebec schools to become a part in the modernized Quebec society. In 1997, the Quebec National Assembly voted to replace the denominational school boards with French and English ones.

This secularized school system produced a new kind of graduate: one with less knowledge of philosophy, French poets and Catholic scholasticism, but with more technical and business training. This system produced a much larger middle class, with the kinds of technical skills that would enable young *Québécois* to operate in the province's business elite and to enter the civil service. Because a large portion of these graduates was unable to find jobs in the private economy, they became employees of the state, either as teachers, civil servants, or managers in newly nationalized corporations.

During the Quiet Revolution, the public sector swelled, as the Quebec state took on more and more responsibilities. This "state middle class," as it was often called, became the motor and backbone for the continuing Quiet Revolution and, as we shall see, for that separatist party which gained power in 1976: The *Parti Québécois* or Quebec Party (PQ).

The activism of the Quebec state was apparent in the province's economy. The basic rationale was that if Quebecers were to be "masters in their own house," they would have to have more influence within the economy, which was largely controlled by anglophone Canadians and Americans.

The Lesage government tackled this objective head-on by creating and expanding state economic enterprises. The most successful of these, Hydro-Quebec, created in 1962, was the project of one of Lesage's cabinet ministers, René Lévesque. This new state-owned enterprise integrated Quebec's many hydro-electric facilities and became the province's largest employer. Its cheap electricity became essential for the industrial rebirth and revival of business confidence in Quebec during the late 1980s and 1990s.

More important for Quebec nationalists was the fact that the working language within Hydro-Quebec was made exclusively French because this insured that the management of the enterprise would be solely in the hands of francophones. In order to demonstrate further that successful economic undertakings need not be directed by anglophones, French was made the exclusive working language of the Manicougan Dam construction, the largest such structure in the world, even though the capital for this mega-project had to be raised in the U.S. French was also the working language of the later massive hydro-electric project at James Bay in the 1970s. Even though francophone ownership of and management positions within the economy grew by leaps and bounds in the 1960s and 1970s, the goal of wresting control over the province's economy from anglophone hands never succeeded.

In 1966, the *Union Nationale* defeated the Liberal Lesage government and experienced its last chance to hold the reins of Quebec provincial power before disappearing from the political scene. The event most remembered during this four-year period was the Montreal Expo-

sition in 1967. The federal government in Ottawa gave full support for this world fair, which commemorated the centennial of the founding of the Canadian confederation in 1867. This massive event was to underscore the success in creating a unified Canada. But the aftermath of this Expo would reveal and widen the rifts existing in the confederation.

The Expo 67, arguably the most successful of all world fairs, was a source of great pride for Quebecers, one-third of whom live in Montreal. Expo displayed to the world that the Quebecers could successfully manage a large, glittering project the people of many nations could enjoy. The fair attracted the world's attention to the accomplishments and the aspirations of a province that had changed so much in less than a decade while also alerting it to the festering wound right in the heart of Canada.

The unpredictable French president, Charles de Gaulle, traveled to Montreal to visit the Expo in July of 1967. There were signs of trouble when his cruiser, the *Colbert*, picked him up on the French island of Saint Pierre and sailed up the St Laurence, dispensing with the customary naval courtesy of flying the Canadian flag. de Gaulle's enthusiasm was whetted during his 10-hour motor trip to Montreal through 22 communities along the St. Lawrence River. He noted: "I have encountered an atmosphere the same as at the Liberation" (of France in 1944-5). Prime Minister Lester Pearson commented: "Canadians do not need to be liberated." The irony was that during World War II, anglophone Canadians were much more sympathetic to de Gaulle's Free French mission than were francophone Canadians, many of whom were staunch supporters of Marshall Pétain.

The French president went to Montreal intending to make trouble. de Gaulle told his son-in-law before leaving for Quebec, "I will hit hard. Hell will happen, but it has to be done." Further, he told his aide that his visit "will make waves" and that he would "make history." de Gaulle was right as he gave an unforgettable speech from the balcony of Montreal's City Hall in which he repeated the separatist slogan: *Vive le Québec libre*, "Long live free Quebec." This utterance unleashed chants among the thousands of Quebecers who heard it: *Québec libre! Oui, Oui, Oui! De Gaulle l'a dit! Oui, oui!* Or "A free Quebec! Yes, yes, yes! De Gaulle said it! Yes, yes!" The Canadian government immediately and indignantly announced that such support for the separatists on the part of a foreign chief of state was "unacceptable." The proud Frenchman left the country within hours.

Some of de Gaulle cabinet thought he went too far. Foreign Minister Couve de

Canada

Murville called his speech "bloody stupid." Yet, de Gaulle showed no remorse. In a November 1967 press conference, de Gaulle hailed Quebec as a "sovereign state, master of its national independence." A decade later, René Lévesque admitted, "we owe him enormous recognition for having made us known throughout the world with this fortunate blunder." Yet, Lévesque and other cooler heads were aware that such pronouncements could propel irresponsible forces that become difficult to control and that thereby endanger, rather than facilitate, the achievement of important goals.

It is important to note that it was not until two decades later, in 1987, that a French president again visited Canada. This time the tone of the visit was very different. President François Mitterrand made a point of arriving in Ottawa, not Quebec, and his toast to his Canadian hosts was: *Vive le Canada! Vive la France!*

The political developments and the violence that were taking place in Quebec toughened the will of the political leaders in Ottawa and Quebec to seek solutions that went to the very roots of the problem. The Liberal government in Ottawa intensified its efforts to so change Canada that francophones could not help but recognize Canada as a congenial home for all of them.

Pierre Elliott Trudeau is often incorrectly credited with having ushered in the kinds of changes in Canada that ultimately undercut the separatist movement in Quebec. He was later to lend his prestige and intellect to bridging the huge gulf that had developed between Quebec and the rest of Canada. Even so, Trudeau had not yet joined the Liberal Party in 1963 when the new Liberal government of Lester Pearson appointed a Royal Commission on Bilingualism and Biculturalism to find and document the causes of the crisis and to propose ways of dealing with the serious frictions that existed between "the two founding races."

The Commission's first report in 1965 left no doubt that francophones were severely limited in their efforts to advance economically and to preserve their language and culture. The report documented the fact that these two aspirations were linked. The conclusion was that "Canada, without being fully conscious of the fact, is passing through the greatest crisis of its history." Many of the subsequent reforms were based on this groundbreaking report. Affectionately called "Mike," Pearson also played the leading role in introducing universal medicare, the Canada–U.S. Auto Pact, and the Canada Pension Plan. In 1965, he also ordered the new Canadian maple leaf flag to be run up parliament's Peace Tower. By getting rid of the remnants of the British flag on Canada's colors, Pearson eliminated another potential irritant in Quebec's adjustment to Canada.

Pearson found an undeniably competent and effective lieutenant and ultimate successor in Trudeau, who joined the Liberal Party in 1965 and was elected to the House of Commons in the same year. Trudeau wanted to demonstrate that the aspirations of francophone Canada could be furthered in Ottawa as well as in Quebec City. He feared that the kind of Quebec nationalism that was emerging would not only destroy Canada but would drive Quebec into isolation. Trudeau believed that only a tolerant federalism could remedy the situation.

In 1966, Trudeau was appointed as Justice Minister, lending his support to enlarging what was called "cooperative federalism." This meant in practice that all ten provinces would be granted their full powers under the BNA and that Ottawa would return to the provinces all the powers that it had assumed during the 1950s. "Cooperative federalism" also led to periodic meetings and consultations between the governments in Ottawa and the ten provincial capitals, so that provincial concerns could be aired and influence on federal policy strengthened. These meetings are still a part of routine Canadian political practice.

The Liberal Party government decided that it would be appropriate to remove a symbol from the country's flag which many francophones found to be insulting: the Union Jack, a reminder of Canada's imperial heritage. The debate over the design of the new flag was bitter and protracted. One proposal, to combine the Union Jack and the *fleur-de-lis*, was

Trudeau and Lévesque

rejected. Finally, the present flag, with a single red maple leaf on a white field, was adopted.

Perhaps the most important measure the Liberal government took to quell the fears of francophones was to create a bilingual Canada, in which francophones would feel equal and at home everywhere. In 1969 the Official Languages Act made Canada officially a bilingual country. The brunt of this new law was felt most immediately in the federal civil service, where more and more jobs were reserved for bilingual Canadians. In coming years this law had a greater and greater impact on many dimensions of Canadian life. The move to transform Canada into a bilingual country was not greeted positively in all quarters of Canadian society. Many anglophones, particularly in the West, found it to be an unnecessary and unjustified imposition while many Quebecers viewed it as not going far enough in protecting French language rights.

War Measures Act: soldiers at the Palais de Justice (police headquarters), Quebec
Public Archives Canada/PA129838

Canada

Lighting the flame at the Summer Olympic Games, Montreal, July 1976
Public Archives Canada/PA115800

The policies which the Liberal governments of Lester Pearson and Pierre Elliott Trudeau introduced were in the long run were important for the salvation of Canada as a unified country. However, in the 1960s and 1970s they were unable to satisfy the ardor of Quebec nationalism. No Canadian needed a reminder in the 1970s that the country faced dangers which threatened to rip it asunder. It was clear that if a peaceful solution could not be found, then Canada could be buffeted by something rather rare in the Canadian experience: violence.

In the early 1960s, a rough separatist group emerged, the *Rassemblement pour l'Independence Nationale,* led by the young socialist firebrand Pierre Bourgault. A few bombing incidents occurred in Montreal in February 1963, and in October 1964 a visit by the British Queen to Quebec City to commemorate the 1864 Confederation Conference ignited frightening riots.

The stakes were raised considerably in the summer and fall of 1970 when an extremist separatist organization, the *Front de Liberation du Québec,* the Front for the Liberation of Quebec, or FLQ perpetrated a series of violent deeds, beginning with bombings and robberies, culminating in the twin kidnapping of Richard Cross, senior British trade commissioner in Montreal, and Pierre Laporte, Quebec's minister of labor and immigration. Because flurry of police and political activity could not defuse the crisis, Premier Bourassa requested Ottawa to send in the army. In a now famous television confrontation on the steps of Parliament on October 13, Trudeau scornfully noted, "bleeding hearts just don't like to see people with guns and helmets. Go on and bleed. It is more important to keep law and order." When queried about how far he would go to maintain order, he snapped "just watch me!"

On October 16, Canadians held their breath as Prime Minister Trudeau proclaimed the War Measures Act and outlawed the FLQ and any organization promoting the use of force. Extremists wasted no time in responding to Ottawa's sternness; the next day they murdered Pierre Laporte and left his bloodied body in the trunk of an abandoned car.

Political assassinations are rare in Canadian history; only two have occurred since 1867. When they do occur though, the federal government acts with an energy and determination to which Americans are unaccustomed. For instance, when the political leader, D'Arcy McGee, was assassinated on the steps of his Ottawa boardinghouse in 1868, the government suspended Habeas Corpus, arrested 70 suspects and held them for four months without charging them or permitting them to speak to lawyers.

A century later, Trudeau had the full support of his countrymen to respond to the Laporte murder by whatever means, signaling that he was willing to take full advantage of that support. After a wave of searches and arrests, Cross was located alive and he was freed in return for allowing his kidnapers to fly off to Cuba. This frightening crisis reminded Canadians that they were not free of the scourge of violence that was afflicting other democratic countries at the time. Still, it demonstrated the willingness of Canadian governments to act with great energy and determination against overt threats to undermine the constitutional order in Canada. Between 1963 and 1970, the FLQ ignited over 200 bombs in Montreal, killing at least five and wounding dozens. Terrorism never entrenched itself in the Quebec separatist movement.

From 1970 to 1976, Quebec was again governed by the *Liberal Party* under the leadership of Robert Bourassa. Bourassa and his Liberal government sought to maintain many of the gains that transpired since the Quiet Revolution, but they were leery of the central assumption of the revolution that a continuing expansion of the government's powers and activities was necessary or good for Quebec. The Liberals were concerned that excessive confrontations with anglophones who were well-entrenched in the province's economy would damage the investment climate in the province and thereby hurt Quebecers more than help.

Bourassa was not convinced that much good could flow from Quebec's separation from Canada. Consequently, he by and large supported Canada's federal system. Under his administration there were no major transfers of powers or resources from the federal capital to Quebec City. Critics contended that Bourassa had not pressed Quebec's demands energetically enough.

The Bourassa government did become the first in Quebec to pass comprehensive legislation dealing with the status of French in Quebec. His government did not believe that the federal Official Languages Act of 1969 was strong enough to shore up the French language in Quebec and to satisfy nationalist sentiments. Bill 22 declared that French alone is the province's "official language."

Bill 22 bitterly angered Quebec's anglophones, some of whom went so far as to accuse the government of using "Nazi-like tactics" and committing "cultural genocide." Still, by the standards of language legislation that was to come later, Bill 22 was mild. For instance, it did not require that English-language schools in the province be restricted exclusively to children whose mother tongue was English. Because the majority of immigrant children continued to go to English-language schools, many francophones viewed the bill as a farce that would not really change their status within Quebec.

On the occasion of the second gala event in Montreal within a single decade, the 1976 Olympic Games, the world again had the opportunity to witness the political and economic turmoil in a province so deeply in process of change. The opening of the games was preceded by bitter labor strikes and protests which had strong Quebec nationalist overtones. Many labor union leaders and members had clearly become militant and nationalist. All was not in order in *la belle province*, and in 1976 important challenges to Canadian unity were again on the horizon.

Both Ottawa and Quebec City had sought in different ways to satisfy francophone desires. The result is a tug-of-war that will dominate Canadian politics for

Canada

the rest of the century. Many *Québécois* remained frustrated and political forces were emerging within Quebec that steered toward independence. In the 1960s, a heterogeneous coalition of Quebecers who wanted to push the Quiet Revolution further sought a fairer relationship between Quebec and the rest of Canada or who wanted a totally separate Quebec took shape. This diversity was never easy to manage, but for at least two decades it was held together by the only Quebecer who possessed the necessary charisma, political skill and patience to be its leader: René Lévesque.

The son of a French-speaking country lawyer in New Carlisle, a predominantly English-speaking town of about a thousand inhabitants surrounded by the French-speaking world of Quebec's Gaspé Peninsula, Lévesque grew up bilingually. Therefore, as an adult who could speak perfect English, he personally suffered neither discrimination for being a francophone nor the trauma of having to learn English as a foreign language. Nevertheless, he remembers the taunts exchanged by bands of French and English Canadians: "They used to call us 'pea-soupers'; we called them 'crawfish'."

Lévesque's Quebec nationalism flowered early; while a student in the Jesuit-run Garnier College prep school, he wrote in one of his papers: "Never forget that you are French Canadians, that your own people have been stagnating for generations, and that if they, the people, *your* people do not act, they are lost!" In the early 1940s he abandoned his law studies, or, as he remembers it, "they began to abandon me." Because it was wartime, Lévesque was under the threat of being drafted into the Canadian army. His attitude about this prospect was vintage *Québécois:* "Though I was willing to go overseas, I was not willing to go in the uniform of His Majesty. I therefore went to New York in 1943 and managed to join an information office, and then to be appointed war correspondent in the American Seventh Army. I went to war on a purely intuitive impulse."

Lévesque sailed from Halifax to London early in 1944 on a ship that was not a part of a convoy, a voyage understandably resulting in ten days of "acute anxiety, especially during the night," as he recalls. At the age of 21, Lévesque edited and announced messages to occupied France.

In February 1945, Lévesque was attached to the Sixth Army and moved with this unit and the First French Army eastward through France to the Rhineland, Bavaria and Austria. Lévesque was present at the battle of Nuremberg and was among the first to discover the horrors of Dachau concentration camp a few miles outside of Munich and to speak with the liberated French leaders, including Edouard Daladier, Leon Jouraux, Paul Reynaud, and General Weygand, whom the Germans had imprisoned in comfortable confinement in a castle. Lévesque saw Mussolini's mutilated body and he was one of the few journalists to hear Hermann Goering a few minutes after his surrender.

After the war, Lévesque became a political journalist, a job that took him across Canada and the U.S., to Korea and back to Europe. In the mid-1950s, he switched from radio journalism to become one of Canada's first TV journalists. Lévesque's half-hour Sunday evening program, *Point de Mire*, "Focal Point," first aired in October 1957 and made him a celebrity as it focused on international issues. Because most Quebecers at that time had little schooling and exposure outside of French Canada, this became their window to the world. Moreover, because Radio-Canada, the Quebec equivalent to the Canadian Broadcasting Corporation, had a TV monopoly in Quebec at that time, he became extremely popular with his ratings sometimes reaching 100%. The show made Lévesque's diminutive figure, his gravelly voice, and his well-informed opinions familiar to millions of Canadians.

Lévesque's program consisted of a study of one event or one problem occupying a central point in the news. This focus enabled him to make the transition from international problems, which had occupied him for more than a decade, to domestic politics. The federal government's rough handling of a 68-day strike at Radio Canada greatly angered Lévesque. "I was scared, even traumatized by that experience, so that sooner or later I felt I would have to enter politics."

In politics, Lévesque served in the Liberal Party cabinet of Jean Lesage for six years as the minister of natural resources and came to incorporate the aspirations of the Quiet Revolution. However, he gradually grew impatient with the Liberal provincial government, which, he believed, did not press vigorously enough for an independent Quebec. Lévesque was unable to persuade the Liberals to adopt a manifesto he had published calling for sovereignty for Quebec within a common market association with Canada. Therefore, Lévesque and a group of moderate, but disgruntled, Liberals left their party in 1967 and formed the *Mouvement Souverainete-Association*, the Movement for Sovereignty-Association or MSA. A year later, the *MSA* merged with other smaller separatist parties, the right-wing *Ralliement national* or National Rally (RN) and the somewhat demagogic, "grass roots" *Rassemblement pour l'independence nationale* or Rally for National Independence (RIN) to form the *Parti Québécois (PQ)*. Because the precise objectives of these three parties were never the same, the internal strains would always plague the larger group, weakening and fragmenting it in the 1980s.

The *PQ* became a basket for a diverse collection of Quebecers who wanted to see the Quiet Revolution carried on with greater energy even though they disagreed on how radical the political and economic changes should be and who wished to see some kind of sovereign Quebec even though they could not agree about just how sovereign. Only René Lévesque could hold such a movement together.

Lévesque was a cautious leader who insisted that the party be democratic and respectable. His notion of sovereignty-association was a compromise around which party members could unify. Although Lévesque was always careful not

Young Quebecers with the provincial flag

Canada

to define this notion too concretely, he said that "we do not want to end, but rather to radically transform, our union with the rest of Canada, so that, in the future, our relations will be based on full and complete equality." Quebec was only a "half-fledged state" in conflict with the rest of Canada; "in order to end once and for all the struggle of wills, the costly dividing up of energies and resources, the system must be replaced."

The finished product Lévesque envisaged was not a francophone nation that would completely turn its back on Canada. For him, sovereignty-association "means a sovereign State of Quebec which will accept, or rather offer in advance, new links of interdependence with Canada, but links which will this time be negotiated between equal peoples, as a function of their geographic and other unquestionable common interest." Thus, although the "obsolete constitutional links" would have to be cut, there would still be links of free trade, free travel without passports between Quebec and Canada, a common currency, a joint administration of the St. Lawrence Seaway and a military alliance with Canada, the U.S., and NATO.

Although Quebecers were not unified insofar as their precise expectations for a new relationship with Canada were concerned, many of them were drawn to the PQ, which appealed to all the diverse values which francophones in Quebec considered important. The reward was 30% of the popular vote in 1973 and a stunning electoral victory for the PQ in the Quebec provincial elections in November 1976. Lévesque's party won only 41% of the vote in Quebec, and as a government without a majority of the inhabitants behind it, he had to move cautiously. However, Lévesque had won an absolute majority of francophones' votes, winning in every region in Quebec except in the anglophone-dominated West Montreal. He drew votes from all classes of *Québécois*, but his showing was particularly strong among the young and the professional and semi-professional middle class, especially teachers.

With the support of a majority of francophones, Lévesque perceived that he had a mandate for change. However, the terms for that mandate were not clear. The PQ voters who wanted sovereignty did not agreement on exactly what form it should take. Many Quebecers voted for the PQ because they wanted "clean government" after Bourassa's administration was tainted by scandals. Their vote was by no means an endorsement of Quebec sovereignty. What most PQ voters did agree on, though, was that the protections for the French language should be even tighter than those provided in Bill 22.

The late Hon. René Lévesque

The result was Bill 101, which required that all public signs, including road signs, and every form of commercial advertising be exclusively in French. Thus, Eaton's and Ogilvy's department stores were compelled to remove the apostrophe from their name. In contrast, McDonald's survived in Quebec with its apostrophe. Yet, a greasy spoon diner in Montreal, "Irv's Light Lunch," had to be renamed "Chez Irv."

Quebec's language officials ruled in 2000 that companies with English-language registered trademark names cannot be forced to use French versions in Quebec. The officials argued that international law protects the use of such names. This did not help Quebec-born race driver Jacques Villeneuve who was reported to the language police in 2001 for naming his new Montreal restaurant "Newtown," the English translation of his last name and his nickname in racing circles. Villeneuve responded to those who complained: "You have to look further than the tip of your nose. It's a big world!"

Another change was that access to English-language schools was restricted to children with at least one parent who was educated in English in Quebec. That meant that not only immigrant children, but the offspring of anglophones from other Canadian provinces were required to attend French-language schools. Thanks to a decision by the Supreme Court of Canada, the last provision was softened to permit children with a parent who was educated in English anywhere in Canada to attend English-language schools.

By 2007, 80% of immigrant children learned in French and more than half of those whose mother tongue was neither French nor English could converse in both languages. However, in 2000 a Superior Court in Quebec upheld legislation forbidding francophone children from attending English schools. The judge ruled that Quebec has a responsibility to protect French. The Supreme Court of Canada by a vote of 7–0 reached the same outcome in 2005.

Bill 101 went beyond Bill 22 by requiring that French alone be used for provincial legislation, public administration, the judicial system, most public institutions. It originally required that laws and tribunals would be in French only, but that was later struck down. Ultimately, Bill 101 would have to be used as the working language in all businesses within the province. Employers were obligated to write all communications to their employees in French and they could not dismiss or demote employees simply because they spoke no English.

A watch-dog *Office de la langue française*, the Office of the French Language, was set up to settle disputes arising from this law. It could be anticipated that this office would be overly vigilant in protecting the French language. Perhaps the most widely publicized and most regrettable instance of overreaction was the 1983 case of an elderly patient in Montreal's St. Mary's hospital. Officials in this Office determined that a patient was denied her "right to die in French." The investigator maintained that the patient's nurses spoke little or no French in the intensive care ward during 34% of the time she was dying. The official waived off the hospital's objections that services were always available in French, arguing that humane and legal treatment required that all contact and every sound uttered within hearing distance of a francophone patient had to be in French.

Bill 101 understandably antagonized many anglophones in Quebec. The Lévesque government dismissed the demand of anglophones that the language rights of the minority be respected; the government correctly pointed out that the language rights of the French minority in other provinces had never been effectively guaranteed. The law created new opportunities for francophones and forced the anglophone minority, not the francophone majority, to pay the economic price for unilinguallism.

The *PQ* made little headway in bringing more of Quebec's economy under state domination and in wresting control from anglophones in the rest of Canada or the U.S. Some members of Lévesque's party were demanding that the government break the anglophone capitalists' hold over the province's economy, no matter what the costs. Yet, Lévesque believed that the economic recession that led to growing unemployment in the 1970s

Canada

made any such moves risky. Instead, he focused in the late 1970s on finding the right moment to fulfill a promise he and his party had made during the 1976 election campaign: to conduct a referendum in order to establish Quebec as a sovereign state. This finally happened in May 1980.

Remembering that the bloodiest war in American history was fought from 1861 to 1865 in order to deny states the right to secede from the Union, an American is likely to be amazed by the fact that a Canadian government would permit the citizens of a province to hold a vote over whether they wished to destroy the country's unity. It is true that the prime minister made a veiled threat that he would resort to force if Quebec tried anything "illegal," but he never clarified what action might be illegal.

During the entire campaign, Lévesque and his party stressed the peaceful and democratic nature of their cause. He had amply demonstrated in the past that he wanted nothing to do with firebrands willing to depart from democratic terrain. In any case, the entire campaign proceeded without violence, and there is absolutely no evidence that any kind of fear of civil war influenced the outcome of the vote. This forbearance and absence of violence indicated how different the political temperaments of Canadians and Americans are.

Lévesque had always been aware of how sensitive the question of Quebec independence had always been. He knew well that while many *Québécois* were dissatisfied with the federal structure as it existed, they were not in favor of complete independence. Lévesque therefore was ambivalent and hesitating as he preferred to proceed toward his goal in stages which he termed *étapisme*, thereby reaping scorn from the separatists who wanted immediate and decisive action.

The wording of the referendum revealed Lévesque's sensitivity for a wavering francophone attitude about independence: "The Government of Quebec has made public its proposal to negotiate a new agreement with the rest of Canada, based on the equality of nations; this agreement would enable Quebec to acquire the exclusive powers to make its laws, levy its taxes and establish relations abroad—in other words, sovereignty—and at the same time, to maintain with Canada an economic association including a common currency; no change in political status resulting from these negotiations will be affected without approval from the people through another referendum; on these terms, do you give the Government of Quebec the mandate to negotiate the proposed agreement between Quebec and Canada?"

Clearly, the premier feared a "once and for all" vote to secede and merely asked for the right to talk to Ottawa about a new kind of arrangement. By watering down the gravity of the choice, Lévesque hoped to gather in as large a flock of *Québécois* as possible.

The Trudeau government in Ottawa campaigned enthusiastically against the question, and it no doubt influenced the vote. For one thing, it was difficult for the *PQ* to argue persuasively that Quebecers were an exploited and degraded race within the Canadian federation when the government in Ottawa was led by a prime minister, Trudeau, a finance minister, Marc Lalonde, and a justice minister, Jean Chrétien, all of whom were Quebecers. Also, the long-standing differences in income and opportunity that existed between anglophones and francophones in Quebec had largely disappeared.

As debate continued, the government of Canada and of all other provinces announced they would not negotiate any form of sovereignty-association with Quebec, including an economic common market. Finally, the Trudeau government promised that a *non* vote would result in the BNA's being replaced by a new constitution which could be amended at home and which would bring about a kind of "renewed federalism" which would be satisfactory to all of Canada's ten provinces.

The results of the vote stunned the *PQ*: 59.5% of Quebecers voted against Lévesque's proposal. As anticipated, an overwhelming majority of Quebec's anglophone population voted against the proposition. However, his followers were shocked that a narrow majority of 52% of francophone *Québécois* also voted against the proposition. Quebecers under the age of 40 voted overwhelmingly for the proposition, but their votes could not salvage the battered dreams of Quebec separatism. In provincial parliamentary elections on April 13, 1981, less than a year later, 49% of Quebecers voted for the PQ, giving the party a majority of 80 of 122 seats in the Quebec National Assembly. Nevertheless, the road to a separate, sovereign Quebec had become hopelessly blocked. The 1980 referendum brought a palpable change in Quebecers' political attitudes toward the *PQ* and separatism.

By the end of 1984, it was clear to Lévesque that separatism had reached a dead end and that it would be disastrous for the *PQ* to make this issue the centerpiece of the next provincial election. Already, polls were indicating that only a fifth to a third of Quebecers would vote for the *PQ*. Since 1981, the *PQ* has suffered a distressing loss of members, down to 113,000 from an all-time high in 1982 of 300,000. Without the belief in Quebec sovereignty, which had united the party's faithful in the past, the PQ had increasingly become a loose coalition of social democrats and conservatives who had little in common.

A deep economic recession in 1982–3, which drove unemployment figures upwards to 15%, prompted a series of severe government austerity measures to roll back the salaries of provincial civil servants and halted labor negotiations in the public sector. These measures, to which Lévesque saw no alternative, eroded the *PQ's* image as a social democratic movement and alienated Quebec's public sector employees, labor union members and young people, who had been among the PQ's staunchest supporters. Also, a series of embarrassing scandals in the highest leadership levels of the PQ rocked the party's image as a party of honesty and clean government; these included the conviction of one leader on charges of sexually molesting young girls and of another for shoplifting in a Montreal department store.

Paradoxically, a major reason why separatism had ebbed temporarily as a mainstream political force was that the nationalist thrust had accomplished so much in the preceding quarter of a century. These successes convinced many Quebecers that they could advance their social and cultural causes within the Canadian Confederation. Because of the Official Languages Act of 1969, the use of French has been expanded throughout Canada, and the number of bilingual Canadians has greatly increased.

Québécois also made gigantic strides that were obvious to almost everyone. In the 1960s only 4% of *Québécois* went to universities, compared with 20% in the 1980s. One in six of these students studies business or economics now, as compared with one in ten in the rest of Canada. Francophones have become more comfortable in the boardrooms of Quebec's businesses. In the 1960s they owned only 20% of the province's economy; by the 1980s that figure had doubled to 40%.

The government in Ottawa did, in fact, produce a new constitution for Canada after tireless discussions with provincial governments. The 1982 constitution spells out provincial rights more accurately than did the BNA, and it contains a bill of rights that can be invoked by those who perceive language discrimination anywhere in Canada.

Feeling that he had been out-maneuvered in the negotiations leading up to the new constitution, Lévesque refused to sign the new document. Instead, he indicated in 1984 that he would not require as a condition for his signature a Quebec veto over future amendments. His willingness to cooperate with Ottawa on this

Canada

Former Prime Minister Chrétien meeting with provincial premiers

Photo: J.M. Carisse

important issue was not only due to the fact that the air had gone out of the separatist balloon. Lévesque was then dealing with a prime minister in Ottawa, Brian Mulroney, a Quebecer himself, and whom Lévesque found much more con genial and sympathetic than Trudeau.

Bill 101 made French the sole official language and greatly expanded its use in all sectors of Quebec society, despite the judicial restrictions that have been placed on it. The bill prompted scores of anglophone firms, such as the Sun Life Assurance Company's huge corporate headquarters, and thousands of English-speaking citizens to leave the province, reducing the percentage of Quebecers who listed English as their mother tongue from 14.7 in 1971 to 12.7 in 1981. In fact, a University of Montreal demographer, Jacques Henripin, even predicted that if anglophones continued to leave the province at the rate that they did during the 1970s, the English community would disappear within 50 years. This result is unlikely.

Just as Quebec City, which was once 40% English, is now almost wholly French, so Quebec province has become more French and will probably continue to do so. The problem remains in Montreal, though, where the percentage of French-speaking residents declined from 64% in 1951 to 60% in 1992. This is partly because 90% of all immigrants in Quebec settle there, and two-thirds of them do not speak French. The anglophone exodus opened new economic opportunities for francophones. Francophone businesses supplied 61.6% of the jobs in 1987, compared with 54.8% in 1978. Many formerly anglophone neighborhoods opened to francophones, a fact which helps break down the "Two Solitudes" which had long characterized these groups' lack of contact with each other.

Quebecers seemed to be tired of language battles but have unmistakably heard the message that Quebec is a French-speaking province, at least on the surface. Yet, numerous appeals to the Supreme Courts of Quebec and Canada progressively weakened the application of Act 101. At the end of 1986, the Quebec Court of Appeal declared that those parts of Act 101 mandating French-only signs violated Quebecer's rights to freedom of expression and were therefore unconstitutional. This decision provoked a storm among nationalists just when the new premier, Bourassa, and new mayor, Jean Doré, were trying to put the linguistic wars behind them and revitalize Montreal as an international finance center. Businesses taking advantage of the new ruling faced a rash of bomb threats, window smashing and a fire-bombing. Language tension reentered *"la belle province."*

In the long run, more and more *Québécois* are becoming bilingual. One prominent advocate of English rights noted: "There is linguistic peace. . . . We have evolved from perceiving ourselves as part of the English-Canadian majority to learning to live naturally and willingly as a minority."

Even though polls in 1985 indicated that only four percent of Quebecers favored the complete independence of the province, the dream of such a future died hard. The radical separatist and professor at the University of Quebec at Montreal, Pierre Bourgault, called this development an "end of a dream. End of an era . . . Today it is possible to see that all along Lévesque was on the wrong track with the wrong people. He was still pursuing the Quiet Revolution while his troops wanted something else . . . It all goes back to a big mistake that happened at the beginning: separatists had an idea about Quebec, and it came to fruition in René Lévesque. But he had different ideas at different times. The truth is that Lévesque flirted with separatism because the idea seduced him, but in the end, he lacked the will to promote separatism. And in the end, he betrayed himself. What now?"

Also, the Montreal playwright Michel Tremblay declared: "It took us 200 years to wake up, and now we seem to be going back to sleep. I don't even dare consider the future, things are so bad. We had promised our children a country, and we haven't delivered."

With an eye to Quebec's history, it would be safe to say that Quebec nationalism never dies; it just dies down temporarily. Nevertheless, Lévesque decided that the time was not ripe for independence. In 1984, at the end of a bitter intra-party debate that raged since 1982, he declared that in the next provincial election "sovereignty must not be at stake, neither wholly nor in parts that are more or less disguised." This pronouncement prompted the resignation of seven of his cabinet members, and further resignations and by-election losses reduced his party's majority in the National Assembly from 80 to 65. But in an extraordinary *PQ* convention held in 1985, a majority of delegates (869 to 453) voted to shelve the issue of Quebec sovereignty. This caused such an uproar within the party that Lévesque himself announced his resignation in mid-1985.

At the end of 1985, the *PQ* handed the reins of power back to the man and the party from whom it had wrested them in 1976, Robert Bourassa and the *Liberal Party*. A freelance journalist, Benoit Aubin wrote: "Quebecers, for better or for worse, seem to have decided to join the rest of North America." Yet, in 1989 separatism roared back on the political agenda when the *PQ*,

Canada

led by Jacques Parizeau and running again on an independence platform, won 40% of the votes in the provincial elections.

MEECH LAKE ACCORD

Thus, 1987 appeared to be a good time for the Canadian government to take audacious steps toward securing language harmony and finally winning Quebec endorsement of the 1982 Constitution, introducing legislation to revise and update the 1969 Official Languages Act. The aim was to bring it in line with the 1982 Charter of Rights and Freedoms by stating that federal services will be provided in both official languages where there is "significant demand." It also reached a groundbreaking "Meech Lake Accord" with the 10 provincial premiers at an isolated Quebec retreat north of Ottawa.

The agreement they struck would have become a part of the Constitution and would have made Quebec "a distinct society." The agreement would have explicitly recognized the coexistence of French and English language groups as "a fundamental characteristic of Canada," and given Parliament and the provincial legislatures the role of preserving—but not promoting—the francophone and anglophone character of Canada. The Prime Minister sought a settlement that, in his words, would reflect "a country organized and governed in a manner that corresponds to the diversity of the Canadian people" and end "Quebec's estrangement from the Canadian constitutional family, on terms that are good for Quebec, good for our other regions and good for Canada." It is no surprise that Quebec was the first province to ratify the accord.

What were good for all provinces were the decentralizing clauses which would permit them to opt out of shared-cost programs as long as their own conformed to "national objectives," had more say on the nomination of senators and Supreme Court justices and determined their own immigration policy. Most importantly, each province would have an absolute veto on future constitutional amendments.

This accord reflected Mulroney's belief in government decentralization, local initiative, and power sharing as well as his attachment to cultural and linguistic rights. There were many critics of the accord, the most noted of which was Pierre Elliott Trudeau, who feared a dangerous weakening of Ottawa's power: "Those Canadians who fought for a single Canada, bilingual and multicultural, can say goodbye to their dream." His close associate and later prime minister, Jean Chrétien, shared this view, and women and native peoples found in it no protection of their particular rights.

Constitutional expert Eugene Forsey called it riddled with "ambiguities and obscurities," which could actually limit the rights of linguistic minorities. His warning seemed to be borne out by events in Saskatchewan in the spring of 1988, which threatened to open wide the language wounds in Canada, which seemed to have been healed. The origin of this dispute goes back to 1980, when a francophone priest insisted on using French to enter his plea for a speeding ticket. This demand was based on Section 110 of the North-West Territories Act of 1886, which stipulated that both languages could be used in courts and assemblies and that all statutes had to be in both languages. The Canadian Supreme Court ruled in February 1988 that that statute was still valid in Saskatchewan but that the province was free to repeal Section 110 of the act.

Faced with the same problem in 1985, Manitoba chose to comply by beginning the laborious and expensive process of translating all past and present laws. Still, despite pleas from Prime Minister Mulroney, Saskatchewan's premier, Grant Devine, chose a different route. His government introduced legislation to repeal the bilingual provision of the old law. Devine argued that he had to pay attention to anglophone sentiment and to the budgetary strains that would result from translating thousands of prior laws for only 2.3% of the province's population that is francophone.

Minority language groups throughout all of Canada were incensed, despite Devine's promises to translate some of the more important laws and to provide some French-language services at an undetermined time in the future. Quebec Premier Bourassa supported Devine, but this did not quiet the storm. Coming at a time when the Meech Lake agreement was under growing attack, critics charged that Saskatchewan's actions made the agreement's commitment to "preserve" minority language rights worthless and made it clear that nobody knows exactly what the accord would do for minorities.

In 1989–90, the gulf of understanding between anglophones and francophones was widened in a way which endangered the delicate Accord. English Canadians reacted angrily in 1988 when Bourassa, faced with an intense resurgence of separatist sentiment in Quebec, prohibited the use of English on outdoor commercial signs, an action that seemed to violate the rights of Quebec's anglophones. This struck critics as a foretaste of how Quebec would use the powers implied by the "distinct society" clause in the accord, provoking a backlash and making bilingualism harder to sell in the rest of Canada. Moreover, the political storm increasingly focused on Meech Lake, as momentum against the accord gathered force in English Canada, especially in the West, New Brunswick, and Newfoundland. As the clock turned midnight on June 23, 1990, Meech Lake was dead.

In the Manitoba legislative assembly, the only native member, Elijah Harper, who wanted the accord to fail because it did not address native issues, stalled debate by procedural tricks and prevented a vote from being taken. Newfoundland's premier, Clyde Wells, objected to the "fabricated precipice" which the deadline created, and called off his own legislature's vote. Mulroney's feverish last-minute efforts to find a compromise merely antagonized opponents even more.

The outcome ignited a new wave of Quebec nationalism which, in turn, stirred up even more anti-*Québécois* resentment in anglophone Canada. It helped nurture a new sense of alienation in the West and sparked native assertiveness throughout Canada. In addition, this left a legacy of polarization and volatility and brought to the surface stresses and strains in the very fabric of Canadian society. It put wind in the sails of a new party, the *Bloc Québécois*, and carried the *PQ*, which opposed Meech Lake, to victory in the two succeeding Quebec provincial elections and perhaps more in the new century. A rising Reform Party, renamed the Canadian Alliance in 2000, thrived in the West. Because of Trudeau's and Chrétien's opposition to Meech, the federal *Liberals* became near pariahs in Quebec, but they became more popular in English Canada.

Perhaps most important, this vent left Quebec's signature off the Canadian constitution and thereby rendered Canada vulnerable to calls for Quebec separation, sending Mulroney's approval rating into the cellar at 14%. One pollster noted in 1991 that in terms of popularity, he "is tied with Fidel Castro, but higher than Saddam Hussein." The conflict alienated Mulroney from his old friend, Lucien Bouchard, and from Chrétien, with whom he shared a courteous relationship. A cover story in *Maclean's* commemorating the tenth anniversary of the Meech Lake Accord was entitled, "June 23, 1990: The Day that Changed Canada." Canada was never the same again.

A NEW CONSTITUTION FOR CANADA?

Many Quebecers interpreted the downfall of Meech Lake as their being rejected by the rest of Canada and they acted accordingly. Polls in 1991 revealed that more than two-thirds favored full sovereignty. Premier Bourassa named a "Belanger-Campeau Commission" to conduct four

Canada

months of public hearings to gather opinions from Quebecers on the province's future. In March 1991, the Commission issued its report, calling for a plebiscite no later than October 26, 1992, to determine its future status, unless the federal government could present an acceptable alternative. Bourassa favored continued links with Canada, but envisaged a country that would leave the federal government with little more responsibilities than protecting the borders, managing the currency, and repaying the federal debt.

Seeing that his countrymen were unnerved, uncertain, and pessimistic, Mulroney asserted, "a sense of hurt over a constitutional failure—however real—is insufficient reason for Quebecers to give up on Canada." He promised that his government would put forward its own proposals for constitutional change to build "a new and stronger Canada. We have every intention of restructuring Canada. We have no intention of dismantling it." Mulroney added: "Let me be clear: Canada is not up for grabs. Either you have a country, or you don't. You can't have it both ways."

Mulroney's problem was to devise constitutional reforms far more comprehensive than the Meech Lake Accord in only 18 months to satisfy Quebec and all the other groups clamoring for greater autonomy from the central government. Remembering how many Canadians resented the secretive way the Meech Lake talks had been conducted behind closed doors and the fact that they had focused on Quebec's demands, the government opened up the debate and negotiations to the public and interest groups and to include something for the anglophone provinces and native peoples as well.

Mulroney's action was a radical shift in constitutional talks which had always been tugs of war between Ottawa and the provinces over who controls. To sound out the wishes of all those groups and to try to understand the deep malaise in Canada, Mulroney created a Citizens' Forum on Canada's Future, led by Keith Spicer. It organized hearings throughout the land to hear the complaints and suggestions of hundreds of thousands of Canadians, and it reported them to the government. Six provincial commissions were simultaneously held traveling hearings.

In 1991, Mulroney turned to former Prime Minister Joe Clark to head a new Ministry for Constitutional Affairs and a cabinet committee which would produce a draft proposal for amending the constitution. The challenge, in Mulroney's words, was to come up with "a new, modern and dynamic Constitution that will be accepted by all the provinces."

A bilingual Westerner, Clark's job was to turn around Westerners' and other anglophones' anti-Quebec sentiment and to get them to accept a constitutional plan that would also be compatible with Quebec's demands for recognition as a "distinct society." He had at the same time to offer Quebecers a palatable alternative to sovereignty. No one envied his task, but his performance gained him almost universal trust and respect. Clark's secret was patience, fairness, and elegant, well-crafted speeches "We can be the first generation of Canadians to pass on to the next less than was passed on to us. There is nothing automatic about this country. Canada was not here at the beginning of the last century. There is no logic that says it must be here at the beginning of the next. We have to work to keep it. We always have. This is a large and diverse country. Keeping it large without destroying its diversity has always been our challenge."

A process was set into motion that would have dramatically reduced the federal government's role in the country's affairs and enlarged the powers and responsibilities of the provinces. This was already taking place, but a constitutional change would have given added authority to the on-going shift in the balance of federal and provincial powers, which is reversing a decades-old trend toward an ever more powerful central government. The center seemed to no longer be holding and the parts defined the whole. Ontario's premier, Bob Rae, declared "we cannot just turn the federal government into a post office. It leaves out the soul of Canada."

After two years of intense work, the premiers of the nine anglophone provinces, native leaders, and the prime minister agreed to the "Charlottetown Accord" on August 28, 1992. It included:

1. **Senate reform:** The existing appointed body would be replaced by a more powerful one elected by proportional representation at a different time than the House of Commons in which Quebec would be guaranteed one-fourth of the seats. In response to Western demands, each province would have six seats. The territories, aboriginal groups, and women would also be represented.

2. **Aboriginal rights:** The inherent native right to self-government was accepted, subject to the Charter of Rights and Freedoms, with aboriginal governments recognized as one of three orders of government, alongside Ottawa and the provinces.

3. **Division of powers:** Ottawa would recognize the provinces' exclusive power over such areas as tourism, forestry, housing, and culture. Powers would be divided more efficiently.

4. **Social and economic issues:** Commitments to preserve universal health care, the equalization between richer and poorer provinces, and the free flow of goods, capital and services throughout Canada would be enshrined in the constitution.

5. **Quebec:** It would be recognized as a "distinct society," characterized by its language, culture, and civil-law tradition, and it would choose three Supreme Court justices.

6. **Minorities:** Anglophone communities in Quebec and francophone communities elsewhere would be protected.

Every mainstream political party and institution supported the package except the Reform Party and the *Parti Québécois*. Former Prime Minister Trudeau also opposed it. On October 26, 1992, 54% of the voters, six provinces, and the Yukon Territory said no to the accord. Only

Quebec's Parliament Building

Canada

Newfoundland, New Brunswick, Prince Edward Island, and, by the closest of margins, Ontario, said yes.

Insofar as the package needed the ratification of every province and the federal government, the rejection could not have been more decisive. One drinker in a Montreal bar reportedly called it "horrendously Canadian: a populist revolt in favor of the status quo." It was a popular vote against Canada's leaders. Westerners thought the accord gave too much to Quebec, and Quebecers thought it did not do enough for them. For Quebec separatists, the Western no-vote confirmed that Canada would never recognize Quebec's special character. Parizeau said, "with Meech they said no to Quebec; this time we said it to each other."

Looking back on his dramatic 1993 election victory, Prime Minister Jean Chrétien declared that the *Tories* had "spent too much time on constitutional affairs and not enough on the economy. So I want to do exactly the reverse." He did not have that luxury. Many Canadians seemed to sense an imminent challenge to their country's unity. Canadians saw the separatist *Bloc Québécois* functioning as the official opposition in the federal parliament and the *PQ* emerging victorious in the 1994 Quebec provincial elections.

PQ leader Jacques Parizeau ordered a referendum on October 30, 1995 to clear the way for an independent Quebec. This time, the separatists came closer to victory than ever before, winning 49.4% of the votes in a huge 94% turnout. This was a gain of 10 percentage points since 1980; 60% of Quebec's francophones voted "*oui*," while nearly all anglophones and immigrants voted *non*.

Subsequent investigation revealed that many "no" ballots had been declared invalid for mysterious and trivial reasons, leading to charges of possible *PQ* election rigging. Nevertheless, Quebecers never displayed such deep dissatisfaction with the status quo. Regarding the outcome as a moral victory, Quebec's new leader, Lucien Bouchard, evoked the memory of Lévesque by proclaiming: "Let us keep the faith. The next time will be the right one. And the next time may come sooner than people think." Parizeau, who resigned as premier after the disappointing defeat, was correct in saying that for many Canadians "this Quebec problem is like a never-ending visit to the dentist."

In the midst of the 1997 federal parliamentary elections, Parizeau showed that he, himself, was that dentist. After Prime Minister Chrétien called early elections to focus on the country's economic success and challenges, Parizeau published his memoirs, *For a Sovereign Québec,* in which he admitted that he had been prepared to declare Quebec's independence immediately after a yes-vote in 1995, not after negotiations with Ottawa, as his party had proposed during the referendum campaign. The PQ government had also set aside $17 million to buy up provincial bonds it feared nervous investors might dump on the market.

This reminded Canadians that those who support Quebec sovereignty, though divided among themselves on tactics and on the definition of the term, are dead serious about Quebec independence. Quebec Premier Lucien Bouchard promised another referendum by the year 2000, but flagging interest in Quebec for complete separation has caused it to be postponed indefinitely. Polls continue to show that *Québécois* are divided on the question and that a majority continues to oppose independence. The uproar caused by Parizeau brought the issue of unity back into the center of Canadian politics

In 1995, Chrétien promised to reexamine Quebec's constitutional demands. Yet, resistance to that in anglophone Canada and in the *Reform Party*, as well as Premier Bouchard's and the *Bloc Québécois'* rejection of another round of constitutional talks, limited the prime minister to a meaningless resolution in parliament recognizing the distinct nature of Que-

Quebec lures tourists

Canada

Quebec City

bec. His then finance minister, Paul Martin, and most of his closest advisers were *Québécois*, and he appointed Montreal political scientist Stéphane Dion as Canada's first minister of intergovernmental affairs.

Dion, who in 2006 became party leader, helped the Liberal government in Ottawa formulate a two-pronged approach to Quebec, known as "Plan A" and "Plan B." Plan A was a national unity strategy of economic growth and job creation that would have benefited Quebec and won support throughout Canada for the notion that Quebec is a "distinct society." Plan B was hardball involving tough talk designed to disabuse *Québécois* of illusions about what life would be like if they voted for independence. Under Plan B, *Québécois* could not expect to continue using Canadian passports or money, to remain in the North American Free Trade Agreement (NAFTA), or even retain all the territory within Quebec's current borders. In Chrétien's words, "if Canada is divisible, Quebec is divisible."

The message was clear: if anglophones, Indians, or Inuit in Quebec wanted the areas in which they live to remain in Canada, they could do so. At the end of 1997, it was clear that any abrupt move by Quebec to secede, even after a big "Yes" vote to separate, would be illegal. "There will be a negotiation with the federal government . . . no doubt about that." Federal lawyers asked the Supreme Court in 1997 to rule on the legality of a unilateral Quebec secession. Dion emphasized: Plan A was "the plan is reconciliation;" Plan B involved "the rules of secession." "We are not governing an ordinary country. We are governing a great federation that is in danger of collapse."

On August 20, 1998, the nine Supreme Court justices issued a unanimous ruling: Quebec did not have the right under the constitution to declare independence unilaterally. The Court held that insofar as Quebec was neither a victim of "alien subjugation" nor an "oppressed people," provincial leaders had no automatic right to self-determination under international law. The Court explained that any referendum would have to offer a "clear question," such as Chrétien's proposed "Do you want to separate from Canada?" and that if a "clear majority" voted in favor of independence, then negotiations with the rest of Canada would be "necessary" and a constitutional amendment would be required. Federalists rejoiced at the ruling. The Quebec government unexpectedly joined the celebration.

Seeing much room for interpretation, Bouchard emphasized the requirement that Ottawa negotiate with Quebec after a successful referendum and read the "clear majority" mandate narrowly. Bouchard pointed out that Newfoundland had entered Canada in 1949 with only 52% support in a referendum. In its headline the *Ottawa Citizen* summed up the differing interpretations: "One ruling, two solitudes."

After initially greeting the 1998 Supreme Court decision, the *PQ* let it be known in October 1999 that it no longer felt bound to follow an interpretation of a judiciary whose judges were appointed by Ottawa. In the words of Joseph Facal, the *PQ's* intergovernmental affairs minister, "all rules governing the next referendum will be determined by the national assembly of Quebec." This declaration, along with polling results indicating that a third of those who had voted "Yes" in the 1995 referendum had thought Quebec would still be a province of Canada even if the "Yes" side won, prompted the federal government to take the initiative over the secession question for the first time in three decades.

Bill C-20, known as the "clarity bill," was introduced in December 1999. For the first time the legislation legitimizes the right of any province to hold a referendum on secession but it establishes stringent conditions. First, the question would have to be direct and concise and make no mention of future economic or political partnerships with Canada. To ensure that any future question would be sufficiently clear, it would first have to be vetted by the federal parliament and get its approval. Second, a referendum majority itself must be clear. The bill does not clearly spell out what the word "clear" means, but only that the traditional 50%-plus-one would not be sufficient. Not until the House of Commons had determined that "a clear expression of the will of the population" had been given would the federal government enter negotiations about a secession agreement.

According to former Prime Minister Chrétien, "we are forcing them to be honest." It goes without saying that the *PQ* seethed over the clarity bill. However, voters in Quebec supported the concept. In a 1999 poll, seven out of ten believed 60% represents the clear majority required by the court; 93% favored a clear question, and 61% did not think the 1995 question was clear.

Canada

Constitution Act, 1867

Constitution Act, 1982

Canadian Charter of Rights and Freedoms (1982)

POLITICAL SYSTEM

For a person interested in comparing different governmental systems, Canada is an extraordinarily intriguing case conceived over concern it might be swallowed up by its southern neighbor and born of compromise. In the 19th century a majority of Canadians wanted to retain ties with Britain and have a parliamentary system of government influenced by the political experiences of the British, French, and American nations but that was adapted to Canada.

In 1867, the British Parliament passed the British North America Act (BNA), granting the Canadian government the authority "to make Laws for Peace, Order and Good Government" which was in stark contrast to the United States (U.S.) constitutional document stating the individual's right to" life, liberty and the pursuit of happiness." Typically Canadian, the BNA was a short, sober, legalistic document, focusing on a pragmatic communitarian view of society not the individualistic liberal view seen in the Declaration of Independence, penned almost a century earlier by Thomas Jefferson.

The BNA was written exclusively by Canadians at conferences that no British delegates attended. When it was presented to the British government for formal approval, the latter objected to only two minor points: it was nervous about calling the new country "the Kingdom of Canada" as the Canadians wanted because such a name might be offensive to the Americans, who reacted violently to the notion of monarchy 90 years earlier. The Canadians therefore settled on the word "Dominion," taken from the 72nd Psalm, "He shall have dominion also from sea to sea and from the river unto the ends of the earth." To the "Fathers of the Constitution," as Canada's founders were called, this term, which had never been used before to describe a nation, embodied the monarchial principle so subtly that the Americans would not even notice it.

The second minor point on which the British insisted was a provision for breaking a deadlock between the two houses of parliament. Other than these two points, the BNA was purely a Canadian creation in prescribing "a Constitution similar in principle to that of the United Kingdom." This meant that Canada would have a parliamentary democracy in which the cabinet, called the "Privy Council," would be responsible to the House of Commons, not to the British monarch.

It also meant that custom and tradition, together called "constitutional conventions" would be an unwritten but essential part of the country's constitution. Thus, such fundamental constitutional principles and practices as "responsible government," "collective responsibility," "parliamentary supremacy," the fusion of executive powers and legislative powers as opposed to "separation of powers," "votes of confidence" for the government, with regard to budgetary matters as well as the need for both prime minister (PM) and cabinet, to be appointed by the Governor General (the Queen's representative to the federal parliament) and although a member of Cabinet may not be a member of parliament – indeed at least one member of the Senate is normally a member of cabinet, the norm is that a cabinet member should have been elected to the House of Commons. These matters are not written into the BNA Act.

The trappings of Canadian politics evoke the strong British heritage: Privy Council, governor general, the House of Commons, the position of prime Minister, Throne Speech, Parliament meeting only on royal summons, and Crown corporations. After they arrest criminals, the Royal Canadian Mounted Police turn them over to Crown prosecutors to charge them. In the United States, criminal charges are stated as the People versus the accused individual, whereas in Canada it is the King or Queen, as the case may be, versus the individual reflecting the difference between a Republic and the Dominion. America has military colleges such West Point or Annapolis, and in Canada, military Officers are educated at the Royal Military College of Canada, in Kingston, Ontario (English) and its French-speaking equivalent, the Royal Military College Saint-Jean, 40 km south of Quebec city. In 2011, after 43 years as the unified "Canadian Forces," the word "Royal" was again added to the Canadian Air Force and to the Canadian Navy; the land forces became the "Canadian Army."

All federal acts begin with the words: "Her Majesty, by and with the advice and consent of the Senate and the House of Commons, enacts as follows." Provincial laws commence with similar wording and all bills need "Royal Assent" to be enacted. Even the Canada Act, 1982 requested "that Her Majesty may graciously be pleased to cause a Bill to be laid before the Parliament of the United Kingdom . . . by and with the advice and consent of the Lords Spiritual and Temporal, and Commons. . . ." Immigrants who become citizens pledge their "loyalty and allegiance to Canada and Her Majesty Elizabeth II, queen of Canada."

While the vestiges of the British heritage are still visible, there have been recent reminders that Britain has only a limited hold on the hearts and minds of many Canadians. In 1965, Britannia's stripes were removed from Canada's flag with a simple maple leaf replacing the Union Jack. In 1970 the "E II R" cipher, meaning "Elizabeth II Regina." was removed from Canadian mailboxes. In 1980 the country adopted a new anthem, "O Canada," which can be sung in two languages, to replace "God Save the Queen," which, it need not be said, was only sung in English. Twenty-first-century political correctness objected to the words "all thy sons command" in O Canada which seem to exclude that 50% of the population which is female which caused the anthem to be changed to "in all of us command".

Shortly thereafter, the 12,000-member Monarchist League lost other battles: the country's major holiday, Dominion Day, celebrated July 1st, was rechristened "Canada Day," and even the BNA was renamed the "Constitution Act 1867." One member of the Royal Commonwealth Society rudely referred to each of these changes as a "sop to Quebec." A more accurate explanation is that each of those symbols rubbed salt in the unhealed wound with which Canada was born: the English-French division. Each was a brick in the wall that separated the majority of Canadians from the third of their countrymen who were francophones.

Perhaps no country in the world has been more successful than Canada in reconciling the claims of two founding colonial peoples who are determined to preserve their languages and cultures. It has not been easy, but the English-speaking majority has recognized the "French fact" in Canada. Canadian politics has been significantly influenced by that fact. In Quebec itself, French civil law prevails, and Quebec's anglophones have accepted the necessity of speaking French in their native province. In other provinces, such as New Brunswick, French and English are both used in public life, and everywhere in Canada a francophone can deal with the federal government in French. In Ottawa, French and English are both used on the street and in Parliament. Every PM, governor general, and speaker of the House of Commons, as well as at least three of nine Supreme Court justices, must speak both languages and parliamentary debates are freely conducted in both.

Primarily because of the "French fact," Canada had to be created as a federal state. This means that law-making authority is divided between the central government and the provinces. It was unthinkable that Canada be a unitary state like Britain. Quebec's persistent assertion of provincial rights also benefited other provinces, especially in the West, which wanted to lighten Ottawa's hand on their shoulders. Indeed, in 2019 the premier of Alberta seeks a modus vinendi with Quebec in order to stop federal legislation which threatens to block the creation of resource-based businesses in Canada. Further, Quebec prevented Canada from ever being a "melting pot," like the U.S. where many now prefer the analogy of a "salad bowl" where the ingredients remain as they were originally even as they are part of something larger. Canada has adopted a policy of multiculturalism, overseen by a cabinet minister. In other words, other minority groups in Canada owe the official recognition and legislative protections largely to the existence of the *Québécois*.

The influence of the British and French heritages on Canadian political life is obvious. Even so, another nation has had a powerful influence on Canada, the United States. Much of the Canadian experience was an attempt to survive as a sovereign country and as a unique cultural product in the face of powerful challenges by the American neighbors. In 1812, the Americans were beaten back after a half-hearted attempt to spread their "Manifest Destiny" northward. In 1837, the rebellions in Upper and Lower Canada, which resulted in the Durham Report and ultimate independence, were led by men infected by the idea of rule by the people. These were populist notions that had come alive again during the Jacksonian era of the 1830s. Canadians could learn about them right across the border in the U.S.

Canadians adopted federalism for reasons of their own size and diversity. However, their brand was shaped by their horror of the American Civil War, which seemed to have resulted from the South's concept of states' rights. The "Fathers of Confederation" did create an upper house called a Senate which was supposed to defend regional interests, something that it utterly failed to do. Today, such things as the hoopla of Party conventions where leaders are selected, the increasing observance of four years as a long enough time between national elections, a written bill of rights, and a written constitution, are a but four of many examples of America's impact on Canadian politics.

Even though they heavy borrowed from the other countries' political traditions and practices, it has been Canadians themselves who have shaped their own political system. It is they who have adapted to their unique situation as a huge, regionally and culturally diverse country. The Canadian regime may be a hybrid, but the mix is uniquely Canadian. Its basic outline is as follows: voters elect 338 members of the House of Commons, the lower house of Parliament; the Harper government's 2011 Fair Representation Bill added 30 seats to this total. The leader of the party that wins a majority of seats or can get a majority of votes in the House of Commons on important issues becomes the PM, the most powerful political figure in the land. Queen Elizabeth II, the Queen of Canada, is the head of state, but neither she, nor her representative, the governor general, makes any important political decisions.

The PM selects other ministers who are also usually experienced parliamentary leaders in the Party, to sit in the cabinet. Together, the PM and cabinet are called "the government," which rules "collectively." Put another way, all members of

Canada

the government must publicly support its policies or resign from office. Also, the entire team assumes responsibility for the overall policy. The government rules as long as it maintains a majority in the House of Commons or until it loses a "vote of confidence" on an important bill. The PM must call an election at least five years after the preceding election, but can announce one earlier if that would be to his or her party's advantage.

Unlike in the U.S., where both houses of Congress are equally powerful, the Canadian upper house, the Senate, has far less power than the House of Commons. Moreover, unlike in the U.S., there is no "separation of powers" among the executive, legislative, or judicial branches. Executive and legislative powers are fused, making the PM both the chief executive and chief legislator of the land. Through a tightly disciplined party, the PM controls the House of Commons. Finally, as in the U.S., but unlike in Britain, with the exception of the European courts where the UK has given jurisdiction, laws can be judged unconstitutional by the Supreme Court of Canada. In Canada "parliamentary supremacy" is subject to provincial legislative supremacy in issues reserved in the Constitution Act, 1867 for the provinces and matters touching upon the Canadian Charter of Rights and Freedoms, where such jurisdiction is applicable.

CONSTITUTION

The government in Canada is both democratic, insofar as the people elect the representatives who govern them, and constitutional, in that rules that bind all political actors, limit the exercise of governmental power, impose obligations on the governments, and provide for the judicial enforcement of the rules. In a federal state such as Canada, a constitution has an additional function: it distributes legal power to the central and the provincial legislatures; in the words of Canadian political scientist David Milne, it "forms a master power grid from which all the governmental players get their authority", subject to the federal constitutional power of disallowance.

It should not be surprising that any effort to change the constitution, such as took place in Canada in the early 1980s, would expose the very nerves of government. A change of this nature would inevitably reveal the tensions and power struggles in federal-provincial, inter-provincial, and ethnic group relations.

As to the form of its constitution, Canada stands between the United Kingdom and the U.S. The British constitution remains unwritten; it is a collection of clearly defined documents, such as the Magna Carta of 1215, the Statute of Westminster of 1931, as well as of important customs and traditions that no government would dare violate. However, any portion of the constitution could be changed by Parliament, which is "supreme." How this interrelates with the power of the courts of Europe is an interesting topic itself and indeed how will be altered with Brexit makes the reversion of all authority to the British Parliament a complex issue.

At the other democratic continuum is the U.S., which has a written constitution to spell out the powers of the institutions of governments, with a few prominent omissions, such as political parties. The American constitution is intentionally difficult to change and has been amended only 27 times in more than 200 years. Congress cannot change the constitution because it rather, than Congress, is "supreme." Unlike Britain and Canada, which had not experienced revolutions, the U.S. fought for its independence. After successful revolutions, winners are far more inclined to put in writing the kind of guarantees and rights their former rulers denied them.

The BNA called for a political system like that of Britain. This included customs and traditions, such as the need for the PM to have the confidence of the House of Commons, or the understanding that the monarch "reigns but does not rule." In typical British fashion, these things were not written down, and most of them are still unwritten but are referred to in law as constitutional conventions.

Canada's founders faced a challenge that could not be met by merely adopting British practices. The founders had to create a form of government that was sufficiently strong to hold such a huge, sparsely populated, country together, while at the same time decentralizing it in a way so as to meet the aspirations of different regions and peoples. In so doing, the founders were able to coax the various strong-willed colonies into the new union by promising them that they could share the responsibility for ruling the country with the central government. The founders even used a misnomer to describe the new governmental structure: a "confederation," a loose alliance of sovereign nations. Actually, the founders created a federation which does not recognize the provinces as sovereign states, but which divides authority between the central and provincial governments.

Since 1867, the written portion of the BNA has been supplemented by other important documents with constitutional standing. In all, 24 documents, called "organic laws," make up the constitution; there are 13 acts of the British Parliament, amendments to the BNA, also called British North America Acts; seven acts of the Canadian Parliament; and four British orders-in-council, government declarations permitted by law. This collection includes such statutes as the acts admitting other provinces to Canada after 1867, provincial constitutions, the Supreme Court Act of 1875, the War Powers Act of 1914, the Statute of Westminster of 1931, the Elections Acts, the House of Commons Act, the Legislative Assembly Acts, the Public Service Acts, the Bill of Rights of 1960, and the Official Languages Act of 1969. With all these acts and the many customs that provided the ground rules for Canadian politics, one might think that all the bases had been touched and that Canadians could settle down and live by their voluminous, complicated constitution. Yet, they could not because some important items were missing.

The 1970s and 1980s were decades of both nationalist and regional resurgence in Canada. Many *Québécois* demanded separation from Canada, or at least a radically different kind of federal structure that would enable them largely to govern themselves. Discontent was also reaching the boiling point in the energy-rich western provinces which believed that their economic development was being seriously threatened by Ottawa's policy toward their natural resources. The western premiers banded together to form the first regional bloc in Canadian history that could seriously threaten the predominance of Ontario and Quebec. The Atlantic provinces always resented Central Canada's dominance, fearing that it would find a way of depriving them of the benefits from the oil and gas discovered off of their shores and which, they hoped, could finally enable them to catch up economically with the rest of Canada.

On top of this regional turmoil, the Trudeau government in Ottawa embarked on a nationalist campaign to increase the Canadian hold over the country's own economy and energy resources. The joints of the Canadian state began to creak under the weight of competing visions of federalism, nationalism and regionalism. Because Canada was in crisis, its political and legal minds set out to find a constitutional solution that could save the country from tearing apart.

The result was the Canada Act 1982, which served as the basis for the Constitution Act. Canada did not adopt an entirely new constitution. Instead it refined many existing arrangements and added important provisions to the existing constitution. It was a compromise, but one that was reached only after an enormous hue and cry and some of the most determined political maneuvering in Canadian history. It was a high-stakes intergovernmental struggle among giants. In David

Canada

Milne's words, "because the battle concerned the kind of state (or states) Canada was to be, it challenged every Canadian to define his sense of country more sharply than ever before. Predictably there was no consensus among Canadians as a whole."

The struggle involved many twists and turns before it was resolved; it also revealed how many power centers must be dealt with in Canadian politics. The Trudeau government had been voted back into power in February 1980 after a nine-month breather. It fought a successful battle against the *Parti Québécois'* effort to win a provincial referendum in May 1980 that could have paved the way to some form of separatism.

In order to undercut the *PQ's* appeals during the campaign, Trudeau promised a new federal arrangement. In July 1908, intergovernmental negotiations began but reached an impasse by September 13. On October 6, Trudeau placed a unilateral proposal before Parliament to force the provinces back into action. The latter wasted no time by challenging Trudeau's move in court. By November 1980, Britain's Select Committee on Foreign Affairs began to study the UK's role in the constitutional debate and concluded two months later that "Westminster cannot act as a mere rubberstamp on all requests coming from Parliament to Canada."

After months of further debate, deliberation, and challenges in provincial high courts, the Supreme Court of Canada rendered its judgment on September 28, 1981, declaring that Trudeau's resolution in Parliament was legal and that a province did not have a veto over the entire process. This order practically forced the premiers to reenter negotiations with the Canadian government, culminating a substantial agreement among all parties, except Quebec, in 1980. In December 1981, the constitutional resolution cleared both houses of the Canadian Parliament, was signed by the governor general, and delivered to Buckingham Palace in London.

Premier Lévesque, who felt betrayed and outmaneuvered by Trudeau and the other premiers, unsuccessfully appealed to Prime Minister Margaret Thatcher to delay the proceedings until Quebec's veto power could be established by the Quebec Court of Appeal. Also, Canadian Indigenous people appealed unsuccessfully to the British Court of Appeals, claiming that their full rights had not been secured in the new agreement. In March 1982 the Canada Act breezed through both houses of the British Parliament.

On April 17, 1982, while thousands of *Québécois* and Indigenous people publicly protested and mourned, Queen Elizabeth proclaimed the Canada Act in a signing ceremony in front of the Canadian Parliament. This act terminated the British Parliament's power over Canada and transferred the entire Canadian constitution to the Canadians themselves. Bitter about having been deprived of an absolute veto power, the Quebec government never accepted the validity of the act. The Meech Lake Accord sought to resolve this deadlock.

Under the terms of this Canada Act, the national government was able to proclaim the Constitution Act, 1982. This act lumped together and renamed the BNA and all its amendments the "Constitution Acts, 1867–1975." Canada's major holiday, July 1, was renamed "Canada Day."

In adopting a new constitution, Canada had entered a new age. Canadian government was changed in a variety of important ways. Perhaps the most significant change was that Canada could now amend every part of its constitution without having to secure British approval. This is surely a power any truly sovereign country must possess. Because it is so important, Canadians spoke of the patriation or bringing home of their constitution. In 1927, the first attempts had been made to secure this right. However, for more than a half-century all such efforts foundered due to inability of the federal and provincial governments to agree on a method of amendment. This inability should not be surprising if one remembers that the power to amend a constitution is the power to change the political rules of the game. It is therefore a matter of utmost importance.

The American constitution provides for only one feasible amending process other than an untried new constitutional convention, but the Constitution Act, 1982, elaborates four different formulae or processes, depending on the issue. Important changes dealing with such matters as the monarchy, the governor general, the use of the French and English languages in the federal government or the Supreme Court of Canada, require the ultimate approval of the House of Commons and every provincial legislature.

In other matters, a single province would not have a veto; two-thirds of the provinces need to approve. There are two prominent exceptions which reveal the extent to which provincial powers were respected. First, a proposed change impacting one or more provinces, but not such matters as boundary changes or the use of French or English in a particular province, affords the affected provinces the right of veto. Also under this provision, a province can "opt out" of any amendment seeking to take away any of its powers, rights, or privileges. Fourth, and final, an amending formula deals with most changes in Canada's executive, Senate, or House of Commons; in these instances, changes can be made by an ordinary act of Parliament.

A second important change under the Constitution Act, 1982, is that it "entrenches" certain parts of the written constitution, making it impossible for Parliament or any provincial legislature

Queen Elizabeth II signs the Canadian Constitution, 1982. Prime Minister Trudeau is seated at left. Public Archives Canada/PA/140705 Photo by Bob Cooper

Canada

Rideau Hall, residence of the Governor General

to change them by simple legislative acts. This applies to the monarchy, the governor general, the composition of the Supreme Court, or the amending formulae themselves. The existence of such "entrenched" portions of the constitution that are out of Parliament's reach is a conscious departure from the British doctrine of "parliamentary supremacy," which gives Parliament the right to decide anything in the political realm.

Pursuant to the third change, the provinces were granted more control over the taxing and exportation of their own natural resources. The fourth change was that the Constitution Act, 1982, included a Charter of Rights and Freedoms to strengthen the liberty of individual Canadian citizens. This was also a break from the tradition in Britain under which to the extent that individual liberties are protected adequately by common law, they were never written down as they were in the American Bill of Rights in 1791.

The "Charter" also allows the federal or provincial governments to suspend rights, be they freedom of conscience, religion, thought, belief, opinion, expression, freedom of the press, and/ or association as well as other rights under section 33 for five years. This applies to statutes passed with reference to section 33 of the Charter. Quebec, Saskatchewan, and Alberta have used section 33 to override Charter rights. Without section 33 the provinces would not have agreed to having the Charter become part of the Constitution Act, 1982,

The Constitution Act, 1982, was a carefully constructed compromise between the central and provincial governments containing some significant innovations. Even so, much of it consolidated and refined many existing arrangements in the political system. It left intact the main structure of government, including the division of powers between Ottawa and the provinces, including the federal power of disallowance of any provincial act under the Constitution Act 1867, section 90.

GOVERNMENTAL STRUCTURE

As in the United Kingdom, Canada distinguishes between a "formal executive," who is the head of state, and the PM, who really wields the political power. Americans make no such distinction. Their president must not only be the chief policy maker, but he must also spend many hours meeting visiting heads of state, pinning badges on scouts, congratulating winning athletic teams, posing with and reprieving Thanksgiving turkeys, and smiling at cameras while turning on Christmas tree lights. In Canada, such ceremonial functions are performed by the representatives of the political figure in whom executive authority is still theoretically vested: the King of Canada, who spends most of his time being the British monarch.

The Monarch

The King and his representatives, the governor general and the lieutenant governors in the 10 provinces, are surrounded by a glittering group of advisers known as the King's Privy Council in Canada. This is composed of present and former prime ministers, cabinet members, speakers of both houses of Parliament, chief justices of the Supreme Court, and various other prominent citizens.

This large group of people in King's Privy Council in Canada rarely assembles and only at such ceremonial occasions as the accession of a new monarch. The only people among these advisers who actually wield any power are the PM and cabinet, referred to in the constitution as "the Committee of the Privy Council." All cabinet decisions are issued as decisions of the Privy Council. Even though no federal or provincial bill could be enacted without Royal Assent, no monarch would make a decision without being having the PM offer advice bout what to do. Despite the sweeping powers which the constitution seems to give him, the King "reigns but does not rule."

If the King and his representatives have so little power, a question remains about why Canada retains the monarchy. Monarchs have often served useful functions in countries that have become democracies. In Britain, for example, the King symbolizes national as part of a continuous thread through English history, thereby making him the focus of national pride. In Canada, though, the monarch often symbolizes and exacerbates the disunity of the nation. Québécois have seldom revered the monarch of a nation that conquered New France in 1760. When Queen Elizabeth II visited Quebec during the Quiet Revolution, her presence sparked serious riots. While at one time it might have been true that the monarch seldom set foot in the "la belle province," that has been changing.

In 1987, Queen Elizabeth II made her first tour of Quebec in almost a quarter century but was greeted with polite indifference. To most Quebecers, she is no longer a hated symbol of English oppression. As Pierre Bourgault, a former radical who organized the 1964 protests against her visit, noted, speaking of Queen Elizzabeth II: "Our problems are with the English in Quebec who still refuse to speak French, not with the Queen. She simply comes for a short visit, speaks French while she's here and then goes back to England." In the tense weeks following the failure of Meech Lake in 1990, nationalists made it clear that she was not welcome in Quebec. When Prince Charles and Camilla (since 2022, King Charles III and Queen Camilla) visited Montreal in 2009, hun-

Canada

dreds of nationalist rowdies turned the affair into a tear-gas spectacle of riot police and protesters.

The spectacularly successful July 2011 visit of Prince William and Princess Catherine (since 2022, the Prince and Princess of Wales) to Quebec showed how much of an emotional hold the British royals actually have in a province where 74% said at the time that the monarchy was irrelevant. A half a million Queberers tuned in to see the pair's wedding in the wee hours of an April morning. Then, the glamorous pair accepted the invitation of the Quebec and federal governments, taking part in a cooking lesson and dining on their self-cooked Quebec meal. The prince gave a public address entirely in French, praising Quebecers' vigor and vitality. Although he apologized for his language skills, the prince spoke it better than do most anglophone Canadians. Chants of "Kate and Will" drowned out the dozens who were yelling "royals go home."

Many young anglophone Canadians are no longer stirred by the monarch. One 18-year-old who joined the crowd to see Queen Elizabeth II and Prince Phillip during a visit to Canada in 1984 confessed, "I'm here because she's famous, I guess." Quipped one young lady when Prince Andrew and Princess Sarah visited Canada in 1989, "I don't see why we should have to curtsy to a person who a few years ago was living with a race-car driver!"

In 1982, a CBC TV journalist dared not to curtsy before Elizabeth II and continued her work unrepentant and unscathed. If one compares the yawning public response to that act with that toward another CBC interviewer in 1959, one can see just how much monarchical sentiments had weakened in Canada the last quarter of a century: when Joyce Davidson remarked on the air that "like most Canadians, I am indifferent to the Queen's visit," she required police protection from irate viewers and finally was forced to leave the country in order to find further employment.

Today, most Canadians ignore Commonwealth Day, which is commemorated on differing dates in late winter or early spring, when the King traditionally gives a broadcast message. Prince Charles (now Charles III) experienced the spirit of Canadian equality in 2001 when he was required to wipe his shoes on a special disinfectant mat like every other passenger when stepping off a plane from the UK, which was plagued by hoof and mouth disease.

In a poll after the passage of the Constitution Act, 1982, three-fourths of the Canadian respondents thought that the importance of the monarchy was declining. Asked at the end of the twentieth century to name the symbols that are important for the Canadian nation, the monarchy was at the bottom of the list. Only 41% of respondents cited it, 34% of men and 48% of women; the figure in Quebec was 20%. While some historians argue that the splendid royal visit in 1939, nostalgically reenacted by the Queen Elizabeth the Queen Mother in July 1989, helped solidify Canadian support for Britain when Hitler invaded Poland a few weeks later. It is all but unthinkable that British royalty could sway an important Canadian political decision today.

The royal family can still electrify crowds. Many older anglophone Canadians regard the King as a regal symbol of Canadian patriotism. As one 60-year-old Royal Canadian Air Force veteran in New Brunswick admitted, speaking of Queen Elizabeth II, "Whenever a band plays 'God Save the Queen,' I drop my cigar and stand up straight as wood."

When Queen Elizabeth, the Queen Mother, died in April 2002, a cry of disgust rang out throughout the country when the most widely read weekly Canadian newsmagazine, Maclean's, inadvertently placed the address labels across the photo of her face on the cover. The embarrassed editor had to send a letter of apology to all subscribers assuring them that the magazine meant no disrespect to the deceased monarch.

Warm crowds greeted Queen Elizabeth II wherever she went in Canada, including Nunavut, during her triumphant 12-day Jubilee tour in October 2002. However, the visit elicited a variety of public thoughts about the monarchy. The most prominent was then Deputy PM John Manley, who repeatedly expressed his preference for "an entirely Canadian institution" to replace the monarchy after Elizabeth's reign. Journalist Allan Fotheringham wrote: "She's a magnificent monarch. But she's not ours." Peter Donolo tactfully suggested: "What better gift could we give ourselves on the occasion of this Golden Jubilee year than to give the Queen a hearty handshake, thank her for all her services, wish her the best, and do what any self-respecting nation does: choose our own head of state?" The Queen's nine-day return visit in mid-summer 2010, her 22nd official tour of Canada, elicited little such commentary.

Elizabeth herself was well-liked: 84% of Canadians polled in 2005 thought she has done a good job. In 2010, 69% had a "mostly favorable" opinion of the Queen, but in a March 2005 poll taken two months before her visits to the centennials in Alberta and Saskatchewan, 46% supported replacing the monarch as Canada's head of state, while 37% opposed such a move. At the same time, 49% believed Elizabeth should remain the monarch until she dies. Only 6% thought she should abdicate in favor of Prince Charles, and 18% wanted her to cede the throne to Prince William. Perhaps because of the popularity of William and Catherine, the monarchy ascends in the polls: 56% in 2017 wanted to keep it, but only 34% of Québécois agreed.

Another poll taken four years later, on the eve of the first visit by Prince Charles and his wife Camilla (now King Charles III and Queen Camilla) as a couple, found that 65% were in favor of cutting ties to the Crown and only 35% wanted her successor to rule Canada. Six in 10 Canadians agree that the Queen and the royal family should not have any formal role in Canadian society, up two points since 2016. According to a 2019 poll, 31% of Canadians believe that Canada should remain a monarchy. The royal couple's unenthusiastic reception during this 10-day visit in November 2009 seemed to back up these polling figures. The constitutional difficulty of abolishing the monarchy ensures that this would not happen quickly or easily.

William's glittering wedding to Catherine Middleton on April 29, 2011, sent a current of excitement through Canada. The PM could not attend because he faced an election a few days later. Toronto's venerable King Edward Hotel opened its Sovereign Ballroom at 5 AM to broadcast the wedding live, accompanied by a "royal breakfast" costing $68 a head. When this event sold out, the overflow was invited to afternoon tea to watch a taped rebroadcast of the nuptial event for a fee of $69 per person.

The couple chose Canada for their first official foreign visit in July 2011. The outpouring of affection for them was so overwhelming that Maclean's selected them as the "newsmakers of the year." Their ap-

Queen Mother, an unintended cover up

Canada

pearance on Parliament Hill on Canada Day, July 1, attracted 300,000 well-wishers, many shouting "Will and Kate." Ordinarily, about 50,000 show up as Will and Kate set aside much of the usual royal etiquette: the duchess greeted a group of veterans in Ottawa by telling them to "call me Kate." They hugged each other openly, and they ate in public, something that would once have horrified royal watchers. William flew a Sea King helicopter on Prince Edward Island, landing it on water, a tricky maneuver known as waterbirding.

In Calgary, the couple attended a stampede in cowboy garb. In the Northwest Territories, they played street hockey with youngsters and canoed on Blachford Lake. Will ended his speeches there by adding his thanks in the languages of the Dene and Inuit. Before the 9-day visit, two out of three Canadians said they would follow the royal tour; it is almost certain that many more were drawn into the magic.

In 2016, William and Kate took their children on a successful tour of the West. They were politely confronted with misdeeds committed by the British toward the indigenous people. No offense was taken when Prince George rebuffed the Prime Minister's attempt to give him a high-five.

The royal wedding of 2018 between Prince Harry and Meghan Markle delighted Canadians as it reflected an acceptance of a divorced woman of colour, and an American actress, into the Royal family. The addition of the song "Stand by Me" by an American gospel choir showed the modern nature of the British monarchy.

When Elizabeth II died on 8 September 2022, her heir and successor, Prince Charles, automatically assumed the throne of the United Kingdom and became the head of the Commonwealth of Nations. By operation of law pursuant to the Constitution Act of Canada, at that moment, Charles III also became King of Canada. On 6 May 2023, King Charles III and Queen Camilla were crowned according to the ancient order of service in Westminster Abbey, London, the church in which every English monarch has been crowned since William I the Conqueror (1066–1087).

For some Canadians, the monarchy is still an emotional and nostalgic link with their country's and the British Empire's heritage. The Queen's photo adorns the currency and hockey rinks while toasts are offered in her honor. As a democratic country without a revolutionary tradition, Canada has always taken an evolutionary view of the future and has never turned its back abruptly on its past.

It is certain that the British monarch will remain in Canada's constitution, as well as on its currency, well into the 21st century. Even if a constitutional amendment were proposed, passage would require the unanimous consent of the federal government, both houses of parliament and each of the ten provinces. Any sensible politician would prefer to jump off a cliff than to attempt to achieve such a degree of unanimity in a country like Canada.

The same procedure applies to changing the rules of royal succession. Still, none one anticipated difficulties or opposition when the government submitted legislation in February 2013 to permit the eldest born to ascend to the throne regardless of sex. The amendment, which conforms to the change in Britain and the 15 other royal realms, also allows the monarch and his or her heirs to marry a Roman Catholic, although a Catholic is still excluded from becoming sovereign.

The Governor General

Inside Canada, the Queen is represented by the governor general. The governor general normally holds office for five years, a term that can be extended for up to two years. For about 60 years, the British government decided who would occupy this post, but in 1926 the Canadian government assumed the right to select the person. Consequently, since 1952 the governor general has always been a Canadian. The position alternates between an anglophone and a francophone although by custom all must be bilingual. For example, an anglophone, Edward Schreyer, was succeeded by Madame Jeanne Sauvé. In 1990 she was followed by Ramon Hnatyshyn, who, in a break from the norm, was not fluently bilingual. His successor in 1995 was an Acadian francophone from New Brunswick, Roméo LeBlanc. In October 2010, anglophone David Johnston replaced Michaëlle Jean.

Throne Speech 2006

There is an equivalent of the governor general, called a lieutenant governor, in each of the ten provinces. This official is also nominally appointed by the Queen, but, in fact, is selected by the PM after seeking the advice of the appropriate provincial government.

In defining the job of the governor general, one only looks at the written part of the Canadian constitution, one would have the impression that this individual wields enormous power. According to the job description for governor general, this person must approve all legislative acts, appoint the PM, hire and fire cabinet members, dissolve or convoke Parliament, decide when elections are to be held and, since 1947, command Canada's armed forces. Former Governor General Michaëlle Jean provided a reminder of this latter honor in the Re-

Their Excellencies the Rt. Hon. Adrienne Clarkson, former Governor General of Canada, and her husband, Mr. John Ralston Saul   Photo: Sgt. Michel Roy

Canada

Their Excellencies the Rt. Hon. Michaëlle Jean, former Governor General of Canada, and her husband, Mr. Jean-Daniel Lafond, and daughter

membrance Day ceremony in November 2009. Standing next to Prince Charles, she presided wearing a resplendent uniform, visited Afghanistan twice, and regularly attended repatriation ceremonies to honor those soldiers killed in combat.

The governor general has almost never exercised any of the powers just delineated; paradoxically, these powers exist only as long as they are never used. This person usually acts on the "advice" of the PM, a nice way of saying that she or he almost always does what she or he is told to do. Never in Canadian history has a governor general rejected a federal bill. When delivering the Throne Speech laying out the government's policy at the beginning of each parliamentary session, the governor general merely reads word for word a speech written by the PM and cabinet and put into his or her hands. There has never been a constitutional crisis with Canada's governor generals as occurred in Australia in 1975 when Sir John Kerr dismissed the PM and commissioned the opposition leader to form the government.

At the same time, the governor general does perform a function that some Canadians still consider to be important, possessing a residue of powers called "prerogative power" that could be used in times of crisis. For example, if a group attempt to seize power unconstitutionally, the governor general could serve as a rallying point for Canadians who support the democratic form of government.

The governor general can also be useful in a time when no party leader could get enough support in the House of Commons to form a government, a collective term in Canada to refer to the PM and the cabinet, similar to what Americans mean when they speak of "the administration." In such a situation, the governor general would be charged with finding a person who could gain such support or calling a new election. When there is a government, this person invariably follows its advice; when there is none, the individual is free to act independently. When the Conservative or Tory government lost a vote of confidence in December 1979, Prime Minister Joe Clark went to the governor general to ask that a new election be called. Edward Schreyer discussed the various alternatives with Clark for almost an hour, informing him in a later phone call that he would approve of a new election.

This important role in the formation of government became the topic of intense discussion in 2004 when it became clear that no party would win a parliamentary majority. Suddenly Canadians realized that then Governor General Adrienne Clarkson's position could be more than mere pomp and ceremony. Clarkson became the one who would decide which party leader would be capable of commanding enough support in the House of Commons to conduct government business and win sufficient parliamentary votes for the longest possible time before new elections would be necessary.

If no party wins a majority of seats, it is normally the incumbent PM's privilege to approach the governor general and explain why he or she would like to continue to rule along with how this could be done. The PM would inform the governor general of the plan and commitments from other parties for support, having the authority to require such commitments be in writing or set conditions and a time limit for such commitments to be acquired.

Acting in a non-partisan manner and stressing loyalty is to Parliament, not to any particular party, a PM could turn to the head of another party with fewer seats if she or he concluded that a different leader would have a better chance of creating a stable government. Finally, a PM can defer or refuse to make last-minute patronage appointments such as ambassadorships or Senate seats that outgoing PMs often make before leaving office.

In December 2008, Governor General Michaëlle Jean had to cut short a foreign visit and return home quickly to deal with one of the biggest and most unexpected political crises in the country's history. Prime Minister Harper's minority government had strengthened its position in early elections in October 2008 only to face a possible vote of confidence on its budget because it contained no stimulus spending and sought to cut public financing for parties that the three opposition parties need more than the Conservatives. By tradition, a lost budget vote invariably leads to new elections. In an attempt to prevent such a vote, the PM sought the governor general's permission to prorogue parliament, meaning to prevent it from acting on bills or other business.

Harper's move was not unprecedented and never in history has a governor general rejected a request to prorogue. However, this was the first time such a measure was used in the midst of a political crisis over the objections of a majority in parliament. While a passionate constitutional debate throughout Canada ensued, Jean decided to allow the PM to do what he wanted. A month later the Liberals supported a revised Tory budget and the crisis subsided.

This happened again on December 30, 2009, when Harper prorogued parliament for two months ostensibly to prepare the budget. Opponents charged that it was intended to end embarrassing inquiries into charges that Canadian soldiers turned detainees over to Afghan authorities who might have then tortured them. Such a shutdown means that all committees in both houses are disbanded, and government bills die. This was a break with tradition because such proroguing usually occurs only after most of the legislative business has been completed.

A letter signed by over 200 political and constitutional experts alleged that the PM sought to evade democratic accountability." Subsequently, a March 2010 poll revealed that 57% of Canadians thought parliament should limit the prime minister's powers. A further break in tradition was that the PM phoned the governor general to get her permission rather than appearing before her in person. This was interpreted as gravely insulting.

In performing the duties of the office, a governor general has the same right as the British Queen "to be informed, to advise and to warn." As a rule, the PM meets with the governor general least every other week to provide an update on the political situation. Every three months the governor general dutifully sends the Queen a report on the political and economic situation in Canada. The extent to which a governor general could influence a PM would, of course, depend on the rapport they share. Because the governor general was not a member of the same political party as Brian Mulroney, Jeanne Sauvé was said to have had little influence. In one celebrated snub, she was even excluded from the ceremonies surrounding the American president's visit to Quebec City in March 1985. By contrast, because Hnatyshyn was Mulroney's leader in the House of Commons from 1984–86 and his justice minister from 1986–88, when he lost his seat in parliament, he therefore had more influence on the PM.

Canada

Canadian governors general are usually leading politicians in their own right who have been appointed because of their political service to the country. Schreyer was one of the *New Democratic Party's* (NDP) most successful politicians and had been the premier of Manitoba. He was the first westerner to be appointed, a symbol of the West's rising importance in Canadian politics. He was also a non-white Anglo-Saxon Protestant such that his appointment was a form of recognition that Canadians of British descent are a minority today.

Jeanne Sauvé was perhaps the most successful female politician in Canadian history whose appointment in 1983 was greeted by all major parties. She was almost too good to be true: born in the francophone community of Prud'homme, Saskatchewan, she was the second westerner in a row to serve. Sauvé rose to prominence as a journalist and Liberal Party politician in Quebec, and in the 1970s she had held various portfolios in Trudeau's cabinet; she was only the third female and the first Quebec woman ever to sit in the cabinet. In 1980, Sauvé became the first woman ever to serve as speaker of the House of Commons. Her impartial and competent performance in that trying job marked her as an ideal candidate for the position of governor general. In 1988 she became the first governor general ever to make a state visit to France.

The governor general's most frequent role is a ceremonial one demonstrated by having to entertain important foreign dignitaries, support many worthy causes and events, confer honors and awards Canadians who have distinguished themselves in various walks of life, cut ribbons, and opens new hospitals and museums. For these functions, the governor general is housed in Rideau Hall, an estate on 88 acres, across from the PM's residence at 24 Sussex Drive, a building "guarded" by red-coated soldiers wearing bearskin hats and is surrounded by woods, a park, a skating rink, toboggan slide, cricket field, tennis courts and three greenhouses. A governor general conducts a great deal of business in the main ballroom underneath a 12,000-piece crystal chandelier with two massive paintings on each end of the room: one a portrait of Queen Elizabeth II and the Duke of Edinburgh and the other of the Fathers of Confederation, entitled *Charlottetown Revisited*. The governor general also has a secondary residence inside The Citadel in Quebec City with a staff of about 100 and a budget of about $5,00,000.

A governor general's ceremonial activities are a full-time job and unquestionably take a heavy burden from the shoulders of the PM. For instance, Adrienne Clarkson participated in 908 events during 2003,

President Obama and former Governor General Jean in Ottawa, February 2009

three times as many as her predecessors, an average of 17 per week. For some Canadians, though, a governor general's most important function is to link Canada with the majesty of its past.

Few people can fail to be impressed with the spectacle of a governor general riding in a brilliant carriage to Parliament who then proceeds with much fanfare to the throne in the ornate Senate chamber; in British tradition, she or he is not permitted to set foot in the House of Commons. A governor general then sends a messenger to the House, instructing it to choose a speaker. Later in the day the governor general invites the Members of Parliament (MPs) to come to the bar of the door to the Senate to hear a speech in both English and French, even though everybody knows that it was written by the PM's staff.

Queen's University historian David Mitchell argues that the job of the governor general is actually harder than it looks because the individual faces two contradictory expectations: if one presents oneself royally, then the governor general appears to be embracing the lofty position too enthusiastically. Conversely, if a governor general fails to read the Throne Speech with verve, then he or she is perceived of demeaning the institution.

At the conclusion of the speech, the governor general leaves and the MPs return to the House of Commons. There, again in accordance with three centuries of British parliamentary tradition, the PM promptly introduces a dummy bill, usually a "Bill Respecting the Administration of the Oaths of Office," which is then forgotten by all. This is done to prove that the House has the right to discuss anything it wishes before turning to the monarch's concerns. The MPs then begin to discuss the points made in the governor general's speech.

A governor general is expected to be absolutely impartial, a frustrating experience for politicians. As a former incumbent, Earl Grey, once said, the essential task is walking "the tightrope of platitudinous generalities." *Maclean's* even wrote about "the governor of generality." Canada's 15th governor general, Lord Tweedsmuir, counted the days when he could again be "a free and independent politician" to "liberate my mind on any subject, anywhere, at any time, at any length I please."

Schreyer had wanted to change this by speaking out on the country's pressing issues, but he found himself in a minefield every time he did so. His press conference in 1981, the first ever for a governor general, was not well received, and the Prime Minister's Office (PMO) insisted on absolute control over any of his formal statements. When he indicated that he would have forced an election if Trudeau had attempted to ram his constitutional changes through Parliament in the face of provincial opposition, he was criticized by virtually everybody.

The idea that Schreyer might actually use any of his formal powers was unthinkable. Even Quebec Premier René Lévesque, who did not like at all what Trudeau was doing, told Schreyer in 1982 to return to his "normal occupation—sleeping." From every direction, he was consistently criticized for either not saying enough, for saying too much or for saying the wrong thing. As one of Schreyer's aides noted, the job would drive anyone "stark raving mad from boredom."

In a classic text, *The Government of Canada*, Professor R. MacGregor Dawson wrote that the governor general is "the social head of the country and has always been supposed to exercise moral leadership as well." It is difficult to exercise moral leadership when one is not permitted to express opinions. There is another problem in knowing what it means to be the "social head of the country." Canada is a predominantly middle-class country. Many Canadians preferred Schreyer's kind of down-to-earth style which did not restrain children and dogs from charging through the ballroom or which permitted him and his wife to invite ordinary Cana-

Canada

dians, friends, and family to Rideau Hall for a party or an overnight stay.

Richard Gwyn, columnist for the *Ottawa Citizen*, spoke for many Canadians when he said of all the regal glitter and dressy tea parties: *c'est magnifique, mais ce n'est pas le Canada!* or "It's magnificent, but it's not Canada!" Others preferred the sophisticated elegance and impeccable propriety the gracious and polished Sauvé brought to Rideau Hall. The only certainty is that no matter what kind of style the governor general sets, it will not be right for all Canadians. After completing his "damned if you do, damned if you don't" job, Schreyer sardonically thanked all those who had given him "free advice" on his shortcomings as in his role and took his leave.

The next governor general, Roméo LeBlanc, was a former journalist, fisheries minister, Senate speaker, and political ally of former Prime Minister Jean Chrétien. One of seven children of subsistence farmers, he was the first Acadian to occupy the position. LeBlanc's appointment was intended to send a clear political message to *Québécois* at a critical juncture in Canadian history: Acadians and their culture have prospered *within* the Canadian Confederation.

In 1999, LeBlanc was succeeded by the very embodiment of the immigrant success story, Adrienne Clarkson. Born in Hong Kong, she escaped with her family in 1942. Clarkson made her mark in Canada as a talented and strong-willed broadcaster, writer, publisher and diplomat. She is the first member of a visible minority to hold the position and only the second woman. In her inauguration, she described a Canada that is a work in progress that was originally built on the French, English, and aboriginal cultures, but was expanding to include all colors and religions, with immigrant parents like hers "dreaming their children into being Canadians."

Most agree that Clarkson performed her duties with elegance, intelligence, diligence, and a sense of purpose. She even criticized America in her regal style: "Our cold climate has created our character, that sense of solidarity. America isn't as cold as we are." In describing her performance in office, *Maclean's* called Clarkson "simply the best." At the end of her five-year term in October 2004, Prime Minister Paul Martin secured the Queen's consent and asked the much-loved governor-general to remain in office for an unusual sixth year. He wanted the experienced Clarkson on hand during the experiment with minority government after the June 2004 elections.

Canadians are somewhat ambivalent about the post of governor general; in a 2010 poll, a quarter of them considered the position to be "useless." It is difficult for an incumbent to exercise moral authority and leadership when the public questions the position's legitimacy. This is why outgoing Governor General Adrienne Clarkson proposed that the choice be subject to public review and ratification by Parliament. Clarkson suggested that the PM present a name to a parliamentary committee, which would study the candidate's suitability for the position. Then the committee's recommendation would be put to a vote of the entire Parliament. Without such a reform, there is no consultation or review; a PM simply decides whom to select wants, and the Queen always approves.

In September 2005, a young, charismatic, soft-spoken, multilingual woman who spoke French, Creole, English, Spanish, Portuguese, and Italian, a former TV journalist in Quebec, Michaëlle Jean, became Clarkson's successor. The story of her life is remarkable, coming to Quebec as a young Haitian refugee, working with battered women and supporting causes to improve the lot of the downtrodden.

Jean had some frantic explaining to do when a separatist magazine, *Le Québécois*, claimed that she and her controversial award-winning French filmmaker husband, Jean-Daniel Lafond, had supported Quebec independence. The evidence came from one of his documentaries in 1991, *La Manière Nègre*, showing him and Jean toasting Quebec separatists. He also wrote in a book soon thereafter: "So, a sovereign Quebec? An independent Quebec. Yes, I applaud with both hands." Only after Jean issued a formal statement that she and her husband had "never belonged to a political party or the separatist movement" and were "fully committed to Canada" could majority public opinion accept her, and her appointment could move forward.

In her installation speech to parliament, Jean declared that the earlier "two solitudes" were over a last, and she called for an end to ethnic and linguistic divisions. The *Globe and Mail* applauded her for personifying "the free and open country Canada wants to be." Jean was a good listener, and in office she agreed to pass on to the PM concerns expressed to her by such advocacy groups as those supporting the homeless and subsidized housing in Quebec. Given her reportedly strained relationship with Prime Minister Harper, it is uncertain how this information was received.

Some Canadians questioned whether such activity is compatible with her largely neutral ceremonial role. Queen's University constitutional expert Ned Franks argued that such actions are indeed within the bounds of the governor general's functions. In his words, a governor general has the often ignored role "to represent Canada and Canadians to government." In 2014, Jean was chosen as secretary-general of La Francophonie.

On October 1, 2010, David Johnston was sworn in as governor general at age 69. Born in a small town in northern Ontario, he went on to become a two-time All-American and Hall of Fame hockey player at Harvard. Johnston was also educated at Cambridge and Queen's Universities. The long-time principal, or second in charge, of McGill University in Montreal and then president of another of Canada's best universities, Waterloo, he is regarded as one of Canada's leading advocates of higher education, possessing 13 honorary degrees to prove it. In 1995, Johnston took leave from McGill to head up the "no" campaign during the cliff-hanging Quebec referendum. "I guess I was driven by the sense of this marvelous country breaking up."

Johnston is also a former law professor, making him especially qualified to deal with the kind of tough constitutional issues a governor general must now tackle such as when it is legitimate for a PM to prorogue parliament, at what time can one say a government has lost the confidence of the House of Commons, and whether governor general always follow a PM's advice? His predecessor had to call in expert advice on these questions; Johnson is himself a constitutional expert.

In order to ensure that the new governor general would have unquestioned authority in the office and be independent of party, the Harper government appointed an independent expert committee to vet and recommend the best candidates. Political staffers were kept out of the process. Harper's spokesman made it clear: "This is not about politics." Commenting on the result, a former Liberal Justice Minister, Irwin Cotler, admitted: "I can't think of a better choice." A near majority (49.3%) of respondents agreed that "he's an impeccable choice."

Maclean's described the position in these terms: "The job is, by turns, ceremonial and essential, powerless and unifying. Governors General must assert themselves, but not too much. They can rally us to causes, but they mustn't get involved in the politics of the day. They represent the Crown, but may also speak on behalf of the people. Whoever they were before, they suddenly have medals pinned to their chest and people are compelled to stand when His (or Her) Excellency enters a room. It is an odd job."

On July 26, 2021, Mary Simon became Canada's 30th governor general. Her biography reads (Retrieved from: www.gg.ca/en/governor-general/governor-general-mary-may-simon/biography):

Her Excellency the Right Honourable Mary May Simon was sworn in on July 26, 2021, as Canada's first Indigenous governor general. She is the 30th governor general since Confederation. Mary Simon

Canada

Her Excellency the Right Honourable Mary Simon, C.C., C.M.M., C.O.M., O.Q., C.D., Governor General and Commander-in-Chief of Canada
Photo credit: Sgt Johanie Maheu, Rideau Hall
© OSGG-BSGG, 202

was born on August 21, 1947, in Kangiqsualujjuaq, Nunavik (Quebec), to Nancy May (Angnatuk-Askew), her Inuk mother, and Bob Mardon May, her father, who moved to the Arctic to work for the Hudson's Bay Company. Ms. Simon gained national and international recognition for her work on Arctic and Indigenous issues and for her efforts in advocating for Inuit rights, youth, education and culture. Ms. Simon began her career as a radio broadcaster with the CBC Northern Service (now CBC North) in the 1970s. Following this, she held a series of executive positions with the Northern Quebec Inuit Association (now Makivik Corporation) and Inuit Tapiriit Kanatami, which centred on negotiating the first land claims agreement in Canada, the James Bay and Northern Quebec Agreement.

As president of Makivik Corporation, she was directly involved with the implementation of the agreement, along with the protection and promotion of Inuit rights. Along with fellow Indigenous leaders, Ms. Simon was also actively involved in the negotiations leading to the 1982 patriation of the Canadian Constitution, which formally entrenched Aboriginal and treaty rights in the supreme law of Canada.

Ms. Simon later joined the executive council of the Inuit Circumpolar Conference (now the Inuit Circumpolar Council), for which she served two terms as president. In addition, she was commissioner of the Nunavut Implementation Commission and policy co-director of the Royal Commission on Aboriginal Peoples. From 1994 to 2003, Ms. Simon served as ambassador for Circumpolar Affairs, becoming the first Inuk to hold an ambassadorial position.

During this time, Ms. Simon negotiated the creation of the Arctic Council. Concurrently, she served as ambassador of Canada to Denmark from 1999 to 2001. Beginning in 2006, Ms. Simon served two terms as president of Inuit Tapiriit Kanatami. In 2008, in the House of Commons, she delivered a response on behalf of Inuit to the formal apology on residential schools. She is the founder of the Arctic Children and Youth Foundation and, until 2014, she was the chairperson of the National Committee on Inuit Education.

In 2017, as the Minister's Special Representative, Ms. Simon delivered a report to the Minister of Indigenous and Northern Affairs on A New Shared Arctic Leadership Model, setting the stage for important policy and program development in support of the Arctic and its residents. Among other distinctions, Ms. Simon is an Officer of the Ordre national du Québec. She is also a recipient of the Governor General's Northern Medal, the Gold Order of Greenland, the National Aboriginal Achievement Award, the Gold Medal of the Canadian Geographical Society and the Symons Medal. Upon becoming governor general, Ms. Simon was promoted by Her Majesty The Queen as Companion of the Order of Canada (C.C.), and invested as Commander of the Order of Military Merit (C.M.M.) and Commander of the Order of Merit for Police Forces (C.O.M.). Her Majesty The Queen is the Sovereign of these Orders.

Ms. Simon plays the accordion and loves nature and berry picking. She is anaana (mother) to a daughter and two sons, anaanatsiaq (grandmother) to 12 children and amauq (great-grandmother) to four children. She also has three stepchildren from her marriage in 1994 to Mr. Whit Grant Fraser, former head of the Canadian Polar Commission, former executive director of Inuit Tapiriit Kanatami and a long-time former CBC journalist.

THE POLITICAL EXECUTIVE

On an official visit to Paris in October 2009, Governor General Jean twice referred to herself as Canada's "head of state." The PMO and the Monarchist League of Canada reminded her immediately that that title belonged to Queen Elizabeth II (and now belongs to King Charles III), not to the governor general. Surprisingly, a December 2008 poll revealed that only 24% of Canadians knew this. Almost twice that percentage thought the PM was head of state, and one-third thought it was the governor general. Almost a year later, 30% of respondents in another poll answered that they could not care less about such ceremonial titles.

There is obviously some confusion in Canada about the precise distinction between a formal executive or head of state, who has a largely ceremonial function, and a political executive or head of government who actually makes policy and wields power. The confusion about these roles stems no doubt from the fact that the PM is the undisputed nerve center of the entire Canadian political system. Within the government, the PM is far more than "first among equals" as he used to be called, the towering political figure. Indeed, in federal elections, many Canadians vote according to whom they want as PM, not for whom they wish to be their local representatives in the House of Commons. Most PM serve a long time in office. Those who can survive the first few months have averaged eight years; four were in power for 15 years or more.

Since 1951, the PM and family are housed in an imposing residence at 24

24 Sussex Drive, residence of the prime minister
Photo: J.M. Carisse

Canada

Sussex Drive on the bluffs overlooking the Ottawa River, built in 1868 by a lumber baron named Joseph Merrill Currier, a member of parliament (MP). Not having been built to house the country's top leader, it is said to oppress those who live there. The building was drafty, its walls were lined with asbestos, lacked fire sprinklers, and was in desperate need of repairs to the tune of $12 million. Prime Minister Justin Trudeau's family had to move into another government house, the Rideau Cottage behind Rideau Hall, while waiting for completion of the repairs. Not far away is Stornaway, the official residence of the opposition leader. The PM has an official summer residence at Harington Lake in Gatineau Park, Quebec.

The PM's immense power comes from six sources. First, the PM is the head of his party. Second, the PM's party either has a majority of seats or more seats than any other party in the House of Commons. In the U.S., it is possible for the president to be of one party and for one or both houses of congress to be controlled by the other party, a situation that reduces the ability to enact policy. This is never the case in Canada, where a person is PM by virtue of being the leader of the party with the majority of votes in the lower house. The majority in the House expresses confidence in a PM by voting in favor of bills the PM supports. PMs who lose "a vote of confidence" are replaced or new elections are called, a matter that is resolved within a matter of weeks.

The Canadian leader can control a party for various reasons. At election time the "coat-tails" effect is strong in Canada, and many MPs are elected because of the popularity of their leader. This was especially true in the 2015 elections in which over a hundred Liberals were swept into office by the popularity of Justin Trudeau. Many MPs elected that way depend on the leader's success to advance their own political careers.

The PM, who by tradition must have a seat in the House of Commons or get one within a reasonable time, can also rely on "party discipline" to keep party members in the House of Commons loyal. A government stands or falls depending on whether it retains its majority in the House of Commons. Therefore, it is a serious matter when a MP votes against the party on an important vote. The party could halt an MP's political advancement and deny the member a variety of perks. Therefore, most MPs would never consider voting against their party. Historian Christopher Moore wrote: "The night they are elected you know what an MP is going to do for the next four years: vote how the government tells it, whenever it needs it. They should just fax in their votes if that's all they're going to do."

The third source of the PM's power is the fact that this person is not only the country's chief executive, but its chief legislator as well. The PM and the cabinet draft all the important legislation the two houses of Parliament, the House of Commons and the Senate, consider. Until 2002, the PM could also appoint all committee chairmen. However, in a rare backbench rebellion against Prime Minister Chrétien, many in his own party supported an opposition motion to give MPs the right to elect committee chairmen of their own choice.

For Americans who value the notion of "separation of powers" as a necessary safeguard against tyranny, the Canadian fusion of executive and legislative powers seems surprising. Still, the benefit of such fusion, inherited from Britain, is a much greater degree of government efficiency. The kind of prolonged deadlocks between the president and congress are unknown in Canada, whose governments are given much power and are expected to get on with their work. For example, if a PM's party could win as many votes as President Barack Obama did in 2008 at 52.5%, the government could command an overwhelming majority of seats in Commons. In 2015, the Liberals won only 39.5% of the votes, but were awarded 184 out 338 seats allowing it to achieve most of its legislative goals.

The fourth source of a PM's authority is the power to appoint all Senators, Supreme Court justices, federal judges, the governor general, the chief of the defense staff, and the RCMP commissioner. The PM has the final approval over the placement of every senior public servant and controls thousands of appointments to public agencies and commissions. In addition, the PM has the exclusive right to deal with the governor general; any member of the government can have access to the formal executive only through the PM.

At the same time, the PM can determine when elections will be held as long as one is held within five years and with the approval of the governor general, which is not necessarily automatic. Unlike in the U.S., where congressmen and Senators are elected for fixed terms, in Canada nobody above the level of mayor is ever elected for a fixed term. In some cases, the cabinet can help influence a PM on when to call an election, as it did when John Turner announced an early election in 1984. Even so, PMs usually reserves this privilege for themselves; this is a powerful weapon not only for keeping the opposition off guard, but also for securing the loyalty of one's own party members in Parliament, who dread having to go on the hustings too often.

Former Prime Minister Stephen Harper was committed to democratizing governmental institutions. Under Harper's leadership, Supreme Court nominees were supposed to have been subject to review by a parliamentary committee' Further, he proposed filling vacant Senate seats by elections and limiting Senatorial terms to eight years. Yet, he found it expedient to violate these pledges.

Three months after taking office in February 2006, Harper announced bills allowing elections to take place at fixed four-yearly intervals and this became law but because this did not amend the constitution, it could always be changed. The PM could also call an election on losing a vote of confidence. All parties supported this but the Liberals, who accused Harper of trying to make Canada be like the U.S., always a potent charge. A majority of Canadians told pollsters they favored this reform. Three provinces had already adopted fixed election dates. Harper decided on his own, though, to strengthen his mandate by calling new elections a year earlier, on October 14, 2008, and again on

Chamber of the House of Commons
Public Archives Canada/PA51823

Canada

Justin Trudeau

May 2, 2011. The 2006 election laws were no obstacle. The October 2015 voting was the first fixed-term election.

The fifth source of power is the fact that the PM is the center of publicity. Especially in the era of television, the PM is always in the limelight; in fact, the enormous growth of the modern PM's awesome political power has coincided with the advancement of television. No other political figure can begin to compete with him in terms of media exposure, except during election campaigns, which in Canada normally last only seven or eight weeks. Today, a successful PM must learn to use television effectively and to cultivate his image carefully. Mulroney was reported to be particularly obsessed with and adept at this. He read dozens of newspapers and magazines each week and watched all national news broadcasts in both English and French to monitor what kind of image he was projecting.

The sixth, and final, source of power for a PM is the ability to select, and dominate, the cabinet, which is the real executive of Canada. Cabinet members are usually prominent political figures. Unlike in the U.S., cabinet members do meet and decide on overall policy. Because they must be familiar with many different issues, from foreign, defense and economic policy, to the state's treatment of aboriginal peoples, they are normally "generalists," rather than specialists in one field. Nevertheless, the PM decides what the political agenda will be along with a sense of the cabinet on a particular issue.

Members of the cabinet cannot publicly criticize the PM due to the principle of "collective responsibility." This means that once a decision has been made, all members of the government are obligated to support it. The whole cabinet takes public responsibility for a policy, regardless of whether each individual member agrees with it. Even if cabinet member were to resign voluntarily, they are not permitted to reveal their grounds for doing so unless the PM freed them from the oath of secrecy they took on assuming office cabinet members are protected from removal by the House of Commons by the fact that if a single member were to lose the confidence of the House, then the entire government would have to resign. Only once in Canada's history, in 1896, has a cabinet ever forced a PM to resign.

Much more important, the PM hires and fires cabinet members. Also, as evidenced by Prime Minister Justin Trudeau's removal of two former cabinet ministers, Jody Wilson-Raybould and Jane Philpott, he can unilaterally remove members from the Liberal caucus. Their resignations from the Liberal cabinet were principiated by what former solicitor general and minister of justice Raybould saw as undue influence from the PM office regarding a criminal case about a Quebec multinational business. That business was a SNC-Lavalin, which was seeking a remediation agreement to pay fines and agree to other terms in order to end the prosecution against it which was based on corruption, the payment of funds to the Gaddafi family for contracts in Libya.

Both ministers were later dismissed from the Liberal caucus. This was a huge scandal where, due to cabinet confidentiality and solicitor-client privilege, former minister Raybould was only able to give a partial accounting of events and where due to cabinet confidentiality, former minister Philpott was also unable to "speak all of her truth" in public. The PM's office stropped a complete investigation by the House of Commons Justice Committee and the Ethics Committee.

This case raised serious concerns in Canada's legal community as it goes to the root of an independent justice system in Canada which means that all politicians must not attempt to influence Crown Prosecutors when they exercise their judgment after due deliberation and a final decision having been made. This would not preclude discussion prior to a final decision having been made by the Solicitor General but not thereafter. Clearly, the Canadian political system must follow the lead from the United Kingdom and separate the two portfolios of Minister of Justice, a political position, and Solicitor general, an independent judicial position).

A PM can select how many members to include in the cabinet; in 1984 Mulroney chose 40 while Prime Minister Jean Chrétien appointed only 22 because he wanted to underscore his seriousness about tightening federal government operations. Paul Martin chose in 2004 to appoint 39 to his cabinet. In 2015, Justin Trudeau appointed 30 ministers; half were women, four were Sikhs, two were aboriginal, two were disabled, one is openly gay, and one was an Afghan female Muslim. Former Liberal leader Stéphane Dion was named foreign minister.

In a key duty, because a PM determines which assignments, or portfolios, cabinet members receive, these decisions can make or break political careers. A minister of state for fitness, for instance, will have far less visibility and influence than a justice minister. Also, some posts are extremely important but are so exposed to public scrutiny and criticism that they are considered to be professional suicide. The most prominent of these is the Ministry of Finance. Few PM were ever finance ministers. Recent exceptions were Jean Chrétien, who had been entrusted with all major portfolios at one time or other during the Trudeau era, and Paul Martin. Certain portfolios are traditionally reserved for specific regions: fisheries are usually cared for by someone from the Maritimes or British Columbia and agriculture is for a westerner. The finance minister is usually an MP from Ontario with good business connections.

Despite the power of PMs to select cabinet members, they must observe certain traditions which do restrict choices somewhat. Because Canada's major parties are large, they include members of diverse ideological persuasions. Most PMs try to include all such directions in their cabinets in order to maintain party unity. It is also a wise move for PMs to muzzle certain vocal critics from within their parties by including them in the cabinet and thereby throwing the blanket of collective responsibility over their heads.

A far more important restraint, though, is the "representation principle." This is natural for a country as geographically and demographically diverse as Canada. Although there are no hard and fast rules, most regional, provincial, territorial, social, and economic interests in the country are represented in the cabinet. Each province

Canada

should have at least one representative, although tiny Prince Edward Island has often gone without one. If a ruling party did not elect a single MP in a given province, as was the case for years with the Liberal Party in the West and in Nova Scotia in 1997, then Senators from those provinces can be included in the cabinet.

The two giants in the federation, Ontario and Quebec, which have two-thirds of the seats in the House of Commons, usually receive about ten cabinet seats. These members are chosen from different regions and cities from within those provinces to make representation as dispersed as possible. Major cities like Montreal and Toronto usually have more people in the cabinet than do all the Atlantic provinces put together.

In Jean Chrétien's cabinet that was sworn in after his reelection victory in 1997, for example, there were 27 senior and eight junior ministers, called secretaries of state. Twelve were from Ontario and four, plus Chrétien, from Quebec. He appointed four of the 11 Liberal MPs elected in Atlantic Canada. In an effort to reach out to the restless western provinces, he tapped nine of the 15 Liberal MPs elected in the West.

In 2006, Stephen Harper named a cabinet of 27 ministers reflecting a broad geographic distribution rather than over-representing the West, from where the majority of his government's seats came. The Tories won none of the 48 seats in Montreal, Toronto and Vancouver. Yet, he wanted someone in his cabinet from Montreal, so he appointed an unelected Tory co-chairman, Michael Fortier, to the Senate and brought him into his cabinet as public works minister. In order to have someone from Vancouver, he lured David Emerson from the preceding Liberal Party cabinet, pronounced him a Tory and made him minister for trade and the "Pacific Gateway." Harper selected six women and two Asian-Canadians for his cabinet. Justin Trudeau named 15.

The "representational principle" obviously has its advantages and disadvantages. In a country as diverse as Canada, every tool of unity is beneficial. Cabinet members are expected to support the interests of their region and social group. This is particularly important because the Senate cannot effectively perform this function. Some critics of Canadian government have argued that the provinces have far too little influence over federal politics; the cabinet is a place where at least some attention is paid to their interests.

At the same time, some cabinet members are named as "political ministers," charged with the responsibility to help organize the provincial parties and to oversee patronage appointments in the provinces. This means that the central government tries to influence the provinces, just as the provinces try to influence it. Disadvantages also include the growth of the cabinet to accommodate so many representatives. Some people fear that this makes the cabinets unwieldy. Finally, a PM is unable to choose the best person for a particular job; it may be more important to select a person for a ministry because he is an English-speaking Quebecer rather than because he is an expert in the portfolio he is assigned.

A seventh source of a PM's power is the ability to command of a multifaceted staff. Since Pierre Elliot Trudeau became PM in 1968, two offices have grown enormously in power: the PMO and the Privy Council Office (PCO). He increased their size and importance in order to get policy recommendations independent of the more entrenched civil service. The PMO, made up of the leader's major advisers and aides, who are political appointees, not civil servants, became the more powerful of the two. Its members do everything from answering mail and making travel arrangements to making policy recommendations and ensuring governmental unity.

Many Canadians, including Brian Mulroney, criticized the size and power of the PMO, charging that it was too costly and undercut the power of the cabinet and Parliament. Once in power, though, Mulroney made it even larger, costlier, and more powerful. In 1985 it had 114 members, as opposed to 90 under Pierre Trudeau and 57 under John Turner. It included a special office and two aides for the PM's wife, Mila. More significant, the political operations of the office have been strengthened, employing 13 policy advisers, instead of the three under Pierre Trudeau. It had the added responsibility of reviewing all cabinet members' major press statements before they were released and also cleared all patronage appointments and senior hiring by cabinet members. Some critics in the opposition and bureaucracy charged that this powerful center had become almost like a presidential White House staff.

The PMO lost none of its power under Prime Minister Jean Chrétien whose popularity had always been bolstered by his image as a humble man of the people. Former top civil servant, Gordon Robertson, who served PMs from Mackenzie King to Trudeau, said in 1998, "the concentration of power in the hands of this prime minister is as great as I have ever seen it."

Traditionally, the PCO has been the clearinghouse and coordinating agency for proposals and ideas from the cabinet and various committees. The most important are cabinet committees, which are smaller than the full cabinet. They can discuss matters more informally before they are brought to the attention of the full cabinet. The names, membership, precise organization and functions of these committees change with PMs. They usually deal with such matters as priorities and legislative planning, federal-provincial relations, economic and social policy and government operations.

The work of cabinet committees was normally supported by about 350 civil servants and employees in the PCO who prepared and circulated documents to ministers and the committees. Moreover, the PCO provides clerical and record-keeping back-up to ministers. It used to be almost exclusively responsible for briefing the PM on matters that were about to be discussed by the cabinet. Chrétien selected a bilingual microbiologist, Jocelyne Bourgon, to be clerk of the PCO. The first woman to hold the job, she was responsible for over 200,000 civil servants.

In addition to selecting his inner staff, the PM can make at least 3,500 "order-in-council" appointments, including about 500 high-level positions, such as ambassadors, Senators, judges and heads of key government agencies. PMs are technically free to hand out patronage appointments as they please, but both Trudeau and Mulroney were frequently criticized for their lavish hand-outs. Mulroney had made a campaign promise to give Parliament some say in the process, but only after much public grumbling about his own appointment practices did he consent to a procedure whereby all-party parliamentary committees would be permitted to review all appointees' qualifications.

The largest reservoir of support and information for the PM is the federal civil service, which has grown so fast in modern times that now one million Canadians, or one out of ten persons of working age, are employed by a government at some level. One of 50 Canadians works directly for a federal department or agency. Since Confederation in 1867, the Canadian population has increased seven-fold while the civil service has increased a hundred-fold. This growth reflects the fact that Canadian government has become far more active in such fields as social welfare, the economy, education, and language rights. Many people are skeptical that such a gigantic body of workers can be effectively controlled by anybody. People are particularly skeptical about the possibility of controlling the many Crown corporations which are wholly or partially owned by the state and whose directors are appointed by the PM and his government. Few would doubt, though, that the PM has more influence over the civil service than any other Canadian.

At the head of each department is a cabinet minister. The minister brings with some aides who are responsible to him or her. Ministers are also assisted by some

Canada

"parliamentary secretaries," who are MPs without cabinet seats. Since these latter positions are excellent opportunities for newer MPs to demonstrate their talent, a minister can usually count on good work from them. The second highest positions within ministries are the deputy ministers, career civil servant at the top of the promotion ladder. They are so important that they are often referred to as "Mandarins," reminiscent of the wise and powerful advisers to the Chinese emperors.

Deputy ministers are appointed, and can be removed, by the PM. Even so, they are supposed to serve any government and are usually non-partisan, even though they are active participants in policy making. The deputy ministers have usually directed the day-to-day operations of the department for years, so their expertise is badly needed by the cabinet ministers who, most often, are not specialists in the field for which they are responsible.

When a government changes, PMs usually replace a few deputy ministers. They are merely transferred to other civil service posts, because they cannot be fired. Still, the number of such changes is usually low. For instance, after coming out of the wilderness of 16 years in opposition, the Conservatives, under Prime Minister Joe Clark, replaced only three deputy ministers. Far fewer heads roll in Ottawa after a parliamentary election than in Washington after a presidential election. There is no "revolving door" in Canadian politics.

Entry based on competitive examinations and promotion based on performance and bilingualism has placed severe limits on the spoils system. These criteria have helped to produce civil servants who, by comparison with most other countries, are efficient, impartial, and able. Civil servants are kept honest and incorruptible by being paid better than their counterparts anywhere else in the world. They have handsome fringe benefits, have almost complete job security, and can retire as early as age 55 with pensions indexed to inflation. A sign of the high quality of Canada's civil service is shown by the fact that few Canadians propose radical changes in it, even though some often complain, that the government has grown too large. Finally, to the disappointment of gossip columnists, financial and sexual scandals involving civil servants are almost unknown in Ottawa.

PARLIAMENT

Canada has a bicameral parliament, but unlike in the American system, both houses are not equal in power. The House of Commons is by far the more important chamber. In parliamentary elections, which must be held at least every five years, citizens who are 18 or older vote for an MP in each of 338 constituencies, called "ridings" and increased from 295 in 1997 and 301 in 2004 to 308 in 2006 and 338 in 2015. Voters in Canada do not vote directly for PMs; only voters in their own ridings vote for them.

Counting the votes is not as complicated as in the U.S. Canadians have a uniform voting system in the entire country. Citizens vote with pencil and paper, marking an "X" next to the name of the desired candidate. All votes are counted by hand with results being known within hours, not weeks.

The system of election is the single member district or "first past the post," an electoral method now used only in the UK, the U.S., and New Zealand. The candidate with the most votes in each riding is elected, even if the individual wins fewer than 50% of the votes. This electoral system has the advantage of preventing many parties from gaining seats in Parliament, therefore enhances political stability. Insofar as one or the other of the large parties usually has a majority in the House of Commons, there has never been the need for a coalition government to rule in Canada. Even if one party does not win a majority of seats, the custom is for the one with the most seats to form a "minority government." This leads a precarious existence for a while, relying on votes from another party.

SEATS IN THE HOUSE OF COMMONS

Some critics rightly point out that this electoral system enables the two larger parties to win a far higher percentage of parliamentary seats than the percentage of votes they win nationally. Elections are usually won or lost by a three to four percent shift to one party or the other.

If one focuses only on the parliamentary seats which are won or change hands, rather than on the popular vote, one gets an exaggerated impression of voter volatility; sweeps are seldom as massive as they seem. For instance, Mulroney's Tories barely received 50% of votes in all of Canada in September 1984 but won 211 out of the 282 seats in the House of Commons. In 1993, the PC Party won 16% of the votes but received only two seats; the Reform Party won 18% of the votes but captured 52 seats. The Liberals captured only 38% of the votes in 1997 but still won a majority of seats with 155. The same applied in 2011 to the Conservatives, who won only 39.6% of the votes, but secured a parliamentary majority with 167 seats. In 2008, the Greens captured 6.8% of the votes but not a single seat. in 2015, the Liberals garnered only 39.5% of the votes but won 184 of 338 seats.

The same thing can happen on the provincial level. In 1985, the Liberals won more votes than the Conservatives in the Ontario provincial elections. Because of the electoral system, the Conservative Party ended up with four more seats in the provincial

Canada

legislature. Ontario's Liberals won only 46.5% of the votes in 2003, but captured 70% of the seats. In the 1998 Quebec provincial elections, the Liberals won 43.7% of the votes but captured only 48 of 125 seats. The PQ received 42.7% of the votes but garnered 76 seats and remained the governing party. In 2015, the Liberals garnered only 39.5% of the votes but won 184 of 338 seats.

Almost never does a governing party win more popular votes than the combined opposition. For example, in 2000 the Liberals won a landslide victory of 173 seats, 57% of the total by winning 41% of the votes. If Canada had a proportional representation (PR) electoral system, the Liberals would have captured 123 seats, not a majority. In June 2004 the Liberals won 36.7% of the votes and 135 seats, 44% of the total; under PR it would have earned only 116 seats. The newly formed Conservative Party captured 29.6% of the votes and was awarded 99 seats, 32% of the total; under PR 92. The *Bloc Québécois* received 12.4% of the votes in Canada and 54 seats on 17.5% because it dominated Quebec; under PR it would have had only 37. Things were worse for the NDP, which won 15.7% of the votes, but earned a mere 19 seats, 6% of the total; under PR it would have had 49. It is understandable that smaller parties do not like this system.

Precisely because the largest parties benefit from it, it is unlikely that the system will be changed. During the 2015 campaign, the Liberals promised to reform the electoral system, but there is little public support this proposition. Only 9% favored a complete overhaul. Indeed, as of 2019 it appears that this promise has been withdrawn, perhaps a wise decision by a government in power.

The distribution of seats is based on provinces' populations and is adjusted according to census figures. As of 2016, there are 338 seats in the House of Commons. Only Quebec's minimum of 75 seats are always guaranteed in order to protect the interests of the country's francophone minority; it now has 78. Ontario has 121 seats, a third of the total. Added together, both provinces' have about two-thirds of all the seats. The remaining seats are distributed approximately as follows: British Columbia 36, Alberta 28, Manitoba approximately 14, Saskatchewan 14, Nova Scotia 11, New Brunswick 10, Newfoundland 7, PEI 4, Northwest Territories 1, The Yukon 1, and Nunavut 1.

In 2011, the ruling Conservative government introduced the Fair Representation Bill, which raised the total number of seats by 30. Every ten years following a national census, redistricting changes the ridings' boundaries to reflect demographic changes. The constitution provides that no province can have fewer House seats than it had in 1986 or than it has in the Senate. This protects the smaller provinces. Alberta and British Columbia each received six more seats, Ontario thirteen and Quebec three.

Each province is represented fairly, but some ridings have more voters than others. For instance, cities, on the whole, are under-represented; in the 1979 election 81,000 persons voted in York–Scarborough, 45,000 in Vancouver Centre and only 28,000 in Gaspé, Quebec. The chief argument against making all districts equal in population is that some northern ridings would be even greater in size than they already are, thus making an MP's travel through the riding to keep in touch with his constituents almost impossible. In other words, some Canadians in such districts would be practically cut off from their government.

Election campaigns are much shorter and cheaper than in the U.S. For example, the 2000 campaign lasted only 36 days, but the one in 2015 went 78 days. Races are also more competitive. The chances for reelection were 72.5% in Canada and 98% in the U.S. Candidates for a House of Commons seat face a spending limit of about $50,000 and each national party must restrict its spending to about $8.5 million. The Harper government reduced the amount donors can give and eliminated public financing to the parties.

Salaries for the members Parliament are adjusted on the first of April each year. As 2017, members of the House of Commons in earned $172,700 salary plus tax-free benefits, Senators, who by federal law must receive $25,000 less than members of the House of Commons, received $147,700 plus benefits for Senators. and cabinet ministers earned $255,300 plus benefits. According to the 2018 budget, the PM's salary is $347,400 plus tax-free benefits.

It is often said that money is the "mother's milk of politics." Yet, money cannot ensure victories. For example, the 1993 federal parliamentary elections, the Tories spent $10.4 million to win two seats, the Liberals $9.9 million for 177, the NDP $7.4 million for nine, the *Bloc Québécois* $1.9 million for 54, and the Reform Party $1.5 million for 52.

The physical layout of the House is similar to the British House of Commons. The governing party sits to the right of the robed Speaker, directly across from the opposition parties. The government and the opposition leaders occupy the center seats in the front rows on each side of the aisles. The latter are known as the "shadow cabinet" because each cabinet member has a counterpart in the opposition. The "shadow cabinet" is ready to take office at any time.

The fact that the two sides face each other across an aisle, which, by British tradition, is the width of two sword lengths, is intended to underscore the antagonistic relationship the government and the opposition have. Observers in the galleries notice, though, that this is only political, not personal, antagonism. MPs freely cross the aisle to chat with colleagues in other parties and it is entirely normal for an MP to stand up and publicly wish a member of an opposite party good health after a serious operation or illness. This also applies to the parties' headquarters staffs, which maintain cordial relations with their counterparts in other headquarters and even provide each other with complimentary tickets to their party conferences. The fact that domestic political opponents are not regarded as enemies is one reason why democracy has functioned so well in Canada.

The PM recommends the Speaker of the House of Commons from among his party's MPs, and since 1985 must be elected by the House. All MPs except party leaders and cabinet members are automatically considered to be standing for election unless they remove their names from the list. Individuals are usually prominent members of the governing party who were passed over for cabinet posts. The speakers in both chambers normally alternate between anglophones and francophones; in the House, the deputy speaker is always be a francophone if the speaker is an anglophone and vice versa.

By tradition, the PM and the opposition leader pretend to drag a resisting new Speaker down the aisle to the ornate Speaker's chair. This quaint custom was inherited from Britain. From the 14th century, the commoners' chosen spokesman risked the ire of the monarch and was sometimes even punished on reporting what the Commons wanted.

In Canada today, the Speaker is "punished" with a high salary of $255,300 in 2017, a rambling Kingsmere estate in the Gatineau Hills 15 kilometers or 10 miles from Ottawa, and a personal staff of about 15. This includes a chauffeur for his official limousine and a *maitre d'* to provide for the constant flow of visiting foreign members of Parliament who must be entertained. Most insiders would agree that the Speaker must earn these benefits. Speakers are expected to referee parliamentary debates impartially and even to call the PM plus the government to order when they seem to be playing fast and loose with the rules. The Speaker sets the tone of the daily debates and decides whether they will be spontaneous and scrappy or formal and stiff.

Former Speaker Gilbert Parent described the House as "like a huge animal. Sometimes it lies dormant. Sometimes you prod it and it will jump up and bite you, and it's a wise Speaker who knows when

Canada

to prod and when to let it sleep." Finally, the Speaker must manage the Commons' staff of 3,000 aides, pages, police and janitors. Along with the House leaders, who are usually different from the national party leaders in order that the latter can be absent from the Commons without disrupting the House's business, and whips, which each party selects, the Speaker is a crucial participant in shaping the House's law-making process.

The Speaker breaks tie votes in the House of Commons. On May 19, 2005, a no-confidence vote to determine whether then Prime Minister Paul Martin's government would fall resulted in a 152–152 tie. Speaker Peter Milliken, a Liberal, put the government over the top with his vote. This was the first time in Canadian history that a Speaker broke a tie in a vote of no-confidence. On October 12, 2009, Milliken became the longest-serving speaker in history.

Milliken stepped down June 2, 2011, after nine years in office when then Deputy Speaker Andrew Scheer of the Conservative party was selected in his place following his party's victory in the May 2011 federal elections. At age 32, Scheer was the youngest Speaker in Canadian history and the first to hail from Saskatchewan although he grew up in Ottawa. He cracked down on hecklers, time-wasters, and MPs who demonstrate rude behavior. He became Tory party leader in 2017. In December 2015, a Liberal from Nova Scotia, Geoff Regan, became Speaker, the first person chosen from Atlantic Canada for this post in almost a century. On December 5, 2019, Anthony Rota was elected by the House of Commons to be the speaker in the 43rd Parliament. He is a member of the Liberal Party and is the MP for the district of Nipissing-Timiskaming.

The House is free to establish its own working procedures and it is carefully examining and changing the way it does its work. Many MPs travel to and from their ridings on Mondays and Fridays. Its number of sitting days has declined gradually from as many as 163 days in a year to a low of just 105 in 2008. Traditionally, the average day would unfold something like this: when Parliament is in session, the usual day begins at 2 PM, 11 AM on Fridays, when the Speaker takes the chair and the sergeant-at-arms lays the mace, a gold-plated war club and symbol of the House's authority and of continuity in an ever-changing world, on the long table in front of the Speaker's chair.

The sergeant-at-arms is usually a mere adornment. However, in October 2014 the sergeant-at-arms became a hero when a Canadian-born Islamic jihadist fatally shot a soldier guarding the National War Monument outside Parliament, entered

**The Honourable Greg Fergus, P.C., M.P
Speaker of the House of Commons**

the building with gun blazing, and terrorized the MPs, who were meeting in their weekly caucuses. Kevin Vickers crept up on the assailant outside the entrance of the parliamentary library and shot him dead. Vickers was rewarded with an ambassadorship to Ireland..

A woman trapped for hours in the parliament spoke for millions of her fellow citizens: "I never thought this would happen. This is Canada." On February 8, 2016, Vickers was presented with the Star of Courage along with six others involved in bringing the incident under control.

On March 15, 2019, Vickers announced he would run for the leadership of the New Brunswick Liberal Association to replace Brian Gallant. He was acclaimed as leader and the Liberal Party's executive board acclaimed Vickers on the recommendation by the leadership convention's steering committee on April 16, 2019, effective April 24, 2019.

After a few routine matters are completed, the question hour begins. This takes place from Mondays through Thursdays and is usually the liveliest part of the day, when the entire government and shadow cabinet are present, about 250 in all. This period, which lasts 45 minutes, is the most watched portion of each day in Ottawa. It is controlled by the opposition, which can pose any questions to any member of the government. Questions are intended to elicit information and often to embarrass the PM or cabinet members. One veteran MP confided, "the unwritten rule is never to ask a question unless you know the answer."

Sitting in his spectacular oak chair, the Speaker has a hidden computer screen in front of him with various camera angles to display the action in the House. In addition, the Speaker has a countdown clock to help limit questions and answers to 35 seconds and keep things moving briskly so that as many MPs as possible can participate. Most have no involvement, limiting their role to standing, clapping, and cheering for their party while heckling

and sneering at the other. So important is question hour for a government that Stephen Harper's cabinet became the first in history to meet every weekday after lunch to rehearse the ordeal together..

A few rules are generally observed. MPs are never to be addressed by their family names and all remarks are technically directed to the Speaker. Sometimes civility does break down. Former Prime Minister Pierre Trudeau once was likened to Hitler, a comparison that prompted the PM to invite the MP to step outside for a fight, one the MP declined. He was also compared to an organ grinder; whose cabinet members are like monkeys. Trudeau was a past master at repartee who dubbed opponents as "nobodies" and as "the honorable stinker." MPs can ask questions in either English or French, and the answers should be given in the same language, if the cabinet member can manage to do so.

The overall purpose of the rules is to keep the government responsible and responsive to the opposition and to the country. The answers the government gives during question hour are widely reported in the press. Since 1977 question hour has been televised. It is broadcast live in Ottawa from 2:15 to 3 PM, and in many parts of the huge country it appears at prime time. News programs frequently show excerpts. It is an opportune time for MPs to impress the folks back home, and the government must prepare in advance for potentially damaging questions. Question hour can be raucous at times. Asked in a 2010 poll if it had become so uncivil that it needed to be reformed, two-thirds of respondents said "yes, it's a daily embarrassment"; 21% admitted they had stopped paying attention, and only 14% said "this is politics—it's not meant to be pretty."

MPs do not pose questions to members of their own parties. Backbenchers, MPs who are in neither the government nor the shadow government, have that opportunity only in the weekly party caucuses, which are held behind closed doors and in which genuine debate occurs. The question hour is usually cut off promptly at 3 PM with the rest of day devoted to bills before a mostly deserted House. Former Prime Minister Stephen Harper, who was picked in 2012 as the best-informed MP, seldom bothered to speak in the House, except during question hour.

Most bills have been introduced by the government and must survive three separate readings in the House before they are sent to the Senate for consideration. Debates are often lively and can be conducted in either English or French. Earphones with simultaneous translations are provided for MPs and spectators needing them. MPs are generally articulate and, as in Britain, feel free to bring humor into

Canada

Senate Chamber
Public Archives Canada/PA34219

their remarks. About a third of the MPs are lawyers, with many of the rest drawn from business and the professions.

An increasing amount of legislative work is done in committees. This is in response to the growing legislative workload. The "Striking Committee" decides on the committees' membership although it takes its cues from the assignments agreed on by the parties themselves. There are "standing committees" which roughly correspond to the various cabinet portfolios such as the External Affairs and National Defence Committee.

There are usually 20 MPs on each standing committee, and the composition is determined by parties' proportionate strength in the House. These committees help refine and improve legislation, and they often call in outside experts to testify or provide opinions. Until the rules were changed in 2002, committees were never led by powerful and independent chairs who could defy their party's leadership and prevent legislation from ever getting to the whole House. Chairs are now elected by the whole House rather than being appointed by the PM.

The party leaders' control on all MPs is so strong and their claim to party discipline so sure that the government's legislation will survive all the legislative hurdles, no matter what. Debates in the whole House are lively, but the outcome of votes is seldom in doubt so long as a government maintains its majority. If the government does not maintain its majority, then it can experience some real surprises. The Canadian political system hinges on a government elected by the people which can legitimate its program in Parliament and then enact it until voted out of office.

Senate

The upper house of Parliament, the Senate, was designed in 1867 to serve two purposes: to serve as a check against "hasty or ill-considered legislation" coming from the House of Commons and to represent regional interests in the federal government. Members of the Senate come from the various regions of Canada and have the constitutional power to veto or amend legislation but lacks the authority to bring down a government by defeating a bill.

As in so many other aspects of Canadian politics, powers on paper cannot always be exercised. In fact, the Senate has never performed the two functions given it in 1867. Canada's first PM, John A. Macdonald, swore that the Senate "will never set itself in opposition against the deliberate and understood wishes of the people." It has not dared veto legislation from the House of Commons since the Second World War. In fact, the Senate has rarely amended a House bill in such a way that its principle is touched. Its legislative role has deteriorated, and its debates are seldom reported in the news media. It is not even held in high esteem.

The first reason why the Senate is not held in high esteem is that it is an appointed, not an elected body. This means that its composition does not reflect the prevailing political power in the country. For example, in 1990 Liberals outnumbered Conservatives in the Upper House by two-to-one, even though the Liberals commanded only half as many seats in the House of Commons as the PC Party. Senators are appointed by the PM, not by the provincial governments. Because the Liberals ruled almost constantly throughout the 20th century, they understandably packed the Senate with their own people. Tory Prime Minister Harper did the same in the 105-seat body. Appointments are almost invariably made on the basis of party loyalty and past service to the party in power.

A ruling party thus can dangle attractive patronage appointments to the Senate,

Canada

which promise good pay until age 75 for work which need not be terribly taxing or time-consuming. One reporter observed, "being named to the Senate in Canada is a lot like winning the cash-for-life lottery." Other cynics have called an appointment "a taskless thanks."

Liberal Senator Andrew Thompson demonstrated just how cushy the life of a Senator can be. Claiming that his health would be endangered by Ottawa's winter weather, he spent most of his time at his home in La Paz, Mexico, attending sessions only 12 times from 1990 to 1998. Astonished critics computed that his pay amounted to about $43,000 per appearance, more than his secretary earned in a year. Senate records in 1997 revealed rampant absenteeism on the part of about two dozen other members and approximately a quarter of all Senators missed at least 40% of the chamber's sessions. A furious Prime Minister Chrétien stripped Thompson of his office space, secretary, travel privileges, and seat in the Liberal caucus. But the truant legislator could not be fired.

Unlike an elected MP, a Senator can seldom be held to account. An attempt was made in 2011 when a Liberal Senator, Raymond Lavigne, sent a staffer to chop down trees at his cottage and claimed more than $30,000 in work-related expenses during a three-month period in the preceding year. After years of resistance, every Senator's expenditures are now posted online and public criticism of expense accounts remains. In 2013 four Senators were caught claiming housing and travel allowances to which they were not entitled. The PM's chief-of-staff, Nigel Wright, had to resign when it was learned that he had given one of them a personal check to cover his $92,000 reimbursement and get him off the hook.

The trend has been to appoint people in the middle, rather than at the end, of their careers. An example of a Trudeau appointment was Ann Cools, who lost her bid for a seat in the House of Commons. A former student radical, who spent time in prison for her part in the destruction of a university computer in Montreal in 1969, she was quickly pardoned before being named to the Senate. The government can also ease a cabinet member gracefully out of governmental business by appointing the person to the Red Chamber, so named after the color of its interior decor. It can even appoint a member of the opposition party in order to free a riding of an unbeatable incumbent or to sow discord in the opponents' ranks. This does not mean that Senators are not talented people; it means that they need not be so as a condition of appointment.

Senators are chosen from the various regions of the country. The Fathers of Confederation gave equal representation of 24 members to Ontario, Quebec, and the Maritime provinces, 10 from Nova Scotia, 10 from New Brunswick, and 4 from Prince Edward Island. Newfoundland was awarded six when it entered the Confederation in 1949. The West was also given 24 Senators, with each of four provinces getting six. The Yukon, Northwest Territories, and Nunavut are also represented. Quebec's allotment must be selected from each of 24 Senatorial districts.

Unlike in the U.S., where all states are represented equally in the Senate, a provision that gives enhanced power to the smaller states, senate seats in Canada are distributed to provinces roughly on the basis of population. Even though appointees are residents of the various provinces, they cannot be said to "represent" them because they were appointed by the PM on the basis of their service to the party. No doubt, it is the absence of a true provincial voice in the federal governmental institutions in Ottawa that forced the provincial premiers to be so assertive about provincial rights and powers.

It cannot be said that the Senate performs no useful function. It does make minor amendments to bills that clarify some points. Some eminent lawyers or former premiers or cabinet members have the time to give a longer look at some bills in committee than the more harried MPs in the House have. Amendments made by the Senate are almost always accepted by the Commons, so long as those amendments are not seen as challenges to the deliberate will of the House. Senators are also invited to attend the weekly party caucuses with the MPs and try to influence their party's policies. The Senate has performed increasingly useful investigative work into a variety of topics ranging from defense policy to poverty and unemployment. It can thus sometimes produce useful reports much less expensively than could a Royal commission or task force, since its staff is already in place and Senators are already being paid. Finally, Senators are sometimes appointed to the cabinet.

For a long time there have been many voices saying that the upper house must be reformed. Over a half century ago the Quebec nationalist, Henri Bourassa, quipped that demands for Senatorial reform tend to break out "periodically, like other forms of epidemics and current fevers." The proposals have included allowing the provincial governments to appoint Senators, fixing the terms to, say, five, nine, or ten years, opening appointments up to a larger group of people than merely party loyalists, or changing its role in the legislative process. Unfortunately, these reforms do not get around the fact that an appointed body simply cannot enjoy the same legitimacy in the citizens' eyes as an elected one. Also, an increase in its governmental role could diminish the power of the PM, the cabinet, the House of Commons, and provincial governments. These power centers cannot be expected to be accommodating to any such proposals. This is especially true because there is nothing resembling a consensus over the functions the Senate could or should perform in the political system.

Controversies involving the Senate occur most frequently when different parties form a majority in each house. Thus, the public eye was again directed toward the Liberal-dominated Senate when it delayed approval of the Mulroney government's bills for months at a time. A seriously miffed Mulroney demanded a curbing or abolition of the Senate even though each time its assent was finally given. His ire came to a boil in the fall of 1988 when John Turner instructed the Liberal majority in the Senate, led by Allan MacEachen, to reject the Free Trade Agreement that his government had negotiated with the U.S. Although the Liberal majority shrunk through death or retirement since 1984 from 74 to 59, that was still enough to reject the bill. The Liberals knew that this would make it impossible for the Mulroney government to ratify the accord before the December 31, 1988, deadline and would therefore force the PM to call new elections which would serve as a kind of referendum on that landmark agreement.

This maneuver was perfectly legal, but some constitutional experts argued that it violated Parliament's unwritten conventions. There was no doubt about Mulroney's interpretation: "The leader of the Liberal Party has asked the Senate of Canada, a bunch of appointed people, to hijack the most fundamental rights of the Canadian House of Commons!" The tables were turned in 1994. The Conservatives, who had been reduced to only two seats in the House of Commons and whose remaining federal power base was in the Senate, used their upper house majority to overturn legislation that would have prevented Canada's election boundaries from being revised before the next federal elections. The Tories charged that this would have protected the seats of Liberal MPs.

In 1990, the question of whether an unelected Senate should have the power to veto legislation adopted in the elected House of Commons again grabbed headlines. When the Liberal-dominated Senate blocked passage of the government's highly unpopular value-added tax (GST), Mulroney appointed 24 new Tory Senators in one month. This included Nova Scotia's Premier John Buchanan, who was under investigation for financial impropriety and who became the first sitting premier to leave provincial politics directly for a Senate seat. This raised the total number of Senators to 112, eight more than normal. In order do this, Mulroney invoked an almost forgotten procedure in the BNA, unused for 123 years, which empowers the British monarch, as Canada's head of state, to permit a PM to pack the Senate in order to break a legislative deadlock. When the Queen agreed to this, Mulroney had his majority.

The Liberal Senators reacted with an angry walk-out, a filibuster while court challenges were prepared and chaotic scenes on the floor of the dignified house which cast Canadians into disbelief: journalists were invited to enter the chamber floor; pandemonium broke out and vitriolic epithets were flung. One Liberal Senator called his best friend across the aisle a "despicable little bugger." After cool heads were prevailed, he went to his friend, embraced him, and apologized. Canadians rubbed their eyes and asked themselves again whether this institution, which many consider a constitutional relic, should be reformed or abolished. A poll at the time revealed that 80% favored reform.

Some provincial premiers, particularly those from the West and New Brunswick, have called for the election of Senators, but they often disagree on details. Alberta's former Premier Don Getty argued that western interests were being trampled by the Senate's central Canadian majority and called for a "Triple E" solution: an elected, equal and effective upper house, in which each province would have the same number of representatives. After a seat was vacated in 1987, Getty refused to nominate a replacement on the grounds that it should have been filled by election. In 1989 his government organized the first-ever Senatorial election, despite opposition from Ottawa. Mulroney took perhaps the most significant step. In the Meech Lake Accord of 1987 he struck a deal with the premiers by agreeing to give up his prime-ministerial prerogatives to appoint new Senators and instead to select them on an interim basis from a list of candidates agreed on with the provinces.

Then Meech Lake failed, as did the later Charlottetown accords. Because they failed spectacularly, Canadians shy away from attempting to change anything, including the Senate, by amending the constitution. Although 2013 polls showed that two-thirds of Canadians preferred Senatorial elections, and only a third, rising to 43% in Quebec, favored abolition, any change would have to be incremental. A 2014 poll revealed that two-thirds think the Senate serves no "necessary and useful political function."

In 2006, Stephen Harper from Alberta violated the long-standing principle of his own western-based party by appointing unelected Michael Fortier to the Senate in order to have somebody from Montreal in his cabinet. Even so, he brought the upper house back into the heart of the debate over Canadian democracy, proposing significant reform of the Senate in 2006 but electing Senators and limiting their terms were not among his suggestions. Harper promised that his government would create "a new national process for choosing elected Senators from each province and territory."

Harper wanted to reform the Senate incrementally. In 2011, his government's Senate Reform Act was more specific, starting with nine-year non-renewable terms. Provinces and territories would be encouraged, but not forced, to conduct elections to produce lists of winners from which the PM could pick Senator. Thus, these would be "consultative" votes. Harper still looked for ways of redressing the kind of imbalance that allows New Brunswick and Nova Scotia to have 10 Senators each but provides mighty Alberta and British Columbia only six each.

Polls showed that three-fourths of voters care who gets appointed to the Senate and would like to see it reformed but they do not want a powerful American-like Senate which could introduce gridlock into Canadian federal politics. A majority supports term limits and election of Senators.

The prospects of successful reform are not good; 13 attempts since 1900 to reform the Senate failed. Harper, who called the Senate "a relic of the 19th century," admitted during the 2008 election campaign: "I'll be honest with you. I'm disappointed we haven't made at least some progress on Senate reform." He appointed 59 new Conservative members between 2008 and 2013, 18 in one day. These appointments finally gave his party a majority in the upper chamber. He enlarged that majority as more Senators retired. In a 2013 survey, three in five Canadians called Harper hypocritical for naming so many new Senators despite his public talk about reform. Yet efforts to reform the Senate are paying off. According to a 2019 Nanos poll, 77% of Canadians prefer a more independent appointment process.

The NDP, which became the official opposition in 2011, is traditionally staunchly anti-Senate and does not allow its members to sit there. former leader Tom Mulcair called it "an absurdity" and proposed that the chamber be converted to a daycare center.

Hoping to end partisanship and patronage in the upper chamber, Liberal party leader Justin Trudeau announced in 2014 that its 32 Senators would leave the party and sit as Independents. In the 2015 campaign, he promised to introduce some form of independent selection process to propose nominees. Trying something new in 2016, Trudeau selected seven Senators from a slate of non-partisan candidates put forward by civic groups.

Any reform would require the approval of all provinces or seven provinces comprising at least half of Canada's population. When Harper asked the Supreme Court in 2013 whether his reform is constitutional and if the federal government can introduce it unilaterally or only with provincial approval, its answer was "no." Premiers would almost certainly oppose a new and more powerful Senate because it would replace them in Ottawa as the main voices of the provinces and regions in national affairs. Former premier Saskatchewan premier Brad Wall and former premiers Dalton McGuinty of Ontario, Gordon Campbell of British Columbia, Lorne Calvert of Saskatchewan, and Gary Doer of Manitoba, as well as the NDP and *Bloc Québécois*, favored abolishing the Senate altogether.

In the complex mechanism of Confederation, reform would diminish the importance of the provincial governments and those clubs of all premiers, the Conference of First Ministers, including the PM, and the Council of the Federation. There are many other problems: the convention that the upper house must normally pass bills the House sends to it would have to change. It was unclear how this transition might work when the chamber would be a mix of appointed and elected members Not until 2015 did forty-nine Senators reach mandatory retirement age. Fundamental Senate reform appears to be simply too complicated and too political for a federal government to address the issue.

The Senate stepped up to tackle such important issues as defense, Canada–U.S., and Canada–Mexico relations and health care reform. Finally granted $127,500 each for office and research expenses, Senators increasingly treat their positions as full-time jobs. One committee chairman, Michael Kirby, noted: "People forget that there is a lot of talent in the Senate."

THE LEGAL SYSTEM

Based on British common law and legislation, this section examines the two other key elements in Canadian criminal law is based on English common law. This means that the law is derived from previous judicial decisions which together produce a fabric of rules, precedents, and their application to categories of situations. Common law is thus judge made law.

Criminal law involves such things as murder and theft which are considered to be crimes against the state even though

Canada

The Supreme Court Building in Ottawa

they may be directed toward individuals. All criminal law is contained in the federal statute, the Criminal Code.. By contrast, civil law involves matters that are private to the individual citizen and have to do with property and civil rights, excepting divorce law which is governed by the federal Divorce Act.

Because the federal and provincial governments share responsibility for civil law, it differs from province to the next: for example, each province has its own statutes dealing with education because this topic is a provincial responsibility under the Constitution Act of 1867. Quebec has retained its French Civil Code which means that its property or civil rights were established by law-makers, rather than by judicial precedent dealing with concrete cases and specific sets of facts.

Canada has a single court system organized hierarchically. There are three court levels: lesser provincial courts such as family courts; provincial courts composed of a provincial Supreme Court and superior, county, and district courts; and federal courts namely the Supreme Court and Federal Court of Canada. This organization is not as simple as it appears on paper, though. The federal and provincial governments share judicial functions and responsibilities. Insofar as the provinces have the power to determine the organization of their own court systems, there is considerable variation in the kinds of courts within the provinces. The federal government appoints all federal judges, meaning the PM, with the assistance of the minister of justice. There is no parliamentary confirmation of judges.

It should not be surprising to discover that the appointment of judges is, to some extent, based on political considerations. Any federal government would want to be certain that an appointee shares its general view on, for instance, gay marriage, defendants' rights or the distribution of powers between the federal and provincial governments. Judicial Advisory Committees in every province to vet nominees for the 1,100 federally appointed judge positions. During the Chrétien years, the Liberals filled these committees with their own party members.

Judgeships are been given to persons who had been active supporters or donors of the party in power. For example, half of the Liberal government's 2003 judicial appointments had donated to the party, 60% of those appointed in Ontario, Alberta, and Saskatchewan. Despite such politicization of the appointment process, the Supreme Court of Canada is not as ideologically divided as is its American counterpart.

Rt. Hon. Richard Wagner,
Chief Justice of the Supreme Court
https://www.macleans.ca/politics/
the-other-political-son/

The Canadian selection process relies more heavily than the American on the advice of peers in the legal profession. Traditionally, before the PM selects individuals, the justice minister and ministry, Canadian Bar Association, law societies, and provincial governments are consulted. Consequently, selections are based more on judicial abilities and peer respect than on personal opinions.

Change is in the offing, though. In 2004, former Prime Minister Paul Martin promised more public and parliamentary scrutiny of judicial appointments. When he appointed two women from the Ontario Court of Appeal, Rosalie Abella and Louise Charron, to fill vacancies on the Supreme Court, for the first time the justice minister defended the nominations before a parliamentary committee although the appointees themselves were not present. Abella is a well-known and outspoken advocate of feminist, minority, and gay rights causes. A judicial activist, she dismisses it as "unrealistic to say that judges should not impose their values or make law." It is "better to court controversy than to court irrelevance, and better to court criticism than to court injustice." Her appointment at a time of intense public discussion over same-sex marriage was significant.

Martin's last appointment to the Supreme Court before vacating office in February 2006 was Marshall Rothstein, a judge and former law professor at the University of Manitoba. He was renowned as the hardest working judge in the land, working seven days a week and refusing to hire clerks who did not do the same. For the first time in Canadian history, Rothstein was required to appear before an all-party panel of MPs for a televised grilling of his legal views. All was in English because he is the only justice who is not bilingual.

Former Prime Minister Harper wanted to strengthen the practice of allowing a parliamentary committee to interview potential justices. After all, justices are among the most powerful people in Canada and PMs choose people who may in the long run turn out to be more important than they ever will have been. This is because judicial decisions can change the country's social fabric; they can be so immense as to throws into serious question the whole notion of parliamentary supremacy. Nevertheless, when Stephen Harper tapped bilingual Nova Scotia judge Tom Cromwell to fill a Supreme Court vacancy in September 2008, he decided there was no time for the procedures he himself approved because he called an election two days later. Harper did not come back to it until he announced Cromwell's appointment on December 22. Cromwell was sworn in on January 5, 2009.

Canada

By 2016, Harper had appointed five of the Supreme Court's justices. As such, his government decided that an improved selection process should be firmly in place. Beginning in 2011, the justice minister invites members of the public, provincial officials, judges, and prominent lawyers to recommend long lists of candidates. A parliamentary panel composed of five MPs, including one each from the opposition New Democrat and Liberal parties, creates a short list of six candidates, from which the PM and justice minister pick two.

The two finalists then answer questions before an ad hoc House of Commons Committee, and the majority in parliament selects the judge. Harper explained that "overall, what you're looking for is record, experience, judgment, judicial temperament. These people sit on the bench a long time. We will choose very carefully." By 2013, Harper had appointed 439 judges to senior courts. Prime Minister Justin Trudeau tweaked this slightly in 2016 by choosing from a shortlist of bilingual jurists drawn up by worthies. Legislators can question, but not vote on, appointees.

One constitutional requirement with which few people quarrel is that three of the nine judges appointed to the Supreme Court of Canada, established in 1875, must be from Quebec. By law, the three must be appointed from Quebec's court of appeal or superior court or be lawyers who work in the province. There is an unwritten tradition that the office of Chief Justice alternates between an anglophone and a francophone.

There was considerable controversy over Bill C-232, which parliament adopted in 2010, requiring all Supreme Court appointees to be fluent in both languages and be able to hear cases in both without the aid of an interpreter. The court had always been bilingual in the sense that anyone appearing before it could plead his case in either official language. Critics fear that this new requirement would dangerously reduce the pool of potential appointees, especially from the West. Harper ignored it in 2011 when he appointed the unilingual Michael Moldaver. The Court is just as sensitive about gender balance, so he tapped a second justice from the Ontario Court of Appeal, Andromache Karakatsanis, who is fluent in both languages and Greek.

In 1999, the first woman to be appointed Chief Justice was Beverley McLachlin. Born and educated in Alberta, she moved to British Columbia, where she became chief justice of the province's Supreme Court in 1988. She was appointed to the Supreme Court of Canada a year later. Also, in 1999, Louise Arbour, who won international recognition as head of the U.N. tribunal on war crimes, joined McLachlin on Canada's highest court by. Arbour re-

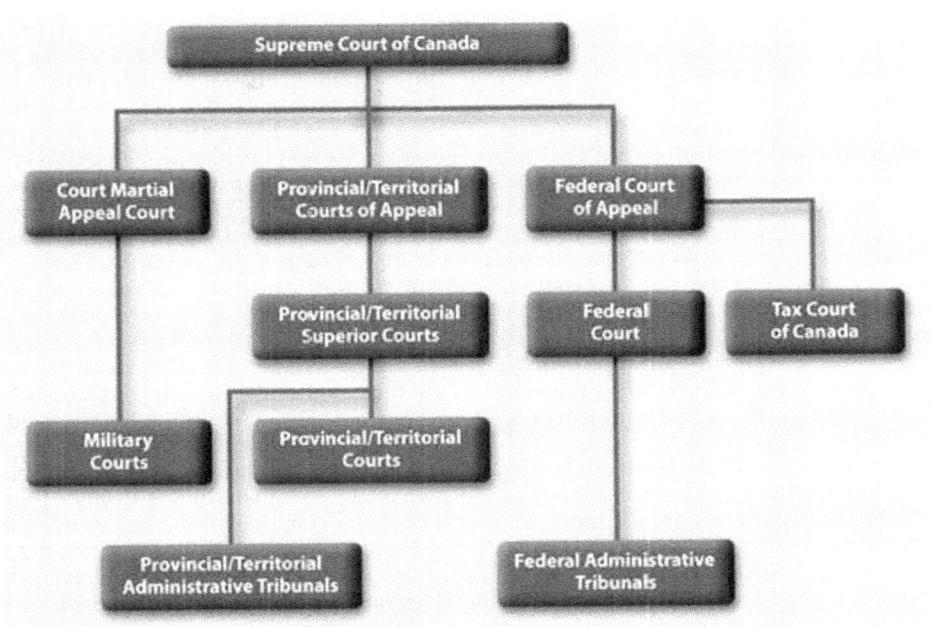

Retrieved from: https://www.justice.gc.ca/eng/csj-sjc/just/07.html

signed from the Supreme Court in 2004 to become the U.N. High Commissioner for Human Rights.

A former law professor, McLachlin was universally acknowledged for her intellect, scholarship, and persuasive powers as her Court produces an increasing number of unanimous decisions (82% in 2001). McLachlin takes a more cautious, centrist view of the law compared with her two predecessors, both of whom were regarded as activists. She is more deferential to Parliament and less open to charges of judicial activism although her court delivered some significant defeats to the government. In her words, "I'm not a politician. I'm not there to vote for this law or that. My job is to decide each case fairly, according to the law."

The formal powers of the Chief Justice are limited. The most important is to determine the size of the panel as five, seven, or nine judges to hear a case. However, people speak increasingly of the "McLachlin court." She is more available to the media and open to defending the court's actions in public. Chief Justice McLachlin retired after serving as Chief Justice for 17 years and 341 days in 2017. Prime Minister Justin Trudeau then appointed Justice Richard Wagner Chief Justice; he took office on December 18, 2017.

Gabrielle Giroday writing in the *Canadian Lawyer* magazine provided the following information on Chief Justice Wagner.

Wagner, a graduate of the University of Ottawa's Faculty of Law, was called to the Quebec bar in 1980. He practised at Lavery, de Billy SENCRL / LLP (formerly known as Lavery, O'Brien and Lavery, Johnston, Clark, Carrière, Mason & Associés), from 1980 to 2004, when he was appointed to the bench at the Quebec Superior Court.

"There is a great deal of respect for Justice Wagner in terms of what he's done as a lawyer, his involvement in the community and his career as a judge. There was a lot of pride when he was appointed to the Supreme Court and all the much more so now that he's appointed chief justice," says Louis Charette, a partner at Lavery lawyers who worked with Wagner on construction and professional liability litigation files in the litigation team at the firm until Wagner was appointed to the bench in 2004.

Charette says Wagner brings a passion for the law but is more "reserved" in his approach than McLachlin.

"I think he's going to bring the same passion and rigour that Justice McLachlin brought, I think that's undeniable. In terms of his qualities he was passionate about what he did, he was rigorous and hardworking and that will continue. I think Richard is more reserved as a personality. Justice McLachlin had an ease with people and it was easy to speak with her. Justice Wagner is very reserved and perhaps that is a difference Canadians will see in terms of his approach in public speaking."

Wagner served as a judge of the Quebec Superior Court for the District of Montreal until 2011, when he was appointed to the Quebec Court of Appeal.

Wagner's appointment ends months of speculation about who would take McLachlin's place at the court. On Dec. 18, he took an oath of office as chief justice.

"I have the utmost confidence in his ability to lead the highest court of Canada,

Canada

an institution with a long and respected history of judicial independence and excellence," said Prime Minister Justin Trudeau, in a news release from the PMO.

"The judiciary, the legal profession, and all Canadians will be well served by his dedication to upholding the laws and Constitution on which this country is founded."

Emmett Macfarlane, an associate professor of political scienceat the University of Waterloo and author of *Governing from the Bench: The Supreme Court of Canada and the Judicial Role*, says in the short time Wagner has been with the SCC, he has carved out a reputation for being "straight-forward" and "clear."

"In some ways, it's the obvious choice. I also think it's the correct choice," he says.

According to Macfarlane, Wagner displays the potential for "consensus building" among the justices, similar to the retiring McLachlin. "It hasn't been that long since he was appointed to the court," says Macfarlane, who adds that in that time Wagner has shown he has a "collegial personality."

"He's very forthright in his public statements," says Macfarlane. Macfarlane says the other name most commonly floated as the potential Chief Justice was Rosalie Abella, but she faces a mandatory retirement in 2021, which could be problematic.

"This decision allows for a little bit of stability," says Macfarlane. He also said the decision to appoint Wagner follows a pattern of PM's elevating someone to the position of Chief Justice, who was appointed by a PM of a different partisan stripe. In this case, Wagner was appointed by former Prime Minister Stephen Harper.

"This is not a partisan institution," he says. He says an interesting issue to watch for will be if there are divisions that emerge amongst the justices in their decisions, as it's a "fairly young court."

Prime Minister Justin Trudeau made a deeply significant appointment to the Supreme Court in 2022. On August 19, 2022, the prime minister nominated Justice Michelle O'Bonsawin of the Ontario Superior Court of Justice to be a justice of the Supreme Court of Canada (replacing Justice Michael Moldaver, who was retiring). Following a hearing before the Canadian Parliamentary Standing Committee on Justice and Human Rights on August 26, 2022, the Prime Minister's Office formally confirmed her appointment to the Supreme Court of Canada and Justice O'Bonsawin joined the court on September 1, 2022. A former law professor, Justice O'Bonsawin is the first Indigenous person to sit on Canada's highest court.

In November 2023, Prime Minister Trudeau appointed Mary Moreau, at the time of her appointment the Chief Justice of the Court of King's Bench of Alberta, to the Supreme Court of Canada. This was the third woman Trudea appointed to the Supreme Court, significant for the fact that for the first time its history, that court now has a 5-4 majority of female justices. That, with Justice O'Bonsawin's appointment in 2022, meant that the Supreme Court is the most diverse in its history— as a result of constitutional requirements and conventions, it is already politically regionally diverse, but it is also now both culturally diverse, including members for the three founding cultures of Canada— French, English, and First Nations, Inuit, and Metis—and gender diverse.

The political nature of some appointments, aside, Canada holds firmly to the basic legal principle of the independence of the judiciary, a tradition inherited from Britain. This means that the government does not remove judge, even if it dislikes their decisions. Even though there are constitutional provisions for removing judges, no judge of any federal or provincial superior court has ever been removed since 1867. This principle of independence is also underscored by the appointment of judges who can remain on the bench until they are 75.

Two other important principles are limited judicial review and judicial restraint. Canadian courts have the responsibility for delineating between federal and provincial jurisdiction. Therefore, the Supreme Court of Canada can determine which level of government has jurisdiction over which powers. The Court can rule that a parliament cannot enact a law because the authority for such issues resides with another legislature. That is, the Court can overrule laws but, unlike Parliament, cannot propose new ones.

The Canadian government can refer hypothetical questions, called a "reference," to the Supreme Court concerning the constitutionality of Constitution Acts or of federal or provincial jurisdiction and powers. Ottawa did this in 1997 when the Court responded no when asked whether Quebec had the right to declare independence from Canada unilaterally . The Court did so again in 2013 when asked if the federal government could reform the Senate without the provinces' approval. Such advisory opinions are issued in the form of judgments that have always been treated as binding.

The referee role in federal-provincial jurisdiction is only a limited form of judicial review. It is more than British courts have, but less than that possessed by the U.S. Supreme Court, which can deem any law null and void because it violates the constitution. Former Chief Justice Antonio Lamer noted: "Since the charter came into effect, we no longer only rule on cases. Now, we rule on the laws themselves."

Until 1949, some cases could be appealed from the Supreme Court of Canada to the Judicial Committee of the Privy Council, the highest court in Britain. Now the Supreme Court of Canada is indisputably the last court of appeal for Canadians. The country's courts have had a long tradition of "legal restraint," meaning that they have been hesitant to use all the powers the constitution had granted them. After 1949, though, the Supreme Court dealt increasingly with contentious issues, such as boundaries of free speech. Since the early 1970s, it has rendered important decisions such as that hanging is not "cruel and unusual punishment," that offshore minerals belong to the central government, that the provinces are free to censor entertainment, and that Quebec's ban on the use of English in the courts was unconstitutional.

The influence of the American model is clear. As James Snell, a Canadian history professor at the University of Guelph, noted: "There is no doubt that the high profile of the Warren court in the United States did influence us in terms of what we expect from the court. Canadian citizens are now expecting them to make decisions that would before have been left to politicians." Former Chief Justice Brian Dickson also spoke about his American counterparts on the Supreme Court: "Increasingly, we look to their experience, not to follow it slavishly but simply as a starting point with which we may agree or disagree. They have made some mistakes that we don't have to make." There are two clear differences: unlike American high court justices, Canadian judges keep a low public profile and they are far more scrupulous in avoiding visible ideological partisanship. Their decisions rarely give evidence of justices' personal philosophies.

The Canadian Charter of Rights and Freedoms, enacted in 1982, gave the courts an additional watchdog role over citizens' rights. Some Canadians had thought that the tradition of "judicial restraint" would dissuade judges from becoming fully immersed in the legally difficult issues of individual rights. They were badly mistaken. The Charter of Rights has, in fact, greatly stimulated the activity of the courts and significantly changed Canadian political life in the process.

About half of the Constitution Act, 1982, was devoted to basic civil and political liberties. This Charter was a dramatic break from British and Canadian tradition. For a long time, Canadians believed that there was no need to write down basic individual rights because they were already adequately protected by Parliament and common law. There was therefore no mention of them in the BNA.

Canada

National Anthem

O Canada! Our home and native land!
True patriot love in all thy sons command.
With glowing hearts we see thee rise,
The True North strong and free!
From far and wide, O Canada,
We stand on guard for thee.
God keep our land glorious and free!
O Canada, we stand on guard for thee.
O Canada, we stand on guard for thee.

 Canadian Heritage / Patrimoine canadien

http://www.pch.gc.ca

Hymne National

O Canada! Terre de nos aïeux,
Ton front est ceint de fleurons glorieux!
Car ton bras sait porter l'épée,
Il sait porter la croix!
Ton histoire est une épopée
Des plus brillants exploits.
Et ta valeur, de foi trempée,
Protégera nos foyers et nos droits.
Protégera nos foyers et nos droits.

Canada

Over the years, though, there have been incidents that made some Canadians wonder whether their rights were indeed adequately protected. The 1914 War Measures Act struck many as perhaps allowing the government too many sweeping powers. The government could rule by decree, usurping the powers of both federal and provincial parliaments. In 1917 the government prohibited naturalized citizens of German origin from voting. Further, in 1960 the federal government passed a Bill of Rights, a normal legislative act which applied only to the federal government and which could have been invalidated by another simple act of Parliament. Just how little it could restrain the federal government was demonstrated in October 1970 when shocking kidnappings by Quebec nationalists took place. The Trudeau government invoked the War Measures Act and made membership in the *Front de Liberation du Québec*, Liberation Front of Quebec, illegal, then arresting those who had belonged to it before it was a crime to do so.

In the wake of a wiretapping scandal in 1986 involving the deputy PM, a legal commission reported that twice as many wire taps are permitted by Canadian judges than by American jurists. The report continued "It is astounding that this country has recorded on a per capita basis more than twenty times the number of authorizations [as] our massive American neighbor." Criticism of an overly-intrusive RCMP prompted the creation in 1984 of a special counterespionage agency, the Canadian Security Intelligence Service in order to reduce the RCMP's powers. In 1989, the second-ranking RCMP officer was forced to resign amid charges of political interference in two high-profile investigations involving a leak of the government's budget.

The Charter of Rights entrenches in the Constitution the rights of Canadian citizens, meaning that they cannot be done away with by a simple act of Parliament. The Charter, along with federalism, is yet another blow to the principle of "parliamentary supremacy." It applies to all levels of government while expanding Canadians' rights to include such things as equality of women and the right to use either of the two official languages.

In provisions, the Charter confers constitutional status to the guarantees in the 1969 Official Languages Act. Moreover, it spells out many of the same rights as are contained in the Bill of Rights which has been so important in the American political experience. Traditionally, Canada has placed more emphasis on group rights than have Americans. Yet, since the Constitution and Charter have been in place, legal scholars have noticed a convergence in the legal reasoning of the Supreme Courts of both countries when ruling on matters of rights. In this regard, former president of the Israeli Supreme Court, Aaron Barak, wrote in the *Harvard Law Review* that "Canadian law serves as a source of inspiration for many countries around the world" and may now be more influential than its American counterpart.

As in the U.S., Canadian courts must decide what the various freedoms mean in practice. Judges must give precise meaning to such phrases as "unreasonable search," "arbitrarily imprisoned," and/or "informed promptly." The Charter requires that any limitations on Canadians' rights must be "reasonable," but the courts must wrestle with the question of what kind of a line this draws. Further, the Charter affirms the existing aboriginal and treaty rights of native peoples even though its language is vague simply because there is no consensus in Canada as to the nature of these rights.

In 2024, the Supreme Court of Canada handed down its decision in *Reference re An Act respecting First Nations, Inuit and Métis children, youth and families*, 2024 SCC 5, an important decision concerning the rights of First Nations, Inuit, and Metis children, youth, and families. In a unanimous judgment, the Court held that the federal government has the power to enact legislation affirming Indigenous peoples' right of self-government with respect to child and family services under section 35 of the *Constitution Act, 1982* and section 91(24) of the *Constitution Act, 1867*. The court found that the legislation enacted by the federal government protected the wellbeing of Indigenous children, youth, and families by promoting the delivery of culturally appropriate child and family services and, in so doing, advancing the process of reconciliation with Indigenous peoples. The Court noted that "[u]nder this framework created by the Act, Indigenous governing bodies and the Government of Canada will work together to remedy the harms of the past and create a solid foundation for a renewed nation to nation relationship in the area of child and family services."

The courts have also found themselves in the middle of the emotionally charged abortion question. In 1988, the Supreme Court struck down the restrictive federal abortion law as unconstitutional because it interfered with a woman's "bodily integrity." In July 1989, the Supreme Court of Quebec countered by ruling that the rights of the father and the fetus, which it considered to be a human being entitled to the right to life, must be respected. Following passionate debate across the country, though, the Supreme Court of Canada responded in August 1989 by permitting a Quebec woman to have an abortion after she had had one. Trying to take the issue out of the courts, the Mulroney government received parliamentary approval in 1989 for a new law permitting abortion if one doctor believes a mother's health is threatened.

In 2003, the courts demonstrated how their interpretation of the Charter can affect sensitive social issues. The Supreme Court ruled that there is no constitutional right to smoke marijuana for recreational purposes, but left open the possibility that parliament could decriminalize it. In 2005, Canada became the first country in

Canada

the world to approve a marijuana-based painkiller for multiple sclerosis patients. Attitudes against the recreational use of marijuana hardened when the Conservatives came into power in 2006. One of its first acts was to declare that the liberalization of the drug was a dead issue. Justin Trudeau's government legalized the recreational use of cannabis in 2018.

In June 2003, an appellate court in Ontario entered more controversial terrain by declaring that denying same-sex couples the right to marry violated their rights and offended "the dignity of same-sex relationships." Because the judgment took immediate effect, hundreds of gay couples rushed to Ontario, one-third of whom from the U.S., to marry. The then PM, Jean Chrétien, announced that the government would not appeal the decision, citing "an evolution in society."

In September 2003, then opposition leader Stephen Harper introduced a motion in Parliament that the Liberals overwhelmingly supported in 1999 defining marriage as the union of one man and one woman. This time it was narrowly defeated 137 to 132, a vote that accurately reflected the 50–50 split on the issue in Canadian society. Many Liberals said their switch was influenced by the case from Ontario. The PM, Jean Chretian, sent draft legislation legalizing gay unions to the Supreme Court to get an assessment of its constitutionality. Chief Justice Beverley McLachlin rebuked the government from for referring the matter straight to the court, which usually only addresses appeals of earlier orders. Nevertheless, with the Liberals split on the issue and constituting only a minority in parliament, the PM left the matter in the Supreme Court and appointed two new justices who might support same-sex marriages.

In 2003, the highest court rejected requests by religious and family groups to appeal the Ontario court ruling, letting it stand as the law of the land. Within a year gay marriage was legal in most Canadian provinces and territories. In 2004 the Supreme Court of Canada, acting on the government's request for a ruling on the constitutionality of eventual legislation, thought that same-sex marriage is consistent with the constitution and did not violate the rights of religious Canadians who desire to uphold the traditional definition of marriage. The Court did say that the guarantee of religious freedom protects clergymen from being forced to perform same-sex marriages. In sweeping language, the court pronounced that the constitution "is a living tree which, by way of progressive interpretation, accommodates and addresses the realities of modern life."

The Alberta premier threatened to invoke the "notwithstanding," or opt-out, provision to prevent the order from taking effect in his province. Nevertheless, the Martin government vowed to pass a law permitting gay marriage, with all MPs except cabinet members free to vote according to their consciences. When it came to a vote in 2005, more than 30 Liberal MPs joined the opposition to reject the bill recognizing same-sex marriage. Many Canadians felt they had been railroaded on this. Still, polls indicated that those who opposed such unions would overwhelmingly accept the Conservative opposition's alternative of civil unions granting gays the same rights, benefits, and obligations as any married couples, with or without the title of marriage. By 2009, two-thirds of Canadians accepted same-sex relationships. In 2007, when Scott Brison became the first MP to marry a same-sex partner, two former PMs, Joe Clark and Paul Martin attended the ceremony.

In 2017, the PM apologized to gays who had been the victims of government discrimination, known as the "gay purge," granting them compensation. In that same year polls indicated that 85% of Canadians were willing to vote for a party led by someone who was gay.

In 2009, another unconventional form of family, polygamy, entered the spotlight. According to section 293 of the criminal code, polygamy is punishable by up to five years in prison. At this time, a poll revealed that 82% of Canadians opposed legalizing polygamy. When the government of British Columbia sought to end the practice in its borders, especially in a Mormon commune called Bountiful, where one former "bishop" had 26 wives and 108 children, in a lengthy decision in 2011 the province's highest upheld the prohibition against polygamy. The court reasoned that the inherent harms in polygamy justified limiting the religious freedom rights underpinning polygamy. Subsequently, in 2017, two men in Ontario, one of whom had 25 wives and 146 children in the first test of the 127 year old section 293 of the criminal code.

THE CHARTER OF RIGHTS AND FREEDOMS

The Canada and Constitution Acts had to be careful compromises in order to gain the backing of the provinces which, for a hundred years, were unable to agree on these matters. Most provinces would agree to give the courts a clear mandate to strike down laws which violate the Charter only by securing a political safety-hatch in return but their officials wished to protect themselves from a flood of court cases attacking their laws.

In order to minimize the dangers of "judicial lawmaking," the Charter contains a clause in Section 33 which says that Parliament or the legislature of a province may expressly declare that their law would still operate "notwithstanding" or despite the Charter's provisions. When a legislature disregards a provision of the Charter, it must declare openly that it is doing so, and thereby bear whatever public onus such a declaration would cause; such noncompliance could only last five years but could be renewed.

Many Canadians were convinced that provinces would be hesitant to use this "notwithstanding" provision because that would be a public statement that they intended to deny rights guaranteed in the Charter. However, no sooner was the ink on the Charter dry when Quebec, which for years rejected the entire constitutional change and which fears that its efforts to make Quebec more French could be frustrated by the Charter, put a "notwithstanding" clause in all of its provincial laws. Quebec invoked the clause again in December 1988 to invalidate a ruling of the Supreme Court of Canada ruling restricting the province's French-only language legislation.

Many critics understandably see this escape-hatch as a serious weakening of the Charter. Yet, it is important to bear in mind that without such compromises, there would have been no Canada and Constitution Acts in the first place.

Since the Charter came into force in 1982, Canadian courts have been inundated with cases relating to individual rights. In the first two years alone, lower courts resolved more than 1,000 Charter-based cases, covering issues ranging from an accused person's right to counsel and Parliament's authority to keep stores closed on Sundays to anglophones' right to have their own schools in Quebec. Thousands more such cases are on the dockets. Of the 100 cases heard annually by the Supreme Court, constitutional cases are usually the most time-consuming. Canada's former chief justice, Brian Dickson, said in 1984: "When there is a breach of the fundamental rights and freedoms under the Charter of Rights, we have been given the right, the duty and the responsibility to deal with it—and it is our duty to strike [the violation] down."

In 1985, Canada entered yet another era when the so-called "equity clauses" of Section 15 of the Charter took effect. This clause insures that every individual is equal before and under the law "without discrimination based on color, religion, sex, age, or mental or physical disability." Such protection had been postponed three years from the enactment of the Charter to give the federal and provincial governments sufficient time to amend any discriminatory laws or regulations. Capital punishment is outlawed even though 53% of respondents in 2009 approved of its use.

Canada

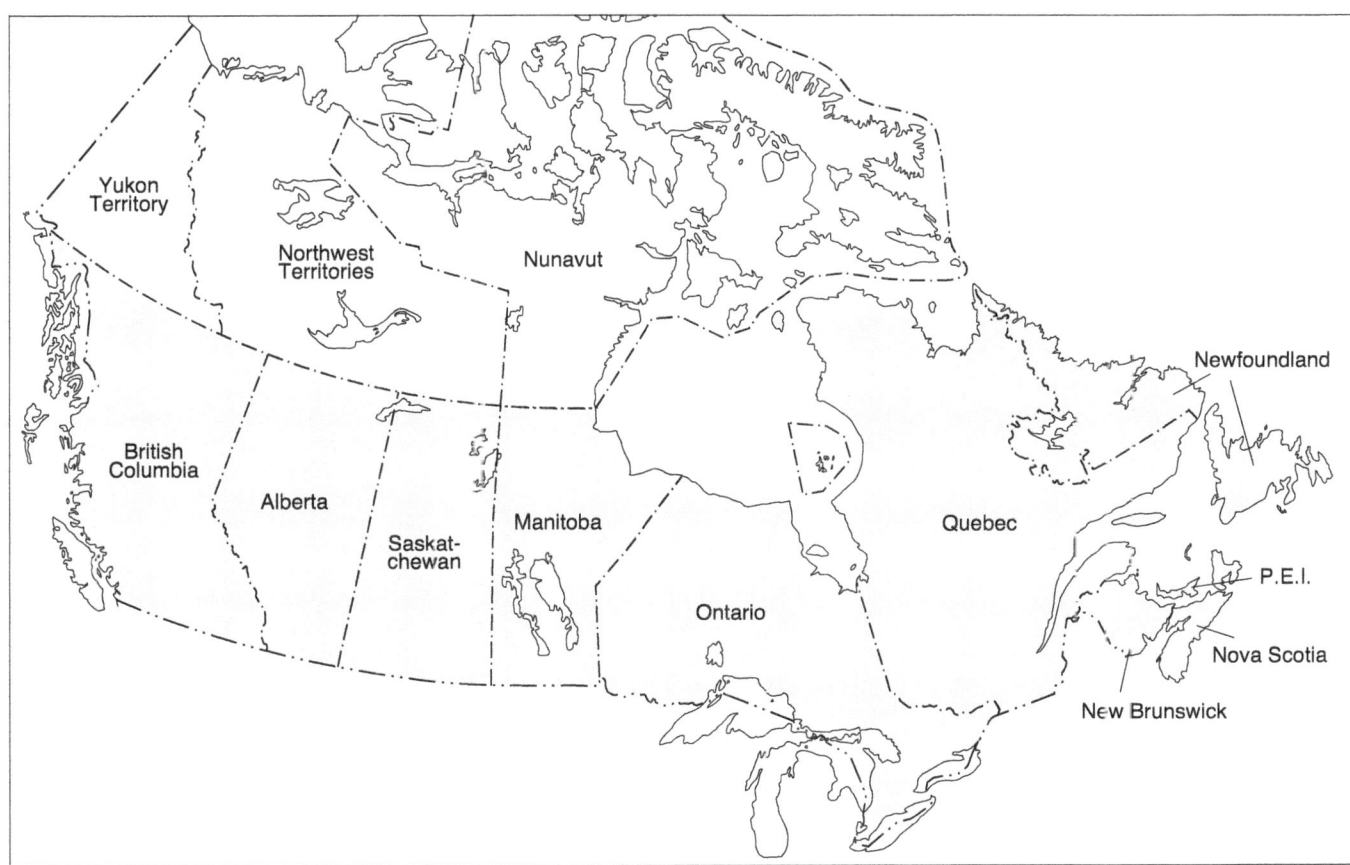

All provincial governments were slow to respond to this task, in part because they were not sure what precisely constituted discrimination. It was unclear whether age could be used for such questions as when a person may drive a car, consume alcohol, serve in the army, get married or be forced to retire or whether women be barred from combat roles in the military, and what "equal pay for equal work" means.

Section 1 of the Charter says that all of Canadians' rights and freedoms are subject "to reasonable limits prescribed by law," but it is unclear precisely what this means in concrete cases. The social and legal consequences of Section 15 remain unclear, but one thing which is certain is the revolutionary power that has been given to the Canadian courts. In the words of Brian Dickson: "The Charter has replaced parliamentary supremacy with constitutional supremacy." No wonder Brian Mulroney joked that one of the first things he intended to do with his new-born son was to enroll him in law school.

Ontario experimented with allowing Muslims to mediate some civil disputes by permitting tribunals that included imams, Muslim elders and lawyers to apply Islamic sharia law to family disagreements, inheritances, and/ or business and divorce matters. This possibility was provided for under the Arbitration Act of the Province of Ontario which grants religious and cultural groups the authority to resolve such disputes through private and binding arbitration. Catholics and Protestants never resorted to the act, but Jews had since 1991. By 2004, Muslim leaders had set up an Islamic Court of Civil Justice that had chosen arbitrators who had undergone training in sharia and Canadian civil law.

Much of the Canadian public was dismayed and incensed that such courts could be permitted to operate in a secular country. Even the Canadian Council of Muslim Women feared that they could undermine women's rights: "Sanctioning the use of religious laws under the Arbitration Act will provide legitimacy to practices that are abhorred by fair-minded Canadians, including Muslim women." Public opinion is enflamed by such a horrific crime in Quebec as the honor killing by drowning of three Muslim sisters and their aunt in 2011 who allegedly dishonored the family by dressing up, wearing makeup, and flirting with boys.

In June 2005, Quebec banned Islamic law. In the words of Premier Jean Charest: "It's important to send a very clear message that there is one rule of law in Quebec." In September 2005, there were demonstrations in a dozen Canadian and European cities against Ontario's legal experiment. The government in Toronto quickly scrapped the use of sharia law and moved to outlaw religious tribunals by Christians and Jews.

FEDERALISM AND THE PROVINCES

In 1867, the Fathers of Confederation intended to create a federation in which the central government would be more powerful than the provinces. The BNA therefore granted the provinces only restricted powers that would enable them to maintain their cultural identity, including powers over local government, property, social welfare, education, health, language, and culture. These were not exclusive powers, though, because the federal government was given the power to protect the educational rights of religious minorities, which meant primarily the English Protestants in Quebec and the Catholic francophones outside of Quebec. The BNA even spoke of "concurrent powers," such as agriculture and immigration, and contained a "supremacy clause" which made the central government's claim on these shared powers supreme.

The BNA granted a limited number of specific powers to the provinces. Conversely, it earmarked 29 kinds of powers for the federal government such as defense,

Canada

Source: *Maclean's*

finance, criminal law, transportation, postal services, coinage of money, banking, and Indian affairs. It also granted Ottawa the most lucrative sources of revenue. Unlike in the U.S. Constitution's Tenth Amendment, any powers not specifically granted to the provinces accrue to the central government in Canada. Further, the BNA contained a "declaratory power," which permitted the central government to usurp provincial powers if the reason for such action were "for the general Advantage of Canada or for the Advantage of Two or more of the Provinces." This power is seldomly used.

Ottawa can also "disallow" a provincial law within a year of passage, or can "reserve" such a law for federal governmental review before such a law goes into force. None of these powers has been exercised since 1961. The hefty central powers the founders built into the BNA explain why the regional units were called "provinces" rather than "states." The latter term denotes dignified sovereignty, while the word "province" implies a rural hinterland outside the limits of the metropolis. Almost everywhere else, "provincial" seems to be an insult. Yet over time, the provinces are entities that have drawn away some important powers from Ottawa and have become more powerful than American states.

Ottawa's power on paper is most impressive. Even so, political practice in Canada can differ greatly from documentary powers. While the founders fully intended to create a Canada with a stronger central government and weaker provincial governments than the U.S., the exact opposite has actually occurred. Today, Canadian provinces are considerably stronger than are American states and the provincial premiers are potentates whose strength can hardly be exaggerated. While it is true that the courts, including the Judicial Committee of the British Privy Council, tended to judge more often in the provinces' favor than in Ottawa's, the strengthening of provincial rights has come primarily from the provincial leaders themselves. In good Canadian style, change has come chiefly by custom and convention. Today's reality is the result of political accommodation, not judicial decision and constitutional change.

The forces of decentralization and centralization are always at work in Canada. Author Peter C. Newman put it this way: "Few land masses of such outrageous dimensions can withstand the tensions of democracy." The stresses and strains of stretching the rule of law across 88 degrees of longitude and 42 degrees of latitude virtually guarantee inefficient central government.

The powers of both levels of government have ebbed and flowed over the years. To summarize these evolutionary changes, because the provinces were quickly dissatisfied with their limited powers, they began almost immediately to strengthen their position through hard bargaining. Yet, two world wars, during which Ottawa ruled by means of expanded emergency powers, and the Great Depression in the 1930s brought a resurgence of central powers. In the mid-1950s, though, the provinces reasserted themselves with a vengeance, first in Quebec, and then in the energy-rich West.

In the 20th century, Canada had become a predominantly urbanized country as provincial leaders faced the task of managing the growth of cities. The "minor powers" which the BNA granted provinces, such as social welfare, health, and education, became salient issues in a country that had become committed to expanding services in these areas. These maters now claim half the budgets of most provinces, requiring their leaders to put heavy pressure on Ottawa, with its greater taxing power, to help finance them. By the 1980s close to half of some provinces' budgets came from the federal government.

By means of a system that some authorities have called "co-operative federalism," the two levels of government share the cost of many programs. The usual practice for such cooperation is that Ottawa sends financial support such as for health insurance or pensions on the condition that the provinces' programs meet federal standards. Ottawa also sends some funds on an unconditional basis.

The dilemma remains: the constitution confers on provinces the responsibility for most public services, including justice, education, health, and the management of natural resources. Yet, the central government has more cash and can run up surpluses while the provinces struggle to pat for expensive services. Canadian politics is largely about chronic jurisdictional quarrels between different levels of government over transfers of money.

In the 1960s, provincial leaders even challenged the federal government's exclusive power to conduct foreign relations. Quebec created a department of intergovernmental relations which acts much like a foreign ministry and seeks to be represented in international conferences along with opening trade and cultural missions in a variety of foreign countries, including the U.S. and France. Many other provinces rapidly followed suit as Ontario alone maintains a dozen similar missions abroad. Prime Minister Pierre Trudeau set out to reverse the trend toward decentralization because the Constitution Act itself puts limits on the provinces' power to veto some constitutional amendments.

Of course, competition between Ottawa and the provinces is as old as the Confederation itself. The BNA granted the central government control over major 19th-century concerns, such as trade, banks, postal service and criminal law. Still, the provinces had control over matters that rose to greater prominence in the late 20th and early 21st century such as health care and education.

The provinces accept money from Ottawa but resist federal intrusion into their jurisdictions. This is especially true of Quebec. Even Ontario has withdrawn from its traditional stance as the natural ally of Ottawa. Having been officially categorized temporarily as a "have-not" province, Ontario complains like the other provinces that it is being cheated by Ottawa politically and economically. It is a messy process. When asked in 2010 if federalism "has more advantages than disadvantages,"

Canada

48% of respondents agreed, including in Quebec, and only 33% disagreed with 42% in Quebec joining this response.

Contemporary Canadian federalism involves close and frequent cooperation and negotiation between provincial and federal governments. This has been called "executive federalism" because the executive branches facilitate the highly interpenetrated relationships. Civil servants from both levels meet and talk by phone daily while cabinet members frequently meet to discuss common problems. Since the 1960s, the premiers and the PM meet in Conferences of First Ministers. These are convened and chaired by the PM.

Such "summit meetings" usually occur at least once a year although PMs often elect not to have them. former Prime Minister Harper never convened a meeting, but his successor, Justin Trudeau, organized a summit in March 2016. Much of the bargaining at these meetings occurs behind closed doors. To the participants it is known as "the Club," and civility is one of its most rigid conventions. According to one premier, "the clubby atmosphere of the gatherings puts tremendous pressures on each premier to conform." Such a situation discourages political head-on collisions although they sometimes occur. In 2004, the premiers began meeting semi-annually in the Council of the Federation, a forum that excludes the PM.

This form of "executive federalism" was seriously harmed by the failure of the Meech Lake Accord in 1990. Top leaders who were derisively dubbed "11 men in suits" made this agreement in relative secrecy. The result was a political disaster. Former Manitoba premier Gary Filmon learned the indelible lesson that if politicians indulge in top-down, brokerage politics, the voters will punish them. "When you look at the names and the faces that were associated with Meech Lake, every single person who signed that agreement was gone from office within a very few short years." Since 1990, federal-provincial agreements tend to be more painstakingly and publicly constructed over years of meetings and with much outside consultation.

The PM can decide whether to have more or fewer meetings with the premiers. Stephen Harper, who led minority governments from 2006–2011 and a majority until October 2015, chose to be as conciliatory as possible with the powerful provincial barons. He bought peace by increasing transfer payments by billions of dollars and avoiding policy clashes. Harper was careful not to intrude on spheres chiefly under provincial jurisdiction. However, by October 2015, when the Conservatives were voted out of power, Harper had not met the premiers as a group since November 2008. Prime Minister Justin Trudeau vowed to change this.

The federal cabinet has a Standing Committee on Federal-Provincial Relations and the Privy Council Office has a Federal-Provincial Relations Secretariat; both help prepare the PM and the PM's retinue for meetings. In addition to these conferences, the premiers and territorial leaders conduct an annual summer meeting among themselves, and frequently the Western or Atlantic premiers will gather. Starting in 2004 a Council of the Federation brings premiers and territorial leaders together twice a year. It has an Ottawa-based secretariat, and the federal government is not a member. Finally, bilateral meetings among premiers are a frequent occurrence.

PROVINCIAL GOVERNMENTS

Canada's provinces have governmental systems similar to that of the federal government in Ottawa except that none has an upper house. All have parliamentary systems meaning that the party leader with majority support in the legislative assembly forms the government led by a powerful premier. Don Braid, political columnist for the *Edmonton Journal* once described the premiers: "They recall the medieval barons who armed against the king while demanding his protection. Their interests are purely regional, but fate has given them a huge role in the national melodrama. On this stage they cavort like off-Broadway Falstaffs shoved into King Lear's shoes. And yet, their subjects love them for it." While premiers are important movers and shakers in Canadian politics, their strong regional power bases have always prevented them from rising to the pinnacle of Canadian political power in Ottawa. No premier has ever become PM of Canada.

The PM appoints a lieutenant governor in each province on the advice of the provincial premier; this person usually performs only ceremonial functions. In 2000, six of the ten lieutenant governors were women after then Prime Minister Chrétien appointed Myra Freeman, a sixth-grade Halifax teacher; she was the first woman and first member of the province's Jewish community to serve as the Queen's representative in Nova Scotia.

The members of the legislative assembly, called "MLAs" in all provinces but Ontario, Newfoundland and Quebec, where they are referred to as MPP, MHA and deputy respectively, are elected by the same kind of single-member district electoral system used in federal elections. There are three exceptions: on Prince Edward Island, MLAs are elected in two-member districts, with each voter casting two votes. Also, Nova Scotia has three such two-member districts and British Columbia seven. Three provinces have adopted fixed election dates. Each province establishes its own voter requirements for provincial elections. Thus, in British Columbia one must be age 19 to vote and in some provinces' citizens of the British Commonwealth and the Republic of Ireland are permitted to vote.

One of the provincial government's main responsibilities is to oversee local governments. Because the provinces are organized and granted authority by the provinces, their specific organization and responsibilities vary from one to the next.

Harbor outside St. John's, Newfoundland

Canada

All provinces provide such services as elementary and secondary schools, to which 40% of the cities' budgets are devoted; such cultural and recreational facilities as parks, pools and ice rinks, libraries and art galleries; health and welfare including public health services, ambulances and welfare administration; housing for the aged and poor, and issuance of building permits, standards, planning and zoning; police and fire protection; public transportation and road repair; and a variety of utilities such as water, garbage collection, sewage, and electricity.

The cities' demands for more powers to cope with their responsibilities have fallen on deaf ears in provincial capitals. Even though the provinces have successfully demanded increased power from Ottawa, their premieres have stubbornly refused to share any of theirs with local governments. Nevertheless, the mayors of major cities such as Toronto, Montreal, or Vancouver can be powerful political figures in provincial and Canadian politics.

Of all the taxes Canadians pay, 50% goes to the federal government, 42% to the provincial governments, and 8% to the cities. To fund their activities, local governments rely primarily on provincial grants of 44%, property taxes of 34%, business taxes of 4%, plus sales and services of 8%. Cities find themselves continuously strapped for finances, made worse by budget cuts by the central government and high provincial debt. As demands for services have risen, property taxes can no longer cover municipal needs. With inadequate funding, cities, which generate most of the country's wealth, are experiencing deteriorating urban infrastructure and cuts in services. The debates over how to use limited funds does not seem to stimulate strong municipal electoral interest; voter turn-out averages only 30% in city elections, 68% in the 2015 federal elections, and 66% in the 2019 federal elections.

It has always been difficult to forge and maintain a unified country out of 13 different provinces and territories. This is made particularly challenging because insofar as Canada's major parties are highly decentralized, they tend not to be strong in every part of the country. The parties can thus do little to help hold the country together. Insofar as the provinces have unique political scenes and problems and play such important roles in Canadian politics, it is worthy examining each in some detail.

Newfoundland and Labrador: Newfoundland and Labrador represent (Newfoundland) Canada's most recent province, having entered the Confederation in 1949 after a close vote in a referendum. In 2001, it was officially renamed Newfoundland and Labrador to recognize the latter's importance. In 2003 decades of negotiations culminated in agreement on a 29,000-square mile new Inuit-governed territory created in Labrador, called Nunatsiavut, "our beautiful land."

Newfoundland has the lowest percentage of French-speakers in all of Canada. French is the mother tongue of only 0.05% of the population, while 5% are bilingual. It also has its own dialect of English, having grown out of an archaic English spoken by seafarers and having been preserved by the province's relative isolation from the rest of Canada. So different is their language that a dictionary of Newfoundland English sells well. In it, one can learn, for example, that a female companion was once called a "friendgirl." Heavily Irish, while a third of Newfoundlanders are Roman Catholic, in an effort to raise the educational level of their fellow citizens, in 1997 Newfoundlanders overwhelmingly voted to replace all church-run schools with a state-run educational system.

Newfoundland has faced knotty economic challenges, with the main one devastated fishing industry which its main

Hon. Andrew Furey
Premier of Newfoundland

source of employment in the over 700 communities around its 6,000-mile coastline. This occurred because in 1977 Canada declared a 200-mile limit in the sea and began subsidizing boats and fish processing plants, many of which now stand idle. Bowing to foreign and domestic political pressure, Canada banned the unrestricted killing of seals thereby enabling the seal population to triple since the 1970s. Each animal consumes an average of 45 pounds of fish a day. This, as well as overfishing, combined almost to destroy the fish stocks, especially cod. Seal hunting with clear quotas is permitted annually as about 6,000 Canadians in outlying areas benefit from this part-time employment.

In 1989, Canada granted France the right to fish an extra 11,000 tons of cod from the waters off Newfoundland in return for its agreement to submit a dispute about the

Government House, residence of the Lieutenant Governor of Newfoundland, St. John's

Canada

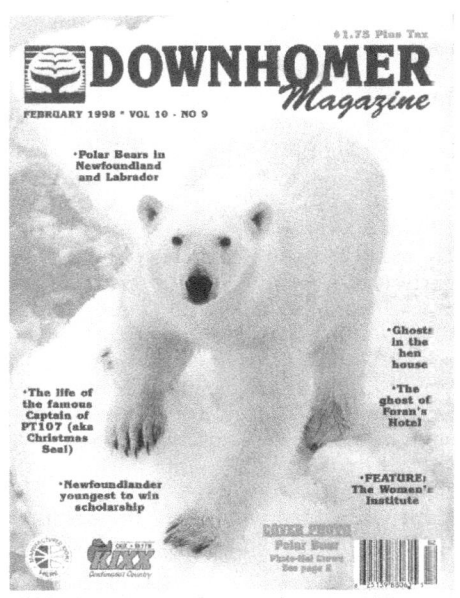

maritime boundaries around the French islands of St. Pierre and Miquelon, which have a population of only 6,000 and are located 16 miles off the coast of Newfoundland, to international arbitration. In 1992 an international tribunal awarded France only a fourth of the area it claimed. In 2009 France announced that it would file a new claim with the UN to an area of the continental shelf south of the two islands in an attempt to procure some of the oil and gas that is enriching Newfoundland.

Also in 2009, Ottawa slapped a moratorium on all northern cod fishing to allow the dwindling stocks to replenish themselves. This bitter decision sent thousands of fishermen and fishery workers into unemployment lines. Of the 42,000 who had once worked in the province's fishing industry, 27,000 were employed by 1999. Revenues from cod fishing had fallen from $136 million in 1988 to only $1 million a decade later. Former Premier Tobin acknowledged, "they know that the fish are gone, they know that the income support won't last forever."

In 2003, the federal fisheries minister announced the closure of most of the remaining Atlantic cod fishing industry because of the depleted stocks. Responding to former Premier Roger Grimes' angry demand for a constitutional change to give the province more control over the industry, former federal Liberal Party leader Stéphane Dion noted sadly: "No amendment would bring back the fish." There are some experts, such as George Rose of St. John's Memorial University, who think the cod will come back, but patience is needed.

There are some hopes that aquaculture, using the cold, unpolluted waters to raise seafood products such as scallops, salmon, mussels, whelk, and sea urchins, can provide work for some of them. In 1998, huge increases in crab and shrimp catches pushed the value of fish landings to an all-time high. Even so, the industry employs far fewer people, about 2,000 in boats and 4,000 in processing plants, compared with about 18,000 in boats and up to 20,000 in plants earlier.

The EU agreed temporarily to suspend fishing in the area. When pirate fishermen from Europe continued to overfish the dwindling stocks, Canada acted in 1995. The government sent a frigate, fired a shot over the bow of a Spanish trawler outside the 200-mile fishing zone, boarded the vessel, and ordered it to St. John's. There officials found illegal nets on board and doctored records proving that the fishermen had violated international agreements. After much acrimony, a settlement was reached calling for closer monitoring and enforcement of fish catches. The then Fisheries Minister Brian Tobin, a former TV anchor from Newfoundland, became a national hero overnight. A year later he was premier.

In October 2003, Conservative Danny Williams, a former Rhodes Scholar, crusading lawyer, and multi-millionaire after selling his cable-TV business for $232 million in 2000, hence his nickname "Danny Millions," was elected premier with 34 of 48 legislative seats. He was scrappy, articulate and prone to the dramatic, and he has made a career out of tough talk and a knack for the well-chosen fight. His antics get Ottawa's attention. Williams faced a huge budget deficit, with $1 billion going annually to servicing a debt that amounts to $23,000 per person, Canada's largest. The population of 527,000 shrunk by 10% from 1994–2003 and is projected to plunge to 482,000 by 2035 despite the oil and gas boom. In only three years Williams turned his province's fortunes around.

In the 1960s, great reserves of off-shore oil and gas were discovered in the Grand Banks. The Hibernia field on the edge of this trove, 200 miles offshore, contains large quantities of oil. The province fought a furious battle with Ottawa over who owns and controls those reserves. According to a 1984 ruling of the Supreme Court of Canada, the federal government owns offshore resources. However, in 1985, the Mulroney government signed an "Atlantic Accord" with Newfoundland, granting it most of the powers over the Hibernia field. In 1993, the federal government agreed to buy an 8.5% share in order that the project could continue and begin producing oil in 1997. The provincial government is trying to buy back that federal equity stake. It is Canada's highest producing field and helped make the province Canada's second-largest oil producer and for a while one of the richer "have" provinces.

The Terra Nova field, 20 miles southeast of Hibernia, produced its first oil in 2000 although its output did not materialize as expected. White Rose, in 2006, and other fields followed. The southern extension of Hibernia was delayed. Nevertheless, Newfoundland expected to receive as much as $4.9 billion in oil revenues for the eight years following 2005. That was not to be. Plunging oil and gas prices, as well as a collapse of the mining sector drove the government deficit close to two billion dollars and pushed the province's unemployment rate up over 11%, the country's highest. Oil and gas account for 30% of the economy, and one-third are employed by the provincial government.

Williams was determined to gain even more of the proceeds for his province, and he succeeded. In 2007 he risked a multi-billion-dollar deal with the oil companies by demanding a 4.9% ownership share in the Hebron offshore project and a generous royalty system. He signed a multi-year agreement with Chevron, ExxonMobil, Petro-Canada, and StatoilHydro to develop Hebron, located south of the lucrative Hibernia fields. He was guided by his simple principle of "no more giveaways," and he won. He had tapped the sense of aggrieved nationalism "the Rock," the province's nickname, pledging to make the half a million Newfoundlanders "masters in our own house."

Voters rewarded Williams richly with a landslide reelection victory in 2007. His party won almost 70% of the votes and all but four of the 48 seats. This was not necessarily good news for the federal Tories. Williams was the first premier to urge Canadians to vote for any other party but his own in federal elections because he believed a Conservative majority would be dangerous.

In 2002, a federal tribunal settled the 37-year boundary dispute between Newfoundland and Nova Scotia about 170 kilometers or about 105 miles, offshore. Newfoundland received 75% of the potentially oil-rich offshore region, known as the Laurentian sub-basin, which could hold nearly a billion barrels of oil. Nova Scotia was awarded only 16%, while the French islands of St. Pierre and Miquelon, home to 6,000 French citizens using euros, received 9%.

Leaders in St. John's bargained hard for maximum benefits from one of the world's richest nickel deposits at Voisey's Bay in Labrador's rugged interior. The mine has the potential of supplying 13% of the world's nickel. After years of negotiations the provincial government and two Aboriginal peoples, the 5,000 Inuit and 1,500 Innu, agreed to allow nickel mining at an open-pit

Canada

site starting in 2006, while a pilot processing plant is built at Argentia. The project should create hundreds of permanent jobs, a hoped-for Can$11 billion in revenue for the government over 30 years, $255 million to the Inuit, who claim the land around the mine, and a percentage of the mine's profits to the two Aboriginal groups. A major problem is that it is so remote: there are no roads to it and sea ice closes it off for six months a year. Ice breakers must make a dozen trips per year to and from the mine. Premier Williams revived an earlier plan to build an 11 mile or 17-km tunnel under the Strait of Belle Isle to connect Newfoundland and Labrador's population of 28,000.

Newfoundland was Canada's poorest province and had its highest cost-of-living, lowest per capita income, and highest unemployment rate, 14.9% in 2017, more than double the national average of 5.9%. It also was heavily dependent on Ottawa, which in 2002 was the source of 39% of the province's revenues. In 2004–5, the central government sent $674 million or $1,304 per person in the form of federal equalization payments.

The situation changed for Newfoundland considering its rising oil revenues. Tens of billions of dollars poured into major developmental projects as the government surplus grew to $755 million in 2011. One unfamiliar problem emerged from this boom, an acute shortage of skilled labor in the midst of high overall joblessness.

In light of Newfoundland's prior condition, Ottawa awarded it equalization payments. These monies are designed to help poorer provinces that are less able to afford basic services so they can achieve an established standard. In 2009, Newfoundland joined Alberta, Saskatchewan, and British Columbia in not qualifying for such payments.

Williams quarreled with the federal government's view that Newfoundland's equalization payments should decline as revenues from offshore oil increase. He became popular at home, with an astounding approval rating of 92% by the time of his retirement in 2010 as his stand against big oil and his arguments that it's high time that Newfoundlanders be "masters of our own destiny" only heightened his popularity. However, he was unpopular everywhere else in Canada because of his insistence that Newfoundland receive every penny of its equalization funds while getting a bigger and fairer share of offshore oil wealth. Williams argued that this was Newfoundland's last and best chance to become a "have" rather than a perpetual "have-not" province. "This is our one shot. . . . We will invest in social programs, in infrastructure, we will lower our debt." He had already eliminated his province's budget deficit.

In 2009, the province still had a debt of $11.6 billion, the highest per capita in Canada. Nevertheless, Williams created the foundation for a more prosperous province, with housing prices soaring resulting in a shortage of affordable housing, higher wages, and lower unemployment. Williams continued to attract much investment capital to "the Rock," prompting local wits to call the province "Dannyland" or "Williamsburg." A film, *Danny*, portrayed his eventful life.

High unemployment continued to stimulate some emigration annually from Newfoundland to more lucrative pastures in Canada although increasing prosperity at home and hard times in the West reduced such movement. Three-fourths of those departing were between the ages of 15 and 34. According to the government of Newfoundland, out migration reached 2,700 in 2019. So many worked in the oil sand industry of Fort McMurray that locals jokingly called their town Fort Mc-Newfoundland. The out migration was particularly distressing because Newfoundland's birthrate is Canada's lowest despite polls at the turn of the century citing its people as the most sexually active Canadians. Almost a half million Newfoundland emigrés live in southern Ontario and even have their own monthly newspaper, The *Downhomer*.

An enduring irritant is the 65-year contract which Newfoundland's former Liberal premier, Joey Smallwood, signed with Quebec in 1969. He needed Quebec's support of development loans to construct one of the world's largest hydroelectric plants at Churchill Falls, in the wilderness of Labrador. In exchange, Newfoundland agreed to sell Quebec almost all the electricity produced by the plant for 65 years at 1969 prices. There was no provision for renegotiating the contract. No one anticipated the skyrocketing of energy prices following the 1973 energy crisis.

Today, Quebec buys the Churchill Falls electricity for one tenth the prevailing market price and turns around and exports it to New England for ten times what it pays Newfoundland for it. Newfoundland loses $800 million annually. Quebec claims that its exported electricity actually comes from its huge James Bay project, and that Quebec uses Newfoundland's electricity at home. Few Newfoundlanders can accept that argument.

To rub salt into the wounds, Newfoundland has had to construct four additional power plants to supply its own electrical needs because it receives only a small portion of Churchill Falls' production. A much-trumpeted deal with Quebec to develop another hydroelectric project on the Lower Churchill River in Labrador collapsed in 2000. In 2005, Ontario and Quebec joined forces to bid for the development of the Lower Churchill River, one of the last remaining large untapped hydroelectricity sites in North America.

All efforts to renegotiate the original contract failed. The Supreme Court of Canada ruled that a deal is a deal. This issue seriously burdened relations with Newfoundland's western neighbor, giving Quebec political leverage. For example, when Newfoundland's premier announced his opposition to the Meech Lake Accord, Quebec Premier Robert Bourassa tartly responded that renegotiation of hydroelectric and other deals with Quebec would be easier in a climate of "cordial relations." Newfoundland continues to badger Quebec for a change to no avail.

That 1969 Churchill Falls deal still haunts the province. The boldness in negotiating high royalties and partial ownership in the Hebron field in 2007 offered the opportunity to put that painful and humiliating history behind them. The future holds even greater frustration regarding Churchill Falls. It was rediscovered that Quebec has the right to a 25-year extension of the contract at even lower pre-set rates after the current 44-year term runs out in 2016. Newfoundlanders groan that the new rate is "barely distinguishable from being free." A week before a new premier took office in December 2010, the province signed a $6.2 billion deal for a hydro mega-project on the Lower Churchill.

Hon. Tim Houston

Canada

The World Trade and Convention Centre, Halifax, Nova Scotia

Williams was succeeded by his former minister of natural resources, Kathy Dunderdale. Not only was she Newfoundland's first female leader, but she entered the 2011 provincial election as the favorite in a field consisting only of women: Lorraine Michaels of the NDP and Yvonne Jones of the Liberals. Born one of 11 children of a trawlerman in Placentia Bay, Dunderdale never finished her degree at Memorial University in St. John's. Dunderdale worked her way up the political ladder, starting as a Liberal before switching to the Tories, and became Williams' right-hand person. Dunderdale was just as feisty as he was and became almost as popular: in 2011 she enjoyed Canada's second highest approval rating at 55%.

The economic shambles on the Rock opened the door for a Liberal landslide in November 2015. Dwight Ball, who called for more deficit spending, became premier, but retired from politics in 2020, replaced by Andrew Furey. In the election of 2021 (which had been delayed due to the global COVID-19 pandemic), Furey was returned to government with a majority of his own. Still, the Rock "have-not" status as oil royalties have declined by a third, the budget deficit grows, the economy shrinks, and megaprojects wind down. Newfoundlanders will return to the polls no later than November 24, 2025.

Human residents share the island with 120,000 to 200,000 moose, the world's highest-density moose population that increasingly make nuisances of themselves. Brought from the mainland a century ago to help attract tourists and hunters to the then British colony, they have no predators since the native wolf became extinct. Moose are unpredictable, can run 35 miles or 56 kilometers per hour, swim as fast as two grown men paddling a canoe, and worse, are inclined to wander out on highways at night and cause about 600 collisions each year. On a different note, sightseers were delighted in 2017 when a 15,000-year-old, 15-story iceberg bumped up against Newfoundland's shore.

Nova Scotia: Like Newfoundland and Labrador, Nova Scotia staked great hopes on an economic resurgence stimulated by offshore energy resources, especially on the natural gas reserves in the Sable Is-

land area 180 miles east of Halifax. With both offshore and onshore facilities for producing and processing natural gas, it is the largest industrial undertaking in the province's history and Canada's biggest construction project entering the 21st century. Delivery of gas began in 1999, with New England as the principal market. There were hopes of even more gas outside the Sable development, but they have been disappointed by a series of dry wells and expired exploration licenses. Many analysts now conclude that there is not as much gas or oil as some had believed. Despite sizable investments offshore by energy giants, no oil was found.

In 2002, Nova Scotia lost an offshore boundary dispute with Newfoundland over possession of potentially vast reserves of gas and oil. Newfoundland claimed it had never signed a 1964 deal drawing a line. The financial stakes were raised for Nova Scotia in 2001 when Ottawa announced the closure of the Prince colliery, the island's last working underground coal mine. The province's Irving Shipbuilding yard supplies the navy with 15 frigates and eight Arctic patrol boats worth about $25 billion. Nova Scotia is the most populous of the four Atlantic Provinces but has one of Canada's oldest and most stagnant populations. It needs 10,000 immigrants to avoid a labor crunch.

In October 2013, the voters replaced the first NDP government in Atlantic Canada after a decade of Tory rule. Led by former Premier Darrell Dexter, who lost his own riding, the New Democrats came in third place winning only 26.84% of the votes, down from 45.26%, and 7 seats, down from 31. Riding on the coattails of popular federal Liberal leader, Justin Trudeau, the Liberals emerged the big winners, led by Premier Stephen McNeil. Following McNeil's resignation in 2020, Iain Rankin became leader of the Liberals and premier, only to lose at the 2021 election. The Progressive Conservatives returned to power, with their leader, Tim Houston, becoming premier; in the 65th General Election, held on November 26, 2024, Tim Houston was returned to power with a huge majority government (43 seats to the New Democrats 9 and the Liberals 2).

Prince Edward Island: The tiny, beautiful Prince Edward Island, which strives to maintain its unique culture and pace of life, saw the Tories end 10 years of Liberal rule in an electoral upset in 1996. The Liberal Party, whose former leader, Catherine Callbeck, had been the first elected female premier in Canadian history, captured only eight seats in the 27-seat Legislative Assembly.

Enjoying a 75% approval rating after three and one-half years, the Tories call new elections in 2000. The results were staggering. Running on the slogan, "Let's continue," they captured 58% of the votes and 26 of 27 seats. This was the Liberals'

Canada

Province House in Charlottetown, P.E.I., where the Canadian federation was born

worst defeat in provincial history. Led in 2003 by Robert Ghiz, whose father Joe had been premier from 1986 to 1993, the Liberals did better, winning 43% of the votes, but only four seats. An astonishing 83% of eligible voters turned out to return the Tories to their third consecutive term.

Pat Binns became premier. His success was especially remarkable on an island where family connections can make or break a political career. Binns, born in Saskatchewan and having grown up in Alberta, first came to Prince Edward Island in 1970 on a student exchange program and married a local woman. Returning in 1978, he became a bean farmer and

Hon. Dennis King—Premier of Prince Edward Island
Retrieved from: http://www.peipc.ca/dennisking

plunged right into politics. One of his Tory colleagues noted: "Pat is the kind of politician they go for out here. He grew up on a farm, he always returns phone calls, he never loses his temper." He successfully met the unenviable task of helping PEI adjust to the shocks of steady reductions in transfer payments from Ottawa.

Under Robert Ghiz's able leadership, the Liberals won dramatic victories in both 2007 and October 2011. In 2011, voters again witnessed the effects of the single-member electoral system. With 51.4% of the popular votes, the Liberals won 22 seats. The Conservatives, led by Olive Crane, captured 40.2%, but garnered only five seats. The Greens, with 4.4%, and the NDP, with 3.2%, earned no seats in the legislature.

Ghiz, born in Charlottetown in 1974, became the country's youngest premier. He had studied political science at Bishops University in Quebec before going to Ottawa to work for the ruling Liberal Party. Ghiz ended up as Prime Minister Jean Chrétien's adviser on the Atlantic provinces, returning home in 2003 to compete successfully for the Liberal Party leadership. Liked for his collegial style and willingness to give credit to his team, Ghiz was succeeded as premier by Wade MacLauchlan.

Agriculture remains the island's main source of income, especially potato farming. Nevertheless, the number of family farms declined from around 5,000 in 1970 to only 2,200 in 2001, and most islanders work in offices. PEI was also the first province to provide internet access in all schools and public libraries.

In 1996, the last concrete span of the 13-kilometer, about 8-mile, Confederation Bridge was lowered into place, opening on May 31, 1997. At a cost of about $25, cars can cross it in 12 minutes. This is Prince Edward Island's first physical link with the outside world since the ice age. Fears of disrupting the island's peaceful style of living had erupted in 1987 when plans for this bridge across the frigid waters of the Northumberland Strait from Borden to Cape Tormentine, New Brunswick, were announced. In a 1988 referendum on the issue, 59% of voters approved the link with the mainland, despite protests from fishermen, ferry employees, and other islanders who feared that outsiders, particularly Americans, would be encouraged to buy up more land on their island.

In an effort to quiet the fear of voters, legislation was passed forbidding non-islanders from purchasing more than five acres without cabinet approval or from

having a shorefront more than 50 meters or about 165 feet). In 2018, the Island Regulatory and Appeals Commission conducted a major review to determine how land is owned by nonresidents and corporations. In 2016, people were required to live in the province for at least 365 days over a two-year period to be considered a resident instead of the prior six months. Som islanders believe that the bridge and foreign ownership threaten something fundamental to the psyche of residents, the sense that they are separate and different from the rest of Canada.

The Confederation Bridge attracts more tourists. In fact, Prince Edward Island's license plates feature the bridge instead of the pigtailed and freckled Anne of Green Gables, the island's most famous fictional resident and most popular tourist site. With a population of only 153,244 (2018) PEI already draws over one million tourists annually, outnumbering the islanders by almost ten to one. To boost its population, it avidly invites immigration. Ottawa rewarded the island for its royalist sentiments by providing $170,000 for tea parties, concerts, and

Canada

Elephant Rock, Hopewell Cape near Moncton, was about 200 feet high until it collapsed in 2016.

picnics to celebrate Queen Elizabeth II's Diamond Jubilee in 2012.

In April 2019, voters ousted the Liberal government of Premier Wade MacLauchlan in favor of a minority Progressive Conservative led by Dennis King. Interestingly the Green Party became the official opposition. Progressive Conservative won 12 seats, the Green Party 8, and the Liberal Party 6.

King called an early election and, on 3 April 2023, voters returned the Progressive Conservatives to government with a majority, increasing from 15 to 22 seats, to the Liberals 3 and the Greens 2. Voter turnout of 68.5%, though, was the lowest recorded for a general election since Elections PEI began keeping records in 1966.

New Brunswick: One of the New Brunswick's oldest political problems is how to accommodate the Acadian French minority. There are 242,000 French Acadians, only 8% of whom no longer speak French at home; they account for 35% of the province's population. This is proportionately the biggest francophone community in any province outside Quebec. The Université de Moncton opened its doors in 1963 and rapidly became North America's largest French-speaking university outside of Quebec. For a while, it was a hotbed of activism for bilingualism and equal rights for francophones. As life on New Brunswick improved, most of the anger disappeared. In 1969, New Brunswick became the only bilingual province in Canada as the government moved to make itself, courts, and public institutions bilingual. Francophone leaders, organized in such groups as the Societé des Acadiens du Nouveau Brunswick, pushed for faster progress.

The government's efforts to increase the number of bilingual civil servants, the bulk of whom are Acadian, aroused charges that unilingual anglophones could no longer be hired or promoted in government service, a claim that was incorrect. So angry were many anglophones that they pressed their demands through a New Brunswick Association of English-Speaking Canadians and a vocally anti-bilingual party, the Confederation of Regions (COR). COR's capture of 30% of anglophone votes risked inflaming language tensions, but in the 1995 elections it was wiped out of the legislature.

In a bid for language reconciliation, the Saint John Theatre Company adopted New Brunswick as the backdrop for its 2012 production of William Shakespeare's *Romeo and Juliet*. In the production Romeo's family spoke English while Juliet's spoke French.

During an Acadian world conference in 1994 author Antoine Maillet, whose play, *La Sagouine*, portrays Acadian resilience, could boast that "we don't need to fight for survival any more, we did it." Former Prime Minister Jean Chrétien savored the opportunity to take a swipe at Quebec separatists by complimenting Acadians for finding "concrete ways to live in harmony instead of remaining prisoners of old grudges." In 1999, he chose Moncton, which is on the verge of replacing St. John as the province's most vibrant economy, as the site for a Francophonie conference of leaders from 49 nations where a majority or sizable minority speak French. This was the first time a French president visited the nearly 290,000 Acadians spread out among the provinces of New Brunswick with 242,000 residents while Nova Scotia's 35,000, Prince Edward Island's 5,500, and Newfoundland's 2,300). In August 2005, tens of thousands of Acadians celebrated their survival of the deportation 250 years earlier.

New Brunswick's bilingualism still creates tension, but it is now regarded as an asset instead of a liability. Moncton is the fastest-growing region in Atlantic Canada largely because it is bilingual. The percentage of anglophone children enrolling in French immersion courses is an impressive 11%, Canada's highest rate of such enrollment at the grade school level. New Brunswick adopted language reforms to guarantee francophones more powers and rights, allowing them to attend French-language schools and receive health care in their mother tongue. Fifteen percent of anglophones are bilingual, compared with 71% of francophones.

In October 2014, 32-year-old Bryan Gallant, an athletic Moncton lawyer, became premier as his Liberal Party captured 43% of the votes and 27 of 49 seats. The Conservatives won 21 and the Greens 1. In 2018, Premier Gallant and the Liberal Party lost at the polls as Blaine Myron

Hon. Blaine Myron Higgs

Retrieved from: https://www.macleans.ca/politics/new-brunswick-election-deadlocked-the-morning-after/

Canada

Baking bread in New Brunswick: an Acadian village woman in traditional garb

Higgs, the leader of the New Brunswick Progressive Conservative party became the 34th Premier of New Brunswick. He had been a member of the legislature since 2010 and served as Minister of Finance from 2010-2014 in the government of David Alward. Higgs' new government has 22 seats and on November 2, 2018 when combined with another party, the People's Alliance, passed a non-confidence vote against the Liberal Party minority government's 21 seats. At the 40th General Election since Confederation in 2020, Higgs was returned to government, this time with 27 seats, two more than required to form a majority. In the General Election of October 21, 2024, however, Susan Holt led the Liberals to power, with a majority of 15 seats over Higgs's Progressive Conservatives. Higgs was defeated in his own riding, and Holt became the first ever woman premier of New Brunswick.

As had previous governments, however, the new government continued to face significant challenges in a province with an aging population and from which the young continue to leave. Services are more expensive in a province where half the people live in rural areas. Still, it sees a bright spot in exploration for shale gas deposits in the south as it finds itself in the middle of a sovereignty dispute with the U.S. over Machias Seal Island and North Rock, a tiny, rocky, treeless uninhabited islands in the Bay of Fundy whose only inhabitants are 5,800 pairs of nesting puffins. Located almost equidistant between Maine and New Brunswick, these islands are the last land mass contested by Canada and the U.S.

Quebec: In 1985, nine years after it had ascended to power, the Parti Québécois (PQ) had to relinquish it. In 2007 it suffered an especially devastating electoral defeat, surpassed by two other Quebec parties. In a way, the PQ was the victim of its own success. French language and cultural rights within the province of 8.1 million inhabitants, and 70,000 French citizens, had been secured, and Canada had been prodded to become bilingual. Quebec had also modernized itself almost beyond recognition. As "masters in their own house," Québécois were ready to turn their attention more to personal achievement and to the down-to-earth problems of unemployment and economic revival. The PQ itself became divided over whether to cling to the dream of sovereignty. Neither the Tories nor the New Democrats are political forces in Quebec provincial politics.

Commenting on the Liberals' 1985 election victory, Lysiane Gagnon, columnist for *La Presse* of Montreal wrote: "Quebecers changed governments the way one changes banks—without passion, as a business decision. There are neither dreams nor exultation nor broken hopes." Dreams and passions were reawakened in 1987 when René Lévesque died of a heart attack. The emotional outpouring sparked comparisons of the charismatic spiritual father of the PQ and his successor, the aloof Pierre Marc Johnson. The latter's replacement in 1987 was future PQ premier, Jacques Parizeau, whose wit, energy, professorial air, and economic record were only outdone by his fervor for Quebec sovereignty.

The Quebec Liberals are staunchly pro-federalist. Consequently, Bourassa met many times with Brian Mulroney to negotiate the Meech Lake Accord. In 1987 he broke with almost a quarter century of Quebec tradition and hosted a banquet for the Queen, presiding over an enviable improvement in the economy of Quebec.

Bourassa's party had promised to relax restrictions on bilingual signs. However, in office Bourassa did nothing because the courts were reviewing the issue. After a temporary respite from language tensions, the flames were rekindled in 1988. The Supreme Court of Canada ruled that Bill 101 violated the freedom-of-expression guarantees in Quebec's own charter of rights by banning the use of non-French words on commercial signs. Nationalist groups immediately rose up against the Court's decision, showing just how volatile the language issue remains. Wishing to avoid a confrontation with Quebec nationalists, Bourassa announced Bill 178, which prohibits English on outside signs while permitting it on inside signs, providing that French is used more prominently. He also invoked the so-called "notwithstanding clause" in the 1982 Constitution to prevent any further court challenge.

Bourassa saw this move as a compromise, but it pleased almost nobody and detonated the most serious English-French confrontation since 1980. Hard-line *Québécois*, who were infuriated that English could again be used on some signs, demonstrated and threw fire bombs into the Montreal offices of the English-rights lobby group called Alliance Quebec, which later imploded in 2005 when the federal government cut off its funds. One young man climbed the large cross on top of Montreal's Mount Royal and sat there for 13 freezing hours in protest. Three anglophone cabinet members resigned, including Clifford Lincoln, who asserted: "rights are rights are rights. There are no inside and outside rights." Anglophone Quebecers felt betrayed and became uneasy again, while Anglophones all over Canada protested. Fears of emigration were reawakened. During the nine-year PQ rule, 140,000 left Quebec, and more than 400,000 departed over a two-decade span from 1976 and 1996.

The Meech Lake Accord was former Prime Minister Brian Mulroney's attempt to create harmony by granting Quebec the status of "a distinct society" and by protecting minority language rights everywhere in Canada; it also would have secured Quebec's ratification of the 1982 Constitution. Its rejection angered Quebecers and reignited powerful nationalist sentiments. A saddened Hugh MacLennan, whose 1945 novel *Two Solitudes* chronicled the cultural divide between francophones and anglophones, mused in 1989, one year before

Canada

his death, about his French-speaking countrymen: "I wish we could get along with them . . . I just don't know if they want us anymore." There remains much ignorance about Quebec. A 1989 study showed that only 5% of the stories in CBC or the *Globe and Mail* came from Quebec.

In making an unambiguous appeal for final and complete separation from Canada and in rejecting federalism of any kind as an option, which is why he rejected Meech Lake, the self-confident Parizeau differed from the humble populist, Lévesque, who always couched his pitch for sovereignty in the context of an undefined association with the rest of Canada. Parizeau, who speaks perfect English and has a doctorate in economics from the London School of Economics, argued that new social and economic conditions make independence more viable now. "I can rely on new strengths that Quebec did not have 20 years ago, when it was not at all obvious that Quebec entrepreneurs were capable of competing internationally. Now it is."

By improving the province's access to American markets, NAFTA further reduces Quebec's economic dependence on the rest of Canada. An independent Quebec would have to negotiate with Canada, the U.S., and Mexico to gain entry into the trilateral agreement. As an independent country it would be the U.S.'s sixth-largest trading partner. However, one of the most protected businesses in Quebec is the milk industry through a system of supply management which the federal government has had to, in part, open up to American competition due to the 2018 USMCA, which replaced NAFTA; a revised version of the USMCA took effect on July 1, 2020.

Both supporters and opponents of sovereignty rest their plans on economic prowess in Quebec. There have been some setbacks. The complex and expensive James Bay project was to be financed largely by exporting electricity to northeastern U.S. to supply cheap energy to companies lured into Quebec. Even so, the province suffered a severe setback in 1992 when its development plans collided with environmentalists and native claims. The 13,500 Cree living in Quebec maintained that the project is on their land and would poison their fish. Indeed, in 1912 the federal government devolved present-day northern Quebec, known to Indigenous people as Ungava, to the province as an administrative convenience.

The Crees' opposition to the James Bay project, which would reduce the flow in the Great Whale and other rivers, found support among American environmental groups. This resulted in New York State's cancellation of its power contract with Quebec, devastating news for the province. In 1994, Parizeau had to put the project on hold indefinitely. In 2002, the Cree agreed to drop their suits against the hydro plans on the Rupert and Eastmain rivers in perhaps the most important treaty signed with an Aboriginal group. They opened up their territory to mining, logging, and industrial development by Hydro-Québec. In return, Quebec paid the Cree a minimum of $3.5 billion over 50 years, granting them a say in any development in order to protect traditional hunting and trapping rights. This deal was calculated to create 8,000 jobs and increase electricity production by about 8%.

In 2011, the Quebec government announced an ambitious 25-year plan to develop a large part of its vast northern and Arctic region, an area where, in former Premier Jean Charest's words, "we have every resource imaginable." While industrial activity will be banned in some of the region, mining and industry will be allowed in other parts, all in close coordination with the local aboriginal populations. Not since the northern Alberta oil sands were exploited has there been such a grandiose attempt to develop the sparsely populated north. Charest argued that this "Plan Nord" will strengthen Canada's disputed claims to the Northwest Passage. It "is an affirmation of sovereignty." Charest's successor as premier, Pauline Marois, vowed to continue this project. Quebec created a sovereign-wealth fund, the Generations Fund, similar to Alberta's, into which royalties from mining and hydropower concessions, as well as profits from Hydro-Quebec, a provincially owned utility, can be deposited; it is managed by an independent agency.

An independent Quebec would have to face the prospect that the Cree and the Inuit, supported by Ottawa, would take back more than half the present province. Quebec's relations with its 60,000 aboriginal peoples, most of whom prefer to speak English, were already strained over their claims also to be a "distinct society." Quebec's aboriginals find their most compelling arguments in the PQ's rhetoric. Cree Grand Chief Matthew Coon Come asserts: "If Canada is divisible, so is Quebec," a concept endorsed by Prime Minister Chrétien in 1996.

Inuit leaders have also put Quebec on notice that "we are not coming with you on a journey toward independence," as Zebedee Nungak put it. The Inuit of the northern third of Quebec moved a step closer to self-government in November 1999. They signed a political accord with Ottawa and Quebec setting up a commission to facilitate discussions leading to a government in their region called Nunavik. There are no roads linking Nunavik to the rest of the province. In an effort to

Cree lands

bring the two parts closer together, the Quebec government is working on plans to construct roads to a few Nunavik communities. In 2016, the Quebec government announced a five-year, $100 million investment in municipal infrastructure.

Numerous anglophone groups in Quebec, supported by the federal government, picked up on the idea of partition if Quebec breaks away from Canada. Examples include the Quebec Committee for Canada and the Committee for a New Quebec. Both proposed that any area in which francophones are not prominent, including suburbs of Montreal, remain with Canada. PQ leaders dismissed such warnings and proposals as nonsense.

Parizeau shrewdly played on the frictions between Quebec and the rest of Canada in rejecting what he saw as a flawed federalism. His solution: a series of referenda to take over powers from Ottawa, on the way to a sovereign Quebec. The political equation was further complicated by the formation in the federal parliament of a *Bloc Québécois*, led initially by Lucien Bouchard. The PQ supported it in the 1993 federal elections rather than Mulroney's Tories, as it had done in the prior two campaigns. This cost Mulroney valuable backing in Quebec and enabled the *Bloc Québécois* to become the second-largest party and official opposition in Ottawa.

In 1994, Quebecers had their clearest choice ever. Gone was the fuzzy middle ground of "sovereignty-association" *à la* Lévesque. The PQ now called for nothing short of separation, declaring that a victory would be interpreted as a mandate to have the National Assembly make a "solemn declaration" of Quebec's intention to become independent. The PQ would then approach Ottawa to negotiate terms and

Canada

put the result to Quebec voters within 10 months of the election. A narrow plurality of Quebec's voters decided to give the PQ that chance.

The PQ noted with uneasiness that it received only 44.7% of the popular votes, compared with the pro-federal Liberals' impressive 44.3%. This bode ill for the referendum Parizeau had pledged to hold in 1995. Even if he could woo many of the 6.5% of voters who supported the *Action Démocratique du Quebec* (ADQ), led by Mario Dumont and composed of moderate former Liberals of a separatist tinge, he faced an uphill struggle. Bouchard, who lost a leg in 1994 to a frightening flesh-eating disease, began to express his opinion publicly that the separatist option should include close ties with Canada.

Quebec and Canada changed significantly since the referendum on Quebec sovereignty in 1980. The presence of the *Bloc Québécois* as the official opposition in the House of Commons gave separatism a new respectability and boost. Bouchard was able to persuade Parizeau and Dumont to agree on a "soft" referendum question calling for negotiating with Ottawa an economic and political partnership with an independent Quebec. The results of the 1995 referendum demonstrated that a majority of Quebec francophones supported that concept.

This is one reason why there was such an outcry throughout Canada in the midst of the 1997 federal parliamentary elections when Parizeau published his memoirs, *For A Sovereign Quebec*. In these memoirs, he admitted that he prepared to declare Quebec's independence immediately after a yes-vote in 1995, not after negotiations with Ottawa, as his party had proposed during the referendum campaign. Many think he deceived Quebec voters. In 2004 Parizeau published a letter in *La Presse* demanding that referenda be done away with and that the next PQ electoral victory be considered a mandate in itself to prepare for succession. Even within the PQ such ideas are scorned.

In the campaign, Parizeau stepped aside to allow Bouchard to energize it. A charismatic master of lofty emotion, he became a hero and savior in Quebec, the most popular figure since Lévesque. His oratorical skill brought separatists within a whisker of victory, winning 49.4% of the votes in a huge 94% turnout. This was 10 percentage points higher than in 1980. As in 1980, the difference was made by anglophones and immigrants, who voted overwhelmingly against independence, while 60% of francophones voted "yes."

Until the final days before the October 30, 1995, referendum the then Prime Minister Jean Chrétien chose to stand aloof from the debates in Quebec over separation, declar-

Trompe l'oeil in Old Town Quebec

ing that "I was elected not to talk about the constitution" and that "everybody knows where I stand. I come from Shawinigan. My province is Quebec. My country is Canada. My language is French. And they are all compatible." This aloofness was a serious blunder that hurt him in Canadian politics. Jean Charest was correct in saying that "winning a referendum doesn't mean you have solved the problem."

A confident Bouchard, who took over the premiership of Quebec from Parizeau in 1996, promised a new referendum by the year 2000, but had to back off from that. He defiantly rejected any option but sovereignty, asserting: "no one is going to get us into sterile discussions we've been having for 30 years. No longer will sovereigntists be begging for anything from the rest of Canada." This attitude guaranteed that Quebec would vigorously test Canada's fragile unity for many years. Perhaps Bouchard 's mother best captured the mood of many *Québécois* at that time: "I've never met an English-speaking Canadian. But I'm sure they are as nice as any other foreigners."

The Quebec economy, although vigorous in general, has Canada's highest per capita debt, highest tax burden (43% of GDP, vs. 37.2% elsewhere), shortest work week, and oldest population, as well as aggressive unionization and a determined unwillingness to change its generous but expensive social system. The safety net used to be offered by the Church and large families, but that was replaced by the most interventionist government in North America. Quebec's GDP in 2020 was 43%, continuing a downward trend from a peak of 54.3% from six years ago. Business interests solidly oppose sovereignty with many withholding investments in the province until its political future was clarified. While investment grew by 2.7% annually in Quebec, the other provinces experienced a 4.2% rise. By 2007, Quebec's share of Canadian private investment declined dramatically from 23% in 1987 to below 18%.

Quebec economist Pierre Cléroux lamented: "we are not going in the same direction as the other provinces." University tuition was frozen for 13 years until Premier Charest vowed in 2007 to raise it slightly. Despite the freeze, Quebec had the lowest university attendance and degree-completion record in all of Canada.

The governing PQ resurrected the Commission to Protect the French Language, abolished in 1993, derisively known among anglophones as the "language police" or "tongue troopers" because of their linguistic repression. It pledged to enforce language laws strictly, which had been diluted since 1993 because of constitutional standoffs in the Supreme Court of Canada and international pressure, including from the U.N. English became permissible on outdoor signs, as long as it appeared at half the size of the equivalent French words. A Superior Court in Quebec upheld this law in 2000 when two anglophone storeowners erected signs featuring

Canada

equal-sized French and English lettering.

In 2017, the legislature unanimously passed a non-binding resolution calling on shopkeepers to stop greeting customers with "bon jour hi" instead of "bon jour." A customer reportedly threatened a pet store owner for trying to sell a parrot that could not chatter in French. Yet, authorities permitted the use of "grilled cheese," "softball," and "drag queen."

The issue re-emerged after the PQ's electoral victory in September 2012. For 35 years the use of brand names by large American companies such as ostco, Walmart, Toys "R" Us, Best Buy, Pizza Hut, Linen Chest, Comfort Inn, and some Canadian ones, such as Canadian Tire, were tolerated. They sued the province, which wanted to require the businesses to add a slogan or description in French to their signs indicating what they sell. Some avoided problems by changing their names in Quebec, such as KFC to PFK and Staples to Bureau en Gros.

English-speaking Canadians who move to Montreal can send their children to English-language schools, but francophone and immigrant parents are not permitted to do so. Quebec immigration ministry figures revealed in 2011 that two-thirds of immigrants to the province speak French. A slight majority of immigrants whose native tongue is neither French nor English now choose French over English.

Just how secular Quebec has become, especially in Montreal, was demonstrated in 1999 when the province replaced its Catholic and Protestant confessional school boards with 60 French-language, nine English-language, and three aboriginal boards. A constitutional amendment made its school system entirely secular.

This seems logical in a province where church attendance among Catholics stands at 15%, the lowest rate in North America. The average age of priests was nearly 65, with empty seminaries providing few replacements. While 88% of *Québécois* say they believe in God, less than a third assert that they believe in the God portrayed by the Church. Only 34% believe there is a hell, compared with 49% in the rest of Canada. Despite this secularity, Canada's cardinal and former archbishop of Quebec City, Marc Ouellet, was a leading candidate for the papacy in 2013.

The 1999 *MacLean's*/CBC Poll revealed that Quebecers value individual rights and freedom to define one's own morality more highly than other Canadians; 70% strongly believe no one has the right to impose morality on others as opposed to 52% in the rest of Canada, and 29% say they would support a 17-year-old daughter's decision to have an abortion, compared with 15% elsewhere. Sexual permissiveness is widespread, with 53% of births out of wedlock.

The province's share of Canada's population has shrunk from 27.9% in the early 1970s to 23.23% in 2016. While Quebec has one of the lowest birth rates in the western world, its situation is improving, and the province has gained a reputation as "parent-friendly. The first step was "bucks for babies;" parents were paid $500 and $1,000 for the first two offspring respectively; subsequent children brought in as much as $8,000. The next was 200,000 subsidized day-care places. This costs parents only $7 per day. A parental leave policy that allows parents to take almost a year off at up to three-quarters of their salary is North America's most generous.

The results are impressive: an 8% increase in the birth rate in 2006, and 2.6% in 2007. The fertility rate has risen to 1.66, which is higher than the national average, even if still under the replacement rate of 2.1. Yet, the Canadian Broadcasting Corporation noted that in 2015 the Quebec birth rate had dropped for the sixth straight year and that the average number of children born to a woman between 15 and 49 years of age was 1.60.

Former Language Minister Louise Beaudoin lashed out at what she called "rampant bilingualism" in the public service and proclaimed 30 new measures to send the message of "French first!" Civil servants are required to get permission from superiors before making speeches in English. They may speak only French in meetings with Quebec-based companies and in dealing with the public by telephone or in person. The government no longer deals with Quebec-based companies that do not meet French language requirements in the workplace. More than eight of 10 franco-

Hon. Lucien Bouchard

phones and over half of anglophones in Montreal already speak French on the job. All computer software must be available in French unless no French version exists.

In 1998, a new challenge emerged: Jean Charest resigned as federal chairman of the Progressive Conservative Party to assume the leadership of Quebec's Liberals. It was not easy for him to fight in Quebec for the cause of a united Canada. One cannot be so aggressive as to alienate the province's "soft nationalists," those who regard Canada as a sensible arrangement but give their emotional attachment to French Quebec. They are the voters who make the difference in provincial elections and referenda.

In 2001, Bouchard resigned as premier saying that he had failed to accomplish the PQ's dream of making Quebec an independent country. A decade later, in 2010, he remained extremely popular, but he had given up on Quebec sovereignty: "There's no referendum in sight, and I don't want any more defeats. . . . It remains just a dream."

Bouchard's successor was Bernard Landry. A former optometrist from Joliette, Quebec, Landry was drawn into the separatist movement by Lévesque's vision and charisma and has embraced the sovereigntist gospel most of his adult life: "I am convinced not only that Canada has no use, but that it has been harmful." He vowed that his government's priority would be secession. However, Bouchard discovered that the province's foundering economy and a changed environment in North America made it necessary to put his pet project on the back burner. PQ party membership dropped to 65,000 although the party contended that the number is still close to 100,000.

The late Dr. Jacques Parizeau

Canada

In April 2003, a political earthquake occurred in Quebec. The PQ was buried in a Liberal landslide in provincial elections. Led by Jean Charest, the Liberals won a solid majority in the 125-seat National Assembly. The PQ under Landry, who predicted that Quebec would become a sovereign state within 1,000 days after his party's victory, fell to 33.2% and only 45 seats. It was hurt by Mario Dumont's ADQ, a center-right party that pledged to postpone referenda. Dumont described his party's goal as autonomy for Quebec while rejecting a complete rupture with Canada. "Old-fashioned separatism has little appeal for younger voters."

The turning point was a televised debate two weeks before the election in which Landry was unable to counter Charest's question why former Premier Jacques Parizeau was again blaming the loss of the 1995 referendum on "money and the ethnic vote," a code for Jews and immigrants. The PQ declined steadily thereafter.

Parizeau's reference to the importance of immigrants backfired, but it points to an important demographic development in Quebec that is distressing for the PQ. About one in ten voters in Quebec, as compared with 27% in Ontario, is an immigrant, and roughly 90% live in Montreal. With the birthrate plummeting, they make up a growing segment of the province's population. Although Quebec has for decades exercised its power to select its immigrants and to require that their children be educated in French, they feel little sympathy for the PQ's nationalist strivings. They have no stake in the historic English–French divide. But they have difficulties finding jobs.

Equally important is the fact that nearly 70% of the province's 918,000 anglophones are bilingual, an increase of roughly 12% since 1991; they do not fight against the language laws any more, and indeed the majority accepts them. The anglophones are willing to marry Quebecers outside their suburbs but overwhelmingly continue to support the Liberal party, Quebec's only outright federalist party. At the same, time more and more francophones believe that the goal to protect their language has been achieved. They are coming out of their Montreal ghettos. Teenagers are no longer inclined to speak the old *joual* dialect and often find English-sounding names for bars and restaurants "cool." The result is that more and more Quebecers are tired of the old passionate language disputes, and this affects politics.

The long-term result of Bill 101 is that two-thirds of anglophones in Quebec are now bilingual, and more than half of those persons whose mother tongue is neither French nor English can now speak both. Francophones are no longer underdogs. When the bill was first introduced, the median income of anglophone households was 20% to 30% higher than the provincial average. Wealth is spread more evenly in today's Quebec. Sponsors of Bill 101 thought it would generate momentum toward independence, but it had the opposite effect. By demonstrating that such a radical reform was possible within Confederation, it deflated the separatist movement more than any measure Ottawa could have taken. Nevertheless, language remains a touchy subject in Quebec. Jean Charest exploited language fatigue, knowing that a political system based on the former lingual divisions was overdue for a shakeup.

Charest's Liberals were not helped by a damaging federal Liberal scandal that provided tens of millions of dollars in taxpayers' money to friendly advertising companies in the province to sway Quebec opinion away from independence after 1995. Most of the money was simply pocketed by the businesses. Yet, the *Québécois* were insulted that anglophone Canadians, who accuse them often unfairly of blatant corruption, would engage in such sordid tactics themselves. Even though the *Bloc Québécois* assured Quebec voters that a vote for it was not a vote for independence, the party benefited from the scandal in the 2004 federal elections. It captured 54 of the province's 75 seats, now 78 seats, and forced the federal Liberals into a minority government. In 2006 it slipped to 51 seats and only 42% of the votes, far short of the majority it would need to secure independence for the province.

The 2006 federal elections caused a political earthquake in Quebec. The Conservatives gained a foothold in the province, rocketing from 9% to 24.6% of the vote as opposed the Liberals' 20.7%. By promising such things as flexible federalism, decentralization, and Quebec's own representation in international organizations such as UNESCO as well as by beginning practically every speech in Ottawa in French, Prime Minister Stephen Harper won a great deal of support, not just in Montreal, but in the eastern hinterland, including Quebec City, where nationalists were traditionally strong. Harper moved the Conservatives into the broad middle ground that formed after the federal Liberals and the separatists radicalized their positions between centralizing federalism and outright separation. The separatists no longer had an easily identifiable enemy.

It was ironic that *Québécois*, who had been unhappy during a 39-year period when PMs from Quebec ruled them for 36 years, were generally pleased with a western anglophone at the helm in Ottawa. Stephen Harper gave them much to be happy about. In 2006 he brought his entire cabinet to Quebec City to celebrate his close relationship with the people there; this was the first time since the 1950s that this had happened.

Later in 2006, Harper outmaneuvered both the *Bloc Québécois* and the federal Liberals to persuade an overwhelming majority in Parliament, including all four federal parties, to adopt a historic resolution declaring that Quebecers, not Quebec, "form a nation within a united Canada." Harper's words referred to a people, not a government or a state. Although this formulation had no constitutional significance and did not imply that Canada was a union of "two founding peoples," it was the first time Ottawa recognized the people of Quebec as a "nation."

Harper met with Premier Charest more frequently than with any other premier and more than any Canadian PM since the 1960s. Harper's 2007 federal budget

Quebec City in winter

Canada

corrected what he called "fiscal imbalance" by awarding an extra $2.1 billion transfer payment to Quebec, which already received $2.2 billion more each year from Ottawa than it contributed. He also steered a $900 million Strategic Aerospace and Defence Initiative to Montreal and permitted Quebec the prestige of occupying its own seat at UNESCO.

In November 2005, the PQ elected dashing young, 39 year-old André Boisclair as its new leader. He was the first PQ leader not belonging to the generation that had founded the party in the 1960s. Boisclair advocated a radical program for a quick referendum after the PQ returned to power, followed, "as soon as possible," by a unilateral "declaration of national sovereignty" if even the barest majority voted yes. He pledged to ignore the Clarity Act, parting with the party's former promises of a "partnership" with Canada and a year of negotiations leading to secession.

Boisclair's radical program was out of touch with the province's majority. To make things worse for the PQ, two of Quebec's cultural icons, playwrights Michel Tremblay and Robert Lepage, admitted in 2006 to have lost some of their faith in the separatist cause. In Tremblay's words, "it was a beautiful dream, and one must respect such dreams, but it will never be more than a dream if we keep looking at it in economic terms first." He remembered that "the driving force was our pride in being the beacon of francophone culture in America—not the economy."

The uproar and panicked bickering that followed revealed a real dilemma for the PQ. It had downplayed culture to broaden its appeal to include immigrant groups and not just francophones but had to assume power before it could achieve sovereignty. Yet, it had to soften its platform in order to win that power but lacked the strong mandate needed to proceed toward separation. It also competed in a greatly changed Quebec where language inequalities were eliminated. The PQ and Boisclair had trouble finding new arguments to fire up supporters for a new push for secession. This was especially hard with a conciliatory PM and a *Québécoise* governor general in Ottawa. The smoother the relations between Ottawa and Quebec, the greater the decline for the separatists. Prime Minister Harper astutely adjusted his policy to the shifting ground in Quebec politics.

Noticing the PQ's disorientation and shaky leadership, the unpopular Premier Charest called an early election in 2007 in which his Liberal party lost its majority. This produced Quebec's first minority government since 1878. Even so, the PQ fared much worse, declining from 45 to 36

François Legault
Retrieved from: http://inroadsjournal.ca/coalition-avenir-quebec-co-founder-francois-legault-speaks-during-a-news-conference-at-the-palais-montcalm-in-quebec-city/

seats and only 28.3% of the votes, down from 33.2%. Both parties experienced their worst results since 1976, in the case of the Liberals, and 1970 for the PQ.

The primary victim of the PQ's electoral failure was Boisclair, who was promptly replaced as PQ leader by former social worker and former cabinet member in various PQ governments, Pauline Marois. Her condition for acceptance was that the party stop its squabbling over a timetable for a future referendum and get back in touch with the real-life concerns of many voters. A pragmatist, she argued that radicalizing the PQ "would be a recipe for marginalization, or even extinction."

The real surprise was Mario Dumont's conservative and moderately nationalist ADQ, which surged to within seven seats of Charest's minority government. A 36-year-old economics graduate from Concordia University, Dumont led a walk-out from the Liberal party in 1992 because it did not favor an independent Quebec. However, after the failed referendum in 1995, in which he gave lukewarm support for sovereignty, Dumont shifted his position between the extremes of federalism and hardline separation. By 2012 the coalition Avenir du Québec (CAQ) absorbed the ADQ.

According to an election-time poll in September 2012, only 28% of provincial voters supported separation, and 68% did not want another referendum. In another poll a month before the election, sovereignty ranked tenth on a list of priorities among Quebecers. In the wake of the fabulously successful Vancouver Winter Olympic Games in February 2010, fewer than a third of Québécois supported the notion of having their own Olympic team. That was wonderful news for Canadian unity. Support for sovereignty was at its lowest ebb in four decades. Although sovereignty is the PQ's raison d'être, it is an electoral non-starter.

Election year 2008 reflected this in Quebec. In the October federal elections, the Bloc Québécois won the most seats in Quebec, but saw its vote decrease by 4%, the second lowest in its history, after a campaign in which it did not say a single word about independence.

In Quebec's December provincial elections, only seven weeks later, in which the economy was the main issue, the PQ, led for the first time by Pauline Marois, Quebec's first female leader, did better than predicted. One reason was that sovereignty was banished from her campaign. Marois noted in an interview: "We might well have a referendum someday. I'm keeping the door open." Her party captured 35.15% of the votes and 51 seats, while the ADQ crashed to only 16.35% of the votes and a mere seven seats.

Pauline Marois's cold feet about advocating concrete steps and timetables toward sovereignty made the PQ ranks restive. She earned a 93% endorsement as leader in the party's April 2011 national congress in return for allowing the hardliners to put language and sovereignty front and center again. If they get their way, Bill 101 would have expanded to cover post-secondary schools and businesses with fewer than 50 employees would have to obey the French Language Charter. This was tricky terrain for the PQ: polls in 2011 indicated that two-thirds of Quebecers thought parents

Canada

should have the right to school their children in the language of their choice.

These objectives also became grist for the May 2, 2011, federal elections, when the Bloc Québécois was practically wiped out in Quebec, losing all but four of its 49 seats. In the 2015 federal elections, it fell below 20% of the votes in Quebec. Such near-extinction of the *Bloc Québécois* was the most startling sign of the change occurring in the province. Open intraparty warfare broke out within the PQ.

Jean Charest became the first Quebec premier since the 1950s to win three terms in a row. He won the majority he was seeking in the 2008 elections, with 42% of the votes and 66 of the 125 seats. His government was beset by scandals in the construction industry, though. Montreal seemed unable to deal with an endemic culture of corruption and organized crime that drove more and more citizens to the suburbs and increasing numbers of businesses out of the province.

When *Maclean's* published a cover story on October 4, 2010, calling Quebec "The Most Corrupt Province in Canada," Charest condemned such "Quebec bashing" and demanded an apology to Quebecers. The House of Commons expressed its "profound sadness at the prejudice displayed and the stereotypes employed by *Maclean's* magazine to denigrate the Quebec nation." Nevertheless, *La Presse* termed the claim "undeniable." Political columnist Vincent Marissal, supported this notion, writing that "every Quebec media outlet has drawn similar conclusions."

The corruption charges led to the resignations of the mayors of both Montreal and Laval while compelling an increasingly unpopular Charest to call for early elections September 4, 2012. He was helped by the distraction of six months of unpopular demonstrations by students protesting a doubling of university tuition, the lowest in Canada and half the national average. Tuition had long been kept low in order to encourage young Quebecers to study but few did so. A quarter of students drop out of high school and only 30% attend the university. About a third of students boycotted classes to oppose the increase. Striking students in Montreal harangued those who wanted to complete their courses, blocked roads, smashed windows, lit fires, tossed Molotov cocktails, vandalized government buildings, and clashed with police. The PQ allied itself with the protesters.

The PQ secured a narrow victory in the 2012 elections, winning 54 seats, up from 51, enough to form a minority government in the 125-seat National Assembly. Pauline Marois became Quebec's first female leader. The Liberals came within a whisker of overtaking PQ, capturing 50 seats, down from 66. Charest lost his own Sherbrooke seat he held for 28 years and resigned as party leader. ADQ fell on hard times and won only seven seats. It joined a larger grouping, the CAQ, the Coalition for the Future of Quebec, which won 19 seats. Led by Francçois Legault, this new party focused on education, health, culture, public finances, and a more efficient state, rather than Quebec sovereignty or Canadian unity. *Québec solidaire*, Quebec Solidarity, led by Françoise David, which believed the PQ drifted too far to the right, won two seats, up from one. The success of the smaller parties prevented PQ from winning a majority of seats.

A bloody incident on election evening served as a reminder of the passions language and independence can still rouse. Marois was in the middle of congratulating her supporters, vowing that "we want a country and we will have one!" when a hooded gunman entered the hall, screaming in French, "The English are awakening!" He shot two people, one of whom died. He then poured gasoline around the back door and set fire to the building as he fled. He was quickly apprehended.

In office Marois tried to wave the flag of sovereignty, declaring to the PQ's 90,000 members that Quebec's need for sovereignty had become an "emergency." The party was aware that it could not win elections by waving that banner. Marois' agenda included new restrictions on the public use of the English language, Bill 14, and on public displays of religious affiliation, known as the Charter of Quebec Values. It prohibits government employees from wearing "overt and conspicuous" religious symbols while on the job. This means no headscarves, hijabs, kippas, niqabs, turbans, and outsized crucifixes. It permitted small crosses and symbols. In 2017, women who provide or receive public services were prohibited from wearing face coverings. The most recent Quebec general election was held on October 1, 2018. The CAQ won 74 out of 125 seats, giving the party a majority and unseating the Quebec Liberal Party.

By way of background, in 2016 Quebec's Muslim population was 5.5%. In 2011 the percentage had grown to 3.1 % making the Muslim population much more visible. There has certainly been a backlash against all religious visibility in Quebec as the fruits of the Quiet Revolution continue to blossom in Quebec society.

This 2017 proposed law divided traditional Quebecers from new immigrants and multicultural Montreal, where most immigrants to Quebec settle, from the rest of Quebec. It also divided PQ members. Three former PQ premiers, including the late Jacques Parizeau, opposed it publicly. Nevertheless, Marois tried to use the issue in the April 2014 provincial elections to increase the PQ's poll numbers even though voters were more interested in the economy and in fighting corruption. Quebec ranked seventh out of the 10 provinces in terms of per capita GDP. The PQ and the Liberals, led by brain surgeon and former Quebec health minister, Philippe Couillard, entered the contest neck-and-neck, with the CAQ poised to capture many votes.

Polls suggested the PQ would win a majority of seats, but that was not to be. The PQ had hoped to ride to victory by the popular ban on religious symbols and to say as little as possible about a sovereignty referendum. After all, only a third of Quebecers wanted to separate from Canada. When one PQ candidate, billionaire media mogul Pierre Karl Péladeau, called for an independent Quebec and reinforced his point by pumping his fist in the air, he pushed the PQ campaign off a cliff. The PQ lead evaporated in an instant, and its results were a disaster. The Liberals captured 41.5% of the votes and 70 seats, an absolute majority. The PQ plummeted to 25.37% of the votes and only 30 seats. CAQ rose to 23% and 22 seats, while QS slipped in with 7.63% and 3 seats.

Despite being publicly associated with the PQ for only one year, Péladeau assumed the party leadership in the spring of 2015. The wealthy businessman related poorly to a core membership that was largely leftist and union-dominated. He alienated many members and caused a string of departures. Péladeau was mistaken in claiming that separatism was more alive than ever because it was a Baby Boomer dream that was less inspiring to young Québécois. After less than a year, Péladeau relinquished his leadership of the PQ and was succeeded by Jean-François Lisée, a former journalist and close advisor to Jacques Parizeau and Lucien Bouchard.

Couillard promised to concentrate on the real issues of concern to Quebecers and to bring them together rather than to divide them, as the PQ does. Separatism had been deflated as a political force in the foreseeable future. Throughout the campaign Couillard repeatedly made it clear: "We have a homeland—it's Quebec. It's the homeland of every Quebecer. And we have a country, Canada. We want it all! You won't take any of it from us! It's the homeland of every Quebecer. And we have a country, Canada. We want it all! You won't take any of it from us!'"

Most recently, the government of Premier Francois Legault, leader of the CAQ who was sworn in on October 18, 2018, proposed a radical new law to promote Quebec secularism. The new law pro-

Canada

hibits civil servants from displaying any religious symbols. The law, entitled *An Act Respecting the Laicity of the State*, was enacted on June 16, 2019, and bans public employees including the minister of justice, attorney general, teachers, school principals and vice principals, Crown prosecutors, judges, police officers, labor arbitrators and court clerks from wearing religious symbols at work. Employees currently working for the government are allowed to continue wearing religious symbols as long as they are in the job they hold as of Thursday. If they change jobs within the public service, they are no longer be able to wear their religious symbols. That means someone who is a teacher now but becomes a school principal loses the right to wear their religious symbol. The law does not define what a religious symbol is. Immigration Minister Simon Jolin-Barrette said tattoos will not be considered to be religious symbols. He said employees will not be searched to see if they are wearing hidden religious symbols. The law bans people from delivering or receiving services with their faces covered from certain government agencies. They include members of the National Assembly, elected municipal officers, school board commissioners, people working at the National Assembly and for the provincial lieutenant-governor, police officers, some doctors, dentists, and midwives and home childcare providers. The law invokes the notwithstanding clauses in the Canadian and Quebec charters of rights to override religious rights.

The reaction across Canada was immediate, with the Prime Minister and others claiming that this is not an action consistent with Canadian values. The secularism law failed, however, to damage the electoral position of the CAQ. In the election of October 3, 2022, François Legault was returned to power with an increased majority, gaining 14 seats over the 2018 total of 76, leaving the Liberals with only 21 seats, Québec solidaire 11, and the Parti Quebecois with 3. The Conservatives lost the only seat they had entering the election. It seems that for the time being, the nationalist-sovereigntist movement, so strong through the latter half of the twentieth century, has receded from Quebec politics.

Ontario: Ontario has traditionally been Canada's political pivot and economic motor, despite the growth of the West, the ambitions of the Maritimes, and the assertiveness of Quebec. Ontario houses 38% of Canada's population and produces about a third of the nation's wealth. Toronto's massive economy alone is equal to or larger than that of every province. Former Premier David Peterson was once asked if he was uncomfortable about Ontario's becoming wealthier while other regions were suffering. He answered: "One of the things that keeps this country together is that everybody hates Ontario, and what keeps Ontario together is that everybody hates Toronto, and what keeps Toronto together is that everybody hates Bay Street" (Canada's Wall Street).

Ontario's its preeminence is being challenged by Canada's new economic power centers: Alberta, British Columbia, oil and resource-rich Saskatchewan, Newfoundland, and Labrador. Ontario does not play the kind of leadership role in Canada it once did. Although it is by no means a

Toronto's Rogers Centre (formerly SkyDome), one of the most modern sports facility in the world

Photo: Ian Steer

Canada

poor province, Ontario's economy has performed sluggishly for a long time and much of the troubled manufacturing and auto industry is within its borders. In the decade from 2001, its per capita GDP remained virtually unchanged. The surging West's combined GDP surpassed that of Ontario for the first time in 2008. Ontario embarrassingly received equalization payments as a "have-not" province.

Toronto's status as the country's premier city was challenged for the first time in over a century, this time by Calgary. Toronto has budget and infrastructure problems and its manufacturing sector is not in good condition, having shed 100,000 jobs in the five years up to 2008. Still, Ontario continues to attract 40% of all immigrants to Canada; 44% of its residents are foreign-born, well above the province's 27%. It also remains the country's financial center. Private wealth is pouring into art galleries, theaters and new museums as Toronto tries hard to retain its image as a "city on the rise."

Canada's largest province is not officially bilingual even though its government extends French-language services to Ontario's half million francophones, about 5% of the population). When a court in Ontario ruled that under the Charter of Rights francophones are entitled to an education in French, the province quickly complied. Toronto is the most ethnically diverse city in North America. In 2002 Ontario received its first Aboriginal lieutenant-governor in Canada: James Bartleman, a Minjikanig Indian and former Canadian ambassador to the EU.

In 1999, a reform compressed high school from five to four years while stressing more mathematics and science, a kind of pre STEM (Science, Technology, Engineering, and Mathematics) initiative. Since 2000, students are subject to a code of conduct that includes reciting the Oath of Citizenship and pledging allegiance to the Queen. Official hoped that the oath and code would instill respect for Canada and make schools safer. In 2001 vouchers were offered granting tax credits to parents who send their child to a private school.

For many voters the pace of the changes was too fast. In 1997, the provincial government stepped into a political minefield by introducing Bill 103. This unified the Toronto area's six municipalities and created a regional government of Metropolitan Toronto for a city of about 4.6 million. The idea was to eliminate inefficient redundancy in urban services while reducing the public payroll. Suddenly, signs reading "Vote No to megacity" appeared everywhere as three-quarters of voters opposed the merger in separate referenda in the six municipalities. The cost-cutting

Hon. Doug Ford, Premier of Ontario
Retrieved from: https://www.dailyxtra.com/doug-fords-confusing-case-against-sex-ed-138583

government ignored the results and enacted the reform.

In a 2007 referendum, voters turned down the proportional representation electoral system. Legislation now mandates that elections be held on fixed dates every four years, though. The defining issue in the 2007 election's was the funding of religious schools. Ontario is the only province that pays the whole cost for attendance to Roman Catholic Schools, reflecting the fact that one-third of its residents are Catholic, but does not covers expenses for schools of any other religion. Voters reelected the Liberal party in 2007 and again in 2011 albeit five seats short of a majority.

In 2012, Dalton McGuinty, Canada's longest-serving premier, suddenly resigned and handed the reins of power

to Kathleen Wynne, not only the first female premier of Ontario but also its first openly gay leader. McGuinty became the sixth woman heading provincial governments in 2012; more than 87% of Canadians were served by female premiers at that time. McGuinty led her Liberal Party to its fourth consecutive victory, this time with an absolute majority.

Ontario's greatest embarrassment in 2013–14 was the self-destruction of Toronto's Tory mayor, Rob Ford, who became an international laughingstock. He came into office in 2010 on a populist wave of anti-elite suburban rage despite a well-known history of intemperate and profane outbursts. After months of denying allegations, Ford finally admitted to having smoked crack cocaine "probably in one of my drunken stupors." Ford showed up raging drunk at a function honoring Canadian soldiers, frequently drove drunk, assaulted his staff mentions, and entertained prostitutes in his city hall office. Since Ford had not been convicted of a crime, the city council was unable to take away his title, even temporarily but did remove most of his powers. Incredibly, Ford remained popular.

Ford vowed to run again for mayor in the October 2014 municipal elections. However, he was diagnosed with cancer and turned the candidacy over to his brother Doug. Emerging victorious was Conservative John Tory. A wealthy businessman, Tory personified the city as it imagines itself: smart, compassionate, clean-cut, and powerful. Ford passed away in 2016 at the age of 46.

In a surprise to many, the late Rob Ford's brother, Doug Ford, became Ontario's Progressive Conservative Premier on June 29, 2018. He secured the leadership of the Party after a political coup which saw the then leader, Patrick Brown facing allegations of "troubling conduct" and precipitously losing the support of his colleagues. Ford's campaign was built around conservative values of home, religion, the traditional family, and economic rationality after the huge deficits, identity politics, and education reform promulgated by the Ontario Liberal Party. Ford went to the polls as leader of the Progressive Conservatives in his own right on June 7, 2018, defeating Wynn's Liberal government and gaining a majority. Premier Ford was widely seen as having met the challenges of the first wave of the Covid-19 pandemic and, while that view would change by the time of the third wave, in the election of June 2, 2022, he was returned with another majority, increasing the Progressive Conservatives' seats from 67 to 83. The New Democrats won 31 seats, the Liberals 8, and the Greens retained the one seat they held prior to the election. In a surprise, on January 24, 2025, Ford asked the Lieutenant-Governor to dissolve the legislature, and called a snap election. In the ensuing election of February 27, 2025, Ford increased his majority by one seat over the New Democrats.

Manitoba: Manitoba was traditionally one of the few Canadian provinces in which

Canada

Portage Avenue looking east to Main Street, Winnipeg   Photo: Henry Kalen

there were real ideological differences between the two main parties that alternate in power: the NDP and the Conservatives. The divisions were created in the Winnipeg General Strike in 1919. Manitoba enjoys one of the country's highest economic growth rates and the lowest unemployment rate. Moreover, Manitoba has Western Canada's most diversified economy. It is increasingly shifting away from agriculture, constituting a mere 5% of its economy, and food-related industries into manufacturing, financial services, transportation, mining, and petroleum production. Sharing in the West's economic renaissance, this makes Manitoba well-equipped to deal with economic downturns.

Despite an $800-million expansion of the Red River floodway is designed to minimize the danger of flooding in the future, disaster struck in May 2011. The Manitoba government declared a state of emergency to deal with "unprecedented and historic" flooding of the Assiniboine River. About 2,000 people were displaced; 800 soldiers were sent to top up existing dikes, fortify unprotected properties, and deploy mobile flood protection equipment. It happened again in June 2014, necessitating assistance from the military. The year 2015 brought dangerous wildfires to all four western provinces.

On October 2009, Gary Doer passed the premiership to Greg Selinger, MLA from St. Boniface. Doer earned a Ph.D. from the London School of Economics and led the NDP to its fourth consecutive term in the 2011 provincial election. In 2014, Doer faced an open rebellion in his cabinet against his leadership, as five NDP cabinet members protested their inability to speak their minds.

Doer was named as Canada's ambassador to the U.S., a post that benefited from his well-developed negotiation skills and the fact that he had been in the U.S. more than any other premier. He personally knew all four former governors in President Barack Obama's cabinet. Doer was replaced as Canada's ambassador on March 4, 2016 by David MacNaughton, the co-chair of the Liberal election campaign in Ontario.

In the election of 2016, the New Democrats were ousted by the Progressive Conservatives led by Brian Pallister, who became Premier with a decisive majority, and was returned with a second, although slightly decreased, majority in 2019. 2021, however, became the year of three premiers for Manitoba. On August 10, 2021, Pallister announced that he would resign the leadership of the Progressive Conservatives on 1 September and that he would not seek re-election in the next provincial election. Deputy Premier Kelvin Goertzen

Hon. Wab Kinew, Premier of Manitoba
Province of Manitoba, Office of the Premier

was chosen as interim leader and served as Premier from 1 September until 2 November. The party elected Heather Stefanson as leader on October 30, and she was sworn in as premier, the province's first female leader, on November 2. The Progressive Conservatives led by Premier Stefanson will face the voters in a general election scheduled for October 3, 2023.

The Manitoba general election of October 3, 2023, saw the incumbent Progressive Conservatives, led by Premier Stefanson and attempting to win a third term defeated by the New Democratic Party, led by Wab Kinew, which formed a majority government. Premier Kinew is the first First Nations premier of a Canadian province, and will face the voters again no later than October 5, 2027.

The capital city of Winnipeg, where 60% of the province's population lives, is experiencing a worrying loss in population, especially by the young, educated and well-trained. In 2005 alone, 22,000 left Manitoba, the highest number since 1990, despite relatively low unemployment. Enrollment has dramatically fallen in some neighborhood schools.

Winnipeg has the highest crime rate of any large Canadian city, double the national average. Manitobans' disposable income lags $2,400 behind that of Saskatchewan and $10,000 behind that of Alberta. Winnipeg has a growing indigenous population that experiences discrimination and poverty. *Maclean's* wrote that it is "arguably becoming Canada's most racist city." The indigenous account for 16.7% of the total population, 4 times the national average. However, it has a Métis Mayor (Brian Bowman) and a Museum for Human Rights in Winnipeg, the only national museum outside of Ottawa.

The question of extending francophone language rights in Manitoba has been an enduring problem with a long and bitter history. In the 1870 Manitoba Act that brought the province into the Confederation, guaranteed the use of French in the courts, legislature, and law. The percentage of anglophones climbed steadily and in 1890 the provincial government declared that English was the only official language. The once vibrant francophone population became gradually assimilated until, by the late 1970s, only about 50,000, or about 5% of the population, remained, scattered in 30 communities across the province conducting most of their daily affairs in English. Only in tiny Ste-Anne, near Winnipeg, did French survive as the main language. Due to immersion schools, adult language education, and offspring of marriages between anglophones and francophones, the number of French speakers doubled to over 100,000 by the end of the century.

Canada

In 1979, the Supreme Court of Canada invalidated the 1890 law as unconstitutional. This ruling raised serious questions about the validity of 4,500 provincial laws that were passed only in English. The then Conservative government in Manitoba began translating some of the laws. The issue took center stage in 1981 when a francophone lawyer from Winnipeg, Roger Bilodeau, challenged the constitutionality of a speeding ticket that was written in English only. Faced with the mind-boggling threat that a court might declare most of the province's laws to be invalid, the government worked out a deal with the *Societé Franco-Manitobaine:* 400 laws would be translated into French, at the federal government's expense, and some French language services in government agencies would be expanded. The government put the substance of this agreement into legislation and introduced it into the assembly.

The Conservatives in Manitoba were willing to allow the translation of 400 laws, but fought against any constitutional recognition of French as an official language in the province. Their opposition and a deafening anglophone outcry against the legislation prevented it from being enacted. Francophone activists vowed to continue the long struggle in the courts. The situation was most uncomfortable for former Prime Minister Brian Mulroney, a bilingual Quebecer, whose firm support of French language rights was essential to his Conservative party's electoral chances in Quebec. Mulroney went to Winnipeg to argue strongly in favor of francophone rights, a move which alienated many Manitoban Tories.

The year 1985 witnessed a dramatic turn-around in Manitoba. The Supreme Court of Canada decided unanimously that all laws enacted in the province since 1890 were invalid. To head off legal chaos, the government engineered an agreement on a timetable for translating the existing laws. As a result, the entire French-language controversy wilted in importance and ceased for the time being to plague the province's political life.

The French language controversy reappeared in 1998 with a vengeance in response to Quebec's decision to disregard a Supreme Court ruling permitting English-language signs. Manitoba's government immediately announced that it would rescind its support of the Meech Lake Accord, a move that ultimately killed the accord. In 1992, the Supreme Court ordered the creation of a Manitoba-wide all-francophone school district in which 75% of the instruction would be in French. Perhaps a retired liquor board manager best captured the mood of more and more Westerners when he said: "Bilingualism is a bunch of horse manure. I don't accept this business of us being bilingual and Quebec being French only."

Saskatchewan: Only seven decades ago, Saskatchewan, which is the size of Texas, depended almost entirely on a one-crop economy. One of Saskatchewan's few claims to fame was that all Royal Canadian Mounted Police are trained at a depot founded on a creek crossing known originally as Pile of Bones. It was made the capital of the Northwest Territories and soon thereafter renamed Regina after Queen Victoria.

Today, Saskatchewan accounts for 40% of all cultivated land in Canada. Its average farm size has risen from 400 to 1,152 acres since 1936, producing 60% of Canada's wheat, 80% of its durum, a third of its oats and barley, and about a third of its oil seeds. Still, by 2005 agriculture represented only 7% of the province's GDP, down from an earlier 50%.

Saskatchewan also has impressive mineral resources, which now contribute more to its economy than does farming. It has oil, including bitumen-like oil sands in the northwest, which are part of the same geological formation as those found in neighboring Alberta. Oil-sands Quest from Calgary had, by 2008, invested $160 million in exploration of Saskatchewan's oil sands. The province became the ninth

Regina, with the Legislative Building (upper portion) set in beautiful Wascana Park
Government of Saskatchewan

Canada

Scott Moe
Premier of Saskatchewan
Retrieved from: https://www.saskatchewan.ca/
government/government-structure/cabinet/
honourable-scott-moe

biggest supplier of oil to the U.S. In fact, the U.S. bought more oil from the province than from Kuwait.

Saskatchewan possesses natural gas and low-grade brown lignite coal as well as the world's largest carbon sequestration project near Weyburn. Six thousand tons of carbon dioxide emissions from a synthetic fuel plant in North Dakota are piped across the border each day and pumped underground. Saskatchewan has the world's largest recoverable supply of potash, over 40%, which is used for fertilizer. Backed by the federal government in 2010, Premier Wall blocked the hostile takeover of Potash Corporation of Saskatchewan, which had been privatized in 1989, by the Anglo-Australian mining giant, BHP Billiton. This would have been Canada's biggest-ever corporate takeover. BHP Billiton was already building the world's largest potash mine near the village of Jansen, 100 miles, or 150 kilometers, east of Saskatoon.

Saskatchewan has some of the globe's highest-grade uranium deposits, producing more than one-quarter of the world's supply. Former Premier Brad Wall boasted: "We are the Saudi Arabia of uranium." Even so, Saskatchewan's industries cannot enrich uranium because Canada is not one of the few countries an international treaty permits to do so. In 1997, Saskatoon-based Cameco, the world's largest uranium processor, began to process nuclear material from former Soviet warheads as part of an international accord to reduce atomic weapons after the Cold War ended.

The province's dependence on the prices of grain and other commodities such as oil, potash, and uranium, means that its economy booms when prices are high and suffers when they are low. Prices were low for a long time, necessitating government overspending and a large deficit, which officials had to confront by slashing public spending and jobs, freezing wages, and selling off some of the province's largest publicly owned corporations, including Potash Corporation of Saskatchewan and the gas utility, SaskEnergy.

Saskatchewan had always been fertile ground for the NDP, which grew out of radical farmer movements that bloomed during the Great Depression. The NDP governed off and on for over a half century. It was the NDP which first brought socialized medicine to Canada and which became the model for Canadian Medicare. The province was shaken in 1988 when officials repealed a law requiring the use of both French and English in the courts and provincial assembly as well as the translation of all past and present laws into French. This upset Saskatchewan's francophones who constitute 2.3% of the total population.

The NDP governed over a prospering province as its population was growing and stood at over one million. Saskatchewan agriculture was more diversified than ever. The number of oil and gas wells drilled rose steadily and its potash sector did well. The subsequent collapse of commodity and oil prices hurt Saskatchewan.

For a while the province was in deep trouble. After 1986, the number of small farms dropped by more than 20,000 because of shrinking farm subsidies, forfeitures, and drought. Many were bought up by large, intensive farm operations with hired management. The rural population was leaving the villages in droves and moving into Regina, Saskatoon, and neighboring Alberta. The overall population fell from 1,134,000 in 2002 to 994,843 in 2003. One saw abandoned buildings all along Saskatchewan's highways.

By 2018, Saskatchewan's population rose to about 1,620,000 with the fastest population growth and lowest unemployment rate of any province. A commodities-fueled boom brought greater prosperity to the entire province reversing the decades-long population exodus. Investments poured in. Perhaps most unexpectedly, Saskatchewan joined Alberta, British Columbia, and Newfoundland as "have" provinces, no longer entitled to federal equalization payments. Ontario slipped to embarrassing "have-not" status and had a per capita GDP lower than Saskatchewan's.

The inner city of Regina was in particular trouble because it was one of the poorest areas in urban Canada with almost a third of its residents depending on government aid. Its poorest people are Aboriginals who are fleeing reservations and now constitute 42% of North Central Regina's population. While Statistics Canada reports that Aboriginals are doing better in most urban centers; Regina remains a conspicuous exception.

There were noticeable improvements by 2008, though. A new sense of optimism had taken hold in the city, as new funding was found for youth employment and skills training programs and other initiatives. There was also greater interaction between city hall and the aboriginal community. Creeland Mini-mart, the downtown reserve's first business, began pumping gas and selling snacks. By 2011 Saskatchewan was booming economically as affordable housing and rental properties became extremely tight. Rent became a key election issue with one desperate new formation even naming itself "The Rent Is Too Damn High" party.

The last NDP premier was Lorne Calvert, a United Church minister, who grew up in a working-class neighborhood of Moose Jaw. In 2007 he faced a much strengthened Saskatchewan Party, which was created in 1997 by Tories who were joined by some Liberals and Reformers. It is the dominant conservative alternative to the NDP. Brad Wall, a young lawyer, moderated the party.

In the April 2016 election, Wall's Saskatchewan Party won a historic third term by a landslide, capturing 51, up from 49, out of 58, because it earned 63% of the votes, down from 64%. This was the best electoral results in the province's history. The NDP won only 10 seats, up from 9. Wall rode the wave of a booming economy and Canada's lowest unemployment rate at 5.9%. Following his victory Wall proclaimed: "After years of lagging behind the rest of the provinces, we are leading in so very many respects, and we are not going back." In 2016 Wall was the most popular premier in Canada, enjoying a 62% approval rating. Wall was the leader of the Saskatchewan Party and premier of the province from November 21, 2007, until February 2, 2018, at which time he retired and was replaced Scott Moe, a cabinet minister in the Wall government became premier. Moe won his own landslide electoral majority in the elec-

Canada

The exciting Chuck Wagon Race during Calgary's once-a-year (July) celebration of the Old West called The Calgary Stampede

Hon. Danielle Smith, Premier of Alberta

tion of 2020, with the Saskatchewan Party winning 48 of the 61 seats in the Legislative Assembly. In the General Election of October 28, 2024, however, Moe's majority was reduced from 11 seats to 3 to a surging NDP, which won every seat in Regina and all but one in Saskatoon.

Commenting on the province's rising fortunes, Jim Marshall, chief economist at the Saskatchewan Institute of Public Policy, said "we're not your father's Saskatchewan. It's a different place, and that's not well known."

In 2010, Saskatoon brought glory to the province by being named Canada's second "smartest" and second "most cultured" city, after Victoria and right above Regina, in *Maclean's* third annual ranking of Canadian cities. In terms of "social engagement," it topped the list. Thus, the city that has long been the brunt of jokes for being a hick town in the middle of nowhere emerges as a leading center of learning and culture.

Alberta: Alberta, named for Queen Victoria's husband, enjoys the fruits of its oil and gas wealth. Oil revenues swelled the province's treasury and the Alberta Heritage Savings Trust Fund, which is to be used toward the long-term development of the province and toward lightening Albertans' tax burden. Alienation and resentment in western Canada, so familiar in the nation's history, survives. There is little support for secession from Canada at this prosperous time despite a 2006 poll in the *National Post* showing that a third of western Canadians, and 42% of Albertans, thought the western provinces should explore setting up their own country. Basically, Albertans want the federal government to leave them alone. Alberta celebrated its 100th birthday in 2005.

In 1992, Ralph Klein, a former folksy environment minister and mayor of Calgary, began a 14-year run as premier. Son of a professional wrestler known as "Killer Klein," he was one of the most colorful figures in Canadian politics. A one-time high school dropout, he became a celebrated local TV reporter in the 1970s, known for his talent in getting stories from the street level. Klein cultivated contacts with biker gangs, prostitutes, and Indian groups. Sometime called "Red-neck Ralph" because of his undiplomatic language, he benefited considerably from his image as an extroverted down-to-earth man of the people. Klein passed away in March 2013 at age 70.

Klein launched "Ralph's Revolution" with his Albertan agenda dominating Canadian political debates. He demonstrated that governments can cut costs deeply and quickly and still post impressive victories. Klein was determined to resolve the financial crisis without raising taxes, making reductions in almost every kind of government service. By 1997, he reduced government expenditures by 20%, cut thousands of positions from the civil service, closed hospitals, and slashed welfare rolls. Alberta led Canada in deregulation and privatization as car licensing, liquor retailing and electricity distribution are in private hands.

Klein pushed through a law mandating a balanced budget and requiring that three-quarters of any budget surplus be used to pay off debt. Alberta has the lowest provincial personal tax rates, a flat-rate of 10.5%, Canada's first, and is the only province without a provincial sales tax.

Alberta produces two-thirds of Canada's supplies of oil and gas. Fifty-four percent of its crude oil is derived from tar sands. These sources are under increasing scrutiny by its main customer: the U.S. Greenpeace succeeded in putting the oil sands on the green radar screen. And more recently, controversy is emerging between the government of Alberta and the Biden administration as the latter increases imports of oil from the Middle East rather than Canada.

Albertans dismiss the environmental threats, responding that if the Americans and Europeans do not want their oil, provincial leaders would commission a pipeline, called Northern Gateway, to the West Coast and ship it to China. Indeed, in 2009 state-owned Petro-China purchased a majority stake in two tar-sands projects. In 2012 the Canadian government approved the sale of Nexen, a tar-sands producer, to a state-owned Chinese oil company, CNOOC. Both the federal and British Columbia government approved of the transaction. There are local objections to Northern Gateway, though, especially from Aboriginal groups, to such a pipeline to the West Coast. Also, the government of British Columbia wants money for taking the risks presented by such a project. Both governments jointly appointed officials to work on a settlement of their pipeline differences.

The preferred pipeline was the Keystone XL which would take oil from Alberta to Texas and to refineries along the way. In 2015, President Obama rejected the project because of environmental concerns. While President Trump lifted the ban, it was reinstated by President Biden in January 2021. Albertans feel hemmed in, "landlocked." former Premier Redford made clear that other means of transport—rail, truck, river

Canada

Convention Centre, Edmonton, Alberta

barge—are far more expensive and less safe than pipelines.

The Heritage Fund shrank to $15.3 billion by 2014. Sometimes no contributions were made or, worse, funds were raided when the government was short of cash. In order to manage the fund better, the Alberta Investment Management Corporation was set up in 2008 to run it on commercial lines.

Alberta's economy is helped in bad times because it has become increasingly diversified. By 2001, the energy sector represented only 21% of the province's GDP, down from 40% in 1985. The manufacturing, technology, service, and wholesale trade sectors are burgeoning. New industries are pouring in. Buoyed by a prosperous farm economy and rising oil and gas prices until 2014, the province outperformed the Canadian economy in every year since 1990 except one. Alberta has the highest per capita disposable income, the highest GDP per capita, and the highest rate of job creation in Canada.

The most visible sign of Alberta's dynamic economy is Calgary, the country's wealth magnet, second only to Toronto as a corporate head-office center. Toronto has 10 of the largest 20 Canadian companies' head offices, while Calgary has six, all oil and gas firms. Office space is the country's most expensive, and fossil fuel companies plus those doing business with them occupy three-fourths of these locations. Further, Calgary had the lowest unemployment rate of any major city.

Calgary boasts Canada's third most ethnically diverse population and the greatest number of post-high school degrees per capita. In 2010, Calgary voters elected the first Muslim mayor of a major Canadian city, Naheed Nenshi enjoys considerable popularity. Born of immigrant parents, he graduated from the University of Calgary and completed his graduate work at Harvard. The dynamic economy made Calgary a magnet for immigrants, ahead of Montreal, and almost a fourth of the residents are visible minorities. Maclean's ranked it third among Canada's "smartest" cities in 2010. Until the recession, the residential housing market in Calgary was booming.

Alberta built the finest public education system in Canada with its children regularly outscoring peers from other provinces and other countries, according to the 2007 PISA results, on standardized tests. In Maclean's annual college rankings in 2006, Alberta's sole university was rated number one in all of Canada, fifth in 2011. Alberta does need another university in light of its growth.

Albertans increased their tax-deductible charitable giving by more than 15% in 2006, thereby helping transform Calgary into an intellectual and cultural center as well as a business one. Yet, it is still one of the few North American cities of over a million residents that does not have an art museum. In 2016, Calgary opened the National Music Center which hosts events every day of the year.

The province faces serious problems. Canadians poured into Alberta at the rate of 100,000 each year, enough to create a medium size town. Its net migration in 2006 was 62,000, compared with Ontario's net loss of 34,000. This put severe strains on housing, government services and infrastructure, and the labor market. Calgary passed the one million mark in 2006, causing rush-hour traffic to slow to a trickle.

Fort McMurray, where the oil sands are located, needs new water and wastewater treatment plants, a new landfill, better and more roads and bridges and more nurses and doctors. The locals were wary of the boom all around them. One summed up the town's problems: "Too many single men, too much time, too much money, too much trouble." GQ magazine called it "a hellhole of testosterone and tattoos." The high wages also attracted drug dealers with drug abuse in the northern oil area is four times the average in the rest of the province. About 40% of oil workers test positive for cocaine or marijuana in job screening or post-accident tests. Economic hard times have befallen the city and lessened the intensity of these problems.

On another matter, during the summer of 2013, the country was shocked by images of flood waters overflowing the Bow and Elbow Rivers and spilling into Calgary. About 75,000 people had to be evacuated from the city. Three years later, in May 2016, Fort McMurray was engulfed by a such a large fire that all of 88,000 residents were ordered to evacuate. The blaze consumed entire swaths of the town and 2,400 buildings, but most of the city and the oil facilities north of town were saved. In dollar terms this was Canada's most destructive natural disaster.

Health-care reductions were temporarily scaled back due to festering unease about government spending cuts, dramatized by hospital workers' repeated walkouts. Then the government introduced Bill 11 which drew particularly sharp criticism. In order to reduce waiting lists and relieve pressure on the public health system, the legislation allows private clinics to perform all cataract surgery and many hernia, foot, ear, nose, and throat operations. The expenses are fully covered by the provincial health-care plan. Critics contended that Alberta was, in effect, creating private hospitals, which are illegal in Canada, and was paving the way for American-style two-tiered health care. According to a 2006 survey, Alberta and British Columbia offer the best health care in Canada.

Alberta has a unique political culture. Oppositions are always weak with gov-

Canada

ernments routinely reelected by huge majorities. During its existence, it has experienced only four changes of government. Each time an established ruling party was replaced by a new upstart.

Emerging in 2011 as Alberta's first female premier was Justice Minister Alison Redford, the preferred candidate of those who wanted to eliminate the "old boys' network." She entered the April 2012 elections far behind Danielle Smith's Wildrose Alliance in the polls, but was seriously underestimated and proved the pollsters wrong. Redford's Progressive Conservatives captured 44% of the votes and 61 seats in the enlarged 87-seat legislature.

Redford's premiership came to an end in 2014 when it was learned that she had sometimes used Alberta government aircraft for personal reasons. She was replaced by businessman Jim Prentice, who left a seven-digit salary to be premier. Knowing that the provincial economy was getting worse, Prentice called early elections in May 2015. The results were a disaster for the Conservatives, ending their 44 years at the helm. In a setting of large-scale layoffs, empty office towers, plunging house prices, and collapsing oil prices, the NDP surged to a landslide victory, winning 53 seats.

Rachel Notley, a labor lawyer and lifelong New Democrat, became premier. She vowed to change oil royalties, get tough on environmental protection, end coal-fired power generation, enhance aboriginal rights, and reduce the economic dependence on oil.

In April 2019, Premier Notley's NDP lost to the United Conservative Party of Alberta which was led by Jason Kenney, a former federal minister under the Harper government. His Party received 54.88% of the popular vote. The common belief is that Notley was liked personally. However, her policy of not supporting any but one of the three pipelines which were to move Alberta oil to tide water and her siding with the capping of Tar Sands emissions and acceptance of the carbon tax for Alberta, when combined with the terrible down turn in the Alberta economy, were a death knell to term as premier.

Because Kenny was aware of Notley's personal appeal, he fought the election claiming he was opposing the Trudeau-Notley coalition against Alberta jobs. The NDP countered with personal attacks against Kenny about his long-ago statements seen as being not supportive of the LGBTQ+ community and alleging that he used if not illegal, then at least improper, tactics to win the leadership of his party.

Beginning in 2021, Kenney faced significant backlash against his leadership from within his own party, the United Conservative Party (UCP), which ultimately led to a leadership review in the spring of 2022. On May 18, 2022, having narrowly won a party confidence vote, Kenney announced his intention to resign as leader and premier, and that he would not be a candidate in the ensuing leadership election. On October 6, Danielle Smith won the UCP leadership vote and was sworn in as premier on October 11. Smith, who inherited Kenney's majority government, will lead the UCP into the next provincial election on May 29, 2023.

As a strong advocate for provincial power in the long-running battle between the Canadian federal government and Alberta, one of Smith's first actions upon assuming the premiership was to introduce the *Alberta Sovereignty Act*, enacted on December 8, 2022. The act provides protection of Alberta from federal laws and policies that the Alberta legislature deems to be unconstitutional or harmful to Albertans or the province's economic prosperity, in areas such as natural resources, gun control, public health, education, and agriculture. Often overlooked in the concern over Quebec secession is a growing western Canadian secessionist or sovereigntist movement, of which the *Alberta Sovereignty Act* is a high-profile example.

In the election of May 29, 2023, Danielle Smith and the United Conservative Party were returned to power, albeit with a reduced majority. Albertans next go to the polls on or before October 18, 2027.

British Columbia: Since the 1970s, British Columbia, with its 3.8 million inhabitants, has sometimes been referred to as "Lotus Land" because of its economic opportunities and relaxed and experimental life-styles. In Canada it conjured up images of a California in the North. British Columbia is the third largest province in size and population after Ontario and Quebec. About two-fifths of the province's people live in the greater Vancouver area. Facing Asia, its economic reach extends to the Orient.

In the May 2009, provincial elections the Liberals won a historic third straight victory. In a referendum at the same time, the complicated single transferable voting system was again rejected. The method is simply too complicated for voters. Christy Clark, a former talk radio host, became premier had been a scrappy former deputy premier, earning such descriptions as "pit bull" and "acid-tongued Liberal hellcat." Yet, she left politics for six years to be a good mother to her son.

Election day May 17, 2005, was a historic occasion: it was the first serving government in Canada to go to the polls on a date fixed by the legislature almost four years earlier. Henceforth regular elections in British Columbia are conducted every four years, depriving the governing party of the advantage of calling a vote at the most favorable time.

Citizens were also asked to vote on a complicated new electoral system, the single transferable method used in Ireland, which allows voters to rank all the candidates in their riding regardless of party. Those who end up with the most votes win. The measure barely fell short of the required threshold of 60% approval, winning 57%. Voters are excused for being somewhat baffled by their choice among 45 parties that registered for the elections including the Work Less Party of British Columbia, the Sex Party, the British Columbia Marijuana Party, the People of British Columbia Millionaires Party, and two separatist parties.

In the actual May 2017 election, the Liberals won the most seats, 43 of 87, but fell short of a majority. Voters in Vancouver, where half of the province's population lives, flocked to the NPD and Greens, which formed a narrow coalition government with New Democrat John Horgan as premier. This was the first time the Greens experienced real political power in North America. The election of 2020 saw Horgan increase his party's seats, from 41 to 57, with the Liberals the big losers, dropping from 41 to 28 seats. However, the Greens retained both of their seats.

On June 28, 2022, Horgan announced that he would step down as premier and leader of the NDP upon the selection of a new leader. On November 18, 2022, David Eby won the leadership election, thereby becoming the premier. In the General Election of October 19, 2024, Eby won government in his own right, although the NDP suffered a net loss of 8 seats, leaving them with a narrow 3 seat majority.

The British Columbian dream has always had two Achilles heels: its dependence on natural resources and exporting. Although the province has experienced a transformation from a resource-based economy, now only 17% of its GDP, to a more service and manufacturing-based economy, it is still not fully prepared for today's global competition. Operating costs are high, which reflects elevated wages, living costs, and personal tax rates. Labor laws are restrictive and governmental regulation of the economy is excessive by North American standards. Taking pages from the success of neighboring Alberta's government, provincial leaders were pursuing tax cuts and privatizations.

In 2006, British Columbia and Alberta agreed to drop their interprovincial trade barriers and recognize each other's standards in more than 60 professions. This Trade, Investment, and Labour Mobility Agreement, called TILMA, is meant to

Canada

save money and create jobs. Saskatchewan joined TILMA.

Thanks to China's insatiable appetite for natural resources, British Columbia is experiencing an economic upsurge with investment rising and unemployment falling. Chinese imports have saved its coal industry with its 25 billion tons of proven reserves. Three new mines have opened, bringing the total to nine in 2005. Copper, zinc, and molybdenum mining is booming, as is gas and oil production. British Columbia's lumber industry has found a new market in China. This resource boom brings prosperity to some of the province's poorer areas. British Columbia is well positioned for the future as North America increasingly looks toward Asia and as Ontario's manufacturing prowess is waning.

Crime

One export crop that is booming is B.C.'s marijuana, reputed to be three to five times more potent than Mexican or Caribbean varieties, including a popular variety called "B.C. bud." It is reported to be the province's most lucrative export crop, by 2008 worth from $5 billion to $7 billion each year, almost as much as the value of the province's tourist industry. It is estimated that the marijuana industry employs more people than do traditional sectors like forestry. The number of Canadians directly employed by the cannabis cultivation industry has increased by 250% in the past year according to Statistics Canada since the legalization of marijuana in October 2018. Canada has emerged as the dominant export of marijuana which Arcview Market Research and BDS Analytics estimated at 14.9 billion in sales for 2019. Despite the legalization of marijuana, the U.S. still treats it as illegal and ineligible for export. U.S. border officials estimate that marijuana smuggling increased tenfold from 1997 to 1999 and blame the upsurge partly on the leniency of B.C. courts. By 2008, Quebec had overtaken British Columbia both in terms of marijuana production and popularity among American consumers.

In July 2005, police shut down an elaborate 360-foot tunnel from a shed in Canada to a living room 300 feet inside the U.S. border in Washington state that was used to smuggle drugs. This was the first tunnel to be discovered at the Canadian one. Responding to requests by American investigators, Canadian authorities raided the headquarters of the British Columbia Marijuana Party, arresting its leader, Marc Emery, who had been operating a thriving mail-order business selling marijuana seeds over the Internet.

In 1999, the B.C. attorney general, Ujjal Dosanjh, a Sikh born in the Punjab state of

Hon. David Eby, Premier of British Columbia

India, became the first non-white to head a provincial government. He left India at age 17 for England. After four years there, he came to British Columbia in 1968 and earned a law degree. Canada's 400,000-strong Sikh community, concentrated in British Columbia and Ontario, produced an impressive list of leading Canadians. They included former Federal Fisheries Minister Herb Dhaliwal, figure skater Emanuel Sandhu, the federal Tory government's secretary of state for democratic reform Tim Uppal and the defense minister in Justin Trudeau's cabinet, Harjit Sajjan.

Because of their religion, some Sikh men have won the right in court to wear their beards and turbans while pursuing careers as Mounties or as boxers. Many, like Dosanjh, do not do that. In 1985, Dosanjh was attacked and beaten with an iron pipe by religious extremists angry because he had condemned their terror-based campaign for Punjabi independence. British Columbia is plagued by bloody Sikh gang warfare over drugs, money, and women in which most victims are Sikhs themselves. The Sikh gangs are Canada's most murderous.

In 2003, a Sikh separatist in Vancouver was incarcerated for five years after being the first to admit guilt in making the explosives for the 1985 bombing of Air India Flight 182 off the Atlantic coast of Ireland killing all 331 persons aboard, most of them Canadian. The dreadful deed, the worst terrorist act in Canadian history, was committed in revenge for the Indian army's storming of the Sikhs' holiest shrine, the Golden Temple, a year earlier. The publicity about this bloody behavior helps explain why only 30% of Canadians said in a 2009 poll that they had a positive view of Sikhism.

In April 2003, the trial of two other Sikh nationalists began in the Supreme Court of British Columbia. This was the culmination of one of the most exhaustive criminal investigations in Canadian

Aboriginal guide in UBC Museum before "Big Raven"

history, hampered by mysterious deaths of witnesses and the unwillingness of Sikh immigrants to cooperate with investigators. This longest, most complex, and most expensive trial in Canadian history came to an end in March 2005 when the court allowed the two to walk free, concluding that the prosecution had not made its case. The verdict caused a public uproar when it was revealed that Canadian intelligence services destroyed vital evidence. After the trial, the government ordered further inquiries, first conducted by former Ontario premier, Bob Rae, and then by a retired Supreme Court judge. The inquiry released more documents that showed that Indian officials and Air India received frequent threat assessments in advance, but treated them with suspicion, ignoring the information.

A great deal of illicit trade is conducted by brutal immigrant gangs from India and elsewhere. More than half of their trade is inside the U.S., where they often exchange drugs for cocaine, firearms, and cash. They have also tapped the Japanese market. Vancouver's seaport is a point of entry for heroin and cocaine as the province has become a key hub in international organized crime, in part because Western Canada is positioning itself to be North America's most important commercial corridor to Asia. This is ideal for criminal gangs' operations.

Gang warfare in Vancouver goes beyond Sikh and Indian circles. In 2008, 37% of homicides in British Columbia were linked or suspected to be linked to organized crime or street crime. Because the police department is understaffed, there are few arrests and prosecutions. More and more women gang members are involved in criminal activities. In all of Canada, women now make up about 6% of gang membership, 12% in British Columbia.

Perhaps it is not surprising that when *Maclean's* looked at Canada's most dangerous cities, 11 of the top 20 were in

Canada

British Columbia. Police authorities rank Vancouver on a par with Los Angeles and New York in terms of being in the grip of crime syndicates. Their activities amount to about 7% of British Columbia's economy. Vancouver experiences 3.6 times as many breakings and entries as New York City, as measured per 100,000 inhabitants.

The lamentable neglect of the Eastside of Vancouver is the focus of city elections. A coalition of community activists, unionists, pragmatic leftists, and New Democrats, known as the Coalition of Progressive Electors (COPE) captured seats on the city council as well as the school and park boards. Voters decided that they had had enough of people dying of overdoses, disease, and murder in the Eastside. The new city leaders moved to create "safe injection sites," where intravenous heroin users could inject drugs bought elsewhere without the threat of arrest under the supervision of public health care workers who would offer them safe needles and counseling to change their lives.

In 2005, Vancouver launched North America's first trial of heroin maintenance: giving addicts free heroin on the condition they enter treatment. The battered Eastside remains the most concentrated pocket of poverty and crime in Canada, with up to 1,800 homeless in the summer. In 2001, the Supreme Court of Canada found that maintenance and treatment programs pose no threat to public health or safety.

Vancouver became the first Canadian city to legalize marijuana as did neighboring Washington state. Vancouver's change was part of a movement advocating a more lenient approach to drugs until the Tories took power in Ottawa in 2006. Such legalization was in line with Canadians' attitudes about recreational marijuana; a 2006 poll indicated that 63% were in favor. In 2018 marijuana was fully legalized in Canada. The results from a Pew Forum Research Poll indicated that 52% of those approved of legalized marijuana while 41% disapproved.

Officials in both Vancouver and British Columbia promised in their winning bid for the 2010 Winter Olympics that they would build new housing and provide more services for the poor and homeless. Officials later confessed that they budgeted insufficient funds for these initiatives.

Environment and First Nations

British Columbians are statistically Canada's healthiest people. A mere 12%, 9% in Vancouver, are obese. Only 16% smoke, and British Columbia leads a group of provinces seeking to penalize the large tobacco companies for the health damage their products cause. Healthy living is a cultural trademark of the west coast.

Retrieved from: http://mywanderingfamily.com/2016/08/22/island-life-victoria-bc/

One of major challenges facing the government of British Columbia was environmental. It approved continued logging in two-thirds of Clayoquot Sound on the Pacific coast of Vancouver Island. Since this is one of the world's last remaining rainforests, this action infuriated conservationists all over the world. Blockades and arrests along the logging roads kept the issue on the front pages until the government announced a plan to restrict logging and create new parks. The government found itself caught in the middle between the logging industry's demands for reducing some of the requirements of the province's Forest Practices Code, and environmental groups who view the code too lax to protect the forests. A new code was enacted to reduce the size of the blocks of trees cut during harvest, to force stricter environmental practices, and to increase the fees paid by forestry companies. This satisfied nobody, and protests continued.

To stimulate the logging industry, the B.C. government slashed logging royalties. The industry's new focus is the vast, largely undisturbed mid-coast forest between Vancouver Island and southern Alaska that contains a quarter of the world's remaining temperate rain forest. Yet, loggers face a collision with Indian villages, a cross-border alliance of environmentalists, and the tourist industry, which greets a half million tourists each year, most from the U.S.

By contrast, almost everybody approved of the 1997 creation of the 10 million acre Muskwa-Kechika wilderness preserve in the northern Rockies, one of the largest conservation initiatives in Canadian history. Many North American environmentalists greeted this as an essential piece in a possible unbroken seam of protected land running from Yellowstone Park in the South through the Yukon Territory in the North, thus "Yellowstone to Yukon" or "Y2Y."

In 2000, four major logging companies and key environmental groups in British Columbia reached a landmark truce with regard to the Great Bear Rainforest. This rainforest is a remote temperate wilderness of thousand-year-old cedar trees, fjords, inlets, islands, glacial mountains, grizzly bears, and wolves. It is considered to be the world's largest unlogged temperate rain forest. Logging activity was postponed until an unusual alliance of loggers, environmentalists, native groups, and the government of British Columbia agreed in 2006 to create Great Bear Rainforest, a park along the Pacific coast from the mid-point of Vancouver Island to the Alaska border, twice the size of Yellowstone. This area remains off-limits to logging.

In 2007, the government of British Columbia unveiled a program to make the province "the continent's greenest spot." It would close down coal-burning energy plants and help create a Pacific Coast grouping of states and provinces to deal with climate change without waiting for their respective federal governments to act. British Colombia's carbon tax came into effect in 2008. It amounted to about 2.3 cents for every liter of gasoline. Because of its carbon tax, B.C. outpaced the rest of Canada both on emission reduction and GDP group according to Stewart Elgie, a professor of law and economics at the University of Ottawa. On April 1, 2019, B.C.'s rate was $40 per ton of carbon dioxide emissions, which translates to 8.89 cents per liter of gasoline. It's set to top out at $50 tons in 2021.

Canada

British Columbia's economic problems created an uproar over offshore oil and gas development. Muted for decades by moratoria, a panel of experts concluded in 2004 that restrictions were unnecessary.

Another challenge stems from 47 native claims to most of British Columbia's land. It was the only province officially to ignore a 1763 directive by the British Crown requiring land treaties to be signed with aboriginals. It never signed treaties with the approximately 160,000 aboriginal inhabitants, leaving legal title to most of the area in dispute. The government of British Columbia joined with the federal government to try to reach a settlement. Forty of the sixty British Columbia bands have joined the negotiation process.

There is widespread nervousness, even anger, among white British Columbians when the Indian bands begin tallying their losses in modern terms. One band, the Musqueam, claims all of downtown Vancouver and most of its suburbs because their ancestors had hunted and fished there. In 1999, the Musqueam won judicial backing for a 74-fold increase in the land-lease rates it collects from householders in a Vancouver suburb. Residents say they face ruin. As such rulings engender opposition from non-aboriginal groups, bands ponder whether they might win more of their claims in court than in negotiations. The Supreme Court of Canada came to the rescue of the 73 leaseholders in 2000 by order that they pay an annual rent of $10,000, rather than the $23,000 the band had demanded. Band members were outraged.

In 1998, the government reached an agreement with the Nisga'a band, involving 772 square miles in the breathtakingly beautiful Nass Valley on the provinces northwest coast just south of the Alaskan panhandle. In return for relinquishing claims eight times that size, the 5,000 members received $190 million and extensive powers of government: taxation, land use, family, social and health services, police, courts, schools, language, and culture. Amid a storm of protest that the terms were too generous, the legislature of British Columbia approved the treaty in April 1999 as did the federal parliament at the end of the year. Another agreement in April 1999 awarded the Sechelt Indigenous people 2,000 hectares of land 50 kilometers northwest of Vancouver and a $42 million "prosperity fund."

Because British Columbia's Liberals opposed the model of self-government won by the Nisga'a in the 1998 treaty, former-Premier Campbell committed himself to put the native treaty process to a vote. In a July 2002 referendum, an overwhelming percentage of voters gave the government a strong mandate to enter a "new era of reconciliation with First Nations." Voters made it clear, though, that private property should not have been subject to negotiation, parks should have been maintained for all British Columbians, and the inherent right of self-government was not on the table. Voters were further concerned that any aboriginal self-government should have the "characteristics of local government with powers delegated from Canada and BC." Only 36% of eligible voters participated in the referendum.

In 2009, the Nisga'a broke with their tradition of holding their land in common and to permit band members to own private property. Under Canada's Indian Act, aboriginals on reserves are usually given certificates of possession for their houses, which they rent, but they do not own; they cannot even use them as collateral for loans. This Nisga'a decision could have revolutionary implications.

The Canadian government hopes that the basic principles of British Columbia's prior agreements can be applied to negotiations not only with other bands there, but with such groups as Inuit in northern Quebec and the Algonquin band which claims the land in Ottawa on which the Canadian parliament sits. In an attempt to create a better atmosphere for negotiations, the government of British Columbia apologized in 2003 for its past treatment of indigenous peoples; it vowed to resolve unfinished land treaties, acknowledging that its institutions "failed aboriginal peoples across the province." It even admitted later that it had been wrong in the way the Nisga'a were treated and in 2006 announced "A New Relationship with B.C. First Nations."

Stephen Harper's federal government joined the British Columbia government to sign treaties with the Tsawwassen, Maanulth, and Yale First Nations that set a pattern for settling future land claims. These treaties will phase out reserve-based tax exemptions. Progress is being made on the huge backlog of other unresolved treaty claims. In 2012, the Tla'amin, a small tribe on the Sunshine Coast north of Vancouver, approved a deal for self-government, 20,564 acres of land, $30.5 million in cash and a share of natural-resource revenue. In 2014, the Supreme Court of Canada ruled that the Tsilhqot'in First Nation had title to 650 square miles of land, the first time it affirmed title to a specific parcel of land.

The business community blames such native-lands claims for the fact that BC attracted only half as much investment as Alberta during the 1990s. Yet, native leader Stewart Phillip responded that this was an unavoidable reality: "If any development does not enjoy the support of aboriginal people, then it's not going to happen."

A dispute over salmon fishing brought the governments of British Columbia and Canada into direct conflict with the U.S. After a 1985 treaty regulating the size of catches by American and Canadian fishermen expired in 1992, British Columbia claimed that Americans were catching too many salmon in U.S. and international waters, thereby preventing them from spawning in provincial rivers. To underscore its indignation, the provincial government announced that it would cancel a seabed lease to a navy weapons-testing base at Nanoose Bay that American submarines used for torpedo practice. Further, the provincial government suspended British Columbia's participation in about 50 agreements with neighboring American states on various topics.

In response, the U.S. Senate voted 81 to 19 for a resolution calling on the president to send the U.S. navy to protect American ferries. Before this was seriously considered, though, the Canadian government announced that the U.S. would not be forced from the testing base. By 2005, the number of salmon spawning in the Fraser River had fallen to about five million, fewer than half the expected number. The number was reduced due to higher ocean temperatures, overfishing, the destruction of spawning habitats, and, most controversially, diseases spread from open-pen salmon farms. The numbers continue to decline. This prompted federal officials to stop sockeye fishing. The Harper government announced in 2006 an inquiry into the collapse of the Fraser River salmon fishery and its opposition to "racially divided fisheries programs." Threats to the Fraser River continue today. One of the key issues is the Big Bar slide, which blocked salmon returning to key Fraser River tributaries such as the Stuart Quesnel and Chilco river systems.

One-quarter of British Columbia's population consists of immigrants. Some British Columbians are worried about an in-pouring of rich Chinese from Hong Kong, who were resettling their families and fortunes before mainland China assumed control of the colony in 1997. Canada actively tried to lure rich foreigners into the country so they could benefit the economy. Vancouver's Chinese population jumped from 30,000 in the 1960s to more than a quarter million today. Ethnic Chinese comprise a fifth of Vancouver's population; 61% of the children in the public schools speak English as a second language.

In the 1990s, Chinese people from Hong Kong Chinese were entering at the rate of more than 100 per day. Even though migrants from other Canadian provinces outnumbered those from Hong Kong by eight to one, a backlash began against arose against them with some. Many na-

Canada

tives accuse these Chinese of buying up British Columbia's prize real estate, such as the site of Expo 86, and driving up prices for the city's land and housing.

Vancouver's approximately 630,000 residents, 2,400,000 in the larger urban area, are expected to rise to 3.4 million by 2041, pay Canada's highest prices for property: in 2021 the average home cost more than 1.4 million Canadian dollars. Even though this amount declined slightly since 2018, these prices continue to drive away many families with children. This makes Vancouver's housing the third-least affordable among the world's major cities, exceeded only by Hong Kong, and Sydney, Australia. In an effort to hold down prices, the city's government levied a 15% property purchase tax on houses over $750,000 bought by foreigners.

British Columbia's former lieutenant governor, wealthy Vancouver businessman David See-Chai Lam, was Canada's first citizen of Chinese descent to occupy a vice-regal office. Lam, who donated up to $5 million to charitable causes each year, was an ideal man to help deal with this delicate and emotionally charged issue. By 1999, the influx had slowed dramatically, as the number of immigrants dropped by about 30%. Also, the composition changed from wealthy Hong Kong investors to small business owners and young factory workers from Taiwan and China.

In February 2010, Vancouver and the nearby Whistler Resort hosted the Winter Olympics. Nervous organizers had to borrow money, import snow, look for ways to scale back on expenses, and make the event a little less spectacular than they had hoped. There were some miscalculations. One was the assumption that the 737 apartments in the Olympic Village, later named Millennium Water, could be sold without loss after the games finished. Given the economic recession, only half of the homes were sold at expected prices, and for a while the entire village had the air of a ghost town. The city had to assume the loan and sell the remaining apartments for about half the original prices, leaving taxpayers with a $200–$300 million loss. It is usually hard to lose money in Vancouver real estate; in 2011 *The Economist* again named Vancouver the most livable city anywhere.

From the moment, three billion viewers tuned in to the opening ceremonies, it was clear that the Games would be among the best in history. Vancouver was the scene of spectacular Canadian athletic triumphs and an outpouring of Canadian pride.

More recently, the British Columbia government opposed the building of the Trans Mountain Pipeline from Alberta to the provincial coast. The federal government paid the original owner, Kinder Morgan 4.5 billion dollars for ownership of the pipeline after delays by British Columbia threatened that Kinder Morgan would walk away from the project.

Then Premier Notley threatened to shut off oil supplies from Alberta to British Columbia thereby triggering a gas shortage if its government continued to put impediments in the way of building the pipeline. The Federal Court of Appeal held that there had been insufficient consultation with Aboriginal groups in British Columbia and that the pipeline could not proceed until new consultation talks had been completed. It was, as one commentator said, a real mess. The federal government could use its disallowance power under the constitution and section 33 of the Charter if necessary to push the completion of the pipeline but it has chosen to start consultation rather than appeal to the Supreme Court of Canada or to take extraordinary legislative measures. However, on December 31, 2019, the Supreme Court of British Colombia granted an injunction barring member from the Indigenous nation from obstructing work on TransCanada's coastal gaslink pipeline from Burnaby, B.C to Edmonton, Alberta. Protesters continue to express frustration and Indigenous groups have 60 days to appeal the decision.

THE YUKON, NORTHWEST TERRITORIES, AND NUNAVUT

As of 2018, the 35,874 residents of the Yukon, 44,541 inhabitants of the Northwest Territories (NWT), and the 38,396 people living in Nunavut took impressive steps toward self-government that they started in early 1970s. Yet, because these areas lack provincial status, they cannot unilaterally amend their constitutions, which are acts of the Canadian parliament that only the federal government can modify.

Northerners are becoming increasingly assertive, though, thereby making disagreements wider and more numerous. There are many unsettled land and mineral rights claims being made by native groups in the Yukon and Northwest Territories. As a condition for the separation of Nunavut from the NWT in 1999, all aboriginal claims were settled in

**Hon. Ranj Pillai,
Premier of Yukon**

Canada

Nunavut. Since the federal government receives lucrative royalties for resource extraction in the North, it is not easy for Ottawa to relinquish this power. All three depend on federal subsidies, amounting to more than $2,000,000,000 annually and accounting for 60% of budget revenues in the Yukon and Northwest Territories and close to 90% in Nunavut. Aboriginal groups also benefit from a host of other federal programs such as being exempt from taxes even though the Inuit must pay them.

All three territories have developed de facto responsible government. Put another way, the commissioners, formally the chief executives within the areas appointed by Ottawa and answering to the Minister of Indian Affairs and Northern Development, accept the decisions made by the members of elected assemblies. Leaders, who call themselves premier, are selected by their legislative assemblies and are formally appointed by the commissioners. The commissioners behave like provincial lieutenant governors insofar as they do not overrule decisions made by the legislative assemblies.

Yukon

Self-government along the Canadian model proceeded fastest in the Yukon, the formal name of which was changed from Yukon Territory in 2002. The construction of the Alaskan Highway in 1942 brought thousands of immigrants into the Yukon, making the native population a minority. Because there are three times as many non-natives as First Nations people and Inuit in the Yukon, the demand for Canadian institutions was greatest there.

In 1978, party politics replaced a system of loose alliances with party discipline enabling the legislative system to operate more or less like any provincial government in Canada. Of course, it is no simple matter practicing democracy in a territory larger than France with only 16,000 registered voters, scattered in 17 ridings with as few as about residents in the smallest, Old Crow, many of whom are reachable only by airplane or dogsled, and in temperatures as low as minus-50 degrees centigrade on election day.

The government seeks to revive the declining mining industry while at the same time stimulating tourism, presently the Yukon's main industry, drawing 300,000 each year and diversifying the economy. In 2018, $146.1 million, or 5.0% of Yukon's total GDP based on tourism. Gold production was only a tenth of what it was in its heyday, but the discovery of hard-rock deposits in 2011 sparked a gold rush. The 1997 closure of the lead-zinc mine at Faro, which had contributed a fifth of the Yukon's $1 billion GDP, was distressing. A fascinating benefit of mining in the territory is that a treasure of ancient fossils tens of thousands of years old is uncovered as rock layers are blasted.

The social and economic challenges are daunting: almost a third of the workforce is employed by one of the three levels of government, and seasonal unemployment is high. As is true everywhere in the North, prices of products shipped in from the South, including food, are expensive because the Yukon has only about 160 working farms. The Yukon faces a severe housing crunch, as citizens oppose new housing developments at a time when Canadians are migrating to Yukon in great numbers to benefit from high-paying jobs in mining and government. The average price for a single-family home was a record $455,000 in 2012, twice the price only six years earlier. As of 2020, the average cost was $508,300. In Whitehorse, the capital the average price reached $598,800 in 2021, up 13.9% from the previous year.

As dependent on Ottawa financially as the Yukon is, its leadership is gradually taking over more federal powers, such as resources, education, and health. In 2003, after 10 years of negotiations, Ottawa granted it control over its natural resources, one of the final steps on the road toward becoming a province. The two levels of government subsequently tangled over exploiting the Peel Watershed for its huge deposits of coal, gas, and minerals.

Disproportionately high levels of family breakdown and alcohol and drug abuse plague the Yukon. Even former Liberal leader Roger Coles was imprisoned in 1986 for cocaine trafficking. The capital city of Whitehorse, where 70% of the population lives, has a homicide rate 355% higher than the Canadian average. The good news is that the crime rate dropped more than 36% from 2000 to 2010. The crime rate in the Yukon dropped even further 2017-2018, from 183 to 170.34 according to Statistics Canada. In 2020, the Crime Severity Index had risen to 215.7.

In 1992, the Tories, who renamed themselves the Yukon Party to break ties with their unpopular federal counterpart, regained power but relinquished it to the NDP in 1996. The 2000 elections continued the game of musical chairs. For the first time since party politics were introduced to the Yukon in 1978, the Liberals

Aerial view of Whitehorse, capital of the Yukon and home for two-thirds of the Yukon's inhabitants. In the foreground is the S.S. *Klondike*, a national historical site, which saw regular service from the 1930s until the early 1950s, carrying passengers and freight on the Yukon River between Dawson City and Whitehorse.

Canada

Hon. R.J. "Rocky" Simpson
Premier, Northwest Territories, Office of the Premier

Hon. P. J. Akeeagok Premier of Nunavut

won, as their leader, Pat Duncan, formed the government.

In 2002, she handed the reins of power to Dennis Fentie, leader of the Yukon Party. In May 2011, he made way for Darrell Pasloski, a Whitehorse pharmacist and community leader, who led the Yukon party to its third majority government in the 2011 provincial elections. While the 2016 elections produced a liberal majority, with Sandy Silver becoming premier, the 2021 elections produced a hung parliament, with both the Liberals and the Yukon Party capturing 8 seats. In April 2021, the Liberals formed a minority government with the New Democrats entering a formal confidence and supply agreement, for a total of 11 combined seats. Sandy Silver remained premier.

On September 9, 2022, Silver announced he would resign as premier and leader of the Liberal Party. He was succeeded by Ranj Pillai, who was sworn in as premier on January 14, 2023, assuming the minority government previously led by Silver. Pillai will face the voters as leader in the next General Election, scheduled to be held no later than November 3, 2025.

Northwest Territories

In contrast to the Yukon, native people constitute about 48% of the overall population in the Northwest Territories (NWT), a plural name that is likely to be singularized in the future. The various ethnic groups are not spread evenly over this gigantic region extending about 500,000 square miles and located mainly above the tree line. The population of the NWT consists of 52% non-aboriginal, 28% Dene, 9% Métis and smatterings of other aboriginals, speaking nine official aboriginal languages, including North Slavey, South Slavey, Cree, Chipewyan, Dogrib, Gwich'in, Inuvialuktun, plus English and French. One tenth are Inuvialuit or Western Inuit, who face daunting challenges because life expectancy is 10 years shorter than the Canadian average, the youth suicide rate is eight times higher, tuberculosis rates are 17 times higher, and dropping out of school is far more common than earning diplomas.

In 2003, a landmark agreement was reached with the 4,000 Dogrib Indigenous people who call themselves the Tlicho First Nation. Following the treaty with British Columbia's Nisga'a, this was only the second agreement that grants the inherent right to self-government to aboriginals. In the process they gained ownership of an area of 15,000 square miles, or almost as large as Switzerland, around Yellowknife between Great Slave Lake and the Great Bear Lake together with its natural resources. Abutting a diamond industry from which it gains 2% of the royalties, and all from any future mines, the Tlicho could become one of the richest First Nation groups in North America; they make and enforce laws, collect taxes, levy royalties on mines, and regulate land use, education, family, and traditional medicine.

The NWT is a land rich in diamonds, oil, and gas with three operating diamond mines and many more planned. Diamonds now make up more than half of NWT's economic output. The last exhausted gold mine closed in 2005. One abandoned gold mine in Yellowknife, Giant Mine, contains deadly toxic arsenic waste, one of many sites that are the government's responsibility.

To facilitate traffic to and from mines, exploration, sites and remote communities, authorities build a thousand miles, or about 1,450 kilometers, of winter roads each year. The busiest runs about 280 miles or 420 kilometers northeast from Yellowknife, over more than 30 frozen lakes. Others run into neighboring Nunavut. An increasing problem is that global warming is shortening the time that trucks can cross ice, leaving mining operations short of the necessary huge construction equipment and vast quantities of supplies and fuel, which must then be flown in at great expense. Without the full use of these winter roads, the NWT's economic lifeblood is threatened.

Distance and the tenuous road conditions drive food prices up; a head of cabbage can cost $28, and a 24-pack of water can run $65. With prices like this, there can be no wonder why an estimated one-third of children go to bed hungry. Of course, global warming creates problems for the Inuit as they must deal with unpredictable sea ice that can be fatal, snowmobiles must take longer routes, and their buildings are weakened by melting permafrost.

The NWT is more self-sufficient and economically healthier than is Nunavut. The separation of Nunavut from the NWT in 1999 caused some economic suffering for the latter's gritty frontier capital, Yellowknife's population of about 19,500 as of the last available date accounts for the largest share of the NWT's estimated population of 45,136.

On a negative note, the NWT lost about 500 federal and territorial government jobs along with some of its much-needed transfer payments from Ottawa. It also suffers from a chronic shortage of doctors and nurses. From 2000 to 2010, the crime rate in the NWT rose by 35%. Aggravated assault in the capital of Yellowknife is more than 350% higher than the average in Canada. Yet, in the 21st century tourism, especially among Japanese, is thriving. Yellowknife's economy is robust, thanks in large part to the mining boom. While Tiffany's has established a cutting and polishing factory in the town, housing remains tight while drug use and crime are problems.

The prospect of uranium deposits in the north has attracted even more interest in the NWT. In an effort to protect their territory and its Boreal Forest, a huge green swath across North America that is crucial for wildlife, native groups and the Canadian government agreed to move toward preserving an area four times the size of Yellowstone Park from diamond and uranium mining interests.

In the NWT's non-party system, the Legislative Assembly has the chance to review government leaders every two years. Since October 2019 the premier is Caroline Cochrane, who succeded Bob McLeod on his retirement.

By tradition, the NWT's is only one of two legislatures in all of Canada, the other being in Nunavut, that reaches decisions by consensus, rather than by party politics and majority votes. In fact, there is no formal opposition in the NWT legislative assembly. During sessions, members use their own languages, with all remarks be-

Canada

ing translated into the other official languages from interpreter booths. For the time, being the NWT retains its name and territorial government. A new territorial constitution is being written and possible changes in the political system are being considered. During sessions members use their own languages, with all remarks being translated into the other official languages from interpreter booths. For now, the NWT retains its name and territorial government. A new territorial constitution is being written.

Northwest Territorians went to the polls on November 14, 2023; due to Northwest Territories wildfires, which caused evacuations in August, the election was delayed six weeks, from October 3 until November 14. Because the Assembly is run on a consensus system in which all MLAs sit as independents, the next premier was only chosen at its first meeting following the election. Because incumbent Premier Caroline Cochrane had announced prior to the election that she would not seek re-election, she was replaced as premier during the first meeting of the Assembly by Rocky "R.J." Simpson.

Nunavut

The Inuit, "The People," singular: Inuk, called "Eskimo" in Alaska, a term meaning "meat-eater" that these people resent, comprise 85% of the people in a definable area to the northeast of the NWT. In 1976, the Inuit Tapirisat of Canada, the national Inuit organization, asked that the former NWT be split in two. The result was the establishment of a new eastern Arctic territory named Nunavut, "Our Land," on April 1, 1999.

The Inuit disliked sharing power with people who have nothing culturally in common with them. Nunavut is much more homogeneous than the NWT. The Inuit, a gentle maritime people, have a different temperament than the NWT's mixture of "frontier mavericks and fractious aboriginal groups," as Maclean's described them. Inuit found many Canadian institutions alien, and considered Yellowknife to be too far away and too Canadian for their taste. For instance, one Inuit school supervisor in the Baffin region, located 2,500 kilometers and two time zones from Yellowknife, argued that the capital "is so far distant that I don't think they realize the impact of their decisions on our communities."

In 1982, the Inuit persuaded the territorial government to conduct a referendum in the NWT to determine whether there was popular support for such a division. The result was that 56% of voters supported the change. Inuit leaders made the division of the NWT the major item on their political agenda.

The breakthrough was made in 1992 when 54% of NWT voters accepted an agreement with the Canadian government. With a population of only 32,200 at that time, Nunavut's predominantly Inuit population, about 85% of its residents, extend over 772,000 square miles in the Eastern Arctic, almost entirely above the tree line. They are settled in 26 communities, which can be reached only by plane or ship. There are no road connections. The 300 kilometers or 200 miles of roads are mostly gravel streets within the communities and end at the last house, where the wilderness begins. There are only about 20 miles of paved highways. The population has grown 12.7% between 2011 and 2016, reaching 35,944 in 2016. In 2021 the population was 39,285.

Perhaps the largest peaceful land settlement in history, the new territory comprises a fifth of Canada's land area, two-thirds of its coastline, and traverses three time zones. Nunavut is the size of California and Alaska combined. In Canadian terms, it is equivalent to British Columbia, Alberta, and the Yukon combined, or twice as large as Ontario.

Inuit received legal title to 136,000 square miles, mineral rights to 14,000 square miles, and $1,148 billion over 14 years. In return, the Inuit had to renounce their claim to another 640,000 square miles of ancestral terrain, possibly containing rich gas and oil fields, which remain Crown land. Nevertheless, the Inuit receive a share in federal royalties from gas, oil, and mineral deposits on Crown lands, as well as hunting and fishing rights over all of Nunavut. As one participant in the negotiations put it, "We're a small people, but we have big ambitions."

In a plebiscite to choose their capital, the Inuit selected Iqaluit, pronounced ee-KA-loo-eet, formerly called Frobisher Bay, a modern community on the southern tip of Baffin Island. Iqaluit is Canada's fastest-growing capital, with about 7,000 inhabitants as of 2019 but it is so small that there is no need for street names. Buildings simply have numbers.

Iqaluit launched the first Internet web site in the Inuktitut language, the first language for 70% of the territory's people. Along with English and French, it is an official language and the one that is used as much as possible in government. Fearing that Inuktitut will slowly die in the capital, then Premier Okalik ordered

Inuit camp, Baffin Island, Nunavut

Courtesy: Michael J. Hewitt

Canada

senior bureaucrats to learn the language if they want to keep their jobs. Laws are being drafted to make it Nunavut's working language by 2020. Television broadcasting is available in both Inuktitut and English. In Iqaluit one hears more English than Inuktitut, but the latter predominates in the 24 smaller communities. There is a local newspaper called the *Nunatsiaq News*.

Public school instruction is offered in Inuktitut, but parents may opt for English schooling. Increasingly, English is the language of choice among young Inuit, a matter of concern for elders. By 2015 only 63% of Inuit could speak Inuktitut. Instruction is given in Inuktitut until grade 3 or 4 then it tapers off and English is favored. There is also no universally recognized spelling and grammar for the Inuktitut.. In a 2006 poll, only 18% of students responded that they speak more Inuktitut than English in school. Part of the problem is a severe shortage of Inuktitut-speaking teachers. Only about a fourth of Inuit children graduate from high school causing Nunavut to have the lowest literacy rate in Canada.

Another problem is that two-thirds of Inuit children suffer some degree of hearing loss due to chronic ear infections. Teachers wear wireless microphone headsets to amplify their lessons in speaker-equipped classrooms. There is also an acute lack of dental care. Children with braces must fly south twice every two months with a guardian for treatments; the average price to the government of each appointment is $25,806.

Nunavut Arctic College offers some academic courses in both English and Inuktitut, training teachers as well as instructing Inuit artisans who wish to diversify their products. In 2005 a joint effort of the College and University of Victoria trained 11 law graduates in order to afford the territory and its people more professional expertise rooted in native culture. In 2009 work began on an Inuit cultural school in Clyde River, which will have satellite campuses teaching cultural programs in Baker Lake and Igloolik. Since completion in 2011 the school provides full scholarships for 26 students age 18 or over. The school's name, *Piqqusilirivvik*, means "a place that has those things important to us" in Inuktitut.

The NWT and Nunavut each send one MP to the House of Commons in Ottawa and a Senate seat. Nunavut has an Inuit-controlled government with its own legislature, cabinet and court system, representing North America's boldest experiment to give a native group so much self-determination. In elections to their legislative assembly, many of the ballots must be dropped by planes into remote settlements. In the vote for the first legislature, held on February 15, 1999, 88% of eligible voters participated.

Under their nonpartisan political system, in which there are no parties and decisions are made by consensus, the 19 newly elected members meet for days after an election to choose their governmental leader. Their 19 seats are in a circle, not divided by an aisle to separate right and left, government and opposition, surrounded by symbols of their unique environment. The first item one sees on entering the premier's office is a huge polar-bear rug. The upholstery in the legislative chamber one floor below is of seal skin. The door handles are made of walrus tusk, and the shaft of the ceremonial mace that symbolizes legitimacy is the tusk of a narwhal, a small Arctic whale.

The premier must consult with all the Members of the Legislative Assembly (MLAs), not just the cabinet, which the MLAs, not the premier, select. They have become more comfortable with Westminster traditions, such as addressing all comments to the speaker. Still, there have been some critics of this unique government without parties and a loyal opposition. Critics contend that there is no mechanism for accountability, that deals involve too much pork-barrel politics, and that there is no way for voters to "send a message" to the government. Supporters respond that because the nonpartisan, consensual system is the Inuit way, it allows the most talented people in the entire legislature to form the government.

In April 1999, the one female and 18 male deputies selected lawyer Paul Okalik as premier. Easily reelected in 2004, his vision was "that we achieve the same standard of living as other Canadians and at the same time preserve our culture and language." Okalik personally experienced the troubles afflicting his entire Inuit people. Okalik was young enough to be the only premier in Canada still paying off his student loans when he took office. Okalik governed a young region with the continent's highest birth rate and where 40% of the population is under age 15 and half under 22; it is young men aged 15 to 29 who commit two-thirds of the crime. He also survived alcoholism, a term in prison, and a brother's suicide.

In November 2008, Eva Aariak succeeded Okalik as premier, serving until 2013. Peter Taptuna served from 2013 until November 2017, Paul Quassa until November 2018, followed by Joe Savikataaq, who took office on June 14, 2018. The current premier, P. J. Akeeagok, assumed office on November 19, 2021, and was returned to office in the election of October 25, 2021. Nunavummiuts will go to the polls again no later than October 27, 2025.

The rate of heavy drinking in Nunavut is three times the Canadian average, and a quarter of all babies are born with fetal alcohol syndrome. Only six communities, down from eight, are dry. The wet counties have three times the number of homicides and almost double the number of assaults. The head of Nunavut's RCMP said the root of all crime is "alcohol, alcohol, alcohol." Even in places where citizens have voted by plebiscite to prohibit alcohol, these decisions are undermined by bootleggers. This helps make the territories the most dangerous parts of Canada. From 2000 to 2010, the crime rate rose by 38%. The murder rate is ten times higher than the national average. Because jail space is so limited, Nunavut must pay to send some offenders to NWT to serve their sentences.

The suicide rate is seven times higher in Nanavut than the Canadian average.

Dog team on the ice, Simpson Strait, Northwest Territories

Canada

Young men are almost 30 times more likely to commit suicide with young women aged 15 to 24 are 36 times more likely to take their own lives than other Canadian women. Teacher Sheila Levy admitted: "suicide touches everyone here." In an attempt to combat this tragedy, a new mental health center was created in Iqaluit.

Drug addiction is epidemic in Nanavut. The lowest form of substance abuse, solvent sniffing, is 26 times more prevalent than in Canada as a whole; 20% of the people admit doing it. Aggravated assault is 1,033% higher, and sexual assaults are 1,270% more likely than in the rest of Canada. The rate of sexually transmitted disease is 15 times the national average.

A shocking dimension of this horrible crime rate in Nanavut is that some of the territory's political leaders show such bad examples. Levi Barnabas was given a cabinet post despite being convicted for sexual assault while he was Speaker of the House. James Arvaluk became education minister even though he served prison time for rape and assault, having beaten a former girlfriend so brutally that she needed 18 stitches to sew up her mouth and sustained permanent nerve damage. Lorne Kusugak was unanimously appointed to a cabinet post two months after being charged with sexual assault and trying to strangle his victim.

A major contributor to these lamentable social problems in Nanavut is the lack of work. The official unemployment rate in 2004 was 30% among Inuit. Yet, if one includes those who have given up looking for a job, the figure increases to an estimated 37% of Inuit. Due to the extremely high birthrate, many children will never find future jobs. By contrast, unemployment among the non-Inuit minority was only about 4%. Of the 2,789 jobs created in the territory's new public service by 2006, 45% went to Inuit, short of the stated goal of 50%.

Unemployment is especially serious because Nunavut has Canada's highest cost of living and lowest per capita income, a third of that in the NWT. In 2012, a bag of flour cost $33 and 10 pieces of chicken $61.99. It is small wonder that hunger is one of Nunavut's most persistent social ills. Nearly 70% of preschool children in Nanavut live in "food insecure" households. Some provide for their families by going outside the wage economy and engaging in hunting and fishing. The government encourages the consumption of local food such as seal, muskox and ground squirrels. It also subsidizes large-scale hunts to increase the food supply. A third of the residents receive welfare, more than three times the Canadian average. This does not go far for the 60% of adults who smoke; they pay $15 per pack. The government has launched an aggressive anti-smoking campaign.

Most jobs in Nanavut are related to government spending, which accounts for more than half of Nunavut's employment. What little private sector is in Nanavut depends directly on government projects such as construction. Only five communities exist in Nunavut where getting a job is a viable option. Not including the land-claim payments, Ottawa sends Nunavut 90% of the territory's revenues. Per capita handouts amount to $21,622 each year in addition to $40,000 per person in "compensation" payments.

Nunavut has a small tax base. It gets about five times as much revenue from tobacco taxes as from corporate income taxes. Lodging is a serious problem and is expensive: 83% live in government-subsidized housing. This situation stems from the 1950s when the federal government forced the nomadic Inuit to resettle in permanent communities, resorting to such brutal measures as shooting their dogs. In 1992, the Canadian government formally apologized to more than a hundred Inuit who, in the 1950s, had been forced to move from their northern Quebec homes to the desolate high Arctic settlements of Resolute Bay and Grise Fiord. The purpose was to assert Canadian sovereignty over the area where a U.S. military outpost was located.

Prospects for economic development are not encouraging. Nunavut has fewer developed resources than the NWT. The best hope for broadening the tax base is mining although extraction costs of many of its resources are prohibitively high. By century's end, three mines were producing lead, zinc, gold, and silver. The first diamond mine opened, Jericho, just south of the Arctic Circle. Jericho is largely responsible for Nunavut's economic growth rate in 2006 of 5.8%, second only to oil-rich Alberta. Ottawa takes 95% of the revenue on mining riches and all three northern premiers want a bigger share.

A 1993 land claims settlement requires outside investors to draw up "impact benefit agreements" with local communities. Mobility must be by air. This creates obstacles in developing the tourist industry. The federal government is committed to creating three new national parks in the territory and eco-tourism is rising. Still, with round-trip air tickets from Ottawa to Iqaluit costing over $2,000, tourism in Nunavut is for the well-to-do.

The Nunavut government engages in devolution talks with Ottawa while the premier meets independently of the Canadian government with the opposite number in Greenland. The topics of discussion include greater independence and control over natural resources. Greenland Air introduced direct flights between Nuuk and Iqaluit while Iqaluit and Nuuk co-hosted the hockey matches in the 2016 Arctic Winter Games.

Perhaps the highest-level tourists came to town in early February 2010: the finance ministers of the Group of Seven, the world's leading developed nations. Canada's choice of location was inspired by the wish to assert Canadian sovereignty in the Arctic and to take a stand against the European Union's ban on seal products. The ministers were invited to a "community feast" and served seal meat, caribou, char jerky, and muskox along with being given souvenirs of sealskin mittens and waistcoats. In August 2009, then Prime Minister Harper brought his entire cabinet to Iqaluit for a meeting as a part of a five-day visit to the Arctic. While in Iqaluit, cabinet members ate raw seal meat to take a swipe at the EU and to make a gesture of solidarity with the Inuit. Former Governor General Jean made the same gesture by eating a raw seal heart.

Most Canadians must experience the extraordinary light and sweep of the Arctic through films. The first Inuit-language feature in history, *Atanarjuat*, The Fast Runner, about an epic tale of love, jealousy, murder, and revenge, directed by Zacharias Kanuk, was greeted by rave reviews at the 2001 Cannes film festival. Award-winning Canadian filmmaker John Houston, who grew up in the Arctic and speaks fluent Inuktituk, turned his artistic talent to Nunavut. His *Songs in Stone*, about his Inuit art collecting parents in the North, opened in 1999. In 2001, Kanuk followed up with a documentary, *Nuliajuk: Mother of the Sea Beasts*, about a legendary sea deity by that name. No one can view these works without experiencing fascination for the Inuit imagination.

Canada

PARTIES AND ELECTIONS

Like any modern democracy, the Canadian political system could not function without parties. They recruit and select candidates, define issues which are important, educate voters about themselves and the issues, finance and fight electoral campaigns, put up governments which rule at all political levels, and provide well organized opposition parties, which continually remind the electorate of the governments' shortcomings. For the government, the party is an essential tool for maintaining cohesion and discipline among members and thus a parliamentary majority, and for the individual politician it is the ladder to power. For the political activist it is an important means for putting her ideas into practice, and for the voter it is an indispensable label for the set of politicians, policies, sympathies or interests.

Canadian parties emerged even before Confederation and were originally named and modeled after the two major British parties in the 19th century, the Conservatives and Liberals. For a while, they were loose coalitions of various factions with little discipline and almost no organization outside of parliament. By the end of the 19th century, though, they had changed considerably to conform to the nature of the Canadian state and society. They now have distinctive characteristics insofar as they are decentralized, which is exactly what one would expect in such a federal state. At the bottom is the local poll organization, and above that is the riding (district) organization, which selects the candidates for parliamentary elections.

Unlike in the United States, it is not necessary in Canada for a candidate to reside in the riding in which he runs. It is a fairly strong tradition, however, that the candidate be from the constituency. Occasionally higher party officials will ask a riding to allow a certain person to run in that electoral district. This is usually a party leader or cabinet member who desperately needs a parliamentary seat in order to be in a government or be a leader in the parliamentary opposition. An example of this was Brian Mulroney, who had never held an elective office before he was selected as Conservative party leader in 1983. In order to lead his then opposition party in the House of Commons, an MP from Nova Scotia agreed to give up his seat so that Mulroney could win it in a by-election. Since Mulroney had lived in the area as an undergraduate at St. Francis Xavier University, and since the riding organization calculated that it would doubtlessly benefit in the long run by lending a helping hand to a person who was likely to become the country's prime minister, it agreed to the move. However, the point must be reiterated: higher party bosses cannot simply "parachute" outsiders into ridings whenever they wish to do so. If the riding organization says "no!", then that is the answer. However, the leader of a party can stop someone from being a candidate for the party,

Parties also have regional and provincial associations. Most major parties maintain permanent provincial headquarters, which help the federal parties conduct campaigns during federal parliamentary elections. At the top is the national headquarters. Except for the headquarters in Ottawa and the provincial capitals, most of the lower party organizations more or less hibernate between elections. They remain ready to spring into action at a day's notice to wage electoral campaigns. The dates for these elections are never known long in advance. They are almost always determined by premiers and prime ministers to take place at their party's advantage. Provincial elections are never timed to coincide with federal elections. The national headquarters has a staff to support the party in a variety of ways. They hire issue consultants and pollsters, print literature and posters, and order campaign paraphernalia. They also plan party conventions, and generally serve the parliamentary party organizations in any way they can.

Party headquarters help raise money for campaigns. Elections have become very expensive, although Canadian candidates do not yet spend as much as their American counterparts. In 1963, Quebec became the first province to pass spending limits for campaigns. Some other provinces later followed suit and have a variety of spending ceilings. In 1974, the Trudeau government placed limits on federal election expenses. For example, in the 1988 elections, Canadian candidates were limited to spending a total of $6.6 million during the 51-day campaign, whereas American candidates spent $140 million in a campaign lasting two years.

Subsequent 2003 legislation also grants tax deductions for political contributions. Candidates who win more than 10% of the votes in their ridings recoup 60% of their expenses from the government. In addition, the federal government provides to candidates from recognized parties a certain amount of free broadcasting time. These contributions from state coffers have helped all the parties, particularly the NDP, which, unlike the Liberals and Conservatives, always had difficulty obtaining contributions from well-to-do individuals or corporations. It has had to rely more on dues from party members and affiliated labor unions than have the other two parties.

The volatility of public election finance was demonstrated in 2008, when a Tory budget provision that would have eliminated it almost brought the newly re-elected minority government down. This seemed blatantly partisan since the Conservatives were in good financial condition while the other parties' finances were desperate. The measure was withdrawn. But in 2011 reductions in the maximum campaign contribution from $5,000 to $1,000 went into effect. This change prevented Liberals from fully tapping their

Federal Election 2021, Leaders Debate, Montreal, September 2, 2021: Prime Minister Justin Trudeau (Liberal), Yves Blanchet (Bloc Québécois), Jagmeet Singh (New Democratic Party), Erin OToole (Conservative Party), TVA moderator Pierre Bruneau.

Martin Chevalier/Le Journal de Montreal/Pool Reuters

Canada

stable of big donors. Federal election subsidies also began to be phased out from 2011 to 2015. Parties that received at least 2% of the votes received got a subsidy of $2.00 per voter.

Broadcasters are usually prohibited from announcing the results of federal elections in provinces where the polls have not yet closed. Thus, western Canadians would not be influenced in their voting by knowing how their eastern countrymen had voted. That rule was set aside by the Supreme Court in 2004 on the grounds that it is an infringement on the freedom of speech. Of course, the internet makes it impossible to black out results from being disseminated anywhere in Canada. But in 2004 and 2006 western Canadians could watch the returns in the east before deciding whether or how to vote.

Despite a kind of party structure that appears to be hierarchically organized from top to bottom, there are no powerful, country-wide parties that can hold the disparate governmental and party elements together and facilitate compromise or smooth out regional differences. No parties are powerful in all parts of the country; all have their fortresses and deserts. After 2006, the Liberals were weak in the West, the NDP had barely a toehold in the Maritimes, and until 1984 and again after 2006 there was almost nothing more depressing than being a Conservative (Tory) in Quebec. Also, regional parties can differ greatly from the national parties that bear the same names.

Although the overall organization is loose *outside* of legislative assemblies, the *parliamentary parties* are tightly bound and led. MPs or MLAs vote against their party leaders only at risk to their political careers. Indeed, as the SNC-Lavalin Affair demonstrated, those who do not support one issue, which is deemed highly significant to a Party, may be removed from the Party caucus and thus are no longer members of the Party in the House of Commons – being relegated to independent members or they may "walk the floor of the House of Commons" and join another party. Unlike their American counterparts, they seldom refuse to support their leadership, either for reasons of conscience, or to serve better the interests of their constituents in the ridings, or simply to hold their seats. Individual MPs make the concerns of their constituents known in their parliamentary caucuses, committees or debates in the whole House; they also serve their constituents in a variety of other ways.

The reason is that parliamentary democracy is practiced at every level in Canada is that governments stand or fall based on the legislative count – one member one vote. The stakes are therefore too high for a party to be indifferent to how its members vote. Such party discipline had been loosening over the years but as earlier stated, the SNC-Lavalin Affair has certainly changed things in the Liberal Party. When a government lacks a majority in parliament, as was the case for seven years after the 2004 elections, there is a lot of wheeling and dealing to win votes from other parties. Members of Parliament find themselves courted for their vote, and this can strengthen their political influence in parliament. Since the advent of multi-party politics after the First World War, Canada has had 12 minority governments compared with 15 majority ones. Some of those minority ones have been successful governments under such prime ministers as Mackenzie King and Lester Pearson and in the 21st century under Stephen Harper. The requirement to vote as the party leaders demand is lifted on votes of conscience, such as whether to legalize same-sex marriage.

A second major characteristic of Canadian parties is that they are democratic in at least two ways: they willingly relinquish power when they lose elections, and the selection of their leaders is decided on at national leadership conventions of delegates representing party organizations throughout the country. Only about a tenth of adult Canadians actually belong to a political party. But any member who wishes to be active in his local, regional or provincial party organization has the chance to influence the outcome of the leadership race. He or she can speak with aspirants for the national party leadership, who travel around the country soliciting support. The caucus pollings are a bit like primary elections among party activists.

At the party conventions, the candidates make speeches, and the voting is by secret ballot based on the majority principle. The first candidate to win a majority of the delegates' votes, a process usually taking multiple rounds of balloting, wins. In each round of voting a candidate is eliminated.

The losing candidates often openly symbolize their support for one of the stronger candidates by actually going over to that person's section in the stands to shake hands or embrace. Sometimes such gestures pay handsome political dividends. For instance, the first contender to cast his support to Brian Mulroney after the first ballot in 1983 was Michael Wilson, who later became finance minister. In 2006, he was named Canada's ambassador in Washington. The purpose of party conventions is not only to select new party leaders, but also to serve as pep rallies to boost party morale. They bring the party elite together with the grass-roots. Sometimes they also draft or adopt party programs or platforms, which are usually

Sir Wilfrid Laurier

statements of what the party would like to achieve in the best of all worlds.

Such conventions have a certain American air about them. Permeated with the smell of hot dogs and hamburgers and awash with Coca Cola and beer, they are noisy, colorful affairs, with a rainbow of hats, scarves, buttons and signs, and big bands playing such songs as "When the Saints Come Marching In" and "Glory, Glory Hallelujah." Before the candidates deliver their crucial speeches (invariably mixing French and English), their enthusiastic supporters march in carefully orchestrated parades around the convention floor, accompanied by bands playing such unlikely political tunes as "Chariots of Fire" (for the underdog, of course). Bono and Canadian singer Paul Anka performed at the Liberals' 2003 convention. The supporters of Stéphane Dion, who won the Liberals' leadership contest at their December 2006 convention in Montreal, pranced around the arena wearing green T-shirts with his name on them and reminding everyone of Dion's special expertise on the environment.

There are also plenty of unabashed expressions of patriotism, such as "this beautiful country," "the most fortunate cluster of people on the face of the globe" and *Vive le Canada!* In dizzying rounds of expensive receptions, dances (with plenty of rock music for the one-fourth to one-third of the delegates who are under age 25), barbecues and "chuck-wagon breakfasts," candidates have the opportunity to meet delegates directly. One major difference with American conventions, though, is that one does not always know for sure whom the Canadian delegates will select.

Programs and platforms seldom bind the party leaders, who must seek votes and make policy. The reason for this is related to a third characteristic of Canadian

Canada

parties: they are mass, non-ideological coalitions of many diverse groups. From the beginning, their goals are to win elections and divide the spoils of victory. Thus, they are pragmatic, practical and flexible.

Minor or regional parties in Canada usually began outside of legislatures as protest movements and therefore tend to be more ideological in their programs and orientation. The federal system, which fragments the political process, helps such parties to arise and provides them with smaller arenas that are less heterogeneous than Canada as a whole. In such smaller units with fewer groups to appease, it is more feasible to take a more partisan approach. A closer look at each of the major parties will help elucidate the differences that do exist among them.

The Liberal Party

The Liberal Party, which in its earliest days was called the Reform Party, was Canada's most successful federal party in terms of years in power. Indeed, this party's history is in many ways the history of Canada itself. It originally began as a combination of agrarian interests in Western Ontario, anti-clerics from Quebec and reformist elements from Nova Scotia and New Brunswick. The dominant Ontario group lent the entire party its nickname as "Grits," a term which derived from one of its founders, who reportedly said that the party wanted candidates who were "all sand and no dirt, clear grit all the way through."

Sir Wilfrid Laurier was the party's first great leader. By standing firmly against conscription during World War I, he was able to convert Quebec into a powerful pillar of the Liberals. Laurier succeeded in persuading many *Québécois* that Canadian-style liberalism was not as stridently anti-clerical as the European variety. He was thereby able to synthesize Canadian liberalism with French Canadian support. This synthesis has been one of the great strengths of the party. Liberals have traditionally appealed to Roman Catholics, Jews, and other ethnic minority groups, and they generally have been more successful in patching together diverse groups and interests. As Christina McCall-Newman wrote in her book, *Grits*, the party forged powerful "alliances of elites," which was a "marvelously adaptable institution." In every generation, the Liberals succeeded in giving Canadians what they thought they wanted. The party also led Canada into the welfare era. In its Kingston policy conference of 1960, it pledged such innovations as universal medicare, minimum wages, old-age pensions, measures which all major Canadian parties have come to support.

In the 1970s, the party began to stumble because of some important changes in Canadian society. Its base in Quebec was eroded by the struggle over separatism; in the eyes of many *Québécois,* the party no longer was the best vehicle for their aspirations. Clashes with the western provinces almost entirely eliminated the Liberal presence in that increasingly powerful region. The social welfare net was predicated on the assumption that the economy would continue to grow and that the federal government would always have handsome surpluses at its disposal. When the worst recession in 50 years began in the early 1980s, that basic assumption was wiped away. More and more Canadians began to wonder if liberalism was a viable economic doctrine any more.

Trudeau let the party machinery and base wither and seemed to become increasingly aloof and insensitive. He had greatly invigorated the party after 1968, but he became more and more unpopular and a growing liability for his party. The party was in the doldrums and needed a fresh start.

The Liberal Party had dominated federal politics for most of the 20th century, after Sir Wilfrid Laurier created a seldom beatable majority in 1896. By election year 1984, it had ruled all but 22 years in that century. Ruling parties suffer from the declining popularity of leaders, whom a party cannot dismiss gracefully after many years of good service. "Trudeaumania" had long-since disappeared.

Many Canadians still admitted that Trudeau had been, in some important ways, good for Canada after becoming prime minister in 1968. He was a highly intelligent, learned, flamboyant and intriguing man. A completely bilingual Quebecer, he effectively confronted the specter of Quebec separatism by extending French language rights throughout Canada. The Liberal Party suffered in the West for this policy, but Canada's unity as

**Rt. Hon. Jean Chrétien,
former Prime Minister**

a country was preserved. Trudeau's last government nationalized the constitution so that Canadians no longer have to request the British parliament to change it. He was also a very visible figure in the world arena. Some Canadians would say that he "put Canada on the map."

At the same time, many Canadians came to view him as aloof, arrogant, and condescending, a reputation that began to rub off on his party. Also, many saw him as an unpredictable politician who sometimes behaved childishly in public. His banister slides or public displays of "the finger" were neither widely applauded nor appreciated. Finally, he seemed to ignore his party's need for effective organization of sound finances. He stepped down in June 1984 and lived in active retirement in Montreal until his death in October 2000.

His passing ignited an outpouring of grief that his countrymen had never before experienced. Parliament adjourned, the Supreme Court closed its doors, and normally reserved Canadians wept openly. He had clearly retained a hold on the imagination and loyalties of millions at home and abroad. People from all over Canada waited in line at Parliament Hill in Ottawa to see and touch his casket. They left red roses, which he had always worn in his lapel. His coffin was loaded into a hearse, a 19-gun salute was fired, and it was put on a train to Montreal. Along the way it slowed in small towns, and people waved and threw red roses. His body lay in state again in Montreal's City Hall. The doors were left open until 4 AM, when the last mourners left. Eight Mounties dressed in scarlet carried his coffin to his grave.

All Canadian prime ministers have mountains named after them when they die. The only exception is John Diefenbaker, who had a lake in Saskatchewan named for him. When Jean Chrétien, who admired Trudeau as his own mentor, decided to change the country's highest mountain, Mount Logan, to Mount Trudeau, an immediate outcry was heard. William Logan had been a famous geologist who in the mid-19th century had overseen the first comprehensive geological survey of Canada.

John Turner replaced Trudeau in June 1984. The former served as prime minister for 80 days before leading his party in a disastrous electoral defeat in September 1984. The 1984 leadership convention pitted Turner against his chief rival in the party, Jean Chrétien of Quebec. Chrétien was an extraordinarily versatile politician, having held virtually all the major cabinet posts. The 18th of 19 children (only nine survived), he grew up in an economically struggling family in Belgoville in northeast Quebec. After graduating from Laval

Canada

University law school and practicing law in Shawinigan for a while, he went to Ottawa in 1963 as an MP who could barely speak English. He not only mastered the language, but he developed a good sense of humor. A childhood illness had left him able to move only one side of his mouth. But he shrugged this off, saying that unlike many politicians, he could not speak out of both sides of his mouth.

He became party leader in 1990. Chrétien's appeal for Canadian unity was popular in anglophone Canada, but he faced hostility in his native Quebec, where his brand of "renewed federalism" found little resonance. Seldom in history had the Liberals' fortunes been so low in Quebec.

Chrétien led his Liberal Party into the 1993 federal elections ahead of all other parties. No one could have anticipated how massive the Liberal victory would actually be. It won 41.2% of the votes and 177 of 295 seats, all but exterminating its traditional rivals. Chrétien became the first Liberal prime minister ever to win office without a majority of seats in Quebec, where it captured only 19 of 75. This was particularly remarkable considering the fact that Chrétien himself is a *Québécois*.

He entered the June 1997 elections both as the most popular prime minister since polling began a half century ago and as the first federal leader to reduce the budget deficit in modern times. Although his Liberals declined from 174 seats (and 40% of the votes) to 155 seats (and 38%) in the House of Commons, his government was able to hang on to a narrow majority.

The Liberals had expected to win the 2000 elections, but the magnitude of victory was especially gratifying: they captured 173 seats (up from 155) based on 41% of the popular votes. This provided Chrétien with a comfortable majority in parliament and the honor of being the first leader to form three straight majority governments since 1945.

In 2000, Liberals found themselves divided. Finance Minister Paul Martin and his followers made it known that they had waited long enough to take over the party's reins. Martin's and Chrétien's differences went back to their bitter leadership contest in 1990, which Martin lost, and to the Meech Lake controversy, which Chrétien opposed, and Martin supported. Martin had always been more accommodating to Quebec nationalists. The result was profound distrust between the two leaders. Chrétien resisted being pushed out.

By 2002, the party could no longer bear the public feuding. After Chrétien fired Martin in June, the Liberal caucus in parliament put enormous pressure on the prime minister to declare his intentions. He stepped down in December 2003. Martin assumed leadership of the party in the November 2003 convention.

In the June 28, 2004, elections the Liberals failed to capture their fourth parliamentary majority in a row and had to settle for a minority government. They captured only 36.7% of the votes and lost 37 seats, falling from 173 to 135. They did well in Atlantic Canada, fell far behind the *Bloc Québécois* in Quebec, saw their stranglehold in Ontario broken even though they still won the most seats, and did better than expected in the West.

The 2006 elections were a disaster for the Liberals, who were consigned to the opposition for the first time in a dozen years. They fell to 30.2% of the votes and only 103 seats. To no small extent, the outcome was as much a rejection of Martin and the Liberals as an acceptance of Harper and the Conservatives. A defeated Martin resigned as party head, leaving the Liberals leaderless and in disarray. They faced the dual task of choosing a leader and rebuilding their fractured and directionless party.

Its leadership convention took place in Montreal December 3, 2006, following a campaign that lasted almost a year. The most interesting contender was Michael Ignatieff. He is the grandson of Tsar Nicholas II's last minister of education, whose son landed in Montreal as a refugee in 1928. Michael, like his friend Bob Rae, was the son of a top-ranking Canadian diplomat, including an assignment as ambassador to the UN. He spent much of his youth abroad.

After graduation, he left Canada for three decades, earning a PhD in history at Harvard, writing 14 books, including his family memoir that won the Governor General's Award, and gathering seven honorary doctorates. He lectured on genocide and ethnic violence in Britain and the U.S., ending up in a professorship of human rights at Harvard from 2000–5. In 2006 he won a seat in Toronto as a Liberal.

However, he proved to have serious skeletons in his closet. In countless articles in leading American newspapers, he had displayed what became known as the "pronoun problem": using the words "we" and "us" when referring to Americans. Many Canadians did not like that. He had supported the U.S. invasion of Iraq in 2003, and he continued to favor military action in Afghanistan. That left him in Canada with a reputation as a "hawk."

Often compared with Trudeau because of his scholarly nature and unusual path into politics, he lacked parliamentary and cabinet experience, and that showed. He made many gaffes in the campaign. His loss to Stéphane Dion on the fourth ballot 55% to 45% was as much a protest against the Harvard alien carpetbagger as a vote for Dion. The Conservatives soon picked up on this theme by running TV and Internet ads saying "Just Visiting" and contending that Ignatieff has no interest in Canada unless he can rule it.

For more than a century, every elected leader of the Liberal Party eventually became prime minister. History did not repeat itself. Dion came off as a cerebral ex-professor whose strong suit was not political organization. He spoke mangled English, and did not connect with people. He failed both as a party organizer and parliamentary leader. Indeed, under his stewardship the party had gone from $5 million in the bank to $6 million in debt. The Liberal performance in the October 2008 elections was a disaster. Its share of the popular vote fell to 26%, the lowest since the party's founding in 1867. It dropped from 103 to 76 seats.

Dion agreed to go. Ignatieff's only serious rival was his former roommate at the University of Toronto, Bob Rae, the former leader of the New Democratic Party of Ontario prior to becoming a Liberal, but he dropped out without forcing a leadership vote.

The May 2011 federal elections were such a calamity for the Liberal Party that wondered if it would ever recover.

The party and the nation were dumbfounded. The Liberals had fallen to less than 20% of the votes and a mere 34 seats. This was their worst result ever and the first time they were not among the top two parties. It had to relinquish to the NDP its position as official opposition in parliament Ignatieff lost his own seat in Toronto and immediately resigned as party chairman to return to the classroom at the University of Toronto and Harvard.

The party was left to ponder its continued relevancy and to face the many questions about its future and purpose. It selected Rob Rae as interim leader of the Liberal caucus in parliament. He chose not to seek the permanent leadership. He recalled the wisdom a former mayor of Toronto had imparted to him when he was just entering politics: "Bobby, in politics,

Canada

you don't get what you deserve, you get what's coming to you." Any leader would have to be bilingual and know how to maneuver the party back into the political center.

The party chose an official party leader in April 2013. The frontrunner was Justin Trudeau, the son of Canada's longest-serving prime minister, Pierre-Elliot Trudeau. He moved many Canadians when he delivered his father's eulogy in 2000. When he threw his hat in the ring, Justin described his decision: "My father's values and vision of this country obviously form everything I have as values and ideals. But this is not the ghost of my father running for the leadership of the Liberal party. This is me." His father tended to be divisive whereas the son is conciliatory.

He admitted that the timing was not ideal. Age 40, he was 12 years younger than Stephen Harper and has two small children. His youth helps him attract young voters. He wished he had spent more time in parliament although former Prime Minister Jean Chrétien noted that Justin had been elected twice in his Papineau Montreal riding, which is overwhelmingly poor and francophone; "it's one more time than his father when he became leader." "Why am I doing this? Because I can, not because I want to. Because I must." Trudeau received 80% of the votes.

He holds a B.A. in English from McGill and a B.S. in education from the University of British Columbia. He did further graduate study in engineering and environmental studies. He taught English and math at two different Vancouver private schools. As an MP, he was responsible for the party's positions on youth, post-secondary education and amateur sport. He was considered very popular when first elected as Prime Minister but the bloom has somewhat faded off the rose. His party's imposition of a carbon tax, stress on identity politics, and the SNC Lavalin Affair with the, in effect, firing of a hugely popular First Nations Minister of Justice and Solicitor General Jodi Wilson-Raybould and former Minister of Health and Treasury Board member Dr. Jane Philpott, have dogged his time in 2019 as Prime Minister. Indeed, the Affair caused the prime Ministers friend and Principal Secretary, political advisor Gerry Butts, and the chief civil servant in the federal service, the Clerk of the privy Council, Michael Wernick, to resign. Thus, the idea that the Prime Minister was a feminist has been challenged due to his recent actions and with photographs of dozens of women turning their backs to him in the House of Commons in April 2019 as he addressed the Daughters of the Vote, it appears that his "sunny days" motto is long gone. In October 2019, Trudeau was re-elected for a second term as Canada's prime minister, but as a minority government. Justin Trudeau went to the ballot box again in 2021 with a snap election in an attempt to regain a majority; the Liberal were returned to government, but with a second consecutive minority.

Throughout the 43rd and 44th Parliament, ethics and personal difficulties have taken their toll both on Trudeau and on the Liberal Party. As a result, on March 22, 2022, the Liberals and the NDP announced that they had entered a confidence and supply agreement in the Parliament of Canada. The agreement, in which the NDP committed to supporting the Liberals in all votes of confidence. For the NDP, this meant that it could make progress on important objectives; for the Liberals, this averts an early election and allows the current minority government to complete a full term ahead of the 2025 election. Still, since mid-2023, public opinion polls showed the Liberal Party slipping in popular support and, by the start of 2024, the party was consistently trailing the Conservative Party. On June 18, 2024, the Conservatives stood at 42% to the Liberal's 25%.

The Liberals continued to decline in opinion polls and suffered disappointing losses in by-elections following the 2021 general election. As a result, Justin Trudeau's leadership became the subject of opposition; while Trudeau continued to issue public statements assuring Canadians that his government remained "strong and united," 2024 closed with a wave of cabinet resignations, culminating in the resignation, on December 16, 2024, of Deputy Prime Minister Chrystia Freeland. At the same time, the incoming administration of President Donald Trump threatened to impose 25% tariffs on Canada and to make Canada the '51st state' of the United States. Amid continuing cabinet opposition, on January 6, 2025, Trudeau announced his resignation as leader of the Liberal Party and as Prime Minister, to take effect once the party elected his successor. He also announced that Governor General Mary Simon would prorogue Parliament until March 24, 2025 in order to allow the Liberal party to elect its new leader. On January 15, 2025, Trudeau also announced that he will not seek re-election in the riding of Papineau. On March 9, the Liberal Party elected Mark Carney its new leader and, on March 14, 2025, Trudeau delivered his formal resignation to the Governor General and, later that morning, Mark Carney was sworn in as Canada's 24th Prime Minister. Interestingly, Trudeau's strong response to the continuing American threat of tariffs and annexation of Canada at the 51st state of the United States lifted the Liberal Party's polling numbers. By the time Carney asked Governor-General Simon to dissolve Parliament on March 23, 2025, and called an election for April 28, 2025, opinion polls showed the Liberals slightly ahead of the Progressive Conservatives (for the first time in three years), a result almost wholly attributable to President Donald Trump's ongoing threats. It was therefore unclear which of the two major parties would win the election, either with a minority or majority, and the effect of the American threats on the Liberal Party's electoral prospects.

Rt. Hon. Charles Joseph Clark

Canada

The Conservative Party

Until 2004, two parties of the right had offered the Liberals three federal election victories on a platter because they split the opposition vote. For example, in 2000 they won a combined total of 38% of the votes (to the Liberals 41%), but because of the effect of the single-member electoral system, they received a combined total of only 78 seats to the Liberals' 172. They were cutting each other's throats. But "uniting the right" was difficult because the Progressive Conservative Party (PC) and the Canadian Alliance had grown out of different traditions, appealed to different kinds of Canadians, and had much bad blood between them. A look at both pillars of the new Conservative Party shows why their merger in 2004 was difficult but necessary.

Progressive Conservative Party

The Progressive Conservative Party (PC), under the leadership of Sir John A. Macdonald and his Quebec partner, Sir George-Etienne Cartier (then "The Conservative Party"), had dominated Canadian politics for most of the first three decades of confederation. Macdonald revealed a strong partisan approach to politics: "I do not say that all Grits [Liberals] are horse thieves. But I feel quite sure that all horse thieves are Grits." The Conservatives (Tories) suffered devastating political setbacks in the 20th century because of their support of a military draft during the First World War and because they were in power when the Great Depression struck in the early 1930s. At times it seemed almost as if they had been condemned to permanent opposition in federal politics. They traditionally drew much support from Protestants of British ethnic origin, but they needed to broaden their base.

In 1968, their exclusion from Quebec was prolonged by the emergence of the *Parti Québécois* and its antagonist, Pierre Elliott Trudeau. To polish the party's image by underscoring its moderate course and acceptance of Canada's social welfare net, they changed its name to Progressive Conservative, words which are not a contradiction in terms. They did not allow the Liberals either to outdo them in welfare spending by very much or to shove them to the right on the political spectrum. In 1978, Trudeau said that the Liberal position was the "radical center." Six years later, the PC leader defined the position of his own party as "the extreme center."

In the late 1970s, the PC's opportunity to regain power in Ottawa had come. The Liberals had been driven out of power in every Canadian province, and the PC captured control of most provincial parliaments. In 1976, Joe Clark, a young Albertan in his 30s, who had buckled down to learn fluent French, came from behind to capture the party leadership. In 1979, he led his party to victory in the federal parliamentary elections. However, his minority government made some cardinal blunders that ensured that it would be short-lived. Despite the fact that the PC had failed to win a majority of seats in the House of Commons, Clark decided that his government would rule *as if* it had a majority. In other words, he decided on a bold political course, which included such controversial stands as moving the Canadian embassy in Israel from Tel Aviv to Jerusalem, delaying the opening of parliament, and driving a very hard bargain with Conservative-governed Alberta in setting oil prices.

In an important budget vote, he failed to count noses carefully and lost the vote. He thereby prompted a new election in 1980, only eight months after the last one. An electorate that was most unimpressed with Clark's leadership gave the Liberals a new lease on life and voted the Conservatives out of power. Constantly nipped at the heels by critics within his own party, Clark decided to silence them by calling for a new leadership conference in June 1983. The result revealed the magnitude of his miscalculation: he lost on the fourth ballot to his challenger, Brian Mulroney.

Although Mulroney had had a passion for politics since his youth, he had never held elective office before becoming party leader. The oldest son of an Irish working-class family, Mulroney was born in the mill town of Baie Comeau, a predominantly French-speaking community located 265 miles north of Quebec City. His father was an electrician who had to hold down two jobs to make ends meet for a family with six children. He was the first offspring of a working class family ever to become prime minister in Canada.

The biggest asset he derived from his family background was that he grew up speaking French with his friends and English at home. Thus, he had acquired that indispensable advantage of being completely bilingual from childhood. This lingual ability, combined with a deep understanding and sympathy for their concerns and fears, enabled him to break through the distrust that many Quebecers had borne toward anglophones for two centuries.

Mulroney became prime minister in 1984. In 1988, he was the first Tory prime minister since 1891 to receive back-to-back majority governments and the first prime minister of any party in 35 years to win two consecutive victories. The Tories won 43% of the vote (down from 49.9% in 1984) and 169 seats (down from 211).

In many ways, Mulroney was a success. He changed Canada more profoundly than most of his predecessors because of his free trade, tax, and constitutional policies. As a party leader, he held together a fractious mix of anglophone westerners and francophone Quebecers, with only a few defections. He was effective in foreign policy. But his popularity dropped to the lowest of any prime minister in a half century. He was widely mistrusted and disliked, partly because of his manner, which seemed affected and insincere.

Mulroney's reputation was not helped by scandals after leaving office in 1993. He faced allegations that he had received money from Airbus to lobby the government and Air Canada to buy the European planes. He sued the government and won an apology and $2.1 million payment. But in a sensational House of Commons ethics committee inquiry in December 2007, Mulroney admitted that he had indeed received between $225,000 to $300,000, probably Airbus money, from a disreputable jailed dispenser of bribes, Karlheinz Schreiber, a German arms industry lobbyist. The cash was slipped to him in envelopes

Rt. Hon. Brian Mulroney

Canada

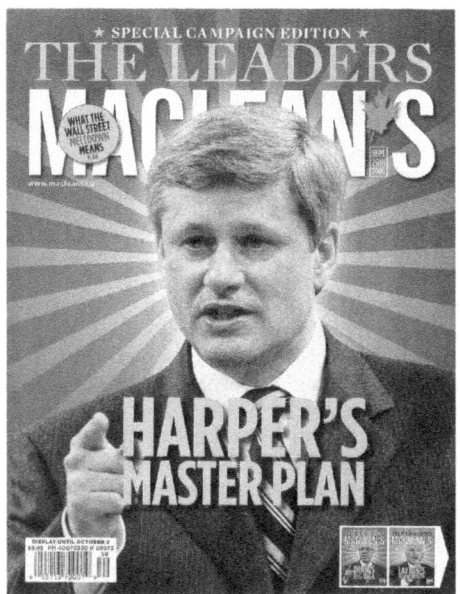

Rt. Hon. Stephen Harper

in hotel rooms, and he issued neither invoices nor receipts. Nor did he pay taxes on the money at the time but sensing trouble he paid them later. He went to great lengths to cover up the payments.

In his testimony to the committee, Mulroney admitted that he had shown an "error in judgment" and had made the biggest mistake of his life. A government enquiry found in 2010 that he had acted inappropriately by accepting the cash. However, he was soon working as a senior partner at the Norton Rose law firm in Montreal, was being feted for his accomplishments and was being sought out for his advice.

Mulroney was disliked because of unpopular policies, such as the Free Trade Agreement, Meech Lake, high interest rates, and the federal 7% goods and services tax (GST), which went into effect in 1991. He faced the twin threats of regional alienation and Quebec nationalism. The rejection of his constitutional reform in October 1992 forced him to make an unpleasant decision in the interest of his party.

Acknowledging his bleak electoral prospects, Mulroney announced in 1993 that he would step down after almost nine years as prime minister. He cleared the way for Kim Campbell, a former justice and defense minister from Vancouver, to take his place in June as party leader and prime minister and to lead the Tories in the October federal elections. Promising to "change the way we do politics in this country," she offered a refreshing candor in public, and her approval rating initially soared. In August, 51% of respondents approved of her performance as prime minister. This was the highest rating for any prime minister in 30 years.

Campbell was an inept campaigner and committed so many gaffes that one cruel reporter wrote that she rarely opened her mouth except to change feet. Although it would have been very difficult for any Tory to have succeeded, given the Mulroney legacy which had spawned severe cynicism in voters' minds, she led her party to the worst defeat in the history of any Canadian party. A group of 25 Canadian historians judged her in 1996 to have been the worst prime minister in Canadian history. After lecturing at Harvard and writing her autobiography, *Time and Change*, she accepted the post of Canadian consul general in Los Angeles. In 2010, she tried her hand at comedy by appearing in promotional clips for a VisionTV sitcom, "She's the Mayor."

The PC experienced a meltdown from 154 to *two* seats in the House of Commons, on the basis of 16% of the votes. The former pillars of Mulroney's strength, Quebec and Western conservatives, crumbled, as voters there streamed to the *Bloc Québécois* and the Reform Party, both protest movements committed to remaking the federal system.

Campbell relinquished leadership to the perfectly bilingual Quebecer, Jean Charest, whom she had narrowly defeated for the leadership in June and who was one of the two Tories to win a seat. During the 1995 Quebec referendum campaign, he displayed far more guts and effectiveness in pleading the federal case than did Prime Minister Chrétien and was the only federal politician who advanced his status during that painful struggle.

The party, which is called the Yukon Party in that territory and the Saskatchewan Party in that province, retained parliamentary influence only in the Senate. Their desperate situation gave rise to black humor: "Why did the Tory cross the road? To meet the other Tory!" Even one longtime Tory strategist remarked: "At least now we know the real meaning of the Conservative ad that said, Think Twice." Under the leadership of the most popular pro-federal politician in Quebec, Jean Charest, the PC fought its way back to respectability in the 1997 elections, winning 19% of the votes and 20 seats. It emerged as the strongest party in the Atlantic provinces.

In 1998, Charest resigned to become the Liberal Party leader in Quebec; in 2003 he became Quebec premier. He was replaced by ex-Prime Minister Joe Clark, who had yearned to return to politics. Since the debt-ridden party could not afford a leadership convention, its 87,000 members were invited to cast ballots. With half voting, he garnered 77% of the second-round votes.

He watched in 2000 as many Tories left the party to join the new Canadian Alliance that grew out of the Reform Party. The Tories were able to win a disappointing 12 seats in the House of Commons, based on 12% of the votes. This was the third consecutive devastating defeat. In only seven years the party had fallen from a majority government to a fifth-place party. It could no longer make its once-proud claim of being a truly national party able to speak for all Canadians in all walks of life. In 2002, Joe Clark told his party to select a new leader, and on June 1, 2003, it chose Peter MacKay in a dramatic convention. In 2006, MacKay became foreign minister and later defense minister.

The Canadian Alliance and Conservative Party of Canada

The second pillar of the new Conservative Party is the Canadian Alliance, which had grown out of the Reform Party of Canada (RPC), led until 2000 by Preston Manning. Founded in 1987, this party viewed itself as carrying on the tradition of earlier western populist movements and promised to integrate its conservative philosophy with a commitment to the disadvantaged. It championed the cause of western Canada without advocating separation. It sought such constitutional changes as an elected Senate with equal regional representation and the possibility of recalling MPs whose performance is questionable to voters. It opposed bilingualism and special treatment for Quebec.

Manning spoke about "One Canada," meaning that Quebec should decide whether it wishes to be a part of Canada as an equal province; if it does not, it should leave. An anti-statist party, it sought a reduction in taxes, the size of government, and immigration. It also demanded more direct democracy in the form of referenda, recalls, and initiatives. Some observers saw its momentum as the "revolt of the middle classes."

It was so successful in exploiting western dissatisfaction that the party decided in 1991 to compete in elections everywhere but Quebec. Manning explained the party's momentum: "People are saying yes to Senate reform, . . . yes to a fair language policy and no to forced bilingualism, yes to candidates responsible to their ridings, no to central Canadian parties that tell their MPs how to vote." An avid student of the American Civil War, he saw the situation in his own country as similar to the U.S. before 1861. An insoluble problem leads to a totally new realignment of parties and the country. And it is an outsider, a "man of the people" from the West, who comes in and picks up the pieces. Whom might Manning have had in mind as Lincoln's Canadian equivalent?

Canada

Hon. Pierre Poilievre, Leader of the Conservative Party of Canada

The Reform Party demonstrated in the 1993 elections that it had become a major political force in Canada. It won 18.7% of the votes and 52 seats, narrowly missing becoming the official opposition in Ottawa. All its seats were from the West. One of its difficult challenges was to expand into eastern Canada. Manning was a folksy, mild-mannered man who sought more decorum in the House of Commons and modestly sat in the second row even though he had front-bench privileges. One of his first motions was to amend official bilingualism. Not surprisingly, the Liberal government and the separatist *Bloc Québécois* handily defeated this. Manning was not an effective parliamentarian.

The BQ and Reform Party actually had much in common, as Manning noted after meeting Lucien Bouchard over pancakes one morning: "I said we were discontented and wanted to reform the system, he said they were discontented and didn't think the system was reformable." In 1995, he told a gathering of conservatives in Washington: "The emerging political axis is: are you a traditionalist defending old systems ... or are you a system changer? I would put us at the changing end. In Canada I would put the traditional parties on the system-defending end." The party capitalized on English Canada's frustration following the 1995 referendum on Quebec independence.

In the 1997 federal elections, the Reform Party dominated the western provinces, winning 60 seats (19% of the votes nationwide) and becoming the official opposition in parliament. Manning showed that he has become a force to be reckoned with in Canadian politics. The Liberal government's deficit cutting and law-and-order policies, as well as its tough approach toward Quebec, were influenced by Manning's popular appeals. His key political objective—to supplant forever the Tory party on the political right—was problematic, not least because Joe Clark adamantly rejected it. The Tory leader refused to attend Manning's "unite-the-right" convention in Ottawa in February 1999, calling it a "media event." No one denied the damage the two parties did to each other by competing in constituencies for the same voters. By fielding separate candidates, they cut each other's throats. But Manning wanted to change central Canada from the outside. Clark wanted to work with the center; he said: "I didn't grow up with the sense, ever, that the rest of the country was against me."

Manning became convinced that Reform was destined to permanent opposition if it remained trapped in the West and if Canada's conservatives remained divided. He was painfully aware that Reform and the Tories together had received as many votes in the 1997 federal elections as had the victorious Liberals (38%). But by competing with each other, they had won only 80 seats to the Liberals' 155. Therefore, in January 2000 his party invited all interested Tories to join them at a conference to discuss unification. By a 75%–25% margin, the delegates voted to create a new, broader party, called the Canadian Alliance. It promised to make some concessions to the center, such as accepting Canada's official bilingualism. It actively raided Tory ranks, and by the middle of the year it had surged to 19% in the polls, leaving the panicked Tories behind at 9%.

Stockwell Day, Alberta's former treasury minister, was elected party leader in July 2000, defeating a stunned Manning by a crushing 2-to-1 margin. He had undergone a dramatic transformation since his days as a marijuana-smoking college dropout who worked as a fisherman, hearse driver, auctioneer, and butcher in a meat packing plant. He became a born-again Christian with a social agenda so conservative that *Maclean's* magazine put his photo on the front cover with the title, "How Scary?" He pledged to reduce the role of government.

In the 2000 elections, the Alliance was all but vanquished in Ontario, winning only two rural seats. This was especially disappointing for Day, who had figured that if Alliance and Conservative voters could unify under one banner in Ontario, a powerful challenge to the Liberals' unassailable federal dominance could be made. That hope was dashed. The Alliance captured 64 seats from Manitoba to British Columbia. Although the Alliance, under Day's leadership, consolidated its hold on the West and its position as official opposition in Ottawa, it did not emerge as a national party that could serious threaten Liberal dominance in federal politics, despite its capture of 66 seats and a fourth of the popular vote nationwide.

In 2001, Day resigned, but he did not disappear. In 2006, his replacement, Stephen Harper from Alberta, who was only 43 years old at the time, put him in charge of the sprawling Department of Public Safety, the Canadian equivalent of the Department of Homeland Security. This had been created by the former Liberal government after September 11, 2001, to give a single minister control over everything from the RCMP and Canadian Security Intelligence Service, to running federal prisons and managing the border with the United States. He is praised for his front-bench survival skills.

An intelligent former policy adviser to Manning, Harper grew up in Toronto the middle-class son of an accountant. He moved to Alberta to do graduate work and had always lived a middle-class life in Calgary suburbs driving ordinary cars and earning a modest salary. Harper was not only a brilliant student, but a walking encyclopedia for hockey trivia subsequently wrote a book on the subject. In fact, he wrote much of the party's early platform. He is an articulate campaigner in both official languages, a fiscal conservative, sure of his convictions, and an evangelical Christian without Day's public displays of born-again Christianity.

Harper demonstrated his negotiating skill throughout 2003 by building a bridge between the two rival parties on the right and then merging them to create a credible alternative to the Liberals. He persuaded the more centrist PC leader, Peter Mackay, that union was their only hope for electoral success. The two parties made the decision to form the Conservative Party in December 2003. The Alliance gave almost unanimous backing for the merger, but PC members had a more difficult time accepting it.

In March 2004, Harper defeated a neophyte politician—telegenic multi-millionaire heiress and Magna CEO, Belinda Stronach, who switched to the Liberal Party in May 2005—and former Tory health minister in Ontario, Tony Clement, for the new party's leadership. Harper declared: "My goal is not only to win an election. It's to create a natural Conservative majority in this country." He admitted that Quebec would be his party's toughest long-term challenge. There were defections, and fault-lines in the new party remained. Some prominent Tories refused to join. For example, Joe Clark not only refused to run for parliament again, but he hinted that he might support Paul Martin, "the devil we know." Many disgruntled Tories gravitated to the Liberals.

Canada

It takes a new party time to gel, and the Conservative Party was not yet a sturdy union when Prime Minister Martin called for new elections in June 2004. It was thrust into an election campaign without a full debate over policy. It still spoke with many contradictory voices. But the Conservatives performed reasonably well, showing in many ways more cohesion than the Liberals, who were licking deep wounds from Martin's bloody unseating of his old rival, Jean Chrétien. They captured 29.6% of the votes (down from the PC-Alliance combined total of 38% in 2000), but received 99 seats in the House of Commons, up from a combined 78. Most important, the Conservative Party now represented a viable political alternative for Canadians. In March 2005 Harper easily won a leadership review, receiving the support of 84% of the delegates at the party conference.

In the January 2006 elections, the Conservatives won an impressive victory, securing 124 of 308 seats in the House of Commons on the basis of 36.3% of the votes. They won big in the West, where they got more than half of their seats, and all the seats in Alberta. Harper proudly proclaimed: "The West is now in." They broke the Liberal stranglehold on Ontario, winning 40 of its 106 seats. However, it was shut out in Toronto, Montreal and Vancouver.

Most dramatically, the Conservatives picked up 10 seats in Quebec, capturing 24.6% of the votes (up from 9%). Harper's openness to *Québécois* concerns, his budgetary gifts to the province, his talk of more flexible federalism, his frequent consultation with Quebec's Premier Charest, and his practice of beginning practically every speech in Ottawa in French, which he commands confidently, offer the prospect of even greater gains in Quebec. According to a 2007 poll, Harper received a good rating on his French from 81% of francophones.

The Conservatives rose steadily to almost 40% in the polls, but its numbers still did not translate into a parliamentary majority. He had to hang on to power in order to have a chance to achieve his real goal: to transform his party into a force capable of replacing the Liberals as the country's natural governing party due to their claim that only they can balance the interests of Quebec and the rest of Canada.

Nevertheless, Harper found himself in an agenda-setting position in Canadian politics. His disciplined control over the party left little room for sentiment or tolerance for failure. He is said to enjoy a comfortable family life that has changed little since his wife and their two children moved into the prime minister's residence. He is an accomplished amateur piano player who is a huge Beatles fan. When in 2009 his wife

Jagmeet Singh

Laureen was the honorary chair for a benefit at the National Arts Center in Ottawa, she turned to him for the starring role. He grudgingly agreed to wear a leather vest and cowboy hat and to accompany himself on the piano while he sang *With a Little Help from my Friends* and *I Need Somebody to Love*. The black-tie crowd loved it and gave him a standing ovation. Four years later he demonstrated his musical versatility at the Conservative convention in Calgary by performing with the Herringbone band, playing Stompin 'Tom Conners's The Hockey Song, as well as some Johnny Cash and BTO songs. The national media all reported the event with delight.

Although ceremonial duties are performed by the Governor General, a prime minister's wife has no official role. She is not officially the "first lady." In fact, Laureen Harper's only public cause is fostering homeless cats for the Humane Society. However, the fact that she is more outgoing and social than her husband is a political asset for him. He is often seen as stiff and arrogant, while Laureen, a farm girl from Alberta who rides motorcycles and hikes mountains, is viewed as more down-to-earth and fun-loving. She softens her husband's image. Having grown up in a political family, she has a sharp political sense. Many Conservatives call her Harper's secret weapon.

Ensconced in their sprawling new campaign headquarters in an Ottawa industrial park and with a winning election team intact after the 2004 and 2006 campaigns, Harper and his party were itching for an election fight. By September 2008 he decided to ignore his own law fixing parliamentary terms and to call new elections for October 14. He failed to win his majority, but his party did increase its popular vote to 37.6% and win 19 additional seats. Disappointingly, it made no gains in Quebec, winning only 22% of the votes.

Through daring, Harper survived an opposition attempt to unseat his government through a vote of confidence shortly after the elections. That would have created an unworkable three-headed government that would have offered neither stability nor popular legitimacy. There was outrage throughout Canada over the prospect that separatists, the BQ, might get their hands on the levers of power in a deal concocted with no respect for the ballot box. Harper instinctively knew this, and polls showed upwards of 60% of the public hostile to the coalition taking power.

The Conservatives continued to rule via a somewhat stronger minority government. However, his large lead in the polls at least temporarily evaporated when he prorogued (sent home) parliament a second time for two months until the throne speech on March 3, 2010. This was a very unpopular decision. Although Harper claimed he needed time to "recalibrate" the budget, it appeared that he was preventing embarrassing documents relating to the treatment of detainees in Afghanistan from being discussed in a parliamentary committee. It seemed the government had something to hide.

Perhaps he was saved politically by the Winter Olympics in Vancouver. He was the chief fan for the victorious Canadian men's and women's hockey teams and basked in the glow of the thrilling sudden-death 3–2 victory of the Canadian men over their American rivals in the last event. Polls showed that he had widened his personal approval ratings over Michael Ignatieff during the Games, and shortly before the hockey final, 37% of voters favored the Conservatives compared with 29% for the Liberals. Only in Canada could this happen.

The Tories and Prime Minister Harper ruled for more than five years as Canada's longest-serving minority government. When the three opposition parties won a no-confidence vote in parliament on March 25, 2011, by a vote of 156 to 145, Harper jumped at the opportunity to call new elections in May that, he hoped, would give his government a stable parliamentary majority. He is a brilliant tactician who, in the words of the *Globe and Mail*, is "nasty, brutish—and competent."

He was not disappointed. The Tories captured 167 seats out of 308, based on 39.6% of the votes.

Canada

Harper's goal was to win a fourth federal election victory, something that had not happened since Wilfried Laurier about a century ago. He faced the October 2015 federal elections with confidence, but the results were a disaster for him and the Tory party. They lost 60 seats falling to 99. They slid to 31.9% of the popular vote. Only three provinces, including Saskatchewan, were still governed by a party associated with the federal Conservatives. Harper resigned as leader.

Not until May 27, 2017, was he replaced by a permanent leader. The decision was made by 85,000 party members, who listed the candidates in their order of preference. Emerging victorious from a field of 14 was 38-year-old Andrew Scheer from Saskatchewan. He campaigned on a platform to unify the party and establish intraparty consensus. A former Speaker of the House of Commons, he is likeable, experienced, and bilingual. On December 12, 2019, Andrew Scheer stepped down as the Conservative leader. Sources told the *National Post* that his resignation was because Scheer was using money from the Conservative Party to pay for his children's private school tuition. On August 24, 2020, the party chose Erin O'Toole as its new leader; he served as Leader of the Official Opposition until February 2, 2022, when he was removed by the party caucus and replaced by Candice Bergen as interim leader. On September 6, 2022, Bergen announced she would not stand at the next federal election; on September 10, 2022, Pierre Poilievre was elected as her successor and was subsequently sworn in as leader of the official opposition of Canada.

The New Democratic Party

The most ideologically oriented Canadian party is the New Democratic Party (NDP), which is an offspring of the Cooperative Commonwealth Federation (CCF). The CCF was a protest party born in the prairies during the Great Depression that frontally attacked capitalism, "with its inherent injustice and inhumanity." Its famous Regina Manifesto of 1933 declared: "No CCF government will rest content until it has eradicated capitalism and put into operation the full program of socialized planning which will lead to the establishment in Canada of the co-operative commonwealth."

The NDP has nothing to do with two long-established parties miles to the left of it, which do consistently poorly throughout Canada. They are the Communist Party of Canada and a Maoist off-shoot called "Marxist-Leninists." The last Communist MP was elected in 1945, but his parliamentary career ended a year later when he was convicted of espionage.

The NDP has never been revolutionary in the sense that it would take power by force; it was always democratic and sought change by means of the ballot box. Since it always sought votes, it has watered down its program throughout the years. In 1961, it changed its name to the New Democratic Party in order to broaden its appeal to non-socialists. However, tension remains between the impulses toward reform and toward electoral victory. It belongs to the Socialist International and remains the only successful social democratic party in North America.

The NDP found most of its support in urban areas in Ontario and the West. It also does well in rural western areas, where it pays attention to farmers' wants. It succeeds in labor union circles, which are a declining reservoir of voters. More men than women give their votes to the NDP. It was vulnerable to Liberals, who sometimes picked up the NDP's ideas, such as medicare, and wrote them onto their own banners. It is very vulnerable to surges of populist conservative parties. In the late 1950s, the Diefenbaker landslide wiped the CCF out nationally. Until the May 2011 elections, the NDP had always been disadvantaged by the single-member district electoral system. This prevented it from having as high a percentage of seats in the House of Commons as its overall popular vote.

In 1989, it chose the first woman ever to become leader of a national political party of any size in North America—Audrey McLaughlin, a former social worker from the Yukon. She inherited a divided and aging party perceived as being adrift on policy and in serious danger of being shunted to periphery of Canadian politics. The western wings of the NDP moved towards the right to capture mainstream voters, but this disappointed many party members who viewed this pragmatic move as a betrayal of cherished social democratic goals.

In the 1993 elections, it captured only 6.8% of the votes and eight seats. It won seats only in the west. McLaughlin admitted that in the rest of Canada, "what we have been putting forward has not struck a chord with many people. That's quite self-evident." The elections were the worst performance since the NDP's founding in 1961. Its Ottawa headquarters were sold, and most of its staff was laid off. While the buzzards circled, a new leader was selected in 1995: Alexa McDonough, a popular former social worker and 14-year

Canada

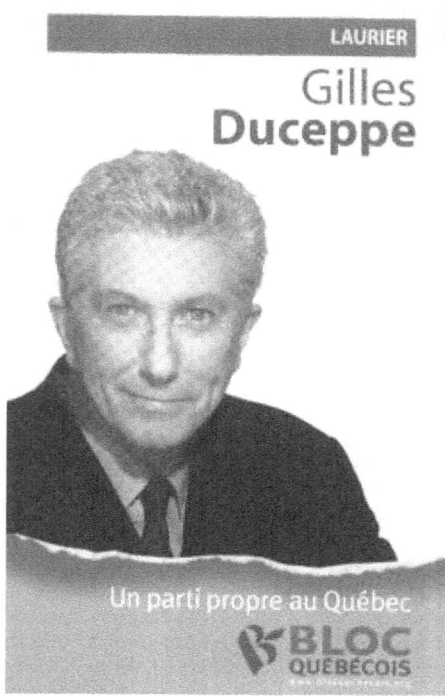

Gilles Duceppe. Clever election slogan: A "clean" party in Quebec or Its "own" party in Quebec

leader of the tiny Nova Scotia NDP. Her selection followed a series of primaries among party members all over Canada intended to revitalize the party. She was chosen because she promised to unify the party's left and right.

In the 1997 elections, the NDP increased its voter harvest to 11% and 21 seats, mainly in the West. At its 1999 national convention delegates backed McDonough's demands by a 2 to 1 majority to move the party toward the political center. In the 2000 elections, the NDP won 8% of the votes and 13 seats, barely qualifying as an official party in Ottawa. McDonough was replaced in 2003 by Jack Layton, a charismatic PhD, fluently bilingual Toronto city councilor and former head of the Federation of Canadian Municipalities. He had a more ideological edge than his predecessor and was not above playing on latent anti-Americanism in Canada.

Layton reenergized the NDP and in the 2004 elections led it to its best result in a decade. Doing well in Ontario and the west, it more than doubled its votes nation-wide to 15.7% and jumped to 19 seats. Its platform called for increased government spending on healthcare and daycare, opposition to Canadian participation in America's missile defense, and especially the adoption of the proportional representation electoral system.

The NDP was the only party other than the Conservatives to improve its standing in the 2006 federal elections. Under the leadership of Jack Layton, who prefered the term "New Democrats" to the NDP acronym, it captured 17.5% of the votes and 29 seats. The NDP picked up a dozen seats in Ontario and 10 in BC. As usual, it was locked out of Quebec. It also had problems appealing to Asians and to other business-friendly immigrants. It did well in the 2008 elections, increasing its votes from 17.5% to 18.2% of the popular total and its seats from 29 to 37.

The NDP prepared well for the May 2011 elections. In an effort to attract Quebec voters, it advocated the separatists' view of the Canadian constitution as unfinished business.

Canadians were left reeling when the election results came in. The NDP captured 31% of the votes and 103 seats, 58 of which in Quebec, up from one in 2008. Because the NDP won seats in eight provinces, for the first time in its history, it became the official opposition in Ottawa and the dominant federal party in Quebec.

After the celebrations on election night were over, the party had to think hard how it would manage such a diverse and largely inexperienced group of MPs that included 58 Québécois, four McGill students (one of whom 19 years old, the youngest ever MP), an ex-communist, teachers and activists, with very few seasoned politicians among them; 19 of its MPs were under age 30. One new NDP MP, Ruth Ellen Brosseau, was working in an Ottawa student bar when a party desperate for candidates from Quebec asked her to run in a Quebec riding. She said yes, but she did not set foot in the riding during the entire six-week campaign. Instead she spent some of her time in Las Vegas celebrating her 27th birthday. Never mind, Brosseau cruised to victory over the incumbent by 7,000 votes. Brosseau displayed good French skills when she visited her riding after the election and went on to defy expectations in Commons, serving as the NDP's deputy agriculture critic.

Jack Layton had made the NDP electable by distancing it from the unions and guiding it toward the political center. He professionalized it much like Stephen Harper had done for the Conservative party. But he slept only one night in Stornoway, the opposition leader's residence in Ottawa. At the top of his career after one of Canada's most dramatic electoral performances, he died of prostate cancer on August 22, 2011. He was the first opposition leader to die in office in more than 90 years, since Sir Wilfried Laurier in 1919. Then Prime Minister Harper offered his family a state funeral in Toronto, a rare honor usually reserved for former prime ministers, governors-general and prominent cabinet members. For six days his country mourned for him.

Thomas Mulcair won a hard-fought election, mostly online, to succeed Layton as party leader. Mulcair grew up in Montreal, the second-oldest of 10 children in a devout Catholic family. He decided at age 14 to become a politician, and he was admitted to McGill's prestigious law school at 18. Although his family spoke English at home and all his education was in English, he polished his French language skills, especially by marrying a French visitor to Quebec, Catherine Pinhas. After the historic 1995 referendum on Quebec independence, Mulcair worked as the only Anglophone bureaucrat on the staff at the *Conseil de la Language Française* (referred to by critics as Quebec's "language police"). Mulcair served as environment minister in the province's Liberal government before switching to the NDP. He acquired the nickname "grizzly bear" for his quick thinking and sharp tongue.

Mulcair sought to shore up the NDP's strong newly won foothold in Quebec. He objected to the party's tradition leftist rhetoric and was determined to move the party toward the center. An example is its approach to the development of oil-sands, which the NDP always opposed. Mulcair declared that the party would be "a partner for the development of Canada's

Fortunately, here, it's the Bloc

Canada

energy resources" although he opposed the Northern Gateway and Keystone XL pipelines. *MacLean's* picked him in 2016 as "parliamentarian of the year." MPs of all parties stood to applaud his service.

Mulcair's influence was significantly diminished by Justin Trudeau's ascent. As reflected by the October 2015 elections, Mulcair was no longer the politician on the opposition benches whom everybody was watching as the NDP dropped from 103 to only 44 seats and from 30.69% of the popular vote to 19.7%. Things became worse in 2019 and 2021, with party, led by its new leader, Jagmeet Singh, taking only 24 and 25 seats, respectively.

The NDP needed a new leader. Jagmeet Singh, whose Indian parents had immigrated to Canada, won the job decisively. A Sikh, he is a lawyer with a degree in biology.

Bloc Québécois

Until the 2011 federal elections, the political landscape was complicated by the *Bloc Québécois (BQ)*, composed originally in 1990 of a break-away group of nine Conservative and Liberal MPs from Quebec. Its first leader was Lucien Bouchard, formerly Canada's ambassador to France. The BQ captured 54 of the 75 seats in Quebec, the only province in which it competes. As the second-largest party in the House of Commons, the BQ became the official opposition. But Bouchard signaled the impermanence of his party in Ottawa by refusing to reside in Stornaway, the mansion at the disposal of the opposition leader. "We don't intend to settle in Ottawa. The presence of the *Bloc* in Ottawa is by definition temporary," he declared.

Most of its MPs were new to Ottawa: 48 of 54. Many spoke no English. As a group, the BQ caucus members have little in common other than their commitment to separation from Canada; they range from left-leaning union activists to moderate lawyers and conservative business owners. They were quick to learn how to operate in Parliament.

Bouchard was an eloquent and passionate speaker in both languages. While leader of the opposition, he made official visits to Paris and Washington to explain his party's separatist agenda. These caused outrage in the rest of Canada; the *Edmonton Sun* described his Paris trip as a "one-finger salute to the country." In 1994, he nearly died from a flesh-eating disease that cost him a leg. Rising from doom, he enjoyed considerable sympathy for his personal courage and support for his milder form of Quebec separatism that allowed for continued economic ties with Canada.

The day after the failed 1995 referendum on Quebec independence, Jacques Parizeau announced his resignation as premier. Bouchard agreed to leave his post as BQ leader and replace him as Quebec's premier in 1996. Gilles Duceppe, a former hospital attendant, Maoist union organizer in his youth, and son of a famous Quebec actor, took over leadership of the BQ. He attributed his separatist leanings partly to having had to hear as a boy "God Save the Queen" played before hockey games.

Quebec nationalist sentiments has weakened considerably since the 1995 referendum, and Quebec sovereignty and constitutional reform has been put on the back burner. In April 2003 the PQ, on whom the BQ relies for organizational support, was ejected from power in Quebec. These developments hurt the BQ, a one-issue left-leaning party.

Its prospects looked dim until the 2004 elections gave it new life. After less than a year in power, the Quebec Liberal government under Jean Charest had become very unpopular. Then a government audit in Ottawa found that the federal government had since 1995 dished out about $75 million to advertising companies friendly to the Liberals to make anti-separatist propaganda in Quebec. Although most of the money had been simply pocketed with little or no work done, *Québécois* were deeply offended. After having cleaned up much of the corruption in their province, this "sponsorship scandal" had been perpetrated by hypocritical federalists in Ottawa.

The results were stunning. The BQ won 50% of the votes. Its 54 seats matched the party's best performance in 1993. Even Jean Chrétien's old riding was picked off by a BQ candidate. The party's slogan was clever: "*Un parti propre au Québec,*" meaning either "a clean party" or "its own party" for Quebec.

Duceppe said repeatedly during the campaign that a vote for the BQ was not necessarily a vote for independence, but after the election he declared: "*Québécois* form a nation. We haven't decided tonight to make Quebec sovereign, but we can say that Quebec has shown it has confidence in sovereigntists." In the run-up to the 2006 federal elections, he argued that an independent Quebec should have its own army and intelligence service, and he reminded Canadians in the televised debates: "Everyone common in Quebec knows Quebec is quite different from the rest of Canada. Not better, not worse. Plain different."

In the October 2008 elections, the PQ did not campaign under the banner of

Canada

Quebec independence, and partly for that reason it was able to block any Conservative advance in the province. It lost one seat for a total of 50.

The BQ experienced near annihilation in the 2011 and 2015 elections, plunging from 47 to a mere four seats, too far below the requisite dozen to qualify as an official party in parliament. It remained as a powerless rump group.

Its membership declined by 17,000 to only 36,000 in 2012. Gilles Duceppe, the longest-serving leader on the federal stage, immediately resigned. Only the most militant advocates of Quebec sovereignty stuck with the BQ, while soft sovereignists and federalists switched to the NDP. Clearly many Quebecers are tired of the BQ and seriously asked themselves if they really wanted to be represented in Ottawa by a party that is in perpetual opposition. Many want to play a more constructive role in federal politics. The fact is that in its two decades of existence, the BQ failed to make a contribution to achieving the goal of separatist destiny. That is why it is a spent force. Federal elections in October 2015 demonstrated that yet again. It captured less than 20% of the votes in Quebec and only 4.7% countrywide. Of the ten seats it won, none was for Duceppe, who lost his riding for the second time. He resigned as leader.

In the October 2019 election, the *BQ* finished in second place in Quebec, taking 32 out of 78 seats, more than triple its haul of 10 in the last election. It achieved the same result in 2021. While the *BQ* was known in the 1990s as a party that would defend Quebec's sovereignty movement, today it is seen as a party that protects Quebec's interests. Yves-Francois Blanchet is the party's current leader.

The Greens

One new party, the Greens, took heart from the ecological protest movement in Germany. In 1983, it formed a movement that views "economic growth as a problem, not as a solution." In 2004, it made its best showing, winning a respectable 4.3% of the votes, up from only 0.8% in 2000. This was too few to win a seat but enough to qualify for federal financing of $1.75 per vote. Rejecting the labels of "right" or "left," the party combines traditional environmental positions, such as banning nuclear power and genetically modified foods, with calls for corporate and income tax cuts. But it has gotten a gust of wind in its sails from the rise of climate change in Canadians' list of concerns.

The party's combative leader, Elizabeth May, is an American activist who left Smith College and accompanied her parents to Nova Scotia in 1972 in protest against the Vietnam War. May became a

Elizabeth May

Canadian citizen in 1980, studied law at Dalhousie, added a Master Degree in Theology, and headed the Sierra Club of Canada for 17 years. The party has never been more popular since being led by May, who once described herself as an "eco bitch." She is earthy and quick-witted. In fact, the Green party more than doubled its membership to 11,000 in only one year.

At the same time, though, Green support has not traditionally translated into votes, in part because the party lacks effective organization. May has not been able to cure the party's backbiting, infighting and defections, and members have differing opinions on whether they belong to a party or a social movement. "Deep greens" suspect all power and are committed to shaking up the status quo. May prefers to work with those in power. For example, she cooperated closely with the Liberals to get the Kyoto Protocol ratified.

By helping to put the environment at the center of Canadian politics, May has spurred all parties to show more ecological commitment. However, electoral success did not quickly materialize. Spurned by voters in Ontario and Nova Scotia, May moved to Saanich-Gulf Islands, British Columbia, to win her long-coveted seat in the House of Commons. Nobody worked harder to win one as May knocked on countless doors and handed out packages of sunflower seeds, the international Greens' symbol. May's efforts paid off, and she won the party's first seat; she won it again in October 2015 although she was the only Green to do so. However, the Green part's popular vote fell from 3.9% to 3.45%, its worst showing in a decade. Her party captured three seats in the 2017 provincial elections in BC and for the first time entered a government.

While she was re-elected to her seat with 54% of the vote in the 2019 election, Elizabeth May stepped down as leader following the 2019 election and, following an interim leader, Annamie Paul, an

Paul Martin replaces Chrétien in 2004

Canada

activist and lawyer, became leader of the party on October 3, 2020. Her tenure was short-lived. Failing to win her own seat in the 2021 election (although the Greens retained their two seats in the Parliament), she resigned as leader on November 14, 2021. Amita Kuttner, an astrophysicist, served as interim leader until November 19, 2022, when Elizabeth May won the leadership of the party. In February 2025, following an amendment to the Green Party Constitution, Jonathan Pedneault became co-leader with May

THE 2000 FEDERAL PARLIAMENTARY ELECTIONS

In 1993, Canadians experienced *three* prime ministers, matched only in 1896 and 1984. Peter C. Newman was right: "Governing Canada in the 1990s is a balancing act—like juggling wet fish while standing on a slippery diving board." The October 1993 elections had brought the biggest political upheaval in Canadian history. Turning against the Tory party of Brian Mulroney and his successor, Kim Campbell, the Conservatives fell to a humiliating two seats in the House of Commons. Rising from the debris were two new parties, the *Bloc Québécois* and the Reform Party. Both were committed to remaking Canadian politics and the country itself. They battled each other in Ottawa over their sharply different visions of Canada's future.

Put in charge was the Liberal Party of Jean Chrétien, who had held every major portfolio during the Trudeau era. Chrétien became the first francophone Quebecer ever to win a majority in the House of Commons without taking a majority of seats in Quebec. This was repeated in 1997, when Liberals captured only 26 seats in Quebec. Chrétien barely hung on to his own seat in his paper mill hometown of Shawinigan against a fiery Quebec separatist.

Against the advice of his aides, he had called new elections for June 2, 1997, after only three and one-half years. The party squeaked through with a 155-seat majority in the newly expanded 301-seat House of Commons. This was the first time since 1953 that a Liberal prime minister had won back-to-back majorities. With the BQ and the Reform Party winning votes by presenting radically conflicting views of Canada, it was difficult for Chrétien to develop a national accord on Quebec. The cracks in the Canadian federation appeared to be wider than ever.

Most Canadians, including members of Prime Minister Jean Chrétien's own Liberal Party, were surprised when he called new elections for November 27, 2000, after only three and one-half years. Chrétien decision was widely criticized, but the results proved that it had been an astute one. The economy was strong, and both the prime minister's and his party's popularity were at their highest level since 1993. The aftermath of an emotional outpouring in the wake of Trudeau's death seemed to indicate that the time was propitious.

The major opposition party to the Liberals, the Canadian Alliance, had just been created in 2000, and its fresh and energetic leader, Stockwell Day, was untested in national politics. He had just won a seat in the House of Commons and was planning to spend the winter parliamentary session to raise money and his profile for the next election. Chrétien also needed to do much work in Ontario to expand his new party's presence there in order to break the Liberal stranglehold that had delivered to Chrétien 101 seats in 1997. Finally, Chrétien's role as party leader was being challenged from within by popular Finance Minister Paul Martin, who was visibly impatient for his turn to be prime minister. By calling a snap election, Chrétien caught Day off guard and forced Martin to demonstrate loyalty in the heat of battle. Winning big, Chrétien silenced calls for him to step down in favor of Martin. "I'm elected and I intend to serve my term," he said.

It was an acrimonious campaign, with personalities playing a more important role than policies. The Liberals succeeded in painting the witty and telegenic Day as a political radical who harbored a secret agenda to endanger important Canadian institutions, such as state-funded one-tier health care, gun control, no capital punishment, and a woman's right to have an abortion under certain circumstances. Even his fundamentalist Christianity, including his belief in creationism, was scorned. Faith is normally considered out of bounds in Canadian elections, but former Ontario Premier David Peterson remarked on TV that Day's creationist views brought his intelligence into question. Such comments made Day a subject of ridicule. Even Conservative leader Joe Clark, who was generally credited with having conducted the best campaign, asked publicly: "Do you trust Stockwell Day's agenda?"

Day turned the heat on the prime minister by accusing him of criminal conduct for securing a loan for a friend in his Quebec constituency. Day rejected Chrétien's characterization of his intervention as a "normal operation" that a representative performs for his constituents and called it "moral rot." Chrétien was cleared of the ethics allegations five days before the election, but the whiff of scandal hung in the air. All participants demonstrated acrimony. Chrétien suggested that the Alliance was out to "destroy Canada." Day once charged that the prime minister put the rights of pedophiles over those of children. Even NDP leader Alexa McDonough compared Day to a cockroach, while the Tories ran negative ads on TV accusing Chrétien of being a "serial liar." It is little wonder

Liberal government runs out of wind

Source: *Globe and Mail*

Canada

that many voters lost interest, and voter turnout fell from 67% in 1997 to 62% in 2000, one of the lowest in Canadian history.

The Liberals had expected to win the elections, but the magnitude of victory was especially gratifying: they captured 173 seats, up from 155, based on 41% of the popular votes. This provided Chrétien with a comfortable majority in Parliament and the acclaim of being the first leader to deliver three straight majority governments since William Lyon Mackenzie King accomplished that feat in 1935, 1940, and 1945. The victory also came embellished with some remarkable gains. In Quebec, where the prime minister was often dismissed as an unpopular federalist, the Liberals increased their seats from 29 to 37, all at the expense of the BQ, which fell from 44 to 37 seats.

These gains and the fact that Chrétien's unity-oriented party won as many seats as did the separatist BQ lent credence to the Chrétien government's hardline policy toward Quebec separatism. The Liberals retained their rock-solid domination of Ontario in federal elections by winning an overwhelming 100 seats, down only one from 1997. They also gained eight extra seats in the Atlantic Provinces.

The performance of the Canadian Alliance demonstrated the gaping divide between the East and West in Canada. It was all but vanquished in Ontario, winning only two rural seats. The party calculated that if only its voters and the Tories' voters could unify under one banner in Ontario, a powerful challenge to the Liberals' unassailable federal dominance could be made; that hope was dashed. The Alliance captured 64 seats from Manitoba to British Columbia, leaving only 14 to the Liberals. Such an outcome again raised the question about national unity and western alienation. Although the Alliance, under Day's leadership, consolidated its hold on the West and its position as official opposition in Ottawa, it did not emerge as a national party that could seriously threaten Liberal dominance in federal politics, despite its capture of 66 seats and a fourth of the popular votes nationwide.

Both the Conservatives and the NDP narrowly escaped extinction and barely won the required dozen seats needed for official recognition as parliamentary parties. Only by winning nine seats in the Atlantic provinces, four fewer than in 1997, were the Tories able to secure a disappointing 12 seats in the House of Commons, based on 12% of the votes. This was the third consecutive devastating defeat. In only seven years the party had fallen from a majority government to a fifth-place party. It could no longer make its once-proud claim of being a truly national party able to speak for all Canadians in all walks of life. The NDP also faced the prospect of spending the next few years on the fringes of Canadian politics. McDonough held on to her Halifax riding, but her party's seats in the Atlantic provinces dropped from seven to four. Overall, the NDP won 8% of the votes and 13 seats, barely qualifying as an official party in Ottawa.

The election campaign was rancorous and personal, with too little serious discussion of issues of importance to Canada's future, such as how the country could remain competitive in the world economy, what to do about the declining value of the Canadian dollar and how to fix the health-care system. Noting that the wrangling about counting votes in Florida had diverted Canadians' already low interest in their own vote, David Rudd, director of the Canadian Institute for Strategic Studies, remarked dejectedly: "Even Mexico is more exciting than we are. I suppose that is what you get when you are a country that is at peace with itself and with its neighbors."

THE 2004 FEDERAL PARLIAMENTARY ELECTIONS

For a decade, Paul Martin had worked to become prime minister and to assemble a formidable political war machine to accomplish his goal. His ruthless unseating of Jean Chrétien in 2003 created a deep rift in the party, and his turfing out and ostracizing of the former prime minister's loyalists added to the bad blood. His heavy-handedness alienated many local Liberal officials and volunteers and left the party vulnerable to a newly united Conservative Party.

Shortly after he gained his coveted top spot, a scandal came to light revealing that $75 million of federal taxpayer money had been funneled to Liberal cronies' advertising firms to be used to undermine the separatist cause in Quebec. As Chrétien's former finance minister, Martin could not escape unscathed. The *National Post* called the scandal "the mother of all Achilles' heels." An Ipson-Reid poll in 2004 found that 61% of voters considered the Liberals corrupt, and only 36% believed their party deserved to be reelected. There was a strong feeling that the Liberals had been in power too long. *Québécois* were furious, and many western Canadians saw it as proof that the Liberals are a profligate party.

Martin's half-year in power had been largely directionless and ineffective, with no overarching new policy agenda. Nevertheless, strongly desiring his own personal mandate, Martin decided to call new elections for June 28. Although many of his advisers thought he had made a mistake, he feared that the scandal might cause even more damage to the party. His poll ratings were falling continually. Also for the first time in over a decade, there was a credible alternative to Liberal rule taking shape in the form of the newly merged Conservative Party. He could have waited another 16 months to call new elections, but the longer he hesitated, the more organized and prepared the new Conservatives would be. For the first time since 1993 Canada had a federal election whose result could not be predicted.

What followed was an ill-tempered and divisive campaign that produced a fractured parliament. There was a heavy dose of negative advertising. Harper tried to swing his new party toward the political center. But the outspoken social conservatism of some of his candidates and advisers fueled charges that Harper had a "hidden agenda," perhaps involving attempts to end abortion rights, alter the sacred medicare, abandon environmental treaties (especially the Kyoto Protocol on global warming) or align Canada more closely with U.S. foreign policy. It is impossible to disprove a "hidden agenda."

Harper fueled these suspicions in the final days of the campaign when he suppressed but refused to apologize for a press release from his party headquarters suggesting that Martin supported child pornography. Until the final week, Martin ran an incompetent and lethargic campaign, and the opinion polls showed the race as neck-and-neck. All three anglophone candidates speak tolerable to good French, and the general impression after the French- and English-language televised debates was that the Conservative leader, Stephen Harper, had done the best.

In the final days of the campaign Martin threw everything he had into the race, flying on the last day from coast to coast and dipping his feet into both oceans. When the votes were counted, the Liberals had succeeded in retaining power, but with a minority of seats in the House of Commons. One out of five voters changed his or her mind on the last day and decided not to take a chance on Harper's new party. Only 60.5% of voters decided to go to the polls, by far the worst turnout ever in federal elections. The Liberals captured 36.7% of the votes and 135 seats, twenty short of a majority. In general, the Liberals dominated Canada's bigger cities, while the Conservatives did well in smaller communities.

The Conservatives overall won 29.6% of the votes, as opposed to a combined total of 38% in 2000, and a respectable 99 seats compared with 78 in 2000. The Conservatives even broke the Liberal stranglehold on Ontario by winning 24 of 108 seats. Atlantic Canada proved to be a Liberal stronghold. Conservatives were disappointed not to have dominated the west, especially BC, more than they did. The NDP made spectacular gains, more than doubling its votes and winning 19 seats.

The biggest surprise was the strong showing of the separatist *Bloc Québécois* in Quebec. It is ironic that a shady financial tactic designed to weaken separatist sentiment in Quebec had precisely the opposite effect. The BQ captured half the votes and 54 of 75 seats, leaving only 19 for the Liberals. The vote was more a protest vote against the Liberals rather than a show of support for Quebec sovereignty. Nevertheless, separatists felt wind again in their sails.

A chastened but relieved Paul Martin admitted, "The message was unmistakable: Canadians expected, and expect, more from us as a party, and as a government we must do better, and we will." Without a parliamentary majority Liberals had to proceed carefully. Martin rejected the option of forming a coalition government, something that Canada has not had since the First World War. Martin instead chose to lead what he called a "stable" minority government, seeking parliamentary votes from different parties for different issues. The last minority government had been formed in 1979 and lasted only eight months. No minority government in Canadian history has survived more than two years, and the average is 18 months. This was to be the fate of the Martin government.

THE 2006 FEDERAL PARLIAMENTARY ELECTIONS

The outgoing Liberal government of Paul Martin was dogged and ultimately dealt a fatal blow by the ever worsening "sponsorship scandal" in Quebec. This involved federal funds directed to Quebec advertising agencies with close ties to the Liberal Party in order to weaken the separatist movement. When the official Gomery inquiry began hearing testimony in Montreal, the information was explosive. Advertising agency executives admitted to kickbacks, payoffs and payroll padding. One head of a firm received $30 million in government contracts and in return paid a "commission" of 17.5% in the form of false invoices and fake bills. Another ad executive secretly kicked back nearly a half million dollars to Liberal Party accounts. He told how he made payments in envelopes left on restaurant tables and put party operatives on his payroll, including relatives of former Prime Minister Chrétien.

These revelations were a political bombshell and a death sentence for the Liberal government, especially in Quebec. Then

Canada

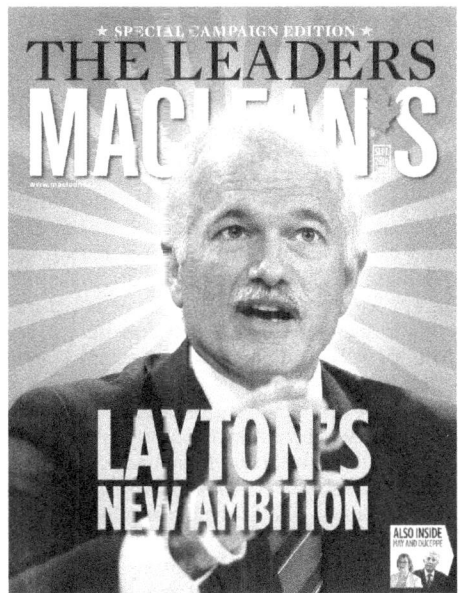

opposition leader Stephen Harper asked publicly: "How can we continue to prop up a government that is under criminal investigation and accusation of criminal conspiracy?"

The Gomery inquiry explicitly exonerated Prime Minister Martin in November 2005 of any blame. The same was not the case for Chrétien and his aides, who were cited for "omissions" and "insufficient oversight" by allowing the slush-fund scheme to be set up and operated under his watch. A beleaguered prime minister ordered his Liberals to repay about $1 million in party contributions and sent the 686-page report to the RCMP for possible criminal investigations. The damage from this sleaze debilitated the Liberal Party and haunted Martin. The then opposition leader Stephen Harper gained enormous credibility for his call: "We have to clean things up."

Martin was forced to focus on survival instead of a clear direction for his government. A successful finance minister, Martin proved to be a disappointing prime minister. Dependent on the demanding and big-spending NDP for its continuation, Martin departed from his decade of careful financial management and doled out public funds with abandon. His minority government nevertheless lost a vote of no-confidence 171 to 133, and new elections were called for January 23, 2006. This was the first winter election in 25 years, and at 56 days, the campaign was long by Canadian standards.

Tory leader Stephen Harper would not allow himself to be painted again as a dogmatic social conservative. He presented an effective blend of traditional conservatism and reassuring moderation. Harper moved pragmatically toward the political

Canada

center as he skirted around emotional social issues, pledged to uphold Medicare, ruled out any change in the abortion law, and tempered both his party's opposition to gay marriage and the Kyoto climate protocol. Instead, Harper focused on such things as cracking down on crime, reducing the sales tax, shortening waiting times for health care, giving parents money for child care and boosting defense spending.

Harper avoided foreign policy issues except for promising to improve relations with the United States, which he called "our best friends." This matter did provide some temporary excitement in an otherwise unexciting campaign. The U.S. ambassador to Canada, David Wilkins, lost patience hearing Martin lecture the U.S. on the subject of greenhouse gas emissions when it was public knowledge that the U.S. was decreasing such emissions, while Canada's were growing. Wilkins made the untimely, if correct, statement: "It may be smart election-year politics to thump your chest and constantly criticize your friend and your No. 1 trading partner. But it is a slippery slope, and all of us should hope that it doesn't have a long-term impact on the relationship."

Martin, who in 2004 had campaigned for a "more sophisticated" relationship with the U.S., jumped on this intrusion into Canadian electoral politics and talked tough against the Yankees: "I'm not going to be dictated to," and "I'm going to call them as I see them." This flap bumped up Martin's poll numbers for a few days, and then they continued on their downward trajectory. When election day arrived, it was no longer a question of whether Harper's Conservatives would win, but whether they would be able to form a majority government.

Voters ended over 12 years of Liberal rule but brought in the country's second minority government in a row. The Conservatives won an impressive victory, securing 124 (up from 99) of 308 seats in the House of Commons on the basis of 36.3% of the votes (up from 29.6% in 2004). Thanks to a defection of a former Liberal minister from Vancouver, David Emerson (who later became foreign minister), the Tories actually command 125 seats.

The Liberals could hardly afford to lose any seats, having declined since 2004 to 30.2% of the votes, down from 36.7%, and only 103 seats, down from 135). To no small extent, the outcome was as much a rejection of Martin and the Liberals as an acceptance of Harper and the Conservatives. A defeated Martin resigned as party head, leaving the Liberals leaderless.

What was remarkable about this comeback was that Harper's party made gains in all parts of this diverse country and became a national party again for the first

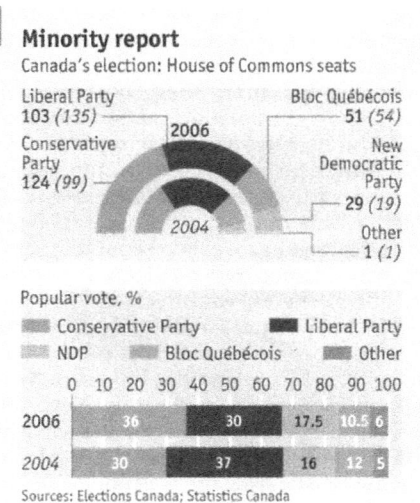

2006 Parliamentary Elections
Source: *The Economist*

time since 1993. Canada returned to a competitive system of two national parties.

The Conservatives won big in the West, where they received more than half of their seats and all the seats in Alberta. Harper proudly proclaimed: "The West is now in." The election gives another nudge to the westward shift of Canada's political center of gravity. The Conservatives broke the Liberal stranglehold on Ontario, winning 40 of its 106 seats. However, none was in Toronto or Ottawa, nor in Montreal or Vancouver; it was shut out in these big cities. Its gains in Atlantic Canada were modest, but the post of foreign minister (later the defense ministry) was given to Peter MacKay to raise this region's visibility in the government. In fact, Harper gave his new cabinet geographical balance, even appointing his party co-chairman, Michael Fortier of Montreal, to the Senate so that he could have someone from Montreal in his cabinet.

Most dramatically, the Conservatives picked up 10 seats in Quebec, capturing 24.6% of the votes, up from 9%, ahead of the Liberals, who with 20.7%, and 13 seats, experienced one of their worst performances in Quebec since Confederation in 1867. It was headline news that many of those Conservative votes were won in nationalist strongholds in the eastern part of Quebec. The *Bloc Québécois* fell short of a majority of votes in Quebec, winning only 42% and slipping from 54 to 51 of the province's 75 seats. Not reaching the magical 50% mark, the BQ offered no prospect of a successful independence referendum any time soon.

Harper's openness to *Québécois* concerns, his talk of more flexible federalism, and his practice of beginning practically every speech in Ottawa in French, which he commands confidently, offers the prospect of even greater gains in *la belle province*. After becoming prime minister, he showered Quebec with attention, promising to recognize "the unique place of a strong, vibrant Quebec in a united Canada." Harper and his party were rewarded for this: within three months as prime minister, polls showed Tory support in Quebec reaching 34%, ahead of both the BQ and the Liberals.

The only other party to improve its standing was Jack Layton's New Democrats, which captured 17.5% of the votes and 29 seats (up from 19). The NDP picked up a dozen seats in Ontario and 10 in BC. As always, it was locked out of Quebec. Despite this strengthening, the NDP does not command the balance of power in Commons it did after the 2004 vote.

Normally a strong economy helps reelect incumbent governments, but that rule did not apply in 2006. Voters opted for a government that had not tarnished itself with corruption and not endangered its perceived moral right to govern in a democracy. Further, voters liked Harper's humility, self-deprecation, moderation and willingness to listen and learn. His first words as prime minister designate were: "Tonight, our great country has voted for change."

THE 2008 FEDERAL PARLIAMENTARY ELECTIONS

In September 2008, Stephen Harper took stock of his two and one-half years in power at the head of a minority government during which he demonstrated considerable skill in managing the House

Victorious Stephen Harper

Canada

of Commons. Harper had been an innovator on Quebec's nationhood and his government was relatively free of scandals. Moreover, Harper put a dramatically new face on Canada's foreign policy. Analysts were writing that it had been a generation since Canada had had such an effective, ambitious and young leader. And the Liberal Party had just elected an ineffective leader, Stéphane Dion. Opinion polls indicated that no major aspect of his agenda bothered the voters and that a majority was within the Conservatives' reach.

Harper's ambition was for the Conservative Party to be the natural governing majority in the country. He was confident in declaring elections for October 14, despite the law he himself had sponsored to have parliamentary elections at fixed times—thus not until a year later—and despite the fact that this would be the third time in little more than four years voters were called to the polls.

For the first three weeks, things went well for Harper's party, which maintained a steady 10-point lead. The situation then turned sour as the global financial crisis that started in the United States changed the mood in Canada overnight to one of foreboding. Canada's economy was relatively good compared with most other rich nations, but suddenly voters doubted Canada's ability to cope with the world downturn. A bewildered Harper came off as insensitive and out-of-touch when he argued that the crashing stock market offered "good buying opportunities." Haper mentioned no government spending to stimulate the economy and save jobs. The polls eroded, and the Conservatives found themselves fighting for their lives.

On election day only 59.1% of registered voters turned out, the lowest in history. The Conservatives increased their share of the popular vote slightly to 37.3%. This translated into 19 additional seats. This meant a somewhat stronger minority government, but not the hoped-for majority. The Tories consolidated their western base and picked up seats in suburban Ontario and the Maritime provinces. The Reform Party elements can be satisfied with the steady, incremental progress, slowly advancing eastward from British Columbia and Alberta election after election, now winning seats in suburban Ontario and the Maritime Provinces. They see a majority in the future.

Their biggest disappointment was Quebec, where the Conservatives won only 22% of the votes and finished third behind the BQ and Liberals. The prime minister had made a serious misstep by making a snide remark about artists who receive government grants. Because many Québécois consider their culture to be the cornerstone of their nation, that was an insult with major symbolism. This rare Harper mistake prompted him immediately after the election to open the Francophonie Summit in Quebec City declaring himself "heir" to Samuel de Champlain and with a pledge of more funding for the international Quebec channel TV5. The *Bloc Québécois* made virtually no mention of Quebec sovereignty during the elections and was able to blunt any Conservative advance. It sacrificed one seat to win 50 of the 75 total Quebec seats.

Disaster befell the Liberals whose share of the popular vote plunged to 26.2%, their lowest since the foundation of the party in 1867. This was the third consecutive election in which their popular vote dropped. Their number of seats dived by a fourth from 103 to only 76. These included a mere seven seats in the entire West, while they lost their dominance of Ontario. The Liberal Party had become largely a Montreal–Toronto party with enclaves in Atlantic Canada. These results raise the serious question about whether it can even be considered a national party. This is a bitter realization for a party that had ruled Canada 55 of the previous 73 years.

Stéphane Dion had chosen to conduct a campaign based on an environmental plan called "Green Shift," that would include a carbon tax, just when Canadians were worrying primarily about the economy. The party's poor performance, along with Dion's clumsy attempt to defeat the government in a vote of no-confidence and take over the prime minister's role himself a few weeks after the election, cost him his leadership. Michael Ignatieff, whose popularity rivaled that of Prime Minister Harper, took the party's reins. Perhaps the only bright spot for the Liberals was the election of Justin Trudeau, son of the former prime minister, in suburban Montreal.

Canada now had a five-party system. The NDP finished no higher in the popular vote than it had in 2006 but did climb from 29 to 37 seats even as it remained as far as ever from its professed goal of replacing the Liberals as the government-in-waiting. The Greens, led by the hard-charging Elizabeth May, fell far below their inflated expectations but did increase their electoral support by 41%, winning 940,000 votes, or 6.8% of the total. Yet, this did not translate into any seats.

The 2011 Federal Parliamentary Elections

In one of the most dramatic federal elections in Canadian history, Canada returned to a three-party political system. The Tories and Prime Minister Stephen Harper had ruled for more than five years as Canada's longest-serving minority government. When the three opposition parties won a no-confidence vote in parliament on March 25, 2011, by a vote of 156 to 145, Harper jumped at the opportunity to call new elections in May that, he hoped, would give his government a stable parliamentary majority. Harper was a brilliant tactician who, in the words of the *Globe and Mail*, was "nasty, brutish—and competent" who correctly predicted that the Liberals and New Democrats would split the vote on the left and the Tories would dominate the center.

Harper was not disappointed as the results transformed Canadian politics. Voters responded to Harper's argument that parliament had become dysfunctional and that his government needed a majority to stop the "socialists and separatists," namely the New Democrats and Bloc Québécois, from endangering the economic recovery and the nation's security. Harper framed the election as a simple choice between a stable Conservative majority in parliament or a "reckless coalition" of Liberals, New Democrats and Quebec separatists as he steered away from social issues, such as abortion and gay marriage, which are controversial and polarizing vote-losers. Instead, Harper focused on the economy, lower taxes, stronger defense and tougher measures against crime.

The Tories captured 167 out of 308 seats, based on 39.6% of the votes. Only seven Tory incumbents lost their seats, compared with 82 from other parties. Although its votes fell below 40% in all of Canada, they totaled 50% in two-thirds of the country, revealing a formula for long-term success by the dominant party.

This was not just a victory. It was a realignment that could make the Conservatives the natural governing party in Canada, as the Liberals were in the 20th century. Their traditional Liberal opponent was crushed. Tory dominance of the West was strengthened: it won 54% of the votes in Manitoba, 56% in Saskatchewan, 67% in Alberta, and 46% in BC. This was an average of 55% in the West, up by 9%.

The most stupefying were the Conservatives' gains in Ontario. In 2000, the Conservatives captured two seats; in 2011, they won 73 seats and 44% of the votes. This was the first time since 1984 they carried this most populated province. The Conservatives even won 30 seats in greater Toronto, including that of Liberal leader Michael Ignatieff. Although they lost ground in Quebec, the Tories made inroads into the influential immigrant community, especially South Asians and Chinese.

There was thus a new governing coalition: the West plus Ontario, one that never existed before. This coalition was destined to grow as those two regions get about 30 more seats in the coming redistricting via

Canada

2008 Parliamentary Elections
Source: *The Economist*

the Tories' redistribution bill. The West now began at the Ottawa River as the Conservatives become Canada's dominant party.

The elections were such a calamity for the Liberal Party that some observers wonder if it could ever recover. Ignatieff had triggered the election in March 2011 by joining the NDP and separatist BQ in bringing about a vote of no-confidence against the Conservative minority government over an issue that voters seemed to care little about: contempt of parliament in concealing the true cost of prisons and new jet fighters. A February poll found that 51% of voters viewed Ignatieff unfavorably, while only 25% viewed him positively. The Conservatives branded Ignatieff as a carpet-bagging elitist, who had no clue about the struggle of ordinary Canadians. They were ready and itching for an election, but the Liberals were not.

By the time the votes were counted, the party and the nation were dumbfounded. The Liberals fell to less than 20% of the votes and a mere 34 seats, the party's worst result ever and the first time it was not among the top two parties. The Libera's turned to the left in desperation, but its voters gravitated to the Tories and New Democrats, who occupied the center. The Liberals lost big in Quebec because they could no longer pretend to be a bridge between the province and the rest of Canada. The Liberal Part was dead in the West and lost much of its foothold in Ontario as it had to step aside and allow the NDP to serve as the official opposition in parliament. Ignatieff lost his own seat in Toronto and immediately resigned as party chairman to return to the classroom at the University of Toronto. The party was left to ponder its continued relevance and to face the many questions about its future and purpose.

The NDP prepared well for the May 2011 elections. Party leader Jack Layton had just undergone prostate surgery and limped with a cane after hip surgery. Neither voters nor Layton could not know that he would die on August 22, 2011, but his party's campaign was anything but lame. In his eight years in charge, Layton overhauled the NDP and sharpened its electoral focus by throwing overboard policies that had cost the party votes in past elections. The NDP no longer spoke of a moratorium on new oil sands development or marijuana decriminalization, and it called for tax cuts for certain businesses. Layton greatly improved the party's technical and fund-raising capabilities, and the party bought a downtown property in Ottawa for its headquarters.

To woo Quebec voters, the NDP advocated the separatists' view of the Canadian constitution as unfinished business as it supported a referendum standard for separation of 50 percent plus one vote. Additionally, the NDP proposed extending French-language protections to federally regulated industries. Yet, the party's biggest drawing card in Quebec was Layton himself: he was born in Montreal in 1950, grew up in Hudson, Quebec, and studied at McGill in Montreal, where he perfected the kind of relaxed, colloquial French that enabled him to perform best in the leaders' French-language TV debate. Layton not only emerged as a likeable street-smart Montrealer but also shined in the English-language debate.

Canadians were left reeling when the election results came in. The NDP captured 31% of the votes and 103 seats, 58 of which in Quebec, up from one in 2008, as it won seats in eight provinces. As noted, for the first time in its history, the NDP became the official opposition in Ottawa and the dominant federal party in Quebec. In fact, Layton was the first anglophone leader of a national party to win in

Canada

Situated halfway between the White House and the Capitol, the splendid Canadian Embassy is the only foreign mission permitted on Pennsylvania Avenue. Courtesy: Embassy of Canada

Quebec when a francophone was heading another party, in this case Gilles Duceppe of the BQ.

Quebec voters have frequently demonstrated massive swings in elections. After the celebrations on election night were over, the party had to think hard how it would manage such a diverse and largely inexperienced group of MPs that included 58 Québécois, four McGill students, one of whom 19 years old, an ex-communist, teachers and activists, with very few seasoned politicians among them.

The BQ experienced near annihilation in the 2011 elections, plunging from 47 to a mere four seats, too few to qualify as an official party in parliament. The BQ remained as a powerless rump group. Gilles Duceppe, the longest-serving leader on the federal stage, immediately resigned. Only the most militant advocates of Quebec sovereignty stuck with the BQ, while soft sovereignists and federalists switched to the NDP. Clearly, many Quebecers are tired of the BQ and seriously asked themselves if they really wanted to be represented in Ottawa by a party that is in perpetual opposition. Many want to play a more constructive role in federal politics. The fact is that in its two decades of existence, the BQ failed to contribute to achieving the goal of separatist destiny, resulting in its becoming a spent force.

Spurned by voters in Ontario and Nova Scotia, Green leader Elizabeth May moved to Saanich-Gulf Islands, British Columbia, to win her long-coveted seat in the House of Commons. Nobody worked harder to win one as May knocked on countless doors and handed out packages of sunflower seeds, the international Greens symbol. May's efforts paid off, and she won the party's first seat. However, after 13 years of being the leader of the Green Party, on November 4, 2019, Elizabeth May stepped down as a follow through on a promise made to her daughter after the 2015 election, that the 2019 campaign would be her last. She remains the leader of the three-person caucus in Parliament.

The 2015 Federal Parliamentary Elections

Against a backdrop of a weakened economy, falling oil and resource prices, controversy over Muslim religious headwear, declining popularity of a Conservative prime minister who had ruled for a decade, and the appearance of a charismatic young Liberal leader with a magic name, Canadians went to the polls on October 19, 2015, to elect a new federal parliament. Excitement was demonstrated by a turnout of over 68%, the highest since 1993. The campaign lasted a record 78 days making it the longest race in modern Canadian history. This was plenty of time for 43-year-old Justin Trudeau to disprove that he was "just not ready," as Tory politicians proclaimed and to move his Liberal party from third place to the top of opinion polls. Although he is not the towering intellect his father was, Justin was was boosted by an outstanding TV debate performance, both in English and French. He was the clear winner and became Canada's 23rd prime minister.

The Liberal Party staged a sweeping victory, its best showing since 1949. It won 39.5% (up from 19%) of the votes enabling it to advance from only 36 seats to an absolute majority of 184 out of 338 seats. This was the biggest seat gain in Canadian history as the Liberal Party captured every riding in Atlantic and Northern Canada, more than doubling its seats in Quebec to 45, winning a majority of seats there, and in Ontario. It even captured four seats in the Tory stronghold of Alberta, taking two in Calgary. Trudeau maintained an optimistic and positive campaign and succeeded in helping bring about a generational shift to young voters. As dramatic as the result was, one perplexed BC voter said: "I see little real change with this election: another PM from Quebec, with central Canada politically controlling the country."

Many voters saw the election as a referendum on Tory leader Stephen Harper, was many Canadians viewed his 10-year rule as stern and divisive. Two-thirds of voters rejected Harper the polls, denying him a rare fourth consecutive victory, something that had not happened since

Canada

1908. Harper was not helped by the weak economy and came off as anti-Muslim by opposing so strongly a woman's insistence that she remain veiled during a ceremony in which she was to be sworn in as a new citizen. The Federal Court of Appeal dismissed his ban on the niqab in the ceremony.

The election was a calamity for the Conservatives as they lost 60 seats, falling to 99, from 39.6% of the popular vote to 31.9%. By the time the votes were counted, only one province, Saskatchewan, was still governed by a party associated with the federal Conservatives. Harper resigned as leader and was replaced by interim leader Rona Ambrose, an MP from Alberta who is forbidden from running for permanent leadership in the race that followed.

The NDP had a disappointing outcome, especially after briefly leading in the polls in the early days of the campaign. The dramatic gains the NDP made in the previous election were wiped away. Led by Tom Mulcair, the NDP dropped from 103 seats and 30.6% of the popular votes to 44 seats and 19.7%. Its largest provincial caucus remained in Quebec. Mulcair had to face a leadership review.

The Bloc Québécois (BQ) disappointingly captured less than a fifth of the vote in Quebec and only 4.7% of country-wide, a loss of 1.4%. Of the ten seats it captured, none was for leader Gilles Duceppe, who lost his riding for the second time resulting in his resignation as leader. The Greens, led by Elizabeth May, did no better, losing one of their two seats and falling from 3.9% of the popular vote to 3.45%. This was the Greens' worst showing in a decade. Other minor parties won 11 seats.

Compared to American campaign spending, the Canadian election was a bargain. Total spending by the parties and the candidates was $39 million for the Conservatives, $34 million for the victorious Liberals, and $27.5 million for the NDP. Canadian law prohibits labor unions and corporations from making political donations and establishes relatively low limits on personal donations.

The parliament that voters elected was as diverse as the country itself as it containd 46 nonwhite members (14.2%), most of them immigrants. Aboriginals made up 3%. Women constituted 26% overall, but the Liberals alone elected 50, and half of the cabinet was female. The average age of the members of Parliament was 49.8 and 58.6% were elected for the first time.

Prime Minister Justin Trudeau made more than 200 promises during the campaign that keep parliament and his cabinet very occupied including more collegial relations within the cabinet and provincial leaders. He asserted that power would be less centralized in the hands of the prime minister and his father's goal of creating a progressive, multicultural and idealistic Canada would be restored. Trudeau said that his foreign policy would put more emphasis on humanitarian aid and peacekeeping, while military forces, including the combat aircraft bombing the brutal Islamic State, would be ended.

As Foreign Minister Stephane Dion noted, though, terrorists "are everywhere" and Canada has to "fight with our allies." Orders for the purchase of F-35 fighter jets would be canceled. Relations would be improved with "our closest friend and partner, the United States." Stopping global warming and carbon emissions would be a much higher priority. Taxes would be lowered for the middle class, and pension improvements would be made. Government deficits would be maintained to pay for infrastructure improvements, including day care and affordable housing. Marijuana would be legalized. Senators would be appointed in a non-partisan way and the first-past-the-post British electoral system for the House of Commons would be replaced by some kind of a new system.

THE 2019 AND 2021 FEDERAL PARLIAMENTARY ELECTIONS

Going into the 2019 federal election, the Liberal Party under Justin Trudeau continued to hold a majority, with 177 seats. Held on October 21, 2019, the Liberals returned to government, but with a minority, gaining 157 seats, 18 seats short of a majority, and 33% of the popular vote. The Conservative Party, while gaining 26 seats, and actually gaining a higher popular vote percentage than the Liberals (34%), still failed to fulfill expectations, and its leader, Andrew Scheer, soon came under pressure to step aside. Sheer did, in fact resign in 2020.

The New Democrats, the Official Opposition of Canada only four years earlier, continued to lose seats, dropping from 39 to 24, and garnered just under 16% of the popular vote. The Bloc Québécois (BQ) went from 10 to 22 seats, while the Green Party retained the 2 seats with which it entered the election. The erosion of support in Quebec, combined with fewer seats in the West and British Columbia, sealed the Liberal Party's fate. Without those key seats, a majority became impossible.

Nothing had changed by the time Trudeau called the snap-election in 2021, only two years into a five-year term. And the electorate punished the Liberal Party for the blatant attempt to gain the seats lost in 2019. Held on September 20, 2021, the Liberals went into the election with 155 seats and came out with 160, up only 3 from the 2019 result. The Conservatives held the 119 seats it entered with, as did the BQ (32) and the Greens (2). The New Democrats had a marginal gain of 1 seat, moving from 24 to 25. The regional voting mirrored 2019. In the result, nothing changed: the Liberals and Trudeau continued with a minority government, the Conservatives formed the Official Opposition, and the BQ taking third party status. The New Democrats and the Greens held the left, barely, with 27 total seats.

Shipping routes at the top of the world

Source: *Maclean's*

Canada

It seems unlikely, given the current political landscape, that any of the major parties can gain sufficient support across the country to be in a position to form a majority government. Indeed, since 2000, only twice have voters given a majority government—in 2011 to the Conservatives and in 2015 to the Liberals. Minority government appears to be the norm for the regionally disparate national landscape found in Canada.

Justin Trudeau resigned as prime minister and leader of the Liberal party at the beginning of 2025, and Mark Carney was elected the leader of the party and sworn in as prime minister. On March 23, 2025, Carney asked Governor-General Simon to dissolve Parliament and called an election for April 28, 2025. On the first day of the campaign, opinion polls showed the Liberals slightly ahead of the Progressive Conservatives (for the first time in three years), a result almost wholly attributable to President Donald Trump's ongoing tariffs threats and rhetoric around annexation of Canada as the 51st state of the United States. Prior to those threats and associated rhetoric, Justin Trudeau and the Liberals trailed the Progressive Conservatives by a wide margin. It was therefore unclear which of the two major parties would win the election, either with a minority or majority.

FOREIGN POLICY

Canada, in the upper half of the North American continent, shares a 5,335-mile border, including Alaska, with the United States. This fact makes each country vital to the other. Canada tried to expand its trade with Asia and view its own security as linked with that of Europe. Yet, Asia and Europe are located far away. Canada's shared values, economic well-being, and proximity to the United States require that it focus much of its foreign policy attention on its southern neighbor.

Canada is involved in innumerable forms of cooperation with the United States. The Nations jointly administer the St. Lawrence Seaway, and their International Joint Commission (IJC) has objectively and far-sightedly dealt with many environmental issues for years. Following a bilateral agreement in 1972, the IJC helped facilitate the cleanup of the Great Lakes, which contain 21% of the world's fresh water. A Permanent Joint Board on Defense coordinates the two countries' security relationship, and they are allies in the North Atlantic Treaty Organization (NATO) and in the North American Aerospace Defense Command (NORAD).

Polls have indicated that Americans are more willing to defend Canada in case of attack than they are to defend any other country. In 2004, 84% of Americans supported their troops being sent to help Canada if attacked, and 75% of Canadians said the same about deploying their troops to defend the U.S. From 1984 to 1994, the top leaders of the two countries met each other at least annually, and the U.S. secretaries of state and Canadian ministers of foreign affairs met four times per year. By tradition, the first foreign leader with whom a new president should meet is the Canadian prime minister.

It was unusual that Bill Clinton waited almost two years to visit Ottawa in 1995. It was even more unusual that George W. Bush visited Mexico first after his inauguration in January 2001.

After his re-election Bush finally made his first bilateral visit to Canada, his third visit there overall, on November 30, 2004 in what was billed as an official, not state, visit. Breaking with precedent, Bush declined the invitation to address a joint session of parliament. Instead Bush delivered his main address in Halifax, Nova Scotia, in order to be closer to those Canadians who had helped thousands of American air passengers stranded after the September 11 terrorist attacks.

Each country is the other's most important trading partner and target for foreign investment. Every day close to US$2 billion in trade and travel pass over the border. Although it imports more from China than from Canada, the U.S. conducts more overall trade with the single province of Ontario than with either Japan or the entire European Union (EU); Canada trades more with California than with Japan. In fact, more international trade passes over the Ambassador Bridge that connects Detroit and Windsor than either the U.S. or Canada conducts with any other country in the world. Every province, except two in the Maritimes, has more trade with the United States than with other Canadian provinces. Overall, exports from Canada to the U.S. fell 1.7% in January 2020, mainly due to passenger cars and light trucks, but exports from the U.S. were up 1.6%, the first increase in five months (Statistics Canada, 2020). Canadian exports to the U.S. were $286.02 billion during 2020.

There always seem to be disagreements in the economic and trade field. In Washington there is a reservoir of good will toward Canada, even though there is often a need for American leaders to be reminded of what Canadians want. While the term is not used often any more, especially after former Prime Minister Chrétien's election in 1993, there is indeed a sort of "special relationship" between the two neighbors. If there were not, then Winston S. Churchill would not have been able to speak of "that long frontier from the Atlantic to the Pacific Oceans, guarded only by neighbourly respect and honourable obligations." It is now the world's longest thinly defended border.

Nevertheless there are differences and difficulties between Canada and the U.S. Former Prime Minister Pierre Trudeau once said that 70% of Canada's foreign policy involves its dealings with the U.S. Far less of America's foreign policy attention is focused on Canada. Some observers have called that kind of relationship "asymmetrical" because Canada is more dependent on the United States than vice versa. The United States has ten times as many people and is economically and militarily more powerful and influential in the world than is Canada. Canada is a "middle power;" the United States is a "superpower." Canadians have problems getting their larger neighbor to pay attention to their concerns.

The Arctic and the Northwest Passage

The differences emerged in the uproar over the American Coast Guard icebreaker *Polar Sea's* voyage in the summer of 1985 through the Northwest Passage without Canada's permission. The U.S. has long held that those are international waters, while Canada's position is that they are territorial waters. At the 1987 summit meeting in Ottawa, Mulroney asserted unmistakably that Canada owns the northern waters "lock, stock and icebergs."

Leaders of both nations reached a compromise in 1988. The Arctic Cooperation Agreement (ACA) permits the U.S. and Canada to increase their collaboration in the region without prejudicing the legal position of either country. The ACA acknowledged American, EU, British, Russian, and all other nations' reject Canada's claim that the waters are within Canadian sovereignty. No country questioned that Canada owns its resources or that it is sovereign over its Arctic islands. However, by requiring Washington to obtain Ottawa's consent for passages through the waters, which was always given, it hopes to prevent future incidents such as that caused by the *Polar Sea*. Canada and the U.S. agree that neither icebreakers nor nuclear submarines need permission to pass. When the U.S announced in 2000 that its new polar icebreaker, *Healy*, would sail through the passage that summer, a team of Canadian navigators and pollution experts went along.

The passage is not yet a reliable commercial route, and until 2013 transit was limited chiefly to research or military craft. In that year the first container ship navigated the route from China. In 2016, no fewer than 25 ships transited. One, Capital Serenity, carried 1,070 passengers. Many more commercial vessels take the Russian-

Canada

controlled Northern Sea Route along the Russian coast. Arctic ice has been declining by an area the size of Britain each year, twice as fast as the rest of the world. The U.S. Navy estimates that the North Pole will be ice-free by 2035; the UN estimate is 2050. Even so, commercial use of the Polar routes remains very expensive.

The routes are only open for a few months a year, and some ships must pay an icebreaker to accompany them. Because the waters are mostly uncharted, it is a problem getting insurance and securing rescue ships. The closest forward base is Halifax, a week's sail from the Northwest Passage. Once the ice is gone, the Bering Strait between Russia and the U.S. could rival the Persian Gulf and the Strait of Malacca in shipping importance. In 2008, Prime Minister Harper announced stricter registration of ships sailing through the Northwest Passage; all ships are required to report to Nordreg, the Canadian Coast Guard agency.

In general, it is tricky for Canada to determine whether to regard its southern neighbor as a friend or rival in the Far North. Former U.S. Ambassador to Canada, Paul Cellucci, once said he agreed with Canada's position on the passageway, he was quickly corrected by his successor, David Wilkins, who restated American insistence that the passage is an international strait. In 2006, Wilkins himself then slipped and called the passage "neutral waters," and the Canadian government jumped to correct his mistake. Wilkins' description was indeed at variance with the official American position, supported by the UK and others, that the waters are a "strait for international navigation."

A State Department official stressed that the U.S. prefers not to make a "big deal" of the navigation issue. The two partners agree to disagree about its legal status. But as a 2007 *Maclean's* poll reveals, 55% of American consider the Northwest Passage to be Canadian waters. This makes Americans the only people in the world besides Canadians, at 66%, to adopt this position. Consequently, it is important for Canadian politicians to be seen on the right side of this sovereignty issue.

Hours before calling a new election in 2008, Prime Minister Harper took selected members of his cabinet to the far North for three days to demonstrate his commitment to defend "Canada's Arctic sovereignty." In fact, after becoming prime minister in 2006, Harper made the Far North one of his signature issues, and he traveled there to inspect the military and its "Op Nanook" and Nunalivut exercises. Harper even held a rally in Yellowknife, Northwest Territories, during his 2011 election campaign.

In the summer of 2010, about 160 reserve soldiers were sent north to train near Yellowknife in "Exercise Sovereign Grizzly" as they helped set up the first reserve unit north of the 60th parallel. This is part of the 20-year Canada First Defence Strategy, announced in 2008, emphasizing domestic defense, especially in the Arctic. He justifies this as "use it or lose it."

Harper's point was to demonstrate to the world that Canada's military forces can operate anywhere on Canadian territory. During the Second World War, the American ally had already demonstrated that it was possible to do that: in 1943, there were more Americans, 33,000 military and civilians, in the Canadian North than Canadians.

In 2009, Harper took the entire cabinet to the Nunavut capital of Iqaluit for a cabinet meeting and even required all the members to join him in eating raw seal meat to show solidarity with the locals. Harper also hosted a Group of Seven meeting of finance ministers in Iqaluit in February 2010 to underscore Canada's presence in the North. In fact, all Arctic powers are boosting their northern presence. Norway moved its operational command north of the Arctic Circle, and Russia is upgrading its northern fleet, which already includes more than 18 icebreakers.

Canadians fear that the issue of sovereignty could become more important because global warming continues to melt the ice to such an extent that thousands

Canada

of ships from all nations could routinely traverse the ecologically vulnerable waterway. Arctic air is warming twice as fast as the atmosphere as a whole. This is especially worrisome because 90% of all goods in the world, measured by tonnage, are transported by sea. China's and India's rapid economic growth promises to increase the overcrowding of existing routes. In the 20th century, Arctic temperatures rose twice as fast as those in the rest of the world. If melting continues at its present rate, there will be no ice cover during the summer by the middle to end of the 21st century. Another powerful magnet is that the region is estimated to contain 13% of the world's undiscovered oil and a third of its gas.

The five various routes are a meandering set of channels through the Northwest Passage. They would offer a shipping channel between Europe and Asia 4,350 miles or 7,000 kilometers shorter than the route through the Panama Canal. For example, a ship traveling from Rotterdam to Yokohama would take 29 days to go around the Cape of Good Hope, 22 days via the Suez Canal, but only 15 days across the Arctic Ocean.

Two other Arctic shipping routes are also inviting: the Northern Sea Route (NSR) along the northern coast of Russia, which is already open part of the year, and the Arctic Bridge from Murmansk in Russia, around the southern tip of Greenland and into the Hudson Bay to Churchill, Manitoba, Canada's northern-most port. It was closed in 2016. As the summer ice melts, more and more ships sail through the Arctic waters. The alternative passages are more accessible than the Northwest Passage because only 10% of it has been charted, there is no infrastructure, and Canada's Arctic islands have special icing effects. The shrinking ice cap also makes mineral deposits more accessible. Some even predict a fishing bonanza, but scientists warn that a warming Arctic will not be full of fish.

A U.S. Navy study in 2002 reported that the ice cover has been shrinking by 3% per year. The Arctic Ocean could be ice-free in the summer by 2040. Western glaciers could shrink by 70% by 2100. As sea ice continues to melt, it can no longer deflect the heat away from land and water and so sped up the warming process. This scares Canadians, especially the Inuit, who urge Ottawa to assert its sovereignty over the waters of the Arctic Archipelago.

Canadians already claim that the 1982 Law of the Sea Convention gives them the right to regulate this area; as of 2019, the U.S. has yet to ratify the Convention but respects it in practice. The Canadian government ordered neither the promised powerful all-season ice-breaker nor the nuclear submarines needed to monitor the Northwest Passage and has no search-and-rescue helicopters permanently based in the North. Further, the Canadian government disbanded the one military unit capable of dropping onto the ice and has no deep-water ports north of Churchill, which is now shut down.

To underline its claims to sovereignty, Canada occasionally sends a coastal patrol boat into the passage during the summer, and every summer the Canadian Forces conduct joint army, naval and air exercises, called Op Nanook, in the Far North. The largest, conducted in 2011 near the hamlet of Resolute on Cornwallis Island, involving 1,200 troops, included a simulated rescue of passengers stranded on a grounded cruise ship. The relevancy of this exercise was soon demonstrated in August 2011 when a cruise ship was stranded in the Northwest Passage for two days until an icebreaker arrived. The vessel had hit a rock shelf, and the owner claimed that the Canadian government had not informed it about the shelf.

Following the practical principle of Arctic sovereignty, "use it or lose it," the Harper government promised to build three armed icebreakers, a deep-water port and a military training center in the Arctic. However, the number of icebreakers was scaled down to one.

While the ships are on hold, permafrost was broken at an abandoned mine in Nanisivik at the northern tip of Baffin Island near the entrance of the Northwest Passage to build a deep-water harbor that would allow Canada to refuel its military patrol ships. At Pangnirtung, with a population of 1,300 on the east coast of Baffin Island, a harbor for the small Inuit fishing fleet is being constructed. The Canadian government also made plans to refurbish an army facility in Resolute Bay in Nunavut to train soldiers year-round. Canada has only 120 year-round soldiers in the military bases to look after a northern region the size of Europe. These bases provide more resources to monitor traffic in the Passage.

In order to keep an eye on the entire Arctic region and to detect incursions, Canada has ordered from Northrop Grumman an unmanned spy aircraft (drone). This allows the kind of full surveillance not possible with the periodic Aurora CP manned flights and one Polar satellite. The Polar Hawk would enable Canada to take a photo of the whole Northwest Passage four times during a mission. The U.S. operates a similar drone over its own Arctic territory.

At Iqaluit, the housing stock is being increased, and a research institute with a polar vessel is being constructed. A problem is that the maritime boundary between Alaska and the Yukon extending northward into a sliver of the oil-rich Beaufort Sea in the western Arctic has never been agreed. Canada protested when the U.S. sold leases for this disputed area.

In 2005, Canada became embroiled with Denmark over ownership of Hans Island, an uninhabited square-mile, or 1.6 kilometer, patch of Arctic rock of no strategic or economic value and of no influence on the maritime boundary between Greenland and Canada's northeast. The island is within the 12-mile territorial limits of both countries, which allows both to claim it. Although largely self-ruling now, Greenland still falls under Danish sovereignty. The minuscule island at one point is only 14.5 miles from Canada.

Reflecting how closely the rock could be related to other Arctic jurisdiction issues, Canadian troops followed by the then defense minister himself, Bill Graham, visited the rock to plant the flag and

Canada

erect an Inuit stone marker. The Danes responded by sending a warship to back up their sovereignty over the island; they also planted their flag. Ottawa responded by dispatching a frigate to keep an eye on Danish fishermen. The two countries soon called a truce and agreed to disagree over its possession. In an act of reconciliation, scientists from both countries proposed in 2007 that a joint weather station be built on the island. In December 2012, Canada and Denmark reached a formal agreement on the maritime border between Greenland and the Canadian Arctic. Hans Island is another dispute between Greenland and Canada. The status of Tartupaluk Island (called Hans Island) has been unresolved since 1973. However, as of May 2018 the Canadian-Danish task force on boundary issues are seeking to resolve a disagreement over the maritime border between the two countries. One of the resolutions they are considering is to name the barren island a shared sovereignty.

In the Arctic, two prominent trends are the speed with which development is going forward and the huge number of political, legal and technical questions that remain unresolved. Unlike the treaty-bound Antarctica, which is a land continent and not an ocean like the Arctic, there is no long-standing supranational body in the Arctic.

An Arctic Council, which in 2013 established its first permanent secretariat in the northern Norwegian city of Tromso, came into being in 1996 with eight members: the U.S., Canada, Denmark, Finland, Iceland, Sweden, Norway, and Russia. Six non-voting representatives of cross-border indigenous Arctic peoples (such as Inuit, Sami, Athabaskan, Gwich'in, and Aleuts), belong. There are more than 26 permanent observers joined later by many more countries, including China and India. No IGOs or NGOs are granted that status. Canada is wary of admitting the European Union because of the latter's ban on commerce in seal products, which is important for the Inuit. The Council began as a talk shop, but it became a decision-making body. Members have signed treaties on joint search-and-rescue missions and on cleaning up oil spills.

The starting gun for a scramble to claim chunks of the region was fired in August 2007 when Russia, using a mini-submarine, planted its flag on the ocean floor four kilometers below the ice of the North Pole. This daring move carried echoes of the Soviet launch of the first satellite, Sputnik, in 1957. In January 2014, Canada announced its intention to claim the North Pole, a surprising move that provoked a sharp response from Russia.

What is driving the polar countries is that according to the 1982 Law of the Sea, which is intended to regulate almost all human uses of the high seas, countries can claim an economic zone up to 200 nautical miles from their coast or even further if they can prove that the area in question is the extension of their own continental shelf. This is the kind of claim Russia made by Russia with regard to the Lomonosov Ridge, which extends 1,800 kilometers or about 1,200 miles from the Russian coast to Greenland and Canada's Ellesmere Island.

The terms of the Law of the Sea require a country to make a claim within a decade of ratifying it. Russia's deadline was 2009, Canada's 2013, and Denmark's 2014. Because Washington has yet to ratify the Convention, the U.S. cannot make a claim. Canada is working together with Denmark and the U.S. to gather information needed to make the ultimate delineations.

In various ways, Canada has little to worry about. No country is actually threatening to invade Canada's North. Although each Arctic state defines its own security policy to safeguard its sovereign rights, most members are allies in NATO and are unlikely to fire at each other. Norwegian Admiral Haakon Bruun Hanssen noted that the region is "probably the most stable area in the world." Legal norms are well established and all countries play by the rules. There is also no large or serious overlap of its claims in the Arctic and those of other contenders.

Falling oil prices and conflicts between Russian and NATO had by 2018 prevented an aggressive scramble for territory and resources in the Arctic. Even the Northern Sea Route was used by only 71 ships in 2013 and 53 in 2014.

Canada must be aware of potential conflict with its Inuit population who claim much of the Arctic coast as their traditional territory. Even so, the Inuit are not against development. However, they insist that development be on their terms, meaning that it respect the environment and provide them with a share of the benefits. They also have banded together in the Inuit Circumpolar Council (ICC), created in 1977 to strengthen their interests and demands.

Canadians are sensitive about maintaining their sovereignty and independence in the world, a sensitivity that is sometimes hard for Americans to understand. Despite all their resemblances, Canadians are *not* Americans and do not think like Americans in all matters of foreign and military policy. The two peoples' activities in world affairs are compatible but distinct.

International Organizations

There are various reasons for such differences. Canada is active in certain political arenas in which the United States is not. One is the British Commonwealth of Nations. Canada maintained close ties with Britain while it gradually cut the apron strings with the mother country. It was Canada's push for greater sovereignty as much as anything else that led to the Statute of Westminster in 1931. That important act eliminated all pretenses that Great Britain made the foreign and defense decisions for the dominions or white-settled colonies. Canada actually helped to shape the kind of relationships with Britain that loosely bind together all Commonwealth countries.

Starting in 2012, Canada shares expenses and administrative duties with some British embassies. The UK offers Canada office space in its embassy in Myanmar while Canada returns the favor in Haiti. Canadian passports still contain instructions to go to the nearest British consulate in case of emergency in a country that lacks a Canadian mission.

Canada also is a leading member in the French Commonwealth of Nations, which loosely binds 49 countries that use French as their first or second language. This is dedicated chiefly to the survival of the French language. Canada's major purpose for supporting *La Francophonie* is to gain another forum for making its foreign policy presence known, as well as to indicate to the world Canada's bilingual character. Because of their bilingual status, the provinces of Quebec, New Brunswick, Ontario, and Manitoba also have the right to send delegations. Another arena of special Canadian activity has long been francophone Africa, where Quebec has sought a more active Canadian role.

A further reason for differences is that Canada is a "middle power." It can neither project military power nor influence international politics, to the extent that the U.S. can. Therefore, Canadians are more inclined to focus on non-military or long-term economic developmental solutions to problems than are Americans, who despite the limits to their power can still project military force to many parts of the globe. Being a medium-sized power does not mean that Canada is of no consequence in world politics. To the contrary, Canada is far more important than one might expect for a country of only 35.5 million people.

Canada is a very active participant in international organizations. It was a founding member of the United Nations and is deeply involved in all aspects of the UN's work. With the largest combined coastline in the world, it took a strong interest in the law of the sea conferences. In 1997, the UN appointed a Canadian, Maurice Strong, to help coordinate the much-needed administrative reform of that world body. In 1998, Canadian diplomat Louise Frechette was named the UN's first deputy secretary general in charge of reform issues. In 2004, Louise Arbour quit the Canadian Supreme Court to serve as UN High Commissioner for Human Rights until 2008. The head of the International Criminal Court (ICC) in 2005 was Canadian.

For the sixth time, Canada assumed a two-year term on the Security Council in 1999 but was rejected in 2010 for the first time since the UN's founding. The two western seats went to Germany and Portugal. It did not help that then opposition leader, Michael Ignatieff, said publicly that Canada had not earned such a prestigious position. Many member states do not like Harper's foreign policy, which gave outspoken support to Israel's government, closed embassies in Africa, and dragged its heels on climate change. Polls indicated that Canadians were indifferent to this setback: 38% said it did not matter, 42% that "it's humiliating and proves we're headed in the wrong direction," and 20% that "it's disappointing, but it shouldn't impact our policies."

The government had hoped that 2010 would be a year in which Canada would play an important role on the international stage. Canada is an important actor in the many international agencies that attempt to create and maintain global economic stability as it aids the World Bank, the International Monetary Fund (IMF) and the World Trade Organization (WTO). In 2000, Donald Johnston, a former Liberal cabinet member, was reelected to a second five-year term as secretary general of the Organization for Economic Cooperation and Development (OECD). He was the first non-European to hold the post.

Because of American insistence, Canada was in 1976 included in that select "group of seven" (G7) advanced industrial nations to meet periodically in "summit meetings" to discuss global economic issues at the highest level. When Russia participates, it is called the G8. In the 21st century that forum was enlarged to include major developing countries like Brazil, China, India and China, called the G20.

In the summer of 2010, Canada hosted both the G8 and G20 summits in Toronto. As always at such gatherings, thousands of anarchists, thugs, and advocates of myriad causes protested, and some turned violent, smashing shop windows, burning police cars and pelting the police with anything that can hurt. Toronto, which has always prided itself as a tolerant city, was shocked by the wanton criminality and destruction in the streets. There was an outcry in Canada about the $1 billion bill for security and clean-up and for what some viewed as overreaction by the police: about 1,100 demonstrators were arrested, including many bystanders, and 278 were ultimately charged.

In 1985, Canada hosted the first meeting in North America of the Organization of Security and Cooperation in Europe (OSCE), to monitor the progress of the so-called Helsinki Accords, signed in 1975 by 33 European nations and the U.S. and Canada. Canad'a role in these accords indicates its interest in and importance for Europe. Then Minister of Foreign Affairs Joe Clark said in opening the conference, "Canada remains firmly convinced that a safe, prosperous and humane Europe is a cornerstone of a safe, prosperous and humane Canada."

Latin America

During the Cold War, Canada was less likely than Americans to see the Soviet Union's hand in most Third-World conflicts. This meant that the U.S. had to do without Canada's support in dealing with such countries or regions as Grenada, Central America, or Cuba.

Canada never broke diplomatic and trade relations with Cuba The Caribbean island has long been a sort of foil for Canada to demonstrate its foreign policy independence from the U.S. It is Cuba's largest trading partner, doing about a half billion dollars of trade each year, not including the sizable revenues from a steady stream of Canadian tourists. Canada is the island's largest source of foreign tourists. With a half billion in investments, it is also Cuba's largest foreign investor after Spain. In 1997, Canada reached an agreement with Cuba on a broad range of cooperation, including protecting human rights, combating drug trafficking and terrorism, and providing Cuba with food and medical aid. This was the broadest commitment yet by a major U.S. ally to work with the Castro regime. The House of Commons also signed an agreement with the Cuban parliament to exchange information and delegations.

Always sensitive to American attempts to place limits on its sovereignty, Canada strongly opposed the Helms-Burton Act, which denied travel rights in the U.S. to companies and individuals that benefit from expropriated property in Cuba. Ottawa dismissed Washington's preference for isolating Cuba, arguing that Canada's policy of engaging Cuba is the best way of achieving human rights and democracy in the long run.

In order to strengthen such "constructive engagement" in 1998, Chrétien became the first leader of a major Western country to visit Castro in Cuba in more than a decade. He made a personal appeal for the release of four prominent dissidents. When they were sentenced 11 months later, the prime minister felt betrayed and ordered a review of Canada's relations with Cuba. In December 2014, the U.S. government announced that it would restore full relations with Cuba. Although Canada did not participate in the negotiations, it hosted seven meetings in Toronto and Ottawa.

Not until 1989 did Canada join the Organization of American States (OAS), and it has still not signed its collective security agreement, the Rio Treaty. For many years, Latin American governments had encouraged Canada to join the OAS in order to mitigate Washington's pervasive influence on the organization. But Ottawa had feared that full membership could limit its independence of action in the region and create a greater risk of putting its foreign policy at odds with positions taken by an OAS dominated by the U.S.

In 1989, Canada accepted a leading role in supporting a UN peacekeeping force in Central America. When the U.S. withdrew its peacekeeping troops from Haiti in 1996, Canada assumed command of the UN force through 1997. Its 750 troops were the key personnel in maintaining peace, training a police force, and improving the judicial system. In 2004, it sent peacekeeping forces to Haiti once again.

When Port-au-Prince, the capital of Haiti, was devastated by a powerful earthquake in January 2010, Canada's response was fast and generous, providing an emergency hospital, air transport and a wide variety of supplies. Canada's financial assistance was the largest per capita of any nation and the second largest in total dollars after the United States. The number of troops Canada deployed to help was nearly as many as it had fighting in Afghanistan. Successfully coordinating its effort was a new secretariat in the Foreign Affairs Department called START (Stabilization and Reconstruction Task Force), which is charged to make sure that all parts of the Canadian government work together in a crisis. Canada's close historical and cultural ties to Haiti center on the large Haitian immigrant community, especially in Quebec. Former Governor General Jean was the most prominent Haitian refugee.

Canada hosted the third Summit of the Americas, a gathering of 34 Western Hemispheric nations every three years, in Quebec in April 2001, where it supported creation of a Free Trade Area of the Americas (FTAA). It sponsored a "democracy clause" for FTAA that would penalize undemocratic regimes. However, little progress has been made for the FTAA. Prime Minister Harper's July 2007 trip through Latin America was a high-profile bid to intensify hemispheric development and trade. While Canada is increasing its two-way trade with Latin America, it amounts to less than 5% of total Canadian trade or

Canada

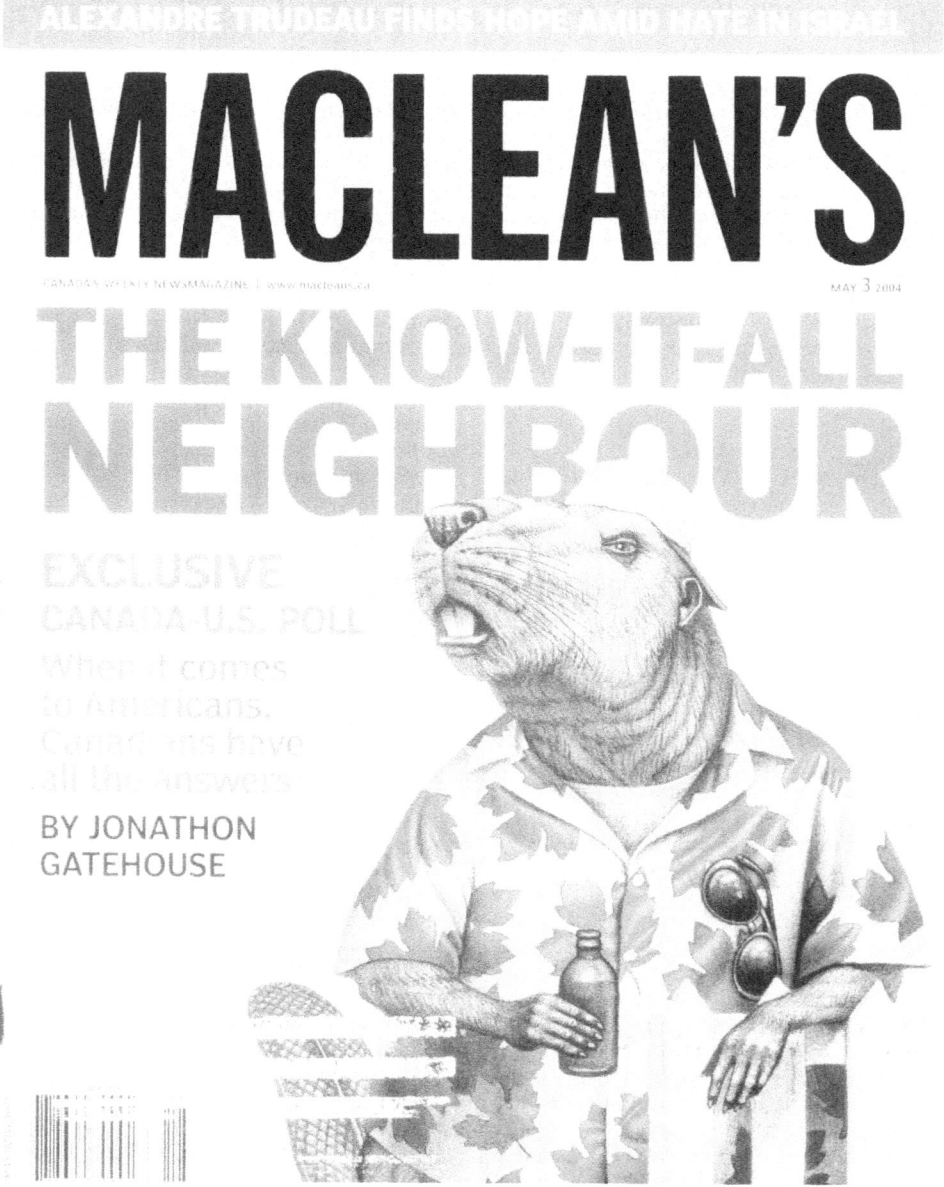

15% of that portion that does not involve the United States.

Through NAFTA Canada's ties with Mexico were significantly tightened. In 2005 it forged with the U.S. and Mexico the Security and Prosperity Partnership of North America (SPP). Its purpose was to facilitate closer cooperation to maximize the flow of goods and services across their borders while minimizing the passage of terrorists and illegal migrants. It aimed to continue North American integration where NAFTA left off. The "Three Amigos," the top leaders of all three member states, were to meet annually.

It achieved little beyond giving rise to countless conspiracy theories about a future "continental union" of all three countries. Of course, North America lacks the historical impetus that the Second World War had on European integration. Also, international terrorism, immigration and the violent drug war in Mexico have prompted Canada and the U.S. to strengthen their border enforcement. Canada imposed visa restrictions on Mexican visitors in 2009, a move that infuriated the Mexican government. The Obama and Harper governments found SPP too rigid and had little enthusiasm for it. They shut down its 20 working groups and cancelled the summits in 2010 and 2011.

Arms Control

Canadians push hard for arms control talks and once had a cabinet post in charge of disarmament affairs. In 1984, the government founded the Canadian Institute for International Peace and Security on the crest of strong public pressure for disarmament and a highly publicized and popular junket by Pierre Elliott Trudeau during his last year in office to world capitals in an unsuccessful attempt to stimulate greater support for the arms control process. Trudeau won the Albert Einstein Peace Prize for this, but his efforts were not appreciated in Washington. American officials saw this as a public relations gimmick to revive his party's declining popularity and as a hindrance to their own efforts to persuade the Soviet Union to negotiate seriously. The Mulroney government later closed the institute.

In 1997, Canada spearheaded the diplomatic campaign to negotiate an international ban on anti-personnel landmines, which killed more than 2,000 non-belligerents each month. In this "Ottawa Process," as the crusade was known, the government tapped a humanitarian tradition in Canadian foreign policy and endorsed the work done by Nobel Peace Prize winner Jody Williams and other private advocates, such as Princess Diana. Canada found huge support in world opinion. An American senator nominated Foreign Minister Axworthy for the Nobel Peace prize even though the U.S. did not support the ban. The Canadians detonated the remnants of their own stockpile, which had not been used since the Korean War and had long since ceased serving a tactical need for their armed forces.

On December 3, 1997, delegates from about 100 countries met in Ottawa to sign the treaty, an example of Canada's "value-added" diplomacy that permits it to play a visible role in world affairs despite acknowledged limits on its resources. Axworthy explained: "With the new fluidity taking place [since the end of the Cold War], there is room for value-added diplomacy. We made a choice that other middle powers have not. We decided to stay global." The view of some Canadians that their country is a kind of "moral superpower" inevitably creates friction with the superpower to the south. Almost two decades later, the treaty's success was obvious: 161 countries had signed on, and deaths and injuries from mines had practically ceased, along with their use and production.

Quebec and France

In any country, domestic political factors strongly influence foreign policy. In Canada, the particularly fragile unity of the country has created difficulties. It has always made Canadians especially wary of what they might interpret as American threats to their sovereignty. Also, the threat of Quebec separatism revealed a potential Achilles heel. It forced Canada to turn its attention even more inwardly than before and to look nervously abroad to see how other countries, especially France and the United States, would respond to Quebec claims of independence.

In 1967, French President Charles de Gaulle gave public support to separatism by saying in a speech in Montreal, "*Vive le Québec libre*" ("Long live free Quebec") which infuriated his host, Prime Minister Pearson. For a while, it seemed as if the French government might even grant Quebec full diplomatic status in Paris, and, in some ways, it did indeed give Quebec's representatives, who outnumber Ottawa's diplomats, the trappings of such status. Such games were played as whose flag could be flown where, and there was some bickering over the titles which Quebec's representatives should be permitted to have. But France concluded, especially after Quebecers rejected sovereignty in 1980, that it should support a unified Canada and has subsequently done so.

In 1985, France's former Prime Minister Laurent Fabius, who went to Canada on his first official visit abroad as head of government, assured the Canadian government that while relations with Quebec were of great importance, "our ambition is vaster and aimed at all Canadians." He even offered a toast designed to undo the damage done in 1967: *Vive le Canada; vive la France!* The French government also turned a cold shoulder to the 10,000 Canadians of French ancestry who submitted a request for dual citizenship in 1989 on the occasion of the 200th anniversary of the French Revolution.

In 1994, *Bloc Québécois* leader Lucien Bouchard, who was once Canadian ambassador to France, made an official visit to Paris to demonstrate to Quebecers that independence would not leave them international pariahs. Bouchard's visit was not reported at all in the French media, and a reserved French foreign minister reminded him that France's position on the Quebec issue is "non-indifference but non-interference."

In 1997, Bouchard returned to the French capital as Premier of Quebec with a bevy of Quebec ministers and received a mixed report: President Jacques Chirac told him, in Bouchard's words, that "whatever road Quebec chooses, France will accompany it." However, ex-Prime Minister Lionel Jospin, who regarded Canada as an important ally in countering American cultural dominance in the world, was less enthusiastic, noting that any decision to recognize Quebec would have to take into account the Canadian government's assessment of the post-referendum situation.

At the 1999 Francophonie summit in New Brunswick, Chirac was restrained. He stressed that France and Canada are partners and that Paris has no wish to interfere in other countries' affairs. But a gaffe made by one of France's presidential candidates in 2007, Ségolène Royal, who said in a speech that Quebec should have the right to self-determination, demonstrated that there remains some ambivalence in Paris concerning Quebec's future in Canada.

On his returning to Canada, Bouchard found himself in a firefight over a proposed agreement between the province and France to enforce child support settlements. Since Canada's constitution limits provincial governments' foreign relations to culture and commerce, Ottawa scuttled the deal because of the contractual language that treated Quebec as a sovereign country.

Even in the cultural sphere Ottawa resists any gesture that seems to treat Quebec as a sovereign state. In March 1999, Canada angrily pulled out of an international meeting of culture ministers in Paris after the French government issued a direct invitation to Quebec. "Only the government of Canada has the right to decide on the presence and representation of Canada and its constituent parts in our relations with other foreign states."

Quebec also tried hard to gain some form of special recognition from the U.S., but American leaders and diplomats were careful always to stress that the U.S. would deal only with Ottawa on diplomatic matters. They prevented Quebec from opening a kind of "embassy" in the U.S. and permitted only trade missions. Quebec has more than 25 representative offices throughout the world.

The consistent American view is that there should be only *one* Canada, not two. This was politely reiterated to Bouchard during his 1994 visit to Washington. U.S. officials expressed this more bluntly to a former American political officer and later ambassador at the U.S. embassy in Ottawa, David T. Jones, who wrote in a 1997 article in the *Washington Quarterly* that the U.S. could "live with" an independent Quebec. The State Department publicly called this statement "an outrageous, undisciplined act."

In order to shore up Canada's relationship with France in 2000, the former prime minister appointed his nephew, Raymond Chrétien, as ambassador in Paris. Quebec's Liberal Premier, Jean Charest, maintained much more cooperative relations with his fellow Liberal government in Ottawa after his election in 2003. At the same time, Chrétien traveled to Paris, flying the Quebec flag and acting like the government leader of a sovereign state. Chrétien initiated discussions to obtain for Quebec a greater presence in the international arena, especially in trade negotiations. "What we are aiming for is to be at the negotiating table with the federal government if the topic of discussion affects Quebec's competence. . . . As French speakers representing 2% of the population of North America, we have always felt the need to maintain external relations." Quebec did secure a seat in the UN Economic Social and Cultural Council (UNESCO), and it announced its desire for more such international memberships.

Charest returned to Paris in 2007 to meet with new French President Nicolas Sarkozy, who was openly pro-Canadian. Charest discovered that nobody talks about separation anymore. But this time he was working closely with the federal government to stimulate Europeans' interest in a transatlantic, Canada-EU free trade agreement. In April 2008, France's leading right-leaning newspaper, *Le Figaro*, described the PQ as "an empty shell" that has "sold its soul" by resigning itself to ruling only a Canadian province, not its own country.

In 2008, there was an unprecedented number of contacts between Canadian and French politicians due to the celebrations surrounding the 400th anniversary of Quebec City's founding. Immediately after the October 2008 elections, Harper raced to Quebec City to open the Francophonie Summit declaring himself "heir" to Samuel de Champlain and pledging more funding for the international Quebec channel TV5.

The prestigious French daily, *Le Monde*, lauded Governor General Michaëlle Jean, the great-great-granddaughter of French-owned Haitian slaves, during a May 2008 visit to Paris as an "almost Queen." Quebec nationalists fumed that she was being feted in France instead of Quebec Premier Jean Charest. President Sarkozy (2007–2012) antagonized them again in February 2009. After ceremoniously awarding Charest the Legion of Honor medal, Sarkozy added: "Do you believe the world, as it faces an unprecedented crisis, needs more divisions?" He favored "deepening in every domain the unique relation that links France to Quebec," but the best way to do that is "in harmony with the relation that France maintains with all of Canada." Quebec nationalists were stunned at such "lack of respect" and "contemptible epithets." PQ leader Pauline Marois was dumbfounded: "What are you talking about, Mr. President?"

Sarkozy was the first modern French president openly to oppose separatism. His successor, François Hollande, returned to the country's earlier official policy toward Quebec's future as "non-indifference and non-interference." Nobody knows precisely what this means. Hollande referred to *"une amitié et un cousinage."* roughly "Canadian friends and its cousins in Quebec." Hollande explained to ex-Prime Minister Harper, who was one

Canada

of the first foreign leaders to congratulate him on his win, that France sees its relations with Quebec and all of Canada to be "parallel, harmonious and essentially synonymous" and that he has no intention of disrupting that state of affairs. Not to be left out, Hollande's conservative opponent, Jean-François Copé, conducted a charm offensive to Ottawa in early 2014.

Complex Relations with the United States

The Canadian domestic political system is complicated. The provinces are very powerful and can sometimes place limits on Ottawa's power. Of course, American states also have the power to act on their own in many matters. Therefore, both countries experience some difficulties in settling bilateral affairs, when state and provincial capitals manage to get into the act.

Canada's parliamentary system simplifies the conduct of foreign policy. Responsibility is clearer, and once the federal government establishes policy, there are fewer obstacles to its implementation than in the U.S. Canada's parliamentary committees in the House of Commons and Senate debate policy and hold hearings. They may also suggest amendments. But Parliament cannot thwart a policy to which the government has committed itself. No majority government that has negotiated a treaty needs to worry about whether Parliament will ratify it.

The American political system works differently. As in Canada, power is divided in a geographic sense. However, unlike in Canada, power is also separated in Washington, and this can create diplomatic nightmares for both American and Canadian leaders. Foreigners have every reason to be mystified by America's large, highly decentralized institutions, which wield power of their own and which often seem to be hostile to each other. Separation of powers is particularly troublesome for foreign policy: it is often impossible for a president to produce what he promises to foreign leaders.

The complicated and extensive interagency bargaining in Washington confuses many Canadians although they expend a greater effort to understand the U.S. system than Americans do the Canadian. The American political system enables relatively unknown persons of various professional backgrounds to rise to the highest national political offices through a painfully long and complicated electoral system, largely unfathomable to Canadians, and to many Americans as well.

Newly elected U.S. presidents such as Donald Trump may have had little experience in foreign affairs and yet have the power to select a multitude of foreign policy advisers, secretaries, and agency chiefs, many with little or no foreign policy background. Such a presidential "team" appears often to operate in an uncoordinated way, frequently sending off widely differing signals. This inevitably creates and fuels doubts about American leadership capabilities and the continuity of U.S. foreign policy. In 1996–7, it took 15 months for the Clinton administration finally to name a new ambassador to Canada, Gordon Giffin, who lived most of his youth in Montreal and Toronto, and months more before the Senate confirm him to his post.

Canadians are particularly frustrated by the powerful U.S. Congress. It has undergone significant changes: the seniority system has weakened, and the number of committees and subcommittees has proliferated. Also, the workload has become so demanding that congressmen and senators are retiring earlier. Therefore, an increasingly high percentage of the legislators are new in Congress. At the same time, committee and personal staffs have grown enormously. What these changes have done is to take much of the power that used to be concentrated in a few key figures and to disperse it within Congress.

In this more decentralized, or, more positively, "democratized," Congress, legislative work has become more complicated. For instance, more than 40 congressional committees and subcommittees deal with the defense budget alone. Absent strong party discipline as in Canada, American congressmen and senators are more protective of their constituents' interests and can safely vote against their party leaders or the president if an issue of great interest in their districts or states is at stake. In December 2000, ex-Foreign Minister John Manley said that it would be easier to work with the new American President George W. Bush than with Congress: "It's always easier for Canada to deal with the

Kirsten Hillman, Ambassador of Canada to the United States

United States when the administration has the strength to deal with issues and can expect congressional support."

Because the approval of the U.S. Senate, by a two-thirds vote, is needed for all treaties, the American upper house can even veto the most painstakingly crafted international agreement. Canadian governments have experienced how this fact can affect their bilateral relations with the United States. The East Coast Fisheries Agreement of 1979, the Tax Treaty of 1980 and the Pacific Salmon Treaty of 1983 were all victims of senatorial opposition. Also galling to Canadian diplomats and governments is the fact that after already making all the concessions it could to secure the president's or State Department's agreement, a president or secretary of state might come back to them and say that yet more concessions are needed in order to secure senatorial approval. Thus, Canada must sometimes go farther than halfway to get a ratified agreement, and that favors the United States.

In an attempt to get around this problem, Canada began to lobby directly in Congress in order to compete with the interest groups that were seeking to stymie agreements important to Canada. Allan Gotlieb, ambassador to the U.S. in the 1980s, wrote in *The Washington Diaries* that "Americans just do not see us as different from themselves. When we do something different, Americans feel betrayed. They don't see us as foreigners but as perverse Americans."

Gotlieb changed the earlier standard practice of working only with the State Department and took his country's concerns directly to Congress and its powerful staffers. When calling on members of Congress, he remembers: "One always feels as though he is begging. One is. The challenge: how to beg and keep one's dignity." Gotlieb noted that diplomatic disputes often arise not as a result of White House decisions but from the rulings of unknown bureaucrats at federal agencies, which Canadian diplomats must not neglect. Gotlieb also worked with journalists: "I would never have dreamed of how important journalists are in Washington. My views were shaped by 20 years in Ottawa dealing with the semi-educated press corps there." Gotlieb concluded that his country has no friends in Washington, only interests. That might be changing: in 2006 a new congressional "Friends of Canada" caucus was created to focus on shared concerns.

In 2004, a new public advocacy and legislative secretariat was created in the Canadian Embassy, which includes provincial representatives, to lobby Congress more effectively. Alberta, which exports close to $90 billion in goods, mainly energy and food, to the U.S. annually, is the

Canada

only province that runs a trade office out of the embassy. Quebec and Manitoba have their own lower-profile representatives to lobby on issues of interest. Quebec also has a tourism office elsewhere in Washington.

Former Ambassador Michael Wilson commented in 2007 that Canada's and Alberta's joint effort to influence the American government is good. Wilson wanted to demonstrate that the bilateral relationship goes much farther than merely dealing with a few irritants and rises to the level of a global "partnership." This struck a positive note with an American diplomat: "It's exactly what we have wanted from Canada: a partner who will work with us together on the 96 per cent of international issues where our goals are the same: defeat terrorism, advance and consolidate democracy and good governance, prevent the proliferation of WMDs, promote economic development through open trade and development."

Canadians also rely on U.S. governors to advocate shared concerns in Washington. Gottlieb said "these governor relationships really matter because the states matter—that is increasingly where the problems come from. And if the governor is our friend, then we are closer to solving them." One governor who was a friend is Vancouver-born Canadian citizen Jennifer Granholm of Michigan. One of the oldest relationships is the Conference of New England Governors and Eastern Canadian Premiers. A major asset of former Manitoba Premier Gary Doer, who was appointed to replace Michael Wilson as ambassador to the U.S. in 2009, was that he had spent much time in the U.S. and knew personally all four former governors in President Obama's cabinet. Of course, mayors and city councils on both sides of the border work closely together.

It is rare that incivility is shown, as it was in 2013 over efforts to expand the plaza on the New York side of the Peace Bridge connecting Buffalo to Fort Erie in Canada. New York Governor Andrew Cuomo stooped to describing his Canadian counterparts in e-mails as "duplicitous" and their behavior as "deceitful, disrespectful and arrogant." Passions ran so high that the ambassadors on both sides had to step in and calm the parties down. The dispute was settled in June 2013.

It also began to try harder to influence the American public directly. In one case, the Canadians produced a film on acid rain to help educate Americans on its consequences for Canadian fish, trees, lakes and public monuments. Some American officials bristled at this attempt by a foreign country to go over their heads in an important diplomatic issue and appeal directly to the American people. U.S. officials temporarily banned the film, a move that predictably heightened Americans' interest in it and spurred them to jam halls in which the film was later shown.

Americans and Canadians have a great deal of practice in settling their disputes peacefully. When they cannot, they have taken their disputes to the International Court of Justice, agreeing in advance to abide by its decision. In 1984, the court rendered a long-awaited decision on a disputed maritime boundary in the Gulf of Maine, giving Canada jurisdiction over about one-sixth of the rich Georges Bank fishing grounds. Canadians were unhappy with this outcome. The countries worked out an agreement as to what should be done to manage the fish stocks that cross the boundary and are caught by both countries' fishermen.

The two countries had a sovereignty dispute over Machias Seal Island and nearby North Rock, which are tiny, as Machias is 20 acres, rocky, remote and uninhabited islands in the Bay of Fundy. They have neither strategic significance nor oil and gas. Bird watchers go there to observe nesting Atlantic puffins. The disagreement stems from differing interpretations of the 1783 Treaty of Paris. Britain built a lighthouse on Machias Seal Island in 1832, and Canada has manned it ever since. Located almost equidistant between Maine and New Brunswick, it is the last land mass contested by Canada and the U.S.

The U.S.–Canadian Border

Even before the September 11, 2001, attacks, there was congressional clamor to tighten up controls along the U.S.–Canadian border. An Algerian with a fake Canadian passport was arrested at the border in December 1999 with enough material in his car to make four powerful bombs. Two other Algerians and a Canadian woman were apprehended at the border to Vermont five days later with traces of explosives that sniffer dogs detected. All were identified as members of a violent Algerian organization called the Armed Islamic Group (GIA).

Members of the U.S. Congress charged that Canada was "soft on terrorism." Months of intense diplomatic and political activity were necessary before a deal could be reached dropping the proposed requirements for Canadians to fill out time-consuming entry forms at the border like all other foreigners. Nevertheless, the U.S. added 600 new customs and special agents along the border, bringing the number to 2,200.

The September 11 attacks changed the way many Americans look at their borders, raising the urgency to secure them. Officials set out to apply technology to create a "smart border" to tighten security and thwart terrorists while keeping the 49th parallel open for the world's largest trading relationship. The longest undefended border became a bit more defended and more complex to traverse.

The challenge is daunting: a truck crosses the Ambassador Bridge between Detroit and Windsor every six seconds. This bridge, with an accompanying tunnel, is the cornerstone of the two neighbors'

Source: *The Economist*

Canada

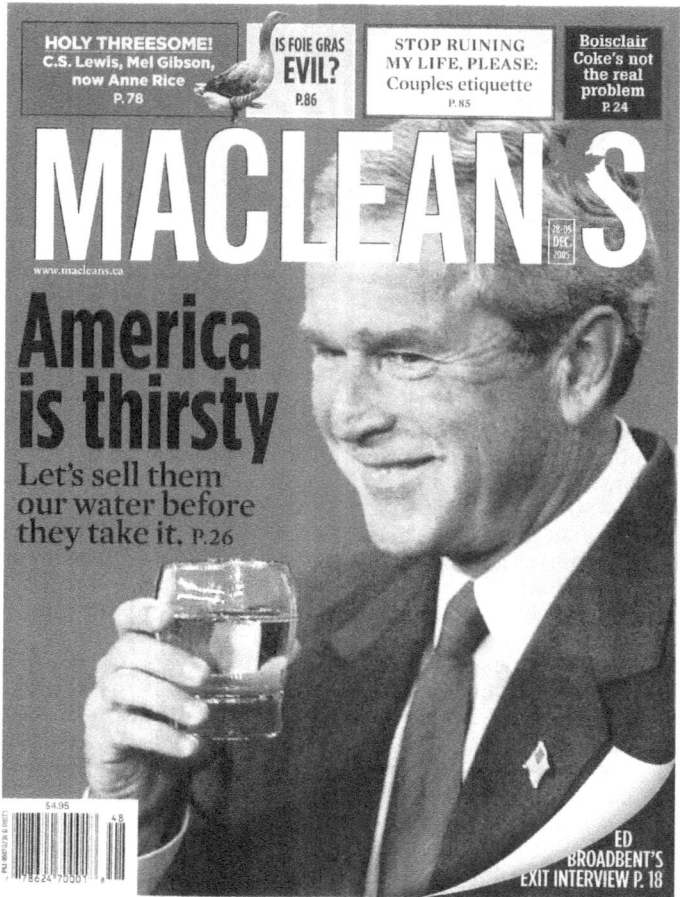

trade, especially that of Canada's export-dependent economy. Even a temporary closing of the 555-meter-long bridge, owned privately by the Manuel Mouroun family and its Detroit International Bridge Company, would be devastating to the two countries' $627 billion annual trade relationship (in 2010) and to Canada's economic future. That is why Michigan voters rejected a ballot initiative in 2012 that would have hindered the construction of a second bridge connecting Detroit and Windsor. It will be located about two miles from the Ambassador Bridge. It will be named the Gordie Howe International Bridge and will be built through a public-private partnership. Canada will bear most of the project's costs. By 2018, the highway on the Canadian side was completed, and Canada had obtained all the required approvals for the crossing.

About 70% of Canada–U.S. trade travels by truck, with 37,000 trucks crossing the border every day; 58% of these cross at only five border crossings—Ambassador Bridge, Sarnia, Fort Erie, Lacolle, and the Pacific Highway. Eight out of ten top crossing points are either bridges or tunnels and have become bottlenecks with long waits. Speed is increasingly important because of growing "just-in-time delivery." Trucks loaded with goods bound for either country are pre-cleared and sealed with electronic sensors that allow them to cross the border in fast lanes. The "Nexus" system of allowing "pre-approved frequent travelers" across the frontier was improved and reintroduced.

Before September 11, half the 126 official crossings were unguarded at night, but they are all protected 24 hours now. The U.S. Coast Guard stops all boats crossing the maritime border in the Great Lakes and escorts all oil and gas tankers. When U.S. Coast Guard vessels in American waters installed machine guns and conducted periodic live-fire exercises in 2006, an outcry was heard all around the lakes. Armaments in the Great Lakes are supposed to be limited, according to an 1817 treaty. Eighty American and Canadian mayors demanded that the shooting stop.

The Canadian–U.S. border has become more secure; it is not as open as it was before September 11. The number of Americans who cross the border dropped by 22% between 1999 and 2005. This hits Ontario the hardest, whose tourist trade is 95% dependent on Americans. BC and Alberta depend more on Asian visitors, and Quebec on Europeans. In the other direction, the opening in Canada of large American retail outlets like Wal-Mart, Best Buy, Pottery Barn, and Home Depot, as well as growing internet purchasing, have contributed to the reduction of Canadian day-trippers into the U.S.

Canadian consumers have complained loudly about the fact that prices for American goods are still higher in Canada than across the border. One can see this in the two prices on book covers: the American price is always lower. The price difference is especially grating for automobiles: in 2007, a Lexus RX350 sold for $52,000 in Canada, but only $37,000 in the United States.

The stronger Canadian dollar and high Canadian gasoline prices helped drive many Canadians southward across the border for shopping. There they can visit certain chain stores, such as Macy's, Saks Fifth Avenue, J. Crew, Kenneth Cole, Anthropologie, and Bath & Body Works, that have not expanded to Canada. Canadians can generally buy products in the U.S. for lower prices than they would pay at home. However, if they buy too much, they may be required to pay sales taxes and other duties when they reenter Canada. The greatest fear on both sides of the frontier is that the $2 billion daily two-way trade will be affected. Already old-style warehousing of goods is being reintroduced in many places to replace the efficiency of just-in-time delivery.

The main factor for slower border crossings is the fear of terrorist attacks; 44 government agencies on both sides have some jurisdiction over border matters, and that means slower crossings. Eight Canadian ministries alone have responsibility for some part of the border. The sprawling Department of Public Safety, the Canadian equivalent of the Department of Homeland Security, was created after September 11, 2001, to give a single minister control over everything from the RCMP and Canadian Security Intelligence Service, to running federal prisons and managing the border with the United States. In 2004, the U.S. began demanding fingerprints and photos at its borders for non-Canadian citizens between the ages of 14 and 80.

From January 2007, all airline passengers arriving in the U.S. had to show a valid passport. For the first time in history that was extended to land and water passengers on June 1, 2009, when the Western Hemisphere Travel Initiative came into effect. The disruption this requirement caused was reportedly modest even though there was a sharp drop in cross-border travel. However, relying on passports is a problem since only an estimated 34% of Americans over age 18 have one, compared to 54% of Canadians.

Where there is real worry, though, is that fire trucks and ambulances are delayed at

Canada

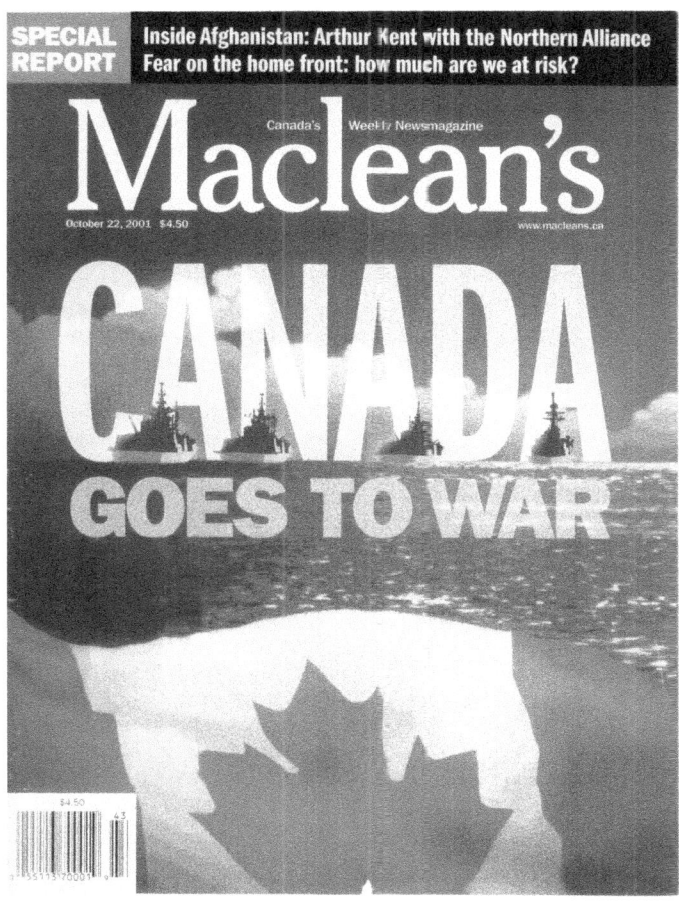

the border, thereby hampering community-level cross-border cooperation. That already happened in 2008 when Quebec volunteer firemen speeding to a hotel blaze in upstate New York were held up so long on the border that the building had burned to the ground by the time they arrived on the scene. Nobody knows what may happen elsewhere in places like Stanstead, Quebec, and Derby Line, Vermont, which are, in effect, a single community. Not only do streets continue unguarded into the other country, but the joint opera house and library building is shared. Most of the interior is in Canada, but one can only enter the building from the U.S. A black line on the floor runs through the library demarcating the two lands.

In the Maclean's 2003–04 year-end poll, 61% of Canadians approved of the idea of a North American perimeter. Prime Ministers Martin and Harper agreed that one of Canada's main challenges is to keep the American border open. After all, three-fourths of its exports head across the U.S. border, accounting for 52% of Canada's GDP.

Given the facts that a truck crosses the Canada–U.S. border every 2.5 seconds and that every minute more than US$1 million in trade passes across it, trade must be kept unimpeded. This is the rationale for the bilateral "Beyond the Border" trade and security plan of 2011–12. The main idea is that American customs and immigration officials will be physically stationed on the Canadian side of the border, and Canadian border officials on the U.S. side to screen people, trucks, and cargo before they cross into the other country. Both countries will share information about people crossing the border, facilitating trade and travel. As it stands, when goods cross the border, 45 authorities in the two countries require data.

Bilateral cooperation has been stepped up, with a growing exchange of intelligence information and criminal records, allowing U.S. law enforcement agents to retrieve records from the Canadian Police Information Centre, consultation on visas as Canada requires no visa for 52 countries, while the U.S. exempts only 32, and collaboration at foreign embassies to stop people smuggling from overseas. At the time of the September 11 attacks, only Canadians worked at the RCMP headquarters in Ottawa. Now Americans from four agencies are based there. Cooperation is reported to be "pervasive." The two countries have acted in concert to plug a hole at St-Bernard-de-Lacolle along the Quebec border with New York. It is now more difficult to arrive in New York with fraudulent passports and then scoot across the border to claim refugee status.

The Mexican and Canadian borders are still different. Whereas the Mexican border is normally divided by walls, the Canadian frontier is in most places no more than a ditch or a cleared area in a forest. By 2015, the U.S. stationed only 2,200 (up from 340 in 2001) border patrol agents along the Canadian border, compared with 18,600 along the shorter boundary with Mexico. Still, the U.S. is creating border security bases like it has along its border with Mexico. Each equipped with two helicopters, an airplane, a high-speed boat, and a staff of about 70, the first was located at Bellingham, Washington, and Plattsburgh, New York, followed by bases near Detroit, Michigan, Grand Forks, North Dakota, and Great Falls, Montana.

President Obama's first homeland-security secretary, Janet Napolitano, wanted controls along the Canadian border to be brought in line with those on the Mexican frontier. She said she wanted everybody to realize that "this is a real border." There are plans to install heat-detecting sensors and additional cameras along the border. The U.S. also now uses aircraft with sensor arrays, thermal cameras, and unmanned surveillance drones to patrol parts of the frontier. Napolitano's replacement, Jeh Johnson, focused more on defense along the border, not the economic issues that matter to Canada.

Both countries are targeting potential terrorists and smuggling. The latter includes marijuana from Canada and cocaine and weapons from the U.S., as well as large amounts of cash in both directions. In order to deal with the dangers of such cross-border criminality, the 4,800 officers of the Canada Border Services Agency were armed with guns. The aim of such cooperation is an even more open and safe U.S.–Canada border.

The election of President Donald J. Trump in November 2024 ushered in significant changes in American trade and foreign policy. Trump was buoyed by a victory in which he ran on a campaign in large part relying on a platform calling for an "America First" strategy. Trump's "America First" strategy included, among other items, helping to secure the border by preventing individuals from entering into the United States illegally along with stopping the large flow of fentanyl that is causing the deaths of many Americans and to end existing trade imbalances with other nations. In line with that policy, Trump announced the imposition of 25% tariffs on various imports from Canada, and other nations, in an effort to help revive the economy in the United States. Combined with this economic policy,

Canada

Trump also made repeated comments about making Canada the 51st state of the United States. The initial 25% tariffs went into effect on March 4, 2025, after Canadian and American officials were unable to reach an agreement to pause or end their being imposed. In response, then Canadian Prime Minister Justin Trudeau announced that Canada would impose its own tariffs on goods from the United States. Also in early March, Trump rescinded what he promised would be even larger tariffs on Canadian steel and aluminum after Ontario Premier Doug Ford walked back a planned 25% surcharge on electricity exports to Michigan, Minnesota, and New York. Not surprisingly Trump's actions has caused significant conflict.

On March 23, 2025, after being in office for only nine days, Prime Minister Mark Carney, who to date neither served in public office nor ran a political campaign, called for a snap election on April 28, 2025. Carney explained that he had called an election because in light of the tariffs Trump has put in place Canada is "facing the most significant crisis of our lifetimes." Tensions thus remain high as this book heads to press as Canadians are responding with am "elbows up" attitude, a phrase coined by all-time hockey Great Gordie Howe who "used his elbows to defend himself when opposing players crowded in" on the ice, meaning that he was willing to use his physical strength as a means of self-defense. It can only be hoped that cooler heads will prevail and a mutually acceptable compromise that is beneficial to both nations can be worked out soon to preserve the long-standing good relations between the governments, and people, of Canada and the United States.

Water Resources and Acid Rain

In 1909, the two countries signed and ratified the Boundary Waters Treaty to preserve the quality and quantity of their shared water, setting up an International Joint Commission to arbitrate disputes. In its century of existence, it has worked well; of 53 joint references, 51 were resolved by mutual agreement. Nevertheless, the two countries seem always to have on-going disagreements over use of North America's water resources.

For decades, American governments have been interested in a project to divert the waters of the Garrison River in order to direct water from the Missouri River basin into 250,000 acres of parched lands in northwestern North Dakota for irrigation purposes. North Dakota long wanted to drain millions of gallons of water from Devil's Lake, which has no natural outlet and is located 60 miles south of the Manitoba border, in order to prevent the rising lake from continuing to flood the surrounding countryside. The problem is that the spill-off waters might carry unwanted invasive species, parasites, disease, and the high concentrations of sulphates, arsenic, phosphorus and other pollutants from Devil's Lake via the Sheyenne River into the Red River across the Canadian border into Lake Winnipeg. From there, they could ultimately pass through Canadian rivers, most of which flow northward, into the Hudson Bay watershed.

Although the projects had actually been started, the determined efforts of environmentalist groups on both sides of the border, as well as the Manitoba provincial government, prevented for a while the projects from getting complete approval. Nevertheless, there continued to be support in Congress for them. After devastating floods along the Red River in North Dakota and Manitoba in 1997, the two countries agreed to work together to minimize future flooding.

In 2000, the North Dakota governor traveled to Manitoba to see firsthand the province's concerns and promised to consult with provincial leaders. A few months later the Manitoba premier and the governors of Minnesota and North Dakota met for the first time and reached an agreement to protect all citizens from Red River flooding. In the same year, Canada sent 200 firefighters to help weary Americans battle a hundred wildfires out of control across the Western United States. For the first time, the U.S. put a foreigner, a Canadian, in command of a unit battling a blaze.

Ultimately, patience ran out in mid-2005. North Dakota officials, who resisted Canadian requests to refer the issue to the commission, announced that the draining of Devil's Lake would begin. This kind of unilateral action could lead to difficulties for both neighbors. Half the 300 transboundary rivers flow southward into the United States. In 2005, Montana challenged BC's plans to mine coal under a vital riverbed. Good will can run thin. In a landmark cross-border pollution case, a Canadian company in BC, Teck Cominco, voluntarily agreed in 2006 to pay for any harm done to Americans or wildlife by the waste products its zinc smelter had dumped into the Columbia River and traveled downstream into the U.S.

With ten times Canada's population, the U.S. is in much greater need of water resources, and American eyes have often looked to Canada's supply as a long-range solution. Canada has always resisted the large-scale transfer of its water resources, though. Its leaders have noted that even though the Canadian Shield has abundant lakes and streams, its water is not easily replenishable. The fact is that the flow of rain, spring water and snowmelt that goes through Canadian waterways represents 7% of the world's renewable water supply.

Of Canada's 18 principal watershed systems, 15 provide less than 10% of their annual renewable supplies to human usage. Canadians have also opposed large-scale

Canada

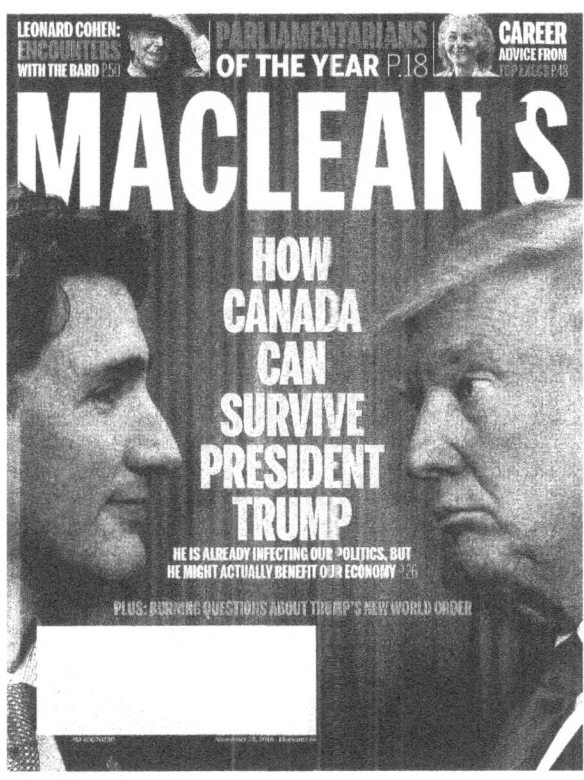

diversion of water from the Great Lakes, which are shared by both countries. Although they have occasionally studied the possibility of siphoning off that water, the Great Lakes states agreed not to initiate any such scheme without Ontario's permission. Forty-five million, including 10 million in Ontario, get their drinking water from the Great Lakes.

In 2002, the International Boundary Waters Treaty Act went into effect banning the bulk removal of water from basins that straddle the border, particularly the Great Lakes. Actually, researchers who sought examples of economically viable ideas for bulk-water exports from Canada have found none. There are neither serious proposals nor realistic prospects for such exports to the U.S. Although NAFTA says nothing about water, ex-Foreign Minister Pierre Pettigrew, made clear: "Water is not a [tradable] good, it is a resource that needs to be managed."

One of the most stubborn problems of both countries was acid rain, pollution caused by the burning of fossil fuels and released into the air via high smokestacks that mixes in the atmosphere with nitrogen oxide from automobile emissions to form an acid moisture. This unhealthy combination sometimes is then carried hundreds of miles before being brought back to earth by rain, killing trees, fish and other animal life and eating away at stone buildings and monuments. For a country whose people are rightly proud of its natural beauty and 10% of whose work force depends on tourism, this is a catastrophic ecological and economic problem.

Much of Canada's acid rain stems from plants in the U.S., particularly in the Midwest. Therefore, any solution to the problem must be an international one. American administrations tended to buy time by calling for "more research" on acid rain. Because of the salience of this issue in Canada, its leaders could not accept this and pushed for more concrete steps. The acid rain issue, which became a sort of litmus test for the two countries' relations, severely tried Canadians' patience.

In 1991, the two signed a landmark accord committing the two countries to curb emissions that cause acid rain and to reduce other pollutants. By 1995, acid rain levels had dropped significantly, and sulfur dioxide emissions had declined in the East by 40% since 1980. Still, work remains to be done on both sides. In 2000, the New York's Attorney General asked the President to put pressure on the Ontario government to clean up coal-burning plants on the Canadian side that are destroying forests and causing respiratory problems in Buffalo and other border areas.

Prime Ministers and Presidents

Brian Mulroney came into office in 1984 determined to improve Canada-U.S. relations. Not since Lester Pearson and John F. Kennedy were in power in the early 1960s was there such a warm personal relationship between the leaders of these two neighbors and allies. Regular summit meetings forced Washington to confront Canadian issues promptly, instead of consigning them to the back burner. The invitation of Mulroney to address the U.S. Congress and to dedicate the newly completed Canadian embassy in Washington, the only foreign embassy to be permitted on Pennsylvania Avenue, demonstrated the two countries' good relations.

Mulroney had to pay a domestic political price for his relationship with Reagan and Bush. He reaped criticism for seeming too eager to please and to impress American presidents even though he was not afraid to say "no" when Canadian interests were at stake: he refused to withdraw from UNESCO, favored tough economic sanctions against South Africa, permitted Nicaragua to open a trade office in Toronto, and refused officially to endorse the Strategic Defense Initiative, or SDI. In fact, Mulroney publicly broke ranks with the U.S. more frequently than did either Pearson or Trudeau, whom President Nixon considered to be an "asshole," according to Watergate tapes. Mulroney merely concluded that a confrontational approach toward the U.S. is less effective than a more conciliatory style.

Former Prime Minister Chrétien decided that his approach toward the U.S. would be less enthusiastic and more formal. He had scorned Mulroney's pledge always to give the Americans the benefit of the doubt, joking that Mulroney would answer the phone from the president before it rang. Chrétien also announced after his election that, unlike Mulroney, he would not be going fishing with the president, fearing that he might end up as the fish. Chrétien played golf with Clinton, but he winced in 1997 when the president introduced him in the Rose Garden by saying that "I don't know of any two world leaders who played golf together more than we have." Chrétien had said in 1992: "Mulroney cares more about getting others to like him than about getting the things that Canada needs. Me, I understand that in politics there is no room for friendship."

Chrétien also knew that Canadian voters do not like overt reverence for the U.S. They have ambivalent feelings toward the U.S. and are alternately drawn to and repelled by American might. Canadians prefer what the *Globe and Mail* called "affected standoffishness" toward Washington. Chrétien expresses that ambivalence well. A 1994 poll showed that 53% of respondents approved his management of the relationship with America, compared with 25% for Mulroney in 1992. Chrétien established comfortable rapport with President Clinton, meeting discreetly with him 16 times leading up to an official visit to Washington in April 1997, his first since taking office in 1993.

Canada

Chrétien described that rapport he had with Clinton as "good, and not cozy," treating him as an equal, not as the ranking world leader. Chrétien thus felt free in 1997 to expound to the leaders of Belgium and Luxembourg that Clinton's views on NATO expansion are "not for reasons of security" but "for short-term political reasons to win elections." As one Canadian political commentator noted, Chrétien's assertion that American foreign policies are driven by domestic interests are about as shocking as the reality that the same is true for Canada.

Chrétien offered swift support for important American policies and appreciated Clinton's pitch for a united Canada during the president's 1995 visit to Ottawa, repeated at the time of the Quebec referendum: "A strong and united Canada has been a wonderful partner for the United States and an incredibly important and constructive citizen throughout the entire world." But when he introduced Clinton to Parliament, he said: "The Americans are our best friends—whether we like it or not." Moreover, Chrétien went out of his way in Washington in 1997 to underline the differences between the two countries, stressing the way Canada values such things as universal health care and gun control.

In Chrétien's words, "it's nice to have a big client like the United States, but you can't have just one. It wouldn't be a good business position." Nevertheless, the two countries' close economic ties and cordial relations remained essentially unchanged. Chrétien's foreign policy had been less outspoken about human rights, more aggressive about promoting Canadian exports and economic interests, and less generous with foreign aid (which it cut to only .28% of GDP by 2018 (the world's 15th highest, ahead of the United States' .21%).

Ex-Foreign Minister Axworthy crusaded visibly and energetically on the world stage under the banners of "soft power" and "human security" that emphasize values and human need. He stepped down in 2000 and was replaced by John Manley, who proclaimed that his first priority was to enhance Canada's privileged relationship with the United States. In September 2003, the government announced that seven new consulates would be opened in the U.S., and two consulates would be upgraded to consulate generals. Twenty honorary consuls would be appointed. Thus, representation in the U.S. grew from 15 to 22. Most new locations were in the Southeast, Southwest, and Midwest. This reflects the government's concern about the shift of American political and economic power to the "Sunbelt" away from the northern states adjacent to Canada.

Prime Minister Paul Martin promised the same thing on taking power in December 2003 and even created a cabinet committee with himself as chairman to explore ways to improve relations with Washington. The business lobby in Ottawa, as well as many other Canadian leaders, encouraged Martin to continue in this direction. Martin appointed a heavy hitter as ambassador to the U.S.: Frank McKenna, former premier of New Brunswick. Despite serious disagreements with the American government over issues like Iraq, there was unease about being estranged from the United States without the backing of a rising regional block like the European Union. If one adds to this an inadequacy of military power, fewer funds for foreign aid, and a declining share of America's imports, Canada was worried about its influence in the world.

Martin shifted the locus for making important decisions on the Canada–U.S. relationship from the Department of Foreign Affairs and International Trade to the Privy Council Office (PCO). Martin's proposal to create a new Department of International Trade, separate from the Department of Foreign Affairs, was rejected by parliament in 2005. The Harper government decided in 2006 to keep the two together, thereby emphasizing the importance of trade with the U.S. After the September 11 terrorist attacks, responsibility for the bilateral border was transferred to the PCO.

Martin ordered major policy reviews in both foreign affairs and defense. In April 2005 the results, entitled "Now is the time to rebuild," were unveiled. The government pledged to bolster its diplomatic corps, beef up the military, and overhaul foreign aid in an attempt to reverse Canada's diminishing influence in foreign affairs. The prime minister asserted: "You cannot have a robust foreign policy if all you're prepared to engage in is empty moralizing." Concrete proposals included raising military spending by C$10 billion over five years, increasing the size of the armed forces by 5,000 to 67,000, instituting a central command, strengthening the special operations forces, purchasing more equipment, such as helicopters and ships, and creating a new emergency response team capable of dealing with disasters anywhere.

After his reelection in 2004, President George W. Bush seized the opportunity to reach out to Canada and to improve the tone of the relationship. With only two weeks' notice, he accepted Martin's invitation to Canada. In his December 1, 2004, speech in Halifax, he thanked all those Canadians who "came out to wave—with all five fingers—for the hospitality." Bush expressed belated gratitude to those who had taken in stranded American passengers after the September 11 terrorist strikes in New York and Washington. Martin admitted that "it's not always easy to sleep next to the elephant," but he spoke a language Canadians like to hear: building multilateral institutions and making international cooperation a top priority. Bush and his Canadian counterpart displayed the warmest personal relationship at the top in over a decade.

Martin's successor as prime minister, Stephen Harper, publicly resisted any opposition efforts to paint him as a Canadian Bush, and he stuck up for Canadian interests whenever they were challenged, such

Canadian Soldiers in Afghanistan

Canada

as in the Arctic. Still, he vowed throughout his leadership of the Conservative Party to transform a bilateral relationship that had turned sour. Noting that Canada's access to the highest governmental circles in Washington had persistently eroded, he named as ambassador investment banker and former finance minister in the Mulroney government, Michael Wilson. The new ambassador promised a respectful but firm approach: "America is a neighbor. You don't throw snow on his driveway." When he left his post in the autumn of 2009, he noted that his best calling card in Washington was the fact that Canadian soldiers were fighting shoulder-to-shoulder with Americans in Afghanistan. "It was highly appreciated and highly admired." He was replaced by former Manitoba Premier Gary Doer.

Doer's American counterpart in Ottawa until 2013 also took office in 2009: David Jacobson, a Chicago-based corporate lawyer and top fund raiser for President Obama. Like most American ambassadors, Jacobson knew little about the country when he was appointed. But in order to understand this huge land, Jacobson embarked on an 8-week coast-to-coast road trip across Canada, avoiding airplanes and getting the feel of the terrain. Jacobson met all the premiers and as many Canadians as he could. H Jacobson successor, Chicago investment banker Bruce Heyman, made similar voyages.

Harper sent some positive signals to Washington: "Canada intends to be a player" and will advance "our shared values." He promised and delivered a large increase in defense spending, and he pledged to strengthen border and port security, renew NORAD, and continue his predecessor's policy of bolstering his country's efforts against the Taliban in Afghanistan. Harper embraced the American-led war on terrorism and asserted Israel's right to protect itself, daring to incur Turkey's ire by calling the killing of Armenians in the First World War a genocide, something his American counterpart, Barack Obama, did not dare do as president. Harper discusses human rights with the Chinese to little avail. In fact, China's leaders lambasted him for his "disgusting conduct" in meeting the Dalai Lama in October 2007. Nevertheless, a 2007 poll revealed that a quarter of Canadians consider China the most important country to their interests.

Harper had seldom traveled outside Canada before becoming prime minister but showed a wide-ranging interest in international affairs. He quickly acquired the confidence to handle foreign policy himself without depending on career diplomats and enjoyed not having no subordinate on foreign policy. At the same time, Harper re-energized relations with Washington. He has his public's support in this. A survey published at the time he entered office showed a slim majority (54%) of Canadians wanting a foreign policy that would bring Canada closer to the U.S. But pollster Michael Adams says this message comes with a warning: "The minute you look like you're kowtowing, as far as we're concerned, you're toast."

The Canadian government is acutely aware of the traditional ambivalence many of its people show toward too extensive cooperation with the U.S. Ex-Foreign Minister Manley noted: "There are two rules in Canadian politics. The first is: don't be too close to the United States. The second is: don't be too far from the United States." In the aftermath of the September 11 attacks, Canadians wanted their leaders to emphasize the second rule.

That was not the case in 2003 when the U.S. led a coalition to end Saddam Hussein's rule in Iraq. Emotions were high, and three-fourths of the Canadian public favored the government's decision to stay out of the war. The media do make a difference, though. Canadians who get most of their news from U.S. television were three times more likely to support the war effort in Iraq. In a 2004 poll, 66% of Canadians said their attitude toward the U.S. had worsened since 11 September; 76% said this was because of their dislike of President Bush. Only 16% of Canadians would have voted for him. Half saw the U.S. as arrogant, bullying or dangerous, and two-thirds thought America's global reputation had worsened over the past decade. Americans did not reciprocate these negative feelings: 74% said their opinion remained unchanged after four years, and 12% said they had improved

American diplomats in Canada revealed some mild irritation of Canadian attitudes in cables publicized by Wikileaks. One is the American perception that Canadians "always carry a chip on their shoulder," apparently because of their feeling that Canada "is condemned to always play 'Robin' to the U.S. 'Batman' " Another is "moral outrage, a Canadian specialty." One diplomat described "soul searching" in Canada about its "decline from 'middle power' status to that of an 'active observer' of global affairs, a trend which some Canadians believe should be reversed." The Americans marveled that "despite the overwhelming importance of the U.S. to Canada for its economy and security," candidates for parliament rarely mention anything about relations with the U.S. The U.S. is like the "900-pound gorilla": "overwhelming but too potentially menacing to acknowledge."

Thousands of Canadian fans booed the American national anthem before two Montreal Canadiens hockey games. Even a pee wee hockey team from Boston was booed and heckled. Such insensitive treatment of young Americans was so appalling to some Canadians that the team was invited back to Fredericton, NB, where it was treated with touching love and respect.

A stream of insults came from Canadian officials and MPs. The prime minister's communications director, Francine Ducros, called President Bush a "moron," a slip that cost Ducros her job. A Liberal MP was overheard to decry the "damn Americans, I hate those bastards"; Carolyn Parrish later apologized for that remark. However, a year later she lapsed into another anti-American tirade by stomping on a Bush doll during a nationally televised satire show. For this she was ousted from the Liberal parliamentary caucus. Another MP was reproached for declaring that the U.S. was leading "the coalition of the idiots" in Iraq. An NDP MP called Bush a "war criminal."

Some Canadians who actually met with President Bush had more complimentary memories of him. Bush was said always to have been well briefed. Former Liberal cabinet member, Anne McLellan, remembered that "he was a person easy to deal with. There is no artifice. He tells you exactly where he is coming from. There are not a lot of surprises—and there are benefits to that." No back-channels were needed to clarify statements or inferences.

Bush's commitment to NAFTA was never in doubt. By contrast, the Democratic Congress was more protectionist. During her campaign Democratic presidential candidate and later Secretary of State Hillary Clinton called NAFTA her husband's "mistake." Barack Obama sought electoral college votes by suggesting that it should be renegotiated. He dropped that pledge after his election, advocating only that the side agreements on labor and the environment should be brought into the main text of the treaty to ensure enforcement. As president he repeatedly emphasized his commitment to open trade between the two northern neighbors. President Donald Trump ordered the resumption of complicated NAFTA negotiations in 2017 and 2018.

President Bush was a more consequential president for Canada than were most of his predecessors. For instance, he created the Department of Homeland Security after September 11, 2001, spurring Canada to reorganize its own government by creating the equivalent Department of Public Safety. He rearranged North American defense by creating a Northern Command. This prompted Ottawa to create its own Canada Command.

Canadians hated Bush's infamous "axis of evil" term. Few were aware that it had been coined by David Frum, a Canadian

Canada

author and pundit who spent 13 months as a speech writer for the American president. Perhaps even fewer know that one of America's hardest-hitting neo-conservative columnists, Charles Krauthammer, also hailed from Canada, as does Tea Party Texas Senator Ted Cruz. The latter's parents worked in Alberta's oil patch before moving to Texas when he was a child.

In 2008, Americans elected a president whom many Canadians greeted as the near-perfect political leader: Barack Obama. They celebrated his inauguration on January 20, 2009, with an outpouring of enthusiasm not even shown to a Canadian prime minister for decades. Busloads of admirers made the nine-hour trip from Toronto and Ottawa to witness his swearing in, and some Canadian schools interrupted their classes to enable pupils to watch the ceremony. For the eight years of the Bush presidency, Canadians felt a kind of moral superiority to Americans, but that almost completely changed with his successor.

By February 19, 2009, when he made his first foreign trip as president, to Ottawa, Obama enjoyed an approval rating in Canada of 82%, higher than in the U.S. where it was 64% and much higher than that of Prime Minister Stephen Harper at 38% and then opposition leader Michael Ignatieff at 42%. Obama was more popular in Canada than Harper would ever be.

From the time he stepped off Air Force One in Ottawa, Obama commanded nonstop TV coverage during his six and a half hours in the country. Canadians clustered on overpasses and along the road to get a glimpse of him, and he greeted 2,500 of them who had gathered outside the Parliament in freezing weather. Obama's welcome by Canada's first black governor general, Michaëlle Jean, was a historic moment for both nations.

Obama's charm never faltered, and he revealed a special attachment to Canada: that he has a brother-in-law who is Canadian and that two of his key staff people are from Canada. "And I love this country and think that we could not have a better friend and ally." An opinion survey at the time revealed that 41% of Canadian respondents desired greater ties with U.S., while 45% thought Canada should maintain the same level of relations. Only 9% wanted the country to distance itself from its southern neighbor.

Within months, many Canadians expressed disappointment that the new American president appeared to be unresponsive to Canada's needs, soft on protectionism and supportive of legislation pending in Congress that could prevent Canadians from selling the oil gained from their western sands in the U.S., the destination for half of it. Obama eased some concerns when in August 2009 he approved a pipeline called the Alberta Clipper to carry 800,000 barrels of oil sands fuel a day to the U.S. Yet, that relief was slashed in 2015 when Obama rejected the much more important Keystone XL Pipeline that would bring Canadian crude all the way through the U.S. to the Gulf of Mexico. The Nebraska state government approved of a new route for the pipeline, and the State Department initially gave the green light, but died because of American environmental and domestic politics. In one of his first acts as president, Donald Trump lifted the ban that his successor, Joseph Biden reinstated on taking office in 2020.

Perhaps expectations had been too great. Magazine headlines began to read: "Canada's Biggest Problem: America" or "Barack Obama. Why He's Bad for Canada." In 2013, *Maclean's* characterized the two leaders' relationship as "growing mutual indifference and incomprehension." *Maclean's* reminded its readers that, though unpopular, "Bush was in fact a strong and committed supporter of many causes dear to our national interest, including trade, open borders and energy."

Donald Trump is unpopular in Canada. In 2019, a New Research Co. poll found that 17% of people think Trump's presidency was good for Canada, and 65% say it was bad or very bad. Conversely, another poll concluded that between 41% and 46% of Canadian conservatives would vote for Trump. An updated poll in 2020 from Maclean's showed that only 14% of Canadians would vote for Trump, while 86% support Biden.

In fact, on January 20, 2021, Joseph R. Biden, who had been elected on November 3, 2020, was sworn-in as 46th President of the United States. President Trump only visited Canada once, on June 8–9, 2018, for the G7 Leaders' Summit in La Malbaie, Quebec. President Biden waited over two years into his presidency before making his first visit, on March 23–24, 2023, for a bilateral visit to Ottawa, during which he addressed the Canadian Parliament.

As noted, President Donald J. Trump's imposition of 25% tariffs on various imports from Canada were met with strong resistance by Canada's leaders. Then Canadian Prime Minister Justin Trudeau announced that Canada would impose its own tariffs on goods from the United States. Also in early March, Trump rescinded what he promised would be even larger tariffs on Canadian steel and aluminum after Ontario Premier Doug Ford walked back a planned 25% surcharge on electricity exports to Michigan, Minnesota, and New York. And on March 23, 2025, new Prime Minister Mark Carney called for a snap election on April 28, 2025, explaining that in light of the tariffs, Canada is "facing the most significant crisis of our lifetimes." Tensions thus remain high as this book heads to press.

Response to September 11 Terrorist Attacks

Canada's prime minister on September 11, 2001, Jean Chrétien, said at the time: "You know, the world will never be the same again," and he was right. The terrorist attacks against the World Trade Center in New York City and the Pentagon in Washington, D.C., gave Americans and Canadians a shared sense of vulnerability. Their feeling of security between two wide oceans disappeared. Foreign Minister John Manley, who became deputy prime minister and was named to lead a powerful new cabinet committee on national security, stated: "The towers in Toronto are just as vulnerable. Canadians want to be safe, too." Not only did Manley show his solidarity with New Yorkers by signing up to run the New York marathon. He led his colleagues in assuming an unapologetic pro-American stance.

President George W. Bush's gaffe in failing to include Canada among 13 other countries he thanked in his September speech to Congress did not alter this. An embarrassed president later explained that the U.S. considers Canada a brother and saw no need to thank family. His ambassador to Ottawa, Paul Celucci, told the 100,000 Canadians who had gathered on Parliament Hill to honor the victims: "You are truly our closest friends." The 2002 annual *Maclean's*/CBC poll revealed that only a tenth of Canadians accept Bush's description of the relationship as "like family." The most frequent description (47%) was "friends but not particularly close"; 23% agreed with the formulation, "the best of friends"; 18% chose "cordial but distant," and only 1% described it as "openly hostile."

Canada's foreign policy shifted in the wake of the attacks from a primary preoccupation on trade and economics to fighting international terrorism. Prime Minister Chrétien vowed a few days after the attacks that Canada would "go every step of the way" with its American neighbors. His people seemed to agree: 84% of Canadians supported joining the U.S. fight against terrorism although only 23% wanted to see their troops directly involved in the fighting. A third favored closer ties with the U.S., compared with only 23% in March 2001. Manley captured the mood: "On the Hill when we had the memorial service, and people had their Canadian and American flags and tears running down their faces, you realized that when it comes to an event like that, forget the border. There is no border in the sharing of that experience."

Canada

Canada's assistance to its hard-pressed southern neighbor included a military contribution to the war effort in Afghanistan. It dispatched the largest fighting flotilla the country sent to sea since the Korean War to join American and British war vessels: three frigates, the HMCS Halifax, the HMCS Charlottetown and the HMCS Vancouver, a destroyer, HMCS Iroquois, one of its two supply ships, HMCS Preserver plus Sea King helicopters that staffed by more than 1,000 sailors. The air force sent three Hercules transport planes, one Airbus and two Aurora maritime patrol planes.

Canada dispatched 100 commandos from the secretive Joint Task Force 2. In 2004, President Bush awarded this elite commando unit a Presidential Unit Citation for "extraordinary heroism in action against the enemy" in rooting out Taliban fighters from caves in Afghanistan. It was the first time since the Korean War in the early 1950s that Canadian soldiers received this rare and prestigious recognition.

Canada's airmen also served on NATO Airborne Warning and Control System (AWACS) crews that patrolled the American east coast. This was the first time since the Revolutionary War that the U.S. needed protection by foreign troops on its soil. A Canadian pilot could scarcely believe what he was doing: "I never, ever imagined that we'd be here. This place in the world that we're now trying to defend has always been the biggest boy in town. It has always been the U.S. protecting everyone else."

Few Canadians or Americans knew at the time that in the minutes before the first hijacked airplane slammed into the World Trade Center, it was senior Canadian officers on duty at NORAD headquarters that morning who gave permission to U.S. Air Force base commanders on the east coast to intercept the aircraft in terrorists' hands.

The neighbors introduced important steps to shift the overall protection of their territory to North American "perimeter security." The Canadian public supported these cooperative measures as long as they did not challenge their country's sovereignty or capacity to act independently.

Both populations support efforts to stop terrorism. When asked in a 2005 poll, 74% of Canadians and 86% of Americans favored closer collaboration to deal with this threat. Canadians were reminded in 2013 that terror can be homegrown. Canadian citizens, under instructions from al-Qaeda, were involved in an attempt to derail a passenger train between Toronto and New York, an attack on a natural-gas plant in Algeria that left 68 dead, and a pressure-cooker bomb attack outside the BC legislature in Victoria, reminiscent of the Boston Marathon bombing. A horrid

reminder of the danger of home-grown terrorism occurred in October 2014, when a terrorist ran over two soldiers at a Quebec mall, killing one, and when another shot dead a guard outside of Parliament and terrorized thousands inside until he was killed. Both were Canadian-born converts to Islam who became radicalized jihadists. Both nations need a more integrated system of military and emergency responses in the event of a catastrophic attack or natural disaster, like Hurricane Katrina in 2005.

Canada was not interested in creating a jointly managed North American perimeter with a common approach to customs, trade, immigration, security and defense, and it worries about talk in the U.S. of registering all travelers entering and leaving the country, including Canadians. Still, Canada agreed in 2002 to allow U.S. troops to cross its border in the event of terrorist attacks or natural disasters, and Canadian troops have the same right to cross into the U.S. When that happens, U.S. forces would serve under Canadian command while in Canada, and Canadian soldiers would be commanded by Americans while on U.S. soil.

In 2002, the U.S. created a new Northern Command to defend North America and coordinate military relations with Canada and Mexico. A joint task force called the "Planning Group," based at NORAD's Colorado Springs headquarters, was created with Canada to work on contingency plans to defend North America. Canadian leadership discussed a new command structure to match this Northern Command. It calls for the integration of the army, navy and air force into six regional commands answering to a single Canada Command headed by an admiral. A new expeditionary force would be created to respond to calls to intervene in failed states, and counter-terrorist special forces would be strengthened.

The common border is not the way Canadian diplomat Hugh Keenleyside defined it in 1929: "It is physically invisible, geographically illogical, militarily indefensible, and emotionally inescapable." It is more guarded today. Nevertheless, this frontier still has only one Border Patrol agent for every 16 miles, compared with the border with Mexico, which has enough agents assigned for one every 1,100 feet.

There is more intelligence sharing. For the first time ever, the FBI provides the RCMP access to its digital fingerprint database; no other foreign police force is granted such information. American law enforcement officers can now gain access to criminal records in the Canadian Police Information Centre. The Canadians introduced more tamper-proof passports and check background references more carefully before issuing travel documents. The partners ended "asylum shopping." They created a common set of standards for asylum and a common list of countries whose citizens must obtain visas before entering either country. Would-be refugees must apply for asylum in the first country they enter and cannot reapply in the other if they are rejected. Those entering at unguarded crossing are exempt from this rule.

Ottawa moved swiftly to erase any impression south of the border that Canada was tolerant toward terrorism. Canada's intelligence agency identified more than 50 terrorist groups that operate and raise money in the country. The government allotted $4.2 billion to fight terror and steered a vigorous anti-terrorist act through both houses of parliament that makes it illegal "to harbor a terrorist" or to collect money to carry out terrorism. Police were granted authority to use electronic surveillance against terrorists and to arrest and detain suspected terrorists without warrants.

Former Justice Minister Anne McLellan answered the objections of civil liberties groups by arguing that "reasonable limits" on citizens' rights "are justified in a free and democratic society." In February 2007, Parliament voted 159 to 124 to allow two anti-terrorism measures to lapse since they had never been used. A week later the Supreme Court of Canada gave Parliament a year to fix a law allowing foreign terrorist suspects to be detained indefinitely without trial while awaiting deportation.

Canada acted energetically in detaining immigrants suspected of involvement in terrorism. In August 2003, it arrested 19

Canada

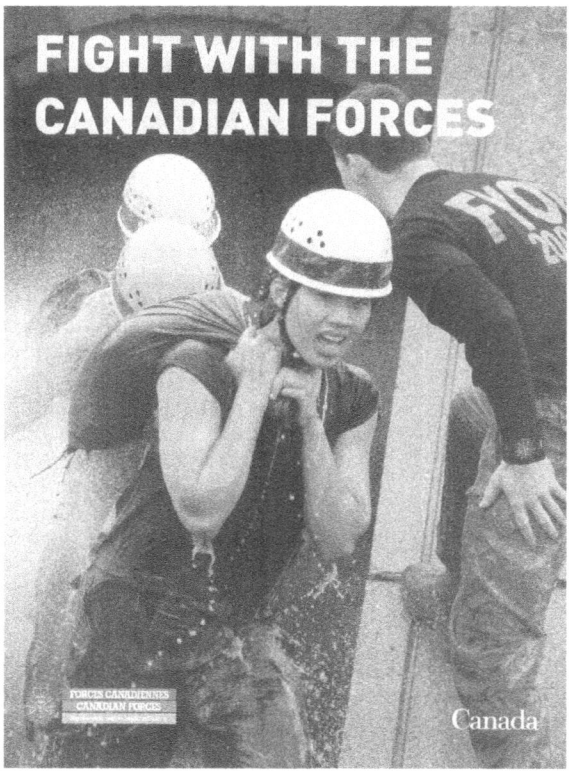

men who could have links with al Qaeda. Its spy agency, the Canadian Security Intelligence Service (CSIS), conducts only domestic security operations, relying on "liaison officers" to gather foreign intelligence from friendly governments. The CSIA does no spying overseas. The CSIS handed over to the U.S. an alleged al Qaeda operative accused in a plot to blow up the American and Israeli embassies in Singapore. These actions keep alive the debate about how the fight against terrorism can be made compatible with the Canadian ideals of tolerance, inclusion and the belief that immigrants should have the same rights as Canadian citizens. Prime Minister Harper underscored Canada's vigilance on terrorism during President Obama's first visit in February 2009: "I just want to make this clear to our American friends. The view of this government is unequivocal: threats to the United States are threats to Canada."

That terrorism is no idle threat to Canada was dramatically demonstrated in June 2006. Working closely together, the RCMP and CSIS uncovered a deadly plot by 18 homegrown Muslim terrorists in the Toronto area to launch a wave of truck-bomb attacks against the Toronto Stock Exchange, the Toronto office of CSIS, an undisclosed military base, and Parliament in Ottawa. The plotters intended to capture politicians and beheading the prime minister if he refused to order the withdrawal of Canadian troops from Afghanistan. Those charged came from a variety of Muslim countries, especially South Asia. Most were born in Canada, and the oldest plotter was an imam who reportedly spewed hatred of Canada in his sermons.

The operation began with police monitoring of internet chat rooms. Soon, 400 intelligence and law-enforcement officers were involved in Canada's largest counterterrorist operation since the often-reviled Anti-Terrorism Act was adopted after the September 11, 2001, attacks. The powers the act granted to the police were crucial in foiling the plot. The RCMP paid two civilian informants $4.4 million to help execute the successful sting operation. One, who received $300,000, was a young, charismatic Muslim with a taste for cocaine. The other, a Muslim businessman, was paid $4.1 million and is in the witness protection program.

Canadian authorities moved in when the group acquired three tons of ammonium nitrate fertilizer, one-third of the amount used in the 1995 Oklahoma City bombing. A Toronto mosque was burned in a backlash. But the roughly 2% of Canada's population that is Muslim, half of whom were born in the country, could be relieved that such a tolerant country did not blame them for the ghastly project of a small minority.

In 2008, charges were dropped against seven of the defendants. The evidence seemed to show that the group was more like a youth gang that loved inflammatory chatter. Even so, the plotters knew little about the means and methods of pulling off an effective attack. Some Canadians had begun to wonder if this entire incredible conspiracy had been fact or fiction. Subsequent testimony and convictions eliminated any doubts that it had been real and dangerous. In September 2008, a young man who had been only 17 years old at the time of his arrest was found guilty of knowingly participating in a plot to behead the prime minister. He was the first to be found guilty of terrorism since the anti-terrorist laws had been enacted in 2001.

In 2009, four more were tried for conspiring to ignite three explosions in southern Ontario. Three of them pleaded guilty, including the 24-year old ringleader of the group, Zakaria Amara. His testimony revealed shocking incompetence. He underestimated the Canadian police, grossly exaggerated his chances for success, and placed faith in the wrong people, including two RCMP informants supported by numerous wiretaps. At his sentencing hearing in January 2010, Amara apologized to Canadians and especially his fellow Muslims for his "naïve and gullible" interpretation of Islam. He faced a life sentence since Canada has no capital punishment.

There have been other warnings about the political radicalization of some young Canadians. Two friends from a Canadian high school were killed while participating in a terrorist attack on an Algerian gas plant in January 2013.

Omar Khadr, who had been born in Toronto, was incarcerated at Guantánamo Bay, Cuba, at age 16 for killing an American soldier in Afghanistan. In September 2012, he was transferred to a Canadian maximum security prison.

In 2017, the Canadian government gave Khadr an apology and Can$10.5 million in damages. This was done quietly without the knowledge of the widow of Sgt. 1st Class Chris Speer, a US special forces medic who died in July 2002, 12 days after shrapnel hit him in the head during a raid on an Afghan compound in which Khadr was with a terrorist cell. Sgt. Speer's widow Tabitha Speer sued Khadr and received a 134 million-dollar US judgment against him. Although she has been unsuccessful to date in recovering against Khadr, many Canadians who are outraged at either the payment to Khadr or the fact that it is not subject to the claim by Ms. Speer, have joined together to provide financial assistance to Ms. Speer's family.

The Canadian intelligence service's web site asserted that "with the exception of the United States, there are more terrorist groups active in Canada today than in any other country in the world." That judgment was confirmed by documents found at Osama bin Laden's Pakistani compound specifically naming Canada as a worthy target for terrorism.

Canada

DEFENSE

Both the U.S. and Canada are blessed with oceans that insulated them from European and Asian conflicts and with a border between themselves that has not had to be defended for more than a century and a half. Therefore, military concerns were never paramount in either country until well into the 20th century. Yet, two world wars forced very different roles on them. With Europe in shambles and near poverty, and with the emergence of the Soviet Union as a dominant force in Europe and Asia, the United States was compelled to play a role as financial, military and political leader of the free world. This role brought increased military responsibility to the United States, and security concerns became very important in America's body politic.

Canada's military role remained minor, compared to that of the U.S.. Therefore, security issues have been much less important in Canadian politics. This low salience was reflected in Canada's low defense budgets, amounting to a mere 1% of GDP, the lowest in the Atlantic Alliance except Iceland and Luxembourg and lower than those of his liberal predecessors. The Harper government promised and produced in 2006 a hefty increase in defense spending that included US$13 billion in equipment purchases. By the May 2011 election, he raised defense spending by 27%, falling back to 1.5% annually after the election. His countrymen have supported this unprecedented increase, which was intended to "revive Canada's leadership in the world."

As in political and economic affairs, Canada is linked with and dependent on the United States in defense. Its close cooperation was first formalized in the Ogdensburg Agreement of 1940, before the U.S. had entered World War II. The Canadian government realized that Britain might be conquered and would therefore be unable to defend Canada. The American government was concerned that the approaches to the North American continent might not be secure if Britain were indeed defeated. Therefore, Prime Minister King met with President Roosevelt to sign a permanent defense agreement. As with all good and lasting treaties, this one was firmly based on mutual interest. A year later at Hyde Park, FDR's New York estate, they agreed to pool their military production. The two countries' wartime cooperation was excellent.

Both nations sacrificed thousands of lives in the bitter global struggle but were spared the destruction of their own homelands and emerged from the war intact and richer than before. Both Canada and the U.S. were among the very few countries in the world that could positively contribute to the reconstruction of war-torn Europe. Both shared the view that the Soviet Union posed a threat to the democracies of Western Europe. Canada agreed that its own security was linked to that of Western Europe. Additionally, Canada wanted to forge military ties with Western Europe in order to counterbalance its necessarily tight defense links with the U.S. Canadian leaders were the first to make public statements about the need for a postwar Atlantic Alliance, and Canada became a founding member of NATO.

Cheyenne Mountain, Colorado. Canadian and American soldiers at NORAD. NOTE: This operation was moved to nearby Peterson Air Force Base in 2006.

It is characteristic of the Canadian understanding of the world that its diplomats insisted on the inclusion of article II of the treaty, which underscored their conviction that the Atlantic Alliance had to be more than a military alliance. This became known as "the Canadian article" and called for a pledge by members to strengthen free institutions and to encourage economic cooperation.

Canada never provided the personnel and equipment to which it had committed itself at NATO's birth. In 1969, the Trudeau government reduced its troop strength in Europe from 10,000 to 5,000, a decision that angered Western European allies, especially Germany. The fact is that Pierre Trudeau, who was despised by many soldiers, spent more on defense than any other prime minister since. His federal budget allotted 13.3% to the Department of National Defence (DND), compared with 8.7% under Harper until 2011. The Mulroney government raised the Canadian contingent in Europe to 7,800 troops.

The end of the Cold War prompted Canada to announce in 1992 the withdrawal of all its troops and airmen from Europe and the closure of its bases in Lahr and Baden-Soellingen. This was completed in 1994. Canada hosted German air force units that trained in Goose Bay, Newfoundland, and army artillery and armor units outside of Winnipeg. The Germans announced in 2004 that they were moving out of Goose Bay.

At home Canada maintains three land combat groups along with two squadrons of aircraft that could be flown quickly with aerial refueling to Europe for close support of NATO forces. Part of Canada's naval forces is also occupied in protecting the North Atlantic approaches. Canada regards NATO as a key part of its defense policy and earmarks 10,000 combat troops for NATO service. Ottawa confirmed at NATO's Prague Summit in 2002 that it would take part in the alliance's new 21,000-strong rapid-response force deployable to all parts of the globe to combat terrorism and contain outlaw regimes.

In 2006, a Canadian general, Ray Henault, occupied the key post of chairman of NATO's military committee; this was the highest NATO post ever held by a Canadian. In April 2009, then Defense Minister Peter MacKay was on the short list to become secretary-general of NATO. Although he lost out to Danish Prime Minister Anders Fogh Rasmussen, MacKay's near success demonstrated that a Canadian could one day occupy NATO's highest political office. This is particularly true since the Conservatives took power in 2006.

The Harper government intended to make Canada a responsible military partner, and Canada's participation in Afghanistan and Libya provide convincing

Canada

Canada's French Military College
Retrieved from: https://commons.wikimedia.org/wiki/File:Flag_of_the_Royal_Military_College_of_Canada.svg

evidence. He was aware of the criticism he gets from some Canadians who prefer to see their country as primarily a peacekeeping country. He responded: "When you're in a dangerous world and countries are from time to time called on to do things to deal with these dangers, if you don't have the capacity to act you are not taken seriously. Nobody takes your views seriously unless you can contribute to solutions . . . including military capabilities."

In an effort to raise the morale of Canadian soldiers and to reconnect with the country's rich military heritage, the Conservative government reintroduced the word "royal," which had been dropped in 1968 when the three branches of the services were unified, and all soldiers wore the same uniform. The Maritime and Air Commands are once again called the Royal Canadian Navy and Royal Canadian Air Force. The Land Force is again the Canadian Army.

As of 2019, Canada's navy consists of about 8,500 sailors and 5,100 primary reservists supported by 5,300 civilians. In 2007, Commodore Jennifer Bennett, who headed an Ontario private school, was given command of the country's 24 naval reserve divisions, a position her father held when she first joined the naval reserves 33 years earlier. She was the first woman to lead a Canadian naval formation

Canada's Pacific fleet is based at CFB Esquimalt on Vancouver Island with a larger fleet is stationed at CFB Halifax. Among its resources, the navy has 12 modern frigates, four submarines, seven support ships, 14 patrol and coastal combatants, and one diving support vessel. With 63 ships in 2019, the Canadian navy is proportionate to the British fleet of 74 commissioned ships and the U.S. navy's 282 combat vessels. Canada has no anti-mine or year-round icebreaking capability and is widely considered to be incapable of adequately protecting its huge coastline.

The Canadian navy has four patrol submarines, two on each coast. In October 2004, after three years of refitting and maddening cost overruns, one of the subs, the HMCS *Chicoutimi*, caught on fire during her maiden voyage, and the first Canadian seaman in 49 years died of smoke inhalation. All four subs were promptly docked until the cause of the tragedy could be determined. The inquiry cast no blame, but part of the subsequent $10–$15 million in repairs was devoted to making the electrical cables much more waterproof. Critics were quick to react, claiming that Canada had bought the outdated subs mainly to engage in cat and mouse training exercises with American nuclear submarines in the North Atlantic. Why, they asked, was $750 million (mainly in trade for the use of Canadian airspace to train British pilots) squandered when Canada could not afford to field armed forces capable of defending the country?

Canada had no reliable naval helicopters or submarine surveillance planes. By 2014, 14 of its Sea King helicopters had self-destructed, killing a dozen crew members. One crashed in 2003 while trying to take off from the deck of the HMCS Iroquois, a destroyer that was heading for the Persian Gulf. The navy could not find a replacement, so the ship had to leave without it.

In 2004, the government selected an American-led consortium, with Canadian participation, to build 28 new Sikorsky H92 Superhawk maritime helicopters for a price tag of Can$3.2 billion (US$2.4 billion). They can fly from the navy's frigates and used for anti-submarine, patrol, rescue and transport tasks. Delays stretched out for years. In 2013 the government threatened to scrap the deal and shop around for an alternative to the Sikorsky. All forces will benefit from the purchase in 2009 of 15 Chinook heavy-lift helicopters built by Boeing and originally scheduled for delivery in 2013. Canada had already received six used Chinooks from the Americans for use in Afghanistan. In 2015, new Cyclone helicopters began to arrive.

In 2011, the government announced a $35-billion investment in new warships and support vessels over the next three decades. Because many of Canada's existing ships are over 40 years old, keeping them operational is very expensive. Promised ships to patrol the Arctic are years behind schedule.

The land and air forces have been slightly better off. In 2019, Canada had more than 60,000 men and women in its army and air force. Canada's army consists of about 23,000 men ans women plus 17,000 reservists. The air force consists of about 14,500 personnel on active duty, backed up by about 2,600 reservists and 2,500 civilians in support of 258 manned aircraft. Women can serve in all combat roles, including submarines. Between 2001 and 2011, 310 women filled combat roles in Afghanistan, and artillery Captain Nichola Goddard became the first female Canadian soldier to die in combat. In 2016, the first woman (Christine Whitecross) was promoted to three-star general, and Jennie Carigman was the first general to emerge from the combat arms.

There are more Canadians trying to get into the all-volunteer military than there are open slots. The result is that the military personnel are carefully selected and well trained. The main problem is in retaining experienced soldiers, not attracting raw recruits. In 2002, the Canadian Forces raised the mandatory retirement age from 55 to 60 in order to head off a manpower shortfall. Canadians fly the aging CF-18 fighter.

In October 2014, Canada began a deployment to Iraq, not Syria, to support the U.S.-led effort to defeat the brutal Islamic State. The mission involved six CF-18 fighters, 600 support personnel, two refueling planes, two surveillance aircraft, and 69 Special Forces to train Kurdish troops. The Liberals and NDP opposed this involvement although 57% of Canadians approved. Nevertheless, newly elected Prime Minister Justin Trudeau kept his campaign promise and ordered the fighter aircraft home because he wished to refocus Canada's military role to peacekeeping and humanitarian operations.

Canada

The Harper government purchased 65 F-35 Joint Strike stealth jet fighters from Lockheed Martin and spend hundreds of millions of dollars helping to develop this plane. There was criticism about the sophistication of the plane and the increasing cost and wisdom of purchasing a one-engine plane for use in the remote Arctic region. The future use of surveillance drones to watch the entire Canadian Arctic also erodes the rational for the F-35. With a price tag of $45 billion over 42 years—much more than the government had promised—it would be the largest military purchase in Canada's history. In 2012, the government stopped funding the project and began to review alternatives to the F-35. A stopgap 18 F-18s will be purchased while the government decides on a permanent solution. In 2019, Canada bid for a F-18 Super Hornet, which will replace its fleet of CF18s, according to *Defense News*.

To save money, the air force had to retire an entire fleet of electronic warfare aircraft. When it decided to send peacekeeping forces to East Timor in Indonesia in 1999, the Canadian government had difficulty transporting them there because it had so little transport capacity that it was compelled to use its only supply ship to service its entire Pacific fleet. The first of its aging transport planes was forced to turn back to base three times because of malfunctions with its compass and tail rudder. Another 34-year-old C-130 Hercules aircraft managed to make the trip, but only by flying below 10,000 feet because of a faulty cabin-pressurization system. Canada subsequently ordered three large C-17 transport aircraft.

Canada is caught between the conflicting realities of declining defense budgets and increasing military conflict around the world. This was apparent in August 2000 when armed Canadian commandos in a dramatic high-seas seizure had to be dropped from a Sea King helicopter onto the deck of a private American freighter to take control of the ship that was transporting 590 military vehicles and 440 containers of small arms, ammunition, communications and surveillance equipment being shipped back on contract from Kosovo. The shipping company had refused to unload it in Canada until a private debt was settled. The capture was flawless, but the embarrassing thing was that the cargo amounted to about 10% of the Canadian army's entire supply of such equipment. A Canadian defense expert, David Rudd, remarked: "There is a definite mismatch between Canada's desire to remain a player on the world stage and the ability of the armed forces to carry it out. They are over-stretched everywhere."

The air force is acquiring new search and rescue helicopters. To hone their capabilities in the Arctic, Canada hosted joint exercises with American and Russian soldiers in 1995. It was the first time in 50 years that Russians trained on Canadian soil. NORAD had a joint exercise with Russia in 2010.

In 1993, the Canadian government created a secret counter-terrorist force called Joint Task Force 2 (JTF2). Well-trained and well-equipped with the latest high-tech weaponry, this commando unit, numbering 1,500 in 2010, is considered to be on a par with the best of Britain's and America's special forces. The JTF2 is especially trained for operations in extreme winter conditions, and in 2001 it was tapped for clandestine service in the Afghan war. The JTF2, which fights effectively alongside U.S. and other allied special operations forces, was granted a prestigious U.S. Presidential unit citation by the U.S. president. The former commander of U.S. Central Command, Gen. Tommy Franks, praised the Canadian soldiers: "They've done an absolutely wonderful job." "We are in their debt. We recognize our friends."

Canada's land forces are good. Because the White Paper designates peacekeeping as the Canadian Forces' main job in an unstable world, Canada acquired additional armored personnel carriers and other equipment needed for that commitment. It purchased 66 soft-armor Strykers, an 8-wheel troop carrier that is lighter and more mobile than tanks.

Public outrage over the murder of a Somali teenager and shockingly crude hazing rituals led to the disbanding in 1995 of the Canadian Airborne Regiment. It was replaced by three separate parachute companies, each serving as the nucleus for a new light infantry battalion. Canada is strained to maintain adequate units for peacekeeping. In 2017, there were only 112 soldiers on peacekeeping assignments.

In order to reduce costs, headquarters staffs were slashed by 50% and the top officer corps by 25%. The civilian workforce was trimmed from 33,000 to 20,000. The three services consolidated their headquarters in Ottawa. In 1999, the defense department endorsed a plan to sell off as much as 10% of its property and buildings to raise funds for equipment.

Sovereignty over the Arctic is enforced by 60 soldiers stationed in Yellowknife, backed by a 100-soldier reserve unit. They are supported by four ageing Twin Otter bush aircraft. The main ground force is 1,600 Canadian Rangers, 80% of whom are Inuit. They are a reserve force based in 165 remote communities composed largely of Inuit and Indians, including women who, transported by snowmobiles, provided by the Rangers themselves, and armed with pre-First World War Lee Enfield rifles and a toll-free 800 number to report any trouble, perform surveillance duty in the Arctic. Their mission is to fly the Canadian flag and assert sovereignty over remote Arctic areas and are the only arm of the military that uses its own transporta-

Helping earthquake victims in Kashmir

Source: *Maclean's*

Canada

Prime Minister Harper visits troops in Afghanistan

tion equipment, such as fishing boats and motorized canoes. The unit, which is organized in over 50 patrols in communities across the North, each limited to 30 members, is widely admired as demonstrated by the fact that there are waiting lists of Inuit hoping to join.

It is no surprise that Canada depends on its alliance with the United States. It is engaged in many forms of military cooperation. The two countries' security relationship is coordinated by the Permanent Joint Board on Defense. There is the Defense Production Sharing Agreement, which exempts Canada from duties and "Buy American" policies. By 2007, Canada had a $7 billion defense industry. Half of it came from sales to the U.S. military and 80% to all NATO allies. Much of the rest came from over 70 countries. In 2005, it was the world's ninth-largest seller of military weapons.

There is also cooperation in anti-submarine warfare (ASW). Since Canada is economically dependent on trading, it is crucial that the seas surrounding it be safe in times of crisis. It does have some ASW destroyers and some long-distance coastal aircraft, but it needs American air cover and nuclear attack submarines to deal with an enemy submarine threat, especially in the Arctic Ocean.

Perhaps the closest form of military collaboration is in the North American Aerospace Command (NORAD), created in 1957 and renewed again for five years in 2006, with a new emphasis on global surveillance from space. NORAD has a joint staff of American and Canadian officers. The only thing that distinguishes the Americans from the Canadians there is the patch on their sleeves. They formerly worked in a well-protected headquarters dug into Cheyenne Mountain in Colorado. But NORAD announced in 2006 the transfer of its surveillance operations to an office building a dozen miles away at Peterson Air Force Base. The mountain facility, composed of 15 underground buildings centered on the war room, is kept on "warm standby," meaning that it could be reopened within hours in case of emergency.

NORAD was a response to the threat posed in the 1950s and 1960s that Soviet bombers could fly across Canadian territory and into the North American heartland. In order to meet this threat, two lines of radar installations were stretched across Canada. The outermost line was called the Distant Early Warning Line (DEW), consisting of 31 radar stations scanning the Arctic region. The second, closer to the U.S. border, was the Pine Tree Line, consisting of 24 stations. Canada supplemented these radar lines with three all-weather fighter squadrons, which fly American F-18 aircraft, a training squadron, an electronic warfare squadron and space sensor units.

By the 1980s, these radar lines were obsolete. Low flying airplanes and cruise missiles could fly past them undetected. Also, the increasing importance of land- and submarine-based missiles (ICBM and SLBM), as opposed to manned bombers, made these radar defenses even less suited to present defense needs. The transition to missiles also made parts of NORAD's defense system, composed of interceptor aircraft and defensive missiles, obsolete. The collapse of the Soviet threat completed the process of obsolescence. The manned DEW stations were converted to unmanned ones.

Nuclear Weapons

The problems of creating a defense against potential air strikes from the Soviet Union were linked with a ticklish issue in Canada: the use of nuclear weapons. From the very beginning, Canadians and their governments have been uneasy about any Canadian role involving atomic weapons. They assumed a commitment in the 1950s to arm their forces ear-marked for NORAD with such weapons for one major reason: in terms of destructive power, nuclear weapons are less expensive than conventional arms. Canadians hosted five kinds of U.S. nuclear weapons from 1950 to 1984: Mark IV air-dropped atomic bombs deployed for use by the Strategic Air Command bombers at Goose Bay; Bomarc surface-to-air missiles; Genie air-launched missiles on CF-101 VanDoo fighters; Falcon air-to-air missiles; and anti-submarine nuclear depth bombs at Argentia Bay, Newfoundland.

The Canadian government under John Diefenbaker stalled Canadian acceptance of nuclear weapons to be used with the military equipment it had purchased. He also hesitated to put NORAD forces, which still lacked nuclear warheads, on alert during the 1962 Cuban Missile Crisis, thereby greatly exacerbating his already strained relationship with President John F. Kennedy.

The leader of the opposition Liberal Party, Lester Pearson, put the issue squarely to the people by promising an end to Diefenbaker's wavering policy by "discharging the commitments [which Canada] has already accepted. . . It can only do this by accepting nuclear warheads for those defensive tactical weapons which cannot effectively be used without them but which we have agreed to use." By the skillful use of press releases that showed that the Canadian prime minister was not being entirely honest with his own people, Kennedy helped bring about Diefenbaker's defeat in the April 1963 election. The vote was, in part, an expression of Canadians' desire to honor their defense commitments and military cooperation with the United States. At the same time, the entire debate was an early reminder of how unenthusiastic and ambiguous Canadians have been concerning their country's part in a defense based on atomic arms.

In 1984, the Canadians deactivated their last nuclear warheads, replacing them with conventional ones. Canada still was linked

Canada

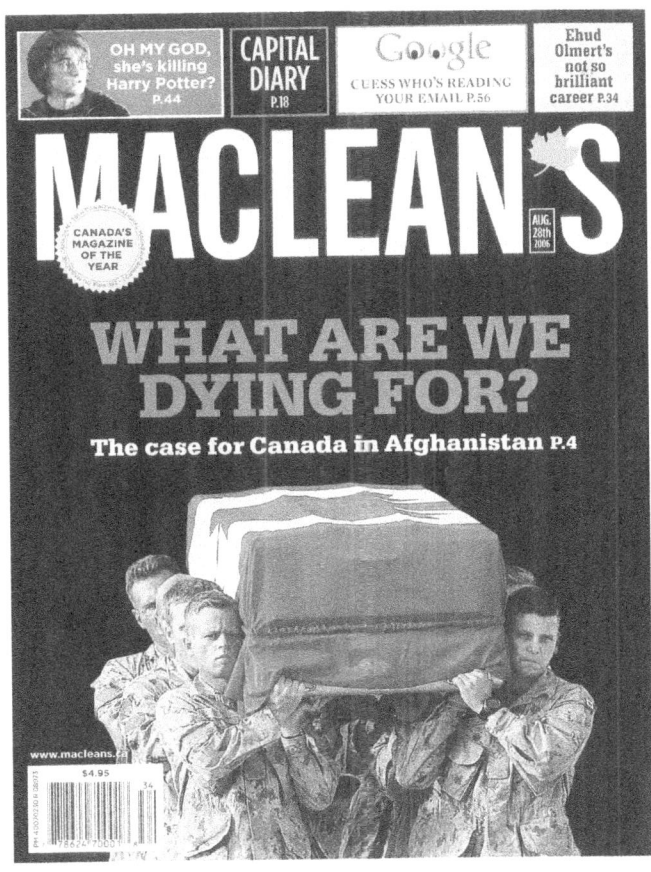

with nuclear deterrence, though. Ottawa permitted experiments with a wide variety of nuclear-related weapons systems on Canadian territory, so long as they did not actually carry nuclear warheads. The most controversial result was that Americans were permitted to test unarmed cruise missiles over Canada. Germany officials actually proposed such testing to their Canadian counterparts as a token gesture in support of the 1979 twin-track decision involving the deployment of medium-range nuclear missiles in Western Europe. Trudeau had committed himself in public to disarmament but accepted NATO's request because he was aware that Canada relied on nuclear deterrence for its defense and therefore had to accept some obligations because of that reliance.

These tests unleashed a loud debate and demonstrations throughout the country. A diverse "peace movement" began to gel. In 1994, the Canadian government grudgingly approved the continuation of U.S. cruise missile tests over Western Canada, but the U.S. announced that such tests are no longer needed. Canada still permits some forms of U.S. testing. In December 1999, it permitted the U.S. Air Force to test an unmanned aerial vehicle (UAV) called Global Hawk, which is used for intelligence purposes.

Remarks by former U.S Secretary of Defense Caspar Weinberger on Canadian television during the Quebec summit meeting in 1985 to the effect that American nuclear weapons could possibly be sent to Canada during a crisis brought down a thunder of protest and prompted an official denial that there were any such plans. A similar outcry erupted over the question of whether Canada should participate in the Strategic Defense Initiative (SDI—dubbed "Star Wars"). Such participation promised hefty contracts to Canadian industries, but the fear that it could unleash a new round of arms competition made it a "hot potato." In 1985, Mulroney announced his government's decision not to participate in SDI, but to permit private Canadians to accept contracts for SDI-related research.

Former Defense Minister Art Eggleton sought in 2000 to lay the groundwork for some kind of limited Canadian participation. He argued that it fits within NORAD and that failure to take part would deprive Canada of important space research and harm Canada's defense relationship with the U.S. While Canada was prepared to assume a certain role as a partner in nuclear deterrence, its leaders stressed that Canada is a nuclear-free country. It was adamantly opposed by the NDP, whose support Martin's minority government needed on certain issues.

In 2004, the Martin government quietly agreed that the joint U.S.–Canada NORAD operations center in Colorado Springs could share incoming missile information with NORTHCOM, the American command that will control the 40 interceptor rockets planned for Alaska, California and at sea. Therefore, technically the Canadians are already in although the Americans do not ask them for land or money for the system. In 2005, Ottawa announced that Canada would not take part in the planned North American ballistic-missile defense system. This decision could be reversed in the future.

There are not many influential voices in Canada calling for withdrawal from NATO or NORAD. These alliances are supported by a solid majority of Canadians. Besides, there has always been an uncomfortable awareness that if Canada did not contribute to its own defense, the United States might defend Canada in its own way in time of crisis. Some have called this possibility an "involuntary American guarantee."

It is doubtful that any enemy would ever consider Canada and the U.S. as totally separate entities, one neutral and one belligerent, in time of war. The two countries are linked so closely economically that no enemy could attack the United States without also affecting Canada's vital interests. Also, Canada's location is so strategically important to the U.S. that no country could attack it without the a response from the U.S. Insofar as this is the case, Canadian governments have always considered it better to cooperate in North American defense arrangements in order to be able to influence or shape that defense. Such a calculation has been gruesomely called, "no incineration without representation." One of Canada's most distinguished diplomats, J. H. Taylor, noted that though many Canadians find it hard to accept, they are "one of the most secure countries in the world . . . defended by the United States in the act of defending itself, whether we choose to defend ourselves or not."

Defense Efforts

Responding to concern over sovereignty in the 1980s, the Mulroney government established a northern training center and five new fighter bases in the high Arctic. Canadians traditionally saw the primary threat to their *security* coming from the Soviet Union and its allies and the primary threat to their *sovereignty* coming from the United States. Both of these threats intersected in the Arctic. No longer is it true, as a Canadian officer said in the 1940s,

Canada

"there's nowhere to go and nothing to do once you get there." It remains an unlikely theater for ground operations, but long-range aircraft and nuclear submarines posed major problems.

Located between both superpowers, the Arctic was the only ocean from which American nuclear subs could hit targets anywhere in the Soviet Union. The USSR was no less committed to the Arctic: half of its nuclear attack and missile-launching subs were deployed there. Soviet subs could trespass in Canadian waters to launch cruise missiles, to lay mines which could block sea access and exits from Canada, to ambush American submarines which might be moving through them, with or without Canada's consent or to pass to the North Atlantic, over which Canadian reinforcements would travel in case of war in Europe.

The frightening thing for Canada is that it does not have a single ship capable of operating in the Arctic outside the summer months. Canada has neither all-season icebreakers nor minesweepers and lacks submarines capable of operating under the ice for more than a few days, even though a third of its territorial waters are covered by ice most of the year. Finally, Canada has no independent way of even knowing what is going on in the Arctic.

In 1989, the government announced budget cuts that canceled orders for more CF-18 aircraft, a new generation of frontline tanks to replace the aging Leopards, and the promised "Polar 8" icebreaker and fleet of nuclear-powered submarines capable of under-ice warfare. This stunning move led some critics to question the government's commitment to Arctic sovereignty. An exasperated Peter Newman wrote in *Maclean's*: "To have Arctic sovereignty protected by the only country [the U.S.] that challenges it means we have become squatters on our own land."

In 1991, Canada faced a dilemma about how to respond to Iraq's invasion of Kuwait. It was torn by conflicting traditions of participation in the Western alliance and of peacekeeping, and polls indicated that Canadians were unsure what to do. The Mulroney government decided that it had to support its allies militarily while assuring Canadians that its participation had not compromised its ability to be a peacekeeper. President George H. W. Bush declared: "The American people knew from Day 1 where Canada stood. We are very, very grateful for that."

Canada sent its crack CF-18 Desert Cats fighter squadron to Bahrain; its 24 planes, refueled by a Canadian tanker based in Qatar, flew 2,700 combat missions. Canada also sent three ships to the Persian Gulf outfitted with weaponry cannibalized from half-completed replacement frigates. In all, 2,200 military personnel participated in the campaign, and for the first time in Canadian history, there was not a single casualty. Canada's Gulf operations captured the attention and admiration of a people normally indifferent to defense. As soon as the hostilities ended, the government dispatched hundreds of troops to the Iraq-Kuwait border as part of a UN peacekeeping mission.

In 1997, Canada won praise at home when it deployed 8,600 troops, three times the combined strength of its UN peacekeepers in Bosnia, Haiti, and the Golan Heights, to try to stop the flooding Red River in Manitoba, which drove 25,000 Canadians from their homes. This was the country's largest single military endeavor since the Korean War. The military's image, tarnished by a series of embarrassments, was reversed by the sight of skilled helicopter pilots plucking desperate countrymen from their rooftops and of mud-caked troops standing in knee-deep water while tossing sandbags.

In 1998, the government mobilized 11,000 troops to help communities across eastern Ontario and southern Quebec, including Ottawa and Montreal, deal with a devastating ice storm and power blackout, called the "Ice Siege of '98." Ex-Defense Minister Eggleton said: "This is by far the biggest deployment in our history to deal with a disaster in Canada."

In 1992, the armed forces lifted the ban against homosexuals in the armed forces, following a court ruling that exclusion violated the Charter of Rights and Freedoms. While there is still a diminishing stigma attached to being gay in the forces, there was little resistance to the new rules. In fact, Pentagon officials had extensive consultations with their Canadian counterparts to discuss the relative success of this transition. Gay partners of Canadian soldiers receive spousal benefits with the first gay marriage at a Canadian Forces base taking place in 2005. In 2008, a Canadian Forces set up a recruiting booth at Toronto's gay pride festival.

By 2017, Canada was spending only 1.29% of its GDP on defense, half the average figure for its NATO partners. Most shocking to many communities was the outright closure of 30 military bases in Canada. The government did not have to take the blame for the 1994 American closure of its naval base in Argenta, Newfoundland, where unemployment was already 20%. A crucial installation during the Second World War, when 20,000 Americans were stationed there; it, too, fell victim to defense cuts following the end of the Cold War. This closing brought to public attention conflicting visions of what the government owes civilian employees, who have claim to much higher severance pay than in the U.S. Insofar as the employer of the 265 newly unemployed Newfoundlanders was the U.S. government, they grudgingly had to accept a far smaller good-bye package than their Canadian counterparts elsewhere.

Canadians suddenly developed a renewed interest in military matters after the September 11, 2001, terrorist attacks in New York and Washington. In the 2002 and 2003 *Maclean's*/CBC polls, two out of three Canadians agreed that "we must substantially increase the amount of money we spend on the Armed Forces" although 57% believed that the main purpose of the military should continue to be peacekeeping. Eggleton argued: "The world is changing, and Canada must adapt its armed forces to the evolving military and security environment." Yet, a 2001 defense study by the Canadian Conference of Defence Associations concluded: "The Canadian Forces currently inhabit the worst of two worlds: conventional military capabilities are in decline; and new capabilities are unaffordable." Prime Minister Harper fulfilled his campaign pledge to raise military spending, with transport helicopters and planes as priority items.

Two military academies were closed: the Collège Militaire Royal (CMR) in St-Jean, Quebec, and the Royal Roads Military College in Victoria, BC, leaving only one military university, the bilingual Royal Military College (RMC) in Kingston, Ontario. The shutdown of the CMR was met by a thunder of protest in Quebec since it had been a major steppingstone for francophone Quebecers into the officer ranks. The government needed to reexamine not only its defense funds, but also its doctrine in a dramatically different world.

The Canadian Armed Forces underwent painful self-examination following a wave of bad publicity from peacekeeping missions in Somalia and Bosnia. In 1997 it was revealed that Canada's first female infantry officer, Captain Sandra Perron, had been the subject of discrimination, had perhaps been brutalized during training exercises, and had "never been totally accepted" despite her good performance record. In 1998, *MacLean's* published three lengthy reports about sexual assaults in the military that prompted many women to come forth with complaints. A scathing report in 2015 concluded that the military culture was hostile to women and that female soldiers were twice as likely as the civilian population to have been victims of sexual assaults. The situation does not seem to be getting better. According to *Statistics Canada* in 2018, the proportion of women in the Regular Force who were sexually assaulted (4.3% of the population) was about four times higher than that of men (1.1%).

Canada

The forces felt compelled to set up a sexual assault hotline and to join in encouraging female soldiers to tell their stories. They were swamped with charges of rape, including from 21-year veteran Deanna Brasseur, one of the first Canadian women to fly a CF-18 fighter. The Ministry of Defence released a damning report that described how women had faced assault, harassment and intimidation for the past decade. For the first time in its 40-year history, the renowned Snowbirds aerobatic squadron was assigned a woman commander, LTC Maryse Carmichael, in 2010.

Peacekeeping and Overseas Deployments

Canada used to be one of the world's most important sources of peacekeeping forces. In 1995, it opened the Lester B. Pearson Canadian International Peacekeeping Centre in Cornwallis, NS, to train soldiers in this kind of service, named after the former prime minister, who won a Nobel Peace Prize for his mediation efforts in the 1956 Suez Crisis. Pearson proposed that forces from nations not involved in the conflict help separate the belligerents. Since that time Canada has supported every peacekeeping venture which the UN has sponsored. Canadians have served in Palestine, Korea, Cyprus, Egypt, India, Pakistan, New Guinea, the Congo, Yemen, Lebanon, Nigeria, West Irian, Cambodia, Iran, Iraq, Kuwait, and East Timor.

In 2004, Canada had more than 4,500 troops serving in a dozen trouble spots, including in Afghanistan and war-torn Bosnia, Kosovo, and the Ethiopian–Eritrean border. In 1997, Major General Lewis Mackenzie commanded all UN forces for four and one-half months in the former Yugoslavia. In 1993, Canada deployed 845 troops to Somalia to assist in a global rescue operation. In 1994, two Canadian generals commanded the UN peacekeeping contingent trying to create order in Rwanda's genocidal civil war. In 1996, Canada again took the lead in central Africa when the UN appointed the ex-Canadian ambassador to the U.S, Raymond Chrétien, as special envoy to deal with the war and refugee crisis. Canada sent 350 troops to prepare the mission. Its publicly visible peacekeeping operations were supported materially and diplomatically by the United States, a sign that they were in line with American interests as well.

Canadians solidly supported their country's involvement in the NATO bombing campaign against Yugoslavia in 1999 to try to bring a halt to ethnic cleansing of Albanians in Kosovo, sending 18 CF-18 Hornets equipped with precision-guided munitions to fly missions. Canadian pilots flew about 10% of the initial NATO strike missions and commanded half the ones in which they participated. It left 800 troops in Kosovo to try to stabilize that traumatized land. It continued to deploy 1,200 troops in Bosnia, turning over its role there to European allies in 2005.

Canada dispatched 800 ground troops to Macedonia to help enforce an eventual peace settlement. This was in line with ex-Foreign Minister Lloyd Axworthy's policy, which he called the "human security agenda" to help suffering individuals. Ex-Prime Minister Chrétien asserted: "As Canadians, as world citizens, we could not sit and watch as people are displaced, their homes looted and burned, and lives taken away." Referring to peacekeeping, he added in 1999: "We are always there, like the Boy Scouts. Canadians love it."

Canada's peacekeeping experience in Somalia and the Balkans was sobering. The worst military scandal in Canada's post-1945 history occurred in Somalia, where a group of elite Canadian soldiers from the Airborne Regiment brutally tortured and killed a frail 16-year old Somali, who entered their camp looking for food. At least 16 other soldiers heard his screams and pleas but did nothing. This seriously tarnished the country's positive self-image as a peacekeeper, as well as the public image of the Canadian Forces themselves. The Airborne Regiment involved in this crime, for which nine soldiers were court-martialed, was disbanded in 1995 when videos were released showing soldiers making racist remarks and engaging in grotesque hazing rituals.

The follow-up inquiry delved deeply into the subtleties of how leadership and organization may have created the atmosphere in which such beatings could occur. They also had to deal with a 1993 occurrence in Bosnia in which Canadian troops were caught engaging in drunkenness, sex, black marketeering, and patient abuse at a mental hospital they were guarding. Officers must now undergo special training in military law, human rights, ethics, and public affairs before assuming command of their own units. In 2017, Canada adapted new rules of war: if a threat comes from Children, shoot first.

The challenges to peacekeepers have increased enormously. This is, in part, because of obsolete equipment. General Mackenzie called his overworked, under-armed and outgunned troops "the poor cousins when it comes to the budget, and they deserve better when we send them abroad to do our dirty work." Also, the days are over when peacekeepers serve at the invitation of a host country to monitor an existing peace. They must deal with belligerents who still want to fight.

Alex Morrison of the Canadian Institute for Strategic Studies noted that today's peacekeeping "is not playing with toys in a sandbox. It's what our men and women in uniform would surely call war." There is an unofficial distinction today between "peacekeeping," which involves wearing a blue UN beret and keeping two groups separate that want peace, and "stabilizing operations," which involves troops who can coerce belligerents with overwhelming military power. In 2017, only 112 Canadian forces were committed to nine UN missions; the rest of the soldiers deployed overseas were in the more dangerous second category. Ex-Defence Minister, and former general, Gordon O'Connor observed in 2006: "It is a shock for many people in our country that we're involved in something that is not blue helmets and no rifles."

Canada seemed to become a warrior nation, not a peacekeeping one although there was some nostalgia for the earlier role. A Canadian's opinion about the country's new role in the world is influenced by his party loyalty. Asked in 2012 if he or she is proud of Canadian's global reputation, 54% of Conservatives said yes, while 60% of Liberals and New Democrats said they were embarrassed by it. Three fourths of Conservatives were "proud of Canada's new military might, whereas 61% of Liberals and 68% of New Democrats were worried about it. Nevertheless, Canada's image abroad has not changed dramatically. In 2011, the Global Peace Index ranked it the eighth-most peaceful nation out of 153, up six places from the year before. Iceland placed first, and the U.S. 82nd.

Canadians tend to have certain beliefs which feed their ambivalence about war: Canada is never the aggressor, never starts a war, and always fights someone else's conflict Canada always goes to war as part of an alliance but has little influence on the strategy. At the same time, Canada is unlikely to be united in war, but when involved, its soldiers show uncommon courage.

Peacekeeping and other more robust military deployments create problems that Canada must confront. Repeated peacekeeping deployments pose severe hardships on soldiers and their families and produce burnout. This aggravates the problem of retention in the armed forces. At its peak in 1993, Canada deployed 4,641 peacekeepers worldwide. If one does not count its soldiers in Kosovo and Afghanistan, Canada had fallen by 2011 to 53th place of 115 nations in terms of total number of troops, police and observers involved in UN peacekeeping operations. Most were in Haiti and Sudan, and 13% were women. The U.S. placed 71st.

In 2019, Canada was the ninth largest contributor to the UN's total peacekeeping budget. Its foreign aid spending, .28%

Canada

of GDP in 2020, compared with 0.19% for the U.S., also ranks 15th in the world as a percentage of GDP with the U.S. 22d; this is among the lowest within the OECD as a percentage of GDP. Canada spends more than 6.1 billion in foreign aid each year, but Conservative Party Leader Andrew Scheer plans to cut 25% of Canada's foreign aid spending "to help Canadians get ahead at home." However, not all Canadians agree with Andrew Scheer's plan. They fear that by cutting aid, Canada would be retreating from the world stage.

In 2004, Canada deployed 170 troops to Haiti to join with U.S., French, and Chilean troops to restore order on that strife-ridden island. Canada left 66 police officers until July 2007 to train the Haitian National Police while sending hundreds of soldiers and tons of supplies and an emergency hospital back to Haiti in January 2010 to help relieve the suffering after the catastrophic earthquake that devastated the capital of Port-au-Prince and killed tens of thousands of Haitians. Further, Canada permanently deploys 303 military personnel in the United States with Northcom and NORAD. It also maintains troops in Germany and Kosovo.

COVID-19 and the Economy

A virus of uncertain cause in China in December 2019 led to what is now called the COVID-19. This has affected 199 countries with the numbers of sick and dying increasing rapidly as this book heads to press.

The World Health Organization declared the virus a pandemic on March 11, 2020. According to the National Post, Minister Karina Goud says that Canada will spend 50 million to help the world's most desperate people fight COVID-19 because it is in the country's long-term security interest and because it is the right thing to do. Gould says the government must spend $50 million globally to protect Canada's future security and economic prosperity from a virus that knows no border.

On March 29, 2020, the federal government passed emergency COVID-19 legislation providing for $52 billion of support to help workers, families, and employers to cope with the pandemic.

Iraq

Canadian diplomats had worked in vain to achieve a compromise in the UN Security Council that would have avoided war with Iraq. Two days before the bombing in Iraq began in March 2003, Prime Minister Chrétien announced that no Canadian troops would fight because the war was not backed by a UN mandate. Opposition leader Stephen Harper of the Canadian Alliance publicly apologized to Americans, writing: "For the first time in history, the Canadian government has not stood beside its key British and American allies in their time of need."

Nevertheless, Canada left its more than 50 technicians and liaison officers at allied headquarters in Qatar, at sea with U.S. ships, and as exchange soldiers in U.S. units in Iraq. One was Major-General Walter Natyncyk, who had been seconded to the U.S. Third Armored Corps in Fort Hood, Texas, as deputy commander. When his unit shipped out to Iraq, Ottawa gave him the green light to go too. "The Canadian government sent me to Fort Hood, bottom line, to show in a tangible way the close affiliation between the U.S. and Canada."

Canadian soldiers in Iraq under the cover of various "liaison" programs are more numerous than some of the contingents in the coalition of the willing. Thus, in a December 2007 *Maclean's* poll that determined that Americans know more about Canada than any other people, the half of Americans who thought Canadian soldiers were fighting on their side in Iraq were not entirely wrong.

Canadians still make up the largest contingent of foreign nationals serving in the American military, and hundreds of them were in Iraq. A Canadian commodore commanded a flotilla of a dozen American, British, French, Italian and other nations' ships, including two Halifax-class frigates and the HMCS Iroquois destroyer, in the Persian Gulf in case of "an emergency." Canada also trained Iraqi police and troops in Jordan. In 2009, Canada dispatched a warship, *Winnipeg*, to the Indian Ocean waters off the coast of Somalia to be part of an international flotilla formed to combat down pirates.

Canada had delivered $215 (US$166) million in humanitarian and reconstruction aid to Iraq, and it distinguished itself as the fastest disburser of aid. It deployed a small mobile medical team to save lives in the recapture of Mosul in 2017. This quiet effort was far more than that of most nations explicitly backing the war. This is why Canada was hurt by the U.S. decision to grant primary contracts in Iraq only to allies who were supporting the war effort, thereby excluding Canadian companies. This slight was rectified when President Bush assured ex-Prime Minister Martin that Canadian companies could bid on a new round of contracts. Ottawa announced that it would send troops back to Afghanistan, thereby freeing American soldiers for operations in the Persian Gulf.

Tempers gradually cooled. Chrétien called on his countrymen to respect the American decision. He tried to explain his stand in the least offensive way, saying that he did not support the war effort, but hoped for victory, that he did not support regime change in Iraq, but was glad Saddam was gone. Chrétien's deputy, John Manley, made it clear that "at the end of the day, governments come and go, different people are in different offices, but at an institutional level we've got to make sure the continental relationship works."

Quebec singer Celine Dion was flown to the USS *Truman* to sing "God Bless America" to the troops. In 2005, she donated US$1 million to aid Katrina hurricane victims, while her government offered whatever assistance the U.S. might need. American ambassador Paul Cellucci, who had earlier expressed his "disappointment" in Canada's lack of support, joined in the conciliation: "We are friends, we are allies, we are neighbors, and we are family. And nothing is ever going to change that."

Asked why Canada first sent troops to Afghanistan, General Rick Hillier explained: "As a way to relieve the pressure of saying no to the Americans on Iraq." The Afghanistan deployment was therefore of major political importance for the Canadians, their most conspicuous contribution to the "war on terror" and was therefore significant in Ottawa's attempt to rebuild its credibility in Washington after refusing to participate in the 2003 Iraq war. The Canadian Forces felt a strong need to do something significant for the United States.

Afghanistan

Its major overseas military commitment was to Afghanistan. Ottawa offered 1,000 troops to join the UN peacekeeping force there in 2002. In 2003, it sent a battle group of 1,900 soldiers back to Afghanistan for a further one-year tour of UN duty and assumed command of peacekeeping forces in Kabul. By 2007, Canada's 2,500 soldiers constituted the fourth-largest contingent within the overall peacekeeping force of 32,800 NATO-led troops in Afghanistan. The combat contingent of its 2,830 forces was withdrawn in July 2011. But up to 1,000 were redeployed near Kabul to train Afghan security forces and police and to assist Canada's aid and reconstruction efforts. The Canadians we're responsible for maintaining security in Kandahar, one of the most historically fractious and dangerous parts of the country. The Canadians left a great deal good works behind: a new road, 10 open schools. up from only one, and 600 trained Afghan police officers, up from 100.

In 2004, Canadian forces were commanded by Canadian General Rick Hillier, who was appointed a year later as chief of the defense staff. Hillier overhauled the structure of the Canadian military, restored its morale, and prepared it for a new era of combat missions abroad before his retirement in July 2008, appear-

Canada

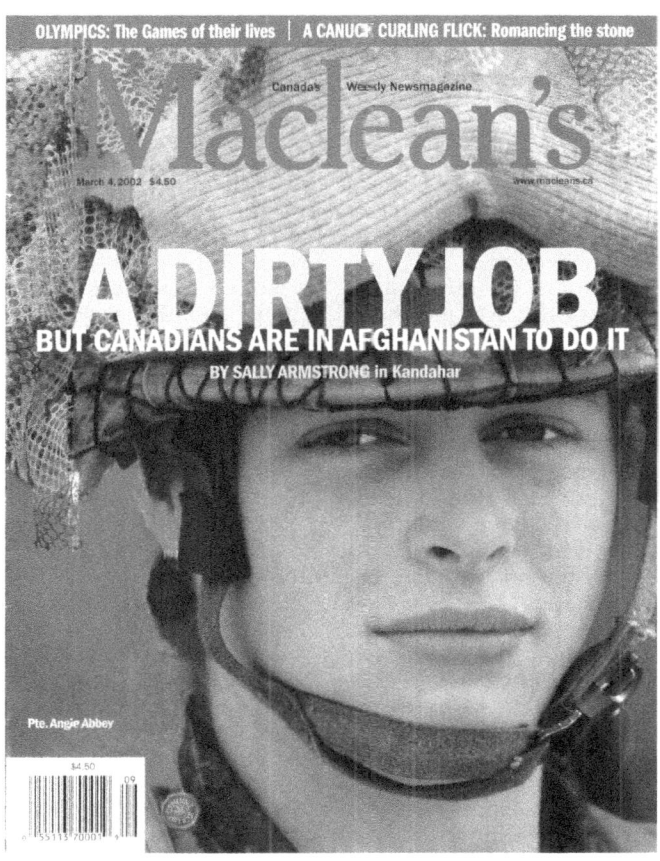

ing on TV regularly, gaining a level of fame theretofore unknown for a Canadian military officer. Hillier regularly took ice hockey players to visit the troops in the field. Moreover, Hillier expressed his view of military power in a very unCanadian way: "We are the Canadian Forces and our job is to be able to kill people." The outspoken General Hillier's experiences with the Taliban left him convinced that they are "detestable murderers and scumbags."

The Afghan engagement enabled Canada to play its part in the post-September 11 world without being at the beck and call of the American president. By taking part in and even commanding the NATO force, which is acting with a UN mandate in Afghanistan, it showed and improved its military competence in difficult anti-insurgency warfare. For Prime Minister Harper, Afghanistan was the defining element in the new face for Canada in the world. He told troops at Kandahar Airfield: "Your work is also about demonstrating an international leadership role for our country."

At the same time, the government was careful not to imply that it was fighting in an "American war" as Canada interests that overlap with other Western nations and that are by nature global and threatened by a totalitarian ideology, represented by the Taliban. It was not easy for the Conservative government to make the point that its troops were serving under a UN and NATO mandate, not a U.S. one.

Its force is proving to be a workable alternative to the traditional blue-bereted UN peacekeeping missions. It is a display of what Ottawa calls "Three D" defense that also includes development and diplomacy. This engagement is Canada's dominant military commitment. Not since the Korean War has Canada been involved in such a large and dangerous wartime effort and suffered so many casualties, 158 deaths, half by roadside bombs, and 800 wounded. To put this in perspective, 211 Canadian police officers and firefighters were killed across Canada during the same period. This is proportionally higher than those of other NATO countries, including the U.S. Only the U.S. and UK suffered more total casualties.

The highest-ranking battle fatality was Colonel Geoff Parker, who had been slated to become NATO's deputy commander in Kandahar. The effort changed the public image of the Canadian Forces to an army engaged in full-scale combat and counterinsurgency warfare and gave the military a chance to transform itself into an efficient fighting machine.

Tragically, four Canadian soldiers were killed by friendly fire when an American F-16 pilot mistakenly dropped a bomb on them during a training exercise in Afghanistan. A high-level Canada-U.S. investigation concluded that the pilots had shown "reckless disregard" for the rules of engagement, but a subsequent American military hearing made a non-binding recommendation against court martial and criminal charges on the ground that administrative punishment would better serve "the interests of good order and discipline." The U.S. army awarded each of the four dead Canadian soldiers a Bronze Star.

Regrettably, this was not the last time such a tragic mistake occurred. In 2006, Canadian troops called in air support during a fierce engagement with the Taliban. But the U.S. jets mistakenly strafed the Canadian soldiers, killing one and wounding 30. The dead soldier was Mark Graham, a former Olympic sprinter at the 1992 Barcelona Games.

The war placed unknown strains on many of the Canadian soldiers who fought in Afghanistan. While on patrol in Helmand province, infantry captain, Robert Semrau, spotted a suffering enemy who he judged to be "98% dead." To end his suffering, he shot the man. But such mercy killing is a violation of the Geneva Conventions and the Canadian Forces Code of Conduct, which obligates soldiers to provide first aid to all casualties, friend or foe. Semrau, the first Canadian soldier to be charged with battlefield murder, was tried and convicted of disgraceful conduct, demoted and released from the army. His case captured the sympathy of thousands of Canadians and of many rank-and-file soldiers.

It is one of the largest donors to Afghanistan, providing $650 million in aid through 2007 and pledging over $1 billion more. This makes Afghanistan by far the largest recipient of Canada's bilateral aid. This assistance is the largest Canadian aid commitment ever made to a single country.

In 2005, the outgoing Liberal government decided to deploy 2,500 troops to Afghanistan to strengthen the anti-insurgency effort in the province of Kandahar, south of Kabul. They fought shoulder-to-shoulder with Americans, British, Dutch and other allies. In all, 37 allies contributed troops to the International Security Assistance Force (ISAF). In March 2006 it took command of the 6,000-strong multinational brigade that operated under aggressive NATO rules of engagement. This force included 100 elusive commandos from the elite Joint Task Force 2 unit. Canada paid for this deployment in lives because this was undeniably dangerous fighting. General Hillier called this "three-block war:" humanitarian assistance, peace support operations, and high-intensity conflict, all within a relatively small area.

Canada

Polls from 2007 to 2012 revealed that half the Canadians, 41% in 2012, thought the mission failed. The end of 2010, 53% of respondents in one poll responded that "it's time to get out." Only 31.6% thought Canada should stay. Many were appalled by the casualties and the brutality: one captain was badly wounded in the head by a young man wielding an ax while attending a meeting of village elders.

One of the first political crises Prime Minister Harper faced in office was its return to the tradition of banning news media coverage of returning coffins from war and the flying of flags at half-staff to mark the death of troops. Harper argued that the families should be able to grieve out of the limelight, but critics accused him of not honoring the dead and forced him o back down. Harper telephoned the family of every soldier killed in action, so he was constantly reminded of the horror of that war.

The ensuing vigorous and emotional debate merely underscores Canadians' uneasiness over this enhanced role in Afghanistan and the government's nervousness about uncertain public support for the war. Some see an Iraq-like quagmire, the wrong cause in the wrong place. Canadians debated what the appropriate global role is for their country and military.

In late 2009, the Harper government was embarrassed by allegations made by a former diplomat in Afghanistan, Richard Colvin, that in 2006 and early 2007, Canadian soldiers handed detainees over to Afghan authorities knowing that the latter use torture and that they did not follow up on the detainees' welfare. Colvin called this practice "un-Canadian, counterproductive and probably illegal." The Harper government allegedly ignored reports of this. When a parliamentary committee of inquiry demanded to see documents relevant to the case, Harper prorogued, or closed, parliament for two months, while Canadians were distracted by the Winter Olympics. It seemed to many that the government had something important to hide. This scandal overshadowed the entire debate of Canada's military role in the country. It eroded further Canadians' fading support for the war effort.

Between 2001 and 2014, more than 40,000 Canadian Armed Forces members served in the Afghanistan theater of operations with 158 of them dying in that conflict. The further sorrow is that on returning to Canada, many soldiers suffered post-traumatic stress syndrome. In a counter intuitive finding, though, the rate of suicide in the Canadian armed forces is higher among those who have not served in Afghanistan and elsewhere.

Harper staunchly supported the war effort to which the previous Liberal government had committed the country. His first foreign trip after becoming prime minister was to visit Canadian troops in Afghanistan for two days. In 2007, he defeated an opposition proposal in Commons to withdraw all Canadian troops. However, Harper could not extend the mission beyond 2011 without parliamentary approval, and all three opposition parties opposed that. There was a strong fear of an open-ended commitment. Harper did not need parliamentary approval to leave up to a thousand troops in Afghanistan to train Afghan security forces and to support humanitarian efforts.

Realizing that this war could go on for years, Harper ordered a substantial increase in military spending, to include the purchase of transport helicopters, three new support ships, transport aircraft and 2,300 supply trucks. His government, which had budgeted $20.6 billion for defense in 2010, wanted to increase the full-time military force from 65,722 to 75,000 and add 10,000 more reservists, constituting 13% of the fighting forces in Afghanistan. However, by 2013 military talk was dominated by cost-cutting; the land force's operating budget shrank by 22%.

The fact that three generals with experience in irregular warfare in the Middle East and Afghanistan, Chief of Defence Staff General Rick Hillier, who stepped down in 2008 after more than three years at the top of the Canadian Forces, his chief of strategic planning, General Andrew Leslie, in 2007 Chief of the Land Staff, and General Walter Natynczyk, who replaced Hillier as Chief of the Defence Staff, had risen to top positions within the Canadian forces brought fresh thinking about modern war-fighting and about the need to reform Canada's military to be fit for more robust requirements. They restored the forces' morale and prepared them for a dangerous new era of combat missions abroad. In 2012, General Tom Lawson, a fighter pilot, became Chief of the Defence Staff. In 2015, newly elected Prime Minister Justin Trudeau named Harjit Sajjan as defense minister. A Sikh, he was a highly decorated Afghanistan veteran and detective in Vancouver. Sikhs are known for their warrior culture.

Between 2001 and 2014, more than 40,000 Canadian Armed Forces members served in the Afghanistan theater of operations with 158 Canadian of them dying in that conflict. The further sorrow is that on returning to Canada, many soldiers suffered post-traumatic stress syndrome. In a counter intuitive finding, though, the rate of suicide in the Canadian Armed forces is higher among those who have not served in Afghanistan and elsewhere.

Canada

ECONOMY

By world standards, Canada is a rich country. Measured in terms of gross national product or GDP, the total value of the goods and services a country produces annually, Canada ranks eleventh in the world, despite the fact that it has only 37.06 (2018) million inhabitants. As visitors can easily see, the average Canadian has a standard of living as high as the average American. Enjoying the sixth highest per capita GDP in the Organization for Economic Cooperation and Development (OECD), often called a "rich man's club" of nations, Canadians live better than the Japanese, Germans and French. There is less visible poverty than in the U.S. Canadians are well clothed, housed, fed, educated and cared for.

The UN Human Development Report consistently ranks Canada as among the world's best places to live based on standard of living, life expectancy, and educational attainment, usually slightly above the United States. Because of its bountiful natural resources, many people have said that Canada was economically "a solution searching for a problem." However, there are occasional reminders that the large, complex Canadian economy has weaknesses as well as strengths.

Canada has a capitalist, free-market economy, although the state's hand in the economy is considerably greater than in the U.S. Canada's natural beauty attracts millions of tourists each year, mainly from the U.S. although that has slowed since the September 11 attacks; a million Canadians, or about one out of ten jobs, earn their living from the tourist industry.

Canada is a country richly endowed with natural resources of all kinds. Although only 5% of its total territory is arable, Canada possesses enough arable land to be one of the world's largest producers of food. For a long time, natural resources and agriculture were the pillars of Canada's economy. In the 18th and 19th centuries, Canada borrowed and attracted large amounts of capital from abroad, and it imported manufactured goods. It paid for imported goods with raw materials and grain.

In the 20th century, and especially after 1945, the Canadian economy changed considerably. Its services and manufacturing sectors now overshadow the resource and agricultural (primary) sector in terms of contribution to GDP and employment. Services in 2019 provided 71% of employment and 70% of GDP while industry was responsible for 22% of the jobs and 28% of GDP. Only 2% of employment and 2% of GDP were derived from agriculture. This sparsely populated country has a small domestic market of 35.5 million people. Canada must trade in order to maintain its prosperity; foreign trade with the U.S. alone generates 52% of its GDP, as opposed to less than 20% of the U.S.'. One out of three Canadian jobs is linked to trade. This dependence on the international market makes Canada particularly vulnerable to world-wide economic trends and protectionism.

The problem of dependence is compounded by the fact that its international trade is practically dominated by one country: the U.S. Every year Canada sells about three-fourths or 74% (2019) of its exports to the U.S., and approximately 64% (2019) of its imports must be bought from its only neighbor. The two countries' trade is roughly balanced over time. Until 2008, Canada relied on its trade surplus with the U.S. to pay for its trade deficit with the rest of the world. In 2007, China overtook Canada to become the largest source of American imports, and it is now the U.S.'s second-largest overall trading partner after Canada. China buys 4.3% of Canada's exports and provides 11% of its imports. Its trade with Canada doubled in the five years to 2011, and it continues to grow, amounting to nearly US$56.5 billion in 2019, according to the United Nations COMTRADE database on international trade. In 2020, exports to China grew 8.1% while declining internationally 11.9%. Imports from China grew 1.9% during this time.

Foreigners, especially Americans, own a large portion of its economy. The U.S. accounts for 64% of total foreign direct investment (FDI) in Canada and the European Union (EU) for only 29%. In 2000, Americans accounted for 75% of Canada's foreign ownership. Canadian FDI in the U.S. more than trebled between 1989 and 2002, growing to US$92 billion in 2002 and multiple times that by 2005. Half of its outbound foreign direct investment (FDI) goes to the U.S. and a fourth of it to the EU countries.

Because the Canadian and American economies are so tightly linked, when the U.S. sneezes, Canada catches pneumonia. *Maclean's* went even farther in 2008: "If the U.S. catches a cold, well, call up the undertaker." U.S. economic growth is too important and its ties to other economies too complex for the effects of an American downturn not to be felt beyond its borders. When the American economy slips into recession, the Canadian economy normally follows the same downward path, but it usually takes a little longer to recover. The good news is that when the U.S. economy booms, it can pull Canada along in its slipstream.

Lacking the size and diversity of the U.S. economy, Canada is normally not as resilient as the U.S. when faced with economic adversity. However, in the 21st century the high world demand for natural resources, especially oil, gas, and mining, gave the Canadian economy much needed

Canada

stability and predictability. In the 1970s and 1980s, the dependence on the U.S. stimulated economic nationalism again, which has always been close to the surface of most Canadians. As reasonable as the calls for "Canada for the Canadians" seem to be, they brought serious problems to the Canadian economy.

On November 19, 2018, Canada launched its new $10 vertical note, which features the portrai of social justic icon Viola Desmond. She is honored as the first woman to appear on a Canadian bank note. In 2019. it was named Banknote of the Year by the International Banknote Society.

Geography has so closely linked the two countries' economies that cooperation, not conflict, is in their mutual interest. Also, Canada is too open a country, with too vulnerable an economy, to pursue a consistent policy of economic nationalism. The U.S. and Canada are each other's most important trading partners and form the world's largest bilateral trade relationship. Since the Free Trade Agreement (FTA) went into effect in 1989, the value of two-way trade had trebled by 2013, surpassing US$680 billion, making this the world's largest bilateral trading relationship. If services are added, the total is about $800 billion. Total trade equals $2 billion each day. In the process, the FTA has reoriented Canada's economic axis from east-west to north-south. Since 2000, trade with non-U.S. partners grew faster than trade with the U.S.

Trade with Canada is of increasing importance for the U.S.; a fifth of America's exports and 15% of its imports flow to and from Canada. One-third of all transborder trade takes place within companies having a presence on both sides of the border. Cross-border trade supports 221,500 jobs in Michigan alone. The Canadian foreign ministry estimates that more than 7 million American jobs depend on Canada–U.S. free trade. America's trade with Canada is, in dollar value, about three times its trade with Japan. Canada's second largest partner is China, which provides 11% of Canadian imports. Canada runs a large trade deficit with it, and until the financial crisis of 2008, that was more than compensated by Canada's trade surplus with the rest of the world. By 2004, 400 companies had established a permanent presence in China, and in 2005 its trade with China soared by 40%.

The U.S. sells more to the single province of Ontario than to either Japan or all of Western Europe. Canada sells more to a single American company, Home Depot, than it does to all of France. Canada is the largest trading partner for 36 of the 50 American states, and Pennsylvania exports more to Canada than to its next seven markets combined.

Motor vehicles and parts represent 14% of Canada's manufacturing output and employ more than 150,000 Canadians, accounting for about 25% of U.S. merchandise exports to Canada and about a quarter of imports. Motor vehicles constitute 23% of Canadian exports to the U.S., and 90% of the vehicles and automotive parts manufactured in Canada are shipped south. In 2011, Canada produced 2.1million vehicles, or about 16% of the North American total. Thus, when the situation of the American automotive industry turns bad, as in 2008–9, this is shared by Canada, and production in Canada plummets. Windsor's jobless rate shot up to 14.4% during the recession, and two-thirds of the jobs lost were in Ontario, most of them in manufacturing. The second largest category of U.S. exports is electronics and telecommunications equipment.

Canada is the U.S.'s largest supplier of imported energy, oil, uranium, natural gas and electricity, sending 99% of its oil exports to America. Consequently, Canada it is vulnerable to the lack of pipeline capacity and an oil glut in America. Canada supplies 21% of U.S. imports of crude and refined oil products, amounting to more than 10% of America's overall oil needs. Over half of Canada's gas production is shipped to the U.S., accounting for 94% of its natural gas imports and 13% of its demand. Much flows through 31 pipelines that cross the U.S. border. Canada is the only country in the Group of Seven, except the UK, that is a net oil exporter. Its people consume per capita roughly twice as much energy as other developed countries. Both countries suffer similar problems, though: high labor costs although the unit cost of production is lower in Canada and a decline of traditional industries.

After this brief overview of the Canadian economy, it is worth looking more closely at its individual components and at the economic policies that the Canadian federal governments have pursued.

The Primary Sector

Any treatment of the Canadian economy must always begin with the primary sector. Throughout the country's history, raw materials and agriculture provided the foundation for Canada's development. Today this sector accounts for only 5% of the workforce and less than 8% of its GDP, and the agricultural portion now amounts to 2% of the value of Canada's total output. In terms of employment, 2% of Canadians now make a living from farming, and the corresponding figure for mining, lumbering, fishing and other forms of primary extraction is only about 2%.

These figures understate the importance of the primary sector for the overall economy. This element is the basis for much of Canada's manufacturing, such as wood and paper products, food and beverages and petroleum products. Even more significant is its contribution to Canada's export trade: about 60% of the country's exports leave in raw or semi-processed form, a high percentage for any developed country.

Canada can be thankful for its natural wealth. A problem with heavy reliance on the export of raw materials, though, is that their prices fluctuate widely on world markets. Therefore, a country becomes excessively vulnerable to the ups and downs of outside market forces. Unfortunately, this has often been the case with Canada. Things go well whenever the voracious demand in the U.S. and developing countries, especially China, for raw materi-

Earlier days in Battle Harbour, Labrador.   Courtesy: Mike Earle

Canada

als keeps the prices for Canada's metals, minerals, lumber and oil up. Canada's economy thrives when the prices of natural resources, especially energy, are high, which has been the case most of the time in the 21st century; it is hurt when prices go down.

Fishing

Most of Canada's earliest European visitors came to fish in the waters off its 241,402-kilometer, or 149,670 miles, coastline, and the success of early settlements in Canada depended greatly on the ability to maintain a subsistence fishery. Canada was once the world's leading exporter of fish and fish products. Canada's formerly rich fishing grounds, extending 200 miles off its coasts, contained 150 fish and shellfish species and was able to maintain more than 900 fish processing plants, which employed over 100,000 people. Most of these plants were located in the Atlantic provinces. In Newfoundland alone, about 15% of the inhabitants found employment in fishing or fish processing.

In 1989, Newfoundland's dependence on a fishing industry was devastated by overfishing and dwindling stocks. A 2005 study concluded that stocks of adult cod off the North American coast had diminished by 96% since the fishing industry took off in the 1850s.

In 1992, Ottawa slapped a moratorium on all northern cod fishing to allow stocks to replenish themselves, thereby provoking a clash with France. The French claimed the right to fish in the Gulf of St. Lawrence because of their tiny island outposts, St. Pierre with a population of about 6,500 and Miquelon and its approximately 600 residents, located just 16 miles off the Newfoundland coast. Fishermen in both Newfoundland and the two French islands feared that French trawlers would further deplete codfish stocks in the Gulf. The feud was settled by treaty in 1995, a year in which Canada used its navy to see that earlier agreements would be respected. A further dispute between the two countries broke out in 2005 over rights to thousands of square miles of Atlantic seabed south of the islands.

The EU agreed temporarily to restrict fishing in the waters inside and outside the 200-mile zone in order to allow stocks to replenish themselves. When pirate fishermen from Europe, especially Spain, continued to overfish the dwindling stocks, the Canadians decided to act in 1995, sending a frigate to fired a shot over the bow of a Spanish trawler outside the 200-mile fishing zone, boarded the vessel, and ordered it to St. John's. There it found illegal nets on board and doctored records proving that the fishermen had indeed violated international agreements.

After a great deal of acrimony, Canada and Spain reached a settlement calling for closer monitoring and enforcement of fish catches. However, in 1998, the UN International Court of Justice decided that it lacked jurisdiction to settle the dispute. Canadians applauded the use of military force to support their national interests. In 2003 the federal government closed down most of the remaining Atlantic cod fishing industry.

Canada also was involved in a festering dispute with the U.S. over the fishing of fragile West Coast salmon stocks, which swim through Alaskan waters into Canadian waters to breed. Both sides accepted mediation, but those talks ended in stalemate in 1997. In June 1999 a landmark agreement was reached establishing a system of flexible catch quotas and a $140 million fund to protect spawning grounds. Aquaculture still threatens to make diplomacy irrelevant, though, despite the emotional tie that British Columbia has with wild salmon. More fish are produced on fish farms within the province than are caught in its waters. The number of wild salmon continues to decline, many from diseases contracted from salmon farms.

No beings overfish more than do seals. Bowing to foreign and domestic political pressure, Canada banned the unrestricted killing of seals, thereby enabling the seal population to triple since the 1970s to about six million on the east coast. Each animal consumes an average of 45 pounds of fish a day. This, as well as overfishing, combined almost to destroy the fish stocks, especially cod.

In order to reduce the seal population to a manageable level, the federal government began in 1994 to support the price of seal meat, which is used for animal feed. Seal over-reproduction and the need for employment in outlying areas are the reasons why people from Quebec and Newfoundland living close to thawing ice floes in the Gulf of St. Laurence are permitted each spring to engage in the world's largest seal slaughter for a few weeks. For those living in rural regions where work is sporadic at best following the disappearance of cod stocks, the hunt supplements their meager winter incomes. One sealer who pocketed $5,000 in one week noted: "When you make $25,000 a year, that's a big boost."

About 6,000 people benefit from seal hunting, and by 1997 they had quadrupled the size of their annual catch, despite the protests of animal rights activists. The largest seal hunt in a half century took place in 2004, with more than 200,000 taken in the first 36 hours. The rest of the 350,000 maximum was hauled in by smaller operations. The quota for 2006 was 335,000 harp seals, not the whitecoat seals, a tiny percentage of the overall population. The 2008 quota was 275,000 harp seals and 8,200 hooded seals. The killing of baby seals remains outlawed, but critics claim that it still happens and that most of the seals killed are only one or two months old.

The business is fraught with dangers. In April 2007, nearly 100 fishing boats became trapped in thick ice caused by a sustained dry Arctic wind. The crushing ice destroyed or damaged some of the boats, and only the country's largest icebreakers could free the boats and rescue the 450 stranded hunters. Due to global warming there are fewer suitable seals to hunt; premature thawing of the ice causes seal pups to fall through the ice and drown.

The sealers are harassed each step of the way by animal rights activists, such as Paul McCartney, Pamela Anderson, and Brigitte Bardot who find such an animal culling cruel. Tempers flare as both sides do what they think has to be done. Opinion polls in 2009 revealed that most Canadians agree with the celebrities: 51% found seal hunting "cruel and inhumane and should be banned;" another 17% regarded it as "ugly and brutal, but that's no reason to ban it." Only 25% had no objections and 7% "don't care."

A major blow to commercial harvesting was delivered in May 2009 by the European Parliament, which banned the importing or sale of furs and other seal products. Canadian officials immediately protested, pointing out that European fur farms growing minks and foxes kill more animals every four or five days than the entire annual hunt does in a year. But, a European animal rights spokesman called the ban the "final nail in the coffin." Products from subsistence hunts by Inuit and other indigenous peoples were exempted. To poke a thumb in the EU's eyes, the prime minister and his entire cabinet flew to Nunavut and nibbled appetizers of raw seal. Governor General Jean helped Inuit cut out the heart of a seal and then ate part of it raw. The parliamentary canteen in Ottawa even served seal meat for the first time ever.

Fur and Timber

Lucrative fishing possibilities had lured Europeans to Canada who then established contact with Indians. These native Canadians had very valuable goods to trade, furs. With its cold climate and rugged timbered terrain, Canada provides a natural habitat for a wide variety of fur-bearing animals, including beaver, wild mink, Arctic fox, muskrat, otter, coyote, timber wolf, red fox, marten, and Canada lynx. As noted earlier, the fur trade dominated the Canadian economy from the early 1600s to the late 1700s, and it

Canada

Largest grain elevator in North America, Thunder Bay, Ontario

powerfully shaped the Canadian destiny. Unlike the fishing industry, which was restricted chiefly to the fringes of Canada, the fur trade directed European attention toward the north and the interior of the huge North American continent. The fur trade broadened the horizon of the early Canadians and provided the initial impetus to expand Canada "from sea to sea."

The fur trade was also an enterprise best conducted by huge trade monopolies, such as the Hudson's Bay and Northwest Companies. It therefore left in Canadians' mouths a good taste of large, state-sanctioned economic monopolies, which still differs somewhat from the American preference for purely private competitive firms. A negative consequence of the fur trade, though, was that for many decades it delayed both permanent settlement in the West and the development of Canadian manufacturing. Profits from fur could simply buy whatever foreign manufactures were needed. Although its significance for Canada's overall economy is minimal today, the sale abroad of raw Canadian furs continues. Despite protests by animal rights activists, the British army admitted in 2003 that it failed after twenty years of searching to find an artificial substitute for the traditional bearskin headdresses worn most famously by guards at Buckingham Palace as only the pelt of the Canadian black bear can survive the 24-hour year-round onslaught of British weather.

An unintended consequence of the severe restrictions on the fur trade is that the traditional livelihood of many Aboriginals disappeared as they have had to replace their lost income by permitting oil, gas, and mining into their previously unspoiled areas. This has contributed to environmental problems. Trappers once killed wolves to protect other animals in their traps. But the wolf population has soared, to the detriment of the caribou and buffalo herds. A national symbol, the beaver, has also multiplied dramatically to an estimated 20 million animals in Canada alone. In their avid pursuit of building dams, they have destroyed many trees and caused unwanted flooding of farmland.

Unlike the fur trade, the timber trade was favorable to settlement in Canada. Ships carrying timber to Europe had excess space for the return passage. Settlers could occupy such space very economically. Indeed, except during the American Revolutionary War, timber provided the first significant boost to the populating of Canada. In addition, timber was conducive to agriculture because logging operations left land cleared for agricultural use. Further, unlike the fur business, timberwork stimulated manufacturing as lumber had to be processed in sawmills, transported in vehicles larger than canoes and ultimately transformed into such goods as ocean-going vessels and furniture.

At the same time, the timber trade created a market for many kinds of metal tools. A fourth of Canada's territory is covered by forest. With 10% of the globe's total forest area, it is the world's premier exporter of timber and forest products and its third largest producer, with about 14% of the total world production. In a good year, almost 250 million trees are felled in Canada.

Four million trees are required to produce the newsprint for *The New York Times* in one year alone. Canada is the world's largest exporter of newsprint. A third of the world's newsprint comes from its forests. Unfortunately for the industry, declining newspaper sales world-wide, smaller newspaper formats, the transfer of many classified ads to the internet, and such modern practices as the "paperless office" have cut seriously into demand. Sales were also harmed by environmentalist policies of such publications as *Victoria's Secret*, which announced in 2006 that it would not print catalogues on paper manufactured from endangered Canadian boreal forests. Sales fell 8.5% in 2005 alone, and 31 pulp and paper mills in Canada (13 of them in Ontario) closed either entirely or partially.

The problem is that trees are being cut faster than they can be replenished. Moreover, mismanagement is so bad that millions of cut trees are cut are never transported out of the forests and are left to rot. To make matters worse, Canadian forests have been ravaged in recent years by acid rain, by fires which have destroyed about six times more forest area than loggers harvested, and by such pests as the spruce budworm, which defoliated about 185 million acres in the eastern half of Canada, and the mountain pine beetle, which kills more trees in BC than wildfires or logging. The latter, which can kill a mature tree in one year, is threatening to cross the Rocky Mountains and sweep across the entire northern continent.

The gradual destruction of Canada's most lucrative natural resource is particularly dangerous because it is Canada's largest employer, employing about 300,000 people as loggers and as workers in sawmills and pulp and paper operations, primarily in outlying communities whose economic stability depends on it. Another 700,000 jobs exist because of it. In British Columbia, which accounts for 60% of Canada's lumber production, one in four persons is at least indirectly dependent on the forest industry. Thus, when this industry experiences hard times, as a result of a decline in the American construction industry, for example, the entire Canadian economy suffers. Canadians control about 75% of the country's total timber production.

For many years, passions on both sides of the border were inflamed by a seemingly interminable dispute over softwood lumber. Canada consistently supplies about a third of the U.S. market. American companies claimed that Canadian producers receive illegal subsidies and should therefore be forced to pay countervailing duties (which amounted to 32% in 2001 and 10% in 2006). Canada retorts that it merely has a different system for granting rights to cut and that American producers are engaging in selfish protectionism. In a nutshell, 95% of the timber in the U.S. is privately owned and is sold by auction at market prices. In Canada, because the provinces own about 94% of the timber, they set the harvest levels and stumpage fees. American producers contend that the fees are below market prices and therefore constitute a subsidy, which is forbidden. Canadians rejected this argument.

In 1996, the two countries signed an agreement granting selected provinces fee-free access to the U.S. market for a certain volume of wood but requiring

Canada

Canada to collect fees on anything above that level. When the agreement expired in 2001, the two countries again found themselves at loggerheads, so to speak. While waiting for the World Trade Organization (WTO) to rule on the dispute, mills in British Columbia, which account for half of lumber exports, and Quebec had to close, and thousands lost their jobs.

In 2002, the U.S. imposed countervailing duties averaging 27% on Canadian lumber exports. Although these duties hurt, the Canadian lumber industry concentrated its production in its most efficient mills thereby lowering average costs and strengthening the industry economically. This unexpected Canadian response hurt both American producers, who faced stiffer competition, and consumers, who must pay higher prices for protected lumber.

In May 2003, the WTO determined that Canada's stumpage is not an unfair subsidy, and a North American Free Trade Agreement (NAFTA) panel decided in September that the U.S. had not proven that Canadian softwood exports threatened to injure American lumber firms. In December the two countries reached a tentative agreement lasting three years that would limit Canadian producers to 31.5% of the U.S. market.

In another judgment in April 2004, the WTO rejected all of Canada's complaints against American anti-dumping duties on softwood lumber. Nevertheless, the deadlock continued, even after a NAFTA panel ruled yet again in September 2004 that Canada's softwood lumber exports are not subsidized, and the U.S. agreed to accept this ruling. A half year later, the WTO established a dispute panel to investigate whether the U.S. has complied with its rulings against tariffs on Canadian softwood lumber. While Canada's annual softwood sales of $7 billion to the U.S. accounted for only about 3% of the trade relationship, the dispute took on oversized political symbolism.

The 20-year dispute seemed to be resolved in April 2006, the first foreign policy success of Prime Minister Harper's government. The U.S. lifted a 10% duty on softwood lumber and agreed to refund $4 billion of the $5 billion collected since 2002, paying about a half billion of the remainder to American softwood lumber producers. However, Canada agreed that if the price of lumber fell below a threshold calculated by a complex formula, or if a surge in exports occurred, it would levy an export tax to be retained by the Canadian provinces or quotas on Canadian shipments, or a combination of the two. Although this settlement departed significantly from the principle of free trade, Canadians greeted it.

In April 2009, the new Obama administration reintroduced a 10% duty on some lumber imports, claiming that the Canadians had not made amends for violating the trade deal. In January 2011, American trade officials asked a London arbitration court to penalize exports from British Columbia arguing that the underpricing of timber from public lands was a subsidy. BC shrugged this off because the U.S. is not its only market now because its exports to China have increased. By 2011, its total sales to China and Japan exceed those to the U.S., which once bought two-thirds of BC's lumber. By 2011, that had fallen to only a third, thanks in part to its housing crisis. This endless dispute arose again in 2017 when Donald Trump became president and has yet to be resolved even under his successor Joseph Biden.

Agriculture

Agriculture provided the livelihood for a large portion of settlers to Canada. When, toward the end of the 19th century, strains of wheat were developed which could thrive in the northern climes of the Prairie regions, settlement in the Western part of Canada was greatly stimulated. This produced a strong demand for metal implements and manufactured supplies and a powerful additional incentive to complete the East–West railway. Newcomers could easily enter farming; a federal governmental homestead policy provided any farmer with 160 acres of land, provided that he lived on it and worked it for five years.

Such family-owned and operated farms remain the backbone of Canadian agriculture, despite the continuing tendency for farms to grow in size and decline in number. The average farm in Canada today is 540 acres; in the Prairie provinces they average over 900 acres. About 7% of the country's total land area is devoted to farming; most is within 300 miles of the U.S. border and is concentrated in only three provinces: Saskatchewan, which has 40% of it, Alberta and Ontario.

The relative importance of agriculture has declined in Canada, although it remains important in its export sector. In 1900 approximately 75% of Canadians were engaged in agriculture; by 1946, this percentage had decreased to 29%, and today it is 2.4%. Its share in GDP has also declined dramatically, from 12% in 1951 to 2%. Nevertheless, agriculture remains important. About 40% of Canada's produce is exported, including about 85% of the wheat crop. Its major buyers are Japan, the U.S., the EU, and China. In 2010, Canada sold three times more wheat to Asia than to EU countries.

Behind only the U.S., Canada is the world's second largest exporter of wheat, 60% of which is grown in Saskatchewan, alone accounts for nearly half of all agricultural export earnings. Canada possesses a fifth of the international market. Any precipitous fall in world wheat prices sends many Saskatchewan family farms into bankruptcy, as occurred at the turn of the century when the cost of production exceeded prices of grain. Also, the widespread rejection in Europe of genetically modified organism (GMO) foods has narrowed Canada's market. Only in North American markets can GMO foods be readily sold. In 2003, Canada joined the U.S. to challenge in the WTO the EU's ban on GMOs. Some Canadian farmers are trying to keep their crops free of GMO pollen in order to be able to sell to non-GMO markets.

Because of its agricultural prowess, Canada is a net exporter of food. However, this fortunate situation is due chiefly to wheat production. Canada runs a deficit in fruit, vegetables, nuts, honey, sugar, tobacco and other products, which may in the future cause Canada to become a net importer of food. Canadians face the same specter as do the American farmers: hard times at best, and bankruptcy at worst.

In 2003, cattle farmers, who sell $7 billion worth of beef each year, were shaken by North America's first case of mad-cow disease (BSE). A single cow in northern

Canada

Alberta tested positive. The U.S., which normally accounts for three-fourths of all Canadian beef exports, and nearly 30 other countries temporarily sealed their borders to Canadian beef, causing severe financial loss to Canadian farmers. Herds in all three western provinces were quarantined and slaughtered. The next shock came in December 2003 when a cow in Washington State also tested positive for BSE. It turned out that it had come from an Alberta herd. In 2007, a 13-year-old beef cow from Alberta was confirmed to have the disease, the 11th case since 2003. Ottawa opted for a partial ban of U.S. beef that was much less restrictive than the one Washington had imposed.

During 2004, the U.S. slowly opened its doors to boneless processed Canadian beef from young animals. President Bush said before his visit to Canada in November 2004 that the ban should be lifted, but the wheels of bureaucracy grind slowly and mysteriously in Washington. Despite the fact that another Canadian cow was found in January 2005 to be infected by BSE, the American door to Canadian cattle under 30 months of age was to be opened in March 2005. However, a federal judge in Montana ordered the border to remain closed. Two months later the U.S. Senate blocked the agriculture department's efforts to open the border and instead voted to block Canada's designation as a "minimal risk" region for BSE. In 2006, Bush vowed to end all BSE-related restrictions.

One product in which Canada does not run a deficit is beer. American beer drinkers have been thirsty for the Molson, Labatt, O'Keefe, and Moosehead beers and ales. In 1992 agreements were reached not only eliminating barriers that prevented beer brewed in one province from being sold in another but opening up the market to American beers. By 2004, the only Canadian-owned beer left after Labatt was bought by Belgium's Interbrew was Molson, which has over 40% of Canada's beer market. Yet, the beer that flaunted nationalism and came up with the rant, "I am Canadian," merged with Coors, the third-largest brewer in the U.S. It had already brewed and sold Coors in Canada. Canadian beers in the U.S. face stiff competition from the rapidly growing number of microbreweries and successfully challenging the old conventional wisdom that Canadian beer tastes better than the American variety.

Canadians purchase about half of California's exported wines. Canadian wines, 90% of which come from Ontario, particularly the Niagara area, and most of the rest from BC, have come into their own and have won hundreds of international awards. Canadian "ice wine" is an expensive dessert wine made from frost-bitten grapes of which Canada has become the world's leading producer. It has a national appellation, which enables it to be sold in the European Union (EU) but faces stiff competition from another Canadian product, cider or "apple ice wine," a beverage with 12% alcohol from Quebec. The domestic market for wine remains somewhat restricted because Canadians are not big wine drinkers although that is slowly changing. Canadians consume on average only 10 liters per year (one-sixth that in France and Italy), compared with 88 liters of beer.

As in other sectors of the Canadian economy, the state's hand has always been involved in agriculture. Since the Great Depression, marketing boards for various types of farm products have regulated markets. They have attempted to keep farm prices up in order to control the chronic problem of low and unstable agricultural prices. In the centralized "supply management" structure, dozens of federal and provincial government boards assign production quotas for dairy, poultry and other farm products.

Wheat growers typically had only one customer, the Canadian Wheat Board (CWB) monopolized the buying and selling of wheat and barley crops, as well as providing quality control. The CWB fixed a guaranteed price, and the government covered any losses. Founded in 1935, the CWB was the only marketer for Prairie grain destined for export or human consumption within Canada and was one of the world's biggest grain exporters. Farmers elected the majority of its 15-member board of directors and the federal government did not control or interfere in day-to-day operations.

The U.S. launched numerous formal complaints claiming that the CWB was a monopolistic state trading organization that broke global trading rules. Believing that farmers should be able to sell their crops freely, Prime Minister Harper moved to eliminate the CWB's "single desk" monopoly as of August 2012, a reform that had been advocated for decades.

The Western Grain Stabilization and the Agricultural Stabilization Act Programs are federal projects designed to enhance stability offering limited subsidies to save Canadian farmers. For example, in 1998, for every $100 of income for a Canadian wheat farmer, $9 came from government subsidies while an American farmer received $38 and a Western European $57.

Governmental protection of agriculture is not as great as in the EU or Japan, but there has been a tendency over the years for it to grow in Canada. As such, these efforts are perpetually surrounded by political controversy. American farmers resent high subsidies and tariffs up to 350% on dairy products. As a result of the tariffs on dairy imports, ranging from 200% to 300%, the Canadian consumer pays 63% more for milk than in the U.S. Quebec holds about half the dairy quota, and younger farmers resent having to pay hundreds of thousands of dollars to purchase a quota share when they go into business. Other farmers contend that without protection, their farms would be taken over by American conglomerates.

The potential Achilles' heel of Canada's agricultural breadbasket has always been transportation of grain from western sources to eastern markets or ports. Western farmers are dependent on the railroads, which take their grain to the port of Thunder Bay on the northern shore of Lake Superior where the grain is deposited in some of the largest grain elevators in the world from which it is loaded into ships and transported through the elaborate locks of Sault Ste. Marie and into the St. Lawrence Seaway system.

Mining

Canada is one of the world's major storehouses for minerals, ranking first in the world in mineral exports and third in terms of mineral production, behind the U.S. and Russia. Canada is the world's largest producer of asbestos, zinc, silver, nickel, and potash and the second largest of gypsum, molybdenum, and sulfur. Plus, Canada is one of the world's major producers of uranium, titanium, aluminum, cobalt, gold, lead, copper, iron, and platinum.

Canada exports of potentially deadly asbestos mainly to poor countries has come under increasing criticism within Canada, especially Quebec, where ca. 1,000 persons still make their living from asbestos mining. In 1981, a huge body of gold ore was discovered at Hemlo in northwestern Ontario. With improved mining technology, Canada is now extracting more gold than ever and is the world's third largest producer, after Russia and South Africa and tied with the U.S.

Diamond production in the Northwest Territories and Nunavut is increasing so dramatically that it has transformed that region into the world's third-biggest producer of high-quality diamonds with 11.4% of the world market, after Botswana's 26% and Russia's 17.8%. The boom has generated commercial and political interest in the Canadian Arctic not experienced since the 19th century. Most diamonds are shipped to London and then to Belgium. A Tiffany diamond-finishing center was established in Yellowknife.

Canada has the potential to threaten De Beers' century-old grip on the industry. For this reason, in 2004, De Beers channeled almost half of its exploration budget to Canada. Further, De Beers signed joint ventures and partnerships while more than four-fifths of its holdings are in Nunavut, leading it to open a mine in 2007.

Canada's mineral wealth is distributed over virtually the entire country. This brings both advantages and disadvantages. It provides some economic activity to regions, especially in the North, which would be otherwise almost completely locked out of the country's economy. On the other hand, the costs of extraction and transportation are very high in the North. Also, mining operations sometimes create unfortunate collisions between the interests of mining companies, on the one hand, and environmental groups and native groups, on the other, whose lands and special rights are largely located in the North.

Industry and Services

For all of Canada's wealth in the primary or agricultural sector, it must be remembered that the country is no longer a rural society composed of farmers, trappers, lumberjacks, and fishermen.

Rather, Canada is a predominantly industrial, highly urbanized country with four out of five in its population living in cities as the largest ten cities produce 51% of Canada's GDP.

Only about 10% of Canada's GDP comes from its primary sector, even though much of its manufacturing is centered on processing primary products. Industry accounts for 28% of GDP, of which manufacturing and mining constitute about a fifth of GDP. Industry creates 22% of employment.

In terms of sales, the largest industry is petroleum and natural gas extraction and refining, followed by the manufacture of motor vehicles, pulp and paper, meat processing and iron and steel. The auto and paper and pulp industries are the leaders, as measured by employment. Over one million jobs depend on the resource sector, making it Canada's second-largest employer.

It is nevertheless true that the soaring world prices of energy and natural resources turned part of Canada's economy on its head in the 21st century as its engines of growth are no longer cars and high-tech industries, which were hurt by the nation's strong dollar and troubles in the North American auto sector, but energy and other natural resources, which by 2005 constituted more than 60% of its exports when imported components are subtracted. The same applies to employment. Young Canadians in rural areas, where jobs are available in oilfields, mines, and forests, have an easier time finding work than youth in big cities. Since 2000 the number of blue-collar jobs has increased faster than white-collar ones. In oil-rich Alberta the unemployment rate is below that in the rest of the country.

A particular characteristic of Canadian manufacturing is that it is highly concentrated in four ways. First, it is mainly located in the two largest provinces: Ontario and Quebec. Second, it tends to be concentrated in the hands of rather few firms. For instance, almost all brewing is concentrated in one company, and the same is true of cane and sugar beet processing. Fifteen of the top 40 industries in Canada had concentration ratios in the hands of single firms of more than 50%. Third, an unusually high percentage of Canadian manufacturing is in the hands of foreign companies.

A fourth, and final, reality is that much of Canada's manufacturing is done by industries that produce semi-processed primary products. Such industries are particularly vulnerable to competitors in developing countries, where labor costs are much lower. In 1970, the manufacturing sector provided 20% of Canada's GDP, but by 2014 that had shrunk to 13%. In part because of the higher value of the Canadian dollar, outsourced manufacturing has not returned to Canada as it is in the U.S. Canada has become the most expensive place in North America for manufacturing.

This is not to say that Canada lacks high-technology industries. In 2006, the World Economic Forum ranked Canada sixth in the world in terms of information technology; the U.S. was first. It produces such sophisticated products as guidance systems for missiles and "smart" weapons, space satellites, and robot arms for American space ships.

"Canadarm" was used on more than 50 shuttle missions, most spectacularly on the repair of the Hubble Space Telescope in 1993. In 1987, it had become the first international partner to reach an agreement on participating in NASA's space station project. In 1999, the company that produced "Canadarm" was sold to the American concern, Macdonald-Rotweiler.

Astronaut Julie Payette
(Governor—General of Canada, 2017–2021)

It supplied a sophisticated computerized manipulator arm, called "Canada Hand," that not only services spacecraft in the sky, but put together sections of the orbiting space station after the U.S. has ferried them into space. In return, Canadian researchers are able to use the full range of capabilities provided on the permanently manned space station. "Canadarm" was retired after NASA launched its last shuttle mission in July 2011, but designers are working on a "next-generation Canadarm."

Canada provides astronauts, such as Chris Hadfield. The U.S. Navy Test Pilot of the Year in 1992, he was the first Canadian to be a part of a shuttle flight crew, as opposed to a scientific team. He commented: "For a Canadian kid, this was just an impossible dream." In 2001, he became the first Canadian to walk in space, doing so twice to help deploy Canadarm2 on the international space station. However, without warning the robotic arm froze and refused to function. This was a dramatic breakdown because the entire multibillion dollar space station depends on the Canadarm2. Fortunately, it was a computer problem that was fixed a tense month later.

In 2010, Hadfield was chosen to lead a NASA underwater mission, which uses the ocean floor to simulate exploration missions to asteroids, moons and Mars; he then commanded the International Space Station for five months. During this time, he shared his experiences by entertaining millions from space with musical performances with his acoustic guitar, many Twitter postings, and publicity stunts like demonstrating how to make a sandwich and brush one's teeth in space. At age 53,

Hard numbers

Rough diamond production, by value, 2005, %

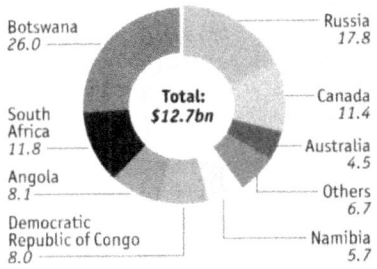

Botswana 26.0
Russia 17.8
South Africa 11.8
Canada 11.4
Angola 8.1
Australia 4.5
Democratic Republic of Congo 8.0
Others 6.7
Namibia 5.7

Total: $12.7bn

Source: *The Economist*

Canada

he announced his retirement at the Canadian Space Agency headquarters in Montreal.

In 1997, a Canadian born in Iceland, Bjarni Tryggvason, took part in an 11-day space shuttle mission. In 1999, Julie Payette (who later became the 29th Governor–General of Canada), was the first Canadian to fly to the international space station, and she returned in May 2009.

On 3 April 2023, NASA announced the crew of the Artemis 2 Mission, scheduled for November 2024, which will be the first crewed mission to fly around the Moon since the last Apollo mission in 1972. The crew will include three American NASA astronauts—commander Reid Wiseman, pilot Victor Glover, and mission specialist Christina Koch—and a Canadian, Jeremy Hansen. Hansen, the mission specialist, will become the first non-American to leave low Earth orbit on a moon mission.

Canada has a mini "Silicon Valley" clustered mainly around Ottawa. Nevertheless, some Canadians are worried that their country's manufacturing activities revolve too much around low-growth industries.

As in most economically advanced countries, the fastest growing sector in Canada's economy is the service one, in which no physical object is produced. If one includes all persons involved in wholesale and retail trade, finance, transportation, recreation and in the wide range of government services, including health and education, then three-fourths of all Canadians are employed in this sector; they produce 76% of GDP. According to the Economic Council of Canada, proportionally more people hold jobs in the civilian service sector in Canada than in any other economically advanced, western nation. This is this area in which most women who are moving into the employment market find jobs but it is also the sector that is hit hardest by unemployment.

Every economically powerful country has its own peculiar problems, vulnerabilities and dependencies. There is no denying that most countries on this earth would be delighted to have the kinds of problems that Canada has. Still, one should not lose sight of the fact that Canada does confront some real challenges, which include its large size, the tensions that plague federal-provincial relations, labor unions that are far more confrontational and ideological than their American counterparts, and heavy economic dependence on a single foreign country, namely the U.S.

Energy

Among Canada's plentiful natural resources are copious energy reserves of all kinds. It is self-sufficient in energy. This

Artemis 2 Mission Specialist Jeremy Hansen *Courtesy of NASA.*

is a particular blessing given the fact that Canada is one of the world leaders in per capita energy consumption, even higher than the U.S. Canada is blessed with large reserves of fossil fuels. In the 21st century, energy in all forms is Canada's number one export as it accounted for more than half its merchandise trade surplus with the U.S. Canada supplies 13% of America's natural gas needs and over 10% of its oil. Canada, with the world's second-largest oil and third-largest gas reserves, after the U.S. and Russia, is by far America's most secure and reliable source of imported energy, considering that the next suppliers, each responsible for 11%–12% of U.S. imports, are Mexico, Saudi Arabia, and Venezuela.

Canada possesses almost a quarter of the world's fresh water and 7% of the planet's renewable water supply. The Canadian government, backed by 69% of the people, according to polls, refuses to export any of it to the U.S., which is dangerously short of water in some regions. It is not surprising that Canada is a major producer of hydroelectricity, which now supplies about three-fifths of its own electrical power needs.

Since 1901, Canada pumps much leftover electricity into American grids. New Brunswick sells power from its Point Lepreau nuclear plant to Maine, and Hydro-Québec has major contracts with New York and New England states. Hydro-Québec took over New Brunswick's power generating plants in 2010 and proceeded to move into the American Midwest market of 66 million people, where electricity rates are three times higher than in Quebec. Manitoba sells ten times more electricity to its American neighbors than to Saskatchewan, and British Columbia exports electricity as far as California.

Canadian electricity companies benefit from American federal legislation mandating electricity suppliers to increase their renewable energy sources by 20% by 2020. The country's vast clean hydroelectricity is in this category. Hydro-Québec is also investing heavily in wind power. Despite its green image, Quebecers are the second biggest energy consumers after Alberta, 31% of whose GDP is derived from oil and gas.

Canada is a major supplier of electricity to New York and Michigan. At peak times, especially in the winter, Canada buys electricity from U.S. utilities. In fact, it was a problem in one of Ontario's relay stations that caused the great blackout in 1965, which paralyzed the entire northeastern U.S. In 1997, Ontario Hydro and Hydro-Québec were told by American regulators that they must open their markets or lose cross-border sales.

The U.S. and Canada have developed an interconnected power grid that is so tight that a problem at one power plant can cascade and cause a massive blackout. This happened August 14, 2003, when a breakdown in an Ohio power plant triggered automatic shutdowns of 100 generating stations, including 18 nuclear power plants, across Ontario and seven American states. It left 50 million Canadians and Americans, including 10 million in Ontario alone, without power. The blackout was six-times more extensive than the one in 1965. Officials on both sides of the border were left to confront estimates that up to $100 billion would be needed to modernize the North American power grid and increase its capability. In the previous decade, American demand for power increased by 30% while capacity grew by only 15%.

Canada produces a fifth of the world's uranium; 15% of its exports go to the U.S. In 2009 Canada had a total of 22 nuclear reactors, many of which are close to the end of their useful service. It had been two and a half decades since a new reactor was commissioned in either Canada or the U.S. Until 1999, Ontario relied on nuclear power for 60% of its electricity, compared with 13% for Canada as a whole and 20% for the U.S. Ontario had earlier announced that eight of its 18 reactors would be shut down after an internal study documented widespread management problems and years of inadequate maintenance and safety practices. This was a severe blow to the Canada Deuterium Uranium (CANDU) reactors, which had been touted as more versatile, cheaper to operate and safer than its competitors. In 40 year‚s CANDU was able to make only 11 sales.

Ontario dominates Canada's nuclear industry but has been in turmoil since an earlier Conservative government in 1998 broke up the now defunct Ontario Hydro, a long-standing monopoly. The province now has less generating capacity than it had in the mid-1990s. The problems with

Canada

Ontario's crumbling power generating system can almost certainly only be solved with more nuclear power in the future. In 2005, Ontario started up two reactors at the Pickering station east of Toronto and restarted two more later.

Environmentalists predictably vow to oppose any further plans to develop nuclear power. Although Ottawa has no say in how provinces supply their power needs, the Harper government supported an expansion of the nuclear option. Atomic power emits almost no greenhouse gasses; only the upfront cost of $5 billion for each nuclear plant is daunting. By 2007, public opinion in favor of nuclear had risen to 44% overall and 63% in Ontario, where people remember the 2003 power grid failure. However, Harper wanted the government out of the nuclear business as his government announced in 2009 that it would privatize the part of the state-owned Atomic Energy of Canada (AECL) that makes and services nuclear-power stations. This means the eventual extinction of CANDU.

Coal supplies only a tenth of Canada's overall energy needs. This is an environmental advantage. Canada is a net exporter of coal, selling more through Vancouver to Asia than it imports into eastern Canada from the nearby Appalachian fields in the U.S. Nova Scotia announced in 2001 that its last underground coal mine, the Prince colliery 25 miles north of Sydney, would shut down, ending a 280-year industry that had sustained a poor region. Ontario vowed to shut down its coal-fired power stations by 2009 although they provide a fifth of its electricity. Alberta is the only province still constructing coal-fired plants. Still, Ottawa and Alberta spend heavily on carbon capture technology.

Coal is a major contributor to global warming, a climatic phenomenon whose signs are obvious in Canada: droughts in the prairies and melting sea-ice and permafrost in the North. Coal is responsible for a fourth of all of Canada's greenhouse gas emissions, while only about 5% are produced by the oil sands. This amounts to one-tenth of one percent of global emissions. In 2002, parliament ratified the Kyoto Accord, which obligated Canada to reduce its greenhouse gas emissions by 6% of its 1990 levels. The federal government had to fight to win agreement among provincial premiers.

Some argued that Kyoto is a costly fiasco that would mean mass layoffs. The earlier Liberal governments endorsed Kyoto but did almost nothing to meet its objectives. By 2009, gas emissions were 20.4% higher than in 1990. The government could have offset this by purchasing emission credits from countries, such as Russia, that have exceeded their targets. But handing billions of dollars over to countries like that for this purpose was hard to sell politically at home.

After assuming power in 2006 the Conservative government acknowledged the obvious fact that painful cuts in jobs and public spending would be necessary to achieve small benefit for the environment. Such a modification would also require wrenching life changes that many Canadians would not make.

Canada uses more energy than any other developed nation in the world except tiny Luxembourg and Iceland. Like their southern neighbors, Canadians burn a large amount of gasoline, which, although more expensive than in the U.S., is still half the price as in Europe. It does not help that global warming sounds good in a country that has long and bitter winters. Some growers, such as grape, maple, corn, wheat and soybean farmers, would see their yields rise, and mining operations in the North would be easier and cheaper. Another bright note is that because of its low population Canada's overall emissions amount to only 2% of the world total.

The government reduced funding for the protocol in 2006 and dropped the targets. The U.S. refused to ratify the original Kyoto Protocol, but it nevertheless managed to reduce its greenhouse gas emissions because of its plentiful natural gas. With the U.S. and China outside of the protocol, the Conservative government announced in 2011 that it was pulling out of it, which every party has a legal right to do. Remaining in would have cost Canada multibillion dollar penalties for failing to comply with the emissions reduction targets. Harper argued that remaining in would have harmed Canada's energy companies without contributing much to saving the planet.

Canada's problems stem in part from the fact that 28% of its increased carbon dioxide emissions come from its oil production, especially from the oil sands, which is responsible for 5% of it. Since Canada produces only 2% of global emissions, the oil sands are responsible for only 0.1% of them. The Obama administration approved the construction of a 1,000-mile Alberta Clipper pipeline to carry 800,000 barrels a day of fuel from the vast oil sands into the U.S.. It was completed in 2014. An existing Keystone pipeline runs from Alberta to the oil crossroads at Cushing, Oklahoma.

Far more important was the fate of the proposed $7-billion 2,000-mile underground Keystone XL pipeline, which opened new capacity for Alberta's crude oil by extending from Cushing to the Texas Gulf Coast with connections to a network of pipelines and refineries elsewhere in the U.S. Since this crosses the U.S. border, the U.S. State Department had to approve. In 2010, it issued a favorable draft environmental impact statement and conducted public hearings along the proposed pipeline route, especially in Nebraska, where opposition was strongest. The pipeline company, TransCanada, submitted a revised route around the sensitive Sand Hills area, and the state's governor approved it in 2013.

The U.S. State Department then issued a new report concluding that the pipeline

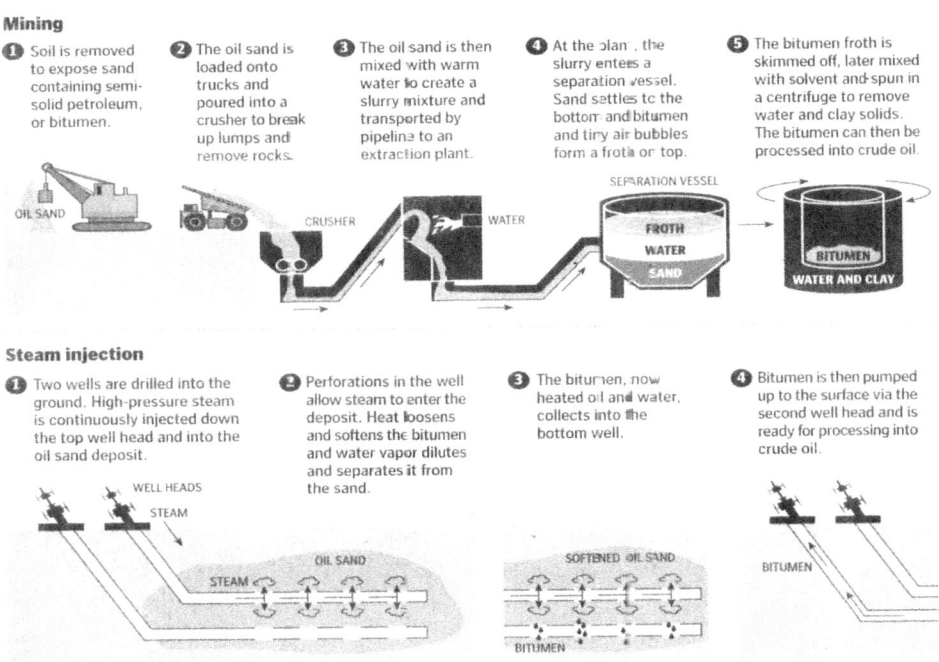

Source: *Washington Post*

Canada

would have little effect on greenhouse-gas emissions, that extraction of oil from the oil sands would continue regardless, and that alternative transportation means by rail or truck would be even dirtier and more dangerous. It approved of the pipeline's new route all the way to Texas. It reiterated this judgment in 2014, reporting again that the pipeline would have little environmental impact. The final approval lay with President Obama, who hesitated to make a decision until he was certain that the project "does not significantly exacerbate the problem of carbon pollution." Vigorous domestic debate and resistance from environmentalists delayed the decision. Finally, in 2015, Obama vetoed the pipeline. One of newly elected President Trump's first acts was to give the go-sign for the pipeline in 2017. With the ban lifted, the work could be completed.

Progress has been made in reducing oil sand pollution, estimated to be 18% higher than conventional extraction. For example, more than 80% of the water is recycled, and some tailing ponds containing wastes are being reclaimed as green land. Steam is being increasingly used in extraction. Still, the proposed pipeline became a lightning rod for discontent about the environmental consequences, especially CO_2 emissions, of exploiting the oil sands in Alberta and elsewhere. Nine Nobel Prize laureates, including the Dalai Lama and Bishop Desmond Tutu, signed an open letter to Obama condemning the project.

The case for the pipeline was not helped by two oil spills in Michigan in 2010 and Arkansas in 2013. Further a spate of crude oil train derailments created doubts about the transport alternatives to pipelines. Crude oil shipments by rail have soared as pipelines fail to keep up with growing supply and pose greater danger and environmental destruction than do pipelines. This was made tragically clear in a small Quebec town, Lac-Mégantic, In July 2013, A runaway train carrying crude oil derailed and exploded, creating a fireball that destroyed the center of the city and killed 47 people, Canada's worst train accident in 149 years. Progress is being made in oil car safety.

Stephen Harper, who considered development of the oil sands as a national strategic priority, was furious about the decision by the president of the country he considered to be Canada's best friend and which is the destination for over 90% of Canada's oil and gas exports. Supported by Trudeau's Liberal government, extraction of oil from the sands continues.

The oil sands, which contain 97% of Canada's oil reserves, became a major political and diplomatic problem for the Conservative government. Canada became a pollution villain in the eyes of many environmental groups. An international Climate Change Performance Index for 2009 placed Canada 59th, one rung higher than Saudi Arabia. The Trudeau government takes a more aggressive role in combatting climate change, an approach favored by two out of three Canadians in 2016.

More than 900 American companies supply Canada's oil sands operations as it is making plans to expand its Asian market for petroleum. Pipeline projects are being considered to transport its oil westward to the Pacific coast for shipment to China and Japan. The most important and controversial is the 728-mile (1,172-km) Northern Gateway Pipeline from Edmonton. Disputes with dozens of aboriginal and green groups complicated and delayed these efforts. Law requires the government to consult indigenous people on such development projects. British Columbians support it 48% to 32%, but the BC government insisted on a share in the royalties and more money from Alberta to cover the risks of such a pipeline. The BC and Albertan governments negotiated over this, and the Harper government supported the agreement reached by the two provincial governments. However, the Trudeau government opposes this. The prime minister did approve the Kinder Morgan Trans Mountain pipeline carrying oil for export from the oil sands to the west coast in BC. Another possibility is Energy East, which would deliver oil by pipeline from Alberta to New Brunswick.

Canada is one of the few developed countries with the potential to be self-sufficient in both crude oil and natural gas, energy sources now supplying about 60% of its current energy consumption. Natural gas accounts for about a fifth of Canada's total energy. Canada is not only self-sufficient in natural gas but is able to export considerable amounts to the U.S. which itself is experiencing a gas boom. In 1999, a natural gas pipeline was completed that transports enough gas from northwestern Canada to Chicago to heat a million American homes each day.

A massive offshore natural gas deposit, estimated to be equal in size to all of the country's known gas reserves, was discovered in 2002 about 120 kilometers (80 miles) west of Vancouver Island in BC. The fuel is frozen in a thick layer of ice, and environmental concerns could postpone extraction for decades.

Until recently, most of Canada's known oil and gas reserves and production were in Western Canada, mainly in Alberta and Saskatchewan. Today, 11 of the 13 provinces and territories, with Quebec and Nunavut being the exceptions, are energy producers and have more of a stake in the energy industry than as mere consumers. Thus, governments all over Canada have welcomed American investment in the Canadian oil and gas industries. During

On the coast of British Columbia Courtesy: Michael J. Hewitt

Canada

ST. LAWRENCE SEAWAY

2001 alone, more than $35 billion in Canadian assets fell into American hands. This brought foreign ownership to 48%, up from 33% in 1999, but below the 74% level in the late 1970s. Of course, energy investments flow both ways across the 49th parallel. Canadian oil and gas giants, such as PanCanadian Energy, Alberta Energy Company, and Nexen have extensive holdings in the U.S.

Canada is the world's sixth largest oil producer. With a 10% share, it is America's largest foreign source of imported petroleum products by far ahead of Mexico, Saudi Arabia and Venezuela. Oil furnishes almost 40% of Canada's own total energy needs. Now that Canada is able to extract oil from oil sands, a molasses-type substance also called tar sands, it has the world's second largest reserves after Saudi Arabia that are predicted to last for 40–50 years.

Investments in the petroleum and gas industries poured into Canada, not only from the U.S. but also from countries including India, France and China. The Canadian government made a rare exception in 2012 by approving a $15.1 billion bid by China National Offshore Oil Corporation, a state-owned, as opposed to a privately owned, Chinese oil company, for oil-sands producer Nexen. The sale means that China's government controls almost 10% of oil-sand extraction. Helped by tax and royalty breaks from the federal and Alberta governments, $51 billion in realized or promised investment in oil-sands development were made for the years 1996 to 2010.

The Athabasca oil sands in Alberta are the chief basis for Canada's energy optimism. They are found in an area about half the size of Colorado in central Alberta, and the formation extends into neighboring Saskatchewan. The commercial center is Fort McMurray with its peak population 88,000, in the northeastern corner of Alberta. Property values in this boom town shot up higher than in Toronto or Vancouver. Although a huge fire in 2016 consumed 2,400 buildings, it spared the oil facilities. The sands are estimated to contain the equivalent of 300 times the known recoverable Canadian liquid oil reserves. Thanks to impressive technological advances in separating the oil from the sand, almost half (46%) of Canada's oil production comes from the sands. Huge investments poured in from Royal Dutch Shell, ExxonMobil, and Total.

Almost needless to say, it presents a technological challenge to dig up raw oil sand using massive power shovels, or in a licuefied form using steam so that bitumen can be pumped to the surface. The process requires large quantities of water and natural gas to boil that water at a great environmental cost. Each barrel of oil produced requires two to five barrels of water and enough natural gas to heat a home for one to five days. Four tons of earth are dug up and the process emits lots of greenhouse gases as it produces two or three times as much carbon dioxide as does a normal well. However, progress has been made to reduce such pollution.

Oil sands production became profitable after the price of oil shot over $50 per barrel; the break-even point for new operations is considered to be $100 as compared to $30 to $65 for existing projects. Oil sand operations are expensive to start and take five to ten years to design. Once up and running, such operations have a 25- to 50-year lifespans with profit margins of about 15% compared to about 30% for conventional oil drilling. Yet, there are advantages: oil from the sands involves no exploration risk because it is definitely there.

Once up and running, the oil from sand production flows for 30 years or more. The crude oil that is extracted in this way is shipped to refineries in the American Midwest and on to Oklahoma and the Gulf coast. It is a hugely valuable future resource for Canada and the rest of North America. The collapse of world oil in 2014–15 hit Canada, especially Alberta, very hard: 40,000 workers were laid off, doubling the province's unemployment. Plunging oil prices dragged the Canadian dollar down as it lost 30% of its value. Canada's dream of becoming an energy superpower has been put on hold.

Other large potential reserves of oil and gas are believed to lie under the Arctic Ocean, especially Beaufort Sea, and under the Atlantic waters off the east coast of Canada. Prospecting and drilling off Canada's coast is expensive and dangerous as demonstrated by the capsizing of the oil rig Ocean Ranger, with 85 men aboard. Operations are also politically delicate, igniting serious disagreements between Ottawa and provincial governments over ownership and pricing of these resources.

Canada is encountering some difficulty in finding new, easily extractable gas reserves, as gas in western Canada is being depleted. The resulting squeeze has heightened interest in two ambitious long-term projects to transport natural gas from Alaska and the Canadian Arctic to the lower 48 states. The all-Canada route would link new gas fields in the Mack-

Canada

enzie River delta to pipelines in Alberta and could provide almost 2% of American consumption. An even larger one extending from Prudhoe Bay in northern Alaska through the Yukon to the Alberta pipelines would yield even more. Both schemes face numerous environmental, technical and financial obstacles.

In 1984, North America's first tidal power plant began to churn out electricity at Annapolis Royal on the Bay of Fundy in Nova Scotia, where the tides are among the largest in the world. Despite its long coastlines, immense forests and bountiful sunlight and wind, these kinds of renewable resources made up less than 5% of Canadians' energy consumption. It will be many years before these kinds of renewable energy sources will make a truly significant contribution to Canada's energy requirements.

The COVID-19 pandemic has significantly affected the oil and gas industry. Canada sends almost all of its oil exports to the U.S. and tens of thousands of energy-sector workers are at risk at losing their jobs. The oil and gas industry has not been good over the past five years and has only gotten worse during the COVID-19 pandemic.

Transportation

As immense as Canada, given the distribution of its population, it should best be viewed as a snakelike country, more than 4,000 miles wide and only 75 to 100 miles deep. The major population clusters are separated not only by such physical barriers as the Gulf of St. Lawrence, the Great Lakes, the Canadian Shield, the Rocky Mountains and sheer distance; they are also separated by lingual barriers. Boston, New York City, Buffalo, Detroit, Chicago, Minneapolis, and Seattle have always exerted an economic pull on Canadians as strong or stronger than that of other Canadian cities or regions. Therefore, Canada must expend enormous sums of money to bind that band of regions together that stretch east to west from coast to coast. From the beginning, constructing and maintaining roads and highways which cut through the Shield and the forests and which must withstand the hostile winter climate have been major undertakings. However, roads alone could never hold together the world's second largest country.

Canada was blessed with long coastlines and a fifth of the world's fresh water, all of which facilitated the cheapest form of transportation: by water. Nevertheless, a complicated and expensive canal system was required to bind these natural waterways together. None is as significant as the St. Lawrence Seaway, a grandiose project lining 56 ports that was undertaken jointly by Canada and the U.S. By means of seven locks, stepping from Montreal to Lake Ontario and eight locks along the Welland Canal, ships can now reach waters 183 meters (617 feet) above sea level and 2,300 miles (3,864 kms) from the Atlantic Ocean to the head of the Great Lakes. Containing a fifth of the world's non-polar fresh water, the five Great Lakes are governed by the Boundary Waters Treaty of 1909, implemented by an independent bi-national joint commission, which has functioned without dispute or political intervention.

Due to successful cooperation between Canada and the U.S., and the local governments around the lakes, they are much cleaner than they were in 1978, when the cleanup was launched. Still, Lake Erie was afflicted anew by a huge thick and growing coat of toxic algae that appears every summer and which covers one-sixth of its waters while killing much of the marine life.

By the 1980s, the St. Lawrence Seaway was losing much cargo traffic to barges down the Mississippi River and container traffic by rail to large Atlantic ports in the U.S. and at Halifax. Maintenance problems and the drop in American steel production have further threatened its major role as a seasonal carrier of grain, coal and iron ore. The result has been severe financial losses. Nevertheless, this bilateral cooperative project, completed in 1959, was a welcomed change from the competition that had existed between the two neighbors from the beginning of the 19th century, with the U.S. always being

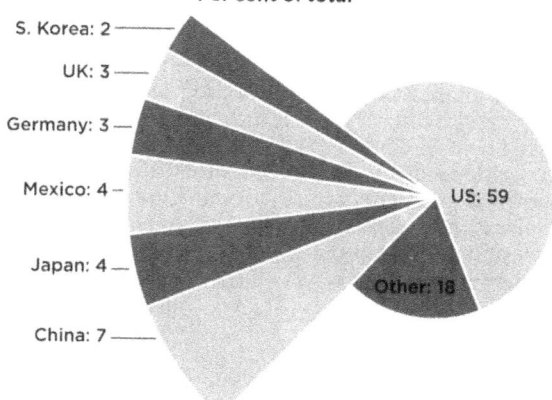

THE U.S. REMAINS our dominant trade relationship, but to prosper, Canada has to focus more on the rest of the world

Source: *Maclean's*

Canada

a step ahead. The problems of proceeding by water from the St. Lawrence River into the Canadian West had been clear since the early part of the 16th century, when Jacques Cartier was rebuffed by the turbulent Lachine Rapids just west of what is now Montreal, thereby frustrating his efforts to find a Northwest Passage to the Far East.

When the fur trade with the Northwest was diverted to the Hudson Bay in 1820, Canadian planners began to devise a way somehow to bring grain from both the U.S. and Canada through the Great Lakes to Montreal. These designs were temporarily foiled by the American construction of the Erie Canal in 1825, which enabled Midwestern grain to be shipped through the Great Lakes to Buffalo or Oswego and then along a relatively inexpensive, two-way, all-season canal through the flat terrain of upstate New York into the Hudson River to New York harbor. In order to build a competitive Canadian canal system required enormous support from governments in both Britain and Canada, and it also required solutions to daunting technical challenges. The first was to soften the abruptness of the 300-foot drop from Lake Erie to Lake Ontario. As demonstrated by numerous adventurers who have gone over the Niagara Falls in barrels, there are certain risks involved with navigating that treacherous watery precipice.

No sooner had the construction of the Welland Canal in 1829 solved this problem when the energetic southern neighbors presented another challenge: they expanded their railroads at a dizzying rate. By 1850, they had over 9,000 miles of track laid, compared with only 100 miles in Canada. This necessitated another Canadian mega project to carve railways, through hostile country from the Atlantic to the Pacific, that were so expensive that the nation was strapped with a huge debt even before it became self-governing in 1867.

The government chartered what became the Canadian Pacific Railroad (CPR), bestowing ultimately on it 26 million acres of prime land, more than $100 million grants and loans and 700 miles of already-built railway in eastern Canada. Pierre Berton wrote in his books, *The National Dream* and *The Last Spike*, that the CPR tied Canada together "like a line of steel from coast to coast." "Our cities and towns popped up along it like beads on a string. Without it we would have developed vertically rather than horizontally. We became the nation we are because of the railroad."

The Canadian Rail Passenger Service or VIA, is heavily subsidized by taxpayers. Prior to establishing this service in 1977, rail passenger service had been provided almost wholly by the two Canadian systems, Canadian Pacific and Canadian National. Both are private since the government privatized CN in 1995. Most shares were bought by Americans and doubled their value in two years. CN's largest shareholder is Bill Gates, who possesses about 10% of its stock. To remain economically viable, CN shed 14,000 of its 36,000 employees and sold off a half billion dollars of real estate holdings, including the CN Tower in Toronto. It abandoned more than a quarter of its track. By 1996, it was earning a profit.

Seeking to cut costs, the CPR requested the government to take over its passenger operations, forgetting about the huge subsidies it had received from the government when it was built. The state's purchase of the passenger business left the CPR as one of the world's most profitable railways, with large holdings in the energy, shipping, trucking and hotel sectors. It moved its headquarters from Montreal to Calgary in 1996.

CP Rail and Canadian National, renamed CN North America with its headquarters in Montreal, entered the north-south freight market in a big way. CP Rail owns two U.S. railways, the Soo Line in the Midwest and Delaware and Hudson in the Northeast. CN North America formed an alliance with the Burlington Northern railway in the West. CN also allied with America's largest long-distance trucking firm, JB Hunt. After NAFTA went into effect, trains started running from Canada through the U.S. into Mexico. In 2000, CN and CP agreed to share track in Canada and the U.S. CN gained access to CP's New York, New Jersey, and Pennsylvania networks, while CP began operating on CN's busy Toronto–Chicago main line. This agreement was historic for such traditional rivals. In 2012, the New York hedge fund Pershing Square Capital Management LP took a 12.2% stake in CP and installed an American boss. The oil sands have sharply boosted both companies' freight revenues. Trains bring supplies and carry out crude oil.

VIA was chartered and the passenger service was amalgamated into a single system calculated to save costs. However, as in the U.S., when it comes to calculating the cost of passenger service, railroad accountants are highly imaginative. The system provides vital service to areas with no roads which otherwise would not be accessible. A few smaller lines supplement this service. Combined, they reach such remote points as Mosoonee on James Bay, where there may be snowstorms in June, and Churchill on Hudson Bay, where polar bears plague the local dumps and trash bins. Canada is home to the world's largest polar bear population, numbering 15,000. In all, the system reaches 450 communities, but 85% of its revenues are generated in the Quebec City-Windsor corridor linking the major cities in Ontario and Quebec.

By 1989, the government had to face squarely the obvious problem that Via simply was not sustainable. Federal subsidies had risen steadily, totaling $1.6 billion from 1992–7 with an increase of $402 million in 2000, and ridership had declined from 55.4 million passengers in 1945 to 6.4 million in 1988, less than 5% of total intercity travel by all means of transportation. Half the track being used was originally built before 1914. Therefore, routes and subsidies were slashed. More than half of Via's service disappeared in 1990, to about 9.5 million kilometers, down from 19 million.

From 1990 to 1998, service had fallen from 810 trains per week to 396, and Via's job force had been slashed from 7,000 to 3,000. Some transcontinental service from Vancouver to Halifax and numerous regional routes, mainly in Central and Eastern Canada, remain. But its southern transcontinental route in the West on the Canadian Pacific was cancelled. Cuts created real hardships for travelers in many rural communities, where services disappeared entirely. Even so, healthy infusions of government money enabled a resurgent VIA in 2003 to offer 139 plush new passenger cars, 21 new locomotives, and renovated stations.

In addition to rivers, canals, lakes, and railways, there is an air link, the only tie to many points in the extreme Canadian North. Two privately-owned airlines competed: Montreal-based Air Canada and Calgary-based PWA, parent of Canadian Airlines International or CAI. Both struggled to survive. After their merger in 1999, Air Canada carried 80% of Canada's air passengers and got 90% of airline revenues.

The situation changed dramatically as

Canada

no-frills discount carriers increasingly snatched market share. Air Canada's fell by 2004 to 51%, and Calgary-based WestJet, modeled on Southwest Airlines in the U.S., steadily increased its share by 2009 to 36%. It hopes to squeeze out Air Canada and control as much as half the domestic market one day. It also signed deals with international carriers to corner a greater share of the lucrative transborder business.

A variety of other low-cost carriers, such as Jetsgo in Montreal and Canjet Airlines of Nova Scotia, have grown rapidly and even started cutting into Air Canada's extensive cross-border network. All of these trends helped force Air Canada into bankruptcy protection in 2003 and into acrimonious litigation with WestJet over suspected industrial espionage. Victor Li, a Canadian citizen and son of a Hong Kong billionaire, acquired a 31% stake in Air Canada. In 2004, it emerged from bankruptcy. It flies smaller aircraft more frequently on domestic routes to compete with low-cost competitors, while expanding its more profitable international routes. America's stricter visa requirements for transit passengers encourage more international passengers to fly over Toronto, Montreal and Vancouver, thereby benefiting Air Canada, enabling it to return to profitability. The rejuvenated airline selected Céline Dion as its main advertising voice.

In 1995, Canada and the U.S. signed an "open skies" agreement allowing their airlines access to any airport on the other side of the border at unregulated prices. For the first time in more than three decades, there is direct service between Washington, DC, and Canadian cities. In the five years after the agreement was signed, air passenger traffic between the two countries went up by two-thirds, as 24 U.S. cities began direct flights to Canada, and Air Canada tripled its American destinations to 45.

Federalism and Labor

A second major concern is the effect on the economy of federal-provincial controversies. Canada is a federal state in which the provinces are more powerful than are American states. The boundaries of jurisdictions between the governments in Ottawa and in the provinces have not yet been as sharply drawn as in the U.S.; the upshot is that these overlapping jurisdiction become very visible in economic disputes. The situation is made more difficult because the two levels of government have become much more economically interdependent since 1945.

In an attempt to even out the economic disparities among the various provinces and to demonstrate to all Canadians the benefits of being a part of Canada, no matter where in the country they might live, the federal government transfers some of its tax revenues directly to the provinces. These "transfer payments" are made on the basis of a hodge-podge of fiscal formulae, laws, regulations, subsidies and traditions, which support such activities as social welfare, health and education.

The allocation formulae inevitably cause serious disagreements between Ottawa and the provincial governments, some of which depend on such payments for half their budgets. Saskatchewan, Alberta and BC receive nothing. Transfers to newly rich Newfoundland and Nova Scotia were supposed to be reduced by 70 to 90 cents for every dollar of provincial revenue for their huge offshore oil and gas reserves. The Newfoundland government retained some of its support, though. An embarrassed Ontario moved into the "have-not" category. Becauseee more than two-thirds of Canadians now live in a province receiving equalization payments, the math no longer works. Ontario's have-not status threatens the sustainability of the system.

It is not clear that these transfer payments significantly improve poorer regions' basic economic structures; some of the Atlantic provinces remain relatively poor, and Alberta is the economic leader. Nevertheless, these transfers sometimes spark criticism from the U.S. because the assistance to exporting industries smacks of export subsidies forbidden by GATT international trade agreements. There are few policy areas where only one government acts.

Intense intergovernmental arguments are raging over transfer payments. The negotiations and compromising necessary to coordinate economic policies greatly delay solutions. In an effort to reduce the federal government deficit, the Liberal government made serious cuts in the transfer payments to the provinces. Between 1990 and 1998 the total value of such payments fell by 5.4%, leaving the provinces to serve more people with less money. In response, they cut services, including in health care, universities, and welfare.

Social welfare is almost entirely a provincial responsibility, with Ottawa providing only 16% of health care costs. Cash transfers to the provinces constituted about 10% of federal program spending in 1997. In 1999, then Prime Minister Chrétien and nine premiers agreed on a "social union" to provide a framework for more power sharing and cooperation on national social programs. Quebec's premier rejected the plan because it did not give Quebec the right to opt out of new federal programs and simply take its proportionate share of federal funding.

A third burden to the economy is the type of labor unions in Canada. Of course, employers' power in Canada needs the same kinds of organized employee checks as in other countries. Workers and civil servants have almost complete freedom to organize in Canada, and the unions perform an essential function of watching out for employee interests. Almost a third, 30%, of private employees compared with less than 10% in the U.S. of all wage-earners are unionized; further, 70% of members belong to unions affiliated with the Canadian Labor Congress (CLC). Private sector union membership in 2008 had declined to 16%, while 71% of public sector workers are unionized, comparable to the situation in the U.S.

As in the U.S., unions negotiate by workplace rather than across an industry. Canadian unions are a blend between American and British and have problems stemming from both connections. A further complication is that many union leaders in Quebec are nationalists who are willing to use their economic clout to further their separatist or provincial political goals.

About half of the Canadian labor movement belongs to unions whose headquarters are in the U.S. and are extensions of large American unions. The AFL-CIO affiliates give their Canadian branches considerable autonomy, but Canadian unionists are nevertheless subject to pressures from south of the border. After a 1984 strike against General Motors of Canada resulted in a settlement more favorable than that received by American workers, Canadian United Auto Workers (UAW) director Robert White decided to sever Canadian auto workers from the American-based UAW. White no doubt hoped that other Canadian unionized workers would follow, but Canadian members of the United Steelworkers refused in 1985 to break their ties with their Pittsburgh headquarters.

The more militant tendency reflects the other labor heritage which Canadian unions share: the British one. As in the United Kingdom, Canadian unions are organized along craft lines. This means that a company must usually deal with multiple unions, rather than with only one. Consequently, if only one union strikes, an entire plant closes down. Canadian unionists tend to regard their American counterparts as too cowardly and too accommodating to employers.

Another difference is the ties unions have to political parties. Although most American unions like to support the candidates of the Democratic Party, it is a moderate, middle-of-the-road party. By contrast, the CLC is directly supportive of the New Democratic Party, much as Brit-

Canada

ish unions are organizationally linked to the British Labour Party. The NDP once wrote class conflict on its banner, and, therefore, Canadian unions share a tempered spirit of class conflict. The CLC is always forced to deal with governing parties in Ottawa and most provinces that it is trying to put out of power. This makes for considerable tension.

In Canada, the unions' political influence has declined, and their support by the general public is waning because they have shown themselves to be impotent in fighting unemployment. On top of their image problems, they are unable to attract white collar and service industry workers. As in the U.S., their traditional base, smokestack industries and mining, are losing jobs due to technological changes. An outgrowth of this more confrontational approach is that Canada has the third-worst strike record among western industrialized countries after Iceland and Spain. When Canadians strike, they tend to strike hard and long. The first national public-service strike in Canadian history almost paralyzed the country in 1991. The frequency of strikes, sometimes with the financial backing of hefty strike funds in the U.S., is one of the factors that make Canadian productivity lower than in the U.S. even though it outperforms the American neighbor in some sectors.

Economic Dependence

A fourth major economic issue with which Canadians have struggled since their inception as a self-governing people is their dependence on the outside world, especially on a single country—the U.S. With a relatively small domestic market, Canada must trade heavily abroad in order to maintain its citizens' high standard of living. Fifty-two percent of Canada's GDP is generated by foreign trade, and the bulk of that trade is with its neighbor to the south. In some sectors of Canada's economy, the dependence on foreign trade is much greater. For newsprint the proportion is 88%; for wheat 85%, and for zinc 61%.

In 1972, the Canadian government decided to try a "third option" to impossible self-reliance and excessive dependence on the U.S.: to diversify its trade with countries other than the U.S., Canadians vigorously sought trade with the EU and Asia.

In 2009, Canada and the EU gave the green light to talks aiming at a trade agreement. Most trade between Canada and the EU was already tariff-free. What remained were farm products, which were the hardest to eliminate. The deal is more ambitious than the Canada–U.S. free trade agreement insofar as it included the provinces and sought to open markets in services, investment, and government procurement. The Comprehensive Economic and Trade Agreement (CETA), completed and put into effect in 2017, is Canada's most important trade agreement since NAFTA and now the USMCA.

China is Canada's second-largest trading partner, accounting in 2019 for $24.4 billion of its exports and $6.48 billion of its imports. The EU is also Canada's second biggest source of investment after the U.S. Ex-Prime Minister Harper hailed the EU as "the biggest deal our country has ever made." The deal opened access to a larger market than does NAFTA and is broad in its sweep as it not only eliminates 99% of tariffs on both sides of the Atlantic, but removes regulations and red tape on services and many other areas. The inclusion of the ten provinces as parties to the negotiations was something new. The CETA agreement had to be approved by all the provinces, the EU's 28 member states and the European Parliament.

The EU, the world's largest trading bloc, trades five times more with China than with Canada. Ottawa wants more of that trade for itself, and Canadians agree. A *Maclean's* poll in 2012 revealed that 72% of respondents believed that American dominance peaked in the 20th century. A third preferred China as the partner for future trade, 22% the EU, 15% India, and only 12% the U.S. While the U.S. remains Canada's main trading partner, popular enthusiasm for continental free trade has plunged from 80% at the turn of the century to 54% in 2012. even though 40% of total North American trade takes place within NAFTA, and Canada's GDP per person has grown faster over the two decades of NAFTA's existence than that of the other two partners. The government emphasizes that Asian trade would not supplant NAFTA but would take the country beyond it.

Canadian efforts to expand diversify trade in Asia bore some fruit. China is Canada's second-largest trading partner, with Japan in fourth place. However, Canada's trade with Asia is little more than 10% of that with the U.S. although it is growing faster. From 2006–2009, Canada signed eight bilateral trade agreements with other countries in a further attempt to lessen its dependence on trade with the U.S.

Vancouver, which is closer to Tokyo than to Halifax, NS, is North America's second busiest port after New York and handles more tonnage than all other Canadian ports put together. The seat of many banks, Vancouver aspires to become North America's gateway to Asia. Of course, the expansion of trade ties with Asia is a two-way street. The challenge to Canadian markets from China, South Korea, Taiwan, and other Asian countries with low labor costs and aggressive marketing strategies is as worrisome to Canada as it is to the U.S. This challenge from the Orient has given the two North American countries even more in common with each other and helped undermine the objective of the 'third option."

Despite the efforts to diversify, Americans still buy and sell about three-quarters of Canada's exports and imports. American-Canadian trade constitutes the largest two-country trade relationship in the world. This trade tie is very important for the U.S., amounting to about a fifth of its exports and 15% of its imports, roughly the same volume of American trade with the entire EU. According to Canadian government estimates, about 7 million American residents are employed, directly or indirectly in the export trade with Canada, and the border states of Michigan, New York, and Ohio are particularly involved in such trade. Clearly, this vibrant trade relationship is mutually beneficial to both neighbors, even though American trade has an overall greater importance for Canada than *vice versa*.

Roughly two-thirds of Canada's $75 billion tourist trade depends on American travelers. Thirteen million American tourists annually and million more from other countries provide jobs for one out of ten Canadians. Due to a tightening of the border since the September 11 terrorist attacks, especially since passports are required since June 1, 2009, tourism from the U.S. slowed down.

Canadians are also ardent foreign travelers. At any given time during the winter, 5% of the Canadian population is vacationing in Florida. Two million Canadian "snowbirds" find their way there, and more than a million vacation in Mexico each year. Francophones have their own free newspaper, *Le Soleil de la Floride*. From early November until the first week in April, Monday through Saturday, all can listen to five-minute news broadcasts on about 20 Florida radio stations, "Canada Calling—the News from Home for Vacationing Canadians," anchored by long-time Toronto newscaster Prior Smith (website: www.canadacalling.com). He is kind to his American listeners by using inches, feet, Fahrenheit and "zee," not "zed."

Francophones tend to congregate on the Atlantic Coast, while anglophones prefer the Gulf Coast. In 1992, the Canadian Snowbird Association was formed and since 1994 Canadians gather in the Florida State Fairgrounds for a couple days in January and flaunt their being Canadian in a "Snowbird Extravaganza," which offers entertainment and a trade show; 80,000 attended in 1997. The yearning for a warmer climate also helped persuade a

Canada

million Canadians to settle permanently in the Los Angeles area. By 2012, Canadian investors were not only snapping up distressed properties in sunny Phoenix, but they were the largest foreign buyers of American real estate, making up about a quarter of international purchasers.

A far more worrisome development than trade dependence, in the minds of many Canadians, has always been the high degree of foreign ownership of their country's economy. No other industrialized country has such a large portion of its economy in foreign hands, and certainly no other industrial country has such a great chunk of its wealth in the hands of *one* foreign nation. This is, of course, not a new problem. From the early 19th century on, investment capital, primarily British, poured into Canada to build canals and railways and to develop paper and mining industries. After World War I, the U.S. replaced Britain as the main source of capital.

John A. Macdonald's "National Policy," which erected a tariff wall against foreign goods in order to encourage manufacturing within Canada, had the unforeseen effect of encouraging foreign producers to scale that tariff wall by creating branch plants in Canada itself. That way, foreign companies could sell in the Canadian market and also, for a long time, even gain favored access to markets in the British Commonwealth due to the British Preferential Tariff. Thus, the high Canadian tariffs had at least two effects: first, they increased foreign ownership; second, manufacturing enterprises within Canada could relax behind the tariff shield, rather than strive for the kind of efficiency which would be required if they had been fully exposed to foreign competition.

In 1947, the discovery of oil in Alberta sparked huge foreign investments in the exploration and development of energy sources. Almost before Canadians realized it, foreign investments in Canada had increased by 800% between 1950 and 1975. At the same time, Canadians are investing more abroad, especially in the U.S., than foreigners are investing in Canada. Measured on a per capita basis, Canadian investment in the U.S. is twice as high as the American investment in Canada. In 1999, it owned 9% of total foreign direct investment (FDI) in the U.S., making it the fifth largest foreign investor, with the United Kingdom as first.

Statistics Canada figured that in 2005 FDI in Canada, primarily from the U.S., was worth $390 billion. By boosting a strong Canadian dollar, Canadian ownership of foreign companies, with the U.S. remaining the most popular place for Canadians to invest, was growing at an even faster rate, now worth $452 billion. In some sectors, such as machine manufacturing and metals, Canadians are already the leaders. Lured by many American chambers of commerce, Canadians are attracted by the political stability, the tax incentives, and the size and proximity of the world's largest market. Such Canadian giants as Alcan, Northern Telecom, Seagram, Bombardier, and Magna International bought companies in the U.S.

Some Canadians cynically refer to their country as a "branch-plant economy," the most important decisions for which being made in a foreign country. They argue American companies are like parasites, drawing huge profits out of Canada, closing their Canadian subsidiaries whenever it pleases them, and saving most of the research and development for their American headquarters and plants. For example, in 2015, Target, which failed to satisfy Canadian tastes, announced the closure of its 133 stores in Canada employing 17,600 people, leaving gaping holes in some prominent shopping centers. In 2018, Sears announced the closure of its stores in Canada, costing 12,000 jobs.

The critics frequently overlook the fact that these American companies created thousands of jobs in Canada, which otherwise would not have existed, introduce much future technology into Canada, and pay staggering amounts of taxes to the federal and provincial governments. In 2014, Burger King purchased financially strapped Tim Hortons, a national icon named after its ice hockey playing founder in 1964. It was the largest chain in Canada. Company headquarters were in Canada, where corporate taxes are lower, but it is managed from the U.S.

The election of President Donald J. Trump in November 2024 ushered in significant changes in American trade and foreign policy. Trump was buoyed by a victory in which he ran on a campaign in large part relying on a platform calling for an "America First" strategy. Trump's "America First" strategy included, among other items, helping to secure the border by preventing individuals from entering into the United States illegally along with stopping the large flow of fentanyl that is causing the deaths of many Americans and to end existing trade imbalances with other Nations. In line with that policy,

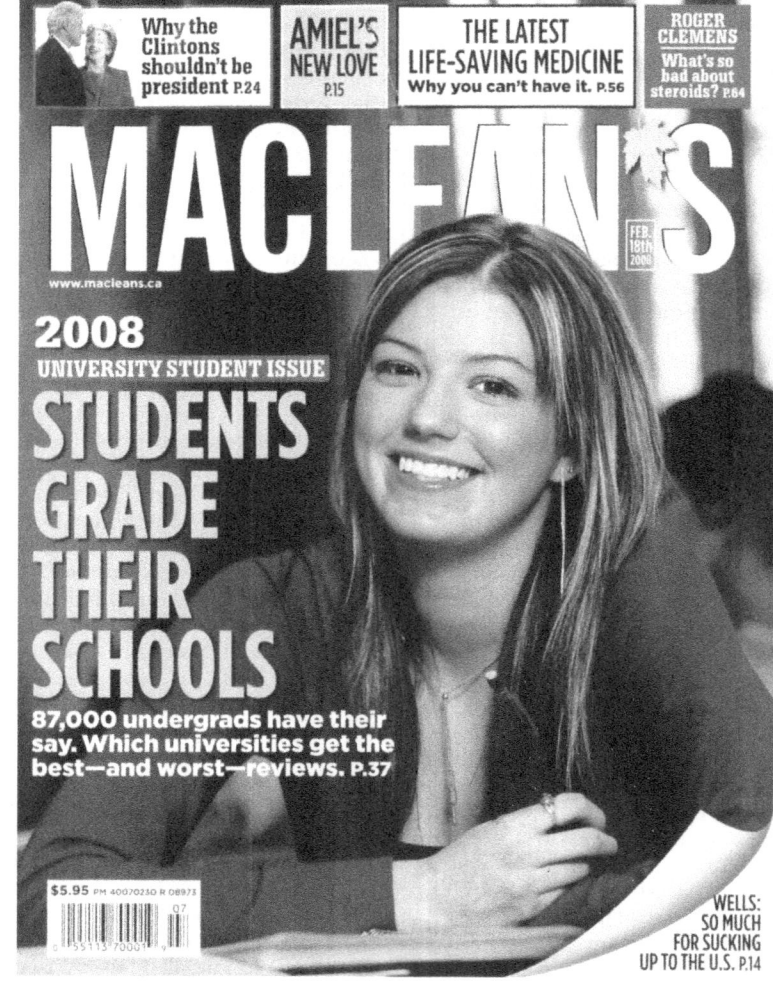

Canada

Trump announced the imposition of 25% tariffs on various imports from Canada, and other nations, in an effort to help revive the economy in the United States. Combined with this economic policy, Trump also made repeated comments about making Canada the 51st state of the United States. The initial 25% tariffs went into effect on March 4, 2025, after Canadian and American officials were unable to reach an agreement to pause or end their being imposed. In response, then Canadian Prime Minister Justin Trudeau announced that Canada would impose its own tariffs on goods from the United States. Also in early March, Trump rescinded what he promised would be even larger tariffs on Canadian steel and aluminum after Ontario Premier Doug Ford walked back a planned 25% surcharge on electricity exports to Michigan, Minnesota and New York. Not surprisingly, Trump's actions has caused significant conflict.

FIRA and the National Energy Policy, 1960–1985

By the 1960s, the question of foreign control over the Canadian economy had become an important and widespread political issue in that country. "Economic nationalism" exercised a formidable influence on Canadian politics from the late 1960s into the 1980s and became a considerable bone of foreign political contention between these two large neighbors. These fears prompted the creation of the Foreign Investment Review Agency (FIRA) to screen investment proposals by foreigners; such an agency actually came into existence in 1974.

FIRA was a red flag waved in the faces of foreign, mainly American, investors. While about 90% of all proposals were ultimately approved, a figure that climbed by 1983 to 97%, a fact that irritated many Canadian nationalists, applications were so expensive and time-consuming that many potential investors decided not even to submit them. In general, applicants had to be able to demonstrate that the American company's presence in Canada would be of "substantial benefit" to the Canadian economy. Moreover, approval often came with numerous conditions, known as "performance criteria" that could include a minimum of jobs to be created or of money to be invested or requiring foreign companies to purchase supplies in Canada, a standard which, on American prompting, was declared impermissible by the General Agreement on Tariffs and Trade (GATT), now enforced by the WTO. These "performance criteria" would not apply to Canadian companies, so a double standard was created.

FIRA and other economic nationalist policies did succeed in the sense that foreign control over the assets of all corporations in Canada did fall from 37% in 1971 to 16% by 1981. On the other hand, foreign investors found FIRA excessively intrusive and began to fear that the Canadian government might change the rules of the game after they had placed their money in Canada. Foreign investments began to dry up. At the same time, inflation and unemployment began to climb. In other words, FIRA coincided with the worst recession in Canada since the 1930s, and unlike in the U.S., Canadian nationalism always tends to become weaker in times of economic distress.

FIRA became a major target of the conservatives who were not ideologically opposed to such regulation of foreign investment, but who concluded that such restrictions seriously threatened Canadians' high standard of living. Therefore, within weeks of becoming prime minister in 1984, Mulroney renamed the agency "Investment Canada," giving it the mandate to encourage, not discourage, foreign investment. Mulroney assured Americans that "there shall be one game, building Canada, and one set of rules. These shall not be changed after the game has started to the detriment of any of the players."

Investment Canada screened only those direct foreign takeovers of firms with more than $5 million in assets. The government continued to watch any foreign investments in the cultural sector closely, though. Almost all Canadians, of whatever political persuasion, are very sensitive to any threat of foreign control over Canadian culture.

Energy was another sector of Canadian concern. In 1980, at the peak of Canada's lucrative production of oil and gas, the government made its most far-reaching economic move, designed to take control of at least 50% of its oil industry by the 1990s. The National Energy Policy (NEP) was a series of legislative acts that, through grants, tax write-offs and various incentives, favored Canadian owned or controlled companies. There were other odious aspects of the NEP, from the standpoint of foreign investors as it operated retroactively to confiscate some of the foreign oil companies' profits. This lowered the book value of the companies and therefore made them prime targets for being bought out by favored Canadian firms.

American businesses that felt forced to sell out did not receive what they considered to be a fair market price. Perhaps worse, the NEP contained a "back-in" clause. This clause required the transfer to the government-owned oil company, Petro-Canada or PETROCAN, created in 1976 with its headquarters in Calgary, of up to 25% of the value of an oil or gas well after a find was made on federal lands; indeed, all land in the Arctic region is owned by the federal government. This clause took no notice of the exploration costs of finding the oil or gas in the first place.

By world standards, the NEP was rather gentle. The nationalization of all foreign energy assets was never considered, even though Canadian provinces earlier had taken over direct control of certain other raw materials: Quebec took control of most of the asbestos industry, while Saskatchewan did the same with the potash within its borders.

The NEP did represent a changing of the "rules of the game" by violating the principle that discriminatory changes in rules should not be applied to foreign investments already in place. This is a dangerous practice for any country that is so dependent on foreign investment, as Canada has always been. Both the FIRA and the NEP moved Canadian–American relations into the spotlight and stimulated intense irritation in the minds of many Americans who had barely thought about Canada before, adding tension to the two countries' dealings. As Andrew Malcolm observed, "it signaled the end, if a formal conclusion was needed, of the quiet old boy network of handling bilateral relations."

The basic objective of the NEP, to "Canadianize" the bulk of Canada's own energy resources, was and remains popular in Canada. In fact, one of the reasons why the Tory Prime Minister Joe Clark was thrown out of office in 1980 was the fact that he wanted to return PETROCAN to private ownership. In one respect, the NEP was succeeding: by 1983, the percentage of the oil industry belonging to Canada had already risen to 35%, an impressive step toward the goal of 50%.

The timing of the policy could not have been worse. In the years leading up to the NEP, oil and gas prices steadily increased, but by the early 1980s, they declined significantly on world markets. This meant that the holdings and profits of PETROCAN and private Canadian oil companies also declined. The government had calculated that rising oil and gas prices would provide the revenues to buy back much of the foreign-owned oil industry. Instead, those prices fell, and interest rates rose to the stratospheric level of 21%.

Canadian oil companies learned that they created serious problems for themselves by going deeply into debt to buy foreign companies at what seemed at the time to be bargain prices. These companies were thrown into a serious economic crisis. The most celebrated case of a Canadian oil company that went on a wild spending and borrowing spree was Dome Petroleum.

Canada

By 1982, Dome Petroleum was on the verge of becoming such a financial disaster that it could have undermined confidence in the country's entire financial system if the federal government and the banks had not given it large amounts of aid to keep it from going bankrupt. By 1983, Dome Petroleum had to take huge losses to sell assets in a depressed market in order to remain solvent. The lowered price of oil, combined with foreign investors' fears of losing any more money in Canada, caused drilling operations in the country to dry up for a while, and it diverted much of that activity to the U.S. The resulting bust severely hit Alberta's economy and temporarily created the first *eastward* shift of population in many years.

The economic costs of the NEP and FIRA brought a political reaction as well. Their introduction roughly coincided with Canada's worst recession in a half century, during which unemployment climbed into double figures. These measures exacerbated Canada's economic woes and actually discouraged the achievement of self-sufficiency. More and more Canadians became convinced that they were more damaging than helpful to the nation in the long term. The debate that ensued did not revolve around matters of principle; Canadians by and large accepted the federal government's right to seek the objectives which FIRA and NEP sought. Indeed, no people can be faulted for wishing to gain control over their own economic resources, and thereby over their own destiny. Instead, the debate involved the question of what is prudent and necessary for Canada.

In Canada, protectionist sentiment is usually strongest in times of economic prosperity but the years leading up to FIRA and the NEP were boom years. In times of economic adversity, Canadians are more likely to look for ways to facilitate the international trade and the in-flow of foreign capital on which their prosperity has always depended. In the U.S., the opposite is true: protectionist sentiment tends to be strongest during threatening economic times and weakest during good times. In Trudeau's final years as prime minister, FIRA's provisions began to be slackened and streamlined, and more attempts were made to assuage the fears of foreign investors. The Conservatives pointed directly at these nationalist measures as villains partially responsible for Canada's hard times.

The Mulroney government moved quickly to dismantle the two programs since the Liberal government had designed them. Most of the teeth were pulled out of FIRA's mouth and the thrust was reversed to encourage, rather than discourage, investment. FIRA was renamed "Investment Canada" and, in the words of one of its advertisements in foreign magazines, "the Canadian Government has placed the welcome mat out to foreign investors." By 1985 the Montreal and Toronto stock exchanges opened electronic trading links with the stock exchanges in Boston, New York and Chicago, facilitating the sale of a number of Canadian stocks to American investors.

In 1985, Mulroney signed an "Atlantic Accord" granting Newfoundland control over its offshore energy resources. He also signed a "Western Accord" with the premiers of British Columbia, Alberta and Saskatchewan that largely freed the Canadian oil industry from federal regulation. In a third step, Mulroney's government adopted a frontier energy policy known as the Canada Petroleum Resources Act, which meant less government intervention in federally controlled northern and offshore areas. Finally, the government deregulated the natural gas market.

Government controls on the exporting and pricing of oil and natural gas have been abolished, and discrimination in tax treatment of exploration spending between Canadian and foreign firms was ended. These accords effectively spelled the end of the NEP. Canadian ownership in its oil industry declined to 42.1% by 1989, down from 47.9% in 1985. In 1991, 15% of PETROCAN's shares were sold to the public, and in 1995 the Chrétien government announced the sale of its remaining 70% stake and eliminated the 25% limit on foreign investment in PETRO-CAN. In 2009 it was acquired by Suncor Energy, which had pioneered the development of Alberta's oil sands.

In 2010, a rare rejection of private foreign investment in Canada took place. BHP Billiton, an Anglo-Australian mining company, made a $39 billion hostile takeover bid for PotashCorp of Saskatchewan. Premier Brad Wall called on Prime Minister Stephen Harper and his fellow Canadians to "stand up for Canada" by opposing this purchase. Canada possesses 53% of the world's reserves of potash, a strategic resource vital to food production. PotashCorp alone accounts for about a third of the world's supply of this food nutrient. They stopped the deal.

Out of 1,600 reviewed foreign purchase requests in the preceding 25 years, this was only the second time one had been turned down. Canada has always been among the world's most open countries to foreign investors although the OECD ranked it in 2011 one of the most restrictive places for foreigners to invest. Still, some sectors that remain off-limits to foreigners: banks, publishing, broadcasting, cable television systems, telecommunications, airlines and one of Canada's two major railways. In 2011, the largest banks and pension funds launched a rival bid to prevent the London Stock Exchange from buying the Toronto stock exchange (TMX), regarded by most Canadians as a strategic asset. The new merger would be branded "Maple."

In light of the the Cornovirus pandemic, there has been a great deal of human suffering and major economic disruption. Global trade was already weak with merchandise trade volumes falling in the declining in 2019. In January 2020, China's decline in production has been felt around the world.

Free Trade Agreement

By 1985, the old, controversial issue of free trade with the U.S. again moved into political center stage. This debate has existed as long as Canada has been an independent country. When the British adopted a policy of free trade in 1846, the colonies of British North America entered into a Reciprocity Treaty with the U.S. This treaty facilitated free trade for many manufactured goods until the U.S. unilaterally abrogated it in 1866. This American move divided Canadians on the question of free trade with the U.S. for the next century and a quarter. After all attempts to reach some kind of agreement had failed, John A. Macdonald declared his National Policy of trade protection in 1878, asserting that "no great nation has ever arisen whose policy was free trade."

In the early 20th century, the Canadian government had second thoughts about this. Prime Minister Laurier reflected on President William Howard Taft's comment and question: "Canada is at the parting of the ways. Shall she be an isolated country, as much separated from us as if she were across an ocean, or shall her people and our people profit by the proximity that our geography furnishes and stimulate trade across the border?" Laurier decided that his country should seek free trade, but Canadian voters had different thoughts and voted him out of power in the 1911 election, which was fought on that issue. The Conservative slogan, "No Truck or Trade with the Yankees!" was a potent one. The arguments for or against free trade have not basically changed since that time.

Two world wars greatly intensified the trade ties between the Canada and the U.S. and after the Second World War they entered sectoral free trade agreements with each other. In 1959 leaders created the Canadian–U.S. Defense Production Sharing Arrangement, which permits unfettered trade in military products. To the chagrin of Canadian peace groups, the government and industries seek to increase their contracts with the Pentagon in

Canada

Prime Minister Harper meets with Presidents Calderón and Obama in Guadalajara

order to have a larger share of American defense spending.

The second milestone in sectoral free trade was the 1965 Canadian–U.S. Automotive Trade Agreement which required the Big Three U.S. automakers to build as many cars in Canada as they sell there. It is responsible for the fact that a third of Canada's exports to the U.S. and more than a fourth of its total exports are in the form of finished vehicles and automotive parts. Auto ownership in the U.S. has reached an astonishing 99.8% in the U.S., compared with 68% in Canada, and 85% of all vehicles assembled in Canada are sold in the U.S. Ontario produced more vehicles than Michigan for the first time in 2004.

The Canadian Autoworkers Union announced in 2005 that 57,500 Canadians were directly employed by carmakers, 10,000 fewer than in 1998; 85% worked for the Big Three. The auto pact did not provide for free trade in replacement parts, tires, batteries, and used cars. In 2000, the WTO accepted Japan's and the EU's argument that the auto pact violates international trade guidelines. The Canadian government unsuccessfully appealed the ruling. Canada's auto industry was responsible directly or indirectly for more than a million jobs in Canada, 11% of the full-time work force. When the Big Three fell into crisis in 2008–9 and Chrysler entered bankruptcy protection in April 2009, many Canadian autoworkers found their employment terminated or curtailed, but the government came to the rescue and acquired Chrysler stock that Fiat was eager to buy.

The Mulroney government was more interested in free trade. Radically reversing the position which John A. Macdonald had taken a century ago, Mulroney asserted in 1984 that efforts to control trade and investment "ignored the basic lesson of our history, namely that free and unfettered access to world markets has been a boon to strong and dynamic economic growth." No doubt the massive Canadian surplus in the trade account with the U.S. helped change some Canadians' minds.

Canadians have always been afraid that free trade with the U.S. would kill their weaker, less efficient manufacturing companies. However, this fear was less justified in an era when Canadians are able to sell more manufactured goods to the U.S. than vice-versa. It also makes less sense at a time when both countries face their greatest trade challenges from Japan, China, and some third world countries, whose lower labor costs help them to undersell American and Canadian products in those two countries' home markets. These challenges give the U.S. and Canada a strong incentive to join efforts to tighten their own trade ties with each other.

The business community is almost unanimously in favor of free trade but the Liberal Party opposed completely it. Some provincial premiers, especially in Ontario, were fearful that an agreement could prevent them from subsidizing or otherwise favoring companies within their boundaries in order to save jobs. Organized labor, supported by the NDP, feared that free trade could destroy the jobs of many Canadian workers. Finally, cultural nationalists argued that such cornerstones of Canadian culture as film-making and book production would be killed by free trade.

In an attempt to assuage all these fears, Mulroney announced that essential Canadian economic, political, cultural, and social features were not negotiable. In a speech in Chicago he said: "Our political sovereignty, our system of social programs, our commitment to fight regional disparities, our unique cultural identity, our special linguistic character—these are the essence of Canada."

Mulroney argued that "the deal is a must for Canada," proceeding to negotiate and sign the Free Trade Agreement (FTA) on January 2, 1988. The following 12 months saw one of the most furious debates and outbursts of nationalism ever to grip Canada. It pitted proponents, who argued that the agreement would protect Canada against American protectionism, keep economic nationalism within Canada in check, and create jobs, against opponents, who feared that Canadian industry and culture would be crushed.

As the smaller European members of the EU or EFTA have seen, distinctive cultures can indeed survive within free trade organizations. Also, some sensitive areas of the economy were exempted from the agreement such as water, east coast fish, most agricultural products, and the "cultural industries."

Free Trade was the crucial issue in the 1988 elections. The fact that Mulroney's Tory government was returned to power was an important sign that Canadians had largely shed their economic inferiority complex toward the U.S. In 1988, both houses of parliament approved of FTA amidst uproarious attempts to show who was the most patriotic: opposition members sang "O Canada," while Tories waved the Canadian flag. The pact went into effect in 1989.

The value of bilateral merchandise trade jumped by 42% in the first four years of FTA's existence. Yet, criticism persisted that it brought job losses to Canada. The issue of subsidies continues to be an explosive matter even while cross-border trade and investment boomed. In 1994, some shoppers were induced to stay in Canada by a lowering of Canadian taxes on cigarettes, as well as by the opening of 136 Wal-Mart stores, purchased from Woolworth Canada. Each has a McDonald's restaurant inside and the trademark low prices, customer service "with a smile," and "greeter" at the door. Wal-Mart promised that 60% of the products in these stores would be produced in Canada. This was necessary at first because of the requirement that every package in Canada be labeled in French and English.

The retailing giant had to learn some hard lessons about doing business in Quebec. Wal-Mart distributed thousands of flyers in English only and sent letters to its middle managers in English, which were violations of the province's language laws. Another problem is the way Wal-Mart 's name sounds in Quebecers'

Canada

ears. A columnist for *Le Journal de Montreal* claimed that "even uttering the word [Wal-Mart] is disgusting, like chewing an old Kleenex that was forgotten in the pocket of a winter coat."

Wal-Mart found itself in a legal thicket in 1997 when, fearing American legal action, it took a line of pajamas off its shelves produced in Cuba. This action was a violation of a Canadian law that forbids companies in Canada from complying with the American trade embargo against Cuba, with which Canada conducts normal relations. This incident merely demonstrated again how sensitive Canada is concerning its sovereignty *vis-à-vis* the U.S; Wal-Mart restocked the pajamas.

The Ontario Labor Relations Board ordered the company's store in Windsor to become the chain's first to have union employees. This did not happen, but in 2004 the Quebec Labour Relations Board approved the United Food and Commercial Workers (UFCW) union's bid to represent the 180 Wal-Mart employees in Jonquière, 250 miles northeast of Montreal. Wal-Mart responded a year later by closing the store, allegedly for economic reasons. Few people believed that explanation, and the union continued to recruit support from a dozen of the 44 stores in Quebec and at twice that number elsewhere in Canada.

In 2006, it faced a union showdown in St. Hyacinthe, 40 miles outside of Montreal, the only Wal-Mart store in North America with broad union representation. In 2009, a Quebec government arbitrator awarded employees at the store a labor agreement including a grievance process and seniority rights. Wal-Mart's struggle is greatest in Quebec, where about 40% of the workforce is unionized, the highest percentage in North America.

Despite such problems of adaptation, by 2005, Wal-Mart captured about 52% of the discount market. By 2014, it was Canada's largest retailer, not only taking business from other department store giants, such as Kmart, which has disappeared, Canada's traditional leader but now American-owned, Zellers with 28% of the market share, and "The Bay," a struggling dowdy department and discount chain that was sold in 2006 to an American company. By offering an 8% reduction in the price of a standard basket of department store goods and by winning customer loyalty through friendly service, it helped force Eaton's, a national institution, to seek bankruptcy in 1997, from which it emerged wounded later in the year; Eaton's market share had dwindled to 7% by 1999.

This was a bitter blow to many Canadians who for generations had grown up mail-ordering from the Eaton's catalogue and staring at its magical Christmas season displays. Eaton's, which French language police forced to drop the English possessive from its signs in Quebec, failed to adjust to a new age of retail competition. In 1999, Sears Canada bought Eaton's corporate entity and 18 of its stores including six downtown stores and the flagship Toronto Eaton Center, which were renamed Eatons, without an apostrophe, and reopened in 2000 after an upscale makeover. The rest were turned into Sears stores. However, this business plan failed and in 2002 five of the remaining stores were converted to Sears outlets while two were closed. Eatons is no more.

Though vilified on both sides of the border, Wal-Mart's success is related to what it offers to areas, consumers, and employees. Most Canadian communities with outlets reached out to and embraced them. Thousands of small suppliers compete to get their products on Wal-Mart's shelves and new stores receive six to ten applicants for every available job. A 2004 survey by the Canadian Imperial Bank of Commerce of more than 1,800 small-business owners in Canada revealed that only 16% claimed to have been hurt by competition from large retailers like Home Depot and Wal-Mart, and 5% said they had benefited from them. The overwhelming majority contended that their presence had little or no impact on their businesses.

The American chains keep coming. In 2013, Target took over leases for up to 220 Zellers stores, the last major Canadian discount chain, which had been owned by the Hudson's Bay Company. This was its first expansion over the U.S. border, but it failed within a year. Safeway also pulled out of Canada in 2013. Other American businesses hoping to make up for declining sales at home by expanding to Canada are J. Crew, Nordstrom, Kohl's, and Marshalls. Hudson's Bay bought Saks.

Canadian firms, seeking lower tax rates, lower wages in anti-union states, and especially market penetration, are the fifth-largest purchaser of American assets, with 9% of the total foreign holdings. Canada's international competitiveness is enhanced by its being one of the cheapest places in the industrialized world to do business despite its high corporate taxes. In 2000, federal corporate rates began to be reduced from 28% to 21% over three years, below the U.S. level. By 2007, it stood at 15%. In 1999, the start-up and operating costs of a business were 7.8% lower in Canada than in the U.S. A World Bank/Harvard study in 2000 placed Canada at the top of the international list for the least amount of red tape in setting up a business.

Canada's strengths are relatively high quality and inexpensive telecommunications, a good transport network, cheap fuel, low total business travel costs, and a lack of corruption. Housing prices used to be generally lower than in the U.S., but the average home in Canada was $449,142 in 2020, higher than in the U.S. Still 69% of Canadian households own their own dwelling. During the housing crash in the U.S. from 2008 on, house prices dropped more than 30% in the U.S. compared with only 8% in Canada. Canadians also have 2.5 rooms per person versus 2.3 rooms per person in America. However, one of Canada's weaknesses is that its manufacturers are only about 80% as productive as their U.S. counterparts.

The FTA helped reorient Canada's economy north–south rather than along the historical east-west lines. British Columbia looks increasingly to Washington and Oregon, Quebec to New York, the Maritimes to the American Northeast. A former Ontario premier said: "We have a stronger relationship with Michigan than any other jurisdiction around."

North American Free Trade Agreement

In 1991, negotiations the U.S. entered negotiations with its southern neighbor, Mexico, to have it sign on to NAFTA. Only a tiny fraction, about 4% of Canada's trade in goods and services was with Mexico. Yet, national leaders feared that the country court be adversely impacted by remaining on the sidelines, that its preferential access to the American market could be eroded, and trade and investment could be diverted. Canada thus joined the talks. The parties reached a trilateral agreement extending from the Yukon to the Yucatan creates an open market of then 435 million people, now almost 600,000,000 with an economic output larger than that of the EU. Proponents say that it increases growth and makes North America more competitive with Asian and European rivals, adding that it could be a step toward a Western Hemisphere free trade area.

The difficulty was to knit together three economies of vastly different sizes and stages of development and with huge disparities in per capita income; in 2007 this was about $41,640 in the U.S., $34,480 in Canada, but only $7,180 in Mexico. Negotiations were concluded in 1992 with the three countries' leaders signing NAFTA in December.

NAFTA, which took effect on January 1, 1994, was phased in over 10 years. In its first year, Canada's trade with the U.S. increased by 12% and with Mexico by 21%. Because U.S.–Canadian bilateral trade doubled from 1988 to 1999, few people in Canadian political circles criticize the principle of free trade. An EKOS poll in 2002 found that three-fourths of Canadians supported free trade with the U.S., up from 30% in 1992. In 2003, two-thirds favored stronger economic integration

Canada

with the U.S, and 57% even supported an economic union along the lines of the EU; 59% of Mexicans agreed while only 44% of Americans liked this idea. By 2013, Canadian support for NAFTA felle to 54%. NAFTA was oversold at its onset: it did not reverse U.S. trade balance, produce Mexican prosperity, or hold down migration to the U.S.

The strains of globalization have cut away at Americans' liking for free trade. Asked in 2007 if America has benefited from foreign trade agreements such as NAFTA, only 15% of Democrats and 20% of Republicans agreed. Hillary Clinton said in her campaign that NAFTA had "hurt a lot of American workers." Barack Obama vowed immediately to call the "president [sic] of Canada to try to amend NAFTA." When one of his staff met a Canadian diplomat in Chicago, though, telling him not to worry about such election rhetoric, the information was leaked and caused confusion in Canada. Both Prime Minister Harper and ex-Mexican President Felipe Calderón made it clear they would not support reopening the agreement. As president, Obama dropped the talk of reopening negotiations and limited his message to bringing side agreements on labor and the environment into the text of the treaty to make them more enforceable.

In the beginning, many Canadians had feared that closer integration with the American economy could threaten their social-welfare model, but that has not happened. Canadians are willing to pay the higher taxes needed to finance their generous public services. Nevertheless, conflicts continued over cultural products, wheat, potatoes, fishing, lumber, beer, steel, and other things. Most trade disputes between Canada and the U.S. involve sectors shielded from NAFTA. These disagreements test the willingness of both countries to live peaceably within the rules they had accepted.

In 1995, Chile was invited to join. In 1996, Canada signed free trade agreements with both Chile and Israel, with which it conducts a modest amount of trade annually, about a half billion dollars each. In 1997, former Prime Minister Chrétien called for more bilateral trade agreements with Latin American countries, beginning with Brazil. Canada entered formal negotiations with Costa Rica in 2000, followed quickly by free trade talks with Guatemala, Honduras, El Salvador, and Nicaragua. A trade deal with Costa Rica was ratified in 2002, and a bilateral free-trade agreement was forged with Colombia in 2009.

Canada also proposed a NAFTA–EU agreement, then a Canadian-EU pact. The EU turned this down in 1999, but agreed in 2009 to begin talks. Discussions with Japan to forge a trade pact remained fruitless. The Canadian market is too small to tempt some non-North American partners. In 2001, Quebec City was host to 34 Western Hemispheric nations to launch the creation of a Free Trade Area of the Americans (FTAA). Canada is one of FTAA's strongest advocates, with a 2003 poll finding that 69% of Canadians supported it. But it had made little progress by the end of the decade.

It may be surprising that although Canada enjoys freer trade with its NAFTA partners, there are still sizable trade barriers between Canadian provinces. Such "balkanization" is cited as an important reason for sluggish productivity growth. Two of them, Alberta and British Columbia, became so frustrated with the lack of progress toward domestic free trade that in 2007 they created the Trade, Investment and Labour Mobility Agreement (TILMA). Within two years, this eliminated most impediments to the free flow of trade, investment, and labor between them. An example of obvious improvement is that a hay wagon from one province that crosses the border into the other no longer has to have its bales restacked in order to comply with two different arcane transportation rules. The two neighbors are the country's fastest-growing region, with 7.7 million people and a GDP of CAN$400 billion. The agreement created Canada's second-largest economic unit after Ontario.

During the 2016 American electoral campaign, Donald Trump blasted NAFTA as "the single worst trade deal" the U.S. ever signed even though it has been a success with trade among the three partners almost quadrupling since 1994. But negotiations in 2017 and 2018 to update the treaty dealt with new problems left out of the earlier agreement, such as the web, e-commerce, and robust labor and environmental protections.

In September 2018, the United States, Mexico, and Canada reached an agreement to replace NAFTA with the United States–Mexico–Canada Agreement (USMCA). Ratified in March 2020, the USMCA took effect on July 1, 2020, replacing NAFTA, but effecting only minor changes to its overall policy direction.

In early 2025, however, the USMCA was itself thrown into disarray following the election of President Donald J. Trump in November 2024. Trump, acting on an "America First" policy, announced the imposition of 25% tariffs on various imports from Canada, and other nations, in an effort to help revive the economy in the United States. Combined with this economic policy, Trump also made repeated comments about making Canada the 51st state of the United States. The initial 25% tariffs went into effect on March 4, 2025, after Canadian and American officials were unable to reach an agreement to pause or end their being imposed. In response, then Canadian Prime Minister Justin Trudeau announced that Canada would impose its own tariffs on goods from the United States. Also in early March, Trump rescinded what he promised would be even larger tariffs on Canadian steel and aluminum after Ontario Premier Doug Ford walked back a planned 25% surcharge on electricity exports to Michigan, Minnesota and New York. Not surprisingly, Trump's actions has caused significant conflict, not least in relation to the ongoing operation of the USMCA.

Strong State Role

The territorial size, low population, and hostile geography of Canada have always necessitated a greater degree of state intervention in the economy than was the case in the U.S. Canadians have always been less receptive to the notion of a *laissez-faire* market in which the government intervenes little and more receptive to strong government control than have Americans.

As Canadian economist Dian Cohen wrote in a column in *Maclean's*, "public policy and public enterprises to activate the policies in the absence of private initiatives are even more Canadian than the beaver and the Maple Leaf. It is ironic that we Canadians spend so much time looking for ways in which we differ from Americans but overlook the one crucial characteristic that has always set us apart—an almost blind belief in the virtues of public enterprise."

Even though they differ among themselves in matters of degree, all Canadian political parties are more supportive of a strong state hand in the society and economy than either the Democratic or Republican parties in the U.S. During his electoral campaign, Mulroney stressed the Conservative welfare tradition. Nevertheless, in its first economic policy statement the Mulroney government had to conclude that in Canada "government has become too big."

This welfare tradition is visible in the large number of nationalized industries, or "Crown corporations," as they are called in Canada that can be found in virtually every aspect of Canadian life: in culture (Canada Council or the CBC, which was founded on the cry: "It's the state or The States!"); trade (earlier the Canadian Wheat Board); housing; transportation (St. Lawrence Seaway Authority, National Harbors Board); utilities (Atomic Energy of Canada, Eldorado Nuclear); industry (Sydney Steel Corporation); development (Canada Development Investment Corporation). Conversely, in the U.S., utili-

Canada

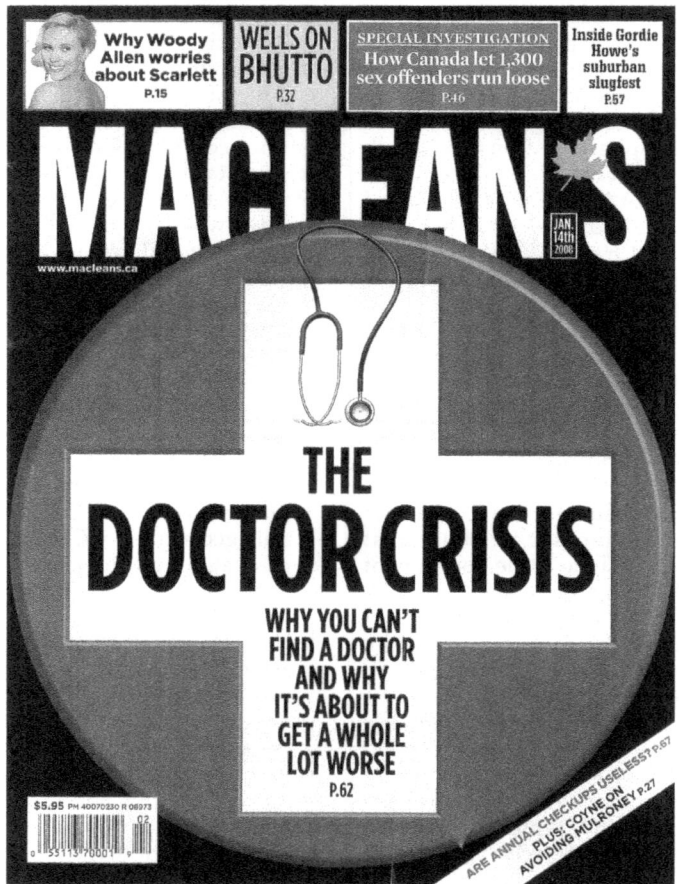

ties are privately owned, but regulated by public commissions, in Canada they are publicly owned and operated.

At the top of Canada's financial world are five banks: the Royal Bank of Canada, the Bank of Montreal, the Canadian Imperial Bank of Commerce, the Bank of Nova Scotia, and Toronto Dominion Bank. Among all North American banks, all five of these are in the top 15 in market value. Although Canadian banks were not immune to the global banking crisis in 2008–9, their value fell less than in the U.S. but no bank failed. In 2008, the World Economic Forum picked the country's banking system as the healthiest in the world; U.S. banks were ranked 40th. Canada's big five control 93% of the assets of the 12 national banks. In 1998, the Canadian government blocked two proposed mergers among four of these giants, calling the links "an unacceptable concentration of economic power." It would have enabled only two banks to control 70% of all bank deposits, especially since U.S. banks are prevented from entering the Canadian market.

In general, Canada has relatively few multinational companies. On the Fortune 500 list of the world's largest companies in 2004, Canada's top entry was George Weston Ltd. in 240th place. While Sweden has Ikea and Finland Nokia, Canada does not have a single global brand.

Some Crown corporations have existed for a long time and are known to some Americans, such as the CBC, 70% of which were created since 1960. Some make a profit, but some of them are perennial money losers and are kept alive chiefly to save jobs; in fact, many were taken over in the first place because they were not able to survive on their own.

Second, Canada has a higher percentage of its GDP in government hands than does the U.S. Of course, defense spending is much greater in the U.S. although it rose in both countries. In 2019, it accounted for 1.3% of GDP in Canada. If one only looks at the civilian sector, then the differences between the two countries would be even greater. Canadians pay higher taxes and have fewer write-offs. Canadians cannot write off the interest they pay on home mortgages, whereas this is perhaps the greatest tax "loophole" in the U.S. Americans can even write off the charitable contributions they give to Canadian charities; Canada is the only country to which the U.S. extends this privilege.

The annual *Maclean's*/CBC polls from 1997 to 2002 revealed that Canadians were less inclined to look to the state to solve their economic problems than they once were: they accepted the message that government deficits must be reduced if the country's long-term prosperity is to be preserved. Canadians are willing to tolerate fundamental changes in the social safety net: 61% accept the evolution of private universities; 53% are resigned to having the government hand over some social services to charities; and 47% find the emergence of a two-tier, state and private, health-care system acceptable. On leaving his job at ABC in New York in 2001, Canadian Broadcaster Kevin Newman recalled a difference that remains between the two peoples: 56% of American adults do some form of volunteer work every year compared with 32% of Canadians.

The growing trend toward individualism was confirmed in the 2002 *Maclean's*/CBC poll: 81%, compared with 71% three years earlier, thought they themselves, as opposed to government, labor unions or business leaders, were best able to take care of their economic interests. In 1997, Canadians gave then Prime Minister Chrétien his second majority in a row even after he declared that they "know that there is nobody who will have a magic wand and solve all the problems [just by] being there."

Health and Welfare

Another key issue is that Canada has a more extensive and expensive social welfare net than does the U.S. It is an ironic fact that many democratic countries that have conservative, elitist political and social traditions also have developed broad nets of social welfare. This is the case with Britain, Germany, and Sweden as well as Canada. In the U.S., equality of opportunity for the individual has been a supreme value, requiring a weaker state that could not place restrictions on the individual. Canada always had a strong state, and when it became democratized, citizens demanded that it intervene on behalf of all of them to secure more *equality of results*. That is, Canadians demanded that the state redistribute the wealth of the country in order to diminish differences among its citizens.

The Great Depression that started in 1929 gave special impetus to this. As Keith Banting observed in his work, *The Welfare State and Canadian Federalism*, "during the last half century, the Canadian state has established a new set of social rights, a set of claims for protection from the insecurities of modern society. It is deeply embedded in the fabric of Canadian life." Social welfare spending in Canada now embraces such things as pensions, disability protection, unemployment insurance, child benefits, maternity welfare, subsidized housing, and free medical care.

Under the Canada Pension Plan, all Ca-

Canada

nadians have the right to receive a government pension on reaching retirement age. This pension includes an automatic entitlement, as well as supplemental benefits for those who can demonstrate need. Almost all employed and self-employed persons are compelled to contribute to this plan, and the payments are financed from the contributions and interest of the invested funds. Like the U.S. social security system, it is a pay-as-you-go system, meaning that current contributions are used to pay current retirees. Unlike America's system, Canada's has been on solid financial footing for at least the next three-quarters of a century. Under the Family Allowances Act of 1944, parents with children under age 18 living at home and with low enough incomes are automatically entitled to a monthly allowance of $29.95, which is taxable, for each child.

Canada's Medicare system, paid largely from tax sources, provides health care to any Canadian in needs. Patients choose their own doctors, who are not employed by the state, and they seldom see large hospital bills. "Medically necessary" hospital treatment and doctor services are paid out of taxpayer dollars making up 71% of spending on health care in 2003. However, other medical goods and services such as drugs dispensed outside hospitals, vision care, dental services and long-term care, are not always covered. About 30% of all health care spending comes from private pockets. Originally the federal government paid one half of the cost but cuts greatly reduced that share to only 16% of its health dollars, with the provinces paying more and more. Within federal guidelines, the provinces operate their own health systems.

Canadians like this system in principle; in 2010, 69% said they were proud of their health care system. Former Governor General Adrienne Clarkson called Medicare "a practical expression of the values that define us as a country." In 2004 a television contest to determine "the greatest Canadian" picked Tommy Douglas, the earlier Saskatchewan premier who pioneered Medicare; a *Maclean's* poll found that Pierre Elliot Trudeau is considered the greatest Canadian, either living or dead with 22% of the votes.

Polling figures in 2002 showed that 85% of Canadians considered their health-care system better than America's with 87% opposed making it more like that of the U.S. However, Canadians argue about its problems and demand more funding. In 2006, the World Health Organization (WHO) ranked Canada 30th in the world, ahead of 37th-placed U.S., in terms of quality of health services. A 2010 comparative study of seven developed countries placed Canada last in terms of effective care and timeliness of care, behind the U.S. The level of government spending per capita on health care twice as high in the U.S.: $7,290 vs. $3,895 in Canada. As in the U.S., the costs of health care have ballooned; by 2005 they had climbed by a third over the past decade.

Canadians say that health care is one of their foremost worries. In 2005, 86% told pollsters that health care was a very or fairly serious problem. In the 2006 federal elections, Prime Minster Stephen Harper did not propose a sweeping overhaul of Medicare, but one of his five chief campaign promises were to guarantee shorter waiting times for services to help the two million Canadians on waiting lists. Yet, because this is a provincial responsibility, Harper was unable to fulfill his promise. Although the situation has improved, a quarter of patients, as opposed to 7% of Americans, waited more than four months for non-emergency, elective surgery.

Canada faces a crisis of spiraling health costs caused by higher pay and benefits for medical personnel, who constitute 7% of Canada's work force, soaring prices for high-tech medical equipment, and a growing number of older persons. To cope with the costs, hospitals everywhere have taken beds out of service, limited the operations performed, cut back on many services and purchases of high-tech diagnostic equipment, and reduced nursing and physician staffs. One result has been lengthening waiting lists and some highly publicized deaths of patients waiting for treatment or surgery. One exasperated patient claimed: "You could die before they know what's wrong with you!"

Asked in 2004 if their confidence in the health system was rising or falling, 6% of respondents said it was rising, and 47% said it was falling; 86% said there were not enough doctors and 81% not enough nurses. In 2005, only 23% of Canadians were able to see a doctor the same day they needed one. A 2014 survey of 11 prosperous countries placed Canada last when it comes to how quickly patients can get an appointment with a regular family doctor. Five million Canadians had no family doctor in 2011. Emergency rooms were maxed out. Part of the problem is that the new generation of physicians is no longer willing to work the many hours their predecessors did. This is related to the large number of women in the healthcare profession, who must juggle work and families: 30% of the workforce is female, as are 52% of physicians under age 35.

More and more Canadians wonder if their country can afford the popular publicly funded universal system that offers one of the highest standards of health care in the world. Few Canadians, even doctors, look to the U.S. for a solution although many Americans turn to the Canadian system as worthy of imitation. Health costs in the U.S. are rising even faster, and Americans pay a higher percentage of their GDP for medical care than do Canadians even though millions of the former long had no medical protection at all prior to the passage of the Affordable health Care Act, commonly called Obamacare. Canadian doctors, who remain in the top 1% of all professional workers in terms of income, must devote a much smaller percentage of their earnings to malpractice insurance.

Canadians are seeing their drug medication prices rise because of a booming cross-border trade in pharmaceuticals. Drug prices are cheaper than in the U.S. because of the lower value of the Canadian dollar and because of price breaks from pharmaceutical companies negotiated by the Canadian government. Ottawa demands lower prices and threatens to strip away patent protection if the manufactures do not give in. Americans who need common medicines, which can often be half the price in Canada, flock across the border or use the internet to acquire at a discount the medications they need. Even many American city and state governments are turning to Canada to purchase drugs although dozens of Canadian internet pharmacies refuse to fill such bulk orders. Thus, medicines mostly produced in the U.S. but intended for Canadians are being resold at a profit in the higher-priced American market. This tightens supplies and increases prices for Canadians. Former Health Minister Ujjal Dosanjh proclaimed: "Canada cannot be the drugstore of the U.S."

By almost any standard, the Canadian system keeps its citizens at least as healthy as does America's. A joint head-to-head survey in 2004 by Statistics Canada and the U.S. National Center for Health Statistics determined that the overall health status of both nations is remarkably similar. The study reported that Americans like their market-based health care system more than Canadians like their own Medicare, which costs less per capita. For-profit U.S. hospitals cost on average 19% more than publicly funded Canadian equivalents.

Life expectancy in Canada of 80.4 for men compared to 76.3. in U.S. and 84.2 years for women as opposed to 80.1 in U.S. At 84.3, Canada ranks 12th highest in the world for life expectancy as opposed to the U.S., which is 32nd at 81.6. Heart disease, the focus of much advanced American medical research, kills Canadians at a rate 20% lower than for Americans, despite similar dietary habits. Americans are more obese: 33% of women and 31% of men, compared with 19% of women and

Canada

17% of men in Canada; 36% of Canadians are merely "overweight," and 8% of kids are obese. At just over five feet eleven, the average Canadian-born male is nearly an inch taller than his American counterpart. More Canadians smoke regularly, but the disparities between the health of rich and poor are more pronounced in the U.S.

The Canadian approach to health care is that it cannot be left to market forces. In 2001, Canada became the first country to allow terminally ill patients to grow and smoke their own marijuana to alleviate their pain as long as they obtain a doctor's certificate. The Canadian government also began gearing up to supply patients and researchers. In 2018, this was extended to recreational use of the drug. Almost two-thirds, or 63%, of Canadians told pollsters in 2006 that they favored legalization. A government report revealed in 2004 that marijuana use in Canada had nearly doubled in the previous 13 years. A law was enacted in 2016 permitting people with terminal illnesses to end their lives with the assistance of a doctor or nurse.

A basic principle in health care benefits, as well as in other benefits such as family allowances, is universality, meaning that all Canadians can receive them, regardless of wealth and/or income. During his 1984 electoral campaign, Mulroney called such universality "a sacred trust." The daunting costs of the social welfare system caused his government to reconsider after the election, but public pressure on the government was so great that Mulroney was forced to back off from any attempt to tamper with this fundamental principle.

The soaring costs and federal cuts sparked demands that fundamental changes be made in health care and the welfare system. In 1994, Ontario ended health coverage for thousands of foreign students and immigrants with temporary residence authorization. Some provinces refuse to cover bills for Canadians visiting from other regions of Canada. Provinces imposed three-month waiting periods before new residents can be covered, and coverage abroad was limited. Specified operations, such as vasectomy reversals, that were once paid, are no longer free.

In 2004, Ontario imposed a new healthcare tax while removing coverage for physiotherapy, chiropractic and eye tests. In the same year Vancouver's St. Paul's Hospital contracted out 947 publicly funded surgeries to three private clinics. Private health care had already slipped into the door. In 2004, almost a third of all money spent on health care had been paid for out of private pockets. Private clinics were springing up everywhere.

The ground was thereby set for the kind of private services and insurance approved by the Supreme Court in a landmark ruling in June 2005. The Justices struck down a law from Quebec that banned private medical insurance and ordered the provincial officials to enact a reform within a year. The Court ruled that long waits for various medical procedures violate patients' lives and freedom and that prohibitions on private health insurance were unconstitutional when the public system failed to deliver "reasonable services."

The Supreme Court of Canada's judgment generated calls for more private clinics and insurance in multiple provinces beyond Quebec, which already had about 50 private health clinics even before the court decision. While there were dozens of such clinics in Alberta and BC, they were primarily limited to services not covered by Medicare.

Polls in 2004 indicated that Canadians are very wary about their health-care system and were open to change as long as there is no resort to higher co-payments and personal wealth to get timely care. A year later, 59% of respondents supported the Supreme Court's order; a further 59% expressed their support for Alberta's proposal permitting payment out-of-pocket for service enhancements, like better prosthetic joints; and a majority believed that private insurance would reduce waiting times and have a positive effect on Medicare as a whole.

BC and Alberta led the way to more private care. The BC government considered a system in which it would pay for essential treatment delivered in both public and private clinics and hospitals. Albertans are discussing legislation to permit doctors to practice simultaneously in private and public institutions and to permit the construction of private hospitals. Even the widely read weekly newsmagazine *Maclean's* devoted an entire issue on May 1, 2006, to advising Canadians on all the private care offerings in their country.

The level of care varies from region to region and from city to rural locales. Attempting to eliminate the federal deficit, Ottawa took billions of dollars out of the system, amounting to an 8.7% reduction from 1985–95. This left the difficult decisions to the provinces, which passed many of them on to local governments. The federal government thereby abdicated its right to insist on maintaining national standards. In effect, there is no longer a national Medicare system.

Because Ottawa was under intense pressure to return to the provinces the money it had taken from health care, so in 2000 the federal budget boosted such spending by 25%.

The biggest health scare in 2003 was the spread of a mysterious respiratory disease, Severe Acute Respiratory Syndrome,

Canada

or SARS, to Canada. Due to its close links with China, Toronto became the population center most affected by the deadly virus outside of Asia.

The WHO thought it necessary to issue a travel advisory twice for Toronto, an embarrassing and economically damaging move the city's mayor called outrageous. Toronto accounts for 20% of Canada's economic growth and tourism is the city's second-largest industry after finance. SARS seriously blemished Toronto's image as a safe place to visit and live even though the city won praise for the way it handled the crisis. The illness claimed 31 lives in Toronto, 44 in Ontario. An investigative commission issued a report in 2007 that SARS spread due to a shoddy public health system and inadequate safety practices insofar as almost three-fourths of the victims became infected in clinics and hospitals.

In 2004, British Columbia experienced an outbreak of an avian influenza, which was fortunately not the kind that could infect humans and animals. Nevertheless, 38 countries, including the U.S., imposed bans on poultry products from BC while 19 million chickens, turkeys, and other poultry had to be killed to prevent the flu from spreading. COVID-19 is the latest outbreak to affect the Canadian health care system.

According to IBISWorld, the challenge for Canadian hospitals is that they are already functioning at a 100% capacity rate or more for the last 20 years. With the increased number of affected people needing health care because of the COVID-19, hospitals will be even more overcrowded and come with added challenges.

The erosion of the Canadian health system shows the risks of making health care dependent on taxes. When budget deficits must reduced, and political pressure makes tax increases impossible, health and welfare programs become targets for cuts. The earlier Reform and Alliance Parties' success since 1993 demonstrated the appeal in Canada of attacking government waste and abuse by overhauling social programs and holding the line on taxes.

The rapid rise in Canadian taxes from 31.6% of GDP in 1980 to 36.8% in 1999, compared with 29% in the U.S., provoked a near tax revolt. The difference is particularly pronounced in income taxes: at middle-income levels, Americans pay about half the income tax Canadians owe. Yet 40% of Canadians pay no income tax at all, and the lowest rate is 15%. Those in the top income bracket pay from 39% in Alberta to 48% in Quebec, compared with a top of 37% in the U.S. The high taxes have driven wealthy Canadians, such as singer Shania Twain, billionaire Michael

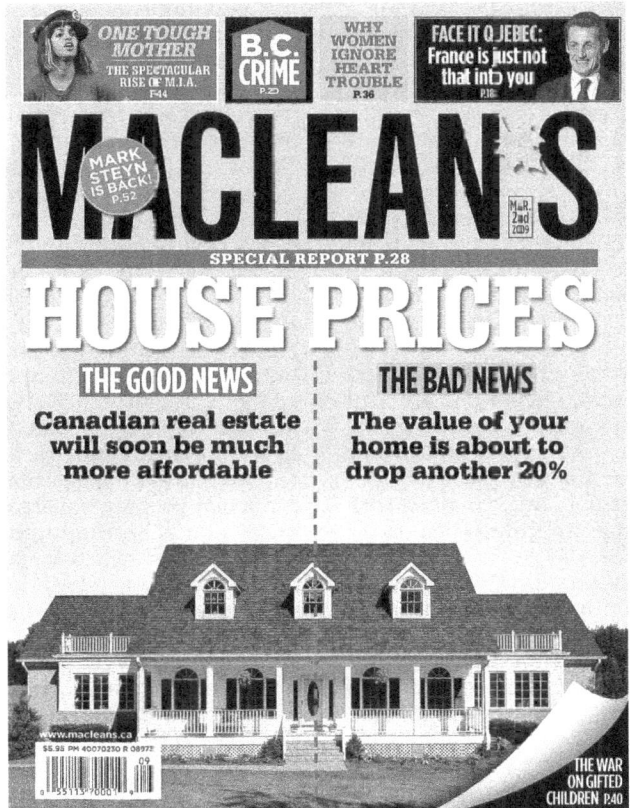

DeGroote and auto magnate Frank Stronach, to establish residency in lower tax jurisdictions, such as Bermuda or Switzerland. In 2008 the federal goods and services tax fell to 5%.

While Canadians remain devoted to their safety net, they are demanding that their governments end what seems to be a built-in incentive for those who resort to welfare and unemployment. In 1999, Ottawa responded by providing a modest tax break. This was continued in 2000, when the federal government announced sweeping tax cuts, indexing tax brackets to inflation to eliminate "bracket creep," and increasing child tax benefits. Canadians often find welfare policy models in the U.S. In 2007, the federal government proposed a Working Income Tax Benefit to make work more appealing than welfare. This is practically a carbon copy of America's Earned Income Tax Credit.

There seems to be an emerging consensus that many social programs have failed to solve the problems of those who need them most, while bestowing benefits on many for whom they were never intended. From 1981 to 1995, the number of Canadians on social assistance doubled. Some programs have perhaps even hurt those whom they were designed to help by fostering dependency. Provincial leaders are clamoring for the right to introduce their own reforms while demanding more federal assistance to pay for them.

Called for reforms seem to undermine a fundamental tenet of Canadian federalism, uniform standards of social services across the country. Because many Canadians regard their social security net as one of the country's hallmarks which helps define their national identity, any attempt to overhaul it arouses fierce opposition and intense struggles among competing interests. With a half-trillion-dollar national debt hanging over their heads, though, politicians find it harder to sweep the problems under the rug.

Canada's social welfare system has not eradicated poverty. As in the U.S., the gap between rich and poor continues to widen. This development challenges deeply held assumptions about Canada as a place where U.S. style extremes of wage and income distribution do not exist and where the safety net is adequate for all. More than one in ten Canadian adults and children lived in 2014 below the poverty line, defined as a household in which income is half the national median; 17.9% live in low-income households. That proportion has remained steady over the preceding 25 years. In 2013, UNICEF ranked Canada in the bottom third of rich countries in regard to relative child poverty.

About 235,000 Canadians are homeless, including families with young children. The number of people using food banks was 900,000 in 2010, a 9% increase in one year and 92% increase from 1991–2001.

Canada

Single mothers are especially hard hit: a federal report in 2001 concluded that it took 75.4 weeks of work, the equivalent of 1.5 full-time jobs at an average wage, to cover a family's basic expenses. Specific goals announced in the 1980s to eliminate child poverty by 2000 are no longer mentioned.

The number of homeless persons who trudge with their few belongings from soup kitchen to hostel has doubled in Canadian cities since the 1980s. Observers estimate that at least 100,000 people lack shelter on any given day. Despite the magnitude of social welfare benefits and income guarantees, Canadians are still vulnerable to the ups and downs of the economy. Poverty has not been a major political issue in Canada, probably because it still does not have a high enough visibility to prompt the government to try to act on it.

The federal and provincial governments share responsibility for social welfare policy; it has therefore become a major source of conflict between Ottawa and the provinces. These issues have been at the heart of many a struggle concerning the distribution of power among the various governments of Canada. Social welfare spending was a major contributor to staggeringly high federal and provincial budget deficits. As the federal and most provincial governments balanced their budgets, welfare spending declined.

Transfer payments sustain public services in all "have-not" provinces. Only British Columbia, Alberta, and more recently Saskatchewan and Newfoundland, qualify as "have" provinces. The preponderance of "have-not" provinces threatens the sustainability of the system. Newfoundland has used some its new-found oil and mining wealth to reduce its poverty rate in half to 6.5%. Ontario slipped into the "have-not" category, but it is unlikely to remain there. Beginning in 1996 federal transfer payments to the provinces for social programs were converted into block grants and reduced by 4%. Provinces, most of which try to balance their budgets, are severely indebted and have no alternative to reducing their services.

COVID-19 Crisis

Almost needless to say, the coronavirus disease of 2019, commonly known as COVID-19, that rocked the global community, had a major impact in Canada. In response to the crisis, officials in the Public Health Agency of Canada continue to work with their counterparts in the provinces, territories, and international partners, including the World Health Organization, as they continue to monitor the situation with a focus on containment outbreak and preventing its further spread. In addition, Canada's Chief Public Health Officer remains in close contact with provincial and territorial Chief Medical Officers of Health to ensure that cases of COVID-19 are identified rapidly and managed in order to protect the health of Canadians.

As of May 12, 2020, the government of Canada reported that there were 3,784,278 confirmed COVID-19 cases in the country resulting in 39,877 deaths and 3,472,555 people who recovered. In addition, 59,791,354 COVID-19 tests were taken and 84,609,785 doses of vaccine administered.

Trucker's Strike

Unhappy with the Canadian government's vaccine mandate that required truckers who crossed the border into the United States to be inoculated against COVID-19 or be subject to two-week quarantines, truckers created what they called the "Freedom Convoy" to demonstrate their unhappiness. As a result, in January 2022, truckers obstructed border crossings while others engaged in noisy demonstrations in various cities. The convoy finally came to an end when Prime Minister Justin Trudeau invoked the Emergencies Act for the first time in Canadian history, thereby allowing police to move against and arrest hundreds of protesters in late February.

Current Economic Situation

The accumulated national debt, including provincial debt, stands at $1.4 trillion (2016/17) sharply up from $833 billion between 2007 and 2008. The COVID-19 pandemic will likely create a global recession as countries shut down non-essential businesses and lock down their citizens. In 2021, combined national and provincial debt is up 65.2% and is expected to climb to $2 trillion by the end of 2021.

At the time of this writing, the federal deficit could spike to $113 billion and the unemployment rate could hit 15%. Paying the interest on this debt is one of the federal government's largest single expenditures, greater than its spending on health care, family allowances, old-age pensions and social assistance combined. When the indebtedness of the 10 provinces is added, the total debt is larger than the economy itself. This is high among industrialized nations, and from a third to half of that debt is in foreign hands. Canada suc-

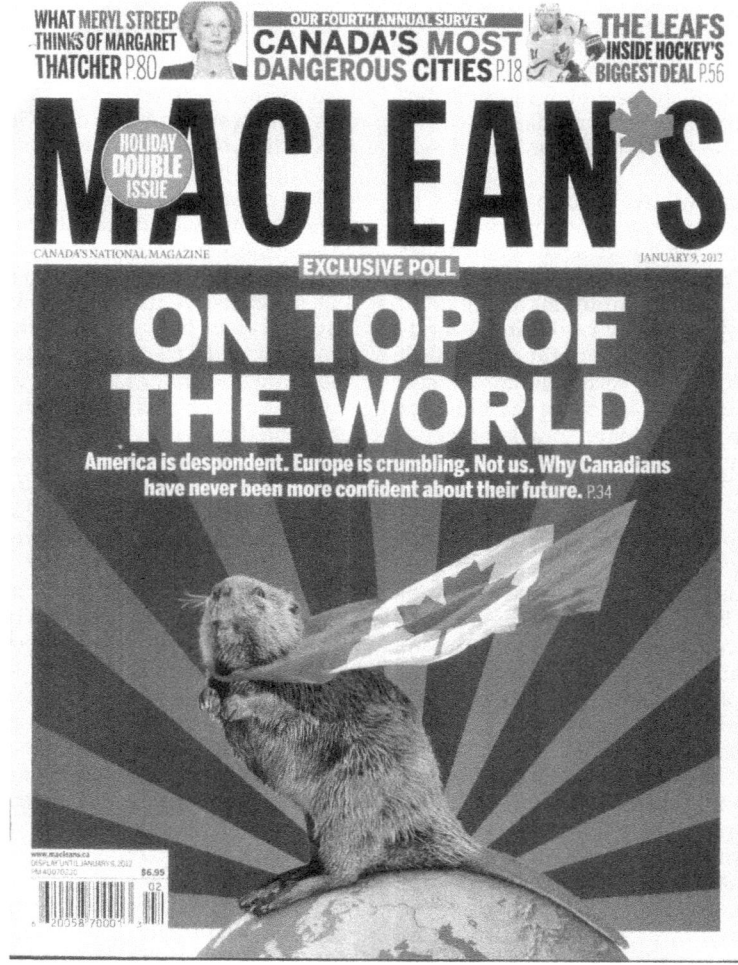

Canada

ceeded in eliminating its budget deficits after 1998, but in 2018 it stood at 1.7% of GDP. The victorious Liberal government promised to run deficits for multiple years to modernize the country's infrastructure.

Due to the global financial crisis that began in 2008, the government was forced in the fiscal year of 2009–10 to end 12 years of budget surpluses. By 2009, the economy had shrunk by an annualized rate of 3.4%, a year later by 1.2%. However, Canada's recession was the mildest downturn in three decades, and by 2018 annual growth was 3%, slightly higher than America's 2.3%. Inflation was 1.4% in 2018. Unemployment sank to 5.9%, higher than 4.1% in the U.S.

Eight thousand jobs were lost when the postal service ended door-to-door letter deliveries in 2018 to concentrate on package deliveries. City dwellers will have to pick up their mail at community mailboxes. Apartment inhabitants must get their mail in their buildings, and country folks continue to use their rural mailboxes.

None of Canada's banks collapsed during the great recession with the then governor of the Bank of Canada, Mark Carney, earning much of the credit for this and the rapid return of the economy to growth. In July 2013, Carney became the Bank of England's governor, arguably the most influential unelected post in Britain. He is the first foreigner to head Britain's central bank in its 318-year history.

By 2012, while American housing was still in the doldrums, the Canadian housing market was soaring on low mortgage rates to a record high median home price of $300,000, up 83% from 1999. Vancouver, which *The Economist* selected in 2011 as the world's most livable city, with Toronto and Calgary also ranked in the top five, was the most expensive housing market, with an average house price in 2017 of around $1 million and $2.5 million in Westside, followed by Toronto at $916,500). About two-thirds, or 69%, of Canadians have their own homes. Recently, in 2018-19, the BC government has taken measures to slow down the real estate market which has caused a significant reduction in home sale prices in Vancouver. In Alberta, the inability to move oil to market has slowed the housing market.

High world prices for oil and gas were a boon for the country with the world's second largest oil reserves and helped increase Canada's diplomatic and economic influence in the world. For instance, these high prices elevated Canada to a higher priority in the eyes of the U.S. government.

Productivity is lower in Canada. In 2007, output per man-hour was 79% of America's, and there are reasons for this. In general, the U.S. economy remains more pro-

The White House from Washington, DC
By Shealah Craighead. https://www.flickr.com/photos/whitehouse/44300765490/, Public Domain. https://commons.wikimedia.org/w/index.php?curid=74766604

ductive in part because of its investments in technology and education. Canada spends less than half as much on research and development; business investment in R&D especially lags. Canada devotes less on higher education and training; since 1993 the U.S. increased the annual spending on education by 3.3%, compared with 0.2% for Canada. Investment per worker in machinery and equipment, especially in information technologies, is only 60% of the American level.

The productivity gap is partly explained by the facts that the average Canadians work 69 fewer hours per year, taking 3.9 weeks of vacation compared with two weeks for their American counterparts. Moreover, Canadians retires earlier at age 61. In the World Economic Forum's annual rankings of most competitive countries, Canada had slipped from sixth in 1998 to tenth in 2008.

Measured in terms of per capita GDP, Canada's living standard is one fifth below that of the U.S. Using purchasing power parity, the gap is 13%. However, this may be changing: Canadian median incomes rose 20% between 2000 and 2010 to $18,700, putting Canadians equal to Americans. Canadians live in slightly smaller houses of about 2,000 vs. 2,434 square feet, but each Canadian has on average 2.5 rooms compared with 2.3 in the U.S. Nevertheless, in 2007 only 19% of Canadians thought that Americans had a better standard of living than they did; 53% did not think that a gap would make any difference in their lives. An impressive 72% were satisfied with their living standard as it was.

That satisfaction did not necessarily extend into the future. In a 2007 poll, 45% of Canadians did not believe the next generation would be able to afford a better standard of living, and only 26% thought it would continue to get better.

Canada tried to rebrand its economy in the 1990s as high-tech. Yet, the contemporary foundation of its economy is a familiar one: natural resources, particularly oil and mining, albeit technologically sophisticated. When world, and especially Chinese, demand keeps commodity prices high, Canada can look forward to a strong economy. One thing Canadians had to get used to was the gradual disappearance of their penny. In other words, because it cost more than one cent to make a copper penny, the last one was struck in May 2012.

Carbon Pricing

In 2018, in order to implement a carbon pricing system designed to assist in combatting climate change pursuant to federal commitments to the Paris Climate Agreement, and in the absence of any provincial regulation, the federal government enacted the *Greenhouse Gas Pollution Pricing Act (GHGPPA)*. On March 25, 2021, the Supreme Court of Canada rejected a provincial challenge to the federal power to enact such legislation brought by Manitoba, Ontario, Alberta, and Saskatchewan; the court, in *Reference re Greenhouse Gas Pollution Pricing Act*, held the GHGPPA to be constitutional. The federal government redistributes revenue raised from the GHGPPA to the provinces; in provinces where it is levied, 90% of the revenues are returned to taxpayers. The Conservative Party of Canada tried, unsuccessfully, to make the carbon tax an issue of the 2019 and 2021 federal elections.. The tax remained deeply unpopular throughout the term of the Trudeau government following the 2021 election. Following Justin Trudeau's resignation as the leader of the

Canada

Liberal Party and Prime Minister on March 14, 2025, and following his swearing-in as the new Prime Minister, and following his first cabinet meeting, Mark Carney signed an Order-in-Council cancelling the consumer carbon price. The Order-in-Counsil provided that Canadians who had been receiving a rebate on the carbon price would receive a final payment in April for the next quarter. Not all were satisfied with the elimination of the consumer carbon price; Danielle Smith, the Premier of Alberta, and Canada's principal oil and gas producer, argued that the real test of the new federal government led by Carney would be not the elimination of the consumer price, but how it would treat industrial polluters. With Carney likely to call an election sometime in the first half of 2025, voters will have the opportunity to have their voices heard on this issue.

FUTURE

In 2017, Canadians celebrated the 150th birthday of their country. A SES survey (SES Research was a Canadian public opinion and research company established in 1987 and later renamed Nanos Research) in 2005 revealed that, despite their political differences, Canadians and Americans think much more alike about important things and are, in fact, closer than one might think. They want to work closely with each other on such matters as counter-terrorism and still define their two nations more by their similarities than by their differences. Asked which country is most like their own in terms of human rights, Canadians picked the U.S. more than any other at 43% while 51% of Americans chose Canada.

Canadians are as determined as ever to preserve their sovereignty and their independence of action. Still, they accept the need for greater security along the border, increased police cooperation with U.S. authorities, common policies on immigration and refugees, and even restrictions on some of their personal freedoms in order to meet the terrorist threat.

Canadians have a developed sense of social justice as most support same-sex marriage and allowing gay and lesbian couples to adopt children. Also, in 2016 after much debate and litigation, the House of Commons amended the Criminal Code of Canada to allow for Medically Assisted Dying (MAID). Initially designed for adults with terminal illness who wished to end their suffering, in 2021, the Criminal Code was modified to include individuals with serious and chronic physical conditions even if non-life threatening. A more recent proposal to extend MAID to those suffering solely from a mental illness has been postponed to March 17, 2024, because, while 60% of Canadians support MAID in its current form, only 30% favor that extension. A recent report indicates that under MAID, 10,000 Canadians voluntarily took their own lives in 2021.

This social liberalism points to an increasingly self-confident country. These social issues join gun control and universal one payer health care in solidifying a Canadian sense of, to some degree, separateness from the U.S.

Dramatic changes have taken place in Quebec. *Québécois* seem to accept Canada more than they used to as only 2% of them considered national unity a major issue. As the most socially liberal Canadians, the majority of *Québécois* approve of gay marriage, abortion, and the legalization of marijuana: 69% endorsed the statement that they are proud of what Canada is becoming "because it shows what a socially progressive and diverse country, we live in." The figure in the rest of Canada was 54%.

A major reason for this unprecedented *Québécois* embrace of Canada is the confidence they now have that their language and culture are more firmly entrenched than ever before. In the 2011 and 2015 federal elections, the separatist *Bloc Québécois* was wiped out in the province, winning only ten lonely seats in the House of Commons, far short of the number required to constitute an official parliamentary party. The *Bloc Québécois* is divided over how bold to be in seeking a separate Quebec. When the issue became dominant for it in the April 2014 provincial election campaign, it spelled disaster for the party, which was thrown out of government. Independence remains unlikely in the foreseeable future.

Looking forward, Canada will keep its door open to refugees and more than 300,000 immigrants each year; this amounts to 1% of its population, 80% of whom will become citizens. Canadians will continue to worry about Islamic terrorism. Reform of the electoral system has fallen along the wayside for lack of popular support.

A growing problem in Canada is vaping by students as a survey of more than 12,00 youth aged 16 to 19 reveled that the use of electronic cigarettes in a two-year period. More specifically, 17.8% of Canadian youth vaped in 2019 within the past month, up from 8.4% in 2017. Further, Statistics Canada (2019) noted that 36% of Canadian youth between the ages of 15–19 tried vaping at some point, a rate more than five times higher than adults aged 25 and older; in addition, this report noted that Statistics Canada 87% of students who vaped used e-liquids containing nicotine, thus risking health problems. Vaping involves the use of individual electronic devices containing a battery, a heating element, and a place to contain liquids such as nicotine, flavorings, and/or other chemicals to produce aerosols, or mixes of small particles in the air, that can be inhaled deep into the lungs of users and those nearby.

Along with possible nicotine dependence, which can lead to disruptions in brain development and chemistry vaping can cause shortness of breath, coughing, fevers, acid reflux. Vaping has also been linked to behavioral changes; cardiac difficulties; cardiovascular disease; heart attacks; mental health issues; nicotine poisoning; and high-risk behaviors by high school students leading to injury, violence, and sexual activity.

Teens vape for six reasons. First, because vaping has become so popular users yield to peer pressure by trying e-cigarettes. Second, students are curious about vaping. Third, through the widespread use of advertising on the internet manufacturers and sellers of vaping devices target teenagers by flavoring their products to increase its appeal. Fourth, teens mistakenly think that vaping causes little or no harm compared to regular cigarettes even though most devices use products containing nicotine. Fifth, because vaping is odorless, it is easier to conceal, combined with the fact that they often look like pens or other electronic devices. Sixth, despite bans against their sales to minors, vaping devices and products are cheaper and easier to purchase than other tobacco products.

While anti-vaping legislation at both the Provincial and Federal levels is in its early stages, a good example of a comprehensive law is the Smoke-Free Ontario Act. This Act bans vaping in public places, forbids the sale of devices to individuals under the age of 19, and prohibits those in this age group from entering Vape Shops or locations where the of smoking tobacco and cannabis is permitted. The law also bans vaping in cars when persons under the age of 16 are present while prohibiting the use of vaping devices at schools or on school grounds, in public areas within 20 meters of schools, on playgrounds within 20 meters of playgrounds, at community recreational facilities, and all public areas within 20 meters of these grounds.

In a controversial move raising concerns for free speech and expression, in February, the government introduced Bill C-63, the Online Harms Act. If adopted, this bill is designed to require social media, user-uploaded adult content and live-streaming services to reduce exposure to online content deemed harmful. The bill defines harmful content as that which incites vio-

Canada

lence; foments hatred; incites violent extremism or terrorism; is used to bully, sexually, victimize or induce children to harm themselves; or intimate content communicated without consent. In addition, the bill would create both a five-member Digital Safety Commission which will be responsible to enforce rules by rendering online services accountable and a Digital Safety Ombudsperson to support and advocate for users while making recommendations to social media services and the government. Proponents of the bill emphasized that the bill would not apply to private message services such as email. The bill would also amend the Criminal Code by adopting a new standalone hate crime offense allowing penalties of up to life imprisonment to deter hateful conduct while raising the maximum punishments for hate propaganda offenses from five years to life imprisonment for advocating genocide. It also decriminalized the recreational use of marijuana. Canada legalized the use of marijuana in 2018.

Still, *Maclean's* 2012 annual poll found a nation that was proud and confident about the future. An overwhelming majority (86%) agreed with the notion that their country is "the greatest in the world"; 97% of Tory voters agreed. Asked if their country is heading in the right direction, 63.5% of Canadians answered yes, while a meager 17% of U.S. voters answered in the affirmative. Was their country the best place to raise a family?: 87% of Canadians but only 61% of Americans thought so. Only 17% of Canadians thought they could get better work in their southern neighbor.

A decade later, in the midst of a great deal of uncertainty in Canada and the world, a Matus Public Poll published in the *Toronto Star* in February 2022 revealed a different picture. According to the poll 66% of Canadians fear for the future in light of the Trucker's Convoy, as 82% thought that the protests never should have been allowed, fearing that there is no longer a common ground for civil discourse.

The election of President Donald J. Trump in November 2024 ushered in significant changes in American trade and foreign policy. Trump was buoyed by a victory in which he ran on a campaign in large part relying on a platform calling for an "America First" strategy. Trump's "America First" strategy included, among other items, helping to secure the border by preventing individuals from entering into the United States illegally along with stopping the large flow of fentanyl that is causing the deaths of many Americans and to end existing trade imbalances with other Nations. In line with that policy, Trump announced the imposition of 25% tariffs on various imports from Canada, and other nations, in an effort to help revive the economy in the United States. Combined with this economic policy, Trump also made repeated comments about making Canada the 51st state of the United States. The initial 25% tariffs went into effect on March 4, 2025, after Canadian and American officials were unable to reach an agreement to pause or end their being imposed. In response, then Canadian Prime Minister Justin Trudeau announced that Canada would impose its own tariffs on goods from the United States. Also in early March, Trump rescinded what he promised would be even larger tariffs on Canadian steel and aluminum after Ontario Premier Doug Ford walked back a planned 25% surcharge on electricity exports to Michigan, Minnesota, and New York. Not surprisingly Trump's actions has caused significant conflict.

On March 23, 2025, after being in office for only nine days, Prime Minister Mark Carney, who to date neither served in public office nor ran a political campaign, called for a snap election on April 28, 2025. Carney explained that he had called an election because in light of the tariffs Trump has put in place Canada is "facing the most significant crisis of our lifetimes." Tensions thus remain high as this book heads to press as Canadians are responding with am "elbows up" attitude, a phrase coined by all-time hockey great Gordie Howe who "used his elbows to defend himself when opposing players crowded in" on the ice, meaning that he was willing to use his physical strength as a means of self-defense. It can only be hoped that cooler heads will prevail and a mutually acceptable compromise that is beneficial to both nations can be worked out soon to preserve the long-standing good relations between the governments and people of Canada and the United States.

Web Sites and Bibliography of Key English-Language Books

https://www.bbc.com/news/world-us-canada-64004329

https://budget.gc.ca/2022/home-accueil-en.html

https://www.canada.ca/en/health-canada/services/canadian-tobacco-nicotine-survey/2019-summary.html

https://www.canada.ca/en/health-canada/services/medical-assistance-dying.html

https://www.cbc.ca/news/health/vaping-injury-youth-canada-health-1.5684342#

https://comtrade.un.org/ (United Nations Comrade Database-detailed global trade data)

https://covid19tracker.ca/ https://premier.novascotia.ca

www.cbsa.asfc.gc.ca (Canada Border Services Agency) https://www.canadapopulation.net/ontario-population/

https://www.canadapopulation.net/quebec-population/

https://www.cbc.ca/news/canada/edmonton/carbon-tax-carney-alberta-1.7484760?

https://www.ctvnews.ca/canada/freedom-convoy-protest-how-did-we-get-here-1.5772901, n.d.

https://www.ctvnews.ca/health/most-canadians-don-t-support-latest-planned-maid-expansion-survey-finds-1.6271104www.defensenews.com (Global website and magazine about the politics, business and technology of defense, serving senior military and industry decisionmakers.)

www.dfait-maeci.gc.ca (Foreign Affairs and International Trade)

https://www.canada.ca/en/canadian-heritage/services/official-languages-bilingualism/publications/statistics.html

https://financialpost.com/news/mark-carney-government-terminates-consumer-carbon-price

https://www.forbes.com/advisor/legal/product-liability/juul-lawsuit-update/

http://www.eco.gov.yk.ca/stats/pdf/real_estate_q219.pdf (Yukon Bureau of Statistics)

https://www.gov.nl.ca/premier/www.gov.nl.ca/fin/economics/pop-overview (Newfoundland)

https://www.ibisworld.com (research on industries worldwide)

https://www.hsph.harvard.edu/news/press-releases/common-e-cigarette-chemical-flavorings-may-impair-lung-function/

https://humanevents.com/2023/04/27/canadas-government-assisted-suicide-took-the-lives-of-10000-2021-new-documentary-reveals-maids-massive-faults

http://www.mapleleafweb.com/main.shtml (Central site for Canadian affairs)

https://www.gov.mb.ca/asset_library/en/executivecouncil/kinew.jpg

https://www.ntlegislativeassembly.ca/sites/default/files/styles/3_4_portrait_profile/public/legacy/r.j._simpson.jpg?

https://www.ntassembly.ca/meet-members/mla/caroline-cochrane

https://nunatsiaq.com/stories/article/nunavut-premier-talks-1st-week-on-the-job/

https://www.ourcommons.ca/Speaker/Assets/Images/StandUpCropped.jpg

https://www.worldatlas.com/articles/religious-composition-of-canada.html

https://worldpopulationreview.com/canadian-provinces/british-columbia-populationlop.parl.ca/About/Parliament/speakers/hoc/sp-37Rota-e.htm

www12.statcan.gc.ca/census-recensement/index-eng.cfm

www.150.statcanada.com (Stats Canada)

www.canoe.ca and www.Yahoo.ca (Canadian search engines)

www.canadianembassy.org (This site is a key source containing a search engine, an issues menu, many links, a virtual reference desk, and a virtual tour of the Canadian embassy in Washington.)

www.ambassadeducanada.org (All of the above functions in French)

www.usembassycanada.org (Site for US embassy in Ottawa with reports and information)

www.canada.gc.ca (General Web site for information on Canada from the Canadian government. See links.)

www.cbc.ca (Web site for the Canadian Broadcasting Corporation. This is an excellent current source for all aspects of Canadian news, with numerous links. See also www.cbc.ca/newsworld/)

www.ctv.ca (Broad Canadian reporting)

www.radio-canada.ca/nouvelles (French-language news)

www.elections.ca (election results. Phone: 1-800-463-6868)

www.pm.gc.ca (Web site for Canadian prime minister's office. By substituting the first letters of other ministries, access to other ministries' Web sites can be gained. See below.)

www.fin.gc.ca (Web site for Canadian Finance Ministry)

www.strategis.ic.gc.ca (Industry Canada)

www.dfait-maeci.gc.ca (Web site for Department of Foreign Affairs and International Trade)

www.cfp-pec.gc.ca (Web site of Canadian Centre for Foreign Policy Development. See many links. For peacekeeping, add: /peacekeeping/menu-e.asp. For additional links, add: /y2k. For magazine, add: /Canada-magazine)

www.cbsa.asfc.gc.ca (Canada Border Services Agency)

www.cic.gc.ca (Citizenship and Immigration Canada)

http://www.mapleleafweb.com/main.shtml (Central site for Canadian affairs)

www.canschool.org (Web site for many aspects of Canadians in the World)

www.citizens.ca (Site for information relating to who Canadians are; description of people)

www.gov.nu.ca (Site for Nunavut)

http://parkscanada.gc.ca (Parks Canada site)

www.travelcanada.ca

www.liberal.ca (Liberal Party site)

www.conservative.ca (Conservative Party site)

www.ndp.ca (National Democratic Party site)

www.bloc.ca (Bloc Québécois party site)

www.greenparty.ca (Green Party site)

www.un.org (Web site for United Nations. Many links.)

www.nato.org (Web site for NATO. Many links.)

www.chatelaine.com (Web site for *Chatelaine* weekly Canadian magazine. In English and French.)

www.macleans.ca (Web site for *Maclean's* weekly Canadian news magazine)

www.macleans.ca/news/canada/the-safest-and-maybe-most-honest-places-to-live-in-canada/ (Poll on safest places to live in Canada)

www.mh-education.com (*Maclean's* educational Web site. See links.)

www.mercer.com (Quality of life)

www.GlobeAndMail.ca (Respected Canadian national newspaper)

www.nationalpost.com (Respected Canadian national newspaper)

www.torontostar.com (Respected Canadian national newspaper)

www.ottawa citizen.com (Respected Canadian national newspaper)

www.montrealgazette.com (Respected Canadian national newspaper)

www.winnipegfreepress.com (Respected Canadian national newspaper)

www.vancouversun.com (Respected Canadian national newspaper)

www.ledevoir.com (Respected Quebec French-language newspaper)

www.candacalling.com (Prior Smith's five-minute Canadian newscasts)

www.cyberpress.com (Canadian news)

www.iam.ca (Humorous Web site for Molson beer's Canadian nationalism commercial)

www.economist.com (Respected British news weekly with some coverage of Canadian affairs)

www.chicagotribune.com (Respected U.S. newspaper with some coverage of Canadian affairs. Named best overall US newspaper online service for newspapers with circulation over 100,000.)

www.csmonitor.com (Respected U.S.

Bibliography

newspaper, *Christian Science Monitor*, with some coverage of Canadian affairs. Named best overall US newspaper online service for newspapers with circulation under 100,000.)

www.nytimes.com (Respected U.S. newspaper, *The New York Times*, with some coverage of Canadian affairs)

www.washingtonpost.com (Respected U.S. newspaper with some coverage of Canadian affairs)

www.washingtontimes.com (Respected U.S. newspaper with some coverage of Canadian affairs)

www.canada.plattsburgh.edu (The Center for the Study of Canada at the State University of New York Plattsburgh maintains the major Web site for Canadian Studies. E-mail address: CANADA-ACSUS@Plattsburgh.EDU. Search also for Association for Canadian Studies in the U.S. –ACSUS.)

philippe.premont@dfait=maeci.gc.ca (New-scan E-mail of Weekly Canadian news summaries)

http://www.eco.gov.yk.ca/stats/pdf/real_estate_q219.pdf (Yukon Bureau of Statistics)

www.gov.nl.ca/fin/economics/pop-overview (Website for Government of Newfoundland)

https://trading economics.com/Canada/imports/china (An online platform that provides historical data, economic forecasts, news, and trading recommendations)

https://www.arctictoday.com/in-the-battle-for-sovereignty-of-a-disputed-arctic-island-canada-and-denmark-use-whisky-and-schnapps (An individual news site reporting on the arctic)

https://www.bbc.com/news/world-us-canada-42586638 (British Broadcast Corporation poll on passports)

www.angusreid.org (Angus Reid Institute is a national, not-for-profit organization commissioning research and opinion polls on issues that matter to Canada)

www.univcan.ca/universities/facts-and-stats/tuition-fees-by-university/ (Universities Canada)

https://comtrade.un.org/ (United Nations Comrade Database-detailed global trade data)

www.defensenews.com (Global website and magazine about the politics, business and technology of defense, serving senior military and industry decision-makers.)

https://www.ibisworld.com (IBISWorld provides trusted industry research on thousands of industries worldwide)

https://www.theblaze.com/news/electoral-college-donald-trump-official

https://www.cnn.com/2025/03/11/business/tariffs-canada-trump/index.htmlhttps://time.com/7205012/justin-trudeau-resigns-liberal-party-leader/

https://www.foxnews.com/politics/president-trump-grover-cleveland-how-presidential-candidates-triumphantly-returned-white-house

https://nypost.com/2025/03/04/us-news/trumps-stiff-new-tariffs-on-canada-mexico-and-china-take-effect/

https://nypost.com/2024/11/07/us-news/trump-first-candidate-in-40-years-to-sweep-key-2024-swing-states/

https://nypost.com/2025/03/23/world-news/canadian-pm-mark-carney-calls-snap-election-slams-trump-trade-war/

https://www.whitehouse.gov/briefings-statements/2025/01/president-trumps-america-first-priorities/

https://www.whitehouse.gov/fact-sheets/2025/03/fact-sheet-president-donald-j-trump-adjusts-tariffs-on-canada-and-mexico-to-minimize-disruption-to-the-automotive-industry/

https://www.usatoday.com/story/news/nation/2025/03/18/elbows-up-canada-gordie-howe-hockey/82525433007/

I. GENERAL

Beach, Richard, ed. *O Canada, Its Geography, History and the People Who Call It Home.*
2nd rev. ed. Plattsburgh, NY: Center for the Study of Canada, 2000.

Berton, Pierre. *Why We Act Like Canadians. A Personal Exploration of Our National Character.* Toronto: McClelland and Stewart, 1982.

———. *Hollywood's Canada.* Nd.

Black, Peter. *Canada Matters: Chronicles of a Northern Neighbour.* Plattsburgh, NY: Center for the Study of Canada, 2002.

Ricker, Darrell and John Wright. *What Canadians Think.* Toronto: Doubleday, 2005.

Callwood, June. *Portrait of Canada.* Garden City, NY: Doubleday, 1981.

The Canadian Encyclopedia, 2nd ed., 4 vols. Edmonton: Hurtig, 1988.

———. *The Canadian Pocket Encyclopedia.* Vancouver, BC: CanExpo, annual edition.

Center for the Study of Canada. *Occasional Paper Series.* See also its annual *Teaching Canada.* Its 2002 volume (21) is entitled *Canada & The World.* Plattsburgh: State University of New York. (Phone: 518-564-2086).

Crowley, Jason Clemons and Niels Veldhuis. *The Canadian Century. Moving Out of America's Shadow.* 2010.

Dermer, Jerry, ed. *The Canadian Profile. People, Institutions, Infrastructure.* North York, Ont.: Captus Press, 1992.

DePalma, Anthony. *Here: A Biography of the North American Continent.* New York: HarperCollins, 2001.

Gould, Karen, Jockel, Joseph T. and Metcalf, William, eds. *Northern Exposures. Scholarship on Canada in the United States.* Washington, D.C.: Association for Canadian Studies in the United States, 1993.

Hobson, Archie. *The Cambridge Gazetteer of the United States and Canada. A Dictionary of Places.* New York: Cambridge University Press, 1995.

Joyce, William W. and Richard Beach. *Introducing Canada. Current Backgrounders, Strategies, and Resources for Educators.* Washington, D.C.: National Council for Social Studies, 1997.

Malcolm, Andrew H. *The Canadians.* New York: Times Books, 1985.

Mathews, Robin. *Canadian Identity. Major Forces Shaping the Life of a People.* Ottawa: Steel Rail Educational Publishing, 1988.

Metcalfe, William, ed. *Understanding Canada. A Multi-disciplinary Introduction to Canadian Studies.* New York: New York University Press, 1982.

Olive, David. *Canada Inside Out: How We See Ourselves/How Others See Us.* New York: Bantam, 1996.

Pryke, Kenneth G. and Soderlund, Walter C. *Profiles of Canada.* Toronto: Copp Clark Pitman, 1992.

Richler, Noah. *This is My Country, What's Yours?* Toronto: McClelland & Stewart, 2006.

Roste, Vaughn. *The Xenophobe's Guide to the Canadians.* London: Oval Books, 2004.

Sabin, Louis. *Canada.* Mahwah, NJ: Troll Associates, 1985.

Sherman, George. *O Canada. Its Geography, History and the People Who Call It Home.* Plattsburgh, NY: Center for the Study of Canada, 1994.

Taras, David, et al. *A Passion for Identity.* 2nd ed. Scarborough, Ont.: Nelson, 1992.

The 1997 Corpus Almanac & Canadian Sourcebook. Don Mills, Ont.: Southam Magazine & Information Group, 1997.

II. BIOGRAPHIES AND AUTOBIOGRAPHIES

Ayre, John. *Northrop Frye.* Vintage Books, 1990.

Boyden, Joseph. *Extraordinary Canadians: Louis Riel and Gabriel Dumont.* Toronto: Penguin, 2009.

Brown, R.C. *Robert Laird Borden: A Biography.* 2 vols. Toronto: 1975, 1980.

Cayley, David. *Northrop Frye in Conversation.* Don Mills, Ont.: Anansi, 1992.

Charlesbois, Peter. *The Life of Louis Riel.* Toronto: NC, 1975.

Chretién, Jean. *Straight from the Heart.* Toronto: Key Porter, 1985.

———. *My Years as Prime Minister.* 2007

Bibliography

Clarkson, Adrienne. *Heart Matters*. Toronto: Penguin, 2006.

Cohen, Andrew and J. L Granatstein, eds. *Trudeau's Shadow. The Life and Legacy of Pierre Elliott Trudeau*. Toronto: Vintage, 1999.

Creighton, Donald. *The Old Chieftain* (Classic biography of Macdonald). 1955.

———. *John A. Macdonald*. 2 vols. Toronto: Macmillan, 1968.

Delacourt, Susan. *Juggernaut: Paul Martin's Campaign for Chrétien's Crown*. Toronto: McClelland & Stewart, 2003.

Diefenbaker, John G. *One Canada*. 3 vols. Toronto: Macmillan, 1975–1977.

English, John. *The Worldly Years of Lester Pearson 1949–1972*. Toronto: Alfred A. Knopt, 1993.

Ferns, Henry and Ostry, Bernard. *The Age of Mackenzie King*. Toronto: James Lorimer, 1976.

Flanagan, Thomas. *Louis "David" Riel: Prophet of the New World*. Toronto: University of Toronto Press, 1979.

———. *Harper's Team: Behind the Scenes in the Conservative Rise to Power*. 2007.

Foran, Charles. *Extraordinary Canadians: Maurice Richard*. Toronto: Penguin, 2011.

Fraser, Graham. *PQ: Réne Lévesque and the Parti Quebecois*.

Garr, Allen. *Tough Guy: Bill Bennett and the Taking of British Columbia*. Toronto: Key Porter, 1985.

Gillen, Mollie. *Lucy Maud Montgomery*. Markham, Ont.: Fitzhenry Whiteside, n.d.

Gwyn, Richard. *The Northern Magnus. Pierre Trudeau and Canadians*. Markham, Ont.: Paper Jacks, 1981.

———. *John A.: The Man Who Made Us*. (About John A. Macdonald). 2007.

———. *Nation Maker*. Second volume of Gwyn's 2007 book above. 2011.

Hadfield, Chris. *An Astronaut's Guide to Life on Earth*. 2013.

Harcourt, Michael, with Wayne Skene. *A Measure of Defiance*. Vancouver, BC: Douglas & McIntyre, 1996.

Ignatieff, Michael. *True Patriot Love. Four Generations in Search of Canada*. Viking Canada, 2009.

———. *Fire and Ashes. Failure in Politics*. Cambridge, MA: Harvard University Press, 2013.

Johnson, William. *Stephen Harper and the Future of Canada*. Toronto: McClelland and Stewart, 2005.

Lam, Vincent. *Extraordinary Canadians: Tommy Douglas*. Toronto: Penguin, 2011.

Lavigne, Brad. *Building the Orange Wave: The Inside Story Behind the Historic Rise of Jack Layton and the NDP*. Douglas & McIntyre. 2013.

Lévesque, Réne. *Memoirs*. Toronto: Cross Canada Books, 1986.

Levine, Allan. *Toronto: Biography of a City*. Toronto: Douglas & McIntyre. 2014

McNaught, Kenneth. *A Prophet in Politics. A Biography of J.S. Woodsworth*, Toronto: University of Toronto Press, 1959.

MacDonald, L. Ian. *Brian Mulroney. The Making of the Prime Minister*. Toronto: McClelland and Stewart, 1987.

MacNeil, Robert. *Looking for my Country. Finding Myself in America*. Toronto: Vintage Canada, 2002.

Martin, Laurence. *The Antagonist: Lucien Bouchard and the Politics of Delusion*. Toronto: Viking, 1997.

Martin, Paul. *Hell or High Water*. 2008.

McIlroy, Thad, ed. *A Rose is a Rose: A Tribute to Pierre Elliott Trudeau in Cartoons and Quotes*. Toronto: Doubleday, 1984.

Morison, Samuel Eliot. *Samuel Champlain, Father of New France*. Boston: Little Brown, 1972.

Mulroney, Brian. *Where I Stand*. Toronto: McClelland and Stewart, 1983.

Myers, Mike. *Canada*. Toronto: Doubleday Canada, 2014

Neatby, H. B. *William Lyon Mackenzie King*. 3 vols. Toronto: 1963, 1976.

Nemni, Max and Monique. *Trudeau Transformed: The Shaping of a Statesman, 1944–1965*. Translated by George Tombs. 2011.

Manning, Preston. *The New Canada*. Toronto: Macmillan, 1992.

Pearson, L. B. *Mike: The Memoirs of the Rt. Hon. Lester B. Pearson*. vol. I, 1897–1948; vol. II, 1948–1957; vol. III, 1957–68. Toronto: 1972–75.

Pelletier, Gerard. *Years of Impatience*. New York: Facts on File, 1984.

Pickersgill, J. W. *My Years with Louis St. Laurent*. Toronto: 1975.

Pratte, André. *Extraordinary Canadians: Wilfrid Laurier*. Toronto: Penguin, 2011.

Radwanski, George. *Trudeau*. Agincourt, Ont.: Signet, 1978.

Rae, Bob. *From Protest to Power: Personal Reflections on a Life in Politics*. Toronto: Viking/Penguin, 1996.

Richards, David Adams. *Lord Beaverbrook*. Toronto: Penguin Group (Canada), 2008.

Ross, Catherine S. *Alice Munro*. Toronto: ECW Press, 1992.

Saul, John Ralson. *Extraordinary Canadians: Louis Hippolyte LaFontaine and Robert Baldwin*. Toronto: Penguin, 2010.

Sawatsky, John. *Mulroney. The Politics of Ambition*. Don Mills, Ont.: Stoddart, 1991.

Schull, J. *Laurier: The First Canadian*. Toronto: 1966.

Stanley, G. *Louis Riel*. Toronto: 1963.

Sweeny, A. *George-Etienne Cartier: A Biography*. Toronto: 1976.

Thomson, D. *Alexander Mackenzie: Clear Grit*. Toronto: 1960.

Thomson, D. C. *Louis St. Laurent: Canadian*. Toronto: 1967.

Troiano, Edna. M. *Uncle Tom's Journey from Maryland to Canada: The Life of Josiah Henson*. Charleston, SC: The History Press. 2019.

Trudeau, Justin. *Common Ground*. 2014.

Trudeau, Pierre Elliott. *Memoirs*. Toronto: McClelland and Steward, 1993.

Urquhart, Jane. *Extraordinary Canadians: L. M. Montgomery*. Penguin Group (Canada), 2009.

Young, B. *George-Etienne Cartier: Montreal Bourgeois*. Montreal and London: 1981.

Penguin Group (Canada) launched in 2008 a three-year *Extraordinary Canadians* series, edited by Ralston Saul and composed of 20 Canadian biographies by notable Canadian novelists and authors. The biographies are lively and important stories told by talented writers, not ponderous academic works.

III. HISTORY

Allan, Ralph. *Ordeal By Fire. Canada, 1910–1945*. Toronto: Doubleday, 1961.

Anderson, Fred. *Crucible of War. The Seven Years War and the Fate of Empire in British North America, 1754–1766*. Toronto: Vintage Books, 2001.

Baldwin, Douglas and Odnyak, Emily. *Canada's Political Heritage*. Regina: Weigl Educational Publishers, Ltd., 1985.

Bailyn, Bernard. *The Barbarous Years: The Peopling of British North America, 1600-1675*. 2012.

Beal, Bob and Macleod, Rod. *Prairie Fire. The 1885 North West Rebellion*. Edmonton, Alb.: Hurtig, 1984.

Bercuson, David J. *Canada and the Burden of Unity*. Toronto: Copp Clark Pittman, Ltd. 1985.

Berger, Carl. *Contemporary Approaches to Canadian History*. Toronto: Copp Clark Pittman, 1987.

Bernier, Serge. *The Royal 22e Regiment, 1919–1999*. Montreal: Art Global, 2000.

Berton, Pierre. *My Country. The Remarkable Past*. Toronto: Seal Books, 1979.

———. *The Invasion of Canada 1812–1813*. Toronto: McClelland and Stewart, 1980.

———. *The Great Depression, 1929–1939*. Markham, Ont.: McClelland Stewart, 1990.

———. *Marching as to War. Canada's Turbulent Years 1899–1953*. Toronto: Doubleday Canada, 2001.

Bird, Harrison. *Attack on Quebec: The American Invasion of Canada 1775*. New York: Oxford University Press, 1968.

Black, Conrad. *Rise to Greatness: The History of Canada from the Vikings to the Present*. Toronto: McClelland & Stewart, 2014.

Bothwell, Robert and Drummond, Ian, and English, John. *Canada Since 1945*. Toronto: University of Toronto Press, 1989.

Bourrie, Mark. *The Fog of War: Censorship of Canada's Media in World War Two*. 2011.

Bibliography

Boyko, John. *Cold Fire. Kennedy's Northern Front*. 2015.

Broadfoot, Barry. *The Pioneer Years 1895–1914. Memories of Settlers Who Opened the West*. Toronto, Garden City, NY: Doubleday, 1976.

Brown, Craig. *The Illustrated History of Canada*. Toronto: Lester, 1991.

Buckner, Phillip A. *The Transition to Responsible Government: British Policy in British North America, 1815–1850*. Westport, CT: Greenwood, 1985.

Budiansky, Stephen. *Perilous Eight: America's Intrepid War with Britain on the High Seas, 1812–1815*. 2010.

Bumstead, J.M., *The Peoples of Canada, 4th ed*. Vol 1: *A Pre-Confederation History*. Vol 2: *A Post-Confederation History*. Don Mills, Ont.: Oxford University Press, 2014.

Butler, Rick and Carrier, Jean-Guy, eds. *The Trudeau Decade*. Toronto and Garden City, NY: Doubleday, 1979.

Canadian History. A Readers Guide. 2 volumes: *Beginnings to Confederation*, ed. by M. Brook Taylor, and *Confederation to the Present*, ed. by Doug Owram. Toronto: University of Toronto Press, 1994.

Canadian Broadcasting Corporation. *Canada: A People's History*. A 16-part film documentary series, 2001.

Careless, J.M.S. *Canada. A Story of Challenge*. Rev. ed. Toronto: Macmillan, 1970.

Carroll, Joy. *Wolfe and Montcalm. Their Life, Their Times, and the Fate of a Continent*. Buffalo, NY: Firefly Books, 2004.

Clarkson, Stephen and McCall, Christina. *Trudeau and Our Times. The Magnificent Obsession*. Vol. 1. Markham, Ont.: McClelland and Stewart, 1991.

Cohen, Andrew. *Lester B. Pearson*. Penguin Extraordinary Canadians, 2008.

Conrad, Margaret and Finkel, Alvin, et al. *History of the Canadian Peoples*. 2 vols. Toronto: Copp Clark Pitman, 1993.

Conrad, Margaret. *A Concise History of Canada*. 2 vols. New York: Cambridge University Press.

Constain, Thomas B. *The White and the Gold. The French Regime in Canada*. Toronto and Garden City, NY: Doubleday, 1970.

Cook, Ramsey. *The Voyages of Jacques Cartier*. Toronto: University of Toronto Press, 1993.

Cook, Tim. *Vinny: The Battle and the Legend*, 2017.

Cross, Michael S. *A Biography of Robert Baldwin: The Morning-Star of Memory*, 2012.

Dempsey, Hugh A., ed. *The CPR West. The Iron Road and the Making of a Nation*. Vancouver, BC: Douglas and McIntyre, 1984.

Douglas, W. A. B. and Greenhous, B. *Out of the Shadows: Canada in the Second World War*. Rev. ed. Toronto: Dundurn Press, 1993.

Ehret, Matthew J. L. & Saunders, Richard. *The Untold History of Canada: The Forgotten Struggle for Progress*. Toronto: Canadian Patriot Press: 2019.

Finkel, A. *Business and Social Reform in the 1930s*. Toronto: 1979.

Flanagan, Thomas. *Riel and the Rebellion: 1885 Reconsidered*. Saskatoon, Sask.: Western Producer Prairie Books, 1983.

Francis, R. Douglas and Smith, Donald B. *Readings in Canadian History*. Vol. 1: Pre-Confederation. vol. 2: Post-Confederation. 4th ed. Toronto: Harcourt Brace, 1994.

Francis, R. Douglas, et. al. *Origins: Canadian History to Confederation. Destinies: Canadian History Since Confederation*. 2 vols. 2nd ed. Toronto: Rinehard Winston, 1992.

———. *Readings in Canadian History*. Vol. 1: Pre-Confederation. vol. 2: Post-Confederation. 4th ed. Toronto: HBJ-Holt, 1994.

Fraser, Blair. *The Search for Identity. Canada: Postwar to the Present*. Garden City, NY, and Toronto: Doubleday, 1967.

Gilbert, A.D., et al. *Reappraisals in Canadian History*. 2 vols. Scarborough, Ont.: Prentice-Hall, 1993.

Granatstein, Jack. *Who Killed Canadian History?* 1999.

———. *The Greatest Victory: Canada's One Hundred Days, 1918*. 2014.

Gray, Charlotte. *Gold Diggers*. 2014 (About the Klondike gold rush).

Gruending, Dennis. *Great Canadian Speeches*. Markham, Ont.: Fitzhenry and White, 2004.

Gwyn, Richard. *Nation Maker*. 2012. (Two-part biography of Sir John A. Macdonald).

Hagan, John. *Northern Passage. American Vietnam War Resisters in Canada*. Cambridge, MA: Harvard University, 2001.

Hardy, W.G. *From Sea unto Sea. The Road to Nationhood 1850–1910*. Toronto and Garden City, NY: Doubleday, 1970.

Harris, R. Cole and Warkentin, John. *Canada Before Confederation. A Study of Historical Geography*. New York: Oxford University Press, 1974.

Hayes, Derrek. *Canada: An Illustrated History: An Illustrated History, Revised and Expanded*. Toronto: Douglas & McIntyre, 2017.

Historica-Dominion Institute. *We Were Freedom*. Contains 65 gripping oral histories by Canadians in World War II. 2010.

The Illustrated History of Canada. Markham, Ont.: Fitzhenry Whiteside, 1988.

Jasanoff, Maya. *Liberty's Exiles. American Loyalists in the Revolutionary World*. New York: Knopf, 2011.

Lanctot, G. *Canada and the American Revolution, 1774–1783*. Toronto: 1967.

Lane, Barry. *Canadian Pacific: The Golden Age of Travel*. Fredericton: Goose Lane Editions, 2015.

Levine, Allan. *King: A Life Guided by the Hand of Destiny*. 2011.

Lussier, Antoine S., ed. *Louis Riel and the Métis*. Winnipeg: Pemmican, 1983.

Mackay, Donald. *The People's Railway. A History of Canadian National*. Vancouver: Douglas McIntyre, 1992.

Masters, Donald C. *A Short History of Canada*. Huntington, NY: Krieger, 1980.

McFadden, Fred, ed. *Origins. A History of Canada*. Markham, Ont.: Fitzhenry Whiteside, 1988.

McInnis, Edgar. *Canada. A Political and Social History*. Toronto: Holt, Rinehart and Winston, 1982.

McNaught, Kenneth. *The Pelican History of Canada*. New York: Penguin, 1982.

Moore, Christopher. *The Loyalist Revolution, Exile, Settlement*. Toronto: McClelland and Stewart, 1994.

Morchain, Janet. *Search for a Nation*. Markham, Ontario: Fitzhenry and Whiteside, Ltd., 1984.

Morton, Desmond. *A Short History of Canada*. 5th rev. ed. Toronto: McClelland and Stewart, 2001.

———. *A Military History of Canada. From Champlain to Kosovo*. Toronto: McClelland and Stewart, 1999.

Morton, W. L *The Canadian Identity*. 2nd ed. Toronto: University of Toronto Press, 1972.

Neatby, Blair. *The Politics of Chaos: Canada in the Thirties*. Toronto: Macmillan, 1972.

Newman, Peter C. *The Canadian Establishment*. 2 vols. Toronto: McClelland and Stewart, 1975 and 1981.

Silver, A. I *An Introduction to Canadian History*. Toronto: Canadian Scholars' Press, 1993.

Sherman, George. *The Canada Connection in American History. A Guide for Teachers*. 3rd rev. ed. Plattsburgh, NY: Center for the Study of Canada, 1994.

Sprague, D. N. *Canada and the Métis, 1869–1885*. Waterloo, Ont.: Wilfrid Laurier Press, 1988.

Stanley, George F. G. *The War of 1812: Land Operations*. Toronto: Macmillan, 1983.

———. *The Birth of Western Canada. A History of the Riel Rebellions*. Toronto: University of Toronto Press, 1992.

Taylor, Charles. *Radical Tories: The Conservative Tradition in Canada*. Toronto: Anansi, 1982.

Taylor, Alan. *The Civil War of 1812*. 2011.

Thompson, John H. *Canada, 1922–1939. Decades of Discord*. Toronto: McClelland and Stewart, 1985.

Vance, Jonathan. *Maple Leaf Empire: Canada, Britain, and Two World Wars*. 2011.

Bibliography

Waiser, Bill and De Brou, Dave, eds. *Documenting Canada. A History of Modern Canada in Documents*. Saskatoon, Sask.: Fifth House, 1991.

Weisbord, Merrily. *The Strangest Dream. Canadian Communists, the Spy Trials, and the Cold War*. Toronto: Lester Orpen Dennys, 1983.

Wise, S. F. and Brown, R. C. *Canada Views the United States: Nineteenth-Century Political Attitudes*. Toronto: Macmillan, 1976.

Zaslow, M., ed. *The Defended Border: Upper Canada and the War of 1812*. Toronto: 1964.

IV. POLITICS

Adams, Michael. *Fire and Ice: The United States, Canada and the Myth of Converging Values*. Toronto: Penguin, 2003.

Archer, Keith, and Alan Whitehorn. *Political Activists. The NDP in Convention*. New York: Oxford University Press, 1998.

Atkinson, Michael M. *Governing Canada. Institutions and Public Policy*. Toronto: Harcourt Brace, 1993.

Bell, David and Teppermann, Lorne. *Roots of Disunity. A Study of Canadian Political Culture*. Rev. ed. New York: Oxford University Press, 1992.

Bickerton, James P., Gagnon, Alain-G., and Smith, Patrick J. *Ties that Bind. Parties and Voters in Canada*. New York: Oxford University, 1999.

Bickerton, James P. and Gagnon, Alain-G. *Canadian Politics. An Introduction to the Discipline*. Peterborough, Ont.: Broadview Press, 1994.

Blair, R. S. and McLeod, J. T., eds. *The Canadian Political Tradition. Basic Readings*. Scarborough, Ont.: Methuen, 1987.

Boydell, Craig L., and Connidis, Ingrid Arnet. *The Canadian Criminal Justice System*. Toronto: Holt, Rinehart Winston, 1982.

Brodie, Janine. *Women and Politics in Canada*. Scarborough, Ont.: McGraw-Hill Reyerson, 1985.

Brooks, Stephen, ed. *Political Thought in Canada. Contemporary Perspectives*. Richmond Hill, Ont.: Irwin, 1984.

———. *Canadian Democracy*. 3rd ed. New York: Oxford University, 2000.

Cairns, Alan C. and Williams, Douglas E. *Constitution, Government and Society in Canada*. Toronto: McClelland and Stewart, 1988.

Cairns, Alan C. *Charter Versus Federalism*. Montreal: McGill-Queens University Press, 1992.

Cameron, Duncan and Smith, Miriam, eds. *Constitutional Politics*. Toronto: James Lorimer, 1993.

Cheffins, Ronald I. and Johnson, Patricia A. *The Revised Canadian Constitution*. Scarborough, Ont.: McGraw-Hill Ryerson Hill, Ltd., 1986.

Conklin, William E. *Images of a Constitution*. Toronto: University of Toronto Press, 1989.

Cook, Ramsay. *Canada, Quebec and the Uses of Nationalism*. Toronto: McClelland and Stewart, 1986.

Courtney, John C., ed. *The Canadian House of Commons*. Univ. of Calgary Press, 1985.

Dawson, R. MacGregor and W. F. Revised by Norman Ward. *Democratic Government in Canada*. Toronto: University of Toronto Press, 1989.

De Palma, Anthony. *Here: A Biography of the New American Continent*, 2001.

Doern, G. Bruce, Leslie A. Pal and Brian W. Tomlin, eds. *Border Crossings. The Internationalization of Canadian Public Policy*. New York: Oxford University Press, 1996.

Donaldson, Gordon. *Eighteen Men: The Prime Ministers of Canada*. Toronto: Doubleday, 1985.

Eagles, Munroe, et al, eds. *The Almanac of Canadian Politics*. 2nd ed. New York: Oxford University Press, 1996.

Flanagan, Tom. *Waiting for the Wave. The Reform Party and Preston Manning*. Don Mills, Ont.: Stoddart, 1995.

Forbes, Hugh Donald, ed. *Canadian Political Thought*. Don Mills, Ont.: Oxford University Press, 1985.

Franks, C. E. S. *The Parliament of Canada*. Toronto: Univ. of Toronto Press, 1987.

Gerecke, Kent, ed. *The Canadian City*. Montreal: Black Rose Books, 1993.

Gollner, Andrew B. and Salée, Daniel, eds. *Canada Under Mulroney. An End-of-Term Report*. Montreal: Véhicule Press, 1988.

Goldenberg, Eddie. *The Way It Works: Inside Ottawa*. 2006.

Granatstein, J. L., et. al. *Sacred Trust: Brian Mulroney and the Conservative Party in Power*. Toronto: Cross Canada Books, 1986.

Grant, George. *Lament for a Nation. The Defeat of Canadian Nationalism*. Ottawa: Carleton University Press, 1982.

Higgins, Donald J. H. *Local and Urban Politics in Canada*. Agincourt, Ont.: Gage, 1986.

Jackson, Robert J. and Jackson, Doreen. *Politics in Canada. Culture, Institutions, Behaviour and Public Policy*. 4th ed. Upper Saddle River, NJ: Prentice-Hall, 1998.

Kealey, Linda and Sangster, Joan. *Beyond the Vote. Canadian Women and Politics*. Toronto: University of Toronto Press, 1989.

Kernaghan, Kenneth, ed. *Public Administration in Canada*. 5th ed. Toronto: Methuen, 1985.

Knopff, Ranier and Morton, F. L. *Charter Politics*. Scarborough, Ont.: Nelson, 1991.

Lagassé, Phillippe. *The Crown and Parliament*. 2015.

Landes, Ronald G. *The Canadian Polity: A Comparative Introduction*. 2nd ed. Scarborough, Ont.: Prentice-Hall, 1987.

Langford, J. Stuart. *A Practical Guide to the New Canadian Constitution*. Toronto: Canadian Broadcasting Corporation, 1982.

Leach, Richard H., ed. *Reshaping Confederation: The 1982 Reform of the Canadian Constitution*. Durham, NC: Duke University Press, 1984.

Levine, Allan. *Scrum Wars. The Prime Ministers and the Media*. Toronto: Dundurn Press, 1993.

MacIvor, Heather. *Women and Politics in Canada*. Peterborough, Ont.: Broadview Press, 1994.

Manfredi, Christopher P. and Rush, Mark. *Judging Democracy*. Peterborough, Ont.: Broadview Press, 2008. This is a comparison of the Canadian and American Supreme Courts.

Manfredi, Christopher P. *Judicial Power and the Charter*. 2nd ed. New York: Oxford University, 2000.

McKenna, M. C. *The Canadian and American Constitutions in Comparative Perspective*. Calgary: University of Calgary Press, 1993.

McKercher, William R., ed. *The U.S. Bill of Rights and the Canadian Charter of Rights and Freedoms*. Toronto: Ontario Economic Council, 1983.

McKercher, Asa. *Camelot and Canada* (about Kennedy and Diefenbaker). 2016.

McMenemy, John. *The Language of Canadian Politics. A Guide to Important Terms and Concepts*. Rev. ed. Waterloo, Ont.: Wilfred Laurier University Press, 1993.

McRoberts, Kenneth, ed. *Misconceiving Canada. The Struggle for National Unity*. New York: Oxford University Press, 1997.

———. and Patrick J. Monahan, eds. *The Charlottetown Accord, the Referendum, and the Future of Canada*. Toronto, 1993.

McWhinney, Edward. *Canada and the Constitution 1979–1982: Patriation and the Charter of Rights*. Toronto: University of Toronto Press, 1982.

Megyery, Kathy, ed. *Women in Canadian Politics*. Toronto: Dundurn, 1992.

Milne, David. *The New Canadian Constitution*. Toronto: James Lorimer, 1982.

Monahan, Patrick. *Politics and the Constitution. The Charter, Federalism and The Supreme Court of Canada*. Agincourt, Ont.: Carswell, 1987.

Morton, Desmond. *The New Democrats 1961–1986*. Toronto: Copp Clark Pitman, 1986.

Morton, E. L. *Law, Politics and the Judicial Process in Canada*. 2nd ed. Calgary: University of Calgary Press, 1992.

Bibliography

Pal, Leslie A., ed. *How Ottawa Spends 2000–2001. Redefining the Federal Role.* New York: Oxford University, 2000.

Pal, Leslie and Taras, David, eds. *Prime Ministers and Premiers. Political Leadership and Public Policy in Canada.* Scarborough, Ont.: Prentice-Hall, 1988.

Pammett, J., et al. *The Absent Mandate: The Politics of Discontent in Canada.* Agincourt, Ont.: 1984.

Peacock, Anthony A., ed. *Rethinking the Constitution.* New York: Oxford University Press, 1996.

Penner, Norman. *From Protest to Power. Social Democracy in Canada 1900–Present.* Toronto: James Lorimer, 1993.

Perlin, George, ed. *Party Democracy in Canada. The Politics of National Party Conventions.* Scarborough, Ont.: Prentice-Hall, 1988.

Pike, Corinna and Christopher McCreery. *Canadian Symbols of Authority: Maces, Chains and Rods of Office.* 2011.

Rathgeber, Brent. *Irresponsible Government: The Decline of Parliamentary Democracy in Canada.* Dundurn Press, 2014.

Romanow, Roy J. and Whyte, John D. *Canada . . . Notwithstanding.* Toronto: Methuen, 1984.

Russell, Peter H. *Leading Constitutional Decisions.* 3rd ed. Ottawa: Carleton University Press, 1982.

———. *The Judiciary in Canada. The Third Branch of Government.* Scarborough, Ont.: McGraw-Hill Ryerson, 1987.

———. *Constitutional Odyssey. Can Canadians Be a Sovereign People?* Toronto: University of Toronto Press, 1993.

Simpson, Jeffrey. *Faultlines. Struggling for a Canadian Vision.* Scarborough: HarperCollins, 1993.

Snell, James G. and Vaughan, Frederick. *The Supreme Court of Canada.* Toronto: University of Toronto Press, 1985.

The L-Shaped Party: The Liberal Party of Canada, 1958–1980. Toronto: 1981.

Wearing, Joseph. *Strained Relations. Canadian Parties and Voters.* Toronto: McClelland and Stewart, 1988.

Wells, Paul. *Right Side Up. The Fall of Paul Martin and the Rise of Stephen Harper's New Conservatism.* Toronto: McClelland & Stewart, 2007.

———. *The Longer I'm Prime Minister. Stephen Harper and Canada.* Random House Canada, 2014.

Whitehorn, Alan. *Canadian Socialism. Essays of CCF-NDP.* Don Mills, Ont.: Oxford University Press, 1992.

Woods, Shirley E. *Her Excellency Jeanne Sauve.* Toronto: Cross Canada Books, 1986.

Wilson-Smith, Anthony. *Double Vision: The Inside Story of the Liberals in Power.* Toronto: Doubleday, 1996.

Wright, Robert. *Trudeaumania*, 2016.

V. FEDERALISM, REGIONALISM, PROVINCIAL POLITICS AND NATIVE PEOPLES

Alfred, Taiaiake. *Peace, Power, Righteousness. An Indigenous Manifesto.* New York: Oxford University, 1999.

Anderson, Alun. *After the Ice: Life, Death and Geopolitics in the New Arctic.* Washington: Smithsonian (Virgin Books), 2009.

Archer, Keith, and Young, U., eds. *Regionalism and Party Politics in Canada.* New York: Oxford University, 2000.

Asch, Michael. *Home and Native Land: Aboriginal Rights and the Canadian Constitution.* Toronto: Methuen, 1984.

Banting, Keith and Simeon, Richard. *And No One Cheered. Federalism, Democracy and the Constitution Act.* Toronto: Methuen, 1983.

Banting, Keith. *The Welfare State and Canadian Federalism* 2nd ed. Montreal: McGill-Queen's University Press, 1987.

Barman, Jean. *The West beyond the West. A History of British Columbia.* Toronto: University of Toronto Press, 1993.

Bennett, A., et al. *Inuit of the North.* Markham, Ont.: Fitzherry Whiteside, n.d.

Berger, Thomas R. *Northern Frontier, Northern Homeland.* Vancouver: Douglas McIntyre, 1988.

Bolger, F. W. P., ed. *Canada's Smallest Province: A History of P.E.I.* Charlottestown, P.E.I.: 1973.

Bone, Robert M. *The Geography of the Canadian North.* Don Mills, Ont.: Oxford University Press, 1992.

Bothwell, Robert. *Canada since 1945. Power, Politics and Provincialism.* Toronto: University of Toronto Press, 1982.

Brym, Robert J., ed. *Regionalism in Canada.* Richmond Hill, Ont.: Irwin, 1986.

Byers, Michael. *Who Owns the Arctic.* 2013.

Careless, J. M. S. *Toronto to 1918. An Illustrated History.* Toronto: James Lorimer, 1985.

Cassidy, Frank, ed. *Aboriginal Self-Determination.* Lantzville, BC: Colichan Books, 1991.

Coates, Kenneth. *Aboriginal Land Claims in Canada.* Toronto: Copp Clark Pitman, 1992.

Conway, J. F. *The West: The History of a Region in Confederation.* Toronto: James Lorimer, 1983.

Cox, Bruce Alden, ed. *Native People, Native Lands. Canadian Indians, Inuit and Metis.* Ottawa: Carleton Univ. Press, 1987.

Crowe, Keith J. *A History of the Original Peoples of Northern Canada.* Rev. ed. Montreal: McGills-Queens University Press, 1991.

Dickerson, Mark O. *Whose North? Political Change, Political Development, and Self-Government in the Northwest Territories.* Vancouver: University of British Columbia Press, 1992.

Dickason, Olive P. *Canada's First Nations. A History of Founding Peoples from Earliest Times.* Markham, Ont.: McClelland Stewart, 1992.

Duffy, R. Quinn. *The Road to Nunavut. The Progress of the Eastern Arctic Inuit Since the Second World War.* Montreal: McGill-Queen's Univ. Press, 1988.

Elias, Peter D. *Development of Aboriginal People's Communities.* North York, Ont.: Captus Press, 1991.

Ellis, Richard. *On Thin Ice: The Changing World of the Polar Bear.* New York: Knopf, 2009.

Forbes, E. R. and Muise, D. A., eds. *The Atlantic Provinces in Confederation.* Toronto: University of Toronto Press, 1993.

Francis, R. Douglas and Palmer, Howard, eds. *The Prairie West. Historical Readings.* 2nd ed. Edmonton, Alb.: University of Alberta Press, 1992.

Frideres, James. *Native People in Canada: Contemporary Conflicts.* 3rd ed. Scarborough, Ont.: Prentice Hall, 1988. Friesen, Gerald. *The Canadian Prairies. A History.* Toronto: University of Toronto Press, 1984.

Friesen, John W. *The Cultural Maze: Complex Questions on Native Destiny.* Calgary: Temeron Books, 1991.

Gallant, Melvin. *The Country of Acadia.* Toronto: Simon Pierre, 1985.

Gibbins, Roger. *Regionalism. Territorial Politics in Canada and the United States.* Toronto: Butterworths, 1982.

Giraud, Marcel. *The Métis in the Canadian West (Le Métis Canadien).* Translated by George Woodstock. Edmonton: University of Alberta Press, 1986.

Griffiths, N. E. S. *The Acadians: Creation of a People.* Toronto: McGraw-Hill Ryerson, 1973.

Hamilton, John David. *The Arctic Revolution. Social Change in the NWT 1935–1993.* Toronto: Dundurn Press, 1993.

Hiller, J. and Neary, P., eds. *Newfoundland in the Nineteenth and Twentieth Centuries.*

Ibbitson, John. *Promised Land: Inside the Mike Harris Revolution,* 1997.

Johnston, Wayne. *The Colony of Unrequited Dreams.* (Novel about Joe Smallwood and Newfoundland) NY: Anchor Books, 2000.

Lauritzen, Philip. *Oil and Amulets: Inuit— A People at the Top of the World.* St. John's, Newf.: Breakwater Books, 1983.

Lemon, James. *Toronto Since 1918. An Illustrated History.* Toronto: James Lorimer, 1985.

Levine, Allen. *Toronto: Biography of a City,* 2014.

Little Bear, Leroy, et al, eds. *Pathways to Self-Determination. Canadian Indians and the Canadian State.* Toronto: University of Toronto Press, 1984.

Bibliography

Long, Anthony and Boldt, Menno. *Governments in Conflict? Provinces and Indian Nations in Canada.* Toronto: University of Toronto Press, 1989.

Malone, Greg. *Don't Tell the Newfoundlanders: The True Story of Newfoundland's Confederation with Canada.* 2012.

Melnyk, George, et. *Riel to Reform. A History of Protest in Western Canada.* Saskatoon, Sask.: Fifth House, 1991.

Milne, David. *Tug of War. Ottawa and the Provinces under Trudeau and Mulroney.* Toronto: James Lorimer, 1986.

Molyneux, Geoffrey. *British Columbia. An Illustrated History.* Vancouver: Polestar, 1992.

Morley, J. T. *Secular Socialists: The CCF/NDP in Ontario, A Biography.* Montreal: McGill-Queen's University Press, 1984.

Morrison, R. Bruce and Wilson, C. Roderick, eds. *The Native Peoples.* McClelland Stewart, 1986.

Morse, Bradford W., ed. *Aboriginal Peoples and the Law. Indian, Métis and Inuit Rights in Canada.* Ottawa: Carleton University Press, 1984.

Morton, W. L. *Manitoba: A History.* 2nd ed. Toronto: 1967.

Neary, Peter and Hiller, James, eds. *Twentieth Century Newfoundland: Explorations.* St. Johns: Breakwater, 1993.

Nikiforuk, Sheila Pratt and Wanagas, Don, eds. *Running on Empty. Alberta after the Boom.* Edmonton: NeWest Press, 1987.

Olling, Randy and Westmacott, Martin, eds. *Perspectives on Canadian Federalism.* Scarborough, Ont.: Prentice-Hall, 1988.

Ormsby, M. *British Columbia: A History.* Toronto: 1968.

Palmer, Hans and Tamara, eds. *Peoples of Alberta. Portraits of Cultural Diversity.* Saskatoon, Sask.: Western Producer Prairie Books, 1985.

———. *Alberta: A New History.* Markham, Ont.: McClelland Stewart, 1990.

Patterson, E. P., III. *The Canadian Indian: A History since 1500.* Don Mills, Ont.: 1972.

Peterson, Jacqueline and Brown, Jennifer, eds. *The New Peoples: Being and Becoming Métis in North America.* Winnipeg: University of Manitoba Press, 1984.

Purich, Donald. *Our Land, Native Rights in Canada.* Toronto: James Lorimer, 1987.

———. *The Inuit and Their Land. The Story of Nunavut.* Toronto: James Lorimer, 1993.

Rasporich, A. W., ed. *The Making of the Modern West.* Calgary: University of Calgary Press, 1984.

Ray, Arthur. *I Have Lived Here Since the World Began.* General Publishing, 1996.

Riggs, A. R. and Velk, Tom. *Federalism in Peril.* Vancouver: Fraser Institute, 1992.

Robinson, J. Lewis. *Concepts and Themes in the Regional Geography of Canada.* Vancouver: Talon Books, Ltd., 1983.

Rocher, François and Smith, Miriam. *New Trends in Canadian Federalism.* Peterborough, Ont.: Broadview Press, 1994.

Ross, Sally and Deveau, Alphonse. *The Acadians of Nova Scotia.* Halifax: Nimbus, 1992.

Saywell, John T. *The Office of Lieutenant-Governor.* Toronto: Copp Clark Pittman, Ltd., 1985.

Smiley, D. V. *Federal Condition in Canada.* Toronto: McGraw-Hill Ryerson, 1987.

Stelter, Gilbert A. and Artibise, Alan F. J. *The Canadian City. Essays in Urban and Social History.* Ottawa: Carleton University Press, 1984.

Taylor, John H. *Ottawa. An Illustrated History.* Toronto: James Lorimer, 1986.

Trudeau, Pierre Elliott. *Federalism and the French Canadians.* Toronto: Macmillan, 1968.

Tuohy, Carolyn J. *Policy and Politics in Canada. Institutionalized Ambivalence.* Philadelphia: Temple University Press, 1992.

Tupper, Allan and Gibbins, Roger. *Government and Politics in Alberta.* Edmonton: University of Alberta Press, 1992.

Weaver, R. Kent, ed. *The Collapse of Canada?* Washington, D.C.: Brookings Institution, 1992.

Webb, Melody. *Yukon. The Last Frontier.* Vancouver: University of British Columbia Press, 1993.

White, Graham. *The Ontario Legislature. A Political Analysis.* Toronto: University of Toronto Press, 1989.

———. and Levy, Gary, eds. *Provincial and Territorial Assemblies in Canada.* Toronto: Toronto University Press, 1989.

White, Randall. *Ontario 1610–1985. A Political and Economic History.* Toronto: Dundurn, 1985.

Wiseman, Nelson. *Social Democracy in Manitoba: A History of the CCF-NDP 1932–1977.* Winnipeg: University of Manitoba Press, 1984.

Woods, Jr., Shirley E. *Ottawa.* Toronto: Doubleday Canada Ltd., 1985.

Wotherspoon, Terry and Satzewich, Vic. *First Nations: A Struggle for Equality.* Scarborough, Ont.: Nelson, 1992.

Zellen, Barry. *Breaking the Ice. From Land Claims to Tribal Sovereignty in the Arctic.* Lanham, MD: Rowman &Littlefield, 2008.

VI. FOREIGN AND DEFENSE POLICY

Andrew, Arthur. *The Rise and Fall of a Middle Power: Canadian Diplomacy from King to Mulroney.* Toronto: James Lorimer, 1993.

Bercuson, David. *Significant Incident: Canada's Army, the Airborne, and the Murder in Somalia.* Markham, Ont.: McClelland & Stewart, 1996.

——— and J. L. Granatstein. *Dictionary of Canadian Military History.* Toronto: Oxford University, 1992.

Blanchard, James. *Behind the Embassy Door: Canada, Clinton and Quebec,* 1998.

Bothwell, Robert. *Your Country, My Country. A Unified History of the United States and Canada,* 2015.

Cellucci, Paul. *Unquiet Diplomacy.* Toronto: Key Porter, 2005.

Clarkson, Stephen. *Canada and the Reagan Challenge.* Toronto: James Lorimer, 1982.

Cohen, Andrew. *While Canada Slept. How We Lost our Place in the World.* Toronto: McClelland and Steward, 2004.

Cooper, Andrew F. *Tests of Global Governance. Canadian Diplomacy and United Nations World Conferences.* Washington: Brookings, 2004.

Cuff, Robert D. *Ties that Bind: Canadian-American Relations in Wartime from the Great War to the Cold War.* Toronto: Hakkert, 1977.

Curtis, Kenneth M. and Carroll, John E. *Canadian-American Relations. The Promise and the Challenge.* Lexington, MA: Lexington Books, 1983.

Cutler, A. Claire and Zacher, Mark W., eds. *Canadian Foreign Policy and International Economic Regimes.* Vancouver: University of British Columbia Press, 1992.

DeFede, Jim. *The Day the World Came to Town: 9/11 in Gander, Newfoundland,* 2003.

Dewitt, David B. and Kirton, John J. *Canada as a Principal Power. A Study in Foreign Policy and International Relations.* Toronto and New York: John Wiley, 1983.

Diubaldo, Richard J. *A Study of Canadian-American Defence Policy, 1945–1975: Northern Issues and Strategic Resources.* Ottawa: Department of National Defense, 1978.

Doran, Charles F. and Sigler, John H., eds. *Canada and the United States.* Scarborough, Ont.: Prentice-Hall, 1985.

Douglas, W. A. B., ed. *The Royal Canadian Navy in Transition, 1910–1985.* Vancouver: University of British Columbia Press, 1988.

Downton, Eric. *Pacific Challenge. Canada's Future in the New Asia.* Don Mills, Ont.: Stoddart, 1986.

English, John and Hillmer, Norman, eds. *Making a Difference? Canada's Foreign Policy in a Changing World Order.* Toronto, Lester, 1992.

Flaherty, David and McKercher, William. *Southern Exposure.* Scarborough: McGraw-Hill Ryerson, Ltd., 1986.

Fox, William T. R. *A Continent Apart.* Toronto: University of Toronto Press, 1985.

Gotlieb, Allan. *Washington Diaries.* 2006.

Granatstein, J.L. *Canadian Foreign Policy. Historical Readings.* Rev. ed. Toronto: Copp Clark Pitman, 1992.

———. *Torwards a New World. Readings in the History of Canadian Foreign Policy.* Toronto: Copp Clark Pitman, 1992.

Bibliography

———. and Hillmer, Norman. *For Better or For Worse. Canada and the United States in the 1990s*. Toronto: Copp Clark Pitman, 1992.

Grant, Shelagh. *Polar Imperative: A History of Arctic Sovereignty in North America*. 2011.

Griffiths, Franklyn, ed. *Politics of the Northwest Passage*. Montreal: McGill-Queen's Univ. Press, 1987.

Gwyn, Richard. *The 49th Paradox: Canada in North America*. Toronto: McClelland and Stewart, 1985.

Haglund, David. G. and Sokolsky, Joel J. *The U.S.-Canada Security Relationship*. Boulder, CO: Westview Press, 1989.

Haycock, R. G. and Hunt, B. D. *Canada's Defence*. Toronto: Copp Clark Pitman, 1993.

Hillier, Gen. Rich. *A Soldier First: Bullets, Bureaucrats and the Politics of War*, 2009.

Holmes, John W. *Life with Uncle. The Canadian-American Relationship*. Toronto: University of Toronto Press, 1981.

Honderich, John. *Arctic Imperative. Is Canada Losing the North?* Toronto: Univ. of Toronto Press, 1987.

Jockel, Joseph T. *Security to the North. Canada-U.S. Defense Relations in the 1990s*. East Lansing: Michigan State University Press, 1991.

———. *No Boundaries Upstairs. Canada, The United States and the Origins of North American Air Defence, 1945–1958*. Vancouver: Univ. of British Columbia Press, 1987.

——— and Sokolsky, Joel. *Canada and Collective Security. Odd Man Out*. New York: Praeger, 1986.

Jockel, Joseph T. *Canada and International Peacekeeping*. Washington, D.C.: Center for Strategic and International Studies, 1994.

Keating, Tom. *Canada and World Order. The Multilateralist Tradition in Canadian Foreign Policy*. Markham, Ont.: McClelland Stewart, 1993.

Kirton, John. *Canadian Foreign Policy in a Changing World*, 2007.

Laxer, James. *Stalking the Elephant: My Discovery of America*. New York: Viking, 2000.

Mahant, Edelgard E. and Mount, Graeme S. *An Introduction to Canadian-American Relations*. 2nd ed. Toronto: Methuen, 1989.

Martin, Lawrence. *The Presidents and the Prime Ministers. Washington and Ottawa Face to Face: The Myth of Bilateral Bliss 1867–1982*. Markham, Ont.: Paper Jacks, 1984.

McQuaig, Linda. *Holding the Bully's Coat: Canada and the U.S. Empire*. Toronto: Doubleday, 2007.

Middlemiss, Danford W. and Sokolsky, Joel. *Canadian Defence. Decisions and Determinants*. Toronto: HBJ/Holt, 1989.

Molot, Maureen Appel, and Hampson, Fen Osler, eds. *Canada Among Nations 2000*. New York: Oxford University, 2000.

———. eds. *Canada Among Nations 1999. A Big League Player?* New York: Oxford University, 1999.

Morton, Desmond. *A Military History of Canada from Champlain to the Gulf War*. Markham, Ont.: McClelland Stewart, 1992.

Munton, D. and Kirton, J. *Canadian Foreign Policy*. Scarborough, Ont.: Prentice-Hall, 1992.

Nossal, Kim Richard. *The Politics of Canadian Foreign Policy*. 2nd ed. Scarborough, Ont.: Prentice-Hall Canada, 1989.

Orvik, Nils, ed. *Canada and NATO*. Kingston: Queen's University Press, 1982.

Pearson, Geoffrey A.H. *Lester B. Pearson and Crisis Democracy*. Ottawa: Carleton University Press, 1993.

Porter, Gerald. *In Retreat: The Canadian Forces in the Trudeau Years*. Ottawa: Deneau and Greenberg, n.d.

Preston, Richard A. *To Serve Canada. A History of the Royal Military College Since the Second World War*. Ottawa: University of Ottawa Press, 1991.

Reflections from the Past. Perspectives on Canada and on the Canada-U.S. Relationship. Plattsburgh, NY: Center for the Study of Canada, 1991.

Rosenblum, Simon. *Misguided Missiles*. Toronto: James Lorimer Company, 1985.

Shiels, Frederick L. *Ethnic Separatism and World Politics*. Lanham, MD: University Press of America, 1984.

Simpson, Jeffrey. *Star-Spangled Canadians: Canadians Living the American Dream*. New York: HarperCollins, 2000.

Stacey, C.P. *Canada and the Age of Conflict: A History of Canadian External Policies, 1867–1921*, vol. 1, and *The Mackenzie King Era, 1921–1948*, vol. 2. Toronto: Macmillan, 1977.

———. *Arms, Men and Governments: The War Policies of Canada, 1939–1945*. Ottawa: 1970.

Stein, Janice Gross and Lang, Eugene. *The Unexpected War. Canada in Kandahar*. Toronto: Penguin, 2007.

Thomas, David, ed. *Canada and the United States. Differences that Count*. Peterborough, Ont.: Broadview Press, 1993.

Thompson, John Herd and Randall, Stephen J. *Canada and the United States. Ambivalent Allies*. Montreal: McGill-Queens University Press, 1993.

VII. QUEBEC

Arnopoulos, Sheila McLeod and Clift, Dominique. *The English Fact in Quebec*. Montreal: McGill-Queen's Univeristy Press, 1980.

Beach, Richard. *Alliance or Alienation. Québec & Canada as the Century Turns*. Plattsburgh, NY: Center for the Study of Canada. 2000.

Behiels, Michael D., ed. *Quebec Since 1945. Selected Readings*. Toronto: Copp Clark Pitman, 1987.

Bercuson, David. *Deconfederation: Canada Without Quebec*. Toronto: Key Porter, 1991.

Bernier, Luc. *From Paris to Washington: Quebec's Foreign Policy in a Changing World*. Washington, D.C.: Center for Strategic and International Studies, 1994.

Bourhis, Richard Y., ed. *Conflict and Language Planning in Quebec*. Clevedon, Avon, England: Multilingual Matters, 1984.

Center for the Study of Canada. *L'Americanité des Québécois*. Plattsburgh, NY, 2002.

Clift, Dominique. *Quebec Nationalism in Crisis*. Montreal: McGill-Queen's University Press, 1980.

Coleman, William D. *The Independence Movement in Quebec 1945–1980*. Toronto: University of Toronto Press, 1984.

Conologue, Ray. *Impossible Nation: The Longing for Homeland in Canada and Quebec*. General Publishing, 1996.

Dickinson, John and Young, Brian. *A Short History of Quebec*. 2nd rev. ed. Toronto: Copp Clark Pitman, 1993.

Dodge, William, ed. *Boundaries of Identity. A Quebec Reader*. Toronto: Lester, 1992.

Drache, D. and Perin, R. *Negotiating with a Sovereign Quebec*. Toronto: James Lorimer, 1993.

Eccles, W. J. *The French in North America, 1500–1782*. Rev. ed. Markham, Ont.: Fitzhenry Whiteside, 1998.

Fidler, Richard. *Canada, Adieu? Quebec Debates its Future*. Latzville, BC: Oolichan Books, 1991.

Fitzmaurice, John. *Quebec and Canada: Past, Present, and Future*. New York: St. Martin's, 1985.

Fournier, Pierre. *The Quebec Establishment. The Ruling Class and the State*. Montreal: Black Rose Books, 1988.

Ganon, Alain G., ed. *Quebec: State and Society in Crisis*. Toronto: Methuen, 1984.

Gilbert, Paula Ruth, et al. *Women Writers in Quebec. Essays in Honor of Jeanne Kissner*. Plattsburgh, NY: Center for the Study of Canada, 2002.

Griffin, Anne. *Quebec. The Challenge of Independence*. Cranbury, NJ: Associated University Presses, 1984.

Guindon, Hubert. *Tradition, Modernity, and Nationhood. Essays on Quebec Society*. Toronto: University of Toronto Press, 1989.

Hero, A. O., Jr. and Balthazar, Louis. *Contemporary Quebec the United States*. Lanham, MD: University Press of America, 1988.

Jacobs, Jane. *The Question of Separatism. Quebec and the Struggle over Sovereignty*. New York: Vintage Books, 1981.

Bibliography

Lachapelle, Guy. *The Quebec Democracy. Structures, Processes and Policies.* Toronto: McGraw-Hill Ryerson, 1993.

Laczko, Leslie S. *Pluralism and Inequality in Quebec.* New York: St. Martin's, 1994.

Leonard, Jean-François and Leveillee, Jacques. *Montreal after Drapeau.* Montreal: Black Rose Books, 1988.

Lévesque, Réne. *My Quebec.* Toronto: Totem Books, 1979.

Levine, Marc. *The Reconquest of Montreal: Language Policy and Social Change in a Bilingual City.* Philadelphia: Temple University Press, 1990.

McRoberts, Kenneth. *Quebec. Social Change and Political Crisis.* 3rd ed. Toronto: McClelland and Stewart, 1988.

Milner, Henry. *Politics in the New Quebec.* Toronto: McClelland and Stewart, 1978.

Moniere, D. *Ideologies in Quebec: The Historical Development.* Toronto: 1981.

Nardochhio, Elaine F. *Theatre and Politics in Modern Quebec. A History.* Edmonton: University of Alberta Press, 1985.

Nish, C. *The French Regime.* Scarborough, Ont.: Prentice-Hall, 1965.

Ouellet, Fernand. *Economy, Class, and Nation in Quebec.* Toronto: Copp Clark Pitman, 1991.

Parizeau, Jacques. *For a Sovereign Quebec.* 1997.

Poliquin, Daniel. *Extraordinary Canadians: René Lévesque.* Penguin Group (Canada), 2009.

Quinlan, Don. *Images of French Canada.* Markham, Ont.: Fitzhenry Whiteside, 1988.

Reid, Scott. *Canada Remapped. How the Partition of Quebec Will Reshape the Nation.* Vancouver: Arsenal Pulp Press, 1992.

Richler, Mordecai. *Oh Canada! Oh Quebec! Requiem for a Divided Country.* Toronto: Penguin, 1992.

Robinson, Sinclair and Smith, Donald. *Practical Handbook of Quebec and Acadian French.* Toronto: Anansi, 1984.

Roussopoulos, Dimitrios I, ed. *Quebec and Radical Social Change.* Montreal: Black Rose Books, 1988.

Saywell, John. *The Rise of the Parti Quebecois 1967-1976.* Toronto: University of Toronto Press, 1977.

Shaw, William F. and Albert, Lionel. *Partition. The Price of Quebec's Independence.* Montreal: Thornhill, 1980.

Trofimenkoff, Susan Mann. *The Dream of Nation. A Social and Intellectual History of Quebec.* Toronto: Gage, 1983.

Vallieres, Pierre. *White Niggers of America.* Toronto: McClelland and Stewart, 1971.

———. *The Impossible Quebec. Illusions of Sovereignty-Association.* Montreal: Black Rose Books, 1988.

Wade, M. *The French Canadians.* 2 vols. Rev. ed. Toronto: 1975, 1976.

Walker, Douglas C. *The Pronunciation of Canadian French.* Ottawa: University of Ottawa Press, 1985.

VIII. ECONOMY

Anderson, F. J. *Natural Resources in Canada. Economic Theory and Policy.* Toronto: Methuen, 1985.

Armstrong, Muriel. *The Canadian Economy and Its Problems.* 4th ed. Scarborough, Ont.: Prentice-Hall, 1988.

Brodie, Janine. *The Political Economy of Canadian Regionalism.* Toronto: Harcourt Brace Jovanovich, 1990.

Caloren, Fred, ed. *Is the Canadian Economy Closing Down?* Montreal: Black Rose Books, 1988.

The Canada-U.S. Economic Relationship. Plattsburgh, NY: Center for the Study of Canada, 1991.

Crane, David. *The Next Canadian Century. Building a Competitive Economy.* Don Mills, Ont.: Stoddart, 1993.

Doern, Bruce and Toner, Glen. *The Politics of Energy. The Development and Implementation of the NEP.* Toronto: Methuen, 1985.

Fallis, George. *The Costs of Constitutional Change.* Toronto: James Lorimer, 1993.

French, Richard and van Loon, Richard. *How Ottawa Decides: Planning and Industrial Policy-Making 1968-1983.* Rev. ed. Toronto: James Lorimer, 1984.

Fry, Earl H. *Canada's Unity Crisis. Implications for U.S.-Canada Economic Relations.* Washington, D.C.: Brookings, 1992.

Globerman, Steven and Walker, Michael. *Assessing NAFTA.* Vancouver: Fraser Institute, 1993.

Hoebing, Joyce, et al. *NAFTA and Sovereignty.* Washington, D.C.: CSIS Press, 1996.

Howlett, Michael, Netherton, Alex, and Ramesh, M. *The Political Economy of Canada.* 2nd ed. New York: Oxford University, 1999.

Ismael, Jacqueline S., eds. *Canadian Welfare State. Evolution and Transition.* Edmonton: Univ. of Alberta Press, 1987.

Langdon, Frank. *The Politics of Canadian-Japanese Economic Relations, 1952-1983.* Vancouver: University of British Columbia Press, 1983.

Laxer, James. *Leap of Faith. Free Trade and the Future of Canada.* Edmonton: Hurtig, 1986.

Leslie, Peter. *Federal State, National Economy.* Toronto: Univ. of Toronto Press, 1987.

Levant, Ezra. *Ethical Oil: The Case for Canada's Oil Sands,* 2011.

Levi, Michael A. *The Canadian Oil Sands: Energy Security vs. Climate Change.* Washington, DC: Brookings, 2009.

Muirhead, B. W. *The Development of Postwar Canadian Trade Policy.* Montreal: McGill-Queen's University Press, 1992.

Naylor, C. David, ed. *Canadian Health Care and the State.* Montreal: McGills-Queen's University Press, 1992.

Pomfred, Richard. *The Economic Development of Canada.* 2nd ed. Scarborough, Ont.: Nelson, 1992.

Pritchard, Robert S., ed. *Crown Corporations in Canada.* Toronto: Butterworths, 1983.

Rea, Kenneth. *A Guide to Canadian Economic History.* Toronto: Canadian Scholars' Press, 1993.

Safarian, A. E. *The Canadian Economy in the Great Depression.* Toronto: 1970.

Sarlo, Christopher A. *Poverty in Canada.* Vancouver: Fraser Institute, 1992.

Schott, Jeffrey J. and Smith, Murray G., eds. *The Canada-United States Free Trade Agreement: The Global Impact.* Washington, DC: Institute for International Economics, 1988.

Sitwell, O. F. G. and Seifried, Neil R. M. *The Regional Structure of the Canadian Economy.* Toronto: Methuen, 1984.

Vogt, Roy, et al. *Economics. Understanding the Canadian Economy.* 4th ed. Toronto: HBJ-Holt, 1993.

Watkins, M. H. and Grant, H. M. K. *Canadian Economic History.* Ottawa: Carleton University Press, 1993.

IX. CULTURE AND SOCIETY

Ashworth, Mary. *Children of the Canadian Mosaic. A Brief History to 1950.* Toronto: Oise Press, 1992.

Backhouse, Constance and Flaherty, David H, eds. *Challenging Times. The Women's Movement in Canada and the United States.* Montreal: McGills-Queens University Press, 1992.

Baker, Maureen, ed. *The Family: Changing Trends in Canada.* Scarborough, Ont.: McGraw-Hill Reyerson, 1984.

Balkind, Alvin, et al. *Visions/Contemporary Art in Canada.* Vancouver, B.C.: Douglas and McIntyre, 1983.

Berkowitz, S. D., ed. *Models and Myths in Canadian Sociology.* Toronto: Butterworths, 1984.

Berry, J. W. and Laponce, J. A., eds. *Multiculturalism in Canada. A Review of Research.* Toronto: University of Toronto Press, 1993.

Bibby, Reginald W. and Poterski, Donald C. *The Emerging Generation.* Irwin Publishing, Inc., 1985.

Bibby, Reginald W. *Restless Gods: The Renaissance of Religion in Canada.* Don Mills, Ont.: Stoddart, 2002.

Bird, Michael. *Canadian Folk Art. Old Ways in a New Land.* Don Mills, Ont.: Oxford University Press, 1983.

Bolaria, B. Singh, ed. *Social Issues and Contradictions in Canadian Society.* Toronto: Harcourt Brace, 1991.

Brannigan, Augustine. *Crimes, Courts, and Corrections: An Introduction to Crime and*

Bibliography

Social Control in Canada. Toronto: Holt, Rinehart Winston, 1984.

Buchignani, Norman. *Cultures in Canada: Strength in Diversity*. Regina, Sask.: L.A. Weigl Educational Associates, 1984.

Burnet, Jean and Palmer, Howard. *Coming Canadians. An Introduction to a History of Canada's Peoples*. Markham, Ont.: McClelland Stewart, 1988.

Burnett, David and Schiff, Marilyn. *Contemporary Canadian Art*. Edmonton, Alb.: Hurtig, 1983.

Canada in Film and Video. Plattsburgh, NY: Canadian Film Distribution Center (phone: 1-800-388-6784), annually updated.

Chacko, James. *Cultural Sovereignty: Myth or Reality*. Windsor, Ont.: University of Windsor Press, 1986.

Cédilot, André and André Noël. *Mafia Inc.: The Long, Bloody Reign of Canada's Sicilian Clan*, 2011.

Clandfield, David. *Canadian Film*. Don Mills, Ont.: Oxford Univ. Press, 1987.

Clarkson, Adrienne. *Room for All of Us*. Allen Lane, 2012.

Colombo, John Robert. *Canadian Literary Landmarks*. Willowdale, Ont.: Hounslow, 1984.

———. *Contemporary Canadian Photography. From the Collection of the National Film Board*. Edmonton, Alb.: Hurtig, 1984.

The Dictionary of Canadian Quotations. Don Mills, Ont.: Stoddart, 1991.

Crean, Susan and Rioux, Marcel. *Two Nations: An Essay on the Culture and Politics of Canada and Quebec in a World of American Pre-eminence*. Toronto: James Lorimer, 1983.

Cross, Michael S. and Kealey, Gregory S., eds. *Modern Canada. 1930–1980s. Readings in Canadian Social History*. vol. 5. Toronto: McClelland and Stewart, 1984.

Driedger, Leo, ed. *The Canadian Mosaic. A Quest for Identity*. Toronto: McClelland and Stewart, 1978.

———. *Ethnic Canada: Identities and Inequalities*. Mississauga, Ont.: Copp Clark Pitman, 1987.

Elliott, Jean Leonard, ed. *Two Nations, Many Cultures. Ethnic Groups in Canada*. 2nd ed. Scarborough, Ont.: Prentice-Hall, 1983.

Feldman, Seth, ed. *Take Two. A Tribute to Canadian Film*. Richmond Hill, Ont.: Irwin, 1984.

Forcese, Dennis and Richter, Stephen, eds. *Social Issues: Sociological Views of Canada*. Scarborough, Ont.: Prentice-Hall, 1982.

Forcese, Dennis. *The Canadian Class Structure*. Scarborough: McGraw-Hill Ryerson, Ltd., 1986.

Francis, Daniel. *The Imaginary Indian. The Image of the Indian in Canadian Culture*. Vancouver: Arsenal Pulp Press, 1992.

Friesen, John W. *When Cultures Clash. Case Studies in Multiculturalism*. Calgary, Alb.: Temeron Books, 1993.

Frye, Northrop. *Divisions on a Ground: Essays on Canadian Culture*. Toronto: Anansi, 1982.

Globerman, Steven. *The Immigration Dilemma*. Vancouver: Fraser Institute, 1992.

Haas, J., et al. *Shaping Identity in Canadian Society*. Scarborough, Ont.: Prentice-Hall, 1978.

Harper, Stephen. *A Great Game. The Forgotten Leafs & The Rise of Professional Hockey*, 2013.

Herberg, Edward N. *Ethnic Groups in Canada. Adaptations and Transitions*. Scarborough, Ont.: Methuen, 1988.

Huang, Evelyn and Jeffrey, Lawrence. *Chinese Canadians*. Vancouver: Douglas McIntyre, 1992.

Joy, Richard J. *Canada's Official Languages. The Progress of Bilingualism*. Toronto: University of Toronto Press, 1992.

Kallen, Evelyn. *Ethnicity and Human Rights in Canada*. 2nd ed. New York: Oxford University Press, 1995.

Kallmann, Helmut, et al, eds. *Encyclopedia of Music in Canada*. 2nd ed. Toronto: University of Toronto Press, 1992.

Knowles, Valerie. *Strangers at Our Gates. Canadian Immigration and Immigration Policy, 1540–1990*. Toronto: Dundurn Press, 1992.

Kymlicka, Will. *Finding Our Way. Rethinking Ethno-cultural Relations in Canada*. New York: Oxford University Press, 1998.

Link, Eugene P. *The T.B.'s Progress. Norman Bethune as Artist*. Plattsburgh, NY: Center for the Study of Canada, 1991.

MacNeil, Robert. *Burden of Desire*. A Harvest Book, n.d.

Marchak, M. Patricia. *Ideological Perspectives on Canada*. 3rd ed. Scarborough, Ont.: McGraw-Hill Ryerson, 1987.

Marchand, Philip. *Marshall McLuhan: The Medium & the Messenger*. Cambridge: MIT Press, 1998.

Miles, Angela and Finn, Geraldine, eds. *Feminism in Canada. From Pressure to Politics*. Montreal: Black Rose Books, 1982.

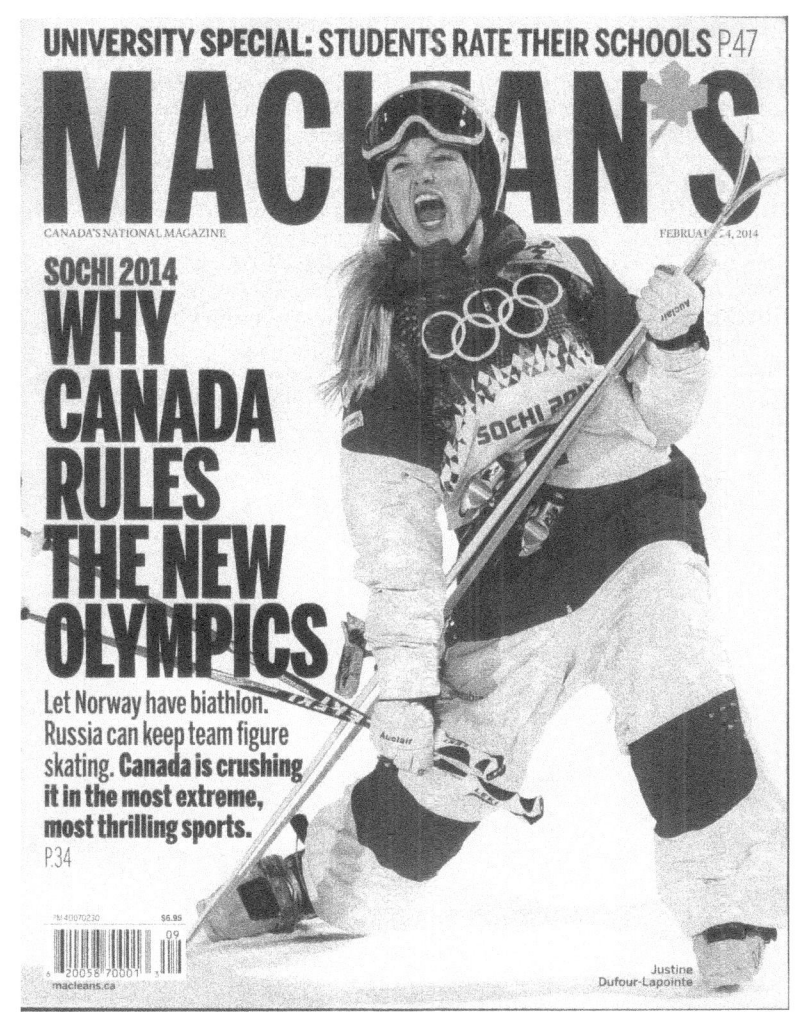

Bibliography

Morris, Peter. *The Film Companion. A Comprehensive Guide to More than 650 Canadian Films and Filmmakers*. Richmond Hill, Ont.: Irwin, 1984.

Murray, Joan. *The Best of the Group of Seven*. Edmonton, Alb.: Hurtig, 1984.

Nemiroff, Diana, et al, eds. *Land Spirit Power. First Nations at the National Gallery of Canada*. Ottawa: National Gallery of Art, 1992.

Porter, John. *The Measure of Canadian Society: Education, Equality, and Opportunity*. Ottawa: Carleton Univ. Press, 1988.

Reid, Dennis. *A Concise History of Canadian Painting*. 2nd ed. Don Mills, Ont.: Oxford University Press, 1988.

Rooney, John F., Jr., et al, eds. *The Remarkable Continent: An Atlas of the United States and Canadian Society and Cultures*. College Station, TX: Texas A&M Press, 1982.

Ross, Jeffrey Ian, ed. *Violence in Canada. Sociological Perspectives*. New York: Oxford University Press, 1996.

Shek, Ben-Z. *French-Canadian and Quebecois Novels*. Oxford: Oxford University Press, 1991.

Story, G.M. et al, eds. *Dictionary of Newfoundland English*. 2nd ed. Toronto: University of Toronto Press, 2002.

Tippett, Maria. *By a Lady. Celebrating Three Centuries of Art by Canadian Women*. Toronto: Penguin, 1992.

Trofimenkoff, Susan Mann and Prentice, Alison, eds. *The Neglected Majority. Volume 2. Essays in Canadian Women's History*. Toronto: McClelland and Stewart, 1985.

Webber, James D. *Reimagining Canada. Language, Culture, Community, and the Canadian Constitution*. Montreal: McGill-Queen's University Press, 1993.

Webster, Judith. *Voices of Canada. An Introduction to Canadian Culture*. Burlington, VT: Assoc. for Canadian Studies in the United States, 1977.

X. FICTION LITERATURE

Atwood, Margaret. *Surfacing*. Toronto: McClelland and Stewart, 1972.

———. *Lady Oracle*. Toronto: McClelland and Stewart, 1976.

———. *Life before Man*. Toronto: McClelland and Stewart, 1979.

———. *Survival: A Thematic Guide to Canadian Literature*.

———. ed. *The New Oxford Book of Canadian Verse in English*. Don Mills, Ont.: Oxford Univ. Press, 1982.

———. and Weaver, Robert, eds. *The Oxford Book of Canadian Short Stories in English*. Don Mills, Ont.: Oxford Univ. Press, 1988.

———. *Alias Grace*. 1996.

———. *The Blind Assassin*. New York: Doubleday, 2000.

———. *The Year of the Flood*. Bloomsbury, 2009.

Carrier, Roch. *La Guerre, yes sir!* Trans. Sheila Fischman. Toronto: Anansi, 1970.

Davidson, Arnold E. *Coyote Country. Fictions of the Canadian West*. Durham, NC: Duke University Press, 1993.

Gustafson, Ralph, ed. *The Penguin Book of Canadian Verse*. Markham, Ont.: Penguin, 1984. Toronto: Anansi, 1972.

Hebert, Anne. *Kamouraska*. Trans. Norman Shapiro. Toronto: Musson, 1973.

Hemon, Louis. *Maria Chapdelaine*. Trans. W. H. Blake. Toronto: Macmillan, 1921.

Keith, W. J. *Canadian Literature in English*. Toronto: Copp Clark Pitman, 1985.

———. *Literary Images of Ontario*. Toronto: University of Toronto Press, 1992.

Kirby, Peter. *The Dead of Winter*, 2012. (A first crime novel in a setting of colorful and gritty Montreal).

Leacock, Stephen. *Sunshine Sketches of a Little Town*. Toronto: McClelland and Stewart, 1970.

Lecker, Robert and David, Jack, eds. *The New Canadian Anthology: Poetry and Short Fiction in English*. Scarborough, Ont.: Methuen, 1988.

Lee, Dennis. ed. *The New Canadian Poets. 1970–1985*. Toronto, Ont.: McClelland and Stewart, 1985.

MacLennan, Hugh. *Two Solitudes*. Toronto: Collins, 1945.

McCombs, Judith and Palmer, Carole. *Margaret Atwood. A Reference Guide*. New York: G. K. Hall, 1991.

Montgomery, Lucy Maud. *The Alpine Path. The Story of My Career*. Markham, Ont.: Fitzhenry Whiteside, n.d.

New, W. H. *A History of Canadian Literature*. Chicago: Ivan R. Dee, 2000.

Norris, Ken. ed. *Canadian Poetry Now. 20 Poets of the '80s*. Toronto: Anansi, 1984.

Nowlan, Michael, ed. *A Land, A People*. St. John's, Newfoundland: Breakwater Books, Ltd., 1986.

Perkyns, Richard, ed. *Major Plays of the Canadian Theater 1934–1984*. Richmond Hill, Ont.: Irwin, 1984.

Roy, Gabrielle. *The Tin Flute*. Trans. Hannah Josephson. NCL, 1957.

———. Translated by Patricia Claxton. *Enchantment and Sorrow. An Autobiography of Gabrielle Roy*. Toronto: Lester Orpen Dennys, 1987.

Toye, William, ed. *The Oxford Companion to Canadian Literature*. Don Mills, Ont.: Oxford University Press, 1983.

Wagner, Anton, ed. *Contemporary Canadian Theatre. New World Visions*. Toronto: Simon Pierre, 1985.

Wasserman, Jerry, ed. *Modern Canadian Plays, Revised Edition*. Vancouver: Talon Books, 1986.

Weaver, Robert, ed. *Canadian Short Stories*. Fourth Series. Oxford University Press, 1985.

Wiebe, Rudy. *The Temptations of Big Bear*. Toronto: McClelland and Stewart, 1973.

———. *The Scorched-Wood People*. Toronto: McClelland and Stewart, 1977.

About the Author

P. T. Babie

P. T. Babie is Bonython Chair and Professor of Law in The University of Adelaide, Australia. He joined the Adelaide Law School in 1999, was promoted to a personal chair in law in 2015, and was named the holder of the Bonython Chair in Law in 2021. He is currently Associate Dean of Law (International) and Director of the Research Unit for the Study of Society, Ethics, and Law, and has previously been Associate Dean of Law (Research) and Associate Dean of Law (Learning and Teaching). He was elected a Fellow of the Australian Academy of Law in 2017 and a Fellow of the Royal Society of Arts in 2021. He received the 2021 Australian Legal Education Awards (ALEA) Excellence in Research Supervision Award, a 2011 Executive Dean's Prize for Excellence in Undergraduate Teaching, the 2007 Adelaide Law School Excellence in Teaching Prize, 2015 and 2016 Executive Dean's Awards for Excellence in Research, and 2014 and 2017 Executive Dean's Commendations for Excellence in Research.

He holds a BA in sociology and political science from the University of Calgary, a BThSt from Flinders University, a LLB from the University of Alberta, a LLM from the University of Melbourne, writing a thesis on the transferability of water entitlements, and a DPhil in law from St Catherine's College, the University of Oxford, completing a thesis on the nature of the Crown (state) interest in Australian land. At Oxford, he was a Viscount Bennett, a Canadian Centennial, and a Landau Scholar.

Following law school, he was an ssociate with Howard, Mackie (now Borden Ladner Gervais (BLG) in Calgary, Canada, specializing in securities and natural resources law. Prior to his appointment to the Adelaide Law School, he was ecturer in Law at St Catherine's and Balliol Colleges, University of Oxford, and the Melbourne Law School, The University of Melbourne. He is a barrister and solicitor of the Court of King's Bench of Alberta (Canada), and an Associate Member of the Law Society of South Australia (of which he is a member of the Property Law Committee). He is frequently consulted on issues relating to real property law and law and religion (especially in relation to the Australian Constitution).

His research, throughout his career, has involved asking what property is and how, if at all, it can be justified. He has explored those questions from legal theoretical and from theological perspectives. He is co-editor in chief of the Australian Property Law Journal, was editor in chief and South Australia editor of the Property Law Review, and is an editorial board member of the Journal of Law and Religion, the Routledge Research Series in Law and Religion, the Springer Research Series in Law and Religion, and of the Forum on Religion & Ecology (FORE) @ Australia (affiliated with FORE, Yale University (USA).

He teaches property law, property theory, law and religion, and Roman law.

Dr. Charles J. Russo

Charles J. Russo, M. Div., J.D., Ed. D., is the Joseph Panzer Chair in Education in the School of Education and Health Sciences, director of its Ph.D. program, and research professor of law in the School of Law at the University of Dayton. The 1998–99 president of the Education Law Association, 2002 recipient of its McGhehey (Achievement) Award, and 2021 recipient of the Distinguished Scholar Award from the Religion and Education Special Interest Group of the American Educational Research Association, he authored or co-authored almost 350 articles in peer-reviewed journals; authored, co-authored, edited, or co-edited 78 books as of this volume, and has more than 1,200 publications. Dr. Russo also speaks extensively on issues in education law in the United States and other nations. In addition, he edits two journals and serves on more than a dozen editorial boards.

Along with having spoken in thirty-four states and thirty nations outside of the United States on all six inhabited continents, Russo taught summer courses in England, Spain, and Thailand. He has served as a visiting professor at Queensland University of Technology in Brisbane, and the University of Newcastle, Australia; the University of Sarajevo, Bosnia and Herzegovina; South East European University, Macedonia; the Potchefstroom and Mafeking Campuses of Northwest University, Potchefstroom, South Africa; the University of Malaya in Kuala Lumpur, Malaysia; the University of Sao Paulo, Brazil; Yeditepe University, Istanbul Turkey; Inner Mongolia University for the Nationalities, Tongliao, Inner Mongolia; and Peking University and Capital Normal University in Beijing. He is presently a visiting professor at the University of Notre Dame of Australia, Faculty of Law, in Sydney, and the College of Education at Capital Normal University in Beijing.

Before joining the faculty at the University of Dayton as professor and chair of the Department of Educational Administration in July 1996, Dr. Russo taught at the University of Kentucky in Lexington, Kentucky, from August 1992 to July 1996 and at Fordham University in his native New York City from September 1989 to July 1992. He taught high school for eight and one half-years, both prior to and after graduation from law school. He received a Bachelor of Arts degree in Classical Civilization (1972), Juris Doctor Degree (1983), and Doctor of Education degrees in Educational Administration and Supervision (1989) from St, John's University in New York City. He received a Master of Divinity degree from the Seminary of the Immaculate Conception in Huntington, New York (1978). He received a Ph.D. Honoris Causa from Potchefstroom University, now the Potchefstroom Campus of Northwest University, in Potchefstroom, South Africa, in May 2004, for his contributions to the field of education law.